New 41st Edition

Self Catering

England's star-rated holiday accommodation

and Camping

2016

Penelope, Viscountess Cobham
Chairman of VisitEngland

Stunning countryside, vibrant cities, open coastlines, history and heritage, accommodation to meet your every need...but let me give you even more great reasons to stay in England in 2016!

Thought by many to be England's greatest landscape-gardener, 2016 sees the 300th anniversary of the birth of Lancelot "Capability" Brown. Brown was born in beautiful Northumberland, in England's north-east, but his legacy includes more than 200 sites across England which claim association with him. Bowood House in Wiltshire, Blenheim Palace in Oxfordshire and Burghley House in Lincolnshire, will all be joined by many other grand houses this summer in celebrating the achievements of this great man with exhibitions and special events throughout the year.

In honour of Brown VisitEngland has designated 2016, "Year of the Garden", and in England they come in all guises. Wonderful Westonbirt Arboretum in Gloucestershire will be offering visitors a "never seen before" perspective when it opens its Treetop Walkway 13 metres up in the canopy; Hampton Court Palace has teamed up with a Chelsea-winning gardener to plan the new "Magic Garden" – an adventure playground with history at its heart featuring a jousting area, five tiltyard towers and a breathing dragon! Magic of another sort will be experienced by visitors to the Derren Brown Psychological Theme Park, the first in the world, when it opens in March at Thorpe Park in Surrey; whilst London's Royal Academy of Arts will be showing a major exhibition: Painting the Modern Garden: Monet to Matisse.

"Exhibitionism" of another sort is on view at the Saatchi Gallery in London where the Rolling Stones will host a comprehensive and immersive insight into the group. National treasures of a different kind will be on view at Durham Cathedral when it opens previously hidden spaces within the Cathedral Cloister and a major restoration project at Rievaulx Abbey in the North Yorks Moors National Park ensures you're guaranteed a fascinating insight into the lives of the people who founded these wonderful sites.

The moors are synonymous with the Bronte sisters and visitors to the Bronte Parsonage Museum in picturesque Haworth can celebrate the 200th anniversary of the birth of Charlotte, best known for her novel, Jane Eyre. Stratford-on-Avon, meanwhile, will mark 400 years of Shakespeare's timeless legacy with many exciting new projects coming to fruition including at his family home, New Place, where the story of Shakespeare's mature years as a successful writer and citizen of his home town will be told.

England's city destinations continue to offer great opportunities to explore and experience new activities. In Bristol, gardens will form the backdrop of a new inland surfing lake, The Wave: Bristol, currently in development and set to bring together people of all ages and abilities. For those seeking coastal waves, Hastings Pier will reopen this summer promising to offer an eclectic range of activities from farmers markets to circus and sport. Brighton sea-front will bring the countryside in range when the British Airways i360 opens. This 162-metre high observation tower is designed, engineered and manufactured by the team responsible for the London Eye and will offer stunning views of the South Downs national park.

As Chairman of VisitEngland I am extremely proud of the constant investment in and development of the tourism experiences in England. I do hope you will enjoy discovering England in 2016 and come to share my passion for it as a destination to holiday and work in.

Contents

How to use this guide

This official VisitEngland guide is packed with information from where to stay, to how to get there and what to see on arrival. In fact, this guide captures everything you need to know when exploring England.

Choose from a wide range of quality-assessed accommodation to suit all budgets and tastes. This guide contains a comprehensive listing of
• Self-catering properties in the VisitEngland Quality Assessment Scheme, including boat accommodation and approved caravans.
• Touring, camping and holiday parks and holiday villages participating in the British Graded Holiday Park Scheme.

Each property has been visited annually by professional assessors, who apply nationally agreed standards, so that you can book with confidence knowing your accommodation has been checked and rated for quality.

Check out the places to visit in each region, from towns and cities to spectacular coast and countryside, plus historic homes, castles and great family attractions! Maps show accommodation locations, selected destinations and some of the National Cycle Networks. For even more ideas go online at www.visitengland.com.

Regional tourism contacts and tourist information centres are listed in each of the regional sections of this guide. Before booking your stay, why not contact them to find out what's going on in the area? You'll also find events, travel information, maps and useful indexes that will help you plan your trip, throughout this guide.

Accommodation entries explained

Each accommodation entry contains detailed information to help you decide if it is right for you. This has been provided by proprietors and our aim is to ensure that it is as objective and factual as possible.

① ② ③ ④ ⑤ ⑩

PORTHTOWAN, Cornwall   Map ref 1B3   S

Rosehill Lodges

Contact: Mr John Barrow, Rosehill Lodges, Porthtowan, Cornwall TR4 8AR
T: (01209) 891920 **F:** 01209 891935 **E:** reception@rosehilllodges.com
W: www.rosehilllodges.com **£ BOOK ONLINE**

Units   10
Sleeps   1-6

PER UNIT PER WEEK
£516.00 - £2229.00

SPECIAL PROMOTIONS
Weekend and mid-week breaks available. Open for Christmas and New Year. Low occupancy discounts available. Free superfast broadband over Wi-Fi. Free cots and highchairs. See website for special offers.

Five Star luxury Gold Award self-catering lodges right on the Cornish coast. Situated in the coastal village of Porthtowan just five minutes walk to a sandy Blue Flag beach, bars and restaurants. Relax and leave your car behind. Each bespoke lodge features super-king size beds, log burners, your own personal hot tub spa and free superfast Wi-Fi. Go green with grass roofs and solar panels and dine al-fresco under glass covered decking whatever the weather. Each lodge has an external drench shower, ideal for washing down after a fun day on the beach. We look forward to giving you a warm welcome.

Open: All year
Nearest Shop: 0.5 miles
Nearest Pub: 0.5 miles

Units: Bespoke luxury timber eco lodges, fully equipped and hand built locally with materials from sustainable sources. Luxur... better together.

Sample entry

Site: ✿ P **Payment:** ☒ **Leisure:** ♿ ♪ ▶ ☺ **Property:** ▦ ☐ ▦ **Children:** ⚲ ▥ ♟
Unit: ☐ ▤ ▣ ☐ ▧ TV DVD ∅ BBQ ☎

⑥ ⑦ ⑧ ⑨

① Listing sorted by town or village, including a map reference

② Rating (and/or) Award, where applicable

③ Prices per unit per week or prices per pitch per night for touring pitches; per unit per week for static holiday units

④ Establishment name, address, telephone number and email address

⑤ Website information

⑥ Accessible rating, Walkers, cyclists, pets and families welcome accolades, where applicable

⑦ Indicates when the property is open

⑧ Accommodation details

⑨ At-a-glance facility symbols

⑩ Accommodation type: S = Self Catering, C = Camping, Touring and Holiday Parks

Key to symbols

Information about many of the accommodation services and facilities is given in the form of symbols.

S *Self Catering*

Site Features

P Private parking
❀ Garden

Booking & Payment Details

€ Euros accepted
£ Visa/Mastercard/Switch accepted

Leisure Facilities

Q Tennis court(s)
↘ Swimming pool – outdoor
↗ Swimming pool – indoor
● Games room
U Riding/pony-trekking nearby
▶ Golf available (on site or nearby)
⌐ Fishing nearby
🚲 Cycles for hire

Children

⅄ High chairs available
▥ Cots available
➤ Children welcome

Property Facilities

⊡ Linen provided
⊞ Linen for hire
⊟ Laundry facilities
⊑ Wi-Fi/Internet access
🐕 Dogs/pets accepted by arrangement
⫽ Cleaning service

Unit Facilities

☎ Telephone
BBQ Barbecue
🔥 Real log/coal fires
📀 DVD player
📺 Satellite/cable/freeview TV
TV Television
🖴 Hairdryer
▤ Washing machine
▭ Microwave cooker
🖥 Dishwasher
🗄 Freezer

C *Camping*

Pitches/Units

🚐 Caravans (number of pitches and rates)
🚐 Motor caravans
   (number of pitches and rates)
A Tents (number of pitches and rates)
▥ Caravan holiday homes
   (number of pitches and rates)
🏠 Log cabins/lodges (number of units and rates
🏠 Chalets/villas (number of units and rates)

Site Features

A🅿 Parking next to pitch
🍺 Public house/Inn

Booking & Payment Details

☼ Booking recommended in summer
€ Euros accepted
£ Visa/Mastercard/Switch accepted

Leisure Facilities

Q Tennis court(s)
↘ Swimming pool – outdoor
↗ Swimming pool – indoor
● Games room
U Riding/pony-trekking nearby
▶ Golf available (on site or nearby)
⌐ Fishing nearby
🚲 Cycles for hire

Children

⋔ Childrens outdoor play area
➤ Children welcome

Catering

🛒 Foodshop/Mobile foodshop
✕ Restaurant on site

Park Facilities

🚿 Showers available
📞 Public telephone
⊟ Laundry facilities
⊑ Wi-Fi/Internet access
♫ Regular evening entertainment
🐕 Dogs/Pets welcome by arrangement

Camping & Touring Facilities

🚰 Water/waste hookup
🔌 Electrical hook-up points
♨ Calor Gas/Camping Gaz purchase/
   exchange service
🚽 Chemical toilet disposal point

6

The symbols below represent the various awards the self catering property, or camping and caravan park has won and schemes they may belong to.

 Visitor Attraction Quality Scheme
Participating attractions are visited by a professional assessor. High standards in welcome, hospitality, services, presentation; standards of the toilets, shop and café (where provided) must be achieved to receive this VisitEngland award.

Visitor Attraction Quality Scheme Accolades

For top-scoring attractions where visitors can expect a really memorable visit.

For 'going the extra mile', ensuring that visitors are really well looked after.

For small, well run attractions that deserve a special mention.

For innovative and effective interpretation or tour, telling the story to capture visitors' imaginations.

For attractions with cafes and restaurants that consistently exceed expectations.

 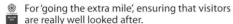 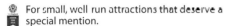 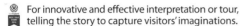 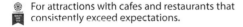

Pets Come Too - accommodation displaying this symbol offer a special welcome to pets. Please check for any restrictions before booking.

Businesses displaying this logo have undergone a rigorous verification process to ensure that they are sustainable (green). See page 25 for further information.

National Accessible Scheme
The National Accessible Scheme includes standards for hearing and visual impairment as well as mobility impairment – see pages 10-11 for further information.

Welcome Schemes
Walkers, cyclists, families and pet owners are warmly welcomed where you see these signs – see page 8 for further information.

Motorway Service Area Assessment Scheme
The star ratings cover a wide range of aspects of each operation including cleanliness, the quality and range of catering and also the quality of the physical aspects, as well as the service provided. – See page 344 for further information.

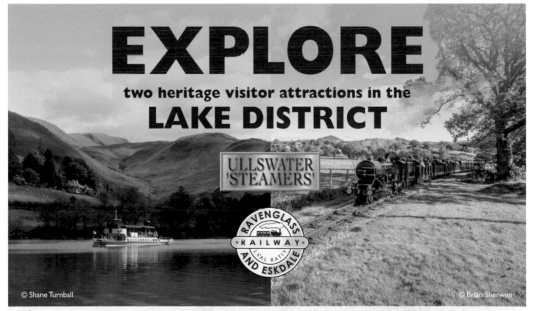

© Shane Turnball   © Brian Sherwen

Explore Ullswater onboard the 'Steamers', that link to some of the most famous and spectacular walking routes in the National Park or climb aboard La'al Ratty and take a journey from the coast to the mountains. Visit one and get 50% off the other*

*on full fare day tickets only

01229 717171 ravenglass-railway.co.uk   017684 82229 ullswater-steamers.co.uk

A special welcome

To help make booking your accommodation easier, VisitEngland has four special Welcome schemes which accommodation in England can be assessed against. Owners participating in these schemes go the extra mile to welcome walkers, cyclists, families or pet owners to their accommodation and provide additional facilities and services to make your stay even more comfortable.

For further information go online at www.qualityintourism.com/quality-schemes/welcome-schemes

Families Welcome

If you are searching for the perfect family holiday, look out for the Families Welcome sign. The sign indicates that the proprietor offers additional facilities and services catering for a range of ages and family units. For families with young children, the accommodation will have special facilities such as cots and highchairs, storage for push-chairs and somewhere to heat baby food or milk. Where meals are provided, children's choices will be clearly indicated, with healthy options also available. They'll have information on local walks, attractions, activities or events suitable for children, as well as local child-friendly pubs and restaurants. However, not all accommodation is able to cater for all ages or combinations of family units, so do remember to check for any restrictions before confirming your booking.

Welcome Pets!

Do you want to travel with your faithful companion? To do so with ease make sure you look out for accommodation displaying the Welcome Pets! sign. Participants in this scheme go out of their way to meet the needs of guests bringing dogs, cats and/or small birds. In addition to providing water and food bowls, torches or nightlights, spare leads and pet washing facilities, they'll buy in pet food on request and offer toys, treats and bedding. They'll also have information on pet-friendly attractions, pubs, restaurants and recreation. Of course, not everyone is able to offer suitable facilities for every pet, so do check if there are any restrictions on the type, size and number of animals before you confirm your booking.

Walkers Welcome

If walking is your passion, seek out accommodation participating in the Walkers Welcome scheme. Facilities include a place for drying clothes and boots, maps and books for reference and a first-aid kit. Packed breakfasts and lunches are available on request in hotels and guesthouses, and you have the option to pre-order basic groceries in self-catering accommodation. On top of this, proprietors provide a wide range of information including public transport, weather forecasts, details of the nearest bank, all night chemists and local restaurants and nearby attractions.

Cyclists Welcome

Are you an explorer on two wheels? If so, seek out accommodation displaying the Cyclists Welcome symbol. Facilities at these properties include a lockable undercover area, a place to dry outdoor clothing and footwear, an evening meal if there are no eating facilities available within one mile and a packed breakfast or lunch on request. Information is also available on cycle hire, cycle repair shops, maps and books for reference, weather forecasts, details of the nearest bank, all night chemists and much much more.

National Accessible Scheme

Finding suitable accommodation is not always easy, especially if you have to seek out rooms with level entry or large print menus. Use the National Accessible Scheme to help you make your choice.

Additional help and guidance on accessible tourism can be obtained from the national charity Tourism for All:

Tourism for All

Tourism for All UK
7A Pixel Mill
44 Appleby Road
Kendal, Cumbria LA9 6ES

Information helpline
0845 124 9971
(lines open 9-5 Mon-Fri)
E info@tourismforall.org.uk
W www.tourismforall.org.uk
   www.openbritain.net

Proprietors of accommodation taking part in the National Accessible Scheme have gone out of their way to ensure a comfortable stay for guests with hearing, visual or mobility needs. These exceptional places are full of extra touches to make everyone's visit trouble-free, from handrails, ramps and step-free entrances (ideal for buggies too) to level-access showers and colour contrast in the bathrooms. Members of staff may have attended a disability awareness course and will know what assistance will really be appreciated.

Appropriate National Accessible Scheme symbols are included in the guide entries (shown opposite). If you have additional needs or specific requirements, we strongly recommend that you make sure these can be met by your chosen establishment before you confirm your reservation. The index at the back of the guide gives a list of accommodation that has received a National Accessible Scheme rating.

For more information on the NAS and tips and ideas on holiday travel in England go to: **www.visitengland.com/accessforall**

The criteria VisitEngland has adopted does not necessarily conform to British Standards or to Building Regulations. They reflect what the organisation understands to be acceptable to meet the practical needs of guests with mobility or sensory impairments and encourage the industry to increase access to all.

England

Mobility Impairment Symbols

Older and less mobile guests
Typically suitable for a person with sufficient mobility to climb a flight of steps but who would benefit from fixtures and fittings to aid balance.

Part-time wheelchair users
Typically suitable for a person with restricted walking ability and for those who may need to use a wheelchair some of the time and can negotiate a maximum of three steps.

Independent wheelchair users
Typically suitable for a person who depends on the use of a wheelchair and transfers unaided to and from the wheelchair in a seated position. This person may be an independent traveller.

Assisted wheelchair users
Typically suitable for a person who depends on the use of a wheelchair and needs assistance when transferring to and from the wheelchair in a seated position.

Access Exceptional is awarded to establishments that meet the requirements of independent wheelchair users or assisted wheelchair users shown above and also fulfil more demanding requirements with reference to the British Standards BS8300.

....

Visual Impairment Symbols

Typically provides key additional services and facilities to meet the needs of visually impaired guests.

Typically provides a higher level of additional services and facilities to meet the needs of visually impaired guests.

....

Hearing Loss Symbols

Typically provides key additional services and facilities to meet the needs of guests with hearing loss.

Typically provides a higher level of additional services and facilities to meet the needs of guests with hearing loss.

Peace of Mind with Star Ratings

Many self-catering properties and camping and caravan parks in England are star rated by VisitEngland. We annually check that our standards are comparable with other British tourist boards to ensure that wherever you visit you receive the same facilities and services at any star rated accommodation.

All the accommodation in this guide is annually checked by VisitEngland assessors and an on site assessment is made every year. This means that when you see the Quality Rose marque promoting the star rating of the property, you can be confident that we've checked it out.

The national standards used to assess accommodation are based on VisitEngland research of consumer expectations. The independent assessors work to strict criteria to check the available facilities. For self-catering, a quality score is awarded for every aspect of the layout and design, ease of use of all the appliances, comfort of the beds, range and quality of kitchen equipment and, most importantly, cleanliness. They also score the range and presentation of the visitor information on offer. For properties that exceed the already high expectations of assessors, a Gold Award may be awarded to recognise the accommodation's excellence.

For Camping, Touring and Holiday Parks, the assessors decide the type (classification) of park – for example if it's a 'touring park', 'holiday park', 'holiday village', etc. – and award a star rating based on over fifty separate aspects, from landscaping and layout to maintenance, customer care and, most importantly, cleanliness.

The Quality Rose marque helps you decide where to stay, giving you peace of mind that the accommodation has been thoroughly checked out before you check in.

Self Catering Accommodation in this Guide

Within this guide you'll find a wide range of accommodation.

A requirement of this category is to be self-contained and have a kitchen so you will always have the option of eating in. NB: this requirement only applies to self-catering accommodation rated 4 star and above and therefore is not applicable to every property listed in this guide.

Holiday Cottages, Houses and Lodges – from cosy country cottages, smart town-centre apartments, seaside villas, grand country houses for large family gatherings, and even quirky windmills, railway carriages and lighthouse conversions. Most take bookings by the week, generally from Friday to Saturdays, but as short breaks are increasing in popularity, accommodation providers often take bookings for shorter periods, particularly outside of the main season.

Holiday Cottage Agencies – these range from small local organisations to large Britain-wide operators. Some agencies organise their own assessments, but the majority use national tourist board quality standards and are gradually bringing all their properties into the star-rating scheme. Many agencies have also been assessed and accredited by VisitEngland to ensure they are well-run and provide excellent customer care. For full details of Holiday Cottage Agencies, see pages 346 to 349.

Boat Accommodation – quality-assessed boats in small and large fleets across England's waterways also offer accommodation. Narrowboats are purpose-built, traditionally decorated boats on canals and rivers and can sleep up to 12 people; Cruisers operate mainly on the Norfolk Broads and the Thames and can range from practical affordable craft, to modern, stylish boats with accessories such as dishwashers, DVD players and flat-screen TV's.

Approved Caravan – approved caravan holiday homes are let as individual self-catering units and can be located on farms or holiday parks. All the facilities, including a bathroom and toilet, are contained within the caravan and all main services are provided. There are no star ratings for these caravans, however, they are assessed annually to check they meet the minimum quality standards.

Alternative Accommodation – Self-catering accommodation with a twist. Alternative accommodation ranges from wigwams or tipis to shepherds' trailers, treehouses or camper vans. Usually located in rural environments this unique style of accommodation allows you to get back to nature. Most proprietors will take bookings for short breaks as well as longer holidays and all facilities are checked to ensure that they meet minimum quality standards, but many are surprisingly luxurious due to the rise in the term 'glamping' (glamorous camping).

All self-catering accommodation is awarded a rating from 1 to 5 stars (apart from Approved Caravans and Alternative Accommodation). All will meet the minimum standards shown below:

- Clear information prior to booking on all aspects of the accommodation including location, facilities, prices, deposit, policies on smoking, children, cancellation, etc.
- No shared facilities, with the exception of a laundry room in multi-unit sites.
- All appliances and furnishings will meet product safety standards for self-catering accommodation, particularly regarding fire safety.
- Clear information on emergency procedures, including who to contact.
- Contact details for the local doctor, dentist, chemist, etc.
- All statutory obligations will be met, including an annual gas safety check and public liability insurance.

The more stars, the higher the quality and the greater the range of facilities and services on offer. For example, a 3-star accommodation must offer bed linen (with or without additional charge) while at a 4-star, all advertised sleeping space will be in bedrooms (unless a studio) and beds will be made up on arrival.

Some self-catering establishments offer a choice of accommodation units that may have different star ratings. In this case, the entry in this guide indicates the star range available.

Always look at or ask for the type of accommodation as each offers a very distinct experience. The parks you'll find in this guide are:

Camping Park – these sites only have pitches available for tents.

Touring Park – sites for your own caravan, motor home or tent.

Holiday Park – sites where you can hire a caravan holiday home for a short break or longer holiday, or even buy your own holiday home. Sites range from small, rural sites to larger parks with added extras, such as a swimming pool.

Many of the above parks will offer a combination of these classifications.

Holiday Villages – usually comprise of a variety of types of accommodation, with the majority in custom-built rooms, for example, chalets. The option to book on a bed and breakfast, or dinner, bed and breakfast basis is normally available. A range of facilities, entertainment and activities are also provided, which may, or may not, be included in the tariff. Holiday Villages must meet minimum requirements for provision and quality of facilities and services, including fixtures, fittings, furnishings, décor and any other extra facilities.

Forest Holiday Village – a holiday village situated in a forest setting with conservation and sustainable tourism being a key feature. Usually offering a variety of accommodation, often purpose built and with a range of entertainment, activities and facilities on site, free of charge or at extra cost.

Star ratings are based on a combination of the range of facilities, level of service offered and quality - if a park offers the facilities required to achieve a certain star rating but does not achieve the quality score required for that rating, a lower star rating is awarded.

A random check is made of a sample of accommodation provided for hire (caravans, chalets, etc) and the quality of the accommodation itself is included in the grading assessment.

Holiday Villages in England are assessed under a separate rating scheme (for details see www.qualityintourism.com).

Also included in this guide are Bunkhouses and Camping Barns – safe, budget-priced, short-term accommodation for individuals and groups.

The more stars, the higher the quality and the greater the range of facilities and level of service. For example, a 2-star park must be clean with good standards of maintenance and customer care, plus improved level of landscaping, lighting, maintenance and refuse disposal. May be less expensive than more highly rated parks. 5-star parks offer the highest level of customer care provided. All facilities will be maintained in pristine condition in attractive surroundings.

Gold Awards

How can you find those special places to stay? VisitEngland's Gold Awards highlight excellence and are given to self-catering accommodation and caravan parks that offer the highest level of quality within their particular star rating. Those that, regardless of the range of facilities and services, achieve exceptional scores for quality. VisitEngland professional assessors make recommendations for Gold Awards during assessments.

For self-catering particular attention is paid to the bedrooms and bathrooms, kitchen, public areas and most importantly the cleanliness. For Camping, Touring and Holiday Parks they look for aspects of exceptional quality in all areas, in particular, cleanliness, facilities and reception.

High star ratings mean top quality in all areas and all the services expected of that classification. Lower star ratings with a Gold Award indicate limited facilities or services, delivered to a standard of high quality.

For self-catering accommodation, Gold Awards are given to individual units on sites with multiple lettings, therefore you should check with the owner before booking if you wish to stay in the unit which has been given the Gold Award.

An index to Gold Award winning self-catering accommodation and camping, touring and holiday parks featured in this guide is given on pages 372 to 373.

VisitEngland
Gold
AWARD

Gold Awards

VisitEngland's unique Gold Awards are given in recognition of exceptional quality in self-catering accommodation.

VisitEngland professional assessors make recommendations for Gold Awards during assessments. They look for aspects of exceptional quality in all areas.

While star ratings are based on a combination of quality, the range of facilities and the level of service offered, Gold Awards are based solely on quality.

For Example a 2 star property with limited facilities but exceptional quality could still achieve the Gold Award status.

Establishments with a Gold Award are featured below. Detailed entries for these properties are also included in the regional pages and can be found using the property index on page 382.

Gold Award Accommodation
with entries in the regional pages

Woodthorpe Hall Country Cottages
Alford, Lincolnshire

Blythe Farmhouse
Alton, Staffordshire

The Old Windmill, Aylsham
Aylsham, Norfolk

Outchester & Ross Farm Cottages
Bamburgh, Northumberland

Greyfield Farm Cottages
Bath, Somerset

Heron Lakes
Beverley, East Yorkshire

Horseshoe Cottage & Bay Tree
Beverley, East Yorkshire

Apartment 5, Burgh Island Causeway
Bigbury-on-Sea, Devon

The Pump House Apartment
Billericay, Essex

Spindle Cottage Holidays
Binegar, Somerset

Rookery Farm Norfolk
Bodham, Norfolk

Over Brandelhow
Borrowdale, Cumbria

Mellwaters Barn
Bowes, Co Durham

Thornthwaite
Broughton-in-Furness, Cumbria

Tamar Valley Cottages
Bude, Cornwall

Whalesborough Cottages & Spa
Bude, Cornwall

Wooldown Holiday
Cottages
Bude, Cornwall

Wychnor Park
Country Club
Burton Upon Trent,
Staffordshire

Lackford Lakes Barns
Bury St. Edmunds,
Suffolk

Pyegreave Cottage
Buxton, Derbyshire

Highfield Farm
Touring Park
Cambridge,
Cambridgeshire

Brackenhill Tower &
Jacobean Cottage
Carlisle, Cumbria

Riding House Farm
Cottages
Castleton, Derbyshire

4* Gold Wharton
Lock Apartment
Chester, Cheshire

Pottery Flat
Chesterfield
Chesterfield,
Derbyshire

Honer Cottage
Chichester, Sussex

Laneside
Chichester, Sussex

The Stables
Cirencester,
Gloucestershire

Craster Tower
Penthouse Apartment
Craster,
Northumberland

Coach Cottage
Cromer, Norfolk

Cromer Country Club
Cromer, Norfolk

Hodges
Crowborough, Sussex

Medley Court -
Hever Castle
Edenbridge, Kent

Log Cabin Holidays
Eye, Suffolk

2 Westgate Barns
Fakenham, Norfolk

Budock Vean
Cottages & Holiday
Homes
Falmouth, Cornwall

Hard Farm Barns
Field Dalling, Norfolk

Prestwick
Self Catering
Godalming, Surrey

Owls roost
Gorran, Cornwall

Mudgeon Vean Farm
Holiday Cottages
Helford, Cornwall

Woodford Bridge
Country Club
Holsworthy, Devon

Cornerside
Hunstanton, Norfolk

Ingleby Manor
Ingleby Greenhow,
North Yorkshire

San Ging Keswick
Keswick, Cumbria

White Heron
Properties
Kington, Herefordshire

Piccadilly
Caravan Park Ltd
Lacock, Wiltshire

Dickman's Cottage
Lambley,
Nottinghamshire

Drws Nesaf,
Metheringham
Lincoln, Lincolnshire

Old Vicarage
Cottages
Lincoln, Lincolnshire

The Apartments
- Chelsea &
Marylebone
London SW3,
Inner London

Church Cottage
Louth, Lincolnshire

Louth Barn
Louth, Lincolnshire

Castle House
Lodgings
Ludlow, Shropshire

Glebe Barn
Ludlow, Shropshire

The Silver Pear
Apartments
Ludlow, Shropshire

Westcott Farm
Holiday Cottages
Luxborough,
Somerset

Home Farm Holiday
Cottages
Malton,
North Yorkshire

Walnut Garth
Malton,
North Yorkshire

Holywell Suite
Malvern,
Worcestershire

Rhydd Barn
Malvern,
Worcestershire

1 The Green
Melton Mowbray,
Leicestershire

Holme House Barn
Mitcheldean,
Gloucestershire

Summer Cottage
Moreton-In-Marsh,
Gloucestershire

Link House Farm
Holiday Cottages
Newton-by-the-Sea,
Northumberland

Woodview Cottages
Nottingham,
Nottinghamshire

Blackthorn Gate
Nunthorpe, North
Yorkshire

Peartree Cottage
Okehampton, Devon

Sunday &
School Cottages
Padstow, Cornwall

Yellow Sands
Cottages
Padstow, Cornwall

Hall Farm Kings
Cliffe
Peterborough,
Northamptonshire

Kale Pot Cottage
Pickering,
North Yorkshire

South Winchester Lodges
Pitt, Hampshire

Rosehill Lodges
Porthtowan, Cornwall

Admiralty Apartments
Portsmouth and Southsea, Hampshire

Mount Pleasant Farm Cottages
Richmond, North Yorkshire

Natural Retreats - Yorkshire Dales
Richmond, North Yorkshire

Upton Grange Holiday Cottages
Ringstead, Dorset

Bruisyard Hall
Saxmundham, Suffolk

Harbourside Apartments
Scarborough, North Yorkshire

The Sands Sea Front Apartments
Scarborough, North Yorkshire

Mount Brioni Holiday Apartments
Seaton, Cornwall

Solely Southwold
Southwold, Suffolk

Trewince Farm Holiday Park
St. Issey, Cornwall

Trethem Mill Touring Park
St. Just in Roseland, Cornwall

20 The Barons
St Margaret's, Outer London

Roundhouse Barn Holidays
St Mawes, Cornwall

Natural Retreats - Trewhiddle
St. Austell, Cornwall

Cornish Holiday Lodges
St. Columb, Cornwall

Larch Loft Self Catering Apartment
Stockbridge, Hampshire

Broad Oak Cottages
Stow-on-the-Wold, Gloucestershire

Stretton Lakes
Stretton, Rutland

Long Cover Cottage & The Coach House
Sutton, Worcestershire

Rochford Park Cottages
Tenbury Wells, Worcestershire

Long Barn Luxury Holiday Cottages
Torquay, Devon

Aish Cross Holiday Cottages
Totnes, Devon

Hartsop Fold Holiday Lodges
Ullswater, Cumbria

Pear Tree Cottages
Wedmore, Somerset

Seascape
Westward Ho!, Devon

Forest Lodge Farm
Whitby, North Yorkshire

Lemon Cottage
Whitby, North Yorkshire

Church Farm Barns
Wickmere, Norfolk

Park Cliffe Camping & Caravan Estate
Windermere, Cumbria

Hop Pickers Rural Retreats
Worcester, Worcestershire

The Blue Rooms
York, North Yorkshire

Minster's Reach Apartments
York, North Yorkshire

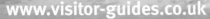

CARBIS BAY
HOTEL, SPA & ESTATE

WINNER - BEST LARGE HOTEL OF THE YEAR
Cornwall Tourism Awards 2015/16

LUXURY HOTEL & SPA

Carbis Bay Hotel, Spa & Estate, Carbis Bay, St Ives, Cornwall, TR26 2NP
01736 795311   info@carbisbayhotel.co.uk   www.carbisbayhotel.co.uk

Cornwall Tourism Awards 2015/16
GOLD LARGE HOTEL OF THE YEAR

Cornwall Tourism Awards 2015/16
SILVER VENUE & BUSINESS TOURISM

the good spa guide AWARDS 2015 WINNER Best for Romance

PROFESSIONAL **beauty** 2016 FINALIST *Awards*

5 **bubble** spa 2015

WINNER BUSINESS AWARDS

CORNWALL LIFE food & drink AWARDS **2014** WINNER Best Hotel Restaurant

VisitEngland Awards for Excellence

A warm welcome and a great night out was anticipated when it was announced that NewcastleGateshead were set to host VisitEngland's 2015 Awards for Excellence and guests at this prestigious annual celebration were not disappointed. The coming together of a signature destination, the Sage Gateshead, and the best that tourism in England can offer was a heady mix. With fifteen categories featuring amazing experiences and top quality establishments the winners epitomised the care, attention and customer-centric approach that England's tourism businesses deliver in droves.

The Awards are open to all businesses that meet the category criteria and operators from across the country compete for a place on a roll of honour which spans 26 years of excellence in tourism. This year a panel of expert judges considered 345 entries and you can find a full list of the winners at www.visitenglandawards.org

Self-catering accommodation has come of age in England with a quality experience to suit every occasion.

Silver Award winning Millbrook Cottages in North Devon offer wonderfully romantic breaks for couples in four sumptuous 5* Gold cottages sitting in a 32 acre estate which comes complete with nature trails, flower meadows, fishing lakes, a magical woodland hot tub and a summer house perfect for private dining or even weddings. Magical memories are guaranteed for families staying at Bronze Award Winner: The Dandelion Hideaway in Leicestershire's Market Bosworth. Luxury glamping in canvas cottages with country home interiors and ensuite roll top baths all set in picturesque countryside evoke halcyon days and the complementary programme of hands-on activities, including hen keeping, milking goats and grooming Shetland ponies make this a unique stay.

Close to York, The Dovecote Barns offer self-catering for larger groups. With a commitment to continuous improvement, a stay at this beautiful environmentally friendly location guarantees comfort without compromise to guests or the environment. Yorkshires Heritage Coast is renowned for headlands, coves and sandy beaches and all this is within reach for guests choosing to stay at High Barn in Bempton, East Yorkshire. This fifth generation family business combines farming and tourism and offers superb cottages in delightful surroundings. Assured comfort, top end luxury and tranquillity underpinned by attentive customer care are offered in beautifully restored historic buildings.

This year's Gold Award winner, Bosinver Farm Cottages, offer 20 detached luxurious cottages, lovingly furnished and equipped with everything needed for carefree family holidays. Guests say that it's the attention to detail and passion for outdoor play which sets them apart and with an indoor pool and Wild Kids adventures on offer lifetime memories are guaranteed to be made.

This year's Caravan and Holiday Park Gold Award winner is set in the glorious Golden Valley in Herefordshire. Catering for all types of holiday from a one man tent, caravan, motor home self-catering or your own luxury Holiday Home Postin Mill Park, set in 35 acres, offers a luxury 5 star Gold holiday experience.

Trenthem Mill Touring Park is a multi-award winning tourism park which nestles in a valley on the Roseland Peninsula, an area of outstanding natural beauty, at St Just-in-Roseland in Cornwall. Owned and run by three generations of the same family the emphasis is on providing a safe, quiet and peaceful park with spotlessly clean and modern facilities all of which earned them the Silver Award for Excellence.

The much loved Seafield Caravan Park at Seahouses in Northumberland, which took the Bronze Award for Excellence, offers peace, tranquillity, stunning coastal scenery, breath-taking sea views and miles of golden, sandy beaches. Providing 5 star luxury accommodation, a pool, spa, gym and fitness studio, this family operated park aims to offer guests richer, longer lasting experiences.

For over 80 years Searles Leisure Resort in Hunstanton, Norfolk, has developed and invested in premier tourism, camping and holiday home facilities. Two on

resort golf courses, bowls and fishing lakes along with an adjacent safe sandy beach affords Searles a super location and the excellent service which ensure guests return year after year.

Celebrating 40 years of providing a warm welcome, Cofton Country Holidays near Dawlish, Devon ensures its loyal guests continue to enjoy the best of facilities. Recent investment in the park includes new all-weather touring pitches and the addition of an indoor leisure, dining and events complex. Cofton is also known for its on-site fishing lakes and wide range of accommodation options.

Cofton Country Holiday Park

Holiday Park/Holiday Village of the Year – Highly Commended

Set within 80 acres of glorious Devon countryside, the family-run Cofton Country Holiday Park celebrated its 40th anniversary in 2015, safe in the knowledge that guests return year after year to enjoy the beautiful and convenient location, extensive facilities and wide choice of accommodation.

The award-winning 4-star graded park is 20 minutes from the M5 motorway, making it the ideal place for family holidays in Devon. Dawlish Warren beach is a 30-minute walk away through scenic nature trails, and the many attractions of South Devon, Exeter and Dartmoor are all within easy reach.

Valerie and George Jeffery purchased the park in 1975 when it was an old dairy farm and the camping and touring caravan site was just a sideline. The couple have since retired and their four children – Roger, Chris, Helen, and Mellony – now run the business.

"The holiday park has grown so much and is very different from when my parents bought it," said Mellony Kirby. *"Back then it really was just a farmhouse with sheds and fields."*

Today there are 72 holiday homes for letting and another 10 privately owned ones, plus 450 touring and camping pitches. The site also has 17 cottages and holiday apartments located within Eastdon House, a Georgian building set away from the main park yet close enough to still enjoy its facilities and entertainment.

The task of running such a successful holiday park like Cofton takes a lot of hard work and planning by the Jeffery family. Roger is the eldest and he heads up the grounds with his wife Lynda helping. Helen works in reception, overseeing the important task of greeting and checking-in visitors, and also deals with HR matters. Mellony looks after the accounts and marketing, while Chris oversees the leisure complex and kitchens.

"We all have our own areas but we make sure we work alongside each other so we can make decisions together," adds Mellony.

"Being a family-run business is one of our strengths. We are all passionate about Cofton and making sure we give our customers a great experience whilst on holiday. Being able to make decisions and changes that are important to us is key and allows us to be flexible without having to answer to anybody else."

> "The holiday park has grown so much and is very different from when my parents bought it, back then it really was just a farmhouse with sheds and fields"
>
> Mellony Kirby

The range of facilities available is another of strength of the park and the family is always looking for more things to add to the Cofton Experience. The leisure complex, completed in July 2012, has an indoor pool, sauna, steam room and gym. The building also houses Amelia's Café and the Warren Retreat Restaurant, children's soft play area and arcade complete with bowling and pool. Elsewhere on site there are outdoor swimming pools, coarse fishing lakes, shop, pub, take-away and laundrettes.

Being highly commended in the Holiday Park/Holiday Village of the Year in the VisitEngland Excellence Awards was a huge boost for Cofton.

"It gave us and our staff recognition for all the hard work we put in and to be recognised as one of the best from across the country is an amazing feeling," says Mellony. "To be able to put this on our marketing gives us a seal of approval that we feel our customers will appreciate and help them make that decision to choose us for their next holiday."

Cofton was the choice of Kirsty Nickson, from Chippenham in Wiltshire, when she won a £500 Golden Ticket competition in last year's VisitEngland Camping, Touring & Holiday Parks Guide.

Kirsty took her family and touring caravan to Cofton in August and had a fantastic holiday. "We had a wonderful time," admits Kirsty. "The site was very clean and tidy, and the new indoor pool was one of the best we have experienced – lovely and warm, with clean changing rooms."

"The clubhouse had a good range of entertainment for all ages, and the food in the restaurant was reasonably priced, well presented and very tasty."

"The star of the site for us was Rolly, the park's fishing instructor. He was wonderful. As a family we spent a whole day learning to fish."

"We loved our stay at Cofton and are already planning to return."

Contact details: Cofton Country Holiday Park, tel 01626 890111, www.coftonholidays.co.uk

David Bellamy *Conservation Award*

2015/16
DAVID BELLAMY
CONSERVATION AWARD
GOLD

'These well-deserved awards are a signpost to parks which are making real achievements in protecting our environment. Go there and experience wrap-around nature ... you could be amazed at what you find!' says Professor David Bellamy.

541gold, silver and bronze parks were named in the 2015/16 David Bellamy Conservation Awards, organised in conjunction with the British Holiday and Home Parks Association.

These parks are recognised for their commitment to conservation and the environment through their management of landscaping, recycling policies, waste management, the cultivation of flora and fauna and the creation of habitats designed to encourage a variety of wildlife onto the park. Links with the local community and the use of local materials are also important considerations.

Parks wishing to enter for a David Bellamy Conservation Award must complete a detailed questionnaire covering different aspects of their environmental policies, and describe what positive conservation steps they have taken. The park must also undergo an independent audit from a local wildlife or conservation body which is familiar with the area. Final assessments and the appropriate level of any award are then made personally by Professor Bellamy.

An index of award-winning parks featured in the regional pages of this guide can be found on page 368.

Sustainable Tourism in England

More and more operators of accommodation, attractions and events in England are becoming aware of sustainable or "green" issues and are acting more responsibly in their businesses. But how can you be sure that businesses that 'say' they're green, really are?

Who certifies green businesses?

There are a number of green certification schemes that assess businesses for their green credentials. VisitEngland only promotes those that have been checked out to ensure they reach the high standards expected. The members of those schemes we have validated are truly sustainable (green) businesses and appear amongst the pages of this guide with our heart-flower logo on their entry.

 Businesses displaying this logo have undergone a rigorous verification process to ensure that they are sustainable (green) and that a qualified assessor has visited the premises.

At the moment we promote the largest green scheme in the world - Green Tourism Business Scheme (GTBS) - and the Peak District Environmental Quality Mark.

Peak District Environmental Quality Mark

This certification mark can only be achieved by businesses that actively support good environmental practices in the Peak District National Park. When you buy a product or service that has been awarded the Environmental Quality Mark, you can be confident that your purchase directly supports the high-quality management of the special environment of the Peak District National Park.

Green Tourism Business Scheme

 Green Tourism is the market leading sustainable certification programme for the tourism sector in the UK and Internationally. From small bed and breakfasts to large visitor attractions and activity holiday providers. A Green Tourism Award means that a business works responsibly, ethically and sustainably, contributes to their community, is reducing their impact on the environment and aims to be accessible and inclusive to all visitors and staff.

With over 2,100 Green Tourism businesses all independently inspected graded Bronze, Silver or Gold they identify businesses that are really making a difference, so you can choose the greenest option with confidence.

How are these businesses being green?

Any business that has been certified 'green' will have implemented initiatives that contribute to reducing their negative environmental and social impacts whilst trying to enhance the economic and community benefits to their local area.

Many of these things may be behind the scenes such as energy efficient boilers, insulated lofts or grey water recycling, but there are many fun activities that you can expect to find too. For example, your green business should be able to advise you about traditional activities nearby, the best places to sample local food and buy craft products, or even help you to enjoy a 'car-free' day out.

The Dovecote Barns

The Dovecote Barns is the perfect place to combine a spot of idylic countryside living with a cultural trip to the historic city of York. The property, owned and run by husband and wife team Richard and Brigita Bramley, was previously derelict farm buildings, but now offers guests *"comfort without compromise"* during their self-catering holiday break.

The five-star accommodation consists of three barns adjacent to a working arable farm and quiet open countryside, and is located 20 minutes from York city centre. The barns sleep two, four and six people, and one of them is equipped to dine a large group of 12 adults when all the accommodation is rented together.

There is an ongoing commitment by the owners to provide an exceptional and welcoming customer service, which promotes the wellbeing of the guests.

"We aim to offer a beautiful place to stay plus a break tailored to guests' individual needs - whether that be homemade gluten free bread in our Yorkshire themed welcome basket, mobility aids for guests or hand-chopped kindling and logs for the wood burners," says Brigita.

The husband and wife team live on-site and are on hand 24/7 to cater for every need. They operate a 'continuous improvement' ethos, which is demonstrated in their multi-award winning history since opening seven years ago.

"We really enjoy what we do," adds Brigita. *"We genuinely love meeting people and welcoming them to stay with us. We want them to enjoy themselves and unwind and get the best out of their stay. That is why we see a high percentage of repeat business."*

"We place a lot of importance on attention to detail. The expectation from guests when booking a five-star property these days is that they will experience a five-star stay. We cater for every eventuality and make sure all fixtures and fittings are in top working order and condition."

Brigita and Richard encourage feedback from guests because it helps them to judge whether they are doing the right thing.

Brigita is involved day-to-day with all the activities that help promote and maintain the business, from website management and marketing, to cleaning and laundering. She employs two helpers on changeover days, which are normally twice weekly.

Her typical day involves dipping into many activities. She starts by checking and replying to emails first thing, before making homemade bread for the welcome baskets twice a week. Then there's the cleaning and making up of the barns, doing the laundering and ironing, and shopping for supplies for the next changeover. At the end of the day she will take care of the accounts, and process enquiries, bookings, receipts and invoices.

The Dovecote Barns are at the forefront of sustainable tourism, having been awarded Green Tourism Gold status. Features include recycling and composting facilities, an electric car charging station, and a purpose-built communal eco-laundry room. The welcome baskets also include a selection of Yorkshire and locally grown produce as well as the homemade brown bread.

The property was Highly Commended in the Self Catering Holiday Provider of the Year category at the VisitEngland Awards for Excellence, recognition that means a lot to the owners.

"It not only reassures us that we have got a winning recipe for what we offer, but also displays publicly that our high standards have been maintained over the years," says Brigita.

"Having monitored our web traffic, the hits received to our site from the visitenglandawards.org website are in our top five referrals list."

"For guests searching for luxury places to stay, it gives us the credibility factor. They know they will not be disappointed."

Contact details:
The Dovecote Barns York, tel 01757 249332; email enquiries@dovecotebarnsyork.co.uk; website www.dovecotebarnsyork.co.uk

Don't Miss...

Eden Project

St. Austell, Cornwall PL24 2SG
(01726) 811911
www.edenproject.com
Explore your relationship with nature at the world famous Eden Project, packed with projects and exhibits about climate and the environment, regeneration, conservation and sustainable living. Be inspired by cutting-edge buildings, stunning year round garden displays, world-class sculpture and art, as well as fabulous music and arts events. See all the sights and immerse yourself in nature with a walk among the the treetops on the Rainforest Canopy Walk or a ride on the land train.

Paignton Zoo

Paignton, Devon TQ4 7EU
(0844) 474 2222
www.paigntonzoo.org.uk
One of Britain's top wildilfe attractions, Paignton Zoo has all the usual suspects with an impressive collection of lions, tigers, gorillas, orangutans, rhinos and giraffes. It is also home to some of the planet's rarest creatures and plants too. For a day jam-packed with family fun and adventure there's Monkey Heights, the crocodile swamp, an amphibian ark and a miniature train, as well as the hands-on interactve Discovery Centre.

Roman Bath

Bath, Somerset BA1 1LZ
(01225) 477785
www.romanbaths.co.uk
Bathe in the naturally hot spa water at the magnificent baths built by the romans, indulge in a gourmet getaway, or enjoy a romantic weekend exploring the wealth of historic architecture. You can find all of this in the beautiful city of Bath and attractions such as Longleat Safari Park and Stonehenge are all within easy reach too.

Sherborne Castle & Gardens

Sherborne, Dorset DT9 5NR
(01935) 812072
www.sherbornecastle.com
Built by Sir Walter Raleigh in c1594, the castle reflects various styles from the Elizabethan hall to the Victorian solarium, with splendid collections of art, furniture and porcelain. The grounds around the 50-acre lake were landscaped by 'Capability' Brown and the 30 acres of tranquil lakeside gardens are the perfect place to escape.

Stonehenge

Amesbury, Wiltshire SP4 7DE
(0870) 333 1181
www.english-heritage.org.uk/stonehenge
The Neolithic site of Stonehenge in Wiltshire is one of the most famous megalithic monuments in the world, the purpose of which is still largely only guessed at. This imposing archaeological site is often ascribed mystical or spiritual associations and receives thousands of visitors from all over the world each year.

South West

Cornwall & Isles of Scilly, Devon, Dorset,
Gloucestershire, Somerset, Wiltshire

A spectacular combination of ancient countryside and glorious coastline, Britain's South West is its most popular holiday area. It stretches from the soft stone and undulating hills of the Cotswolds in the north, through Wiltshire with its historic monuments, to the wild moors, turquoise waters, golden sands and pretty harbours of Dorset, Devon and Cornwall. The beauty of this region and all it has to offer never fails to delight.

Gloucestershire

Wiltshire

Somerset

Devon   Dorset

Cornwall

Explore – South West

Cornwall

Spectacular turquoise seas and white sands dotted with fishing harbours, beautiful gardens and the remnants of Cornwall's fascinating industrial heritage draw visitors from far and wide. The pounding waves to be found along the coastline attract surfers from all over to the world famous beaches around Newquay and make Cornwall a mecca for watersports enthusiasts of all kinds.

The majestic and largely untouched wilderness of Bodmin Moor is only one example of the rich natural environment that can be found here, with miles of walking paths criss-crossing the impressive landscape. This walkers paradise has something for everyone, with The Cornish Way - over 200 miles of inter-linking trails connecting Bude to Land's End – and the spectacular 300 mile long South West Coast Path National Trail with its beautiful views of secluded coves, sandy beaches and jaw-dropping cliffs.

West Cornwall's captivating light and landscape has intrigued and inspired artists since the early 19th century. St Ives is at the heart of today's vibrant art scene, with local arts and crafts galleries rubbing shoulders with international stars such as the Tate St Ives and the Barbara Hepworth Museum and Sculpture Garden.

Cornwall also has a diverse history reaching back to prehistoric, Celtic and medieval roots and there are a huge number of heritage attractions in this corner of the country. St Michael's Mount is an ancient island of myth and legend, Tintagel Castle overlooks the dramatic windswept Atlantic coast, while Grade I listed Port Eliot House & Gardens is a hidden gem nestling beside a secret estuary near Saltash.

Devon

Take a hike or a mountain bike and discover the rugged beauty of Exmoor, explore the drama of the craggy coastline, or catch a wave on some of the region's best surf beaches. North Devon is also rich in heritage with many stately homes and historic attractions including Hartland Abbey and the picturesque Clovelly village, where the steep pedestrianised cobbled main street, takes you to a beautiful deep-blue harbour.

Stunningly beautiful, Dartmoor is perhaps the most famous of Devon's National Parks and offers miles of purple, heather-clad moorland, rushing rivers and stone tors. Walk the length and breadth of the moor or cycle the Drake's Trail, where you'll come across wild ponies and plenty of moorland pubs, perfect for a well earned rest. Head east and discover the imposing Blackdown Hills Area of Outstanding Natural Beauty, stopping off in one of the area's picture-postcard villages for a delicious Devon Cream Tea.

Plymouth is famous for its seafaring heritage, with Plymouth Hoe as the backdrop for Sir Francis Drake's legendary game of bowls, as well as being one of the most beautiful natural harbours in the world. Climb Smeaton's Tower for the incredible views if you're feeling energetic, visit the world-famous Plymouth Gin Distillery at Sutton Harbour, or take the kids to the National Marine Aquarium for an afternoon of fishy fun.

Torquay, gateway to the English Riviera, boasts elegant Victorian villas, iconic palm trees, a sweeping sandy beach and a rich maritime history. Paignton offers great days out including its famous zoo, and the traditional fishing harbour of Brixham is awash with seafood restaurants, waterside pubs and cafés. This whole area is also home to a huge selection of beaches from small, romantic coves to larger, award-winning stretches. The Jurassic Coast is a UNESCO World Heritage Site which stretches for 95 miles along the Devon/Dorset coast, revealing 185 million years of geology and is a must for visitors to the South West.

Dorset

Stretching from historic Lyme Regis in the west to Christchurch in the east, and including a number of designated heritage areas, the whole Dorset coastline is a treasure trove of geology. Interesting landforms are plentiful - Durdle Door, Lulworth Cove, the Isle of Portland with the famous Portland Bill lighthouse and the shingle bank of Chesil Beach to name but a few. Weymouth and Portland are two of the best sailing locations in Europe and offer water sports galore, as well as pretty harbours. For traditional English seaside resorts visit Victorian Swanage, or Bournemouth with its fine sandy beach, perfect for families.

Inland, enchanting market towns, quaint villages and rolling countryside play host to delightful shops, museums, family attractions, historic houses and beautiful gardens such as the Sub-Tropical Gardens at Abbotsbury. Explore Dorset's natural beauty on foot or by bicycle at Stoborough Heath and Hartland Moor nature reserves.

Gloucestershire

A perfect base for for touring the Cotswolds, Cheltenham is an elegant spa town of Regency town houses and leafy squares, award winning gardens and an array of impressive sporting and cultural events such as The Cheltenham Gold Cup or The Cheltenham Festival of music.

Tewkesbury, famous for its fine half-timbered buildings, alleyways and 12th Century Norman Abbey, is one of the best medieval townscapes in England. Enjoy a riverside stroll along the River Severn or a boat trip along the Avon. Grade I listed Sudeley Castle & Gardens, set against the dramatic backdrop of the Cotswolds, is well worth a visit and at the centre of the Severn Vale, Gloucester is a vibrant and multicultural city with an impressive cathedral. It combines historic architecture with numerous visitor attractions, quirky shops and mouth-watering tearooms, restaurants and pubs, and is only a stone's throw from the ancient woodlands of Forest of Dean.

Somerset & Bristol

The maritime city of Bristol is packed with historic attractions, exciting events and fabulous festivals. Cabot Circus offers first class shopping, while stylish restaurants and cafés on the Harbourside serve up locally produced food to tempt and delight. Out and about, Isambard Kingdom Brunel's Clifton Suspension Bridge and the Bristol Zoo Gardens are firm favourites.

Topped by the tower of the ruined 15th Century church, Glastonbury Tor is the stuff of myth and legend, rising high above the Somerset Levels near the delightful town of Glastonbury. Believed to be the site of a Saxon fortress, it has breathtaking views reaching to Wells, the Mendips and the Bristol Channel in the North, Shepton Mallet and Wiltshire in the East, South to the Polden Hills and to the Quantocks and Exmoor in the West.

Wiltshire

Surrounded by stunning scenery and home to a magnificent Cathedral, a wealth of heritage and cultural, dining and shopping venues, the medieval city of Salisbury is the jewel in the crown of South West England's rural heartland.

Further afield you can find an abundance of quintessential English market towns and villages. Marlborough, famed for its charming high street and independent shops, is stylish and sophisticated with a cosmopolitan café culture, while Wilton, the ancient capital of Wessex, is home to Wilton House and a beautiful Italianate Church.

OFFICIAL TOURIST BOARD POCKET GUIDE

Walkers & Cyclists Welcome

England's star-rated great places to stay and visit

The **OFFICIAL** and most comprehensive guide to England's independently inspected, star-rated guest accommodation specialising in Walkers and Cyclists.

Hotels • Bed & Breakfast • Self-catering • Camping, Touring & Holiday Parks

- Regional round ups, attractions, ideas and other tourist information
- National Accessible Scheme accommodation at a glance
- Web-friendly features for easy booking

www.visitor-guides.co.uk

Visit – South West

 Attractions with this sign participate in the Visitor Attraction Quality Assurance Scheme.

Cornwall

Blue Reef Aquarium
Newquay, Cornwall TR7 1DU
(01637) 878134
www.bluereefaquarium.co.uk
*Over 40 naturally themed habitats take you on a
fantastic journey from Cornish waters to exotic seas.*

Boardmasters
Trebelsue Farm, Watergate Bay, Cornwall TR8 4AN
www.boardmasters.co.uk
*Europe's largest surf and music festival, takes place
at Fistral Beach and Watergate Bay in early August.*

Cornwall Film Festival
November, Cornwall
www.cornwallfilmfestival.com
A month long festival of fabulous films.

Cornwall's Crealy Great Adventure Park
Wadebridge, Cornwall PL27 7RA
(01841) 540276
www.crealy.co.uk/cornwall
*Enter the magical land of Cornwall's Crealy and hold
on tight for a thrilling ride.*

Crantock Bale Push
September, Crantock, nr Newquay
www.balepush.co.uk
Teams pushing giant hay bales around the village.

Lost Gardens of Heligan
St. Austell, Cornwall PL26 6EN
(01726) 845100
www.heligan.com
*An exploration through Victorian Productive Gardens
& Pleasure Grounds, a sub-tropical Jungle and more.*

Minack Theatre
Porthcurno, Cornwall TR19 6JU
(01736) 810181
www.minack.com
Cornwall's world famous Minack open-air theatre.

National Maritime Museum Cornwall
Falmouth, Cornwall TR11 3QY
(01326) 313388
www.nmmc.co.uk
Award-winning museum with something for everyone.

National Seal Sanctuary
Helston, Cornwall TR12 6UG
(01326) 221361
www.sealsanctuary.co.uk
*The National Seal Sanctuary rescues, rehabilitates and
releases over 40 seal pups a year.*

Newquay Fish Festival
September, Newquay, Cornwall
www.newquayfishfestival.co.uk
*Three days celebrating Newquay harbour and
delightful fresh local produce.*

Newquay Zoo
Newquay, Cornwall TR7 2LZ
(01637) 873342
www.newquayzoo.org.uk
*Multi-award winning Zoo set in sub-tropical lakeside
gardens and home to over 130 species of animals.*

Royal Cornwall Show
June, Wadebridge, Cornwall, PL27 7JE
www.royalcornwallshow.org
*A fascinating glimpse into rural life, enjoy 3 days of
Cornish heritage, entertainment, displays and fairs.*

St Michaels Mount
Marazion, Cornwall TR17 0HS
(01736) 710265
www.stmichaelsmount.co.uk
*Explore the amazing island world and discover legend,
myth and over a thousand years of incredible history.*

Tate St Ives
St. Ives, Cornwall TR26 1TG
(01736) 796226
www.tate.org.uk
*An introduction to modern and contemporary art,
including works from the Tate Collection.*

Devon

The Agatha Christie Festival
September, Torquay, Devon
www.agathachristiefestival.co.uk
Celebrate the world's most famous crime writer, Dame Agatha Christie. A literary festival with a murder mystery twist!

Bicton Park Botanical Gardens
Budleigh Salterton, EX9 7BJ
(01395) 568465
www.bictongardens.co.uk
Magnificent gardens, streams, woodlands and features. Take a walk through the arboretum before a relaxing meal at the Orangery Restaurant.

Bournemouth Air Festival
August, Bournemouth, Devon
www.bournemouthair.co.uk
Free four-day seafront air show.

Brixham Pirate Festival
May, Brixham, Devon
www.brixhampirates.com
Brixham turns pirate with live music, games, re-enactments, skirmishes on the Golden Hind.

Clovelly Village
(01237) 431781
www.clovelly.co.uk
Most visitors consider Clovelly to be unique. Whatever your view, it is a world of difference not to be missed.

Custom House Visitor Centre
Exeter, Devon EX2 4AN
(01392) 271611
www.exeter.gov.uk/customhouse
Discover the history of Exeter in 15 minutes at the Quay House Visitor Centre on Exeter's Historic Quayside.

Dartmouth Castle
Dartmouth, Devon TQ6 0JN
(01803) 833588
www.english-heritage.org.uk/dartmouthcastle
For over six hundred years Dartmouth Castle has guarded the narrow entrance to the Dart Estuary and the busy, vibrant port of Dartmouth.

Dartmouth Steam Railway
Queens Park Station, Torbay Road, Paignton TQ4 6A
(01803) 555872
www.dartmouthrailriver.co.uk
Running Paignton along the spectacular Torbay coast and through the wooded slopes bordering the Dart estuary, with stunning scenery and seascapes.

Escot Gardens, Maze & Forest Adventure
Ottery St. Mary, Devon EX11 1LU
(01404) 822188
www.escot-devon.co.uk
Historical gardens and fantasy woodland surrounding the ancestral home of the Kennaway family.

Fishstock
September, Brixham, Devon
www.fishstockbrixham.co.uk
A one-day festival of seafood and entertainment held in Brixham.

Hartland Abbey & Gardens
(01237) 441496/234
www.hartlandabbey.com
Hartland Abbey is a family home full of history in a beautiful valley leading to a wild Atlantic cove.

Ilfracombe Aquarium
Ilfracombe, Devon EX34 9EQ
(01271) 864533
www.ilfracombeaquarium.co.uk
A fascinating journey of discovery into the aquatic life of North Devon.

Kents Cavern
Torquay TQ1 2JF
01803 215136
www.kents-cavern.co.uk
Kents Cavern is one of Europe's top prehistoric Stone Age caves with an extensive labyrinth of spectacular and easily accessible caverns open daily all year.

Plymouth City Museum and Art Gallery
Devon PL4 8AJ
(01752) 304774
www.plymouth.gov.uk/museumpcmag.htm
The museum presents a diverse range of contemporary exhibitions, from photography to textiles, modern art to natural history.

Dorset

Athelhampton House and Gardens
Athelhampton, Dorchester, Dorset DT2 7LG
(01305) 848363
www.athelhampton.co.uk
One of the finest 15th century Houses in England nestled in the heart of the picturesque Piddle Valley.

Christchurch Food and Wine Festival
May, Christchurch, Dorset BH23 1AS
www.christchurchfoodfest.co.uk
Celebrity chefs, over 100 trade stands, culinary treats, cookery theatres and some eminent food critics.

Corfe Castle Model Village and Gardens
Corfe Castle, Dorset BH20 5EZ
(01929) 481234
www.corfecastlemodelvillage.co.uk
Detailed 1/20th scale model of Corfe Castle and village before its destruction by Cromwell.

Dorset County Museum
Dorchester, Dorset, DT1 1XA
(01305) 257180
www.dorsetcountymuseum.org
Follow Dorset through time; visit the nostalgic Victorian Gallery, walk on real Roman mosaic floors and discover the dinosaurs that roamed the lands and seas.

Dorset Knob Throwing Festival
May, Cattistock, nr Dorchester, Dorset
www.dorsetknobthrowing.com
World famous quirky festival.

Forde Abbey & Gardens
Chard, Dorset TA20 4LU
(01460) 220231
www.fordeabbey.co.uk
Founded 850 years ago, Forde Abbey was converted into a private house in c.1649.

Larmer Tree Festival
July, Cranborne Chase, North Dorset
(01725) 552300
www.larmertreefestival.co.uk
Boutique festival featuring over 70 diverse artists, a comedy club, street theatre, carnival procession.

Lulworth Castle & Park
Wareham, Dorset BH20 5QS
0845 450 1054
www.lulworth.com
Enjoy historic buildings & stunning landscapes.

Lyme Regis Fossil Festival
May, Lyme Regis, Dorset
www.fossilfestival.co.uk
A natural science and arts cultural extravaganza on the UNESCO World Heritage Jurassic Coast.

Portland Castle
Portland, Dorset DT5 1AZ
(01305) 820539
www.english-heritage.org.uk/portland
Coastal fort built by Henry VIII to defend Weymouth.

Sherborne Abbey Music Festival
April - May, Sherborne, Dorset
www.sherborneabbeyfestival.org
Five days of music performed by both nationally acclaimed artists and gifted young musicians.

Sturminster Newton Cheese Festival
September, Sturminster, Dorset
www.cheesefestival.co.uk
A celebration of the region's dairy heritage.

Swanage Regatta
July - August, Swanage, Dorset
www.swanagecarnival.com
The South's premier carnival.

Bristol

At-Bristol
Bristol BS1 5DB
(0845) 345 1235
www.at-bristol.org.uk
21st century science and technology centre, with hands-on activities, interactive exhibits.

Avon Valley Railway
Bristol BS30 6HD
(0117) 932 5538
www.avonvalleyrailway.org
Much more than your average steam train ride. A whole new experience or a nostalgic memory.

The Bristol Hippodrome
Bristol, BS1 4UZ
(01173) 023310
www.atgtickets.com/venues/bristol-hippodrome
One of the country's top provincial theatres, staging major West End and Broadway productions.

Bristol Zoo Gardens
Bristol BS8 3HA
(0117) 974 7300
www.bristolzoo.org.uk
Your passport for a day trip into an amazing world of animals, exhibits and other attractions.

Brunel's SS Great Britain
Bristol BS1 6TY
(0117) 926 0680
www.ssgreatbritain.org
Award-winning attraction showing the world's first great ocean liner and National Brunel Archive.

City Sightseeing The Bristol Tour
Central Bristol BS1 4AH
(03333) 210101
www.citysightseeingbristol.co.uk
Open-top bus tours, with guides and headphones, around the city of Bristol. Runs daily through summer.

Gloucestershire

Chavenage
Chavenage, Tetbury, Gloucestershire GL8 8XP
(01666) 502329
Elizabethan Manor Chavenage House, a TV/ Film location is still a family home, offers unique experiences, with history, ghosts and more.

Corinium Museum
Cirencester, Gloucestershire GL7 2BX
(01285) 655611
www.coriniummuseum.org
Discover the treasures of the Cotswolds as you explore its history at this award winning museum.

Forest Food Showcase
October, Forest of Dean, Gloucestershire
www.forestshowcase.org
A celebration of the foods and fruits of the forest. Held at Speech House on the first Sunday in October.

Gloucester Cathedral
Gloucestershire GL1 2LX
(01452) 528095
www.gloucestercathedral.org.uk
A place of worship and an architectural gem.

Gloucester Waterways Museum
Gloucester GL1 2EH
(01452) 318200
Closed for refurbishment, opens summer 2016. A Victorian warehouse, interactive displays and galleries.

Hidcote Manor Garden
Chipping Campden, Gloucestershire GL55 6LR
(01386) 438333
www.nationaltrust.org.uk/hidcote
Rare trees and shrubs, outstanding herbaceous borders and unusual plants from all over the world.

Painswick Rococo Garden
Painswick, Gloucestershire GL6 6TH
(01452) 813204
www.rococogarden.org.uk
A fascinating step back to a flamboyant and sensual period of English Garden Design

Sudeley Castle Gardens and Exhibition
Winchcombe, Gloucestershire GL54 5JD
(01242) 602308
www.sudeleycastle.co.uk
Award-winning gardens surrounding Castle and medieval ruins.

Westonbirt, The National Arboretum
Tetbury, Gloucestershire GL8 8QS
(01666) 880220
www.forestry.gov.uk/westonbirt
600 acres with one of the finest collections of trees.

Somerset

Bridgwater Arts Centre
Bridgwater, Somerset, TA6 3DD
(01278) 422700
www.bridgwaterartscentre.co.uk
A beautiful Georgian building; be entertained by one of the evening shows, relax in the cosy bar, or stroll through the local gallery.

Glastonbury Abbey
Somerset BA6 9EL
(01458) 832267
www.glastonburyabbey.com
Somewhere for all seasons! From snowdrops and daffodils in the Spring, to family trails and quizzes and Autumn colour on hundreds of trees.

Glastonbury Festival
June, Pilton, Somerset
www.glastonburyfestivals.co.uk
Known for its contemporary music, but also features dance, comedy, theatre, circus, cabaret and other arts.

Haynes International Motor Museum
Yeovil, Somerset BA22 7LH
(01963) 440804
www.haynesmotormuseum.co.uk
More than 400 vehicles displayed in stunning style, dating from 1886 to the present day.

The Jane Austen Centre
Bath, Somerset BA1 2NT
(01225) 443000
www.janeausten.co.uk
Celebrating Bath's most famous resident.

Number One Royal Crescent
Bath, Somerset BA1 2LR
(01225) 428126
www.bath-preservation-trust.org.uk
Restored and authentically furnished town house shows fashionable life in 18th century Bath.

West Somerset Railway
Minehead, Somerset TA24 5BG
(01643) 704996
www.west-somerset-railway.co.uk
Longest independent steam railway in Britain.

Wiltshire

Bowood House and Gardens
Bowood, Calne, Wiltshire, SN11 0LZ
(01249) 812102
www.bowood.org
Stately home with formal grounds and woodlands created by master landscaper Capability Brown.

Longleat
Warminster, Wiltshire BA12 7NW
(01985) 844400
www.longleat.co.uk
A wealth of exciting attractions including Longleat House along with lots of special events to keep you and your family entertained.

Old Sarum
Salisbury, Wiltshire SP1 3SD
(01722) 335398
www.english-heritage.org.uk/oldsarum
Discover the story of the original Salisbury. The mighty Iron Age hill fort where the first cathedral stood and where our ancestors left their mark.

Salisbury Cathedral
Salisbury, Wiltshire SP1 2EJ
(01722) 555120
www.salisburycathedral.org.uk
Britain's finest 13th century cathedral with the tallest spire in Britain. Discover nearly 800 years of history, the world's best preserved Magna Carta (AD 1215).

Stourhead House and Garden
Warminster, Wiltshire BA12 6QD
(01747) 841152
www.nationaltrust.org.uk/stourhead
A breathtaking 18th century landscape garden with lakeside walks, grottoes and classical temples.

Wilton House
Wilton House, Wilton, Wiltshire SP2 0BJ
(01722) 746714
www.wiltonhouse.com
Wilton House has one of the finest art collections in Europe and is set in magnificent landscaped parkland featuring the Palladian Bridge.

Tourist Information Centres

When you arrive at your destination, visit the Tourist Information Centre for quality assured help with accommodation and information about local attractions and events, or email your request before you go.

Axminster	The Old Courthouse	01297 34386	touristinfo@axminsteronline.com
Barnstaple	Museum of North Devon	01271 375000 / 346747	info@staynorthdevon.co.uk
Bath	Abbey Chambers	0906 711 2000	tourism@bathtourism.co.uk
Bideford	Burton Art Gallery	01237 477676	bidefordtic@torridge.gov.uk
Blandford Forum	Riverside House	01258 454770	blandfordtic@btconnect.com
Bodmin	Shire Hall	01208 76616	bodmintic@visit.org.uk
Bourton-on-the-Water	Victoria Street	01451 820211	bourtonvic@btconnect.com
Bradford on Avon	The Greenhouse	01225 865797	tic@bradfordonavon.co.uk
Braunton	The Bakehouse Centre	01271 816688	brauntonmuseum@yahoo.co.uk
Bridport	Bridport Town Hall, Bucky Doo Square	01308 424901	bridport.tic@westdorset-weymouth.gov.uk
Bristol : Harbourside	E Shed	0906 711 2191	ticharbourside@destinationbristol.co.uk
Brixham	Hobb Nobs Gift Shop	01803 211 211	holiday@englishriviera.co.uk
Bude	Bude Visitor Centre	01288 354240	budetic@visitbude.info
Budleigh Salterton	Fore Street	01395 445275	info@visitbudleigh.com
Cartgate	South Somerset TIC	01935 829333	cartgate.tic@southsomerset.gov.uk
Chard	The Guildhall	01460 260051	chard.tic@chard.gov.uk
Cheltenham	Municipal Offices	01242 522878	info@cheltenham.gov.uk
Chippenham	Hight Street	01249 665970	info@chippenham.gov.uk
Chipping Campden	The Old Police Station	01386 841206	info@campdenonline.org
Christchurch	49 High Street	01202 471780	enquiries@christchurchtourism.info
Cirencester	Corinium Museum	01285 654180	cirencestervic@cotswold.gov.uk
Combe Martin	Seacot	01271 883319	mail@visitcombemartin.co.uk
Dartmouth	The Engine House	01803 834224	holidays@discoverdartmouth.com
Dawlish	The Lawn	01626 215665	dawtic@teignbridge.gov.uk
Dorchester	11 Antelope Walk	01305 267992	dorchester.tic@westdorset-weymouth.gov.uk
Exeter	Visitor Information Centre	01392 665700	tic@exeter.gov.uk

Exmouth	Travelworld	01395 222299	tic@travelworldexmouth.co.uk
Falriver	11 Market Strand	0905 325 4534	vic@falriver.co.uk
Fowey	5 South Street	01726 833616	info@fowey.co.uk
Frome	The Library	01373 465757	touristinfo@frome-tc.gov.uk
Glastonbury	The Tribunal	01458 832954	info@glastonburytic.co.uk
Gloucester	28 Southgate Street	01452 396572	tourism@gloucester.gov.uk
Honiton	Lace Walk Car Park	01404 43716	honitontic@btconnect.com
Ilfracombe	The Landmark	01271 863001	marie@visitilfracombe.co.uk
Ivybridge	The Watermark	01752 897035 / 892220	info@ivybridgewatermark.co.uk
Launceston	The White Hart Arcade	01566 772321	info@launcestontic.co.uk
Looe	The Guildhall	01503 262072	looetic@btconnect.com
Lyme Regis	Guildhall Cottage	01297 442138	lymeregis.tic@westdorset-weymouth.gov.uk
Lynton and Lynmouth	Town Hall	01598 752225	info@lyntourism.co.uk
Malmesbury	Town Hall	01666 823748	tic@malmesbury.gov.uk
Melksham	32 Church Street	01225 707424	info@visit-melksham.com
Mere	The Library, Barton Lane	01747 860546	
Minehead	19 The Avenue	01643 702624	minehead.visitor@hotmail.com
Modbury	5 Modbury Court	01548 830159	modburytic@lineone.net
Moreton-in-Marsh	High Street	01608 650881	moreton@cotswold.gov.uk
Newquay	Municipal Offices	01637 854020	newquay.tic@cornwall.gov.uk
Newton Abbot	6 Bridge House	01626 215667	natic@teignbridge.gov.uk
Ottery St Mary	10a Broad Street	01404 813964	info@otterytourism.org.uk
Padstow	Red Brick Building	01841 533449	padstowtic@btconnect.com
Penzance	Station Approach	01736 335530	beth.rose@nationaltrust.org.uk
Plymouth	Plymouth Mayflower Centre	01752 306330	barbicantic@plymouth.gov.uk
Poole	Enefco House	0845 2345560	info@pooletourism.com
Salcombe	Market Street	01548 843927	info@salcombeinformation.co.uk
Salisbury	Fish Row	01722 342860	visitorinfo@salisburycitycouncil.gov.uk
Scilly, Isles Of	Hugh Street, Hugh Town	01720 424031	tic@scilly.gov.uk
Seaton	The Underfleet	01297 21660	visit@seaton.gov.uk
Shaftesbury	8a Bell Street	01747 853514	tourism@shaftesburydorset.com
Shepton Mallet	70 High Street	01749 345258	enquiries@visitsheptonmallet.co.uk
Sherborne	3 Tilton Court	01935 815341	sherborne.tic@westdorset-weymouth.gov.uk
Sidmouth	Ham Lane	01395 516441	ticinfo@sidmouth.gov.uk
Somerset	Sedgemoor Services	01934 750833	somersetvisitorcentre@somerset.gov.uk
South Molton	1 East Street	01769 574122	visitsouthmolton@btconnect.com
St Austell	Southbourne Road	01726 879 500	staustelltic@gmail.com
St Ives	The Guildhall	01736 796297	info@stivestic.co.uk
Street	Clarks Village	01458 447384	info@streettic.co.uk
Stroud	Subscription Rooms	01453 760960	tic@stroud.gov.uk
Swanage	The White House	01929 422885	mail@swanage.gov.uk
Swindon	Central Library	01793 466454	infocentre@swindon.gov.uk
Taunton	Market House	01823 340470	tauntontic@tauntondeane.gov.uk
Tavistock	The Den	01626 215666	teigntic@teignbridge.gov.uk
Tetbury	33 Church Street	01666 503552	tourism@tetbury.org
Tewkesbury	100 Church Street	01684 855040	tewkesburytic@tewkesbury.gov.uk
Tiverton	Tiverton Museum	01884 256295	tivertontic@tivertonmuseum.org.uk
Torquay	The Tourist Centre	01803 211 211	holiday@englishriviera.co.uk
Torrington	Castle Hill	01805 626140	info@great-torrington.com
Totnes	The Town Mill	01803 863168	enquire@totnesinformation.co.uk
Trowbridge	Civic Centre	01225 765072	tic@trowbridge.gov.uk
Truro	Municipal Building	01872 274555	tic@truro.gov.uk
Wareham	Discover Purbeck	01929 552740	tic@purbeck-dc.gov.uk
Warminster	Central Car Park	01985 218548	visitwarminster@btconnect.com
Wellington	30 Fore Street	01823 663379	wellingtontic@tauntondeane.gov.uk
Wells	Wells Museum	01749 671770	visitwellsinfo@gmail.com
Weston-Super-Mare	The Winter Gardens	01934 417117	westontic@parkwood-leisure.co.uk
Wimborne Minster	29 High Street	01202 886116	wimbornetic@eastdorset.gov.uk
Winchcombe	Town Hall	01242 602925	winchcombetic@tewkesbury.gov.uk
Woolacombe	The Esplanade	01271 870553	info@woolacombetourism.co.uk
Yeovil	Petters House	01935 462781	yeoviltic@southsomerset.gov.uk

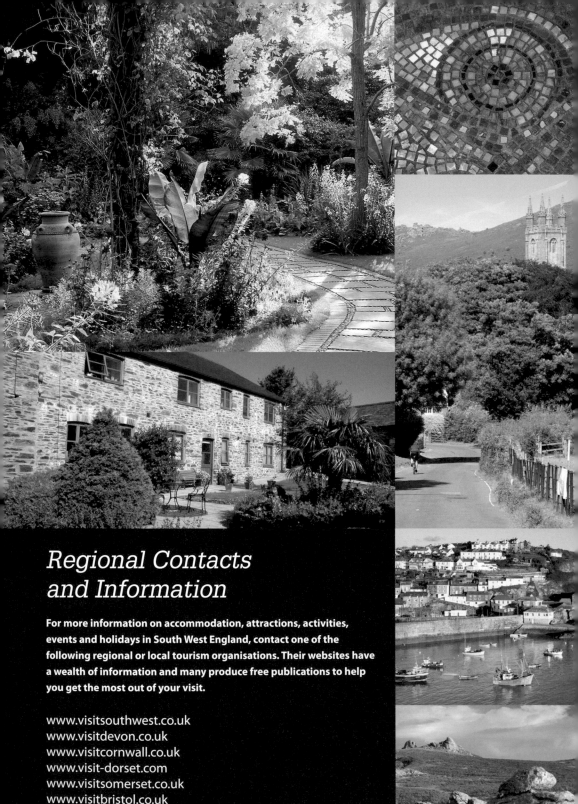

Regional Contacts and Information

For more information on accommodation, attractions, activities, events and holidays in South West England, contact one of the following regional or local tourism organisations. Their websites have a wealth of information and many produce free publications to help you get the most out of your visit.

www.visitsouthwest.co.uk
www.visitdevon.co.uk
www.visitcornwall.co.uk
www.visit-dorset.com
www.visitsomerset.co.uk
www.visitbristol.co.uk
www.visitbath.co.uk
www.southwestcoastpath.org.uk

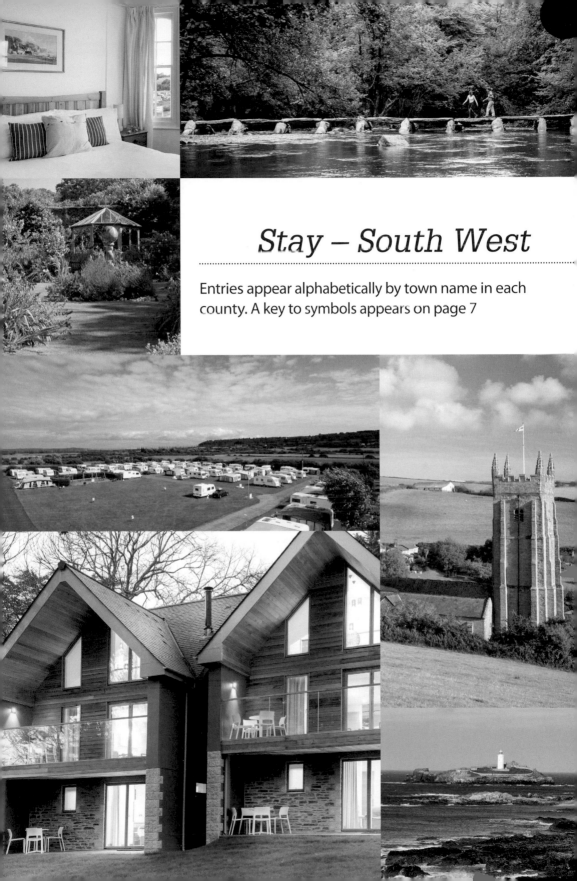

Stay – South West

Entries appear alphabetically by town name in each
county. A key to symbols appears on page 7

BLACKWATER, Cornwall Map ref 1B3 — SatNav TR4 8HR C

VisitEngland ★★★★ HOLIDAY, TOURING & CAMPING PARK

🚐 (30)	£13.00-£21.00
🚛 (30)	£13.00-£21.00
⛺ (30)	£13.00-£21.00
🏠 (20)	£196.00-£700.00

30 touring pitches

Trevarth Holiday Park

Blackwater, Truro TR4 8HR
T: (01872) 560266 **E:** trevarth@btconnect.com
W: www.trevarth.co.uk £ BOOK ONLINE

Luxury caravan holiday homes, touring and camping. A small, quiet park conveniently situated for North and South-coast resorts. Level touring and tent pitches with electric hook-up. Overnight holding area available. Laundry room, games room and play area.

Directions: Leave A30 at Chiverton roundabout (signed St Agnes). At the next roundabout take the road to Blackwater. Park on right after 200m.

Open: April to October 31st.

Payment: 🔲 ☼ Leisure: ♦ Children: ⚲ ⚠ Park: 🖳 🗄 ♟ Touring: 🚰 🚾 🚗

BUDE, Cornwall Map ref 1C2 S

VisitEngland ★★★★ SELF CATERING   **VisitEngland** Gold AWARD

Units	4
Sleeps	4-8

PER UNIT PER WEEK
£255.00 - £1175.00

Tamar Valley Cottages

Contact: David Wright, North Tamerton House, North Tamerton, Cornwall EX22 6SA
T: (01409) 271284 / 07860 726957 **E:** bookings@tamarvalleycottages.co.uk
W: www.tamarvalleycottages.co.uk

Luxury family and dog friendly self-catering cottages at Tamar Valley Cottages offer peace and tranquillity whilst still being within a short drive of some of the West Country's most stunning unspoilt beaches, spectacular coastal paths and wild moors. With great access links to top attractions in both Devon & Cornwall it is easy to explore everything the West Country has to offer. **Open:** All year round **Nearest Shop:** 2.5 miles **Nearest Pub:** 0.5 miles

Site: ❁ P Leisure: ➤ Property: 🐾 🖳 🗄 🍽 Children: ⚲ 🛏 ⚲ Unit: 🗄 🗄 📺 🗄 📺 📀 🍴 BBQ

BUDE, Cornwall Map ref 1C2 S

VisitEngland ★★★★ SELF CATERING

Units	11
Sleeps	2-10

PER UNIT PER WEEK
£433.00 - £2487.00

Treworgie Barton

Contact: St. Gennys, Bude, Cornwall EX23 0NL **T:** (03301) 230 374
E: enquiries@csmaclubretreats.co.uk
W: www.treworgie.co.uk

Set in 36 acres of peaceful farm and woodland, this North Devon accommodation boasts magnificent views over rolling countryside and sea beyond. Whether you are looking to relax, explore or just get away, Treworgie Barton Cottages offer the ideal break. Their beautifully preserved features of the past give each cottage a real feeling of character. **Open:** From 5th Jan throughout 2016 **Nearest Shop:** 2 miles **Nearest Pub:** 2 miles

Site: ❁ P Payment: 🔲 Leisure: ♦ Property: ∥ 🐾 🖳 🗄 🍽 Children: ⚲ 🛏 Unit: 🗄 🗄 📺 🗄 📺 📀 🍴 BBQ 📞

BUDE, Cornwall   Map ref 1C2   **S**

Whalesborough Cottages & Spa

Contact: James & Sharran Proudfoot, Owners, Whalesborough Farm, Marhamchurch, Bude, Cornwall EX23 0JD **T:** (01288) 361626 / 07557 508641 **F:** 01288 361317 **E:** jproudfoot@whalesborough.plus.com **W:** www.whalesborough.co.uk **£ BOOK ONLINE**

Units	20
Sleeps	2-10

PER UNIT PER WEEK
£450.00 - £3750.00

SPECIAL PROMOTIONS
Short breaks between October and Easter. Late availability and offers on our website.

Whalesborough luxury self catering cottages & Spa, near Bude will appeal to visitors looking for contemporary, spacious holiday accommodation surrounded by the natural countryside of North Cornwall. Twenty 5 star gold award winning cottages sleeping 2-10 people with indoor pool/spa, outdoor pool, tennis courts, indoor games barn and onsite cafe/bistro/shop. Walk/cycle from your cottage across the farm to the beach or down the Canal Towpath to Bude or use Whalesborough as a base to explore the rest of Cornwall and North Devon. Cottages all have private, enclosed gardens and are pet friendly too.

Open: All Year
Nearest Shop: 1 mile
Nearest Pub: 1 mile

Units: Most bedrooms have en suite facilities. 5 single storey cottages, all interiors professionally designed. Underfloor heating, woodburners. Enclosed gardens.

Site: ✿ P **Payment:** 💳 **Leisure:** ♪ ▶ 🔍 ⚲ ⚲ ⚲ **Property:** ∥ 🐾 🖥 🗗 🗺 **Children:** 🐤 🛏 🎠
Unit: 🗄 🖵 📺 🖥 🍴 📺 📀 ⚲ BBQ

BUDE, Cornwall   Map ref 1C2   SatNav EX23 9HJ **C**

Wooda Farm Holiday Park

Poughill, Bude, Cornwall EX23 9HJ
T: (01288) 352069 **E:** enquiries@wooda.co.uk
W: www.wooda.co.uk **£ BOOK ONLINE**

🚐	(80)	£20.00-£36.00
🚐	(60)	£14.00-£36.00
⛺	(60)	£14.00-£31.00
🏠	(55)	£287.00-£1043.00
	200 touring pitches	

SPECIAL PROMOTIONS
See our website for special offers.

Stunning views over Bude Bay and countryside; 1.5 miles from safe, sandy beaches. Family-owned and run with excellent facilities for touring and camping and luxury holiday homes for hire. Activities include fishing, sports barn, tennis court, woodland walks and golf. An ideal base for touring the delights of Devon and Cornwall.

Directions: 1.5 miles from Bude, just outside the village of Poughill.

Open: April to October.

Payment: 💳 **Leisure:** ♪ ▶ ♨ 🔍 ⚲ **Property:** 🐾 🖥 🗗 🏠 **Children:** 🐤 🎠 **Catering:** ✕ 🍴

BUDE, Cornwall Map ref 1C2 S

VisitEngland
★★★★
SELF CATERING

Woodland Lodge Holidays

Contact: Chris Pym, Owner, Reservation Office, Tregenna, 10 Oak Tree, Keynsham
BS31 2SA **T:** (0800) 6444 606 / 07973 224287 **E:** info@woodlandlodgeholidays.co.uk
W: www.woodlandlodgeholidays.co.uk **£ BOOK ONLINE**

Units	1
Sleeps	1-4

PER UNIT PER WEEK
£173.00 - £667.00

A luxury lodge to modern standards. Sleeps 4 in double & twin bedrooms. Cozy lounge with TV & DVD player. Open plan kitchen. Modern bathroom with bath & shower. Quiet location with patio overlooking woodland. 2 miles to nearest beach; 4 miles from Bude. 10 minutes stroll to local village. Pets welcome by prior arrangement. Ideal family holiday location. **Open:** 1st March until 31st October **Nearest Shop:** 0.5 miles **Nearest Pub:** 0.5 miles

Site: ❄ P Payment: 💳 € Leisure: 🏊 ⛳ ⛵ 🎣 🚵 ⚓ 🎾 Property: 🐕 📺 🖥 Children: 🚼 🛏 🪑 Unit: 📺 📻 🔥 📺 📀

BUDE, Cornwall Map ref 1C2 S

VisitEngland
4★-5★
SELF CATERING

VisitEngland
Gold
AWARD

Wooldown Holiday Cottages

Contact: Mrs Susan Blewett, Wooldown Holiday Cottages, Sharlands Road, Marhamchurch, Bude, Cornwall EX23 0HP **T:** (01288) 361216 **E:** holidays@wooldown.com
W: www.wooldown.com **£ BOOK ONLINE**

Units	14
Sleeps	2

PER UNIT PER WEEK
£210.00 - £790.00

SPECIAL PROMOTIONS
All year short breaks from 1 night available with any day arrival/ departure.

Enjoy outstanding countryside and sea views in luxury, from cosy country cottages, to ultra-modern, apartment style romantic hideaways.

Featuring copper spa baths, underfloor heating, chunky super-king size beds and walk-in rainfall showers. Perfect for a romantic short break at any time of the year.

Situated on the North Cornish coast on the outskirts of the picturesque village of Marhamchurch with pub/restaurant and shop. Just two miles from the popular seaside town of Bude, with a variety of shops, quality places to eat, walks and beaches.

Open: All year
Nearest Shop: 0.4 mile
Nearest Pub: 0.4 mile

Units: 14 luxury romantic retreats just for two.

Site: ❄ P Payment: 💳 Leisure: 🚴 🏊 ⛳ ⛵ Property: ⚡ 📺 📺 🖥 Unit: 📺 📻 📺 📺 🔥 📺 📀 BBQ

EDMONTON, Cornwall Map ref 1B2 S

Quarrymans Cottages

Contact: Mr Huw Jenkins, Quarrymans Cottages 1 & 20, 17 Granville Terrace, Mountain Ash CF45 4AL **T:** 07866 386611 **E:** jenkins@choicecornishcottages.com **W:** www.choicecornishcottages.com **£ BOOK ONLINE**

Units 2
Sleeps 1-4

PER UNIT PER WEEK
£200.00 - £600.00

SPECIAL PROMOTIONS
Weekend breaks £150 - £250. Please contact for details.

These tastefully decorated, cosy cottages are situated overlooking the Camel Estuary. Originally the homes of 19th century slate quarrymen, they are positioned around a stone-flagged courtyard and adjacent to a traditional Cornish inn. Fifteen-minute drive from Padstow's pretty harbour and sandy beaches.

Open: All year
Nearest Shop: 0.5 miles
Nearest Pub: 40 yards

Units: 2 bedrooms on 1st floor, 1 with double bed, 1 with twin beds.

Site: ❀ P Leisure: 🚣 ♪ ∪ Property: 🖵 Children: 🛝 Unit: 🗄 🖥 📺 ✍

FALMOUTH, Cornwall Map ref 1B3 S

Budock Vean Cottages & Holiday Homes

Contact: Budock Vean Hotel, Helford Passage, Mawnan Smith, Falmouth, Cornwall TR11 5LG **T:** (01326) 250288 **F:** 01326 250892 **E:** relax@budockvean.co.uk **W:** www.budockvean.co.uk

Units 6
Sleeps 2-8

PER UNIT PER WEEK
£470.00 - £2180.00

SPECIAL PROMOTIONS
http://www.budockvean.co.uk/offers

Located in the grounds of the Budock Vean Hotel are 4* traditional self-catering cottages (sleeping 2 - 8, pet friendly) & new 5* contemporary holiday homes (sleeping 6.) Set in 65 acres of gardens & woodland by the spectacular Helford River & coast path, each cottage has a small private garden, all have parking, central heating, wi-fi & guests have full use of the hotels' leisure facilities: 9 hole parkland golf course, tennis courts, large indoor swimming pool, outdoor hot tub, Natural Health Spa, bar and award-winning restaurant. All the freedom of self-catering with 4* hotel services!

Open: 23rd Jan 2016 - 2nd Jan 2017
Nearest Shop: 1.5 miles
Nearest Pub: 1.5 miles

Units: Most rooms have a private bathroom or shower room and toilet. Beavers Lodge, Beavers Dam and Badgers Cottage are all on one level.

Site: ❀ P Payment: 💳 Leisure: 🚣 ♪ ⊦ ∪ 🎣 ❀ ✎ Property: ∥ 🐾 🖼 🗄 🖳 🖵 Children: 🛝 🏠 ♿ Unit: 🗄 🖥 🖳 🍳 📺 ⊚ 📀 ✍ BBQ 📞

VisitEngland
★★★
SELF CATERING

Goodwinds Apartments

Contact: Mrs Jean Goodwin, 3 The Goodwins, Penwerris Lane, Falmouth, Cornwall TR11 2PF **T:** (01326) 313200 / 07772 890999 **E:** Thegoodwinds@gmail.com
W: www.cgoodwin11.wix.com/goodwindsapartments

| Units | 4 |
| Sleeps | 2-5 |

PER UNIT PER WEEK
£285.00 - £550.00

SPECIAL PROMOTIONS
Low season short breaks available, 3 nights or more. Please contact for details.

Goodwinds Holiday Apartments are a modern development of four, self contained two bedroomed apartments all with their own balconies with extensive panoramic views located off of the living/dining room and central heating. All have marvellous views over Falmouth harbour, the Penryn River and the quaint fishing village of Flushing. Close to the marina and town. Falmouth has three beaches. Undercover private parking for two cars.

Fully fitted kitchen, bathroom with bath and shower. All rooms have one double bedroom and one twin bedroom. Some have an extra bed. Flats 4, 5 and 6 are on the first floor.

Open: All Year
Nearest Shop: 0.75 miles
Nearest Pub: 0.75 miles

Units: Two bedrooms, All linens provided, Colour TV's.

Site: P Leisure: ♪ Property: ☈ 🖳 Children: ⛱ ⛏ 🛝 Unit: 🖭 ⚲ 📺

VisitEngland
★★★★
SELF CATERING

Mylor Harbourside Holidays

Contact: Mylor Yacht Harbour, Mylor Churchtown, Falmouth TR11 5UF **T:** (01326) 372121
E: enquiries@mylor.com
W: www.mylor.com/holidays **£ BOOK ONLINE**

| Units | 8 |
| Sleeps | 2-8 |

PER UNIT PER WEEK
£405.00 - £1395.00

SPECIAL PROMOTIONS
We offer short breaks with a minimum stay of three nights. Regular promotions are shown on our website throughout the year.

Our luxury waterside retreats make for the perfect relaxing coastal getaway for couples, families and large groups, offering a variety of 2 storey cottages and single storey apartments. All however, share one thing in common - the stunning harbourside location.

Nestled into the heart of a traditional working harbour in Mylor, Cornwall, these beautiful cottages sit on the banks of the Fal River with views across the estuary and offer the ideal location for those who like to get out and explore the coastline, countryside and not forgetting some of the best sailing waters in the UK.

Open: All year
Nearest Shop: 2 miles
Nearest Pub: On site in the Harbour

Units: We have a range of 1 and 2 storey properties all of which are fully furnished and equipped with modern fitted kitchens, some have en suite bathrooms.

Site: P Property: ∥ ☈ 🖿 🖳 Children: ⛱ ⛏ 🛝 Unit: 🖭 📺 BBQ

FOWEY, Cornwall Map ref 1B3 SatNav PL23 1JU C

VisitEngland ★★★★ HOLIDAY, TOURING & CAMPING PARK

(35) £15.00-£30.00
(16) £15.00-£30.00
(56) £8.00-£30.00
(11) £200.00-£650.00
56 touring pitches

Penhale Caravan & Camping Park

Penhale Caravan & Camping Park, Penhale Farm, Fowey, Cornwall PL23 1JU
T: (01726) 833425 **F:** 01726 833425 **E:** info@penhale-fowey.co.uk
W: www.penhale-fowey.co.uk **£ BOOK ONLINE**

Friendly, uncrowded family run park that overlooks unspoilt farmland and lovely views of the sea. In Area of Outstanding Natural Beauty close to sandy beaches, many scenic walks and the Eden Project. David Bellamy Award. Choice of caravans. Touring pitches, electric hook-ups, free showers. Overnight holding area available. **Directions:** From A30 west from Lostwithiel, on A390 turn left after 1 mile onto B3269, after 3 miles turn right onto A3082. **Open:** Easter or 1st April to End October.

Site: **Payment:** **Leisure:** **Children:** **Catering:** **Park:**
Touring:

GORRAN, Cornwall Map ref 1B3 S

VisitEngland ★★★★ SELF CATERING — VisitEngland Gold AWARD

Units 1
Sleeps 1-4
PER UNIT PER WEEK
£550.00 - £1150.00

Owls roost

Contact: Mrs Myra Welsh, Owner, Owls Roost, Gorran, Saint Austell PL26 6NY
T: (01726) 842295 **F:** 01726 842295 **E:** treveague@btconnect.com
W: www.treveaguefarm.co.uk

Owls Roost is located on our organic farm with far reaching countryside and sea views. A secluded location offering peace and tranquillity, with walks to three local beaches and the chance to relax and swim in our new Swim Spa. Please refer to our website for more information. **Open:** All year including Christmas and New Year **Nearest Shop:** 0.5 miles **Nearest Pub:** 0.5 miles

Site: P **Payment:** € **Leisure:** **Property:** **Children:** **Unit:**
TV DVD

HAYLE, Cornwall Map ref 1B3 SatNav TR27 5AW C

VisitEngland ★★★★ HOLIDAY, TOURING & CAMPING PARK

(80) £13.00-£43.00
(80) £13.00-£43.00
(80) £13.00-£43.00
(33) £365.00-£1530.00
(80) £235.00-£745.00
80 touring pitches

Beachside Holiday Park

Phillack, Hayle TR27 5AW
T: (01736) 753080 **F:** 01736 757252 **E:** reception@beachside.co.uk
W: www.beachside.co.uk **£ BOOK ONLINE**

Beachside is a family holiday park, set amidst sand dunes right on the beach in the famous St Ives Bay. With a range of accommodation and touring pitches, our location is ideally situated in West Cornwall for a touring and beach holiday. **Directions:** Travel west on A30 and turn off into Hayle. Turn right, following the sign to Phillack & Beachside. Our entrance is approximately 400m on right. **Open:** Easter to End October.

Site: **Payment:** **Leisure:** **Children:** **Catering:** **Park:**
Touring:

HELFORD, Cornwall Map ref 1B3 S

VisitEngland 3★-4★ SELF CATERING — VisitEngland Gold AWARD

Units 4
Sleeps 1-6
PER UNIT PER WEEK
£300.00 - £870.00

Mudgeon Vean Farm Holiday Cottages

Contact: Mrs Sarah Trewhella, Proprieter, Mudgeon Vean Farm Holiday Cottages, St Martin, Helston TR12 6DB **T:** (01326) 231341 **E:** mudgeonvean@aol.com
W: www.mudgeonvean.co.uk **£ BOOK ONLINE**

3 & 4* Gold Award. Cosy cottages on small 18th century farm producing apple juice & cyder, near the Helford River. Play area and games room. Peaceful location. Area of Outstanding Natural Beauty. Please contact for individual facilities. **Open:** All year **Nearest Shop:** 2 miles **Nearest Pub:** 2 miles

WALKERS WELCOME — CYCLISTS WELCOME
Site: P **Payment:** **Leisure:** **Property:** **Children:** **Unit:**
TV DVD BBQ

For **key to symbols** see page 7

LOOE, Cornwall   Map ref 1C2   S

VisitEngland ★★★★ SELF CATERING

Talehay Cottages

Contact: Mr & Mrs Dennett, Talehay Farm, Tremaine, Looe, Cornwall PL13 2LT
T: (01503) 220252 **E:** infobookings@talehay.co.uk
W: www.talehay.co.uk

Units   5
Sleeps   2-5
PER UNIT PER WEEK
£220.00 - £895.00

Talehay is situated amidst delightful unspoilt open countryside. The magnificent Cornish coastline with its secluded sandy coves and breath taking views is only 3 miles away. It is ideal as a base to explore the many readily accessible attractions of Cornwall; it's beaches, fishing villages, stately homes, famous gardens, coastal and inland walks as well as the world renowned "Eden Project". **Open:** All Year **Nearest Shop:** 1 mile **Nearest Pub:** 1 mile

Site: ✿ **P** **Payment:** 💷 **Property:** 🐴 🖥 🔟 🕏 **Children:** 🛏 🍽 🎿 **Unit:** 🖥 🔟 📺 🕏 🛝 TV 📀

MARAZION, Cornwall   Map ref 1B3   S

VisitEngland 3★ - 4★ SELF CATERING

Trevarthian Holiday Homes

Contact: Mr Sean Cattran, Trevarthian Holiday Homes, West End, Marazion TR17 0EG
T: (01736) 710100 **F:** 01736 710111 **E:** info@trevarthian.co.uk
W: www.trevarthian.co.uk **£ BOOK ONLINE**

Units   16
Sleeps   1-5
PER UNIT PER WEEK
£240.00 - £960.00

Trevarthian Holiday Homes is a family business focussing on quality self-catering accommodation in the beautiful town of Marazion, Cornwall. All our properties are located opposite the large sandy beach and St Michael's Mount, a must-see for any visit to the South West, and within a five minute walk of the children's playground, village pubs, restaurants, galleries, shops and bus-stops. Accommodation ranges in size from single bedroom apartments to a three-bedroom cottage with a private garden. **Open:** All year **Nearest Shop:** 0.20 miles **Nearest Pub:** 0.20 miles

Site: ✿ **P** **Payment:** 💷 **Leisure:** 🏊 ⚓ ⛳ **Property:** 🖥 🔟 🕏 **Children:** 🛏 🍽 🎿 **Unit:** 🖥 📺 🕏 🛝 📀 🍴

NEWQUAY, Cornwall   Map ref 1B2   S

Green Waters

VisitEngland ★★★★ SELF CATERING

Contact: Mrs R E Pullen, Owner, 19 Riverside Avenue, Pentire, Newquay TR7 1PN
T: (01637) 873551 / 07929725193 **E:** bernruth.pullen@hotmail.co.uk
W: www.greenwaters.co.uk

Units   1
Sleeps   2
PER UNIT PER WEEK
£260.00 - £445.00

A modern, comfortable, self-contained flat for two, in an elevated position with panoramic views of the winding River Gannel tidal estuary. Excellent position for walking and exploring the surrounding beautiful area. **Open:** All year **Nearest Shop:** 2k **Nearest Pub:** 1k

Site: **P** **Property:** ∥ 🖥 🔟 🕏 **Unit:** 🖥 📺 🕏 🛝 TV 📀

NEWQUAY, Cornwall Map ref 1B2
SatNav TR8 4PE **C**

VisitEngland
★★★★
HOLIDAY, TOURING & CAMPING PARK

Riverside Holiday Park

Lane, Newquay TR8 4PE
T: (01637) 873617 **F:** 01637 877051 **E:** info@riversideholidaypark.co.uk
W: www.riversideholidaypark.co.uk

(65)   £19.50-£25.50
(3)   £320.00-£950.00
(1)   £320.00-£950.00
(15)   £235.00-£775.00
65 touring pitches

SPECIAL PROMOTIONS
3 or 4 nights short stay up to the 16th July and from 3rd September.

Welcome to Riverside Holiday Park - Newquay, Cornwall. The park makes an excellent base for exploring the famous seaside resort – just two and half miles away – and the rest of Cornwall too. The park is family owned and run. It's well maintained and caters for families and couples only.

A warm welcome awaits at our reception and information desk which includes a small shop with basic everyday supplies. The park has sheltered, level touring pitches, luxury lodges and caravans. Covered, heated pool and bar.

Directions: Follow A392 for Newquay, at Quintrell Downs go straight over at roundabout, we are first left after Hendra Holiday Park.

Open: Easter to end of October.

Site: ☞ Payment: ▦ ☼ Leisure: ⚓ ♪ ⛨ ∪ ⚭ ☂ Children: ⛄ ⚠ Catering: ✕ ⚑ Park: ⛩ ▤ ⛿ ⚐
Touring: ⚑ ⚬ ⚏

PADSTOW, Cornwall Map ref 1B2
S

VisitEngland
★★★★
SELF CATERING

VisitEngland
Gold
AWARD

Sunday & School Cottages

Contact: Mrs Diane Hoe, Owner, Sunday Cottages, Lower Cottage, Preston-on-Stour, Stratford on Avon, Warwickshire CV37 8NG **T:** (01789) 450214 **E:** di@sundaycottage.co.uk
W: www.sundaycottage.co.uk

Units   2
Sleeps   2-6

PER UNIT PER WEEK
£525.00 - £1360.00

Two beautiful, peaceful and comfortable cottages in old Padstow, with super-fast broadband & off-road parking. Minutes walk to harbour, shops, restaurants, beaches, coastal path, and stunning, unspoilt coastline! Both cottages make an ideal base for walkers.

School Cottage boasts a magical walled garden with summer house, BBQ and lovely old stone wood store, stocked with logs for the wood burner for our winter visits.

We accept children of 8yrs and over. No pets allowed.
Availability can be checked on www.sundaycottage.co.uk

Open: All year except January.
Nearest Shop: 0.10 miles
Nearest Pub: 0.10 miles

Units: Sunday Cottage sleeps 4 in 2 bedrooms.
School Cottage sleeps up to 6 in 3 bedrooms.

Site: ✿ P Property: ⁄⁄ ▤ ▦ ▨ Unit: ▯ ▭ ▬ ▨ ⚑ ⊞ ⧉ BBQ ☎

PADSTOW, Cornwall   Map ref 1B2   S

3★ - 4★
SELF CATERING

Gold
AWARD

VisitEngland
VisitEngland

Units   6
Sleeps   1-7

PER UNIT PER WEEK
£330.00 - £1100.00

SPECIAL PROMOTIONS
We offer Short Breaks
from October through
to end of April.

From £70 per night for
minimum of 3 nights.

We are happy to
discuss any tariffs on
enquiry.

Yellow Sands Cottages

Contact: Sharon Keast, Proprietor, Yellow Sands, Harlyn Bay, Padstow, Cornwall PL28 8SE
T: (01637) 881548 **E:** keast3@btinternet.com
W: www.yellowsands.co.uk

Yellow Sands Cottages are situated just 250 metres from one of North Cornwall's beautiful sandy beaches - Harlyn Bay - access to the shore is via a private pathway through the garden at Yellow Sands or just a short stroll down the road to the bridge, where there is level access, together with the Harlyn Inn, Harlyn Surf school and on a good day, Kelly's ice cream!

Padstow is also close by, just a short 5 minute drive from Harlyn or a public bus trip. Yellow Sands is in an idyllic location - and being local proprietors for over 40 years, we can be there if you need us. A base to visit the County.

Open: All Year
Nearest Shop: 1 mile
Nearest Pub: 250 metres

Units: Our holiday cottages are all ground level with parking adjacent, well kept gardens, high quality fixtures and fittings. Well maintained and serviced.

Site: ✿ P **Leisure:** ▶ **Property:** 🐾 ⛟ 🗄 📠 **Children:** 🛝 🏖 ☗ **Unit:** 🗄 🗄 📺 🎞 📺 DVD BBQ ☎

PENZANCE, Cornwall   Map ref 1A3   SatNav TR20 9AU   C

VisitEngland
HOLIDAY, TOURING
& CAMPING PARK

🚐 (20)   £17.00-£26.00
🚐 (20)   £17.00-£26.00
⛺ (40)   £12.00-£26.00
🏕 (7)   £275.00-£555.00
40 touring pitches

Kenneggy Cove Holiday Park

Higher Kenneggy, Rosudgeon, Penzance, Cornwall TR20 9AU
T: (01736) 763453 **E:** enquiries@kenneggycove.co.uk
W: www.kenneggycove.co.uk

A tranquil park (no noise after 10pm), surrounded by glorious countryside in an Area of Outstanding Natural Beauty. Panoramic sea views. 12 min walk to SW coastpath and secluded coves. Short footpath walks to Prussia Cove and a gastro-pub. **Directions:** We are equidistant from Penzance and Helston off the A394 coast road (3m east of Marazion). At our blue sign, turn down the lane towards to sea. We are near the end of the lane on the left. **Open:** Mid May - End of September.

Site: ♿🅿 **Payment:** € ☼ **Leisure:** ♿ 🎣 ▶ ♺ **Children:** 🛝 🅰 **Catering:** ✗ 🍴 **Park:** 🐾 ⛟ 🗄 🎏
Touring: ☎ 🚻 🚐

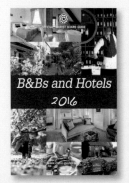

PORTHTOWAN, Cornwall Map ref 1B3 **S**

Rosehill Lodges

Contact: Mr John Barrow, Rosehill Lodges, Porthtowan, Cornwall TR4 8AR
T: (01209) 891920 **F:** 01209 891935 **E:** reception@rosehilllodges.com
W: www.rosehilllodges.com **£ BOOK ONLINE**

Units	10
Sleeps	1-6

PER UNIT PER WEEK
£516.00 - £2229.00

SPECIAL PROMOTIONS
Weekend and mid-week breaks available. Open for Christmas and New Year. Low occupancy discounts available. Free superfast broadband over Wi-Fi. Free cots and highchairs.See website for special offers.

Five Star luxury Gold Award self-catering lodges right on the Cornish coast. Situated in the coastal village of Porthtowan just five minutes walk to a sandy Blue Flag beach, bars and restaurants. Relax and leave your car behind. Each bespoke lodge features super-king size beds, log burners, your own personal hot tub spa and free superfast Wi-Fi. Go green with grass roofs and solar panels and dine al-fresco under glass covered decking whatever the weather. Each lodge has an external drench shower, ideal for washing down after a fun day on the beach. We look forward to giving you a warm welcome.

Open: All year
Nearest Shop: 0.5 miles
Nearest Pub: 0.5 miles

Units: Bespoke luxury timber eco lodges, fully equipped and hand built locally with materials from sustainable sources. Luxury and green better together.

Site: ❀ P **Payment:** 💷 **Leisure:** ⚲ ♪ ♭ ◡ **Property:** ▦ ▣ 🖳 **Children:** ⛱ ▥ 🎠
Unit: ▯ ▤ ▣ ▨ ◵ 📺 📀 ∅ BBQ ☎

REDRUTH, Cornwall Map ref 1B3 SatNav TR16 4JQ **C**

Tehidy Holiday Park

Harris Mill, Illogan, Nr Portreath, Redruth TR16 4JQ
T: (01209) 216489 **F:** 01209 213555 **E:** holiday@tehidy.co.uk
W: www.tehidy.co.uk

🚐	(10)	£16.00-£23.00
🚎	(8)	£16.00-£23.00
⛺	(20)	£16.00-£23.00
🏠	(4)	£410.00-£800.00
🛖	(20)	£270.00-£820.00

30 touring pitches

Cottages, holiday caravans, touring/camping and wigwam cabins, on our multi award winning holiday park, including voted Best Caravan and Lodge Site in UK 2014 - Practical Caravan and Regional Winner 2013, 2014 and 2015 Top 100 Awards. David Bellamy Gold Award 2015. Nestled in a wooded valley, woodland walks, play area and excellent facilities close to beautiful sandy beaches, gardens and cycling.

Directions: Exit A30 to Redruth/Porthtowan. Rigth to Porthtowan. 300m left at corssroads. Straight on over B3300 (Portreath) crossroads. Past Cornish Arms. Site 500m on left.

Open: March to November.

Payment: 💷 **Leisure:** ♭ ♦ **Children:** ⛱ ⚠ **Catering:** 🍴 **Park:** ▦ ▣ ▥

SEATON, Cornwall Map ref 1C2 S

Mount Brioni Holiday Apartments

Contact: Roger & Cathy Stamp, Resident Owners, Mount Brioni, Looe Hill, Seaton, Nr Looe, Cornwall PL11 3JN **T:** (01503) 250251 **E:** holidays@mountbrioni.co.uk
W: www.mountbrioni.co.uk **£ BOOK ONLINE**

Units	25
Sleeps	2-4

PER UNIT PER WEEK
£355.00 - £1018.00

Delightful cluster of 25 self catering apartments on quiet coastline of south Cornwall, near Looe. Luxury 3 & 4 star gold accommodation with free high speed broadband, superb sea views. Beach and ocean just yards away. Special offers always available.
Please phone to book.
Open: All year **Nearest Shop:** 0.10 miles
Nearest Pub: 0.10 miles

Site: ✿ P **Payment:** £ € **Leisure:** ♪ ♭ ☾ **Property:** ♞ 🖳 🖪 🗑 **Children:** ⚲ 🖾 ⚼ **Unit:** 🗄 🗄 🖳 🗑 ⚲ 📺 📀 BBQ

ST. AUSTELL, Cornwall Map ref 1B3 S

Natural Retreats - Trewhiddle

Contact: Natural Retreats, Trewhiddle Park, Pentewan Rd, St Austell, Cornwall PL26 7AD
T: (01625) 416 430 **E:** info@naturalretreats.com
W: www.naturalretreats.com **£ BOOK ONLINE**

Units	34
Sleeps	2-8

PER UNIT PER WEEK
£473.00 - £2426.00

SPECIAL PROMOTIONS
Offers only available at www.naturalretreats.com

Set in a peaceful countryside valley, these luxurious 2, 3 and 4 bedroom self-catering cottages and villas offer privacy and picturesque scenery, yet are ideally located. Trewhiddle is just two miles from Porthpean Beach and three miles from Pentewan Sands, a short drive from Eden Project and Lost Gardens of Heligan, and a stone's throw from the charming towns of Mevagissey and Charlestown. The villas boast spacious and modern interiors, rated Five Star by Visit England. Guests can also discover a private outdoor children's play area, farmland walks and cycling trails all on their doorstep.

Open: All year
Nearest Shop: 1.2 miles
Nearest Pub: 1.6 miles

Units: Spacious and modern villas and cottages. Pets welcome upon arrangement. Properties boast luxurious interiors, private outdoor space and parking.

Site: P **Payment:** £ **Leisure:** ⚲ ♭ **Property:** ⫽ ♞ 🖳 🖪 🗑 **Children:** ⚲ 🖾 ⚼
Unit: 🗄 🗄 🖳 🗑 ⚲ 📺 📀 📀

ST. AUSTELL, Cornwall Map ref 1B3 S

The Old Inn, Pentewan

Contact: Mr & Mrs Robert Haskins, 19 Ullswater Drive, Wetherby LS22 6YF
T: (01937) 580217 / 07802 819409 **E:** rjhaskins@gmail.com
W: www.inncornwall.com

Units	1
Sleeps	1-6

PER UNIT PER WEEK
£260.00 - £790.00

Stone cottage near beach in quiet location, in area of outstanding beauty. Close to Mevagissey (2 miles), the Lost Gardens of Heligan (2 miles) and The Eden Project (7 miles). Once an alehouse for visiting sailors, now a modern 3-star self-catering unit. It retains its character with low beams, pictures and open fireplace. Pentewan has a pub, Post Office stores and restaurant. Country walks.
Open: All year **Nearest Shop:** 500 yards **Nearest Pub:** 200 yards

Site: P **Leisure:** ⚲ ♪ ♭ **Property:** ⫽ 🖪 🗑 **Children:** ⚲ 🖾 ⚼ **Unit:** 🗄 🗄 🖳 🗑 ⚲ 📺 ⌀ BBQ

ST. COLUMB, Cornwall   Map ref 1B2   S

Cornish Holiday Lodges

Contact: Kelly Sharman, Cornish Holiday Lodges - Aspen and Enderley lodges, Retallack Resort & Spa, Winnards Perch, St Columb Major, Cornwall TR9 6DE
T: (01213) 234817 **E:** info@cornishholidaylodges.co.uk **W:** cornishholidaylodges.co.uk

Aspen and Enderley Holiday Lodges are purpose built luxury Scandinavian style self catering lodges in Cornwall. The interiors are exceptionally spacious, remarkably comfortable and beautifully decorated to ensure a relaxing holiday. Set in a rural retreat of the Retallack Resort and Spa a 5* family site with many facilities inc: pool, gym, spa, tennis, golf, bar and restaurant. **Open:** All year

Units 2
Sleeps 1-8
PER UNIT PER WEEK
£485.00 - £1320.00

Site: P Payment: Leisure: Property: Children: Unit:

ST. COLUMB, Cornwall   Map ref 1B2   S

Meadow Rise

Contact: Mrs Helen Grimsey, Proprietor, Cornish Holiday, 24 Valley Mead, Anna Valley, Andover SP11 7SB **T:** (01264) 335527 / 07881 623483 **F:** 01264 335527
E: enquiries@cornishholiday.info **W:** www.cornishholiday.info **£ BOOK ONLINE**

Cosy modern 2 bedroomed house in a quiet village location. An ideal base for all sightseeing and beach holidays. Padstow and Newquay less than 10 miles away. **Open:** All year round **Nearest Shop:** 0.30 miles **Nearest Pub:** 0.5 miles

Units 1
Sleeps 1-4
PER UNIT PER WEEK
£225.00 - £525.00

Site: P Payment: Property: Children: Unit:

ST. ISSEY, Cornwall   Map ref 1B2   SatNav PL27 7RL   C

Trewince Farm Holiday Park

Trewince Farm, Saint Issey PL27 7RL
T: (01208) 812830 **E:** enquiries@trewincefarm-holidaypark.co.uk
W: www.trewincefarm-holidaypark.co.uk

	£14.00-£24.00
	£14.00-£24.00
	£14.00-£24.00
	£290.00-£705.00

A quiet family holiday park, camping, touring and static holidays, set in own working farm. 4 miles from Padstow and beaches. Outdoor heated swimming pool is open during high season. The on site shop is open all season. Whitsun to September, children's play area, pitch and putt green, table tennis. Fully equipped amenity blocks. Natural lake, woodland walk, dogs welcome. Wi-Fi Available. Sea View development for 2015 private static vans.

Directions: From Wadebridge take the A389 signposted Padstow. Turn first left when you see our sign. We are a short distance on the right.

Open: Easter to end of October.

Payment: Leisure: Children: Catering: Park:
Touring:

ST. IVES, Cornwall Map ref 1B3 S

Units   8
Sleeps   1-5
PER UNIT PER WEEK
£295.00 - £750.00

Cheriton Self Catering

Contact: Mr Alec Luke, Owner, Cheriton House, Market Place, St Ives TR26 1RZ
T: (01736) 795083 **E:** alec@cheritonselfcatering.com
W: www.cheritonselfcatering.com

In the centre of beautiful St Ives. Five nice flats and three traditional fisherman's cottages 25 yards from harbour & beach. Also one large flat on Porthminster Point with outstanding views and situated in beautiful gardens. All with parking. Clean and well equipped. Flats sleep two to four. Cottages up to five persons. Short breaks available 'off-season' Oct - May. **Open:** All Year **Nearest Shop:** 20 yards **Nearest Pub:** 20 yards

Site: P Property: 🔌 Children: 🛏 🍴 Unit: 🍳 📺 🛁 📺 📀

ST. IVES, Cornwall Map ref 1B3 S

Units   4
Sleeps   2-6
PER UNIT PER WEEK
£240.00 - £820.00

Trevalgan Holiday Farm

Contact: Mr Russell Osborne, Trevalgan Holiday Farm, Little Trevalgan, Trevalgan Farm, St Ives, Cornwall TR26 3BJ **T:** (01736) 796529 / 07921 450547 **E:** holidays@trevalgan.co.uk
W: www.trevalgan.co.uk **£ BOOK ONLINE**

Expect excellent accommodation, breathtaking scenery and a warm welcome on this family farm. Cottages are child-friendly, decorated, furnished and equipped to a very high standard. Why choose between a beach holiday and a countryside holiday when you can have both? With St Ives just a 5 minute drive our location is ideal for both families and couples to explore wonderful West Cornwall. **Open:** All year **Nearest Shop:** 1.5 miles **Nearest Pub:** 1.5 miles

Site: ✿ P Leisure: ♿ ♪ ♻ ♦ Property: 🐾 🍴 🛁 🔌 Children: 🛏 🍴 🚼 Unit: 🍳 📺 🛁 📺 📀 BBQ

ST. JUST IN ROSELAND, Cornwall Map ref 1B3 SatNav TR2 5JF C

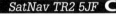

Trethem Mill Touring Park

St. Just in Roseland, Nr St Mawes, Truro, Cornwall TR2 5JF
T: (01872) 580504 **F:** 01872 580968 **E:** reception@trethem.com
W: www.trethem.com

🚐 £20.00-£28.00
🚙 £20.00-£28.00
⛺ £20.00-£28.00
84 touring pitches

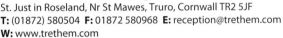

Caravan Park of the Year 2015" South West Tourism Excellence Awards. Nestling in a valley, surrounded by farmland, our multi award winning Park is in the heart of the Roseland Peninsula. **Directions:** A3078 towards Tregony/St Mawes, over Tregony bridge. After 5 miles follow brown caravan and camping signs from Trewithian. Site 2 miles beyond on right-hand side. **Open:** 24th March - 9th October

Payment: 💳 ☀ Leisure: ♿ ♪ ♻ Children: 🛏 🎢 Catering: 🛒 Park: 🐾 🍴 🛁 🔌 🔥 Touring: 🚽 🚿 🔌
🚻

ST. MAWES, Cornwall   Map ref 1B3   S

Roundhouse Barn Holidays

Contact: Barbara Sadler, Owner, Roundhouse Barn Self Catering Holidays, Roundhouse Barn, St Just in Roseland, St Mawes TR2 5JJ **T:** (01872) 580038 / 07977 262342 **E:** info@roundhousebarnholidays.co.uk
W: www.roundhousebarnholidays.co.uk **£ BOOK ONLINE**

Units   3
Sleeps   1-2

PER UNIT PER WEEK
£330.00 - £945.00

SPECIAL PROMOTIONS
We offer short breaks
from November -
Easter every year (3
night minimum stays)

Relax, unwind and escape in our multi-award winning 5 Star Gold Award self catering accommodation. Our 17th Century Cornish stone barns are tucked away on The Roseland Peninsula. Exclusively for adults so you can be sure of a peaceful stay.
Coastal walks, sandy beaches and quaint harbour villages are all close by. We are located in an Area of Outstanding Natural Beauty and surrounded by rolling fields and set within beautifully landscaped tranquil gardens. We have breathtaking views of the Fal Estuary from the top of our driveway.
Ideal base to explore all of Cornwall's attractions.

Open: All year round
Nearest Shop: 4 miles St Mawes or Portscatho
Nearest Pub: 3 miles in Philleigh

Units: Our three cottages are luxuriously appointed offering every home comfort

Site: ✿ P Payment: 🔢 Leisure: ► Property: 🖥 🗐 🔲 Unit: 🗐 🔳 🖥 🎵 📺 🔌 📀 〰 BBQ

TINTAGEL, Cornwall   Map ref 1B2   S

Halgabron Mill Holiday Cottages

Contact: Robin Evans, Manager, The Keep, Halgabron Mill, St. Nectan's Glen, Tintagel, Cornwall PL34 0BB **T:** (01840) 779099 **E:** Robin@halgabronmill.co.uk
W: www.halgabronmill.co.uk

Units   4
Sleeps   2-5
PER UNIT PER WEEK
£289.00 - £925.00

Four well-equipped character stone cottages, with exposed beams and lead latticed windows, surround a former 18th century Water Mill. Situated in St. Nectan's Glen - a densely, wooded valley between Tintagel and Boscastle villages. Coastpath is 10 min walk. Closest Beaches are a 10 min walk or 5 min drive. **Open:** All Year (Millstream Cottage Easter-Oct). **Nearest Shop:** 1 mile **Nearest Pub:** 1 mile

Site: ✿ P Property: 🗐 Children: 🖥 Unit: 🗐 🔳 🔲 🖥 📺 🔌 📀 〰

TRURO, Cornwall   Map ref 1B3   S

Pulla Farm Holidays

Contact: Mrs Mary Richards, Pulla Farm Holidays, Pulla Farm, Pulla Cross, Frogpool, Truro TR4 8SA **T:** (01872) 863143 **E:** info@pullafarmholidays.co.uk
W: www.pullafarmholidays.co.uk **£ BOOK ONLINE**

Units   1
Sleeps   2-4
PER UNIT PER WEEK
£240.00 - £485.00

Traditional accommodation with a warm welcome on a livestock farm between Truro and Falmouth. Ideal for touring, beaches, surfing, walking, cycling and National Trust properties and gardens. Welcome Pack. Cream Tea. **Open:** All year **Nearest Shop:** 2 miles **Nearest Pub:** 1 mile

Site: ✿ P Payment: 🔢 Leisure: & 🎵 ► ♻ Property: 🖥 🗐 Children: 🖥 🖥 Unit: 🗐 🔲 🖥 🎵 📺 📀 〰 BBQ

TRURO, Cornwall   Map ref 1B3   S

VisitEngland
★★★★★
SELF CATERING

The Valley

Contact: Reservations Team, Bissoe Road, Carnon Downs, Truro TR3 6LQ
T: (01872) 862194 **F:** 01872 864343 **E:** info@the-valley.co.uk
W: www.thevalleycornwall.co.uk **£ BOOK ONLINE**

The Valley...Cornwall's hidden secret. Modern and tasteful self-catering accommodation with a personal service and great facilities. Pools, fitness suite, tennis, squash and stylish restaurant all situated in beautiful countryside. **Open:** All year **Nearest Shop:** 0.5 miles **Nearest Pub:** 0.5 miles

Units   46
Sleeps   2-7
PER UNIT PER WEEK
£490.00 - £2215.00

Site: ❀ P **Payment:** 💷 **Leisure:** ♿ ⚐ 🔍 ⚲ ⚲ ⚲ **Property:** ╱ 🐕 💺 🖥 **Children:** 🛝 🍴 🔥 **Unit:** 🖳

WATERGATE BAY, Cornwall   Map ref 1B2   SatNav TR8 4AD   C

VisitEngland
★★★★
HOLIDAY, TOURING
& CAMPING PARK

Watergate Bay Touring Park

Tregurrian, Newquay, Cornwall TR8 4AD
T: (01637) 860387 **F:** 0871 661 7549 **E:** email@watergatebaytouringpark.co.uk
W: www.watergatebaytouringpark.co.uk

🚐 (200)   £11.50-£22.50
🚚 (200)   £11.50-£22.50
⛺ (220)   £11.50-£22.50
🏠 (2)   £250.00-£730.00
200 touring pitches

SPECIAL PROMOTIONS
Outside of the dates 15th July – 29th August, book 7 nights or more and receive a 10% discount.

Half a mile from Watergate Bay's sand, surf and cliff walks. Rural Location in an Area of Outstanding Natural Beauty. Personally run and supervised by resident owners. Heated indoor/outdoor pool, tennis courts, skate park, games room, shop/cafe, licensed clubroom, free entertainment including kids club and kids play area. Overnight holding area available. Free Mini-bus to Watergate Bay.

Directions: From A30 follow signs for Newquay then airport. After passing the airport, turn left onto the B3276. Park 0.5 miles on the right.

Open: 1st March to the 1st November.

Site: ❀ **Payment:** 💷 ☼ **Leisure:** ♪ ∪ 🔍 ⚲ ⚲ ⚲ **Children:** 🛝 🎠 **Catering:** ✕ 🛒
Park: 🐕 ♪ 🖥 🖳 🚻 🚿 **Touring:** ⚐ ⚑ 🔌 ⚡

ST MARY'S, Isles of Scilly   Map ref 1A3   S

VisitEngland
2★ - 3★
SELF CATERING

4 Well Cross

Contact: Ms Marlene Burton, Owner, **T:** 07768 407495 **E:** grannymar1@outlook.com

Situated close to shops and town centre, few hundred yards to the beach. Easy walking distance to harbour. Sky TV available. Please contact for prices.
Open: March - October
Nearest Shop: 0.5 miles
Nearest Pub: Less than 0.5 miles

Units   2
Sleeps   1-7

Site: ❀ P **Leisure:** ♿ ♪ ⚐ ∪ ⚲ **Property:** 🐕 🖥 🖳 **Children:** 🛝 🍴 🔥 **Unit:** 🖳 💺 🖥 📺 💿 📀 🔌

★★★
SELF CATERING

Units   1
Sleeps   2-4
PER UNIT PER WEEK
£415.00 - £825.00

No 9 Harbour Lights

Contact: A. Athawes, Manager, Homeview Cottages Ltd., Thorofare, St Mary's, Isles of Scilly, Cornwall TR21 0JN **T:** (01634) 290 210 **E:** aathawes@convar.co.uk
W: www.stayonscilly.co.uk

Attractive apartment refurbished 2009/10. Accommodates 4 people. Adjacent to the harbour beach, town centre amenities and island ferries and tours. **Open:** All year except Christmas and New Year **Nearest Shop:** 50 yards **Nearest Pub:** 50 yards

Property: ⫽ ▦ ▤ ▣   **Unit:** ▣ 📺

★★★★
SELF CATERING

Units   1
Sleeps   4-8
PER UNIT PER WEEK
£1600.00 - £1800.00

Trevean Holidays

Contact: Mrs Rosemary Sharman, Owner, Trevean, Robinswood Farm, Bere Regis, Wareham, Dorset BH20 7JJ **T:** (01929) 472181 / 07826 865776 **F:** 01929 472182
E: info@treveanholidays.co.uk **W:** www.treveanholidays.co.uk

Trevean is a large, spacious granite town house, sleeps 8. Living accommodation on the top floor with views over the Harbour. It has 4 double bedrooms, 2 shower rooms, bathroom, heating, SkyTV,WiFi and Utility room. Close to shops, restaurants and off island boats. Ideal for the extended family to get together for a holiday to enjoy the beautiful islands. Beaches two minutes from front door. **Open:** Easter - October and Christmas/New Year **Nearest Shop:** 1 mins **Nearest Pub:** 0.10 miles

Leisure: ⅋ ♪ ↑ ☺   **Property:** ▦ ▤ ▣   **Children:** ⛟ ▥ ⚲   **Unit:** ▯ ▤ ▣ ▨ ⚲ 📺 ⑨ ⊚

★★★★★
SELF CATERING

Units   1
Sleeps   1-6

PER UNIT PER WEEK
£475.00 - £1750.00

SPECIAL PROMOTIONS
Bargain weekend and short-stay breaks available in autumn and winter months.

Apartment 5, Burgh Island Causeway

Contact: Mr John Smith, Apartment 5, Burgh Island Causeway, Mill Street, Chagford, Devon TQ13 8AW **T:** (01647) 433593 **F:** 01647 433694 **E:** help@helpfulholidays.com
W: www.burghislandcauseway.com   **£ BOOK ONLINE**

Luxury, modern, ground-floor apartment set into cliff with panoramic southerly views from large patio. Facilities include pool, gym, sauna, cafe/bar, grassy cliff-top grounds and direct access to beautiful large sandy beach and coastal path. Popular for surfing and near golf course and village shop/post office. View www.burghislandcauseway.com. Free Broadband.

Open: All year
Nearest Shop: 2 miles
Nearest Pub: 0.30 miles

Units: 1 double en suite bathroom, 1 twin en suite shower & sofa bed.

Site: ✲ **P**   **Payment:** 🖃   **Leisure:** ♪ ↑ ⚘   **Property:** 🐾 ▦ ▣   **Children:** ⛟ ▥ ⚲
Unit: ▯ ▤ ▣ ▨ ⚲ 📺 ⑨ ⊚ BBQ 📞

BRAUNTON, Devon   Map ref 1C1
SatNav EX33 1HG **C**

Lobb Fields Caravan and Camping Park
Saunton Road, Braunton EX33 1HG
T: (01271) 812090 **E:** info@lobbfields.com
W: www.lobbfields.com

🚐 (60)   £12.00-£32.00
🚚 (30)   £12.00-£32.00
⛺ (90)   £11.00-£32.00
180 touring pitches

South facing park with great views over the sea. On edge of Braunton, with Saunton beach only 1.5 miles away. Excellent bus service. Ideal for all holiday seaside activities. Surf board hire and snack bar on site. Seasonal pitches available. **Directions:** From Barnstaple to Braunton on A361. Then follow B3231 for 1 mile towards Saunton. Lobb Fields is marked on the right of the road. **Open:** 18th March 2016 to 30th October 2016.

Payment: ▢ ☀ Leisure: 🚲 ♪ ⏸ ∪ Children: 🛝 ⚠ Park: 🐾 🚮 ⑤ ⑱ 🅰 Touring: 🅿 🛉 🆒 🏊

BRIXHAM, Devon   Map ref 1D2
S

Harbour Reach
Contact: Jenny Pocock, Owner, 83 North View Road, Brixham TQ5 9TS **T:** (01142) 364761
E: enquiries@harbourreachholidays.co.uk
W: www.harbourreachholidays.co.uk

Units   2
Sleeps   1-11
PER UNIT PER WEEK
£230.00 - £590.00

The amazing views across the harbour, Torbay and out to sea, make this a perfect holiday home at any time of year. Harbour Reach is excellently furnished and equipped and divided into a maisonette and flat which are let separately or jointly thereby sleeping 1 to 11 We are within 10 minutes walk of the harbour side, town and South West coastal footpath. Short breaks available from October to March **Open:** All year including Christmas & New Year. **Nearest Shop:** 500 metres **Nearest Pub:** 200 metres

Site: **P** Property: 🐾 ⑤ 🈺 Children: 🛝 🍴 🚶 Unit: ⑤ 📺 ⑤ 🔆 📺 ⊚

COMBE MARTIN, Devon   Map ref 1C1
S

Manleigh Holiday Park
Contact: Rectory Road, Combe Martin, Devon EX34 0NS **T:** (03301) 230 374
E: enquiries@csmaclubretreats.co.uk
W: www.manleighpark.co.uk

Units   26
Sleeps   4-6
PER UNIT PER WEEK
£269.00 - £858.00

For a great value getaway and an ideal base to explore the beautiful North Devon coast, Manleigh Park is just perfect. Take your pick from Deluxe Static Caravans, Log Cabins and Chalets. **Open:** From 6th Feb. **Nearest Shop:** 1.5 miles **Nearest Pub:** 1.5 miles

Payment: ▢ € Leisure: 🎣 Property: 🐾 ⑤ ⑱

COMBE MARTIN, Devon   Map ref 1C1
S

Wheel Farm Cottages
Contact: Berry Down, Combe Martin, North Devon EX34 0NT **T:** (03301) 230 374
E: enquiries@csmaclubretreats.co.uk
W: www.wheelfarmcottages.co.uk

Units   11
Sleeps   2-8
PER UNIT PER WEEK
£425.00 - £2978.00

A collection of beautiful stone built cottages, Wheel Farm is the perfect choice for a hideaway self-catering country cottage break. The cottages themselves are set in an 'Area of Outstanding Natural Beauty' only a few miles from some of the finest beaches and Exmoor's spectacular coastline. This hidden gem of a retreat also boasts a heated indoor pool with sauna and an outdoor tennis court. **Open:** From 5th Jan throughout 2016 **Nearest Shop:** 1.5 miles **Nearest Pub:** 1.5 miles

Site: ❄ **P** Payment: ▢ Leisure: 🎣 🎾 Property: 〰 🐾 🚮 ⑤ 🈺 ⑤ Children: 🛝 🍴 Unit: ⑤ 📺 ⑤ 📺 ⌀ BBQ 📞

CREDITON, Devon   Map ref 1D2   S

★★★★
SELF CATERING

Units   1
Sleeps   1-2

PER UNIT PER WEEK
£200.00 - £500.00

SPECIAL PROMOTIONS
Short breaks available,
bookings commence
on Friday, other start
days can be
accommodated out of
season and for short
breaks.

Swallows at Falkedon

Contact: Helen Ford, Owner, Falkedon, Spreyton, Nr Whiddon Down, Devon EX17 5EF
T: (01647) 231526 / 07768 342 578 **E:** Helen@falkedon.net
W: www.swallowsholidaycottage.co.uk **£ BOOK ONLINE**

Adjoining a beautiful Georgian farmhouse, this delightful 4 star apartment is situated just off a quiet country lane 1 mile from the pretty village of Spreyton with the famous Tom Cobley Tavern. Located in the center of Devon , close to Dartmoor National Park, 5 minutes from the A.30 highway, Swallows at Falkedon is the perfect base to explore Devon and all it's attractions, National Trust properties, visit the North or South Devon coasts, the Cathedral city of Exeter. Full luxury bed linen and towels are provided together with a welcome hamper.

Open: All year
Nearest Shop: 0.8 miles
Nearest Pub: 1 mile

Units: All on one level, large separate bathroom and bedroom, super king bed, can be two singles, state at booking. Separate lounge, kitchen/diner.

Site: P Payment: 💷 **Leisure:** ► **Property:** 🐕 ▨ ▨ ▨ **Children:** ▥ ⚲ **Unit:** ▯ ▯ ▣ ▨ 📺 📀 BBQ

CROYDE, Devon   Map ref 1C1   S

★★★★★
SELF CATERING

Units   1
Sleeps   2-6
PER UNIT PER WEEK
£750.00 - £1875.00

4 Out of the Blue

Contact: Mr David Royden, Owner, 4 Out of the blue, Moor Lane, Croyde, North Devon
EX33 1FF **T:** 0/711 026889 **E:** david@outoftheblue-croyde.co.uk
W: www.outoftheblue-croyde.co.uk **£ BOOK ONLINE**

The house is right on edge of stunning beach at Croyde Bay on North Devon Coast. It offers luxury five star accommodation in form of a large open plan kitchen/dining /living room, shower room and on first floor three bedrooms and two bathrooms.
However the main attraction is the wonderful south facing views. The sandy bay has something for everyone; surf, rock pools, lovely walks and great pubs **Open:** All Year

Site: ✿ **P Payment:** 💷 **Leisure:** ► **Property:** ▨ ▨ ▨ **Children:** ⛱ ▥ ⚲ **Unit:** ▯ ▯ ▣ ▨ ▨ 📺 📀 BBQ
📞

DARTMOUTH, Devon   Map ref 1D3   S

3★-4★
SELF CATERING

Units   4
Sleeps   2-6
PER UNIT PER WEEK
£315.00 - £685.00

The Old Bakehouse

Contact: Mrs Sylvia Ridalls, The Old Bakehouse, 7 Broadstone, Dartmouth TQ6 9NR
T: (01803) 834585 **F:** 01803 834585 **E:** oldbakehousecottages@yahoo.com
W: www.oldbakehousedartmouth.co.uk

Character cottages beams and old stone fireplaces. Two minutes from historic town centre and river. Beach 15 minutes drive. Free parking. Dogs free. Non smoking. Wi-Fi. Flat-screen TV/DVD with Freeview. Washing machines in all cottages and dishwashers in two. Spring, Autumn and Winter short breaks available. Reduced rates for OAPs Sept 1st - June 30th. Phone for Winter offers and more information. **Open:** All year
Nearest Shop: 0.10 miles **Nearest Pub:** 0.10 miles

Site: P Payment: 💷 **Leisure:** ♪ ► **Property:** 🐕 ▨ ▨ ▨ **Children:** ⛱ ▥ ⚲ **Unit:** ▯ ▣ ▨ 📺 📀 📀

DAWLISH, *Devon* Map ref 1D2 S

Cofton Country Holidays

Contact: Starcross, Nr Dawlish, Exeter, Devon EX6 8RP **T:** (01626) 890111 **F:** 01626 890160
E: info@coftonholidays.co.uk
W: www.coftonholidays.co.uk **£ BOOK ONLINE**

Units	17
Sleeps	4-6

PER UNIT PER WEEK
£385.00 – £1090.00

SPECIAL PROMOTIONS
Special offers and short breaks are available early and late season. Free coarse fishing on site between November and February. Latest offers available via our website.

Twelve cottages and five luxury apartments, located either on our main holiday park or nearby on the Eastdon Estate. Cottages are converted from original farm buildings and apartments are within the 18th century Georgian house. Enjoy views of the Exe Estuary and have acres of countryside to explore. Facilities on the park include swimming pools, indoor leisure complex, shop, takeaway, cafe & bar.

Open: All year
Nearest Shop: 0.10 miles
Nearest Pub: 0.10 miles

Units: Each cottage is individual and comprises of 2 or 3 bedrooms sleeping a maximum of 6 people. Units are fully equipped including bed linen & towels.

Site: ✿ P **Payment:** 💳 **Leisure:** 🚲 ♪ ∪ 🍴 ⚲ ⚒ **Property:** 📺 📻 📲 **Children:** 🛏 🎢 ∱
Unit: 🛏 🍴 📺 🔌 📺 ◎ 📀

DAWLISH, *Devon* Map ref 1D2 SatNav EX6 8RP C

Cofton Country Holidays

Starcross, Nr Dawlish, Devon EX6 8RP
T: (01626) 890111 **F:** 01626 890160 **E:** info@coftonholidays.co.uk
W: www.coftonholidays.co.uk **£ BOOK ONLINE**

🚐 (450)	£17.50-£43.00
🚎 (450)	£17.50-£43.00
⛺ (450)	£17.50-£34.00
🏠 (17)	£395.00-£1060.00
🏕 (70)	£315.00-£960.00

450 touring pitches

SPECIAL PROMOTIONS
Save 25% on touring/ camping in winter, low, mid and high season for advance bookings of 5 or more nights.

A stunning setting surrounded by rolling meadows, mature woods, fishing lakes and just minutes from Dawlish Warren's Blue Flag beach. Superb countryside views. Hardstanding and super pitches available. Fantastic facilities in clean, tidy surroundings with indoor and outdoor swimming pools, play areas, restaurant, bars, park shop, take-away, woodland walks and games room complete with Bowling.

Directions: Leave M5 at junction 30, take A379 towards Dawlish. After passing through harbour village of Cockwood, park is on the left after half a mile.

Open: All year.

Site: 🏞 ⛺🅿 **Payment:** 💳 ☀ **Leisure:** ♪ ▶ ⚲ ⚒ ⚒ **Children:** 🛏 ⛰ **Catering:** ✕ 🛒
Park: ⚘ ♫ 🖥 📻 📲 📶 **Touring:** 🚰 🕁 🔌 ∱

The Eastdon Estate

Contact: Cofton Country Holidays, Starcross, Nr Dawlish, Devon EX6 8RP
T: (01626) 890111 **E:** info@coftonholidays.co.uk
W: www.coftonholidays.co.uk/holiday-cottages **£ BOOK ONLINE**

Units   12
Sleeps   4-6

SPECIAL PROMOTIONS
Short breaks available out of season, otherwise bookings are Saturday to Saturday. Please visit our website for latest special offers.

The Eastdon Estate comprises of Eastdon House, a converted Georgian property and nearby Eastdon Stable Cottages and Woodside Cottages which have been converted from old farm buildings. This is a beautiful, peaceful setting among fields and woodlands overlooking the Exe Estuary. Dawlish Warren beach and nature reserve is just a short walk away plus there is a woodland walk to Cofton Country Holidays whereby you can make use of the parks facilities. For 2016 Woodside Cottages have undergone complete refurbishment and have the added advantage of personal Hot Tubs outside each unit.
Please see website/contact for prices.

Open: All Year
Nearest Shop: 0.3 miles
Nearest Pub: 1.2 miles

Units: A mixture of units with ground floor accommodation available. All units sleep between 4 and 6 people.

Site: ✿ P **Payment:** 💷 **Leisure:** ▸ **Property:** ▦ 🔲 🔳 **Children:** ⛱ 🛏 🚶 **Unit:** 🔲 🔲 📺 🎛 📺 📀

Lady's Mile Touring and Camping Park

Exeter Road, Dawlish, Devon EX7 0LX
T: (01626) 863411 **F:** 01626 888689 **E:** info@ladysmile.co.uk
W: www.ladysmile.co.uk **£ BOOK ONLINE**

🚐 (480)   £15.00
🏕 (200) £260.00-£1155.00

Lady's Mile is an award winning, family run park designed to please everyone! With a fabulous range of indoor and outdoor sports and leisure facilities, you won't have to leave the site to enjoy a holiday full of family fun, come rain or shine! Please contact us for up to date prices.

Directions: Leave the M5 at Junction 30, take A379 to Dawlish, pass the Cockwood harbour for 2 miles over the Sainsburys roundabout, then take 2nd left.

Open: All year - (except for the outdoor pool).

Site: 🏕 🅰️🅿️ **Payment:** 💷 ☀ **Leisure:** ▸ 🎣 🎿 🚣 **Children:** ⛱ ⛰ **Catering:** ✗ 🛒 **Park:** 🎵 🖥 🔲 🛖
Touring: 🚰 🚾 🔌

DAWLISH, Devon   Map ref 1D2   **S**

SELF CATERING

Units   1
Sleeps   2-6

PER UNIT PER WEEK
£345.00 - £605.00

Little Mermaid Cottage

Contact: The Barn House, 3 King Street, Dawlish, South Devon EX7 9LG **T:** (01626) 863881
E: sheilathomas@live.co.uk
W: www.littlemermaidcottage.com

The Little Mermaid holiday Cottage is over 200 years old and will accommodate 6 people comfortably. It is situated by the town centre and is walking distance to the beach and train station. We have WI-FI and parking at the cottage.
Please see our website to view photo's and price list.

Open: All year
Nearest Shop: 5 mins walk

Nearest Pub: 5 mins walk

Units: Spacious lounge, dining room which has a double sofa bed, gallery kitchen which has washer/dryer, microwave,cooker and fridge freezer. Upstairs has a double room, twin room, bathroom and toilet.

Site: P   Unit: ▭ 🗑 ⓒ

DAWLISH, Devon   Map ref 1D2   *SatNav EX7 0ND*   **C**

HOLIDAY PARK

🏕 (50) £145.00-£1005.00

Oakcliff Holiday Park

Mount Pleasant Road, Dawlish Warren, Dawlish, Devon EX7 0ND
T: (01626) 863347 **F:** 01626 888689 **E:** info@ladysmile.co.uk
W: www.oakcliff.co.uk **£ BOOK ONLINE**

Oakcliff is an 8 acre park laid out in lawns and parkland around an elegant Georgian house, complete with a heated outdoor swimming pool and children's playground. Set in a prime location in Devon's premier holiday resort of Dawlish Warren, 600 yards from a Blue Flag beach and nature reserve. Away from the hustle and bustle, Oakcliff offers more peaceful surroundings with views across the estuary.

Directions: Leave M5 at junction 30, take A379 to Dawlish, continue past Cockwood harbour, pass Sainsburys roundabout, then take the 3rd left to Dawlish Warren for 3/4 mile.

Open: Accommodation - All year .
Pool - May to September.

f

Site: A🅿 **Payment:** 💷 **Leisure:** ▸ ⚡ **Children:** ☡ ⛰ **Park:** 🐾 🗑

DAWLISH, Devon   Map ref 1D2   SatNav EX7 0PH   **C**

Welcome Family Holiday Park

Welcome Family Holiday Park, Warren Road, Dawlish Warren, Dawlish, Devon EX7 0PH
T: (0345) 165 6265 **E:** fun@welcomefamily.co.uk
W: www.welcomefamily.co.uk

(60) £240.00–£1070.00
(70) £340.00–£1195.00
(120) £200.00–£940.00

Fantastic entertainment, 4 terrific indoor fun–pools and a truly superb location just a short walk from an award winning Blue Flag beach - these are just a few of the things that make 4* Welcome Family Holiday Park an ideal place for a family seaside holiday. Accommodation is available to suit every taste and pocket and ranges from luxury lodges, to comfortable bungalows and cosy caravans. Welcome Family - Where The Fun Always Shines!
Open: Easter - January (No park facilities from November to January)

Site: Payment: Leisure: Children: Catering: Park:

EXETER, Devon   Map ref 1D2   **S**

Lower Southbrook Farm (LSF) Holiday

Contact: Angela Lang, Owner, Southbrook Lane, Whimple, Exeter, Devon EX5 2PG
T: (01404) 822989 **E:** lowersouthbrookfarm@btinternet.com
W: www.lowersouthbrookfarm.co.uk

Units   3
Sleeps   1-4
PER UNIT PER WEEK
£270.00 - £576.00

We offer quality holiday accommodation set within the beautiful Devon countryside.

The cottages are an ideal base from which to explore the many attractions in and around the wonderful county of Devon. Alternatively if you are looking for somewhere to relax and unwind we are in a rural setting with the benefit of a heated outdoor swimming pool, a children's play area and 3 acres of private land.
Open: All Year **Nearest Shop:** 2 mile **Nearest Pub:** 1 mile

Site: P Payment: Leisure: Property: Children: Unit:

HOLSWORTHY, Devon   Map ref 1C2   **S**

Woodford Bridge Country Club

Contact: Milton Damerel, Nr Holsworthy, Devon EX22 7LL **T:** (0800) 358 6991
E: EuHotels@diamondresorts.com
W: www.DiamondResortsandHotels.com **£ BOOK ONLINE**

Units   103
Sleeps   1-6

PER UNIT PER WEEK
£270.00 - £1414.00

SPECIAL PROMOTIONS
Visit our website or call today for seasonal discounts and great savings.

A quiet haven in the heart of North Devon, this 15th-century former coaching inn is 33 miles from Tintagel Castle, the rumoured birthplace of King Arthur. It has a pool, a gym and free parking on site. Woodford Bridge Country Club is a charming thatched building, with a variety of elegant rooms. Each spacious apartment offers an en suite bathroom, a TV with Freeview, and tea and coffee making facilities.

Guests can enjoy a drink in the bar and breakfast, lunch and dinner in the restaurant. Woodford Bridge has a library where guests can relax with a book in the peaceful garden.

Open: All year
Nearest Shop: On Site
Nearest Pub: On Site

Units: A choice of Studio, one and two bedroom apartments available. All apartments boast a full kitchen, modern bathroom and Television with DVD player.

Site: P Payment: Leisure: Property: Children: Unit:

For **key to symbols** see page 7

Mary's Cottage

Contact: Susan West, Indicknowle Farm, Long Lane, Combe Martin, Ilfracombe, North Devon EX34 0PA **T:** (01271) 883980 **E:** mark.sue@indicknowle.plus.com
W: www.indicknowle.co.uk

Units   1
Sleeps   1-6

PER UNIT PER WEEK
£275.00 - £600.00

SPECIAL PROMOTIONS
Short breaks available. Also butchery, lambing and cider experiences out-of-season. Prices vary, based on the following percentages of the weekly rate; 3 nights 70%, 4 nights 80% and 5 nights 90%.

Adjoining a beautiful eighteenth century farmhouse, this delightful 4 star country cottage lies at the end of its own private lane. Indicknowle is a traditional family farm producing cider, lamb, pork and Ruby Red beef. Located in an area of outstanding natural beauty, close to Exmoor park, it has easy access to the popular North Devon beaches and the South West Coastal Path.
Mary's Cottage is the perfect base for a beach, walking or touring holiday, Christmas or Easter break. We offer peace, tranquility, relaxation and a taste of country life throughout the changing seasons of the farm year.

Open: All year
Nearest Shop: 3 miles
Nearest Pub: 3 miles

Units: Bedrooms en suite with shower & WC. Downstairs cloakroom. Cot/baby bath available on request. Fitted kitchen. Centrally heated with log burner & Wifi.

Site: ✿ P Property: 🖥 🅱 🖳 Children: 🛝 🎠 🏃 Unit: 🗄 🖥 🅱 🔍 📺 📀 🧺 BBQ

Oldaport Farm Cottages

Contact: Miss CM Evans, Owner, Modbury, Ivybridge, Devon PL21 0TG **T:** (01548) 830842
E: cathy@oldaport.com
W: www.oldaport.com **£ BOOK ONLINE**

Units   4
Sleeps   2-6

PER UNIT PER WEEK
£260.00 - £750.00

SPECIAL PROMOTIONS
Short breaks are available from mid - September to May. Please contact for details.

Four comfortable cottages cconverted from redundant stone barns sited on historic, working sheep farm in beautiful South Hams valley, it provides an ideal location for relaxing and absorbing the countryside in an area of outstanding natural beauty. There is an abundance of wildlife in the area, fascinating walks and attractions within easy reach. Dartmoor 8 miles, Plymouth 12 miles.

All cottages are furnished to the high standard of the English Tourism Council. The fitted kitchens are fully equipped with cooker, microwave, refrigerator, toaster, kettle and a comprehensive range of crockery, c

Open: All Year
Nearest Shop: 2.2 Miles
Nearest Pub: 2.2 Miles

Units: One cottage on ground floor

Site: P Property: 🐾 🖥 🅱 🖳 Children: 🛝 🎠 🏃 Unit: 🗄 🖥 🔍 📺 📀 BBQ

MORTEHOE, Devon   Map ref 1C1
SatNav EX34 7EG   **C**

North Morte Farm Caravan & Camping Park
North Morte Road, Mortehoe, Woolacombe EX34 7EG
T: (01271) 870381 **E:** info@northmortefarm.co.uk
W: www.northmortefarm.co.uk

(25)	£15.50-£24.00
	£13.00-£24.00
(150)	£13.00-£19.50
(21)	£296.00-£710.00

25 touring pitches

Set in beautiful countryside overlooking Rockham Bay, close to village of Mortehoe and Woolacombe. **Directions:** Take A361 from Barnstaple, turn left at Mullacott roundabout signed Mortehoe and Woolacombe, head for Mortehoe, turn right at Post Office, park 500m on left. **Open:** April to October.

Payment: ☒ ☀ **Leisure:** ♪ ♨ **Children:** ⚲ ⚠ **Catering:** ⚑ **Park:** ⚡ ☰ ⊟ ⊞ ⌂ **Touring:** ⚑ ⊙ ⚡ ⚿ ⚒

NEWTON ABBOT, Devon   Map ref 1D2
S

Holwell Holiday Cottages
Contact: Debbie Hall, Cottage Manager, Widecombe In The Moor, Newton Abbot, Devon TQ13 7TT **T:** 07746 123878 **E:** info@holwelldartmoor.co.uk
W: www.holwelldartmoor.co.uk **£ BOOK ONLINE**

Units	3
Sleeps	6-8

PER UNIT PER WEEK
£499.00 - £1799.00

Holwell is ideally located for discovering Dartmoor and surrounding area. Stay in one of the three immaculate cottages that have been lovingly and tastefully converted from barns to luxury holiday cottages. Chinkwell Tor 5* - 2 king, 1 double bedroom & two bathrooms, sleeps 6. Hound Tor. Not graded- 1 king, 2 double bedrooms & 2 bathrooms, sleeps 6. Saddle Tor 5* - 4 large bedrooms & 4 bathrooms. **Open:** All year **Nearest Shop:** 5 miles **Nearest Pub:** 2.6 miles

Site: ❋ P **Payment:** ☒ **Leisure:** ⚒ ♪ ♨ **Property:** ⚡ ☰ ⊟ ⊞ **Children:** ⚲ ▥ ⚹ **Unit:** ⊟ ⊟ ▭ ⊡ ⚒ ⊡
⊡ ⌀ BBQ

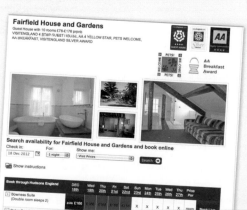

NEWTON ABBOT, Devon Map ref 1D2   SatNav TQ12 6QT **C**

Twelve Oaks Farm Caravan Park

Teigngrace, Newton Abbot TQ12 6QT
T: (01626) 335015 **E:** info@twelveoaksfarm.co.uk
W: www.twelveoaksfarm.co.uk

🚐 (50)	£15.50-£24.00	
🚚 (50)	£15.50-£24.00	
⛺ (30)	£15.50-£24.00	
🏠 (6)	£300.00-£1350.00	
50 touring pitches		

A working farm specialising in Charolais beef cattle. Friendly, personal service. Luxury showers and toilets, heated outdoor swimming pool. Coarse fishing. Good dog walks nearby. Children's play park. Wi-Fi Available. Loo of the Year Platinum 2016 Award. **Directions:** Please come via the A38 south bound exit for Teigngrace straight through the village for two miles Twelve Oaks Farm on left. **Open:** All year.

Payment: 💳 ☼ **Leisure:** 🚲 🎣 ∪ ⚹ **Children:** 🧸 ⚞ **Catering:** 🛒 **Park:** 🐕 📺 🖥 📶 🛝 **Touring:** 🚿 🛁 🚰 🔥

NORTH MOLTON, Devon Map ref 1C1   SatNav EX36 3HQ **C**

Riverside Caravan and Camping Park

Marsh Lane, North Molton Road, South Molton, North Devon EX36 3HQ
T: (01769) 579269 **E:** relax@exmoorriverside.co.uk
W: www.exmoorriverside.co.uk

🚐 (42)	£15.00-£25.00	
🚚 (42)	£15.00-£25.00	
⛺ (40)	£10.00-£24.00	
🏕 (2)	£210.00-£485.00	
42 touring pitches		

SPECIAL PROMOTIONS
For special offers, please visit our website for full details.

70 acres of parkland with lakes and rivers for fishing, woods and meadowland for walking. We are a 4 star park with 5 star facilities. Overnight holding area available.

Directions: M5 turn off on junction 27 onto the A361 turn right when you see North Molton and riverside sign.

Open: All year.

Site: 🏕 **Payment:** 💳 ☼ **Leisure:** 🎣 ∪ **Children:** 🧸 ⚞ **Catering:** ✗ 🛒 **Park:** 🐕 🎵 📺 🖥 📶 🛝 **Touring:** 🚿 🛁 🚰 🔥

OKEHAMPTON, Devon Map ref 1C2   **S**

Peartree Cottage

Contact: Mrs Jacqueline Ellis, Owner, Howards Gorhuish, Northlew, Okehampton, Devon EX20 3BT **T:** (01837) 658750 **E:** jackie.ann.ellis@btinternet.com
W: www.peartreecottage-devon.co.uk

Units	1
Sleeps	4
PER UNIT PER WEEK	
£350.00 - £935.00	

Delightful Gold Award-winning Peartree Cottage stands in the 2 acre grounds of Howards Gorhuish and overlooks a wild flower meadow and small copse. The cottage adjoins the owner's country house standing in a quiet rural position and is well-located to explore the attractions and stunning landscape the south west has to offer, especially Dartmoor and the spectacular North Devon coast. **Open:** All year **Nearest Shop:** 2 miles **Nearest Pub:** 2 miles

f

Site: P **Property:** 🐕 📺 🖥 🍽 **Children:** 🧸 🍽 ⚹ **Unit:** 📺 🖥 📶 🔌 📺 🗑 🍴 BBQ

Ladram Bay Holiday Park

Otterton, Budleigh Salterton, Devon EX9 7BX
T: (01395) 568398 **F:** 01395 568338 **E:** info@ladrambay.co.uk
W: www.ladrambay.co.uk **£ BOOK ONLINE**

🚐 (65)   £15.00-£44.00
🚍 (65)   £15.00-£44.00
⛺ (35)   £15.00-£44.00
🏠 (500) £129.00-£1895.00
160 touring pitches

SPECIAL PROMOTIONS
Short Breaks Available.
Early Booking
Discounts.

Nestled in the rolling Devon Hills overlooking the unspoilt Jurassic Coast, Ladram Bay is the Holiday Park in Devon that has something to offer everyone. Recently awarded 5 star status, you can be assured that your holiday is better than ever before! Whether you choose to stay in one of our luxury holiday homes or your own touring caravan or tent, our extensive range of facilities will suit all.

Directions: M5 Junct 30, follow A376 to Clyst St Mary then A3052 to Newton Poppleford, then B3178 and follow signposts to Ladram Bay.

Open: 11th March 2016 - 31st October 2016

Site: ❀ ⛺🅿 **Payment:** 💷 ☼ **Leisure:** ♪ ▸ ♦ ✑ **Children:** ⛷ ⛰ **Catering:** ✕ 🍴
Park: 🐕 ♫ ▦ 🗐 🛢 🏠 **Touring:** 🚰 🔌

Bolberry House Farm Caravan & Camping

Bolberry, Malborough, Kingsbridge TQ7 3DY
T: (01548) 561251 **F:** enquiries@bolberryparks.co.uk
W: www.bolberryparks.co.uk

🚐 (20)
🚍 (20)
⛺ (50)
🏠 (10)
70 touring pitches

Friendly family-run park between sailing paradise of Salcombe and Hope Cove (old fishing village). Peaceful, mostly level and good facilities. Children's play area. Good access to coastal footpaths. Sandy beaches nearby. Overnight holding area available. Please contact us for prices. **Directions:** A381 from Totnes, ringroad Kingsbridge to Salcombe. At Malborough sharp right through village, signs to Bolberry approx 1m. Do not follow Sat Nav from Totnes. **Open:** Easter to October.

Site: ⛺🅿 **Payment:** ☼ **Leisure:** 🚲 ♪ ▸ ∪ **Children:** ⛷ ⛰ **Catering:** 🍴 **Park:** 🐕 ▦ 🗐 🛢 🏠
Touring: 🚰 🔌

Higher Rew Touring Caravan & Camping

Higher Rew, Malborough, Kingsbridge, Devon TQ7 3BW
T: (01548) 842681 **E:** enquiries@higherrew.co.uk
W: www.higherrew.co.uk

100 touring pitches

Higher Rew is a family run park in an area of outstanding natural beauty close to the beautiful Salcombe Estuary. Three generations of the Squire family have, over many years, created a relaxed caravan and camping park for your enjoyment. We are annually inspected by the English Tourism Council, who have awarded our park four stars and have been featured in both the Lonely Planet and Rough Guides. Please contact or see website for 2016 rates. **Directions:** Some Sat Navs give least suitable route for last 2 miles, please see website. **Open:** March 18th to October 31st.

Site: ⛺🅿 **Leisure:** ♦ ✑ **Catering:** 🍴 **Park:** 🐕 🗐 🛢 🏠 **Touring:** ⌖ 🔌

SEATON, Devon   Map ref 1D2   S

★★★
SELF CATERING

Units   1
Sleeps   1-4
PER UNIT PER WEEK
£225.00 - £595.00

West Ridge Bungalow

Contact: Mrs Hildegard Fox, West Ridge Bungalow, Harepath Hill, Seaton EX12 2TA
T: (01297) 22398 **E:** fox@foxwestridge.co.uk
W: www.cottagesdirect.co.uk/3031758-1/west-ridge-bungalow-devon.aspx
£ BOOK ONLINE

Comfortably furnished bungalow on elevated ground in 1.5 acres of gardens. Beautiful, panoramic views of Axe Estuary and sea. Nearby - Beer, Branscombe, Lyme Regis, Sidmouth. Excellent walking, sailing, fishing, golf. 10% reduction for 2 persons only, throughout booking period. **Open:** March to October
Nearest Shop: 0.5 miles **Nearest Pub:** 1 mile

Site: ✿ P **Leisure:** ⚗ ♪ ▶ ᕫ **Property:** ⌂ ▦ 🖳 **Children:** ⛴ ⊞ ⋔ **Unit:** ⬚ ▭ ℚ 📺 🎰 📀

SOUTH MOLTON, Devon   Map ref 1C1   S

★★★★
SELF CATERING

Units   1
Sleeps   1-6
PER UNIT PER WEEK
£400.00 - £700.00

Dunsley Mill Barn

Contact: Helen Sparrow, Owner, West Anstey, South Molton, North Devon EX36 3PF
T: (01398) 341374 / 07771365951 **E:** helen@dunsleymill.co.uk
W: www.dunsleymill.co.uk

Situated on the edge of the Exmoor National Park Dunsley Mill is surrounded by rolling Devon countryside and there are superb local walks accessible directly from the property. Lovingly restored the barn is brimming with character and charm with restored beams, rich heritage colours and a large wood burning stove that nestles in the corner of the spacious open plan living area.

Three charming double bedrooms on the first floor are each dressed in delicate country fabrics, the two front double bedrooms enjoying wonderful views of the valley. This is an amazing area for walking, riding, fishing, golfing and other amazing country pursuits.

Open: All year
Nearest Shop: 6 mile
Nearest Pub: 2 miles

Units: Detached, stone barn conversion, open-plan, ground floor with host of beams. Three bedrooms, 2 bathrooms. In beautiful secluded valley.

Site: ✿ P **Leisure:** ⚗ ♪ ▶ ᕫ **Property:** ▦ ⬚ 🖳 **Children:** ⛴ **Unit:** ⬚ ⊟ ▭ 🖳 ℚ 📺 🎰 📀 🍴 BBQ

TAVISTOCK, Devon   Map ref 1C2   SatNav - Do Not Use.   C

★★★★★
HOLIDAY, TOURING
& CAMPING PARK

🚐 (15)   £14.50-£19.50
🚙 (15)   £14.50-£19.50
⛺ (15)   £14.50-£19.50
🏠 (12)   £225.00-£599.00
45 touring pitches

Langstone Manor Holiday Park

Moortown, Tavistock, Devon PL19 9JZ
T: (01822) 613371 **F:** 01822 613371 **E:** jane@langstonemanor.co.uk
W: www.langstonemanor.co.uk

Fantastic location with direct access onto moor, offering great walks straight from the park. Peaceful site with beautiful views of the surrounding moorland. Level pitches, some hardstanding with brand new five star facilities. Camping pods also available. The Langstone Bar provides evening meals. A warm welcome awaits! **Directions:** Take the B3357 Princetown road from Tavistock. After approx 1.5 miles, turn right at x-roads, go over cattle grid, up hill, left following signs. **Open:** March 15th to November 15th.

Site: 🏚 **Payment:** 💷 ☀ **Leisure:** ⚗ ♪ ▶ ᕫ 🍴 **Children:** ⛴ ⋔ **Catering:** ✕
Park: 🐾 ▦ ⬚ ⓟ 🅿 **Touring:** 🚽 ⬆ 🚐 ♪

SELF CATERING

Belgravia Holiday Apartments

Contact: Mrs Nadine Green, Owner, Belgravia Holiday Apartments, 31 Belgrave Road, Torquay, Devon TQ2 5HX **T:** (01803) 293417 **E:** info@blha.co.uk
W: www.blha.co.uk **£ BOOK ONLINE**

Units   6
Sleeps   1-6

PER UNIT PER WEEK
£196.00 - £840.00

SPECIAL PROMOTIONS
We offer short and longer stays, free child place with two paying adults plus a discount for a two or more week stay.

Welcome to Belgravia Holiday 4 star awarded self catering apartments situated in the eviable number 1 position in the heart of the premier hotel area on Belgrave Road.
Only 500 meters to the promenade and seafront, and only a few minutes walk to Torquay town centre.
The English Riviera Centre with it's pleasure pool and sports facilities is only 250 meters away, and we are also close to the Princess Theatre, restaurants and bars.

All apartments are kept to a high standard and we offer long or short stays fitting in with the needs of our guests.

Open: All year
Nearest Shop: 0.01 miles
Nearest Pub: 0.01 miles

Units: All apartments have a fully fitted kitchen, central heating and spacious showers plus dining and sofa area.

Payment: **Leisure:** **Property:** **Children:** **Unit:**

Long Barn Luxury Holiday Cottages

Contact: Michael & Sandra Lane, Owners, Long Barn Luxury Holiday Cottages, Long Barn, North Whilborough, Newton Abbot, Torbay TQ12 5LP **T:** (01803) 875044 / 07946 378137
E: stay@longbarncottages.co.uk **W:** www.longbarncottages.co.uk **£ BOOK ONLINE**

Units   4
Sleeps   2-29

PER UNIT PER WEEK
£400.00 - £3500.00

SPECIAL PROMOTIONS
Short breaks available Autumn, Winter and Spring, 3/4/5 nights, subject to availability. View website for prices and availability.

Four Luxury 4* Gold Award Holiday Cottages in the tranquil Devon countryside sleeping 2, 6, 8 and 13 plus cots. Family friendly, each with its own garden as well as the outdoor play area with swings, climbing frames, trampoline and plenty of space for ball games. The cottages share a bookable indoor heated pool and an indoor play area catering for all the family with pool, table tennis and toys.

Open: All year
Nearest Shop: 1.5 miles
Nearest Pub: 0.5 miles

Site: **P Payment:** **Leisure:** **Property:** **Children:**
Unit: BBQ

TOTNES, Devon Map ref 1D2 S

Aish Cross Holiday Cottages

Contact: Mrs Angela Pavey, Aish Cross Holiday Cottages, Aish Cross House, Aish,
Stoke Gabriel, Totnes, Devon TQ9 6PT **T:** (01803) 782022 / 07980 712586 **F:** 01803 782022
E: info@aishcross.co.uk **W:** www.aishcross.co.uk **£ BOOK ONLINE**

Units 3	
Sleeps 1-6	
PER UNIT PER WEEK	
£395.00 - £1479.00	

The cottages are adjoined to Aish Cross House a regency country house. The Coach House, The Stable & The Hayloft are three luxurious cottages which have been lovingly converted to very high standards, each individually styled and full of character. The perfect place to relax and unwind. Close to medieval town of Totnes, amenities of Torbay, South Hams coastline & Dartmoor. **Open:** All year **Nearest Shop:** 1.5 miles **Nearest Pub:** 1.5 miles

Site: ❄ P Payment: 💳 Leisure: ⛷ ♪ ► ☋ Property: 🐾 🖥 🖲 🛏 Children: 👶 🛏 🏃 Unit: 🖥

TOTNES, Devon Map ref 1D2 SatNav TQ9 6PU C

Broadleigh Farm Park

Coombe House Lane, Stoke Gabriel, Totnes TQ9 6PU
T: (01803) 782110 **E:** enquiries@broadleighfarm.co.uk
W: www.broadleighfarm.co.uk

🚐 £12.50-£21.50	
🚗 £12.50-£21.50	
⛺ £12.50-£21.50	
85 touring pitches	

Situated in beautiful South Hams village of Stoke Gabriel, close to River Dart and Torbay's wonderful beaches. Local walks. Bus stop at end of lane. Dartmoor within easy reach. Overnight holding area available. **Directions:** Please visit our website for directions. **Open:** 15th March - 31st October for non-caravan club members. All year for caravan club members.

🌱 Site: ⛺🅿 Payment: 💳 ☀ Leisure: ♪ ► ☋ Children: 👶 Park: 🐾 🖥 🖲 📶 Touring: 🚿 🔌 ⚡

TOTNES, Devon Map ref 1D2 S

Woodpecker Barn

Contact: Louise Baker, Owner, Newhouse Barton, Ipplepen, Nr Totnes, Devon TQ12 5UN
T: 07956 656394 **E:** bookings@woodpeckerbarndevon.co.uk
W: www.woodpeckerbarndevon.co.uk **£ BOOK ONLINE**

Units 1	
Sleeps 2-7	
PER UNIT PER WEEK	
£435.00 - £1668.00	

Detached barn conversion, 3 large bedrooms, sleeping 7 (+2 travel cots), one en-suite and family bathroom. A large lounge with fully working wood burning stove, fully equipped kitchen/diner, cloakroom and private garden with 180 degree panoramic views of South Devon countryside. The complex boasts an indoor heated swimming pool, games room and external children's play area **Open:** Available all year round **Nearest Shop:** 1.5 miles **Nearest Pub:** 1.5 miles

Site: ❄ P Payment: 💳 Leisure: ► ◄ ≈ Property: 🖥 🖲 🛏 Children: 👶 🛏 🏃 Unit: 🖥 📺 📀
 🍺 BBQ 📞

WESTWARD HO!, Devon Map ref 1C1 S

Seascape

Contact: Mr Ian Gibson, 3 Wimborne Grove, Watford WD17 4JE **T:** 07801 916963
E: bookings@ace-holidayhomes.co.uk
W: www.devon-selfcatering-seascape.com **£ BOOK ONLINE**

Units 1	
Sleeps 1-8	
PER UNIT PER WEEK	
£625.00 - £1190.00	

Seascape is a luxurious 5 Star , three-bedroom apartment in Westwood Ho! Waves at high - tide lap below the balcony. Sleeps six plus two plus travel cot. Beautiful views across Bideford Bay towards Lundy. Two-mile sandy beach. Rock pools. Fantastic walks in area. Golf at Royal North Devon Club included in price. **Open:** All year **Nearest Shop:** 0.10 miles **Nearest Pub:** 0.10 miles

Site: P Leisure: ⛷ ♪ ► ☋ Property: 🖥 🛏 Children: 👶 🛏 🏃 Unit: 🖥 📺 📀 📞

WOODBURY, Devon   *Map ref 1D2*   *SatNav EX5 1HA* C

HOLIDAY, TOURING
& CAMPING PARK

Castle Brake Holiday Park
Castle Lane, Woodbury, Exeter EX5 1HA
T: (01395) 232431 **E:** reception@castlebrake.co.uk
W: www.castlebrake.co.uk

🚐 £16.00-£28.00
🚎 £16.00-£28.00
⛺ £14.00-£28.00
🏠 (21) £115.00-£999.00
47 touring pitches

Castle Brake is situated 1.5 miles from the village of Woodbury in the idyllic setting of Woodbury Common. It is a short drive to the Jurassic Coast beaches at Exmouth, Budleigh Salterton & Sidmouth or the city of Exeter. **Directions:** From M5 Jct 30 follow A3052 to Halfway Inn. Turn right onto B3180. Turn right for Woodbury at the sign for Caravan Sites, 500 yards to Castle Brake. **Open:** 11th March 2016 - 11th November 2016

Site: 🏕 Payment: 💳 ☀ Leisure: 🎣 🏊 ∪ 🍴 Children: 🏊 ⚠ Catering: 🍴 Park: 🐾 🚽 🗑 🛢 🚿 ⛲ Touring: ☎ 🚾 🔌 ⚡

BLANDFORD FORUM, Dorset   *Map ref 2D3*   S

SELF CATERING

Dairy Cottage
Contact: Broadlea Farm, Sutton Waldron, Blandford Forum, Dorset DT11 8NS
T: (01747) 811330 **E:** j.s.asbury@btinternet.com

Units   1
Sleeps   4
PER UNIT PER WEEK
£325.00

Fully-equipped cottage amidst lovely countryside, south of Shaftesbury. Two bedrooms, sitting/dining room, separate kitchen and bathroom. Good base for visiting tourist attractions. **Open:** All year **Nearest Shop:** 1.5 miles **Nearest Pub:** 1.5 miles

Site: ❀ P Leisure: ➤ Property: 🚽 🗑 🧺 🔌 Children: 🏊 🎮 🎯 Unit: 🗑 📺 🗑 🍴 📺 📀 📞

BLANDFORD FORUM, Dorset   *Map ref 2B3*   *SatNav DT11 9AD* C

TOURING &
CAMPING PARK

Inside Park
Fairmile Road, Blandford Forum DT11 9AD
T: (01258) 453719 **E:** mail@theinsidepark.co.uk
W: www.theinsidepark.co.uk **£ BOOK ONLINE**

🚐 (90) £14.00-£22.00
🚎 (10) £14.00-£22.00
⛺ (25) £14.00-£22.00
125 touring pitches

Secluded park and woodland with facilities, built into 18th century stable and coach house. Ideal location for touring the county. 1.5 miles south west of Blandford on road to Winterborne Stickland. Country walks, cycling and wildlife. **Directions:** Take Blandford St Mary exit at junction of A350/A354, proceed 1.5 miles SW of Blandford Forum on Fairmile Road. OS Ref: ST 864 052. **Open:** April to October.

Payment: 💳 ☀ Leisure: 🎣 🏊 ∪ 🍴 Children: 🏊 ⚠ Catering: 🍴 Park: 🐾 🗑 🛢 🚿 Touring: ☎ 🚾 🔌

BLANDFORD FORUM, Dorset   *Map ref 2B3*   S

SELF CATERING

Newfield Holiday Cottages
Contact: Lucy Lucas-Rowe, Manager, Newfield Farm, Pimperne, Blandford Forum, Dorset DT11 8BX **T:** (01258) 458623 / 07899 792106 **E:** bookings@newfieldholidays.co.uk
W: www.newfieldholidaysdorset.co.uk **£ BOOK ONLINE**

Units   4
Sleeps   2-19
PER UNIT PER WEEK
£235.00 - £1000.00

Barn conversion with games room and play area on a working farm in a quiet, countryside location. 4 cottages sleeping 2,6,6 and 5 (19 in total). Ideal for family groups or friends get togethers. Woodburner in Rose Cottage, wifi, bedlinen and towels included. Beautiful countryside and plenty to do close by. **Open:** Open all year **Nearest Shop:** 1 mile
Nearest Pub: 1mile

Site: ❀ Leisure: 🎣 Property: 🧺 Unit: 🗑 🗑 📺 🗑 📺 📀 📀 BBQ

Mead Cottage, 17 Bramble Drive

Contact: Mrs Chrissie Fielder, Owner, Erin Lodge, Jigs Lane South, Warfield, Berkshire RG42 3DR **T:** (01344) 303370 / 07974 809736 **E:** mead.cottage@hotmail.co.uk

Units   1
Sleeps   1-4

PER UNIT PER WEEK
£390.00 - £450.00

Situated within the heart of a World Heritage Conservation Area, offering some of best walking and coastal views in the country. Mead Cottage is a delightful, fully equipped modern mid terrace two (twin) bedroom cottage with secluded sunny garden and private car parking for 2 cars.

7 minutes stroll to coastal walks, sandy beach and lively harbour offering excellent fishing, boating and recreational activities. There are a variety of first class restaurants and pubs. It's an ideal touring base.

Approximately 1 mile to the vibrant market town of Bridport and only 10 miles to Lyme Regis.

Open: April-Mid October
Nearest Shop: 0.25 miles
Nearest Pub: 0.25 miles

Units: Lounge, kitchen with dining area, two twined bedded rooms with fitted wardrobes, bathroom with shower over bath.

Site: ✿ P Leisure: 🐾 ♪ ▶ ↻ Property: 🖼 Unit: 🍽 🖥 🖨 🛎 📺 📀 📼

Domineys Cottages

Contact: Mrs Jeanette Gueterbock, Joint owner, Domineys Cottages, Domineys Yard, Buckland Newton, Dorchester DT2 7BS **T:** (01300) 345295 **E:** cottages@domineys.com **W:** www.domineys.com

Units   3
Sleeps   3-4

PER UNIT PER WEEK
£280.00 - £520.00

SPECIAL PROMOTIONS
Short Breaks: 10 June & from 16 September 2016 5% discount, except between 1 July and 2 September 2016. for 2 week visit and return full week visit, and for CSMA members for full week.

Delightful Victorian two-bedroomed cottages, comfortably furnished and equipped and maintained to highest standards. Surrounded by beautiful gardens with patios. Heated summer swimming pool. Peaceful location on village edge in heart of Hardy's Dorset. Well situated for touring Wessex, walking and country pursuits. Regret no pets. Children 5+ and babies welcome. Check availability and book by phone 01300 345 295 or email to cottages@domineys.com; or through freetobook.

Open: All year
Nearest Shop: 1 mile
Nearest Pub: Several pubs within 2/3 miles

Site: ✿ P Payment: € Leisure: ♪ ↻ ⚡ Property: 🖼 Children: 🧸5 🎮 ♿ Unit: 🖥 🛎 📺 📼 ✎

BURTON BRADSTOCK, Dorset   Map ref 2A3   **S**

VisitEngland
3★ - 4★
SELF CATERING

Units   7
Sleeps   4-7
PER UNIT PER WEEK
£300.00 - £650.00

Cogden Cottages

Contact: Mrs Kim Connolly, Cogden Cottages, Old Coastguard Holiday Park, Coast Road, Bridport DT6 4RL **T:** (01308) 897223 / 07530 051517 **E:** oldcoastguard@hotmail.com
W: www.cogdencottages.co.uk **£ BOOK ONLINE**

Cogden Cottages is a former Victorian coastguard station with seven 2/3 bedroom cottages. Outstanding coastal views. All cottages have individual decking or patios. Free wi-fi, dishwasher, towels and linen. **Open:** All year **Nearest Shop:** 0.80 miles
Nearest Pub: 0.80 miles

Site: ✿ **P** **Payment:** 💳 **Leisure:** ♿ 🏌 ⚑ ♻ **Property:** 🐾 🖥 📶 🍴 **Children:** 👶 🛏 ⚐ **Unit:** 🍳 🍽 📺 📻 📟
📀 ⦿

CHRISTCHURCH, Dorset   Map ref 2B3   SatNav BH23 8JE   **C**

VisitEngland
★★★
TOURING &
CAMPING PARK

🚐 (60)   £18.00-£36.00
🚚 (60)   £18.00-£36.00
⛺ (14)   £18.00-£32.00
60 touring pitches

Harrow Wood Farm Caravan Park

Poplar Lane, Bransgore, Christchurch BH23 8JE
T: (01425) 672487 **F:** 01425 672487 **E:** harrowwood@caravan-sites.co.uk
W: www.caravan-sites.co.uk **£ BOOK ONLINE**

Quiet site bordered by woods and meadows. Take A35 from Lyndhurst, turn right at Cat and Fiddle pub, site approximately 1.5 miles into Bransgore, first right after school.
Sorry, no dogs.
Directions: OS: N=97758 E= 19237 GPS: 50.7719 North 1.72872 West **Open:** 1st March to 6th January.

Payment: 💳 ✿ **Leisure:** ♿ 🏌 ⚑ ♻ **Children:** 👶 **Park:** 🖥 📶 🍴 **Touring:** 🚰 🚽 🔌 ⚡

FOLKE, Dorset   Map ref 2B3   **S**

VisitEngland
★★★★
SELF CATERING

Units   4
Sleeps   4-8

PER UNIT PER WEEK
£420.00 - £1500.00

SPECIAL PROMOTIONS
Spring, Autumn and Winter Breaks. 3 nights minimum stay £295-£475 per cottage.

Folke Manor Farm Cottages

Contact: Mr & Mrs John & Carol Perrett, Folke Manor Farm Cottages, Folke Manor Farm, Folke, Sherborne DT9 5HP **T:** (01963) 210731 / 07929 139472
E: stay@folkemanorholidays.co.uk **W:** www.folkemanorholidays.co.uk **£ BOOK ONLINE**

Folke Manor Farm Cottages are spacious barn conversions in a quiet part of the Blackmore Vale area of North Dorset. We are off the beaten track and set within the peaceful grounds of the farm, which has two large ponds and over looks the stunning countryside. There is a heated indoor swimming pool open all year round.

Open: All year
Nearest Shop: 3 miles
Nearest Pub: 0.5 miles

Site: ✿ **P** **Payment:** 💳 **Leisure:** ⚑ ♻ 🎣 🏊 **Property:** 🐾 🖥 🍴 **Children:** 👶 🛏 ⚐
Unit: 🍳 🍽 📺 📻 📟 📀 ⦿ ♨ **BBQ**

LYME REGIS, Dorset   Map ref 1D2   S

Cecilia's Cottage

Contact: Sammie Steepe, 11 Monmouth Street, Georges Square, Lyme Regis, Dorset DT7 3PX **T:** (01865) 297525 **E:** sammie@pennyandsinclair.co.uk
W: www.barkerevansproperties.com

Units   1
Sleeps   6
PER UNIT PER WEEK
£1300.00 - £1500.00

Beautiful, boutique hideaway for romantic couples or small families. Open plan lounge/dining room area with wood burning stove and dining table to seat 6. Master bedroom with en suite bathroom. Further double bedroom and twin bedroom. Large master bathroom with free standing bath and separate shower enclosure. Illuminated decked patio area. Parking for one car with permit in local car park. **Open:** All year **Nearest Shop:** 0.2km **Nearest Pub:** 0.1km

Site: ✿ **Payment:** 💷 **Property:** 🐾 🖥 📺 📶 **Children:** 🍽 🏃 **Unit:** 🛏 🍴 📺 🛁 🍳 📺 📀

LYME REGIS, Dorset   Map ref 1D2   S

Sea Tree House

Contact: Mr David Parker, Sea Tree House, 18 Broad Street, Lyme Regis DT7 3QE
T: (01297) 442244 **F:** 01297 442244 **E:** info@seatreehouse.co.uk
W: www.seatreehouse.co.uk

Units   3
Sleeps   2-4
PER UNIT PER WEEK
£360.00 - £795.00

Spacious, romantic, elegant apartments overlooking the sea and sandy beach just, five minutes walk away. Central yet quiet position giving easy access to restaurants, pubs and walks along Jurassic coast. Warm, friendly welcome from owners. **Open:** All year **Nearest Shop:** 0.1 miles **Nearest Pub:** 0.1 miles

Site: ✿ P **Leisure:** 🎵 ▶ ∪ **Property:** 🐾 🖥 📺 📶 **Children:** 🍽 🏃 **Unit:** 🛏 🍴 📺 🛁 🍳 📺 📀

POOLE, Dorset   Map ref 2B3   S

Wychcott

Contact: K Streeter & Ray Saunders, Proprietor, 29 Churchfield Crescent, Poole, Dorset BH15 2QS **T:** (01202) 743735 / (01202) 741637 / 07720 842099
E: kayestreeter65@btinternet.com

Units   2
Sleeps   2-8
PER UNIT PER WEEK
£320.00 - £850.00

SPECIAL PROMOTIONS
High season saturday-saturday. Other breaks by arrangement.

Wychcott is a 3 bedroom bungalow, situated 200 yards from Poole Park and on the bus route to Sandbanks and Poole town centre, with a delightful sheltered garden and off-road parking for 3 cars. 2 bdrm have a double and a single and third bedroom is a twin. The property lends itself to disabled people as it is all on one level, and there is a ramp to aid wheelchairs. We are happy to welcome well-behaved pets and the garden is enclosed. There are gas/electricity meters which take £1 coins. Please communicate with proprietor for further details.

Open: All year

Nearest Shop: 0.25 miles
Nearest Pub: 0.25 miles

Site: ✿ P **Payment:** € **Leisure:** 🎵 ▶ **Property:** 🐾 📺 📶 **Children:** 🍽 🏃 **Unit:** 🛏 📺 🛁 📺 📀 BBQ ☎

RINGSTEAD, Dorset *Map ref 2B3* **S**

VisitEngland ★★★★ SELF CATERING

VisitEngland *Gold* AWARD

Upton Grange Holiday Cottages

Contact: Mrs Kerrie Webster, Upton Farm, Ringstead, Dorchester, Dorset DT2 8NE
T: (01305) 853970 **E:** uptonfarmholiday@aol.com
W: www.uptongrangedorset.co.uk

| Units | 6 |
| Sleeps | 2-6 |

PER UNIT PER WEEK
£430.00 - £1300.00

SPECIAL PROMOTIONS
Short breaks available from £175.00, minimum 2 nights stay.

Cosseted in the centre of the tiny unspoilt hamlet of Upton, where the World Heritage Jurassic Coastline rejoices in the simplicity of nearby Ringstead Bay, the Tithe barn of Upton Farm stands majestic as it has done, in part, since 1579.

Having been sympathetically converted into a small number of holiday cottages, furnished and equipped to the most exacting standards, these unique properties are guaranteed to incite feelings of nostalgia. We accept all major credit and debit cards.

Open: All year
Nearest Shop: 1 mile (approx)
Nearest Pub: 1 mile (approx)

Units: Some bedrooms feature 4 poster beds and log fires grace the lounges of the larger homes, our cottages can accommodate 2 - 6 persons.

Site: ✿ **Payment:** 💷 **Leisure:** 🚲 ♪ ▶ ♄ **Property:** 🖥 🗺 **Children:** 🐾 🛏 ⚲
Unit: 🗄 🍴 📺 🌀 🍳 📺 🔲 📀 ⬭ BBQ

SWANAGE, Dorset *Map ref 2B3* **S**

Westland Holiday Flats

Contact: Mrs Jackie Hancock, 6 Northbrook Road, Swanage, Dorset BH19 1PS
T: (01929) 422637 **E:** enquiries@westlandflats.co.uk
W: www.westlandflats.co.uk

| Units | 8 |
| Sleeps | 1-6 |

PER UNIT PER WEEK
£160.00 - £560.00

SPECIAL PROMOTIONS
Short breaks available low season (3 days from £105) and often for late bookings in season when available at competitive rates, please check our website or contact us for prices and availability.

Westland is a block of 8 self contained self catering holiday flats sleeping from 2 to 6 people, we are centrally situated for both the beach and shops.
Operated by the same family since 1981 we aim to provide as happy and enjoyable stay as possible for all guests looking for a value holiday, accommodating both couples and families.

* Ground floor flats available
* Private car park (one space per unit) sorry no large vans, 4x4 or large people carriers
* Special Low season rates
* Over 50% returning visitors each year
* Personally attended to by the resident proprietor

Open: All Year

Units: 8 self contained self catering holiday flats (3 Flats, 2 Maisonettes and 3 studio flats) sleeping from 2 to 6.

Site: ✿ **P Payment:** 💷 **Property:** 🐾 🗺 **Children:** 🐾 🛏 ⚲ **Unit:** 🔲 📺 📀

WAREHAM, Dorset   Map ref 2B3   SatNav BH20 5PU   C

HOLIDAY, TOURING & CAMPING PARK

🚐 (58)   £20.00-£52.00
🚎 (16)   £20.00-£52.00
🏠 (19)   £194.00-£851.00
58 touring pitches

SPECIAL PROMOTIONS
Please see website for
further details.

Durdle Door Holiday Park
West Lulworth, Wareham BH20 5PU
T: (01929) 400200 **F:** 01929 400260 **E:** durdle.door@lulworth.com
W: www.lulworth.com **£ BOOK ONLINE**

Ideally situated between Weymouth and Swanage in one of the most accessible parts of the Jurassic Coast. This delightful park has direct access to the South West Coast path, unspoilt beaches, stunning countryside and Jurassic Coast landmarks.

Fully serviced and seafront pitches for tourers and motor homes, pods and holiday homes available. Close to the picturesque Lulworth Cove and many other family attractions.

Directions: Please see website for details.   **Open:** 1st March to 31st October.

Site: ✑ **Payment:** ▦ ☼ **Leisure:** ∪ **Children:** ⅍ ⚠ **Catering:** ✕ 🍴 **Park:** 🐕 🎵 🖥 🗄 🎦 🎰
Touring: 🚰 🕒 🚽 🔌

CHELTENHAM, Gloucestershire   Map ref 2B1   S

SELF CATERING

Units   5
Sleeps   2-5
PER UNIT PER WEEK
£566.00 - £1232.00

Cotswold Cottages
Contact: The Old Mill, Bourton On The Water, Cheltenham, Gloucestershire GL54 2BY
T: (03301) 230 374 **E:** enquiries@csmaclubretreats.co.uk
W: www.retreats.csmaclub.co.uk

Perfect for a romantic getaway or family escape, all four quaint cottage apartments are housed within an old mill building. The self-catering apartments all come with fully equipped kitchens and charming lounges and offer plenty of modern comforts for an unforgettable self-catering getaway. The larger semi-detached cottage 'Stepping Stones' is perfect for bigger groups and families.
Open: From 5th January throughout 2016 **Nearest Shop:** 0.1 Miles
Nearest Pub: 0.1 Miles

Site: ✿ P **Payment:** ▦ **Property:** ∥ 🐕 🖥 🖨 **Children:** ⅍ **Unit:** 🗄 🖵 📺 📀 ☎

CHIPPING CAMPDEN, Gloucestershire   Map ref 2B1   S

SELF CATERING

Units   2
Sleeps   4
PER UNIT PER WEEK
£340.00 - £540.00

Walnut Tree
Contact: Beverley Needham, Director, Barnhaven, Willersey Fields, Worcestershire
WR11 7HF **T:** (01386) 852462 **E:** campdencottages@icloud.com
W: www.campdencottages.co.uk

A honey coloured cotswold stone cottage, without doubt in the idyllic rural setting. Guests can relax in comfort, surrounded by the open countryside whilst still being within reach of tourist attractions, pubs and a village shop.

Open: All Year
Nearest Shop: 1.5 miles
Nearest Pub: 1.5 miles

Site: ✿ P **Payment:** ▦ **Leisure:** 🚴 ♩ ▶ ∪ 🔍 ⚡ 🔍 ⚡ 🔍 **Property:** ∥ 🐕 🖥 🖨 🖨 **Unit:** 🗄 🖥 🖵 🖨 📺 ☎
📀 🔥 BBQ ☎

CIRENCESTER, Gloucestershire   Map ref 2B1   S

Units 1
Sleeps 1-8
PER UNIT PER WEEK
£595.00 - £1950.00

The Stables

Contact: Rowena Paul, Forge House, Limes Road, Kemble, Cirencester, Gloucestershire GL7 6FS **T:** (01285) 771157 / 07787 258758 **F:** 01285 771157
E: info@forgehousekemble.co.uk **W:** www.forgehousekemble.co.uk **£ BOOK ONLINE**

The Stables is a stunning recently converted barn conversion in a delightful courtyard across from the principal house. It has a 40ft beamed open plan living/dining room with contemporary logburner perfect for celebrations or relaxing weekends away. It has a fully-equipped contemporary kitchen. Double patio doors open onto a seating area with teak garden furniture - the perfect place to relax. **Open:** All Year **Nearest Shop:** Kemble Village Stores **Nearest Pub:** 0.5 miles

Site: ☼ P Payment: ⊞ **Property:** ⊞ ⊡ **Children:** ⏣ ⊞ ⚓ **Unit:** ⊡ ⊞ ⊡ ⊞ ⊡ 📺 📀 ⌀ **BBQ**

GLOUCESTER, Gloucestershire   Map ref 2B1   S

Units 2
Sleeps 1-4

Hill Farm Cottages

Contact: Mrs Margaret McLellan, Hill Farm Cottages, Hill Farm, Upton Hill, Upton St Leonards, Gloucester GL4 8DA **T:** (01452) 614081
E: hillfarmcottages@hotmail.co.uk

Two miles from Gloucester with panoramic views of the Cotswolds. Close to the dry ski slope and golfing facilities. Ideal for walking. Country pub nearby providing food. **Open:** All year **Nearest Shop:** 0.25 miles **Nearest Pub:** 0.20 miles

Site: ☼ P Leisure: ♪ ♭ ◡ **Property:** ⌂ ⊡ ⊡ **Children:** ⏣ ⊞ **Unit:** ⊡ ⊡ ⊡ 📺 🄰 📀 **BBQ**

HUNTLEY, Gloucestershire   Map ref 2B1   S

Units 1
Sleeps 6
PER UNIT PER WEEK
£250.00 - £300.00

The Vineary

Contact: Ann Snow, The Vineary, Vine Tree Cottage, Solomons Tump, Huntley, Gloucester GL19 3EB **T:** (01452) 830006

The Vineary is a self-catering annexe to Vinetree Cottage in a quiet country lane with open views. Easy access to shop, post office and country inns.
Open: All year **Nearest Shop:** 0.5 miles **Nearest Pub:** 0.5 miles

Site: ☼ P Leisure: ♪ ♭ **Property:** ⌂ ⊡ **Children:** ⏣ ⊞ ⚓ **Unit:** ⊡ ⊡ 📺 📀

LYDNEY, Gloucestershire   Map ref 2A1   SatNav GL15 4LA   C

🚐 (110) £12.00-£53.00
⛺ (110) £14.00-£38.00
🏠 (29) £306.00-£1540.00

Whitemead Forest Park

Whitemead Forest Park, Parkend, Lydney, Gloucestershire GL15 4LA
T: (03301) 230 374 **F:** 01594 564174 **E:** enquiries@csmaclubretreats.co.uk
W: www.whitemead.co.uk

With a range of woodland lodges, log cabins, and apartments, as well as camping and caravanning pitches in the heart of the forest, you can enjoy the free indoor pool, gym, sauna and Jacuzzis; join in with some great activities and entertainment; explore the acres of ancient woodland right on your doorstep, or simply curl up in your cabin and relax. **Directions:** (M5 headling South) Leave at J11 (signposted Gloucester). Take the A40 and then the A48 towards Lydney. **Open:** 22nd January, throughout 2016.

Site: ⛺🄿 **Payment:** ⊞ **Leisure:** ♪ ♭ ◈ ⚐ **Children:** ⏣ ⛰ **Catering:** ✕ 🍴
Park: ♫ ⊡ 🛢 ⬛ 🞨 **Touring:** 🔌 🕭 🔩

Holme House Barn

Contact: Tim and Diana Bateman, Holme House, Jubilee Road, Mitcheldean, Gloucestershire GL17 0EE **T:** (01594) 543875 **E:** info@holmehousebarn.co.uk
W: www.holmehousebarn.co.uk **£ BOOK ONLINE**

Units	1
Sleeps	1-6

PER UNIT PER WEEK
£450.00 - £840.00

SPECIAL PROMOTIONS
Weekends and short midweek breaks available. Mimimum stay 2 nights.

Holme House Barn is a luxury holiday cottage nestling in rural farmland, surrounded by fields and woodland. It is located 300 metres from a country lane and is only visible from Holme House itself.

Open: All year except January
Nearest Shop: 1 mile
Nearest Pub: 1 mile

Units: Double, twin and bathroom on the ground floor. Open plan kitchen-diner and sitting room upstairs with a sofa bed, easy chairs and freeview TV.

Site: ✿ P **Leisure:** 🔍 **Property:** 🐾 🖥 🔲 **Children:** 🛏 ⬛ ✶ **Unit:** 🗒 🗒 🔲 🖥 🍴 📺 🕔 💿 📻 BBQ 📞

Forget Me Not

Contact: Beverley Needham, Director, Campden Cottages Ltd, 10 Mount Pleasant, Blockley, Gloucestershire GL56 9BU **T:** (01386) 852462 **E:** campdencottages@icloud.com
W: www.campdencottages.co.uk **£ BOOK ONLINE**

Units	1
Sleeps	2

PER UNIT PER WEEK
£340.00 - £560.00

A popular, one bedroom cottage located in the centre of Blockley. Accessed from a footpath, its secluded location makes the cottage a most peaceful retreat. Forget Me Not Cottage provides all the charm and peace expected of a country home.
Open: All year
Nearest Shop: 500 yards
Nearest Pub: 500 yards

Site: ✿ P **Payment:** 💳 **Leisure:** 🚴 ♪ ∪ ✶ **Property:** ∥ 🐾 🖥 🔲 **Children:** 🛏 ⬛ ✶ **Unit:** 🗒 🗒 🔲 🖥 📺 🕔 💿 🍴 BBQ 📞

Old Market Way

Contact: Beverley Needham, Director, GL56 0AJ, Appartment 14, Old Market Way, Moreton In Marsh, Gloucestershrie GL56 0AJ **T:** (01386) 852462
E: campdencottages@icloud.com **W:** www.campdencottages.co.uk

Units	0
Sleeps	4

PER UNIT PER WEEK
£440.00 - £740.00

Old market way is found within the heart of Moreton in Marsh. The traditional Cotswold town itself is attractive and provides comprehensive facilities including restaurants, shops, and a popular Tuesday market. Moreton in Marsh also has its own mainline train station reaching Oxford (40 minutes) and Paddington (92 minutes).
Open: All year **Nearest Shop:** 10 yards **Nearest Pub:** 10 yards

Site: P **Payment:** 💳 **Leisure:** 🚴 ♪ ▶ ∪ 🔍 ✶ **Property:** ∥ 🐾 🖥 🔲 **Children:** 🛏 ⬛ ✶ **Unit:** 🗒 🗒 🔲 🖥 🍴 📺 🕔 💿 BBQ 📞

MORETON-IN-MARSH, Gloucestershire Map ref 2B1 S

Summer Cottage

Contact: 6 John Rushout Court, Northwick Park, Moreton-In-Marsh, Gloucestershire GL56 9RJ **T:** (01214) 451562 **E:** enquiries@summer-cottage.co.uk
W: www.summer-cottage.co.uk **£ BOOK ONLINE**

Units	1
Sleeps	4

PER UNIT PER WEEK
£525.00 - £790.00

This exquisite Cotswold cottage is located in a most enviable and tranquil spot on the Northwick Park Estate, Blockley. Summer cottage has recently been refurbished to a high standard it sleeps 4 has two bathrooms and has a pretty garden. Inside there is a spacious living room, modern and well equipped kitchen, two comfortable bedrooms and immaculate bathrooms all of which provide a fantastic Cotswold haven. **Open:** All year **Nearest Shop:** 2.5 miles **Nearest Pub:** 2 miles

Site: ✿ **P Leisure:** 🚴 ▶ **Property:** 🖥 📶 **Unit:** 🚪 📺 🍳 🧺 TV DVD BBQ 📞

STOW-ON-THE-WOLD, Gloucestershire Map ref 2B1 S

Broad Oak Cottages

Contact: Mrs Mary Wilson, Owner, Broad Oak Cottages, The Counting House, Stow-on-the-Wold GL54 1AL **T:** (01451) 830794 **F:** 01451 830794 **E:** mary@broadoakcottages.co.uk
W: broadoakcottages.co.uk **£ BOOK ONLINE**

Units	1
Sleeps	1-4

PER UNIT PER WEEK
£522.00 - £888.00

May Cottage is a luxury delightful, quiet 2 bedroom cottage all on one level and within a few minutes walk of Stow Square. It includes a Master Suite with luxury bathroom, a conservatory and enlarged sitting room opening onto a patio. Parking and private garden. **Open:** All year **Nearest Shop:** 0.10 miles **Nearest Pub:** 0.02 miles

Site: ✿ **P Payment:** € **Leisure:** 🚴 🎵 ▶ **Property:** 🖥 📶 **Children:** 🍼 🏓 🚼 **Unit:** 🚪 📺 🍳 🧺 TV 📷 DVD 🐾 BBQ 📞

TEWKESBURY, Gloucestershire Map ref 2B1 S

9 Mill Bank

Contact: Bill & Dawn Hunt, Owners, 7 Mill Bank, Tewkesbury, Gloucestershire GL20 5SD
T: (01684) 276190 **F:** 01684 276190 **E:** billhunt@9mb.co.uk
W: www.tewkesbury-cottage.co.uk

Units	1
Sleeps	1-3

PER UNIT PER WEEK
£375.00 - £475.00

A bijou, 16th century, riverside cottage in a delightful medieval town, bordering the Cotswolds. Outstanding location with open views across to the Malvern Hills. Nightly/weekend bookings available. "Peace, quiet and tranquility; it truly is a gem". Alistair Sawday approved. See us on TripAdvisor. Free Wi-Fi. **Open:** All year **Nearest Shop:** 0.1 miles **Nearest Pub:** 0.1 miles

Payment: € **Leisure:** 🚴 🎵 ▶ ⟳ **Property:** 🖥 📶 **Children:** 🍼 🏓 🚼 **Unit:** 📺 🍳 TV 📷 DVD

For **key to symbols** see page 7

WINCHCOMBE, Gloucestershire Map ref 2B1 **S**

VisitEngland
★★★
SELF CATERING

The Old Stables

Contact: Miss Jane Eayrs, Proprietor, The Old Stables, Hill View, Farmcote, Winchcombe GL54 5AU **T:** (01242) 603860 **E:** janeaycote@tesco.net
W: www.cotswolds.info/webpage/the-old-stables.htm

Units   1
Sleeps   1-4
PER UNIT PER WEEK
£300.00 - £390.00

The Old Stables is a delightful conversion situated in an 'Area of Outstanding Natural Beauty' in the hamlet of Farmcote. Farmcote has some of the most beautiful views in Gloucestershire.
Open: All year **Nearest Shop:** 3.5 miles **Nearest Pub:** 2 miles

Site: ✿ P Leisure: ♪ ▶ ⛵ Property: 🖥 Children: 🐾 Unit: 🛏 💻 🖥 🍳 📺 ⓓ 📀 BBQ 📞

WITHINGTON, Gloucestershire Map ref 2B1 **S**

VisitEngland
★★★★
SELF CATERING

Ballingers Farmhouse Cottages

Contact: Ian & Judith Pollard, Ballingers Farmhouse Cottages, Withington, Cheltenham GL54 4BB **T:** (01242) 890335 **F:** 01242 890150 **E:** pollardfam2005@btinternet.com
W: www.ballingersfarmhousecottages.co.uk **£ BOOK ONLINE**

Units   2
Sleeps   2
PER UNIT PER WEEK
£250.00 - £350.00

Delightful single storey cottages, converted from old farm buildings retaining many original features that tastefully combine old and new. Well furnished and equipped to ensure you enjoy your holiday. Set in a village location approximately 8 miles from Cheltenham and Cirencester. Ideal for exploring the Cotswolds and surrounding areas. **Open:** March - October **Nearest Shop:** 3 miles **Nearest Pub:** 0.06 miles

[f]

Site: ✿ P Property: 🐕 🖥 Children: 🐾 🎿 Unit: 💻 🖥 🍳 📺 ⓓ 📀 ✎

WOOLSTONE, Gloucestershire Map ref 2B1 **S**

VisitEngland
★★★★
SELF CATERING

Hill Farm Cottages

Contact: Mrs Diane Andrews, Owner, Woolstone Hill Farm, Woolstone GL52 9RG
T: (01242) 672803 / 07747 758503 **E:** woolstonehillfarm@hotmail.co.uk
W: www.thehillfarmcottage.co.uk **£ BOOK ONLINE**

Units   1
Sleeps   4

PER UNIT PER WEEK
£250.00 - £430.00

SPECIAL PROMOTIONS
Low season £250-300 pw, High season £350-£430pw.

Delightful 3 bedroomed cottage set in a area of outstanding natural beauty overlooking the beautiful cotswold Valley towards Prescott hill climb.
Customers have the privilege of using the hill for walks and can enjoy looking around the large working beef farm.
The cottage is situated 1 mile from the village of Gotherington which has a village shop, Post Office, and local pub. Ideally situated for exploring the Cotswolds and many picturesque towns and villages including Broadway, Chipping Campden, Stow-on-the-Wold and Moreton-in-Marsh. Cheltenham and its racecourse are just 4 miles away while Tewkesbury, Evesham, Stratford-upon-Avon are just a short drive away.

Open: All year
Nearest Shop: 1 mile
Nearest Pub: 1 mile

Units: Fully equipped kitchen/dining room, Lounge with leather sofas, large TV & DVD, log effect gas fire. Ground floor single bedroom with en suite. Upstairs has two bedrooms and a fully fitted shower room.

Site: ✿ P Leisure: ♪ ⛵ Property: 🖥 🖥 🖥 Children: 🐾 Unit: 🛏 🖥 💻 🖥 🍳 📺 ⓓ 📀 BBQ

ALLERFORD, Somerset   Map ref 1D1   **S**

The Pack Horse

Contact: Mr & Mrs Brian & Linda Garner, Proprietors, The Pack Horse, Allerford, Nr Porlock, Exmoor, Somerset TA24 8HW **T:** (01643) 862475 **E:** holidays@thepackhorse.net
W: www.thepackhorse.net **£ BOOK ONLINE**

Units 5	
Sleeps 2-6	
PER UNIT PER WEEK	
£340.00 - £655.00	

Located in the picturesque National Trust village of Allerford, alongside the shallow river and overlooking the ancient Packhorse bridge, you will find our quality 4* Self Catering riverside apartments and detached cottage. Well appointed with quality furnishings, flat-screen TVs / DVDs and bed linen, all situated around a pretty courtyard. Our location gives immediate access to Exmoor and its stunning countryside coast and moor.
Open: All year **Nearest Shop:** 0.1 miles **Nearest Pub:** 0.1 miles

Site: ✿ P Payment: 💷 Leisure: ♿ ♪ ⏐ ☉ Property: ♞ 🖥 🗄 🔒 ♨ Children: ♨ 🍴 ♿ Unit: 🗄 🗄 📺 ♫
📺 🎧 📀 BBQ

BATH, Somerset   Map ref 2B2   **S**

Greyfield Farm Cottages

Contact: Mrs June Merry, Greyfield Farm Cottages, Greyfield Farm, The Gug, High Littleton, Somerset BS39 6YQ **T:** (01761) 471132 **E:** june@greyfieldfarm.com
W: www.greyfieldfarm.com **£ BOOK ONLINE**

Units 5	
Sleeps 2-4	
PER UNIT PER WEEK	
£320.00 - £825.00	

Attractive stone cottages in peaceful, private, 3.5-acre setting overlooking the Mendips. The cottages are spacious, fully equipped, warm and very comfortable. Each enjoys its own garden/patio and adjacent safe parking. Free facilities include hot tub, sauna, mini-gym, information hut and barbecue hut/area.
Open: All year **Nearest Shop:** 0.5 miles **Nearest Pub:** 0.5 miles

 Site: ✿ P Payment: 💷 € Leisure: ♪ ⏐ ☉ Property: ♞ 🖥 🗄 🔒 Children: ♨ 🍴 ♿ Unit: 🗄
🗄 📺 🗄 ♫ 📺 🎧 📀 ⌀ BBQ 📞

BINEGAR, Somerset   Map ref 2B2   **S**

Spindle Cottage Holidays

Contact: Mrs Angela Bunting, Owner, Spindle Cottage self-catering holiday cottage, Spindle Cottage, Binegar, Nr Bath, Somerset BA3 4UE **T:** (01749) 840497 / 07837 782841
E: angela@spindlecottage.co.uk **W:** www.spindlecottage.co.uk **£ BOOK ONLINE**

Units 1	
Sleeps 1-5	
PER UNIT PER WEEK	
£450.00 - £780.00	

Fairytale 17th century cottage, quite magical, on Mendip Hills. Garden, summerhouse, gazebo and conservatory. Full of charm and delight. Lovely sitting room, low ceiling, oak beams. Woodburning stove. Three bedrooms: double with en suite, twin, single. Full of charm. Wells, Glastonbury, Bath, Cheddar, Wookey Hole within easy reach. Holiday of your dreams. 3 unique playhouses for young at heart.
Open: All year **Nearest Shop:** 1 mile **Nearest Pub:** 0.5 miles

Site: ✿ P Leisure: ♪ ⏐ ☉ Property: 🖥 🗄 🔒 Children: ♨ 🍴 ♿ Unit: 🗄 🗄 📺 🗄 ♫ 📺 🎧 📀
⌀ BBQ

BREAN, Somerset   Map ref 1D1   SatNav TA8 2SE   **C**

Northam Farm Holiday Park

South Road, Brean, Somerset TA8 2SE
T: (01278) 751244 **E:** stay@northamfarm.co.uk
W: www.northamfarm.co.uk **£ BOOK ONLINE**

🚐	(350)	£10.00-£28.00
🚍	(350)	£10.00-£28.00
⛺	(150)	£12.25-£23.75
450 touring pitches		

An attractive touring park, situated 200m from a sandy beach. 30-acre park offering children's outdoor play areas, fishing lake, diner, take-away, mini-supermarket, launderette, dog walks, hardstanding and grass pitches. Please contact us for updated prices. **Directions:** M5 jct 22. Follow signs to Burnham-on-Sea, Brean. Continue through Brean and Northam Farm is on the right, 0.5 miles past Brean Leisure Park. **Open:** March to November.

Site: ⚠️🏳 Payment: 💷 ☀ Leisure: ♿ ♪ ⏐ ☉ Children: ♨ ⛰ Catering: ✗ 🛒 Park: ♞ 🗄 🏪 🔥
Touring: 🚿 ⛽ 🚻 ♿ ♪

South West - Somerset

BRISTOL, Somerset   Map ref 2A2 — SatNav BS40 5RB C

TOURING & CAMPING PARK

29 touring pitches

Brook Lodge Farm Camping and Caravan Park (Bristol)

Brook Lodge Farm, Cowslip Green, Redhill, Bristol BS40 5RB
T: (01934) 862311 **F:** 01934 862311 **E:** info@brooklodgefarm.com
W: www.brooklodgefarm.com

Unique rural camping park nestled in Mendip Hills, ideal for visiting Bristol and the surrounding area. Please see website for prices. Bell tents available. **Directions:** From North: M5 jct.18A to A4 to A38, direction Bristol Airport. A38 for 8 miles, Park on left, opposite Holiday Inn. From Bath: A4 to A368 to Churchill, A38 towards Bristol 4 miles park on right opposite Holiday Inn. From Southwest: M5 jct. 22 to A38 to Bristol, travel 14 miles Camping on the right opposite Holiday Inn. Bus: A2 Cowslip Green **Open:** 1st March - 31st October

Site: ❀ A⚑ Payment: 💷 € ☼ Leisure: ✔ ♪ ∪ Children: ⚘ ⚠ Catering: BBQ Park: 🐾 ≡ 🖥 🍴
Touring: ☎ ⏱ ⚡

BURNHAM-ON-SEA, Somerset   Map ref 1D1 S

SELF CATERING

Units   2
Sleeps   2-4
PER UNIT PER WEEK
£220.00 - £435.00

Kings Lynn Holiday Apartments

Contact: Mrs V Young, Kings Lynn Holiday Flat, 18 Oxford Street, Burnham-on-Sea TA8 1LQ **T:** (01278) 786666 **E:** mikevalyoung@btinternet.com

Availability of either a two bedroom, ground floor flat sleeping 2 plus 2 (bunk beds) or a one bedroom, first floor flat sleeping 2 plus 2 (bed settee). Centrally located within sea side town of Burnham-on-Sea within easy walking distance of all amenities and sea front. Easy access to M5 motorway. **Open:** All year **Nearest Shop:** 0.25 miles **Nearest Pub:** 0.25 miles

Site: P Property: 📶 Children: ⚘ Unit: 🍴 📺 🎬

BURNHAM-ON-SEA, Somerset   Map ref 1D1 S

SELF CATERING

Units   2
Sleeps   1-4
PER UNIT PER WEEK
£230.00 - £450.00

Stoddens Farm Cottages

Contact: Mrs Ruth Chambers, Owner, Stoddens Farm, 191 Stoddens Road, Burnham on Sea, Somerset TA8 2DE **T:** 07896 886051 **E:** info@stoddensfarmcottages.com
W: www.stoddensfarmcottages.com **£ BOOK ONLINE**

Located in a Grade II listed barn conversion with plenty of character. Spacious and comfortable accommodation for up to 4 people in each of the 2 cottages. Large private gardens and stunning views over Somerset Levels.

Open: All year
Nearest Shop: 0.5 miles
Nearest Pub: 0.5 miles

Units: One double and one twin bedroom in each cottage. Spacious open plan living area. Bath with electric shower over.

Site: ❀ P Property: 📶 Children: ⚘ Unit: 📺 🎬 BBQ

CHURCHINFORD, Somerset   Map ref 1D2   S

VisitEngland
★★★★
SELF CATERING

South Cleeve Bungalow

Contact: Mr J Manning, South Cleeve Bungalow, Churchinford, Nr Taunton, Somerset TA3 7PR **T:** (01823) 601378 / 07811 362740 **E:** enquiries@timbertopbungalows.co.uk **W:** www.timbertopbungalows.co.uk

Units	2
Sleeps	2-6

PER UNIT PER WEEK
£150.00 - £650.00

SPECIAL PROMOTIONS
Late bookings available at discounted rate. Short breaks available upon request (2 nights minimum stay).

Set in a quiet, rural location in an Area of Outstanding Natural Beauty on the Devon/Somerset border. Within easy reach of National Trust houses, attractions, amenities and north and south coastlines. This fully equipped bungalow is set in its own large, secure lawned garden, that welcomes many wild and birdlife visitors, makes a superb holiday for all the family.
Plenty of walks, fishing, golf and horse riding all close by.
Managed by owners for over 20 years.
Wi-Fi installed.
Disabled friendly, wheelchair and ramp available.
One well behaved pet welcome
Games room

Open: All year
Nearest Shop: 1 mile (Taunton 9 miles)
Nearest Pub: 1 mile

Units: Large, spacious bungalow set in a third of an acre of lawned garden, 2 double rooms (1 en suite) & 1 twin, lounge, kitchen/diner and conservatory.

Site: ✿ P Leisure: ♪ ⏃ ∪ ☎ Property: ⛨ 🖳 Children: ☎ ▥ ⚹ Unit: ⬚ ⬚ ▣ 🗍 🍳 TV ⑩ 🎬 🍴 BBQ

LUXBOROUGH, Somerset   Map ref 1D1   S

VisitEngland ★★★★ SELF CATERING   VisitEngland Gold AWARD

Westcott Farm Holiday Cottages

Contact: Mrs Annette O'Hare, Westcott Farm Partnership, Westcott Farm, Luxborough, Exmoor National Park, Somerset TA23 0ST **T:** (01984) 641285
E: bookings@westcottholidaycottages.co.uk **W:** www.westcottholidaycottages.co.uk

Units	2
Sleeps	2-10

PER UNIT PER WEEK
£375.00 - £895.00

Located in the pretty village of Luxborough, Westcott Farm Holiday Cottages are ideally situated, whether you're looking for an active holiday or simply want to relax in the comfort of your holiday accommodation. We are within the Exmoor National Park, a few miles from the coast and surrounded by picturesque countryside. Our cottages are perfect for families, walkers, cyclists and horse riders. **Open:** All year **Nearest Shop:** 3 miles **Nearest Pub:** 1 mile

WALKERS WELCOME FAMILIES WELCOME CYCLISTS WELCOME

Site: ✿ P Leisure: ⚘ ♪ ⏃ ∪ Property: 🖳 🖥 🗍 Children: ☎ ▥ ⚹ Unit: ⬚ ⬚ ▣ 🗍 🍳 TV ⑩ 🎬 🍴 BBQ ☎

MINEHEAD, Somerset   Map ref 1D1   S

VisitEngland ★★★★ SELF CATERING

Anchor Cottage

Contact: Wendy Steele, Owner, 11 Haven Close, Dunster, Somerset TA24 6RW
T: (01643) 821989 / 07702 985261 **E:** enquiries@anchorcottageminehead.co.uk
W: www.anchorcottageminehead.co.uk

Units	1
Sleeps	2-4

PER UNIT PER WEEK
£295.00 - £630.00

Grade 2 listed 17th century fisherman's cottage in Minehead harbour. Refurbished to a very high standard. Double bedroom, twin bedroom, open fire, central heating, patio with views out to sea. **Open:** All year **Nearest Shop:** 0.5 miles **Nearest Pub:** 0.10 miles

Site: ✿ P Leisure: ⚘ ♪ ⏃ ∪ Property: ⛨ 🖳 🖥 🗍 Children: ☎ Unit: ⬚ ⬚ ▣ 🗍 🍳 TV ⑩ 🎬 🍴 ☎

MINEHEAD, Somerset Map ref 1D1   S

VisitEngland
★★★★
SELF CATERING

Units   8
Sleeps   2-10

PER UNIT PER WEEK
£261.25 - £1650.00

SPECIAL PROMOTIONS
Short breaks available
Oct-Easter, min 3
nights.

Woodcombe Lodges & Cottages

Contact: Mrs Nicola Hanson, Proprietor, Woodcombe Lodges, Bratton Lane, Minehead,
Somerset TA24 8SQ **T:** (01643) 702789 / 07545 271536 **E:** nicola@woodcombelodge.co.uk
W: www.woodcombelodges.co.uk **£ BOOK ONLINE**

Six 4* Lodges and two cottages set in 3 acres of gardens with superb views over the slopes of the
Exmoor National Park. Peaceful rural setting, ideal for walking or family holidays. Within a 5 minute
drive of shops, restaurants, beach and sea front. Games room, putting green. Disabled Access, Wi-Fi.
Dogs welcome. Open all year with short breaks from Oct to May.

Open: All year
Nearest Shop: 1 mile
Nearest Pub: 1 mile

Units: Lodges all single storey, kitchen fully
fitted with all mod cons & flat screen tvs.

Site: ✿ P **Payment:** 💳 **Leisure:** ⚘ ♪ ♭ ♉ 🔍 **Property:** 🐾 ⛟ 🗄 🖥 **Children:** 🐕 🎠 🌲
Unit: 🗄 🖥 📺 🖥 📺 📀 📞

PORLOCK, Somerset Map ref 1D1   SatNav TA24 8HT C

VisitEngland
★★★★
HOLIDAY, TOURING
& CAMPING PARK

🚐 (54)   £18.00-£25.00
🚍 (54)   £18.00-£25.00
🅰 (66)   £15.00-£21.50
🚐 (19)   £220.00-£480.00
139 touring pitches

Burrowhayes Farm Caravan & Camping Site &
Riding Stables

West Luccombe, Porlock, Minehead TA24 8HT
T: (01643) 862463 **E:** info@burrowhayes.co.uk
W: www.burrowhayes.co.uk

Popular family site in delightful National Trust setting on Exmoor, just 2 miles from the Coast.
Surrounding moors and woods provide a walker's paradise. Children can play and explore safely.
Riding stables offer pony-trekking for all abilities. Heated shower block with disabled and baby-
changing facilities, laundrette and pot wash.

Directions: From Minehead, A39 towards
Porlock, 1st left after Allerford to Horner and
West Luccombe, Burrowhayes is 0.25 miles along
on right before hump-backed bridge.

Open: Mid-March to end of October.

Payment: 💳 ☼ **Leisure:** ⚘ ♪ ♉ **Catering:** 🍴 **Park:** 🐾 ⛟ 🗄 🚿 🔥 **Touring:** 🚰 🔌 ♿ 🚽

PORLOCK, Somerset   Map ref 1D1   **S**

Green Chantry

Contact: Mrs Margaret Payton, Owner, Green Chantry, Home Farm, Burrowbridge, Bridgwater TA7 0RF **T:** (01823) 698330 / 07860 135848 **E:** maggie_payton@hotmail.com

A charming Victorian cottage in a tranquil setting yet close to High Street with its range of shops, pubs and cafes and good local bus services. Good walking from cottage. **Open:** All year
Nearest Shop: 0.10 miles **Nearest Pub:** 0.10 miles

Units   1
Sleeps   1-4
PER UNIT PER WEEK
£198.00 - £395.00

Site: ☼ **Leisure:** 🎣 ⚓ ∪ **Property:** 🛏 🏠 **Children:** ⛵ **Unit:** ⬚ 🖥 📻 ❄ 📺 📀

PORLOCK, Somerset   Map ref 1D1   SatNav TA24 8ND   **C**

Porlock Caravan Park

High Bank, Porlock, Somerset TA24 8ND
T: (01643) 862269 **F:** 01643 862269 **E:** info@porlockcaravanpark.co.uk
W: www.porlockcaravanpark.co.uk

🚐 (40)
🚍 (14)
⛺ (6)
40 touring pitches

Delightful, family run, award winning park situated within walking distance of quaint village of Porlock. Luxury holiday homes for hire. Touring caravans, motor homes and tents welcome. Spotless facilities. Prices on Application. **Directions:** A39 from Minehead, in Porlock village take B3225 to Porlock Weir, site signposted. **Open:** March to October.

Payment: 💳 ☼ **Leisure:** 🎣 ∪ **Park:** 🛏 🛒 🖥 🏠 🍴 **Touring:** 🔌 🕒 🏠 🚐 ⚡

SOUTH PETHERTON, Somerset   Map ref 1D2   **S**

Tanwyn

Contact: Mr & Mrs Rodney & Ann Tanswell, Planhigyn, Penylan Road, Saint Brides Major, Vale of Glamorgan CF32 0SB **T:** (01656) 880524 / 07896 892448
E: rodney.tanswell@btinternet.com **W:** www.tanwyncottage.com

Tanwyn is a modernised hamstone cottage situated in a pleasant village with a pub and an award winning restaurant. Ideally located for South coast, Exmoor, Cheddar, Bath, Wells, National Trust gardens etc. Large garden and orchard. **Open:** All year except Christmas and New Year **Nearest Shop:** 1 mile
Nearest Pub: 0.25 miles

Units   1
Sleeps   1-4
PER UNIT PER WEEK
£280.00 - £430.00

Site: ☼ P **Leisure:** 🎣 **Property:** 🖥 🏠 🛒 **Children:** ⛵10 **Unit:** ⬚ 🔥 🖥 📻 ❄ 📺 📀 ☎

TAUNTON, Somerset   Map ref 1D1   SatNav TA3 5NW   **C**

Ashe Farm Caravan and Campsite

Ashe Farm Caravan and Campsite, Thornfalcon, Taunton TA3 5NW
T: (01823) 443764 **E:** info@ashefarm.co.uk
W: www.ashefarm.co.uk

🚐 (20)   £12.00-£15.00
🚍 (10)   £12.00-£15.00
⛺ (10)   £12.00-£15.00
⬚ (3)   £220.00-£280.00
30 touring pitches

Quiet farm site, lovely views, easy access. Central for touring. Easy reach coast and hills. Family run and informal. **Directions:** Leave M5 at Jnt 25, take A358 eastwards for 2.5 miles, turn right at Nags Head pub towards West Hatch. Site 0.25 miles on RHS. **Open:** 1st April to 31st October.

Payment: ☼ **Leisure:** 🎣 🏹 ∪ 🎱 **Children:** ⛵ ⛰ **Park:** 🛏 🖥 🍴 **Touring:** 🔌 ⚡

WEDMORE, Somerset Map ref 1D1 S

SELF CATERING Gold AWARD

Units 2
Sleeps 2-5

PER UNIT PER WEEK
£330.00 - £840.00

SPECIAL PROMOTIONS
Weekend breaks during low and mid season. 2 nights minimum stay.

Pear Tree Cottages

Contact: Mrs P Denbee, Pear Tree Farm, Stoughton Cross, Wedmore, Somerset BS28 4QR
T: (01934) 712243 **E:** info@peartree-cottages.co.uk
W: www.peartree-cottages.co.uk **£ BOOK ONLINE**

In the heart of the Somerset countryside are 2 luxury converted cottages with original features, on a working farm. A mecca for walkers, cyclists, nature lovers and golfers, they are also ideally situated for those who prefer exploring the villages, towns and cities of the area. Private south facing garden/patios.

Open: All year
Nearest Shop: 1.5 miles
Nearest Pub: 0.5 miles

Units: Cottages are furnished and equipped to luxury standard, with underfloor heating and woodburner and many kitchen and entertainment appliances.

Site: ✿ P **Leisure:** ♪ ▶ ∪ **Property:** 🖥 📱 🗔 **Children:** ꕥ 🎮 ⚲ **Unit:** 🗄 🗄 📺 🗄 🔌 📺 📀 🍴 BBQ

WESTON-SUPER-MARE, Somerset Map ref 1D1   SatNav BS22 9UJ C

VisitEngland
HOLIDAY, TOURING & CAMPING PARK

🚐 (90)
🚎 (90)
⛺ (30)
120 touring pitches

Country View Holiday Park

29 Sand Road, Sand Bay, Weston-super-Mare BS22 9UJ
T: (01934) 627595 **E:** info@cvhp.co.uk
W: www.cvhp.co.uk

Country View is surrounded by countryside and just 200yds from Sand Bay Beach. Heated pool, bar, shop and children's play area. Fantastic toilet and shower facilities. Holiday Homes for sale. Please contact us for prices. **Directions:** Exit 21 of M5, follow signs for Sand Bay along Queensway into Lower Norton Lane, take right into Sand Road. **Open:** March to January.

Site: 🏠 **Payment:** 💷 ☼ **Leisure:** 🏊 ♪ ▶ ∪ ⚲ ✦ **Children:** ꕥ ⛰ **Catering:** 🍴 **Park:** 🐾 🗑 💈 🔥 **Touring:** 🚰 🔌 ♪

The Official Tourist Board Guide to **Self Catering & Camping 2016**

WINFORD, Somerset   Map ref 2A2   **S**

Regilbury Farm

Contact: Mrs. Jane Keedwell, Regilbury Farm, The Street, Regil, Winford BS40 8BB
T: (01275) 472369 **E:** stay@regilburyfarm.co.uk
W: www.regilburyfarm.co.uk **£ BOOK ONLINE**

Units   2
Sleeps   2-4

PER UNIT PER WEEK
£230.00 - £490.00

SPECIAL PROMOTIONS
Special offers available.

Working farm with cattle, sheep and chickens, set in a beautiful, quiet hamlet. Wonderful rambling including the mendip hills near by, lots to see. Guided walks available on the farm. Cowshed - double, Parlour - double/twin. No pets. 3 nights 65% / 4 nights 75% / 5 nights 85% of weekly rate. Situated very close to Chew Valley and Blagdon lakes perfect for fly fishing.

Open: All year
Nearest Shop: 2 miles
Nearest Pub: 1 mile

Site: ✿ P Leisure: ♪ Property: ▭ ▣ Children: ➷ ▥ ☆ Unit: ▣ ▤ ◈ TV ▩ BBQ

WINSFORD, Somerset   Map ref 1D1   SatNav TA24 7JL   **C**

Halse Farm Caravan & Tent Park

Halse Farm Caravan & Tent Park, Winsford, Exmoor, Somerset TA24 7JL
T: (01643) 851259 **E:** brit@halsefarm.co.uk
W: www.halsefarm.co.uk

🚐 (22)	£14.00-£19.00
🚎 (22)	£14.00-£19.00
▲ (22)	£14.00-£19.00

44 touring pitches

Exmoor National Park, small, peaceful, working farm with spectacular views. Walkers and country lovers paradise. David Bellamy Gold Conservation Award. One mile to Winsford with shop, thatched pub and tea gardens. Overnight holding area available. **Directions:** Signposted from A396. In Winsford turn left and bear left past Royal Oak Inn. One mile up hill. Entrance immediately after cattle grid on left. **Open:** 18th March to 31st October.

Site: ▲▣ Payment: ⊞ Children: ➷ ⚠ Park: ⌂ ▭ ◈ ▥ Touring: ☂ 🚐

YEOVIL, Somerset   Map ref 2A3   **S**

Little Norton Mill

Contact: Peter & Julie Allard, Owner, Norton-sub-Hamdon, Yeovil, Somerset TA14 6TE
T: (01935) 881337 **E:** p.allard190@btinternet.com
W: www.littlenortonmill.co.uk **£ BOOK ONLINE**

Units   8
Sleeps   2-4
PER UNIT PER WEEK
£249.00 - £698.00

8 Self catering cottages and apartments set in beautiful spacious gardens next to a 18th century watermill. The 2 bedroom cottages overlooking the mill pond sleep 4. The 1 bedroom apartments are a cosy base for 2. Ideal for exploring the beautiful countryside of Somerset, numerous National Trust properties, cider mills and the World heritage coast of Dorset. **Open:** All year **Nearest Shop:** 950 metres **Nearest Pub:** 800 metres

Site: ✿ Payment: ⊞ Property: ▭ ▣ Children: ➷ ▥ ☆ Unit: ▤ ▣ ◈ ◈ TV ▩ BBQ ☎

LACOCK, Wiltshire   Map ref 2B2

SatNav SN15 2LP **C**

Piccadilly Caravan Park Ltd

Folly Lane (West), Lacock, Chippenham, Wiltshire SN15 2LP
T: (01249) 730260 **E:** info@piccadillylacock.co.uk
W: www.piccadillylacock.co.uk

🚐 (39)   £19.00-£21.00
🚗 (39)   £19.00-£21.00
⛺ (4)   £19.00-£24.50
43 touring pitches

This peaceful site stands in countryside 0.5 miles from the historic National Trust village of Lacock. The site is well screened and beautifully maintained. An ideal location for exploring the West Country. **Directions:** Turn off A350 between Chippenham and Melksham, into Folly Lane West signposted Gastard and with Caravan symbol. **Open:** April to October.

Payment: ☼ **Leisure:** ♪ **Children:** 🎠 **Park:** 🐕 🛢 🛏 ☕ **Touring:** 🚿 ⏱ 🚰

MARLBOROUGH, Wiltshire   Map ref 2B2

S

Units   3
Sleeps   1-8

SPECIAL PROMOTIONS
Please contact us for prices.

Dairy Cottage, Cherry & Walnut Lodge

Contact: Mr & Mrs Mark & Hazel Crockford, Dairy Cottage, Cherry & Walnut Lodge, Browns Farm, Marlborough SN8 4ND **T:** (01672) 515129 / 07931 311985
E: crockford@farming.co.uk **W:** www.marlboroughhoilidaycottages.com **£ BOOK ONLINE**

Dairy Cottage is situated on Browns Farm which is a working beef/arable farm set on the edge of Savernake Forest overlooking open farmland. The cottage offers peace and tranquillity for a true North Wiltshire holiday. A modern, spacious, well-equipped bungalow with open fire awaits your arrival.

Open: All year
Nearest Shop: 2 miles
Nearest Pub: 2 miles

Site: ❀ P **Payment:** 🖷 **Leisure:** ♿ ♪ ⚲ ♾ **Property:** 🐕 🛏 🛢 🗒 **Children:** 🎠 🛏 🧍
Unit: 🛢 🔌 📺 🗒 🔧 📺 📻 🍽 BBQ 🔔

SALISBURY, Wiltshire   Map ref 2B3

SatNav SP3 4TQ **C**

🚗   £12.00-£27.00
⛺ (35)   £10.00-£27.00
🏕   £25.00-£85.00
15 touring pitches

Stonehenge Campsite & Glamping Pods

Berwick St James, Salisbury SP3 4TQ
T: (07786) 734 732 **E:** stay@stonehengecampsite.co.uk
W: www.stonehengecampsite.co.uk

Stonehenge Campsite is the most Beautiful Small Gold & Multi Award Winning Glamping Campsite. It is perfectly situated close to Stonehenge, Longleat Safari Park, Bath, Devizes, Wilton, Salisbury, Stourhead & The New Forest. It is the ideal touring base for South Wiltshire. We are a very friendly, well laid out campsite and have over 600+ positive reviews. We are a secluded, rural campsite in a semi woodland setting, with outstanding walking, woods, streams, 2 pubs and a excellent farm & village shop all close by.
Open: 12th February - October

🌱 **Site:** 🏕 ⛺🏴 **Payment:** 🖷 ☼ **Leisure:** ♪ ⚲ **Children:** 🎠 **Park:** 🐕 🛏 🛢 ☕ **Touring:** 🚿 🚰 ♪

Welcome Pets!

Want to travel with your faithful companion? Look out for accommodation displaying the **Welcome Pets!** sign. Participants in this scheme go out of their way to meet the needs of guests bringing dogs, cats and/or small birds. In addition to providing water and food bowls, torches or nightlights, spare leads and pet washing facilities, they'll buy in food on request, and offer toys, treats and bedding. They'll also have information on pet-friendly attractions, pubs, restaurants and recreation. Of course, not everyone is able to offer suitable facilities for every pet, so do check if there are any restrictions on type, size and number of animals when you book.

Look out for the following symbol in the entry.

Don't Miss...

Beaulieu National Motor Museum, House and Garden
Beaulieu, Hampshire SO42 7ZN
(01590) 612345
www.beaulieu.co.uk
In the New Forest, Beaulieu is one of England's top family days out. There's lots to enjoy including the world famous National Motor Museum, home to a stunning and historic collection of automobiles; Palace House, home of the Montagu family; historic Beaulieu Abbey founded in 1204 by Cistercian Monks, and World of Top Gear features vehicles from some of the most ambitious challenges.

Portsmouth Historic Dockyard
Portsmouth, Hampshire PO1 3LJ
(023) 9283 9766
www.historicdockyard.co.uk
Portsmouth Historic Dockyard offers a great day out for all the family and spans over 800 years of British Naval history. The state-of-the-art Mary Rose Museum is home to the remains of Henry VIII's flagship and an astounding collection of 400 year old artefacts recovered from the sea.

The Royal Pavilion Brighton
Brighton, East Sussex BN1 1EE
03000 290900
www.brighton-hove-rpml.org.uk/RoyalPavilion
This spectacularly extravagant seaside palace was built for the Prince Regent, later King George IV, between 1787 and 1823. Housing furniture, works of art and a splendid balconied tearoom overlooking the gardens, it is one the most extraordinary and exotic oriental buildings in the country.

Turner Contemporary Art Gallery
Margate, Kent, CT19 1HG
(01843) 233000
www.turnercontemporary.org
Situated on Margate's seafront, Turner Contemporary is a welcoming space that offers world-class exhibitions of contemporary and historical art, events and activities. Taking inspiration from Britain's best-known painter JMW Turner and designed by internationally acclaimed David Chipperfield Architects, this gleaming structure hovering over the town is the largest exhibtiion space in the South East outside of London and admission to the gallery is free.

Windsor Castle
Windsor, Berkshire SL4 1NJ
(020) 7766 7304
www.royalcollection.org.uk
Built by Edward III in the 14th century and restored by later monarchs, Windsor Castle is the largest and oldest occupied castle in the world and has been the family home of British kings and queens for almost 1,000 years. It is an official residence of Her Majesty the Queen and encapsulates more than 900 years of English history. St George's Chapel within the Castle Precincts is the spiritual home of the Order of the Garter, the oldest order of chivalry in the world.

South East

Berkshire, Buckinghamshire,
Hampshire, Isle of Wight, Kent,
Oxfordshire, Surrey, Sussex

The Thames sweeps eastwards in broad graceful curves, cutting through the beeches of the Chiltern Hills. Miles of glorious countryside and historic cities offer heritage sites, gardens, parks and impressive architecture for you to visit. In the far south, fun-filled resorts and interesting harbours are dotted along 257 miles of delightful coastline and the Isle of Wight is a only a short ferry ride away. The South East of England is an area of great beauty that will entice you to return again and again.

Oxfordshire
Buckinghamshire
Berkshire
Surrey   Kent
Hampshire
Sussex
Isle of Wight

Explore – South East

Berkshire

Renowned for its royal connections, the romantic county of Berkshire counts Windsor Castle as its most famous building. Cliveden House, former seat of the Astor family and now a famous hotel, is nearby. Highclere Castle, the setting for Downton Abbey, as well as Eton College and Ascot Racecourse can be found here too.

For fun-filled days out, explore the models and exciting events at fabulous Legoland in Windsor, or take budding scientists in the family to The Lookout Discovery Centre at Bracknell and The Living Rainforest at Thatcham for plenty of interactive hands-on activities.

Buckinghamshire

Buckinghamshire, to the north east of the region, is home to the most National Trust properties in the country including the magnificent french chateau-style Waddesdon Manor near Aylesbury, idyllic Claydon House near Buckingham and Hughendon in High Wycombe, the former home of Benjamin Disraeli. And don't forget to get some fresh air in the magnificent 'Capability' Brown landscape at Stowe, now a famous public school.

The city of Milton Keynes has its infamous concrete cows and the delights of its vast shopping centre but there's plenty more to see and do in the county. Experience a hands-on history lesson at the fascinating Chiltern Open Air Museum or get your adrenalin pumping and test your head for heights with a zip wire adventure at Go Ape Wendover Woods. For a gentler pace, enjoy a tranquil bike ride through beautiful countryside along the meandering Thames.

Hampshire & Isle Of Wight

Historic Winchester is a must-visit for its charming medieval streets, imposing Cathedral, vibrant galleries and stylish, independent shops. The ancient heaths and woodlands of the New Forest National Park were once a royal hunting ground for William the Conqueror and deer, ponies and cattle continue to roam free. Cycle, walk or go horseriding in this tranquil, car-free environment or visit attractions such as the National Motor Museum at Beaulieu and Exbury Gardens & Steam Railway for a great day out.

Coastal Hampshire, with the Solent, Southampton Water and the Isle of Wight, is one of the sailing playgrounds of England. Nearby Portsmouth Harbour has Nelson's Victory, the Mary Rose and the ironclad HMS Warrior. Stroll gently around the picturesque village of Lymington or explore the cliffs along the coast. The Isle of Wight can be reached by ferry and has amazing beaches, exciting events such as Bestival, or a step back in time, counting Osborne House and Carisbrooke Castle among its historic gems.

Kent

The Garden of England is a diverse county full of romantic villages and unmissable heritage. The opulent Leeds Castle, surrounded by its shimmering lake and set in 500 acres of spectacular parkland and gardens, has attractions and events aplenty. Take a tour of Kent's rural past with a scenic cruise along the River Medway to Kent Life, a museum and working farm with animals galore and a real sense of nostalgia for bygone days.

At the northeast tip of the county, where stunning sea- and sky-scapes famously inspired JMW Turner, Margate is home to the brilliant Turner Contemporary art gallery and the Shell Grotto, a subterranean wonder lined with 4.6 million shells. Broadstairs hosts an acclaimed annual folk festival taking place all over the town, there's hardly a venue that isn't bursting with song, music and dance. Ramsgate is also a firm favourite, with its sophisticated café culture, marina and award-winning sandy beach.

Oxfordshire

Oxford's dreaming spires, echoing quads and cloistered college lawns have a timeless beauty. The Ashmolean Museum, Britain's oldest public museum, opened in 1683 and contains gold and jewellery believed to have belonged to King Alfred, the lantern carried by Guy Fawkes and riches from ancient Egypt and Greece. The Bodleian Library, founded in 1596, contains over one million volumes, including a copy of every book published in the UK since 1900. Just north of Oxford at Woodstock sits magnificent Blenheim Palace, the birthplace of Sir Winston Churchill. Oxfordshire's quiet paths and roads are perfect for cycling, and charming picture postcard villages like Great Tew make excellent rest points.

Surrey

Ashdown Forest, now more of a heath, covers 6400 acres of upland, with a large deer, badger and rare bird population. The heights of Box Hill and Leith Hill rise above the North Downs to overlook large tracts of richly wooded countryside, containing a string of well protected villages. The Devil's Punchbowl, near Hindhead, is a two mile long sandstone valley, overlooked by the 900-ft Gibbet Hill. Farnham, in the west of the country, has Tudor and Georgian houses flanking the 12th century castle. Nearby Aldershot is the home of the British Army and county town Guildford is a contemporary business and shopping centre with a modern cathedral and university. The north of the county borders Greater London and includes the 2400 acre Richmond Park, Hampton Court Palace and Kew Gardens.

Sussex

Sussex is a popular county for those wanting a short break from the hustle and bustle of London. Cosmopolitan Brighton, surely the capital of East Sussex, oozes culture, boutique hotels, marina, shops and 'buzz'. The eccentric Royal Pavilion testifies to its history as the Regency summer capital of Britain.

To the west is the impressive Arundel Castle, with its famous drama festival, nearby popular marinas and Wittering sands. Bognor Regis is a traditional seaside resort with a blue flag beach and the usual attractions. Littlehampton, with its award-winning beaches and architecture including the East Beach Cafe and the Stage by the Sea, is a popular destination and a great base for exploring the beautiful Sussex Coast.

To the east the impressive Beachy Head and Seven Sisters cliffs provide a dramatic backdrop for Eastbourne. The Sussex section of the South Downs National Park stretches from Beachy Head to Harting Down with miles of open chalk grassland, lush river valleys and ancient forests to explore.

If heritage is your thing then Sussex has a plethora of historic houses and gardens and three of the historic cinque ports. Rye in particular, with its cobbled streets, transports the visitor back three centuries. The 1066 Story is told at Battle, near Hastings and Groombridge Place, Great Dixter and Borde Hill all feature stunningly beautiful heritage gardens.

Visit – South East

 Attractions with this sign participate in the Visitor Attraction Quality Assurance Scheme.

Berkshire

Ascot CAMRA Beer Festival
Ascot Racecourse, October
An action packed day of flat racing and an array of over 280 real ales, ciders and perries to sample at the Ascot CAMRA Beer Festival as well as traditional pub games, a quiz and live music.

French Brothers Ltd
Windsor, Berkshire SL4 5JH
(01753) 851900
www.boat-trips.co.uk
Large range of public trips on weather-proof vessels departing from Windsor, Runnymede and Maidenhead.

Go Ape! Bracknell, Swinley Forest
Berkshire RG12 7QW
(0845) 643 9215
www.goape.co.uk
Go Ape! and tackle a high-wire forest adventure course of rope bridges, Tarzan swings and zip slides up to 35 feet above the forest floor.

Highclere Castle and Gardens
Newbury, Berkshire RG20 9RN
(01635) 253210
www.highclerecastle.co.uk
Visit the spectacular Victorian Castle which is currently the setting for Downton Abbey. Splendid State Rooms, Library and Egyptian Exhibition in the Castle Cellars, plus gardens inspired by Capability Brown.

LEGOLAND® Windsor
Berkshire SL4 4AY
(0871) 222 2001
www.legoland.co.uk
A theme park and Lego-themed hotel, with over 55 interactive rides and attractions, there's just too much to experience in one day!

The Look Out Discovery Centre
Bracknell, Berkshire RG12 7QW
(01344) 354400
www.bracknell-forest.gov.uk
A hands-on, interactive science exhibition with over 80 exhibits, set in 1,000 hectares of Crown woodland.

Reading Festival
August, Reading, Berkshire
www.readingfestival.com
The Reading and Leeds Festivals are a pair of annual music festivals that take place simultaneously.

REME Museum of Technology
Reading, Berkshire RG2 9NJ
(0118) 976 3375
www.rememuseum.org.uk
The museum shows the developing technology used by the Royal Electrical and Mechanical Engineers in maintaining and repairing the army's equipment since 1942.

Royal Ascot Races
June, Ascot, Berkshire SL5 7JX
(0844) 346 3000
www.ascot.co.uk
Britain's most valuable race meeting, attracting many of the world's finest racehorses to compete for more than £5.5million in prize money.

Buckinghamshire

Aerial Extreme Milton Keynes
Milton Keynes, Buckinghamshire MK15 0DS
0845 652 1736
www.aerialextreme.co.uk/courses/willen-lake
Amaze yourself as you take each of the challenges head on.

Bekonscot Model Village and Railway
Beaconsfield, Buckinghamshire HP9 2PL
(01494) 672919
www.bekonscot.co.uk
Use your imagination in this unique world of make-believe that has delighted generations of visitors.

Gulliver's Land
Milton Keynes, Buckinghamshire MK15 0DT
(01908) 609001
www.gulliversfun.co.uk
Family theme park with 40 rides aimed at children between 2 and 12 years.

Kop Hill Climb
September, Princes Risborough, Buckinghamshire
www.kophillclimb.org.uk
In the 1900s Kop Hill Climb was one of the most popular hill climbs in the country for cars and motorcycles. Now the spirit of the climb is revived.

Marlow Regatta
June, Eton Dorney, Buckinghamshire
www.themarlowregatta.com
Marlow Regatta is one of the multi-lane regattas in the British Rowing calendar.

Milton Keynes Theatre
Milton Keynes, Bucks MK9 3NZ
www.atgtickets.com/venues/milton-keynes-theatre
Managed by the Ambassador Theatre Group, this modern 1400 seater theatre and entertainment centre offers West End and world class production and events, making every visit memorable.

National Trust Stowe
Buckinghamshire MK18 5DQ
(01280) 817156
www.nationaltrust.org.uk/stowe
Over 40 temples and monuments, laid out against an inspiring backdrop of lakes and valleys.

Reading Real Ale and Jazz Festival
June, Reading, Buckinghamshire
www.readingrealalejazzfest.co.uk
This year's festival is going to be the biggest and best yet, featuring some of the best jazz acts on the circuit.

Roald Dahl Festival
July, Aylesbury Town Centre, Buckinghamshire
www.aylesburyvaledc.gov.uk/dahl
An annual celebration of the famous author, including a 500-strong parade of pupils, teachers and musicians with puppets and artwork based on the Roald Dahl stories.

Roald Dahl Museum and Story Centre
Great Missenden, Buckinghamshire HP16 0AL
(01494) 892192
www.roalddahl.com/museum
Where Roald Dahl (1916-1990) lived and wrote many of his well-loved books.

Waddesdon Manor
Aylesbury, Buckinghamshire HP18 0JH
(01296) 653226
www.waddesdon.org.uk
This National Trust property houses the Rothschild Collection of art treasures and wine cellars. It also features spectacular grounds with an aviary, parterre and woodland playground, licensed restaurants, gift and wine shops.

Xscape
Milton Keynes, Buckinghamshire MK9 3XS
01908 397007
www.xscape.co.uk
Xscape, Milton Keynes offers a unique combination of extreme sports and leisure activities for all ages.

Hampshire & Isle Of Wight

Alton Summer Beer Festival
May, Alton, Hampshire
www.altonbeerfestival.co.uk
Celebrating the cultural heritage of Alton as a traditional area for brewing, based on the clear waters rising from the source of the River Wey, and locally grown hops.

Blackgang Chine
Chale, Isle of Wight PO38 2HN
(01983) 730330
www.blackgangchine.com
The UK's oldest amusement park overlooking the stunning South coast of the Isle of Wight. Great family fun in over 40 acres of spectacular cliff-top gardens.

Cowes Week
August, Cowes, Isle of Wight
www.aamcowesweek.co.uk
Cowes Week is one of the longest-running regular regattas in the world with up to 40 daily races for around 1,000 boats.

Dinosaur Isle
Sandown, Isle of Wight PO36 8QA
(01983) 404344
www.dinosaurisle.com
Britain's first purpose built dinosaur museum and visitor attraction, in a spectacular pterosaur shaped building, on Sandown's blue flag beach. Walk back through fossilised time and meet life sized replica dinosaurs.

Exbury Gardens and Steam Railway
Beaulieu, Hampshire SO45 1AZ
(023) 8089 1203
www.exbury.co.uk
World famous woodland garden, home to the Rothschild Collection of rhododendrons, azaleas, camellias, rare trees and shrubs, with its own steam railway.

Isle of Wight Festival
June, Newport, Isle of Wight
www.isleofwightfestival.com
Annual music festival featuring some of the UK's top acts and bands.

Isle of Wight Walking Festival
May, Isle of Wight
www.isleofwightwalkingfestival.co.uk
The festival boasts 16 days of unbeatable, informative and healthy walks.

Marwell Zoo
Winchester, Hampshire SO21 1JH
(01962) 777407
www.marwell.org.uk
A chance to get close to the wonders of the natural world – and play a big part in helping to save them.

New Forest and Hampshire Show
July, New Park, Brockenhurst, Hampshire
www.newforestshow.co.uk
The show attracts, on average, 95,000 visitors every year and brings together a celebration of traditional country pursuits, crafts, produce and entertainment.

Osborne House
East Cowes, Isle of Wight PO32 6JX
(01983) 200022
www.english-heritage.org.uk/daysout/properties/osborne-house
Step into Queen Victoria's favourite country home and experience a world unchanged since the country's longest reigning monarch died here just over 100 years ago.

Paultons Family Theme Park
Romsey, Hampshire SO51 6AL
(023) 8081 4442
www.paultonspark.co.uk
A great family day out with over 60 different attractions and rides included in the price!

Shanklin Chine
Shanklin, Isle of Wight PO37 6BW
(01983) 866432
www.shanklinchine.co.uk
Historic gorge with dramatic waterfalls and nature trail. The Isle of Wight's oldest tourist attraction, which first opened in 1817.

Southampton Boat Show
September, Southampton, Hampshire
www.southamptonboatshow.com
See the best boats and marine brands gathered together in one fantastic water-based show.

Ventnor Botanic Gardens
St. Lawrence, Isle of Wight PO38 1UL
(01983) 855397
www.botanic.co.uk
Basking in the microclimate of The Undercliff, Ventnor Botanic Garden on the Isle of Wight is one of the great gardens of Britain . A place where the pleasure of plants can be enjoyed to the fullest.

Winchester Hat Fair
July, Winchester, Hampshire
www.hatfair.co.uk
Named after the tradition of throwing donations into performer's hats, it's Britain's longest running festival of street theatre and outdoor arts.

Kent

Bedgebury National Pinetum & Forest
Cranbrook, Kent TN17 2SL
(01580) 879820
www.forestry.gov.uk/bedgebury
Ideal for cycling, walking, running and riding and adventure play. Visit the National Pinetum, one of the world's finest conifer collections, perfect for picnics.

Canterbury Cathedral
Canterbury, Kent
(01227) 762862
www.canterbury-cathedral.org/
One of the oldest and most famous Christian structures in England, stunning Canetrbury Cathedral is a holy place and part of a World Heritage Site.

Deal Castle
Deal, Kent CT14 7BA
(01304) 372762
www.english-heritage.org.uk
One of the finest Tudor artillery castles built by the order of King Henry VIII. Explore the castle's interior and outside, admire the squat, rounded bastions and canons of its defences.

Deal Festival of Music and the Arts
June/July, Deal, Kent
(01304) 370220
www.dealfestival.co.uk
Experience great classical and contemporary music from some of the world's finest music-makers, as well as theatre, opera, cinema and dance .

Dickens Festival
June, Rochester, Kent
www.visitmedway.org/events/festivals
A weekend of colourful celebration honouring one of England's greatest writers with costumed parades, street acts, competitions, readings and fair.

Hever Castle & Gardens
Hever, Edenbridge Kent TN8 7NG
(01732) 865224
www.hevercastle.co.uk
A romantic 13th century moated castle with magnificently furnished interiors, award winning gardens, miniature Model House Exhibition, Yew Maze and a unique Splashing Water Maze.

The Historic Dockyard Chatham
Kent ME4 4TZ
(01634) 823807
www.thedockyard.co.uk
A unique, award-winning maritime heritage destination with a fantastic range of attractions, iconic buildings and historic ships to explore, plus a fabulous programme of touring exhibitions, events and activities.

Kent & East Sussex Railway
Tenterden, Kent TN30 6HE
(01580) 765155
www.kesr.org.uk
Rural light railway enables visitors to experience travel and service from a bygone age aboard restored Victorian coaches and locomotives.

Leeds Castle

Maidstone, Kent ME17 1PL
(01622) 765400
www.leeds-castle.com
With 500 acres of beautiful parkland and gardens, daily activities, flying falconry displays, special events and attractions including a hot air balloon festival and a triathlon, Leeds Castle is one of the best days out in Kent.

Quex Park & Powell-Cotton Museum

Birchington, Kent CT7 0BH
(01843) 842168
www.quexpark.co.uk
Quex Park is home to the Powell-Cotton Museum and the Powell-Cotton family's extraordinary collection of natural history, ethnography and fine and decorative arts.

Rochester Castle

Kent ME1 1SW
(01634) 335882
www.visitmedway.org/site/attractions/rochester-castle-p44583
One of the finest keeps in England. Also the tallest, measures 113 feet high, 70 feet square and has walls 12 feet thick in places, partly built on the Roman city wall. Good views from the battlements over the River Medway.

Oxfordshire

Blenheim Palace

Woodstock, Oxfordshire OX20 1PX
(0800) 849 6500
www.blenheimpalace.com
Birthplace of Sir Winston Churchill and home to the Duke of Marlborough, Blenheim Palace, one of the finest baroque houses in England, is set in over 2,000 acres of landscaped gardens.

Didcot Railway Centre

Oxfordshire OX11 7NJ
(01235) 817200
www.didcotrailwaycentre.org.uk
Living museum recreating the golden age of the Great Western Railway. Steam locomotives and trains, Brunel's broad gauge railway, engine shed and small relics museum.

Henley Royal Regatta

July, Henley, Oxfordshire
www.hrr.co.uk
Attracting thousands of visitors over a five-day period and spectators will be thrilled by over 200 races of international standard.

Oxford Official Guided Walking Tour

owtours@visitoxfordshire.org
A fascinating and entertaining way to explore and learn about this unique city, its history, University, famous people and odd traditions. Covering a wide range of topics from an introduction to the city and its University to Inspector Morse, Harry Potter, J.R.R. Tolkien and more.

Surrey

British Wildlife Centre

Lingfield, Surrey RH7 6LF
(01342) 834658
www.britishwildlifecentre.co.uk
The best place to see and learn about Britain's own wonderful wildlife, with over 40 different species including deer, foxes, otters, badgers, pine martens and red squirrels.

Guildford Cathedral

Surrey GU2 7UP
(01483) 547860
www.guildford-cathedral.org
New Anglican Cathedral, the foundation stone of which was laid in 1936. Notable sandstone interior and marble floors. Restaurant and shops.

Investec Derby

June, Epsom Racecourse, Surrey
www.epsomderby.co.uk
The biggest horse race in the flat-racing calendar.

Loseley Park

Guildford, Surrey GU3 1HS
(01483) 405120
www.loseleypark.co.uk
A beautiful Elizabethan mansion standing in ancient Surrey Parkland. Still the home of the More-Molyneux family, it is remarkably unchanged since 1562 when Sir William More laid the first stones .

RHS Garden Wisley

Woking, Surrey GU23 6QB
(0845) 260 9000
www.rhs.org.uk/wisley
Enjoy a day out at the world-class Wisley garden, stretching over 240 glorious acres. Join in the fun with all year round events.

RHS Hampton Court Palace Flower Show

July, Hampton Court, Surrey
www.rhs.org.uk
One of the biggest events in the horticulture calendar.

Thorpe Park

Chertsey, Surrey KT16 8PN
(0871) 663 1673
www.thorpepark.com
Thorpe Park Resort is an island like no other, with over 30 thrilling rides, attractions and live events.

Wings & Wheels

August, Dunsfold Aerodrome, Surrey
www.wingsandwheels.net
A popular family day out featuring an outstanding variety of dynamic aviation, motoring displays and iconic cars.

Sussex

1066 Battle Abbey and Battlefield

East Sussex TN33 0AD
(01424) 775705
www.english-heritage.org.uk
An abbey founded by William the Conqueror on the site of the Battle of Hastings.

Arundel Festival

August, Arundel, Sussex
www.arundelfestival.co.uk
Ten days of the best music, theatre, art and comedy.

Arundel Wetland Centre

West Sussex BN18 9PB
(01903) 883355
www.wwt.org.uk/visit/arundel
WWT Arundel Wetland Centre is a 65-acre reserve in an idyllic setting, nestled at the base of the South Downs National Park.

Brighton Festival

29 New Road, Brighton BN1 1UG
(01273) 709709
www.brightonfestival.org
A sensational programme of art, theatre, dance, music, literature and family shows starting with a Children's Parade winding its way through the city.

Brighton Lanes

Brighton, East Sussex
www.visitbrighton.com/shopping/the-lanes
From quirky stores, vintage antiques and boutiques to live music, funky restaurants and cutting edge art, Brighton Lanes is crammed with interesting independent shops and watering holes.

Brighton Fringe

May, Brighton, Sussex
www.brightonfestivalfringe.org.uk
One of the largest fringe festivals in the world, offering cabaret, comedy, classical concerts, club nights, theatre and exhibitions, as well as street performances.

British Airways i360

Brighton BN1 2LN
(03337) 720360
www.britishairwaysi360.com
Take a flight into the skies and see Sussex as you've never seen it before. The 450 feet high British Airways i360 will offer breath-taking 360 degree views of up to 26 miles from the world's first vertical cable car. Lift-off summer 2016!

Chichester Cathedral

West Sussex PO19 1RP
(01243) 782595
www.chichestercathedral.org.uk
A magnificent Cathedral with treasures ranging from medieval stone carvings to world famous 20th century artworks.

Denmans Garden

Fontwell, West Sussex BN18 0SU
(01243) 542808
www.denmans-garden.co.uk
Beautiful 4 acre garden designed for year round interest through use of form, colour and texture. Beautiful plant centre, award-winning and fully licensed Garden Café.

Eastbourne Beer Festival
October, Winter Gardens, Eastbourne, Sussex
www.visiteastbourne.com/beer-festival
Eastbourne's annual beer festival features over 120 cask ales, plus wines, international bottled beers, ciders and perries. Each session features live music.

Eastbourne Festival
July, Eastbourne, Sussex
www.eastbournefestival.co.uk
Eastbourne Festival is an Open Access Arts Festival which takes place annually for three weeks. It has become recognised as an annual showcase for local professional and amateur talent.

England's Medieval Festival
August, Herstmonceux Castle, Sussex
www.englandsmedievalfestival.com
A celebration of the Middle Ages.

Fishers Adventure Farm Park
Billingshurst, West Sussex RH14 0EG
(01403) 700063
www.fishersfarmpark.co.uk
Award-winning Adventure Farm Park and open all year. Ideally suited for ages 2-11 years. Huge variety of animals, rides and attractions from the skating rink, to pony rides, toboggan run, bumper boats, theatre shows and more!

Glorious Goodwood
July, Chichester, Sussex
www.goodwood.com
Bursting with fabulous fashions, succulent strawberries, chilled Champagne and top horse racing stars, as well as music and dancing.

Glyndebourne Festival
May - August, Lewes, Sussex
www.glyndebourne.com
An English opera festival held at Glyndebourne, an English country house near Lewes.

Great Dixter House and Gardens
Rye, East Sussex TN31 6PH
(01797) 252878
www.greatdixter.co.uk
An example of a 15th century manor house with antique furniture and needlework. The house is restored and the gardens were designed by Lutyens.

London to Brighton Bike Ride
June, Ends on Madeira Drive, Brighton, Sussex
www.bhf.org.uk/london-brighton
The annual bike ride from the capital to the coast in aid of the British Heart Foundation. The UK's largest charity bike ride with 27,000 riders.

Pashley Manor Gardens
Wadhurst, East Sussex TN5 7HE
(01580) 200888
www.pashleymanorgardens.com
Pashley Manor Gardens offer a blend of romantic landscaping, imaginative plantings, fine old trees, fountains, springs and large ponds plus exciting special events.

Petworth House and Park
West Sussex GU28 0AE
(01798) 342207
www.nationaltrust.org.uk/petworth
Discover the National Trust's finest art collection displayed in a magnificent 17th century mansion within a beautiful 700-acre park. Petworth House contains works by artists such as Van Dyck, Reynolds and Turner.

RSPB Pulborough Brooks
West Sussex RH20 2EL
(01798) 875851
www.rspb.org.uk
Set in the scenic Arun Valley with views to the South Downs, the two mile circular nature trail leads around this beautiful reserve.

Tourist Information Centres

When you arrive at your destination, visit the Tourist Information Centre for quality assured help with accommodation and information about local attractions and events, or email your request before you go.

Aldershot	Prince's Hall	01252 320968	aldershotvic@rushmoor.gov.uk
Ashford	Ashford Gateway Plus	01233 330316	tourism@ashford.gov.uk
Aylesbury	The Kings Head	01296 330559	tic@aylesburyvaledc.gov.uk
Banbury	Castle Quay Shopping Centre	01295 753752	banbury.tic@cherwell-dc.gov.uk
Battle	Yesterdays World	01797 229049	battletic@rother.gov.uk
Bexley (Hall Place)	Central Library	0208 3037777	touristinfo@bexleyheritagetrust.org.uk
Bicester	Unit 86a Bicester Village	01869 369055	bicestervisitorcentre@valueretail.com
Bracknell	The Look Out Discovery Centre	01344 354409	thelookout@bracknell-forest.gov.uk
Brighton	Brighton Centre Box Office	01273 290337	visitor.info@visitbrighton.com
Buckingham	The Old Gaol Museum	01280 823020	buckinghamtic@touismse.com
Burford	33a High Street	01993 823558	burford.vic@westoxon.gov.uk
Burgess Hill	Burgess Hill Town Council	01444 238202	touristinformation@burgesshill.gov.uk
Canterbury	Beaney House	01227 378100	canterburyinformation@canterbury.gov.uk
Chichester	The Novium	01243 775888	chitic@chichester.gov.uk
Deal	The Landmark Centre	01304 369576	info@deal.gov.uk
Dover	Dover Museum	01304 201066	tic@doveruk.com
Eastbourne	Cornfield Road	0871 663 0031	tic@eastbourne.gov.uk

Faringdon	The Corn Exchange	01367 242191	tic@faringdontowncouncil.gov.uk
Faversham	Fleur de Lis Heritage Centre	01795 534542	ticfaversham@btconnect.com
Folkestone	20 Bouverier Place	01303 258594	chris.kirkham@visitkent.co.uk
Fordingbridge	Kings Yard	01425 654560	fordingbridgetic@tourismse.com
Gosport	Gosport TIC, Bus Station Complex	023 9252 2944	tourism@gosport.gov.uk
Gravesend	Towncentric	01474 337600	info@towncentric.co.uk
Guildford	155 High Street	01483 444333	tic@guildford.gov.uk
Hastings	Queens Square	01424 451111	hic@hastings.gov.uk
Hayling Island	Central Beachlands	023 9246 7111	tourism@havant.gov.uk
Henley-on-Thames	Town Hall,	01491 578034	vic@henleytowncouncil.gov.uk
High Wycombe	High Wycombe Library	01494 421892	tourism_enquiries@wycombe.gov.uk
Horsham	9 The Causeway	01403 211661	visitor.information@horsham.gov.uk
Lewes	187 High Street	01273 483448	lewes.tic@lewes.gov.uk
Littlehampton	The Look & Sea Centre	01903 721866	jo-lhvic@hotmail.co.uk
Lymington	St Barbe Museum	01590 676969	office@stbarbe-museum.org.uk
Lyndhurst & New Forest	New Forest Museum	023 8028 2269 / 023 8028 5492	info@thenewforest.co.uk
Maidenhead	Maidenhead Library	01628 796502	maidenhead.tic@rbwm.gov.uk
Maidstone	Maidstone Museum	01622 602169	tourism@maidstone.gov.uk
Marlow	55a High Street	01628 483597	tourism_enquiries@wycombe.gov.uk
Midhurst	North Street	01730 812251	midtic@chichester.gov.uk
Newbury	The Wharf	01635 30267	tourism@westberks.gov.uk
Oxford	Visit Oxfordshire, Oxford Information Centre	01865 252200	info@visitoxfordshire.org
Petersfield	County Library	01730 268829	petersfieldinfo@btconnect.com
Portsmouth	D-Day Museum	023 9282 6722	vis@portsmouthcc.gov.uk
Princes Risborough	Tower Court	01844 274795	risborough_office@wycombe.gov.uk
Ringwood	Ringwood Gateway	01425 473883	town.council@ringwood.gov.uk
Rochester	95 High Street	01634 338141	visitor.centre@medway.gov.uk
Romsey	Museum & Tourist Information Centre	01794 512987	romseytic@testvalley.gov.uk
Royal Tunbridge Wells	Unit 2 The Corn Exchange	01892 515675	touristinformationcentre @tunbridgewells.gov.uk
Sandwich	The Guildhall	01304 613565 / 617197	tourism@sandwichtowncouncil.gov.uk
Seaford	37 Church Street	01323 897426	seaford.tic@lewes.gov.uk
Sevenoaks	Stag Community Arts Centre	01732 450305	tic@sevenoakstown.gov.uk
Swanley	Library & Information Centre	01322 614660	touristinfo@swanley.org.uk
Tenterden	Tenterden Gateway	08458 247 202	
Thame	Town Hall	01844 212833	oss@thametowncouncil.gov.uk
Thanet	The Droit House	01843 577577	visitorinformation@thanet.gov.uk
Tonbridge	Tonbridge Castle	01732 770929	tonbridge.castle@tmbc.gov.uk
Winchester	Guildhall	01962 840500	tourism@winchester.gov.uk
Windsor	Old Booking Hall	01753 743900	windsor.tic@rbwm.gov.uk
Witney	3 Welsh Way	01993 775802 / 861780	witney.vic@westoxon.gov.uk

Regional Contacts and Information

For more information on accommodation, attractions, activities, events and holidays in South East England, contact one of the following regional or local tourism organisations. Their websites have a wealth of information and many produce free publications to help you get the most out of your visit.

www.visitsoutheastengland.com
email enquiries@tourismse.com or
call (023) 8062 5400.

www.visitnewbury.org.uk
www.visitbuckinghamshire.org
www.visit-hampshire.co.uk
www.visitisleofwight.co.uk
www.visitkent.co.uk
www.visitoxfordandoxfordshire.com
www.visitsurrey.com
www.visitbrighton.com

Stay – South East

Entries appear alphabetically by town name in each county. A key to symbols appears on page 7

HURLEY, Berkshire Map ref 2C2

SatNav SL6 5NN

Hurley Riverside Park

Hurley, Near Henley-on-Thames SL6 5NE
T: (01628) 824493 E: info@hurleyriversidepark.co.uk
W: www.hurleyriversidepark.co.uk £ BOOK ONLINE

(138)	£15.00-£30.00
(138)	£15.00-£30.00
(130)	£13.00-£26.00
(10)	£300.00-£550.00

200 touring pitches

SPECIAL PROMOTIONS
Touring Park Loyalty Card. Membership Card. Giveaways and offers on Facebook and Twitter. Short breaks available in Hire Caravan Holiday Homes and ReadyTents one week prior to arrival.

Family-run park alongside the River Thames, ideal for visiting LEGOLAND® Windsor, Henley-on-Thames, Oxford & London. Tents, tourers, motorhomes & RVs are welcome. Caravan Holiday Homes and ReadyTents for hire. Heated shower blocks, laundry, shop, nature trail, children's playground and outdoor table tennis tables , riverside picnic grounds, slipway, fishing in season and free Wi-Fi. 2 day LEGOLAND® tickets available at a great rate and discounts at many other local attractions are also available.

Directions: M4 J8/9 or M40 J4, onto A404(M), third exit to Henley (A4130). Past Hurley Village, turn right into Shepherds Lane.

Open: March to October.

Payment: Leisure: Children: Catering: Park: Touring:

READING, Berkshire Map ref 2C2

SatNav RG7 1SP

Wellington Country Park - Touring Caravan & Campsite

Odiham Road, Riseley, Nr Reading RG7 1SP
T: (0118) 932 6444 F: 0118 932 6445 E: info@wellington-country-park.co.uk
W: www.wellington-country-park.co.uk £ BOOK ONLINE

(56)	£17.00-£37.00
(56)	£17.00-£37.00
(30)	£15.50-£31.00

86 touring pitches

Set within beautiful woodlands, fees include 2 people and unlimited access to Country Park with nature trails, animal farm, play areas, miniature railway, sand pits and mini golf. Easy access from both M3 & M4. Please note: the Sat Nav postcode will not take you to the entrance of the Country Park or Campsite. Please see website for details. **Directions:** Hampshire/Berkshire border between Reading/Basingstoke. Do not use Sat Nav. M4 junction 11 A33 to Basingstoke. M3 junction 5 B3349 to Reading. **Open:** March to November.

Payment: Leisure: Children: Catering: Park: Touring:

The Official Tourist Board Guide to *Self Catering & Camping* 2016

Lower Bassibones Farm

Contact: Anthea and Geoff Hartley, Owners, Lower Bassibones Farm, Ballinger Road, Great Missenden, Buckinghamshire HP16 9LA **T:** (01494) 837798 **F:** 01494 837778
E: lowerbassibones@yahoo.co.uk **W:** www.discover-real-england.com

Units   2
Sleeps   1-5

PER UNIT PER WEEK
£345.00 - £695.00

Lower Bassibones Farm is situated in a rural position in the Chiltern Hills, in an officially designated Area of Outstanding Natural Beauty, but within easy reach of London (40mins) and Heathrow & Luton Airports (50mins). The farm comprises two, completely separate, self-contained, properties.

The Barn: A beautifully restored period barn with a large private garden and parking. Sleeps 4/5 guests. Inglenook Cottage: Situated across the lane from the farm, a cosy period cottage with private garden. Sleeps 4 guests. Both properties have free Wi-Fi access, a TV & DVD player. Both are non-smoking.

Open: All year
Nearest Shop: 0.5 miles
Nearest Pub: 0.75 miles

Units: Both properties furnished to a high standard.

Site: ❀ P Payment: 🔲 € Leisure: ▶ Property: 🐾 🚘 🅖 🗺 Children: 🧸 🛏 🎠
Unit: 🍽 🗄 🖥 🗄 ⚒ 📺 📀 BBQ 📞

Cowes View Coastguard Cottage

Contact: Mel Vennis, Hill Head, Fareham, Hampshire PO14 3JJ **T:** (01329) 664236 / 07712 650805 **E:** enquiries@cowesview.co.uk
W: www.cowesview.co.uk

Units   1
Sleeps   1-5
PER UNIT PER WEEK
£445.00 - £825.00

Welcome to Cowes View, your seaside home from home, a place where smugglers were stopped bringing whisky and tobacco ashore and later where coastguards aided seafaring folk. Now you can soak up the history, the whisky, the sea and fantastic panoramic ever changing views across The Solent. Lay in bed and listen to the sea lapping against the shore, beautiful sunsets, smell the sea, enjoy the air and relax. **Open:** All year **Nearest Shop:** 1 mile **Nearest Pub:** 100m

 Site: ❀ Leisure: 🎣 Property: 🚘 🅖 🗺 Children: 🧸 🛏 🎠 Unit: 🍽 🗄 🖥 🗄 ⚒ 📺 📀 BBQ

Downton Holiday Park

Contact: Shorefield Road, Milford-on Sea, Lymington SO41 0LH
T: (01590) 642515 / (01425) 476131 **F:** 01590 642515 **E:** downtonoffice@btconnect.com
W: www.downtonholidaypark.co.uk

Units   23
Sleeps   1-8
PER UNIT PER WEEK
£150.00 - £685.00

Downton Holiday Park is a small, peaceful park, close to the New Forest and less than 5 minutes drive from the beach Milford-on-Sea. We have a four star rating from Visit England and we are also members of New Forest Tourism, Bournemouth Tourism Services and the British Holiday and Home Parks Association. We have 74 Caravans, of which 23 are available for hire. We are perfectly placed for the ideal holiday, whatever your interests. **Open:** March to October.

Payment: 🔲 Leisure: 🚲 🎣 Property: 🐾 🚘 🅖 🛖 Children: 🧸

OWER, Hampshire   Map ref 2C3

Green Pastures Caravan Park

Green Pastures Farm, Whitemoor Lane, Romsey SO51 6AJ
T: (023) 8081 4444 E: enquiries@greenpasturesfarm.com
W: www.greenpasturesfarm.com

£20.00-£25.00
£20.00-£25.00
£15.00
100 touring pitches

Located within the New Forest, Green Pastures Farm is ideal for families as there is plenty of space for children to play in full view of the caravans and tents. However, it is also peaceful enough to be able to unwind after a busy working week. **Directions:** Drive Off A3090 between Romsey and Cadnam. From M27 junction 2 follow signs for Salisbury until our own brown signs are seen at big roundabout. **Open:** 15th March - 3rd November.

Site: A⊞ Payment: £③ ☼ Leisure: ⚲ ♪ ► ∪ Children: ⚲ Catering: ⚥ Park: ⚹ ▣ ⌘ Touring: ♨ ☺ ♣

PITT, Hampshire   Map ref 2C3

Units   14
Sleeps   1-6
PER UNIT PER WEEK
£575.00 - £1150.00

South Winchester Lodges

Contact: Lesley Ross, South Winchester Golf Club, Romsey Road, Winchester, Hampshire SO22 5SW T: (01962) 820490 E: info@southwinchesterlodges.co.uk
W: www.southwinchesterlodges.co.uk **£ BOOK ONLINE**

Award winning, two and three bedroom, five star lodges, some with hot tubs, beautifully set on South Winchester Golf Course just 3 miles from the city centre of Winchester.
Short breaks available from £380.00.
Open: All year **Nearest Shop:** 0.10 miles
Nearest Pub: 0.10 miles

Site: ✿ P Payment: £③ Leisure: ⚲ ♪ ► ∪ Property: ⚹ ⚏ ▣ ▦ Children: ⚲ ▥ ⚷ Unit: ▢ ▣ ▥ ▣ ▧ ▤ 📺 ⊙ ⊙ BBQ

PORTSMOUTH AND SOUTHSEA, Hampshire   Map ref 2C3

Units   3
Sleeps   2-6
PER UNIT PER WEEK
£900.00 - £1890.00

Admiralty Apartments

Contact: Booking Enquiries, Portsmouth Naval Base Property Trust, 19 College Road, HM Naval Base, Portsmouth PO1 3LJ T: (023) 9282 0921 F: 023 9286 2437
E: admiraltyquarter@pnbpt.co.uk W: www.pnbpropertytrust.org

Admiralty Quarter is ideally located within easy walking distance of the City's historic attractions, overlooking Portsmouth Harbour and the Historic Dockyard. The contemporary apartments are furnished to an exceptionally high standard, offering fast broadband connection, secure parking and most enjoying spectacular views towards the Solent and the Isle of Wight. **Open:** All year **Nearest Shop:** 0.01 miles **Nearest Pub:** 0.01 miles

Site: P Payment: £③ Property: ⚏ ▦ Children: ⚲ ▥ ⚷ Unit: ▢ ▣ ▥ ▣ ▧ 📺 ⊙ ⊙

ROMSEY, Hampshire   Map ref 2C3   SatNav SO51 6FH C

Hill Farm Caravan Park
Branches Lane, Sherfield English, Romsey SO51 6FH
T: (01794) 340402 **E:** gjb@hillfarmpark.com
W: www.hillfarmpark.com

🚐 (70)	£15.00-£35.00	
🚙 (70)	£15.00-£35.00	
⛺ (30)	£15.00-£35.00	
🏠 (6)	£280.00-£550.00	

100 touring pitches

In countryside on the edge of the New Forest, our quiet family-run site provides an ideal base for mature visitors and families with younger children to visit the area. **Directions:** Please see our website. **Open:** Touring & camping: March to October Statics: February to December.

Site: A🅿 **Payment:** 💳 ☀ **Leisure:** 🏊 ♪ ► ∪ **Children:** 🧸 🎢 **Catering:** ✗ 🍴 **Park:** 🐾 🚉 🗄 ⛵ **Touring:** 🚿 ⏱ 🚐 ⚡

STOCKBRIDGE, Hampshire   Map ref 2C2   S

Larch Loft Self Catering Apartment
Contact: Emma Way, Owner, Drove Road, Chilbolton, Stockbridge, Hampshire SO20 6AB
T: (01264) 860649 / 07973 862954 **E:** stay@larchloft.co.uk
W: www.larchloft.co.uk

Units   1
Sleeps   1-2
PER UNIT PER WEEK
£385.00 - £595.00

Larch Loft is a luxury apartment for 2, situated in the beautiful Test Valley village of Chilbolton, Hampshire. WiFi, linen, towels, our welcome hamper and a very cosy and modern apartment, with its own courtyard garden, await your arrival. Quiet village location with River Test, pub and shop in walking distance. Great base from which to explore Cathedral cities of Winchester & Salisbury. **Open:** All Year except Christmas and New Year **Nearest Shop:** 1/2 mile **Nearest Pub:** 1/2 mile

Site: ✿ **Payment:** 💳 **Leisure:** ♪ ► ∪ **Property:** 🖥 **Children:** 🧸

WINCHESTER, Hampshire   Map ref 2C3   S

Mallard Cottage
Contact: Mr David Simpkin, Owner, 64 Chesil Street, Winchester, Hampshire SO23 0HX
T: (01962) 853002 **E:** bookings@mallardcottage.co.uk
W: www.mallardcottage.co.uk

Units   1
Sleeps   1-4
PER UNIT PER WEEK
£500.00 - £650.00

Attractive Grade II listed building, two bedroom, two shower room cottage annexe, accommodating up to 4 people plus travel cot. Based within a five minute walk of the historic heart of the city of Winchester. Peaceful riverside garden with summerhouse. The cottage and garden are both non-smoking throughout. We regret that we cannot accommodate pets. **Open:** All year **Nearest Shop:** 400 yards **Nearest Pub:** 200 yards

Site: ✿ P **Payment:** 💳 **Leisure:** ♪ ► ∪ **Property:** 🖥 🗄 📺 **Children:** 🧸 🛏 🚶 **Unit:** 🗄 🖥 📺 BBQ

NEWPORT, Isle of Wight   Map ref 2C3   S

Newbarn Country Cottages
Contact: Steve Harvey, Newbarn Farm, Newbarn Lane, Gatcombe, Newport, Isle of Wight PO30 3EQ **T:** (01983) 721202 / 07739 868201 **E:** newbarncountrycottages@gmail.com
W: www.newbarncountrycottages.co.uk **£ BOOK ONLINE**

Units   3
Sleeps   2-6
PER UNIT PER WEEK
£250.00 - £800.00

Three beautiful barn conversions in a secluded downland valley in the centre of the Isle of Wight, Parlour Cottage sleeping up to 6 (4 adults and 2 children) and Stable and Dairy Cottages sleeping 4 people. Being centrally located all of the islands attractions are within easy reach and the rural location is ideal for walkers or mountain bikers. **Open:** All year **Nearest Shop:** 2 miles **Nearest Pub:** 3 miles

Site: P **Leisure:** 🏊 ► ∪ **Property:** ♿ 🖥 🗄 **Children:** 🧸 🛏 🚶 **Unit:** 🗄 📺 📀

Claverton House Self Catering

Contact: Mr Harry Metz, Manager, Claverton House Self Catering, Claverton House, 12 The Strand, Ryde PO33 1JE **T:** (01983) 613015 **E:** clavertonhouse@aol.com

Beautiful holiday residence is situated in the idyllic seaside town of Ryde on the seafront. Five minutes walk to town centre and passenger ferries, ten minutes drive to car ferry. **Open:** All year except Christmas and New Year **Nearest Shop:** 0.20 miles **Nearest Pub:** 0.20 miles

Units	2
Sleeps	2-3

PER UNIT PER WEEK
£200.00 - £350.00

Site: ❀ P Payment: € Leisure: ♿ Property: 🖵 📱 🖥 Children: 🧸 🎠 Unit: 🗄 📺 🎮 TV DVD

Whitefield Forest Touring Park

Brading Road, Ryde PO33 1QJ
T: (01983) 617069 **E:** pat&louise@whitefieldforest.co.uk
W: www.whitefieldforest.co.uk

Award winning campsite in the picturesque woodland of Whitefield Forest. Near to the sandy beaches of Ryde & Sandown on a good bus route, ideal for caravans, motor homes and tents. Special offers available on ferry travel & for over 50's. **Directions:** Just off A3055 follow to Brading, at Tesco's roundabout straight across, site approx half mile on left hand side. **Open:** 18th March - 3rd October 2016.

🚐 (50)	£17.50-£26.00
🚗 (50)	£17.50-£26.00
⛺ (50)	£17.50-£26.00

100 touring pitches

Payment: 💷 ☼ Leisure: ♪ ► ∪ Children: 🧸 🎡 Catering: 🍴 Park: 🐕 🖵 🗄 🅿 Touring: 🚰 🛁 🔌 ⚡

Luccombe Villa Holiday Apartments

Contact: Mr & Mrs Miles & Fiona Seymour, Luccombe Villa, 9 Popham Road, Shanklin, Isle of Wight PO37 6RF **T:** (01983) 862825 / 07774 784116 **E:** info@luccombevilla.co.uk
W: www.luccombevilla.co.uk **£ BOOK ONLINE**

Nine apartments in Shanklin Old Village. Wonderful location, close to the town, beach and beautiful walks. Comfortably furnished with well equipped kitchens, digital TV, DVD and free Wi-Fi. Guests' garden with outdoor swimming pool. Plenty of parking. Pets welcome. Tariff includes ferry. **Open:** All year **Nearest Shop:** 0.10 miles **Nearest Pub:** 0.10 miles

Units	9
Sleeps	1-6

PER UNIT PER WEEK
£380.00 - £1235.00

FAMILIES PETS! Site: ❀ P Payment: 💷 Leisure: ♿ ♪ ► ∪ ⚓ Property: 🐕 🗄 🖥 Children: 🧸 🎠 ♿
FAMILIES PETS! Unit: 🗄 📺 🎮 TV 🕹 DVD BBQ

Island Cottage Holidays
Isle of Wight & Dorset Cottages

01983 403377
www.islandcottageholidays.com

ST. HELENS, Isle of Wight   Map ref 2C3 — SatNav PO33 1YN C

VisitEngland
★★★★
TOURING &
CAMPING PARK

100 touring pitches

Carpenters Farm Campsite
Carpenters Road, St Helens PO33 1YN
T: (01983) 874557 **E:** info@carpentersfarms.co.uk
W: www.carpentersfarm.co.uk

Family campsite with beautiful views in picturesque rural setting, adjacent to RSPB Reserve and SSSI. Close to beaches and attractions. Relaxed atmosphere on site. Family groups and pets very welcome. Overnight holding area available. Electric hookup, bookings advised for high season, please check our website for up to date tariffs. **Directions:** Please contact us for directions. **Open:** May - September.

Site: A P Payment: £ ☼ Leisure: & ♪ ▶ ♉ ⚓ Children: ☕ ⛰ Catering: ☕ Park: 🐕 ⛺ 🗄 📮 🎣
Touring: 🚿 🚽 📶

VENTNOR, Isle of Wight   Map ref 2C3 — S

VisitEngland
★★★
SELF CATERING

Units   2
Sleeps   2-4
PER UNIT PER WEEK
£165.00 - £375.00

Little Span Farm S/C
Contact: Felicity Corry, Proprietor, Rew Lane, Wroxall, Ventnor, Isle of Wight PO38 3AU
T: (01983) 855165 **E:** info@littlespanfarm.co.uk
W: www.littlespanfarm.co.uk **£ BOOK ONLINE**

Newly converted cottages with spiral staircase, situated on a working farm in area of outstanding natural beauty on the south-west side of the Island. 2 miles from Ventnor and a golf course. Close to bridle and footpaths, ideal for walking and family holidays, a short drive to the sandy beaches of Ventnor, Shanklin and Sandown. **Open:** All Year **Nearest Shop:** 0.25 miles **Nearest Pub:** 0.5 miles

---

WROXALL, Isle of Wight   Map ref 2C3 — SatNav PO38 3EP C

VisitEngland
★★★★★
HOLIDAY, TOURING
& CAMPING PARK

🚐 (50)   £17.95-£32.95
🚍 (40)   £17.95-£32.95
⛺ (40)   £17.95-£32.95
🚐 (40)   £215.00-£860.00

130 touring pitches

Appuldurcombe Gardens Holiday Park
Appuldurcombe Road, Wroxall, Nr. Ventnor, Isle of Wight PO38 3EP
T: (01983) 852597 **F:** 01983 856225 **E:** info@appuldurcombegardens.co.uk
W: www.appuldurcombegardens.co.uk

Picturesque holiday park within an Area of Outstanding Natural Beauty. Situated within 14 acres of lush secluded grounds & only minutes by car to glorious beaches & attractions. 40 static caravans within a walled orchard & 130 pitches with a selection of pitch options. Prices based on 2 people sharing (excl. static caravans). **Directions:** Head to Newport & take A3020 towards Shanklin & Ventnor. Through Blackwater to Rookley, Godshill & Sandford. Reach Whiteley Bank roundabout, right to Wroxall. **Open:** Feb-Nov

Site: 🐾 A P Payment: £ ☼ Leisure: & ♪ ▶ ♉ ⚓ ☕ Children: ☕ ⛰ Catering: ✕ ☕ Park: 🐕 🎵 ⛺ 🗄 🎣 Touring: 🚿 🚽 📶 ♿

BIRCHINGTON, Kent   Map ref 3C3   S

Raleigh Cottage

Contact: Mrs Jill Edwards, Raleigh Cottage, Band Box, 79 Station Road, Birchington
CT7 9RE **T:** (01843) 841764 - Evening / (01843) 841101 - Day
E: info@birchingtonholidays.co.uk **W:** www.birchingtonholidays.co.uk

Units   1
Sleeps   1-6

PER UNIT PER WEEK
£350.00 - £650.00

SPECIAL PROMOTIONS
Off-season short
breaks available.

Birchington is a delightful seaside town in beautiful Kent, "The Garden of England". Situated on the North Kent coast and within easy reach of London, picturesque Canterbury and the seaside towns of Margate, Broadstairs and Ramsgate, you will find plenty of opportunity to relax, go sightseeing, breathe in some unpolluted sea air and enjoy a break away from it all.

Raleigh Cottage is a comfortable detached house with pleasant enclosed garden. One twin and two double bedrooms. Two large reception rooms, one opening onto a sunny conservatory. Desirable location close to unspoilt sandy beaches, two minutes to sea, shops, station. Linen provided. Off-street parking.

Open: All year
Nearest Shop: 0.25 miles
Nearest Pub: 0.25 miles

Site: ✿ P **Leisure:** ⚓ ♪ ♄ **Property:** ⚘ ▣ ▣ **Children:** ❧ ▥ ✦ **Unit:** ▣ ▭ ▤ ☍ TV ⚇ ⊙ ☎

CANTERBURY, Kent   Map ref 3B3   S

Broome Park Golf and Country Club

Contact: Barham, Canterbury, Kent CT4 6QX **T:** (0800) 358 6991
E: EuHotels@diamondresorts.com
W: www.DiamondResortsandHotels.com **£ BOOK ONLINE**

Units   14
Sleeps   1-6

PER UNIT PER WEEK
£420.00 - £1393.00

SPECIAL PROMOTIONS
Visit our website or call
today for seasonal
discounts and great
savings.

This huge private estate has a historical building at its centre. Broome Park is a relaxing resort with modern log cabins, fine dining, indoor swimming and golf. The 17th-century main house has the restaurant and bar. The accommodation is spread throughout the grounds, in well-equipped woodland cabins. The cabins feature a TV in each bedroom, 2 bathrooms, and a fully-fitted kitchen.

The Broome Park grounds feature a full championship golf course, where there are discounts for hotel guests. The Jacobean Restaurant has an antique crystal chandelier and beautiful countryside views.

Open: All year
Nearest Shop: 2 miles
Nearest Pub: 2 miles

Units: 2 Bedroom Lodges with 1 Double room, 1 twin room and full kitchen unit. Each unit also boasts 2 complete bathroom units.

Site: ✿ P **Payment:** 💳 **Leisure:** ▶ ⚑ ☇ ⚲ **Property:** ▦ ▣ **Children:** ❧ ▥ ✦
Unit: ▣ ▤ ▭ ☍ ☍ TV ⊙ ☎

CRANBROOK, Kent   Map ref 3B4   S

Bakersbarn Annexe

Contact: Mrs Hooper, Owner, Golford Road, Cranbrook, Kent County TN17 3NW
T: (01580) 713344 **E:** hooper.jm@btinternet.com
W: www.bakersbarn.co.uk

Units	1
Sleeps	2

PER UNIT PER WEEK
£300.00 - £350.00

Bakersbarn is a non-smoking accommodation in a quiet rural situation, within seven minutes walk from the town centre of Cranbrook. All rooms overlook the garden and grazing land and are well equipped. The bedroom has optional zipped twin beds and all linen and electricity is included. The bathroom has a bath with overhead shower, toilet and hand basin. Fully furnished kitchen.
Open: All year **Nearest Shop:** 0.25 miles **Nearest Pub:** 0.25 miles

Site: ✿ P Property: 🖥 🔲 Unit: 🖵 🔲 📺 📀

DEAL, Kent   Map ref 3C4   S

Kingsdown Park Holiday Village

Contact: Jo Treadgold, Upper Street, Kingsdown CT14 8EU **T:** (01304) 361205
E: reception@kingsdownpark.net
W: www.kingsdownpark.co.uk

Units	40
Sleeps	2-6

PER UNIT PER WEEK
£229.00 - £799.00

Kingsdown Park is the perfect location for peaceful relaxing breaks or fun family holidays. Whether it's finding shells with the family on the beach, strolling around a pretty fishing village or getting active on the tennis court, Kingsdown Park has a wonderful holiday waiting for you. The lodges are unique looking, built in a charming Scandinavian style but with all the creature comforts of home.
Open: All Year **Nearest Shop:** 200 meters **Nearest Pub:** 200 meters

Site: ✿ P Payment: 💷 Leisure: ⚲ ∪ ☎ ≈ ⚲ Property: ∥ 🖥 🔲 🔲 Children: ☗ 🛏 🚶 Unit: 🖵 📺 🔌

EDENBRIDGE, Kent   Map ref 2D2   S

Medley Court - Hever Castle

Contact: Miss Kate Rowbottom, Sales Manager, Medley Court at Hever Castle, Hever Castle, Hever, Edenbridge TN8 7NG **T:** (01732) 861744 **F:** 01732 867860
E: krowbottom@hevercastle.co.uk
W: www.hevercastle.co.uk/stay/medley-court/ **£ BOOK ONLINE**

Units	1
Sleeps	2-7

PER UNIT PER WEEK
£1785.00 - £3400.00

SPECIAL PROMOTIONS
Short breaks available throughout the year, contact Hever Castle for further information.

Dating back to 1903, Medley Court is a luxurious four bedroom property forming part of the Astor Wing. The charming, double-moated Hever Castle and surrounding formal lawns provide a stunning backdrop to this beautiful holiday cottage in a truly historic location. Although Medley Court is now just over one hundred years old, its appearance is that of a Tudor house, the standard of decoration and comfort is outstanding and it still retains the warm, relaxed feel of a family home.

Open: All year
Nearest Shop: 5 miles
Nearest Pub: 0.5 miles

Site: ✿ P Payment: 💷 Leisure: ♪ ⚲ ∪ ⚲ Property: 🔲 🔲 🔲 Children: ☗ 🛏 🚶
Unit: 🔲 🔲 🖵 ⚲ 📺 🔌 📀 ⚲

MAIDSTONE, Kent   Map ref 3B3 **S**

Coldblow Farm

Contact: Dora Pilkington, Proprietor - Business Owner, Coldblow Lane, Thurnham, Maidstone, Kent ME14 3LR **T:** (01622) 730439 9am-2pm **E:** bookings@coldblowfarm.co.uk **W:** www.coldblowfarm.co.uk

Units 5
Sleeps 2-70

Coldblow Farm is situated on top of the Kent Downs overlooking Maidstone in an Area of Outstanding Natural Beauty. Coldblow has a range of self catering holiday accommodation with two cottages suitable and graded for disabled guests. **Nearest Shop:** 2 miles

Site: ❀ **P** **Payment:** € **Leisure:** ⟩ ∪ **Property:** ⫽ 🐦 🖥 🔲 🍳 🔲
Children: 🐤 ⚡ **Unit:** 🔲 🖥 🔲 🍳 📺 📀 BBQ

ROYAL TUNBRIDGE WELLS, Kent   Map ref 2D2   **S**

Plaisance

Contact: Mrs Angela Worsell, Office Manager, Itaris Properties, 12 Mount Ephraim, Royal Tunbridge Wells, Kent TN4 8AS **T:** (01892) 511065 **E:** enquiries@itaris.co.uk **W:** www.itaris.co.uk

Units 6
Sleeps 2-4

PER UNIT PER WEEK
£310.00 - £500.00

SPECIAL PROMOTIONS
Weekly bookings from Saturday to Saturday.

Royal Tunbridge Wells is surrounded by beautiful and unspoilt countryside and is the ideal location for a short break or relaxing holiday. Our self-contained and fully equipped holiday apartments are situated in the very heart of Tunbridge Wells within walking distance of its many amenities.

Open: All year
Nearest Shop: 0.5 miles
Nearest Pub: 0.10 miles

Units: Gas and electricity are charged as used during the months of October to the end of March.

Site: P **Payment:** 💷 **Leisure:** 🚲 ♪ ⟩ **Property:** 🖥 🔲 🍳 🔲 **Children:** 🐤 🛏 ⚡ **Unit:** 🔲 🔲 🍳 📺 📀

BANBURY, Oxfordshire   Map ref 2C1   SatNav OX17 1AZ **C**

Anita's Touring Caravan Park

The Yews, Church Farm, Banbury OX17 1AZ
T: (01295) 750731 / 07966 171959 **F:** 01295 750731 **E:** bookings@anitascampsite.co.uk **W:** www.oxfordshirecamping.com

🚐 (36) £18.00-£24.00
🚌 (36) £18.00-£24.00
⛺ (20) £14.00-£18.00
🏠 (6) £30.00-£130.00

Anita's is a friendly family run site in North Oxon on the edge of Mollington village. Clean facilities, shop, reception, hard and grass pitches, camping, camping pods and cottages. **Directions:** M40 Junction 11 Banbury take 3rd roundabout to Southam for 4 miles, 150yds past Mollington, turn-off on left. Brown signs. **Open:** All year.

Site: ⚡P **Payment:** 💷 **Leisure:** ♪ ⟩ ∪ **Children:** 🐤 **Catering:** 🍴 **Park:** 🐦 🖥 🎣 **Touring:** 🚾 🚻 🗑

CHARLBURY, Oxfordshire   Map ref 2C1   S

The Stable

Contact: Mrs Christina Pratley, Owner, The Stable, Reeves Barn, Pound Hill, Charlbury, Oxfordshire OX7 3QN **T:** (01608) 810077 / 07903 978798
E: christinapratley@homecall.co.uk **W:** www.cottagesatthecotswolds.co.uk

Units   1
Sleeps   1-2
PER UNIT PER WEEK
£400.00 - £420.00

Situated on the outskirts of the Cotswold town of Charlbury. The Stable is the ideal base for touring the Cotswolds, Stratford-upon-Avon and Warwick. Easy access to Oxford and London. Mainline Train Station only 15 minutes walking distance. Comfortable and cosy. Beautiful countryside in area of outstanding natural beauty. Off road parking. Inns, supermarket and shops within walking distance. **Open:** All year **Nearest Shop:** 500 metres
Nearest Pub: 500 metres

Site: P Payment: Property: Unit:

STANDLAKE, Oxfordshire   Map ref 2C1   SatNav OX29 7PZ   C

Hardwick Parks

Downs Road, Standlake, Witney OX29 7PZ
T: (01865) 300501 **F:** 01865 300037 **E:** info@hardwickparks.co.uk
W: www.hardwickparks.co.uk **£ BOOK ONLINE**

	(196)	£16.00-£26.50
	(196)	£16.00-£26.50
	(196)	£11.00-£19.00
	(7)	£295.00-£600.00

196 touring pitches

Rural park near Witney with lakes and river. Licensed clubhouse serving food and drinks. Shower/toilet block and shop. Tents, caravans and motorhomes welcome. Holiday caravans for hire and sale. Watersports available. Dogs on leads welcome. **Directions:** Four and a half miles from Witney, signposted from the A415. **Open:** April to October.

Site: Payment: Leisure: Children: Catering: Park:
Touring:

WITNEY, Oxfordshire   Map ref 2C1   SatNav OX29 7RH   C

Lincoln Farm Park Oxfordshire

High Street, Standlake, Witney, Oxon OX29 7RH
T: (01865) 300239 **F:** 01865 300127 **E:** info@lincolnfarmpark.co.uk
W: www.lincolnfarmpark.co.uk **£ BOOK ONLINE**

	(90)	£18.30-£33.80
	(44)	£18.30-£33.80
	(16)	£18.30-£30.80

90 touring pitches

Set in eight acres of beautiful Oxfordshire countryside, Lincoln Farm park offers you the opportunity to explore, or simply relax. **Open:** 6th February to Mid November.

Site: Payment: Leisure: Children: Catering: Park:
Touring:

For **key to symbols** see page 7

FARNHAM, Surrey   Map ref 2C2   S

★★★★★
SELF CATERING

Units   1
Sleeps   1-6

PER UNIT PER WEEK
£350.00 - £560.00

Bentley Green Farm

Contact: Mrs Glenda Powell, Bentley Green Farm, The Drift, Bentley, Farnham GU10 5JX
T: (01420) 23246 / 07711 981614 **E:** enquiries@bentleygreenfarm.co.uk
W: www.bentleygreenfarm.co.uk

Luxury self-contained accommodation in purpose-built annexe of listed 16th century farmhouse. Set in 40 acres with outdoor swimming pool, tennis court, and fishing rights. Fully fitted and very spacious. Ideally located between Alton and Farnham with ample parking. Public transport is nearby and London is 55 minutes away by train. Heathrow, Gatwick, Bournemouth and Southampton airports are all an hour away by car. Full details available on website.

Open: All year
Nearest Shop: 0.5 miles
Nearest Pub: 0.5 miles

Units: Beautifully decorated and spacious King sized bedroom. Extra luxury folding beds are available and there is space for an extra bed or cot if needed.

Site: ✿ P **Payment:** € **Leisure:** ♿ ♪ ▶ ∪ ⚲ ⚒ **Property:** ▨ ▣ ▧ **Children:** ⛱ ▥ ♣
Unit: ▤ ▣ ▭ ▨ ⚲ TV ◉ DVD BBQ

FARNHAM, Surrey   Map ref 2C2   S

★★
SELF CATERING

Units   1
Sleeps   2-4
PER UNIT PER WEEK
£280.00 - £350.00

Kilnside Farm

Contact: Mr Bob Milton, Booking Enquiries, Kilnside Farm, Kilnside Farm, Moor Park Lane, Farnham, surrey GU10 1NS **T:** (01252) 710325 / 07860 718464
E: bobmilton@kilnsidefarm.fsnet.co.uk

Self-catering cottage with two single beds and a small fold up upstairs and a 4'6" sofa bed downstairs. Open plan kitchen / dining area. Wi-Fi available. Situated on a sheep / horse farm, 1m east of Farnham. North Downs Way starts only ½ a mile away and runs through the farm. Access from Rock House Lane Runfold. **Open:** All year **Nearest Shop:** 0.5 miles **Nearest Pub:** 0.5 miles

Site: ✿ P **Payment:** € **Leisure:** ♪ **Property:** ▤ ▣ ▧ **Children:** ⛱ ▥ **Unit:** ▤ ▭ TV DVD BBQ

GODALMING, Surrey   Map ref 2D2   S

★★★★
SELF CATERING

Units   1
Sleeps   5-6
PER UNIT PER WEEK
£450.00 - £520.00

Prestwick Self Catering

Contact: Paul Mills, Proprietor, Prestwick Lane, Chiddingfold, Godalming, Surrey GU8 4XP
T: (01428) 654695 / 07966 452256 **E:** prestwick.farm@btconnect.com
W: www.prestwickfarm.co.uk

Prestwick is a working sheep farm, with 500 Ewes set in the picturesque 'Surrey Hills' between Chiddingfold and Haslemere. The bungalow style converted building in 'Area of outstanding Natural Beauty' is ideally located for walkers and provides a comfortable base. Midway between London and the South Coast you really do have access to most of the attractions that the South East has to offer. **Open:** All year **Nearest Shop:** 1.5 miles **Nearest Pub:** 1 mile

Site: ✿ P **Payment:** €£ **Leisure:** ▶ **Property:** ☛ ▤ ▣ ▧ **Children:** ⛱ ▥ ♣ **Unit:** ▤ ▭ ▨ ⚲ TV DVD BBQ

GUILDFORD, Surrey Map ref 2D2 S

VisitEngland
★★★
SELF CATERING

Units 1
Sleeps 5-6
PER UNIT PER WEEK
£620.00

Lavender

Contact: Mr & Mrs Elizabeth Liew, Lavender, 8-10 Martyr Road, Guildford GU1 4LF
T: (01483) 506819 / 07504 574252 **E:** successbee@hotmail.co.uk

Well-presented, fully furnished, comfortable house, conveniently situated in town centre, close to high street shops, river, theatre, leisure facilities and railway station. Airports 40 minutes.
Open: All year **Nearest Shop:** 5 minutes **Nearest Pub:** 3 minutes

Site: ✿ P Payment: € Property: ▨ Children: ⌣ ⊞ ☆ Unit: ⯂ ▣ ▤ ℞ ℡

GUILDFORD, Surrey Map ref 2D2 S

VisitEngland
★★★
SELF CATERING

Units 1
Sleeps 4

Rydes Hill Cottage apartment

Contact: Penny Wilson-Smith, Owner, 176 Aldershot Road, Guildford, Surrey GU2 8BL
T: (01483) 535841 **E:** pjws@btinternet.com
W: www.guildfordapartment.com

Comfortable and up-to-date, newly renovated two bedroom apartment. Ideally located and convenient both for business and leisure visitors. Includes living room, dining area, kitchen and bathroom with bath & power shower. Within easy reach of Guildford town centre and with quick access to Woking, Pirbright, Aldershot, Farnham and the Surrey countryside. Please access website for prices/further info. **Open:** All Year **Nearest Shop:** 0.2 miles
Nearest Pub: 0.2 miles

Site: P Property: ▤ ▣ ▨ Children: ⌣ Unit: ▣ ▤ ℞ ℡ ▤

BARNHAM, Sussex Map ref 2D3 S

VisitEngland
★★★★
SELF CATERING

Units 4
Sleeps 2-4

PER UNIT PER WEEK
£400.00 - £900.00

SPECIAL PROMOTIONS
Short breaks by negotiation.

Orchard Cottage Holidays

Contact: Mrs Lorraine Holden, Owner, Orchard Cottage Holidays, High Ground Orchards, High Ground Lane, Barnham, Nr Bognor Regis, West Sussex PO22 0BT **T:** 07484003978
F: 01243 554568 **E:** lorraine@orchardcottageholidays.org.uk
W: www.orchardcottageholidays.org.uk **£ BOOK ONLINE**

Four-two bedroom flint cottages, newly-built to highest specification. Near to well supplied, popular village close to downs and sea. Perfect base to explore Chichester, Arundel and West Sussex area. Rural outlook, ample parking and easy level access. Both bedrooms en suite (one downstairs). Own sunny conservatory. Private, secure individual gardens with patio.

Open: All year
Nearest Shop: 0.5 miles
Nearest Pub: 0.5 miles

Site: ✿ P Payment: ▦ Leisure: ⅋ ♩ ▸ ↻ Property: ▤ ▣ ▩ ▨ Children: ⌣ ⊞ ☆
Unit: ⯂ ▤ ▣ ▤ ℞ ℡ ◉ ▤

SELF CATERING

Gold AWARD

Honer Cottage

Contact: Mrs Sarah Green, Honer House, Honer Lane, South Mundham, Chichester, W. Sussex PO20 1LZ **T:** (01243) 262299 **E:** info@paghamharbourcottage.co.uk
W: www.paghamharbourcottage.co.uk

Detached single storey 2 bedroom cottage. Open plan modern kitchen/living area. Woodburner. Free WiFi. Enclosed garden. Very rural. Good walking and bird watching. Next to RSPB Pagham Harbour. 5 miles from Chichester. Sleeps 4. Short stays available.

Open: All year **Nearest Shop:** 3 miles **Nearest Pub:** 3 miles

Units	1
Sleeps	2-4

PER UNIT PER WEEK
£380.00 - £700.00

Site: ❀ P Payment: € Leisure: ♪ ▶ ✎ Property: ▦ ▣ Children: ⚓ ♨ ☂ Unit: ▯ ▤ ▣ ▨ ℧ TV ◐ DVD ⌀ BBQ

SELF CATERING

Gold AWARD

Laneside

Contact: Mrs Clare Sherlock, General Manager, Millstream Hotel, Bosham Lane, Bosham, Chichester, West Sussex PO18 8HL **T:** (01243) 573234 **F:** 01243 573459
E: info@millstreamhotel.com **W:** www.millstreamhotel.com

Units	3
Sleeps	2-10

PER UNIT PER WEEK
£350.00 - £750.00

SPECIAL PROMOTIONS
Please contact us for prices.

Three apartments, which are located just 200 metres from the shores of Chichester Harbour. Laneside is owned and managed by the Millstream Hotel - in whose AA 2 Rosette Restaurant dinner can be taken. Sleeps 10 in three units.

Open: All Year
Nearest Shop: 0.6 miles
Nearest Pub: 0.3 miles

Units: Three individual apartments, 2 x two bedroom apartments and 1 x one bedroom apartment with the bedroom on the ground floor. All with seperate bathroom.

Site: ❀ Property: ▦ Unit: TV ◐ DVD BBQ

SELF CATERING

Matchbox Stable Cottage

Contact: Margaret Nightingill, Manager, Woodland Cottage, 21 Orchard Way, Fontwell, West Sussex BN18 0SH **T:** (01243) 814770 / 07990905849
E: margaretnightingill246@btinternet.com
W: www.matchboxstablecottage.co.uk **£ BOOK ONLINE**

Units	1
Sleeps	2

PER UNIT PER WEEK
£300.00 - £475.00

A comfortable cottage for two people nestled in the downland village of Singleton in West Sussex. Originally built as stabling in 1850's the stable has been converted into a delightful flint cottage whilst keeping the unique charm of the old stables.
Ideally placed for visiting many local places of interest. The Weald and Downland Open Air Museum and West Dean gardens are within walking distance. **Open:** All Year round **Nearest Shop:** 2 miles **Nearest Pub:** 900 yds

Site: P Property: ▯ ▣ Unit: ▯ ▤ ▣ ▨ ℧ TV DVD

The Official Tourist Board Guide to **Self Catering & Camping 2016**

CROWBOROUGH, Sussex   Map ref 2D3   S

Hodges

Contact: Mrs Hazel Colliver, Hodges, Eridge Road, Steel Cross TN6 2SS **T:** (01892) 652386 / 07887 505718 **E:** hazel.colliver@hodges.uk.com
W: www.hodges.uk.com

Units	1
Sleeps	1-3

PER UNIT PER WEEK
£365.00 - £395.00

Ground floor luxury accommodation. Kitchen. Large double bed. Superking bed/en suite. Sitting/dining room, triple aspect adjoining small sunny conservatory. Owners plantaholic garden for guest use. Perfect for NT and South Gardens
Longer lets by negotion.
Sleeps 3.
Open: All year **Nearest Shop:** 1 mile **Nearest Pub:** 1mile

Leisure: 🎵 ⚲ ﻝ

EASTBOURNE, Sussex   Map ref 2D3   SatNav BN24 5NG   C

Fairfields Farm Caravan & Camping Park

Eastbourne Road, Westham, Pevensey BN24 5NG
T: (01323) 763165 **F:** 01323 469175 **E:** enquiries@fairfieldsfarm.com
W: www.fairfieldsfarm.com

🚐	(60)	£18.00-£26.00
🚌	(60)	£18.00-£26.00
⛺	(60)	£18.00-£26.00

60 touring pitches

SPECIAL PROMOTIONS
Special promotions available throughout the season, please contact us for more details.

A quiet country touring site on a working farm. Clean facilities, lakeside walk with farm pets and free fishing for campers. Close to the beautiful seaside resort of Eastbourne, and a good base from which to explore the diverse scenery and attractions of South East England. Overnight holding area available. Free Wi-Fi is also available on site.

Directions: From A27 Pevensey roundabout, travel through Pevensey towards castle, then through Westham. Turn left (B2191) towards Eastbourne. Over level crossing and we are on left.

Open: 24th March to 31st October.

Site: ⛺🅿 Payment: 💳 ☀ Leisure: 🎵 ▶ ☋ Children: ⚲ Catering: 🐾 Park: 🐕 🚏 🛢 🏬
Touring: 🚰 🛁 🔌 ♨

FELPHAM, Sussex   Map ref 2C3   S

The Beach Hut

Contact: Mr & Mrs Jackie and Clive Jourdain, Yew Tree Cottage, Church Lane, Rowledge, Farnham GU10 4EN **T:** (01252) 794171 / 07880 731082 **E:** Jackie@thebeachhut.plus.com
W: www.thebeachhut.org.uk

Units	1
Sleeps	4

PER UNIT PER WEEK
£400.00 - £450.00

Cosy bungalow with wood-burning stove. On a quiet private estate. 1 min from sea. Visit our website thebeachhut.org.uk. Within easy reach Goodwood, Chichester and Arundel. **Open:** All year
Nearest Shop: 0.42 miles **Nearest Pub:** 0.25 miles

Site: ❀ P Payment: € Leisure: 🎵 ▶ ⚲ Property: 🛢 🖥 Children: ⚲10 Unit: 🛢 🔌 📺 💿 BBQ

HASTINGS, Sussex   Map ref 3B4   S

VisitEngland
★★★
SELF CATERING

Units   1
Sleeps   1-6
PER UNIT PER WEEK
£320.00 - £630.00

14 Old Humphrey Avenue

Contact: Mrs Chris Nixey, Owner, Merrydown, Main Street, Beckley, Rye, East Sussex TN31 6RS **T:** (01797) 260505 / 07773 641521 **E:** cnixey@aol.com

Victorian end terraced three storey house situated in a peaceful off road position in the Old Town of Hastings. Located approximately 850 yds from the Fisherman's Quarter, Beach, the Jerwood Gallery, independent Shops, Cafes, Restaurants and a selection of Pubs. The Stables Theatre is approximately 100 yds away. The house is well equipped for Families or Couples. There are two large double bedrooms and two singles with flexible sleeping options. Linens are provided. For young Families, in addition to cots and high chairs there are Stair gates, a Stroller, Toys and Games.
Open: All year **Nearest Shop:** 850 Yards **Nearest Pub:** 300 Yards

 Site: ✿ **Payment:** € **Leisure:** ⚙ ♪ **Property:** ∥ ⬚ ⬚ **Children:** ⟲ ⛊ ♣ **Unit:** ⬚ ▣ ⬚ ⬚ TV ⬚ ⬚

HASTINGS, Sussex   Map ref 3B4   SatNav TN35 5DX   C

VisitEngland
★★★★
HOLIDAY PARK

🏠 (26)   £646.00-£819.00
🚐 (3)   £420.00-£672.00

f t

Shearbarn Holiday Park

Barley Lane, Hastings, East Sussex TN35 5DX
T: (01424) 423583 **F:** 01424 718740 **E:** holidays@shearbarn.co.uk
W: www.shearbarnholidaypark.co.uk

A holiday at Shearbarn offers something for everyone. Our guests return year after year, to explore the majestic cliffs and beaches, cafes and bars in Hastings Old Town, and to enjoy the dramatic and rich history of 1066 Country. All of our holiday homes are designed and built to the highest specification by the UK's leading manufacturers and are available in an array of styles, sizes and layouts with state of the art features, fixtures and fittings and sumptuous furnishings. Short breaks available. **Open:** March - Jan.

Site: 🏠 ⚑🅿 **Payment:** 💷 ☼ **Leisure:** ♪ ↺ **Children:** ⟲ ⚠ **Catering:** ✗ **Park:** 🐾 ♫ ☷ ⬚ ⬚ ⬚ ⬚
Touring: 🚾

HORSHAM, Sussex   Map ref 2D3   S

VisitEngland
★★★★
SELF CATERING

Units   1
Sleeps   4-6
PER UNIT PER WEEK
£595.00 - £700.00

Ghyll Cottage

Contact: High Street, Rusper, Horsham, West Sussex RH12 4PX **T:** (03301) 230 371
E: enquiries@ghyllmanor.co.uk
W: www.ghyllmanor.co.uk

The gorgeous authentic Tudor beamed, two bedroom self-catering cottage is set across two floors. With its own private driveway and garden, galley style kitchen, spacious lounge and dining area and family bathroom you'll be delighted by the utterly irresistible mix of original features and modern comforts. Dinner, bed and breakfast options (and even room service) are also available. **Open:** All Year
Nearest Shop: 0.1 miles **Nearest Pub:** 0.1 miles

 Site: ✿ P **Payment:** 💷 **Property:** ∥ ☷ ⬚ **Children:** ⟲ **Unit:** ⬚ ▣ TV ☎

LEWES, Sussex   Map ref 2D3   S

VisitEngland
★★★
SELF CATERING

Units   2
Sleeps   2-4
PER UNIT PER WEEK
£170.00 - £300.00

White Lion Farm Cottages

Contact: Mrs Diana Green, Owner, White Lion Farm, Shortgate, East Sussex BN8 6PJ
T: (01825) 840288 **E:** dgreen384@btinternet.com
W: www.whitelionfarmcottages.co.uk

Two converted holiday cottages, tastefully decorated throughout and provide comfortable accommodation for up to four people in each. Each cottage is completely separate with its own entrance, private patio and small garden with wonderful rural views and parking area. Each cottage has a spacious double bedroom, a good sized bathroom with a shower and large living room with a sofa-bed and a well equipped kitchen area with amenities.
Open: All year **Nearest Shop:** 3 miles **Nearest Pub:** 3 miles

Site: ✿ P Leisure: ♪ ▶ ♻ Property: ▣ ▣ Children: ⛵ ▦ Unit: ▯ ▬ ▣ ▣ TV BBQ

LITTLEHAMPTON, Sussex   Map ref 2D3   S

VisitEngland
★★★
SELF CATERING

Units   1
Sleeps   1-4
PER UNIT PER WEEK
£375.00 - £450.00

Angmering Court

Contact: Mrs Angela Gilmour, Angmering Court, Sea Lane, East Preston, West Sussex BN16 1NF **T:** 07549 522338 **E:** angelagilmour181@btinternet.com
W: www.holidaylettings.co.uk/221336

Angmering Court is situated close to the beach and the vibrant village centre of East Preston which is a "Haven for watersports" and has good public transport links, shops, bars and restaurants. The 1st floor apartment offers deceptively large modern, light, well-equipped accommodation with 2 bedrooms, 2 bathrooms, a kitchen/dining room, sitting room and communal gardens. **Open:** All year **Nearest Shop:** 300 yards **Nearest Pub:** 300 yards

Site: ✿ P Payment: € Leisure: ♪ ▶ ♻ Property: ▬ ▣ ▣ Children: ⛵ ▦ ☨ Unit: ▯ ▤ ▬ ▣ ▣ ▣ TV ◉ DVD

MAYFIELD, Sussex   Map ref 2D3   S

VisitEngland
★★★★
SELF CATERING

Units   1
Sleeps   6
PER UNIT PER WEEK
£400.00 - £800.00

Hoopers Farm Cottage

Contact: Sarah Ratcliffe, Owner, Vale Road, Mayfield, East Sussex TN20 6BD
T: (01435) 873310 / 07721009549 **E:** info@hoopersfarmcottage.co.uk
W: www.hoopersfarmcottage.co.uk

Mayfield, East Sussex - cosy converted barn in secluded location, within walking distance of historic village. Spectacular views across the Weald. **Open:** All year **Nearest Shop:** 5 mins **Nearest Pub:** 5 mins

Site: ✿ P Leisure: ♪ ▶ ♻ Property: 🐕 ▬ ▣ ▣ Children: ⛵ ▦ ☨ Unit: ▯ ▤ ▬ ▣ ▣ TV ◉ DVD ⌁ BBQ

MIDHURST, Sussex   Map ref 2C3   S

VisitEngland
★★★★
SELF CATERING

Units   1
Sleeps   2-6
PER UNIT PER WEEK
£450.00 - £675.00

Long Meadow

Contact: Bridget Adler, Long Meadow, Hoyle Lane, Heyshott, Midhurst GU29 0DX
T: (01798) 867102 / 07885 699479 **E:** mail@bridgetadler.com
W: www.selfcateringinsussex.co.uk

Outstanding views, quiet, rural location, newly refurbished. Close to Midhurst, Petworth, Cowdray Park, Goodwood, Chichester and the Coast. There is an upstairs double bedroom with ensuite shower room and a downstairs twin bedroom with bathroom. Separate well equipped kitchen, sitting room with dining area. Well presented with off road parking.
Open: All year **Nearest Shop:** 4 miles **Nearest Pub:** 1 mile

WALKERS ▣ FAMILIES ▣ CYCLISTS ▣ Site: ✿ P Property: ⋀ 🐕 ▬ ▣ ▣ Unit: ▯ ▤ ▬ ▣ ▣ TV ◉ DVD ⌁ BBQ ☎

RYE, Sussex Map ref 3B4 — S

Units   1
Sleeps   1-4

PER UNIT PER WEEK
£290.00 - £650.00

SPECIAL PROMOTIONS
Short breaks available

The Quarter House

Contact: Sally Bayly, Owner, Rye Cottages, The Mint, Rye TN31 7EN **T:** (01797) 222498 / 07956 280257 **E:** info@ryecottages.net
W: www.ryecottages.net AND www.cottages4you.co.uk/cottages/the-quarter-house-25320

Enchanting Grade II listed 17th century 2-storey apartment in the heart of Medieval Rye. Original beams & floorboards, open log fire, jacuzzi bath & WiFi. Wander Rye's cobbled streets & Church Square, visit its historic pubs, restaurants, tea shops, art galleries, antique & boutique shops, & independent cinema & cafe.

All within easy reach are Kent & Sussex walks & bike paths; beautiful beaches, wind/kite surfing, dinghy sailing/kayaking; Dungeness & Rye Harbour Nature Reserves & Bird Sanctuaries; the historic towns of Battle, Hastings and Canterbury; & Bodiam, Leeds & Dover Castles.

Open: All year
Nearest Shop: 0.01 miles
Nearest Pub: 0.01 miles

Units: Both bedrooms are on the top floor & are separated by a large chimney breast & the stairs, so there is visual privacy but sound may carry.

Leisure: Property: Children: Unit:

SELSEY, Sussex Map ref 2C3 — S

Units   10
Sleeps   6
PER UNIT PER WEEK
£144.00 - £1075.00

Green Lawns Holiday Park (Bunn Leisure)

Contact: Paddock Lane, Selsey, Chichester, West Sussex PO20 9EJ **T:** (01243) 606080
F: 01243 606068 **E:** holidays@bunnleisure.co.uk
W: www.bunnleisure.co.uk **£ BOOK ONLINE**

Offers leafy lanes, duck ponds and open green spaces for privacy, peace and quiet but with access to all Bunn Leisure's facilities and a courtesy bus to take you around. Open 10 months of the year from March to January. **Open:** March to January.

Payment: **Leisure:**   **Property:**   **Children:**

SELSEY, Sussex Map ref 2C3   SatNav PO20 9EL — C

(80)   £20.00-£52.50
(50)   £20.00-£52.50
(120) £20.00-£40.00
250 touring pitches

Warner Farm Camping & Touring Park

Warner Lane, Selsey, Chichester, West Sussex PO20 9EL
T: (01243) 604499 **E:** touring@bunnleisure.co.uk
W: www.warnerfarm.co.uk

Great value, quality, fun filled family camping & touring holidays. Well maintained standed, electric & full service pitches. Stay here & enjoy all Bunn Leisure's great facilities and entertainment. Overnight holding area available. **Directions:** From A27 Chichester by-pass take B2145 to Selsey. Warner Farm is clearly signed on the right once you are in town. **Open:** March to January.

Site: Payment: Leisure: Children: Catering: Park:
  Touring:

SELSEY, Sussex *Map ref 2C3* **S**

West Sands Holiday Park (Bunn Leisure)

Contact: Mill Lane, Selsey, Chichester, West Sussex PO20 9BH **T:** (01243) 606080
F: 01243 606068 **E:** holidays@bunnleisure.co.uk
W: www.bunnleisure.co.uk **£ BOOK ONLINE**

Units 160
Sleeps 6-10
PER UNIT PER WEEK
£144.00 - £1075.00

The liveliest of our parks on the South Coast offering family fun in a fantastic seaside location. Famous for the best entertainment with top acts, live performances and kids entertainment. Directions: From A27 Chichester by-pass take B2145 to Selsey. West Sands is clearly signed on right once you are in the town. **Open:** March to January.

Payment: 🅴 **Leisure:** 🏊 🎵 ⛴ ∪ 🎣 🎿 🏹 ⚲ **Property:** 🐕 🖥 🗄 🖨 **Children:** 🎠

SELSEY, Sussex *Map ref 2C3* **S**

White Horse Holiday Park (Bunn Leisure)

Contact: Paddock Lane, Selsey, Chichester, West Sussex PO20 9EJ **T:** (01243) 606080
F: 01243 606068 **E:** holidays@bunnleisure.co.uk
W: www.bunnleisure.co.uk **£ BOOK ONLINE**

Units 10
Sleeps 6
PER UNIT PER WEEK
£144.00 - £1075.00

With its coveted award for its traditional atmosphere, White Horse Holiday Park is perfect for families. Offering a relaxed holiday, though never far from all the facilities and entertainment. Directions: From A27 Chichester by-pass take B2145 to Selsey. West Sands is clearly signed on right once you are in the town. **Open:** March to January.

Payment: 🅴 **Leisure:** 🏊 🎵 ⛴ ∪ 🎣 🎿 🏹 ⚲ **Property:** 🐕 🖥 🗄 🖨 **Children:** 🎠

Don't Miss...

Buckingham Palace
London, SW1A 1AA
(020) 7766 7300
www.royalcollection.org.uk
Buckingham Palace is the office and London residence of Her Majesty
The Queen. It is one of the few working royal palaces remaining in the
world today. The State Rooms are used extensively by The Queen and
Members of the Royal Family and during August and September, when
The Queen makes her annual visit to Scotland, the Palace's nineteen
state rooms are open to visitors.

Houses of Parliament
Westminster, London SW1A 0AA
020 7219 4565
www.parliament.uk/visiting
Tours offer a unique combination of one thousand years of history,
modern day politics, and stunning art and architecture. Visit the Queen's
Robing Room, the Royal Gallery and the Commons Chamber, scene
of many lively debates. Stylish afternoon tea in the Terrace Pavillion
overlooking the River Thames can be added to many tours.

Madame Tussauds
Marylebone Road, London, NW1 5LR
(0871) 894 3000
www.madametussauds.com/London/
Experience the legendary history, glitz and glamour of Madame
Tussauds London. Visit the 14 exciting, interactive zones and come face-
to-face with some of the world's most famous stars. From Shakespeare to
David Beckham you'll meet leading figures from sport, showbiz, politics
and even royalty. Strike a pose with Usain Bolt, get up close and personal
with One Direction, receive a royal audience with Her Majesty the
Queen, or even plant a cheeky kiss on Prince Harry's cheek.

National Gallery
Westminster WC2N 5DN
(020) 7747 2888
www.nationalgallery.org.uk
Founded in 1824, housing one of the greatest collections of Western
European painting in the world, with over 2,300 paintings dating from
the mid-13th century to 1900. Discover inspiring art by world-class artists
including Botticelli, Caravaggio, Leonardo da Vinci, Monet, Raphael,
Rembrandt, Titian, Vermeer and Van Gogh. The Gallery aims to encourage
the widest possible access to the pictures as well as studying and caring
for the collection, which is on show 361 days a year, free of charge.

Natural History Museum
Kensington and Chelsea SW7 5BD
(020) 7942 5000
www.nhm.ac.uk
The world's most prestigious and pre-eminent museum of natural
history, exhibiting a vast range of specimens from various segments of
natural history. Revealing how the jigsaw of life fits together - animal,
vegetable or mineral, the best of our planet's most amazing treasures are
here for you to see - for free. Alongside the collection, a packed calendar
of year round activities, temporary exhibitions and special events as
diverse as David Attenborough's virtual reality Great Barrier Reef dive
and Crime Scene Live, an interactive night at the museum combining
real science and crime fiction, offers something for everyone.

London

London

Grand landmarks, gorgeous gardens, spectacular shopping, exciting attractions, museums, galleries, theatres, sporting venues and all the buzz and history of the capital - London's treasures are beyond measure. A single trip is never enough and you'll find yourself returning time and again to take in the many unforgettable sights and experiences on offer.

Explore – London

In the Central/West End area the most visited sights are the now public rooms of Buckingham Palace, the National Gallery in Trafalgar Square, Tate Britain on Millbank, Westminster Abbey, Houses of Parliament and Cabinet War Rooms.

Westminster Abbey, nearly a thousand years old, has tombs of many English kings, queens, statesmen and writers. The British Museum in Bloomsbury houses one of the world's largest selections of antiquities, including the Magna Carta, the Elgin Marbles and the first edition of Alice in Wonderland. This entire area can be well viewed from The London Eye on the South Bank.

No visit to London is complete without a spot of shopping. Head for bustling Oxford Street and the stylish shops on Regent Street and Bond Street, check out the trendy boutiques around Carnaby Street, or visit the iconic Liberty store.

For entertainment, enjoy a wide range of theatre, bars, restaurants and culture in Covent Garden and don't forget to take in a musical or an off-beat play and the amazing nightime atmosphere around Leicester Square. Madame Tussauds features all your favourite celebrities and super heroes, or if you fancy an historical fright, visit the London Dungeon near Tower Bridge or explore the streets of old London on a Jack the Ripper tour.

London's parks are its lungs. St James, the oldest, was founded by Henry VIII in 1532. Hyde Park, bordering Kensington, Mayfair and Marylebone, is the largest at 630 acres and one of the greatest city parks in the world. You can enjoy any number of outdoor activities, visit the Serpentine Galleries for contemporary art or Speakers' Corner, the most famous location for free speech in the world. Regents Park, with its zoo and outdoor theatre, lies north of Oxford Circus and was given to the nation by the Prince Regent.

In the North of the capital, trendy Camden is an eclectic mix of intriguing and unique experiences. Locals and visitors alike hunt for vintage treasures in the open air markets at Camden Lock and far-out attire in the alternative shops that line the high street, or spend time celebrity spotting or strolling along Regent's Canal. There's a different kind of food at every turn, from street vendors to swanky sushi restaurants, and Camden is also home to an extraordinary array of bars, live music and arts venues including the Roundhouse.

Heading East, St Pauls Cathedral in the city of London was redesigned by Sir Christopher Wren and the nearby the Tower of London, a medieval fortress dominated by the White Tower and dating from 1097, houses The Crown Jewels, guarded by the famous Beefeaters. Even further East, the Queen Elizabeth Olympic Park is the exciting legacy of the 2012 Olympic Games and is situated at the heart of a new, vibrant East London.

To the South East of the capital, Canary Wharf is one of Londons main financial centres and contains many of Europe's tallest buildings, including the second-tallest in Great Britain, One Canada Square. On the south bank, opposite Docklands, attractions include the National Maritime Museum incorporating the Royal Greenwich Observatory, the Cutty Sark and The O2, one of London's premier entertainment venues.

In November, the Lord Mayors Show will feature a parade of over 6,000 people, military marching bands, acrobats, a procession of decorated floats, a gilded State Coach that the Lord Mayor travels and starts with an RAF flypast. After the procession London's City Guides will be on hand to lead free guided tours of the City's more strange and wonderful corners, and in the evening fireworks will light up the sky over the river.
Visit their website for more information, www.lordmayorsshow.org.

Visit – London

 Attractions with this sign participate in the Visitor Attraction Quality Assurance Scheme.

Apsley House
Westminster W1J 7NT
(020) 7499 5676
www.english-heritage.org.uk
This great 18th century town house pays homage to the Duke's dazzling military career, which culminated in his victory at Waterloo in 1815.

Bank of England Museum
Bartholomew Lane, London EC2R 8AH
(020) 7601 5545
www.bankofengland.co.uk/museum
Housed within the impressive walls of the Bank of England, this fascinating museum takes you through the history of the bank since its foundation in 1694 to its role today as the nation's central bank.

Bateaux London Restaurant Cruisers
Westminster WC2N 6NU
(020) 7695 1800
www.bateauxlondon.com
Bateaux London offers lunch and dinner cruises, combining luxury dining, world-class live entertainment and five-star customer care.

The Boat Race
March, Putney Bridge
www.theboatrace.org
Boat crews from the universities of Oxford and Cambridge battle it out on the Thames.

British Museum
Camden WC1B 3DG
(020) 7323 8299
www.britishmuseum.org.uk
Collections that span over two million years of human history and culture, all under one roof.

Changing the Guard
Buckingham Palace, London SW1A 1AA
www.royalcollection.org.uk
Watch the Changing the Guard ceremony at Buckingham Palace for an impressive display of British pomp and ceremony at 11.30am every day.

Chinese New Year
February, Various venues
www.visitlondon.com
London's Chinese New Year celebrations are the largest outside Asia, with parades, performances and fireworks.

Chiswick House
Chiswick, London W4 2RP
(020) 8995 0508
www.english-heritage.org.uk/visit/places/chiswick-house/
Among the most glorious examples of 18th-century British architecture, the celebrated villa of Lord Burlington with impressive grounds, features Italianate garden with statues, temples, obelisks and urns. The gardens are the birthplace of the English Landscape Movement and have inspired countless gardens.

Churchill Museum and Cabinet War Rooms
Westminster SW1A 2AQ
(020) 7930 6961
www.iwm.org.uk
Learn more about the man who inspired Britain's finest hour at the highly interactive and innovative Churchill Museum, the world's first major museum dedicated to life of the 'greatest Briton'. Step back in time and discover the secret.

City of London Festival
June-July, Various venues
www.visitlondon.com
The City of London Festival is an annual extravaganza of music, dance, art, film, poetry, family and participation events that takes place in the city's Square Mile.

Cutty Sark King
William Walk, London SE10 9HT
www.rmg.co.uk/cutty-sark
Discover what life was like on board the legendary sailing ship Cutty Sark, the world's sole surviving tea clipper, and fastest ship of her time - now an award-winning visitor attraction.

Eltham Palace
Greenwich SE9 5QE
(020) 8294 2548
www.elthampalace.org.uk
A spectacular fusion of 1930s Art Deco villa and magnificent 15th century Great Hall. Surrounded by period gardens.

The Globe Theatre
Bankside, London SE1 9DT
(020) 7902 1400
www.shakespearesglobe.com
Globe Exhibition & Tour and Globe Education seek to further the experience and international understanding of Shakespeare in performance.

Goldsmiths Hall
Foster Lane, London EC2V 6BN
(020) 7606 7010
One of the Twelve Great Livery Companies of the City of London. The Goldsmiths' Company, based at the magnificent Goldsmiths' Hall in the City of London, regularly holds exhibitions and events to promote contemporary jewellers and silversmiths.

Greenwich Heritage Centre
Greenwich SE18 4DX
(020) 8854 2452
www.royalgreenwich.gov.uk
Local history museum with displays of archaeology, natural history and geology. Also temporary exhibitions, schools service, sales point and Saturday club.

Hampton Court Palace
Richmond upon Thames KT8 9AU
(0870) 752 7777
www.hrp.org.uk
This magnificent palace set in delightful gardens was famously one of Henry VIII's favourite palaces.

HMS Belfast
Southwark SE1 2JH
(020) 7940 6300
www.iwm.org.uk
HMS Belfast, launched 1938, served throughout WWII, playing a leading part in the destruction of the German battle cruiser Scharnhorst and in the Normandy Landings.

Hyde Park
London W2 2UH
(0300) 061 2000
www.royalparks.org.uk/parks/hyde-park
Explore one of the greatest city parks in the world, with outdoor sports, a spectacular children's playground, a packed calendar of open air events and a number of fascinating buildings and monuments, such as The Serpentine Bridge, the famous Archiles statue and the Diana Memorial Fountain.

Imperial War Museum
Southwark SE1 6HZ
(020) 7416 5000
www.iwm.org.uk
This award-winning museum tells the story of conflict involving Britain and the Commonwealth since 1914. See thousands of imaginatively displayed exhibits, from art to aircraft, utility clothes to U-boats.

Kensington Palace State Apartments
Kensington and Chelsea W8 4PX
(0844) 482 7777
www.hrp.org.uk
Home to the Royal Ceremonial Dress Collection, which includes some of Queen Elizabeth II's dresses worn throughout her reign, as well as 14 of Diana, Princess of Wales' evening dresses.

Kenwood House
Camden NW3 7JR
(020) 8348 1286
www.english-heritage.org.uk/visit/places/kenwood-house/
Beautiful 18th century villa with fine interiors, and a world class collection of paintings. Also fabulous landscaped gardens and an award-winning restaurant.

London Dungeon
County Hall, Riverside Building SE1 7PB
(020) 7403 7221
www.thedungeons.com/London
Exciting, scary and fun - the London Dungeon has a new home on the Southbank and lots of new scary stories about London's history for you to discover. Steel your nerves for some terrifying new experiences and hrilling new scary rides!

London Eye River Cruise Experience
Lambeth E1 7PB
(0871) 781 3000
www.londoneye.com
See London from a different perspective and enjoy a unique 40 minute circular sightseeing cruise on the river Thames.

London Fashion Weekend
www.londonfashionweekend.co.uk
London's largest and most exclusive designer shopping event. This four-day showcase brings you the ultimate fashion experience.

London Festival of Architecture
June
www.londonfestivalofarchitecture.org
A city-wide celebration of architectural experimentation, thinking and practice. See London's buildings in a new light during the Festival of Architecture.

London Film Festival
October, Various venues
www.bfi.org.uk/lff
A two-week showcase of the world's best new films, the BFI London Film Festival is one of the most anticipated events in London's cultural calendar, screening more than 300 features, documentaries and shorts from almost 50 countries.

London Transport Museum
Westminster WC2E 7BB
(020) 7379 6344
www.ltmuseum.co.uk
The history of transport for everyone, from spectacular vehicles, special exhibitions, actors and guided tours to film shows, gallery talks and children's craft workshops

London Wetland Centre
Richmond upon Thames SW13 9WT
(020) 8409 4400
www.wwt.org.uk
The London Wetland Centre is a unique wildlife visitor attraction just 25 minutes from central London. Run by the Wildfowl and Wetlands Trust (WWT), it is acclaimed as the best urban site in Europe to watch wildlife. Stroll among the lakes, ponds and gardens. The café is perfect for relaxing, and kids will love the play areas.

London Zoo
Regent's Park, London NW1 4RY
(020) 7722 3333
www.zsl.org/zsl-london-zoo
Come face to face with some of the hairiest, scariest, tallest and smallest animals on the planet - right in the heart of the capital.

Lord's Tour
Westminster NW8 8QN
(020) 7616 8595
www.lords.org/history/tours-of-lords/
Guided tour of Lord's Cricket Ground including the Long Room, MCC Museum, Real Tennis Court, Mound Stand and Indoor School.

Museums At Night
May, Various venues
www.visitlondon.com
Explore arts and heritage after dark at museums across London. Packed with special events, from treasure trails to pyjama parties, Museums at Night is a great opportunity to explore culture in a new light.

Museum of London
City of London EC2Y 5HN
(020) 7001 9844
www.museumoflondon.org.uk
Step inside Museum of London for an unforgettable journey through the capital's turbulent past.

National Maritime Museum
Greenwich SE10 9NF
(020) 8858 4422
www.nmm.ac.uk
Britain's seafaring history housed in an impressive modern museum. Themes include exploration, Nelson, trade and empire, passenger shipping, luxury liners, maritime London, costume, art and the sea, the future and environmental issues.

National Portrait Gallery
Westminster WC2H 0HE
(020) 7306 0055
www.npg.org.uk
The National Portrait Gallery houses the world's largest collection of portraits. Visitors come face to face with the people who have shaped British history from Elizabeth I to David Beckham. Entrance is free.

Notting Hill Carnival
August, Various venues
www.thenottinghillcarnival.com
2016 is the 50th anniversary of Europe's biggest street festival – where the streets of London come alive with colourful floats, street performers, music and tempting food stalls. A spectacular event!

RHS Chelsea Flower Show
May, Royal Hospital Chelsea
www.rhs.org.uk/Chelsea-Flower-Show
Experience the greatest flower show in the world at London's Royal Hospital Chelsea. The Chelsea Flower Show has been held in the grounds of the Royal Hospital Chelsea, London every year since 1913, apart from gaps during the two World Wars. Once Britain's largest flower show, it is still the most prestigious.

Ride London 2016
July, London
www.prudentialridelondon.co.uk
RideLondon is the world's greatest festival of cycling and takes place the weekend immediately after the Tour de France. With five events to enjoy on closed roads over a summer weekend in July there's really something for everyone.

Royal Academy of Arts
Piccadilly, London W1J 0BD
(020) 7300 8000
www.royalacademy.org.uk
A varied varied programme of exciting exhibitions and events at the Royal Academy of Arts in 2016. The landmark exhibition Painting the Modern Garden: Monet to Matisse (30 Jan-20 Apr 2016) uses the work of Monet as a starting point to examine the role gardens played in the evolution of art from the early 1860s through to the 1920s.

Royal Air Force Museum Hendon

Barnet NW9 5LL
(020) 8205 2266
www.rafmuseum.org
Take off to the Royal Air Force Museum, located on the former Hendon Aerodrome, and flypast the history of aviation with an exciting display of suspended aircraft, touch screen technology, simulator rides, hands-on section, film shows, licensed restaurant.

Royal Observatory Greenwich
Greenwich SE10 9NF
(020) 8858 4422
www.rmg.co.uk
Stand on the Greenwich Meridian Line, Longitude Zero, which divides East and West. Watch the time-ball fall at 1 o'clock, and explore your place in the universe at London's only planetarium.

Science Museum
Kensington and Chelsea SW7 2DD
0870 870 4868
www.sciencemuseum.org.uk
The Science Museum is world-renowned for its historic collections, awe-inspiring galleries, family activities and exhibitions - and it's free!

Somerset House
Westminster WC2R 1LA
(020) 7845 4670
www.somersethouse.org.uk
This magnificent 18th century building houses the celebrated collections of the Courtauld Institute of Art Gallery, Gilbert Collection and Hermitage Rooms. During summer months 55 fountains dance in the courtyard, and in winter you can skate on one of London's favourite ice rinks.

Southbank Centre
Lambeth SE1 8XX
(020) 7960 4200
www.southbankcentre.co.uk
A unique arts centre with 21 acres of creative space, including the Royal Festival Hall, Queen Elizabeth Hall and The Hayward.

Southwark Cathedral
Southwark SE1 9DA
(020) 7367 6700
http://cathedral.southwark.anglican.org
Oldest Gothic church in London (c.1220) with interesting memorials connected with the Elizabethan theatres of Bankside.

Tate Britain
Westminster SW1P 4RG
(020) 7887 8888
www.tate.org.uk
Presenting the world's greatest collection of British art in a dynamic series of new displays and exhibitions.

Tate Modern
Southwark SE1 9TG
(020) 7887 8888
www.tate.org.uk/modern
The national gallery of international modern art and is one of London's top free attractions. Packed with challenging modern art and housed within a disused power station on the south bank of the River Thames.

Tower Bridge Exhibition
Southwark SE1 2UP
(020) 7403 3761
www.towerbridge.org.uk
Inside Tower Bridge Exhibition you will travel up to the high-level walkways, located 140 feet above the Thames and witness stunning panoramic views of London before visiting the Victorian Engine Rooms.

Tower of London
Tower Hamlets EC3N 4AB
0844 482 7777
www.hrp.org.uk
The Tower of London spans over 900 years of British history. Fortress, palace, prison, arsenal and garrison, it is one of the most famous fortified buildings in the world, and houses the Crown Jewels, armouries, Yeoman Warders and ravens.

Victoria and Albert Museum
Kensington and Chelsea SW7 2RL
(020) 7942 2000
www.vam.ac.uk
The V&A is the world's greatest museum of art and design, with collections unrivalled in their scope and diversity.

The View from The Shard
London SE1 9QU
(08444) 997111
www.theviewfromtheshard.com
The View from The Shard is the premium visitor attraction at the top of Western Europe's tallest building, and London's newest landmark, The Shard, designed by Master Architect Renzo Piano.

Virgin Money London Marathon
April, Various venues
www.virginmoneylondonmarathon.com
Whether you run, walk or cheer from the sidelines, this is a London sporting institution you won't want to miss.

Wembley Stadium Tours
Brent HA9 0WS
0800 169 9933
www.wembleystadium.com
Until your dream comes true, there's only one way to experience what it's like winning at Wembley - take the tour.

William Morris Gallery
Lloyd Park, Forest Road, Walthamstow E17 4PP
(020) 8496 4390
www.wmgallery.org.uk
The William Morris Gallery is devoted to the life and legacy of one of Britain's most remarkable designers and is housed in the grade II* listed Georgian house that was his family home in north-east London from 1848 to 1856.

Wimbledon Lawn Tennis Championships
June - July, Wimbledon
www.wimbledon.com
The world of tennis descends on Wimbledon in South West London every summer for two weeks of tennis, strawberries and cream, and good-natured queuing.

Wimbledon Lawn Tennis Museum
Merton SW19 5AG
(020) 8944 1066
www.wimbledon.com
A collection of memorabilia dating from 1555, including Championship Trophies, Art Gallery, and special exhibitions, reflecting the game and championships of today.

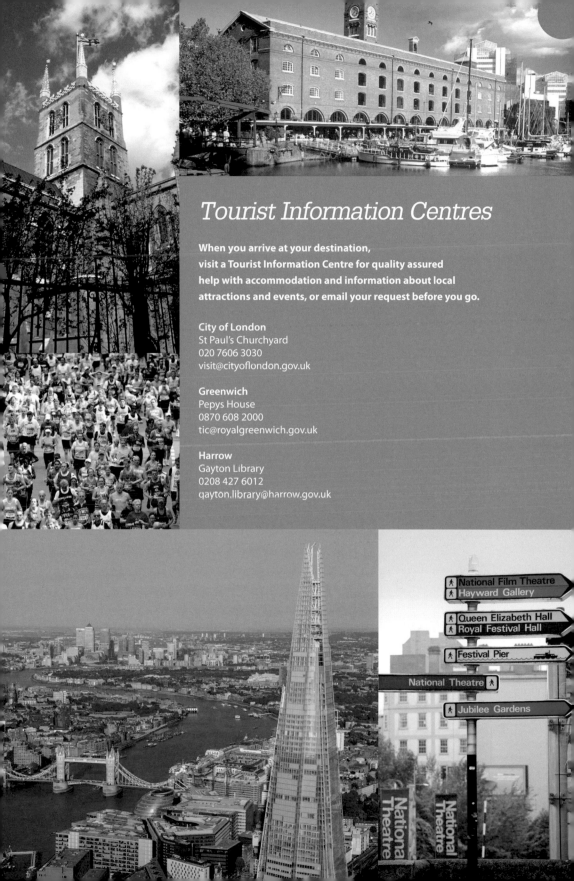

Tourist Information Centres

When you arrive at your destination,
visit a Tourist Information Centre for quality assured
help with accommodation and information about local
attractions and events, or email your request before you go.

City of London
St Paul's Churchyard
020 7606 3030
visit@cityoflondon.gov.uk

Greenwich
Pepys House
0870 608 2000
tic@royalgreenwich.gov.uk

Harrow
Gayton Library
0208 427 6012
gayton.library@harrow.gov.uk

Regional Contacts and Information

Find everything you need to plan your trip on visitlondon.com, the official London website. Here you can download free London maps and guides: transport maps of London, the latest London Planner and the Welcome to London Guide. We do not mail out printed maps and guides as all our London guides, news, editorial and listings are available for free online.

For more information while you're in London, visit one of London's Tourist Information Centres or download our free Official London Cityguide App.

Travel and Transport in London
If you have questions about travelling in London, including Oyster cards, ticket prices, journey planning, booking a taxi and the congestion charge, please visit the Transport for London websitecall 0343 222 1234 or Textphone 020 7918 3015.

Stay – London

Entries appear alphabetically by town name in each county. A key to symbols appears on page 7

Hamlet

Contact: Renata, General Manager, Hamlet, 47 Willian Way, Letchworth SG6 2HJ
T: (01462) 678037 **F:** 01462 679639 **E:** hamlet_uk@globalnet.co.uk
W: www.hamletuk.com

Units   4
Sleeps   4-6

PER UNIT PER WEEK
£675.00 - £929.00

SPECIAL PROMOTIONS
Discounted last-
minute and
long-term lets.

Hamlet was established in 1990 and offers a handful of affordable, excellent value self-catering holiday apartments in a unique and quiet location: St. Katharine Marina is a hidden treasure adjacent to Tower Bridge and the Tower of London on the north bank of the river Thames.

Open: All year
Nearest Shop: 0.10 miles
Nearest Pub: 0.10 miles

Units: One and two bedroom apartments, some overlooking the yachts in St. Katharine Marina.

Site: ✿ P Payment: 💳 Property: 🖥 🔲 📶 Children: 🍼 🛏 🎚 Unit: 📶 📺 🔲 🖥 📺 🎚 💿 ✆

Lee Valley Campsite - Sewardstone

Sewardstone Road, Chingford, London E4 7RA
T: (020) 8529 5689 **F:** 020 8559 4070 **E:** sewardstonecampsite@vibrantpartnerships.co.uk
W: www.visitleevalley.org.uk/wheretostay **£ BOOK ONLINE**

🚐 (65)	£14.50-£22.50
🚚 (65)	£14.50-£22.50
⛺ (35)	£14.50-£22.50
🛖 (17)	£35.00-£45.00

65 touring pitches

Lee Valley Campsite, Sewardstone is less than 40 minutes from central London and is close to the scenic Hertfordshire and Essex countryside. Come camping, caravanning or stay in one of our cosy cocoons or woodland cabins – it's perfect for families, couples or groups of friends looking for affordable accommodation in London.

Directions: The campsite is situated on the A112 between Chingford and Waltham Abbey to the South of the M25. Leave M25 at junction 26 and follow the signs.

Open: 1st March - 31st January.

Site: 🅰🅿 **Payment:** 💳 ☼ **Leisure:** ♿ ♪ ∪ **Children:** 🐎 ⩘ **Catering:** 🍴 **Park:** 🐕 📺 📦 🎣 **Touring:** ♀ ➓ 🔌 ⚡

Lee Valley Camping and Caravan Park - Edmonton

Meridian Way, Edmonton, London N9 0AR
T: (020) 8803 6900 **F:** 020 8884 4975 **E:** edmontoncampsite@vibrantpartnerships.co.uk
W: www.visitleevalley.org.uk/wheretostay **£ BOOK ONLINE**

🚐 (100)	£14.50-£22.50
🚚 (100)	£14.50-£22.50
⛺ (60)	£14.50-£22.50
🛖 (12)	£245.00-£315.00

100 touring pitches

A peaceful site that puts you in easy each of both central London and the many attractions of Lee Valley Regional Park. With excellent facilities including an on-site shop and children's play area, plus a golf course, athletics centre and cinema all located within the complex. Overnight holding area available.

Directions: Leave M25 at J25, follow signs for City. Turn left for Freezywater at traffic lights, follow signs for Lee Valley Leisure Complex.

Open: All year.

Site: 🅰🅿 **Payment:** 💳 ☼ **Leisure:** ♪ ▶ ∪ **Children:** 🐎 ⩘ **Catering:** 🍴 **Park:** 🐕 🚎 📺 📦 🎣 **Touring:** ♀ ➓ 🔌 ⚡

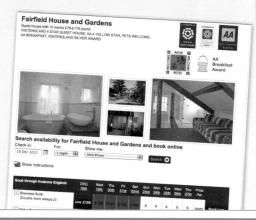

LONDON SW20, Inner London   Map ref 2D2   **S**

VisitEngland
SELF CATERING

Units 1
Sleeps 5-6
PER UNIT PER WEEK
£800.00

Thalia Holiday Home

Contact: Mr Peter & Mrs Ann Briscoe-Smith, Owners, 150 Westway, Raynes Park, Wimbledon, London SW20 9LS **T:** (020) 8542 0505 **E:** info@thaliaholidayhome.co.uk
W: www.thaliaholidayhome.co.uk

Thalia is a three-bedroomed house in the residential suburban area of West Wimbledon. Home from home, with easy access to central London. Wi-Fi/LAN broadband. Special offers: £50 discount on complete 2nd & subsequent weeks of same booking. Bookings can start and end on any day of the week. **Open:** All year **Nearest Shop:** 0.2 miles **Nearest Pub:** 0.5 miles

Site: ✿ P Property: 🖥 🛏 Children: 🛝 🎠 ♿ Unit: 🍳 📺 📷 🎮 ☎

LONDON SW3, Inner London   Map ref 2D2   **S**

VisitEngland
SELF CATERING

VisitEngland
Gold AWARD

Units 41
Sleeps 2-6
PER UNIT PER WEEK
£1092.00 - £2982.00

The Apartments - Chelsea & Marylebone

Contact: Kasia Tymoczko, General Manager, 36 Draycott Place, Chelsea, London SW3 2SA
T: (020) 7589 3271 **F:** 020 7589 3274 **E:** sales@theapartments.co.uk
W: www.theapartments.co.uk **£ BOOK ONLINE**

The Apartments is a family run serviced apartment business with over 15 years experience, offering an elegant selection of studios, one and two-bedroom apartments, in two of London's premier locations. Housed in predominantly prestigious Victorian buildings, each apartment is individually designed with fitted kitchens & bathrooms, with a full range of modern amenities including complimentary Wi-Fi.
Open: All year including Christmas & New Year. **Nearest Shop:** 0.10 miles **Nearest Pub:** 0.10 miles

Payment: 💳 Property: // 🖥 📺 🛏 Children: 🛝 🎠 ♿ Unit: 🍳 📺 🎮 ☎

LONDON W14, Inner London   Map ref 2D2   S

Castletown House

Contact: Mr Mark Poppleton, Manager, Castletown House, 11 Castletown Road, London
W14 9HE **T:** (0207) 386 9423 / 07816 911 471 **F:** 020 7386 0015
E: info@castletownhouse.co.uk **W:** www.castletownhouse.co.uk **£ BOOK ONLINE**

Castletown House offer a small collection of Victorian, modernised
self catering apartments. Ranging from studios to one, two & three
bedroom apartments conveniently located a few minutes away
from West Kensington and Barons Court Tube Station. Our area is
renowned for the annual AEGON Queen's Tennis Championship
and we are perfectly located in between Earls Court and Olympia
Exhibition Centre's **Open:** All year **Nearest Shop:** 0.25 miles
Nearest Pub: 0.25 miles

Units	13
Sleeps	1-6

PER UNIT PER WEEK
£600.00 - £2000.00

ST MARGARET'S, TWICKENHAM, Outer London   Map ref 2D2   S

20 The Barons

Contact: Alison Watts, Proprietor, 20 The Barons Luxury Serviced Apartments,
20 The Barons, St Margarets, Twickenham TW1 2AP **T:** (0208) 241 3153 / 07972 601613
E: enquiries@20thebarons.co.uk **W:** www.20thebarons.co.uk

Luxury serviced apartments - two 1 bedroom apartments, 1 studio
and two 2 bedroom apartments. Located in a splendid Victorian
mansion house situated in a leafy crescent in the London village of
St Margarets. The apartments are all 4 star Gold Quality in Tourism.
Open: All year **Nearest Shop:** 0.3km **Nearest Pub:** 0.3km

Units	6
Sleeps	2-6

PER UNIT PER WEEK
£700.00 - £1600.00

Sign up for our newsletter

Visit our website to sign up for our
e-newsletter and receive regular
information on events, exclusive
competitions and new publications.

www.visitor-guides.co.uk

Don't Miss...

Audley End House & Gardens

Saffron Walden, Essex CB11 4JF
www.english-heritage.org.uk
At Audley End near Saffron Walden, you can discover one of England's grandest stately homes. Explore the impressive mansion house, uncover the story behind the Braybrooke's unique natural history collection, visit an exhibition where you can find out about the workers who lived on the estate in the 1800s and even try dressing the part with dressing up clothes provided.

The Broads

Norfolk
www.broads-authority.gov.uk
The Norfolk Broads with its scenic waterways, rare wildlife and rich history has National Park status. This ancient mosaic of lakes, land and rivers covering 303 square kilometres in the east of England, is the UK's largest protected wetland and boasts a variety of habitats including fen, carr woodland and grazing marshes, as well as pretty villages and no less than 11,000 species of wildlife. Walking, cycling, fishing, boating, wildlife spotting, the list of things to do here is endless and there is something for all ages to enjoy.

Kings College Cambridge

King's Parade, Cambridge CB2 1ST
(0)1223 331212
www.kings.cam.ac.uk
Founded in 1441 by Henry VI (1421-71), King's is one of the 31 colleges in the University of Cambridge. Regarded as one of the greatest examples of late Gothic English architecture, it has the world's largest fan-vault and the chapel's stained-glass windows and wooden chancel screen are considered some of the finest from their era. The chapel's choir, composed of male students at King's and choristers from the nearby King's College School, is one of the most accomplished and renowned in the world and every year on Christmas Eve the Festival of Nine Lessons and Carols is broadcast from the chapel to millions of listeners worldwide.

Holkham Hall

Wells-next- the-Sea, Norfolk, NR23 1AB
(01328) 710227
www.holkham.co.uk
Steeped in history, magnificent Holkham Hall on the North Norfolk Coast, is a stunning Palladian mansion with its own nature reserve. It is home to many rare species of flora and fauna, a deer park and one of the most beautiful, unspoilt beaches in the country. Step back in time in the Bygones Museum or explore the 18th Century walled gardens which are being restored, while the children have fun in the woodland adventure play area.

ZSL Whipsnade Zoo

Dunstable, Bedfordshire LU6 2LF
(020) 7449 6200
www.zsl.org/zsl-whipsnade-zoo
Set on 600 acres in the rolling Chiltern Hills, Whipsnade is home to more than 2500 species and you can get close to some of the world's hairiest, scariest, tallest and smallest animals here. Meet the animals, take a steam train ride, visit the Hullabazoo Farm or even be a keeper for the day.

East of England

Bedfordshire, Cambridgeshire, Essex,
Hertfordshire, Norfolk, Suffolk

Loved for its unspoiled character, rural landscape, architecture and traditions, the East of England is full of beautiful countryside, idyllic seaside, historic cities and vibrant towns. The Norfolk Broads and Suffolk Coast have always been popular with yachtsmen and the North Norfolk Coast has become a fashionable getaway in recent years. Cambridge is steeped in history and oozes sophistication, while Bedfordshire, Hertfordshire and Essex each have their own charms, with pockets of beauty and fascinating heritage. This is a diverse region where you'll find plenty to keep you busy.

Norfolk

Huntingdonshire

Cambridgeshire   Suffolk

Bedfordshire

Essex

Hertfordshire

Explore – East of England

Bedfordshire & Hertfordshire

History, the arts, family entertainment and relaxing, unspoilt countryside - this area has it all. Bedfordshire has plenty of attractions, from exotic animals at Whipsnade Zoo to vintage aeroplanes at The Shuttleworth Collection and notable historic houses. Woburn Abbey, the still inhabited home of the Dukes of Bedford, stands in a 3000-acre park and is part of one of Europe's largest drive-through game reserves. The 18th century mansion's 14 state apartments are open to the public and contain an impressive art collection. Luton Hoo is a fine Robert Adam designed house in a 1200-acre Capability Brown designed park.

Hertfordshire also has its fair share of stately homes, with Hatfield House, built from 1707 by Robert Cecil, first Earl of Salisbury, leading the way. Nearby Knebworth House is the venue for popular summer concerts and events.

Roman walls, mosaic floors and part of an amphitheatre are still visible at Verulanium, St Albans and Much Hadham, where the Bishops of London used to have their country seat, is a showpiece village. Welwyn Garden City, one of Britain's first 20th century new towns retains a certain art deco charm.

Cambridgeshire & Essex

Cambridge is a city of winding streets lined with old houses, world-famous colleges and churches, while the gently flowing Cam provides a serene backdrop to the architectural wonders. Kings College Chapel, started by Henry VI in 1446 should not be missed and the Fitzwilliam Museum is one of Europe's treasure houses, with antiquities from Greece and Rome. First-class shopping can be found in the quirky stores and exquisite boutiques tucked away along cobbled streets, and there's a vast choice of places to eat and drink.

Further afield, Cambridgeshire is a land of lazy waterways, rolling countryside, bustling market towns and quaint villages. Climb grand sweeping staircases in the stately homes of the aristocracy or relax as you chug along in a leisure boat, watching the wildlife in one of the wonderful nature reserves. Peterborough has a fine Norman cathedral with three soaring arches, whilst Ely has had an abbey on its cathedral site since AD 670.

Western Essex is dotted with pretty historic market towns and villages like Thaxted and Saffron Walden and plenty of historic sites. County town Colchester was founded by the Romans and its massive castle keep, built in 1067 on the site of the Roman Temple of Claudius, houses a collection of Roman antiquities. Explore the beautiful gardens and 110ft Norman Keep at Hedingham Castle, which also holds jousting and theatre performances.

Some of the region's loveliest countryside lies to the north, on the Suffolk Border around Dedham Vale where Constable and Turner painted, while further east you can find family seaside resorts such as Walton on the Naze and Clacton-on-Sea. Following the coast south, the Blackwater and Crouch estuaries provide havens for yachts and pleasure craft. Inland, Layer Marney Tower is a Tudor palace with buildings, gardens and parkland dating from 1520 in a beautiful, rural Essex setting. The county city of Chelmsford has a historic 15th century cathedral and Hylands House is a beautiful Grade II* listed neo-classical villa, set in over 500 acres of Hylands Park.

Norfolk

Norfolk is not as flat as Noel Coward would have you believe, as any cyclist will tell you, but cycling or walking is still a great way to see the county. In the west Thetford Forest is said to be the oldest in England while in the east, the county is crisscrossed by waterways and lakes known as The Broads - apparently the remains of medieval man's peat diggings!

The county town of Norfolk and unofficial capital of East Anglia is Norwich, a fine city whose cathedral walls are decorated with biblical scenes dating from 1046. There are 30 medieval churches in central Norwich and many other interesting historic sites, but modern Norwich is a stylish contemporary city with first rate shopping and cultural facilities. Sandringham, near Kings Lynn in the north west of the county, is the royal palace bought by Queen Victoria for the then Prince of Wales and where the present Queen spends many a family holiday.

The North Norfolk coast has become known as 'Chelsea-on-Sea' in recent years and many parts of the region have developed a reputation for fine dining. From Hunstanton in the west to Cromer in the east, this stretch of coastline is home to nature reserves, windswept beaches and quaint coastal villages. Wells-next-the-Sea, with its long sweeping beach bordered by pine woodland has a pretty harbour with small fishing boats where children fish for crabs.

Suffolk

Suffolk is famous for its winding lanes and pastel painted, thatched cottages. The county town of Ipswich has undergone considerable regeneration in recent years, and now boasts a vibrant waterfront and growing arts scene. For history lovers, Framlingham Castle has stood intact since the 13th century and magnificent churches at Lavenham, Sudbury and Long Melford are well worth a visit.

The Suffolk Coast & Heaths Area of Outstanding Natural Beauty has 155 square miles of unspoilt wildlife-rich wetlands, ancient heaths, windswept shingle beaches and historic towns and villages for you to explore. Its inlets and estuaries are extremely popular with yachtsmen. Gems such as Southwold, with its brightly coloured beach huts, and Aldeburgh are home to some excellent restaurants. Snape Maltings near Aldeburgh offers an eclectic programme of events including the world famous Aldeburgh Festival of music. The historic market town of Woodbridge on the River Deben, has a working tide mill, a fabulous riverside walk with an impressive view across the river to Sutton Hoo and an abundance of delightful pubs and restaurants.

In the south of the county, the hills and valleys on the Suffolk-Essex border open up to stunning skies, captured in paintings by Constable, Turner and Gainsborough. At the heart of beautiful Constable Country, Nayland and Dedham Vale Area of Outstanding Natural Beauty are idyllic places for a stroll or leisurely picnic.

Visit – East of England

 Attractions with this sign participate in the Visitor Attraction Quality Assurance Scheme.

Bedfordshire

Dunstable Downs Kite Festival
July, Dunstable, Bedfordshire LU6 2GY
www.dunstablekitefestival.co.uk
Enjoy a fantastic atmosphere as professional kite teams put on show-stopping diplays. With family activities, local artists and entertainment, there's something for everyone.

Luton International Carnival
May, Luton, Bedfordshire
www.luton.gov.uk
The highlight is the spectacular carnival parade – an eye-catching, breathtaking procession through the town centre, superbly reflecting the diverse mix of cultures in Luton. Enjoy the decorated floats, music and dance as you watch the parade go by.

Thurleigh Farm Centre
Thurleigh, Bedfordshire MK44 2EE
(01234) 771597
www.thurleighfarmcentre.co.uk
A wonderful working farm; have excellent fun with indoor activities including trampolines and mini quad biking, and the tea room with delightful homemade cakes.

Woburn Abbey
Woburn, Bedfordshire MK17 9WA
(01525) 290333
www.woburnabbey.co.uk
Home of the Duke of Bedford, a treasure house with outstanding collections of art, furniture, silver, gold and extensive gardens.

Woburn Safari Park
Bedfordshire MK17 9QN
(01525) 290407
www.woburnsafari.co.uk
Drive through the safari park with species such as white rhino, elephants, tigers and black bears in natural groups just a windscreen's width away, or even closer!

Wrest Park
Silsoe, Luton, Bedfordshire, MK45 4HR
(0870) 333 1181
www.english-heritage.org.uk
Enjoy a great day out exploring one of Britain's most spectacular French style mansions and 'secret' gardens. With hidden gems including a thatched-roof Bath house, ornate marble fountain, Chinese Temple and bridge and over 40 statues, as well as a kids audio trail and play area, it's popular with families and garden lovers alike.

Cambridgeshire

Cambridge Folk Festival
July, Cherry Hinton, Cambridgeshire
www.cambridgefolkfestival.co.uk
Top acts make this a must-visit event for folk fans.

Cambridge University Botanic Garden
1 Brookside, Cambridge CB2 1 JE
(01223) 336265
www.botanic.cam.ac.uk/Botanic
Opened to the public in 1846, the Cambridge University Botanic Garden develops & displays over 8,000 plant species in 40 acres of landscapes.

Duxford Air Show
September, Duxford, nr Cambridge, Cambridgeshire
www.iwm.org.uk/duxford
Set within the spacious grounds of the famous former First and Second World War airfield, the Duxford Air Show features an amazing array of aerial displays.

Elton Hall
Elton, Cambridgeshire PE8 6SH
(01832) 280468
www.eltonhall.com
Historic house with a fine collection of paintings, furniture, antiquarian books, bibles and Henry VIII's prayer book, together with beautiful ornate gardens and arboretum.

Imperial War Museum Duxford
Cambridge CB22 4QR
(01223) 835000
www.iwm.org.uk/duxford
Visit this historic airfield and museum of aviation history and discover the stories of people who lived and worked at RAF Duxford. With its air shows, unique history and atmosphere, nowhere else combines the sights, sounds and power of aircraft quite like it.

Kings College Chapel
Cambridge CB2 1ST
(01223) 331212
www.kings.cam.ac.uk
It's part of one of the oldest Cambridge colleges sharing a wonderful sense of history and tradition with the rest of the University. The Chapel is a splendid example of late Gothic architecture.

The National Stud
Newmarket, Cambridgeshire CB8 0XE
(01638) 663464
www.nationalstud.co.uk
The beautiful grounds & facilities are a renowned tourist attraction in the eastern region.

Oliver Cromwell's House
Ely, Cambridgeshire CB7 4HF
(01353) 662062
www.olivercromwellshouse.co.uk
Visit the former Lord Protector's family's home and experience an exhibition on 17th Century life, on the doorstep of Ely Cathedral.

Peterborough Dragon Boat Festival
June, Peterborough Rowing Lake,
Thorpe Meadows, Cambridgeshire
www.peterboroughdragonboatfestival.com
Teams of up to 11 people, dragon boats and all equipment provided, no previous experience required. Family entertainment and catering stalls.

The Raptor Foundation
Huntingdon, Cambridgeshire PE28 3BT
(01487) 741140
www.raptorfoundation.org.uk
Bird of prey centre, offering 3 daily flying displays with audience participation, gift shop, Silent Wings tearoom, Raptor crafts shop.

Essex

Adventure Island
Southend-on-Sea, Essex SS1 1EE
(01702) 443400
www.adventureisland.co.uk
One of the best value 'theme parks' in the South East with over 60 great rides and attractions for all ages. No admission charge, you only 'pay if you play'.

Central Museum and Planetarium
Southend-on-Sea, Essex SS2 6ES
(01702) 212345
www.southendmuseums.co.uk
An Edwardian building housing displays of archaeology, natural history, social and local history.

Clacton Airshow
August, Clacton Seafront, Essex
www.clactonairshow.com
An impressive two days of aerobatic displays taking to the skies whilst a whole host of exhibition, trade stands, food court and on-site entertainment are available at ground level.

Colchester Medieval Festival
June, Lower Castle Park, Colchester, Essex
www.oysterfayre.co.uk
With many of the peripheral activities that this major annual event of the period would have offered. It remembers a time when folk from the countryside and neighbouring villages would travel to the 'Big Fair' in the town.

Colchester Zoo
Essex CO3 0SL
(01206) 331292
www.colchester-zoo.com
As you step inside Colchester Zoo you are transported into a world full of magnificent animals waiting to be discovered. Learn about the animals as you see them up close and why not watch one of many daily displays.

Essex Country Show
September, Billericay, Essex, CM11 2UD
www.barleylands.co.uk
2016 marks the 30th anniversary of the Essex Country Show! A great range of arena shows, rural crafts, agricultural history and more.

Hedingham Castle
Essex CO9 3DJ
(01787) 460261
www.hedinghamcastle.co.uk
Standing in 160 acres of spectacular landscape, Hedingham Castle is a 900 year old Normal castle filled with romance, heritage and history.

Maldon Mud Race
May, Maldon, Essex
www.maldonmudrace.com
The annual Maldon Mud Race is a wacky fun competition in which participants race to become the first to finish a 400m dash over the bed of the River Blackwater.

RHS Garden Hyde Hall
Chelmsford, Essex CM3 8AT
(01245) 400256
www.rhs.org.uk/hydehall
A garden of inspirational beauty with an eclectic range of horticultural styles from traditional to modern providing year round interest.

Royal Gunpowder Mills
Waltham Abbey, Essex EN9 1JY
(01992) 707370
www.royalgunpowdermills.com
A spectacular 170-acre location for a day of family fun. Special events including Spitfire flypast, award winning Secret History exhibition, tranquil wildlife walks, guided land train tours and rocket science gallery.

Sea-Life Adventure
Southend-on-Sea, Essex SS1 2ER
(01702) 442200
www.sealifeadventure.co.uk
With more than 30 display tanks and tunnels to explore, there are loads of fishy residents to discover at Sea-Life Adventure.

Southend Carnival
August, Southend-on-Sea, Essex
www.southendcarnival.weebly.com
A wide range of exciting and enjoyable events for everyone held over eight days. Now one of the largest community events in South East Essex, and includes a thrilling fun fair and the colourful carnival procession along Southend Seafront!

Hertfordshire

Ashridge Gardens
Berkhamsted, Hertfordshire HP4 1NS
(01442) 841300
www.ashridgehouse.org.uk
Originally designed by Humphry Repton in the early 19th century, Ashridge Gardens are 190 acres of pure beauty and tranquillity. Please contact for advice on tours.

Cathedral and Abbey Church of St Alban
St. Albans, Hertfordshire AL1 1BY
(01727) 860780
www.stalbanscathedral.org
St Alban is Britain's first Christian martyr and the Cathedral, with its shrine, is its oldest place of continuous worship. The building's amazing mix of architectural styles bears witness to the many centuries of its life, first as a monastic Abbey and now as a Cathedral.

Chilli Festival
August, Benington Lordship Gardens, Stevenage, Hertfordshire
www.beningtonlordship.co.uk
A popular family event attracting thousands of visitors over two days, offering a chance to buy Chilli plants, products and sample foods from around the world.

Hertfordshire County Show
May, Redbourn, Hertfordshire
www.hertsshow.com
County show with Trade Stands, Award Winning Food Hall, exclusive 'Made in Hertfordshire' marquee, Countryside Arena, and much much more.

Knebworth House
Hertfordshire SG3 6PY
(01438) 812661
www.knebworthhouse.com
Historic house, home to the Lytton family since 1490. Knebworth Park offers a great day out for all the family, with fun activities for children and lots to do for all ages, including Adventure Playground, Dinosaur Trail, a walk through history in Knebworth House and Gardens and special events throughout the summer.

Potters Bar Museum
Hertfordshire EN6 4HN
(01707) 654179
www.pottersbar.org
Go back in time at Potters Bar Museum with pottery and artefacts revealing history from Potters Bar and the surrounding area. See fossils, stones, and even parts of a Zeppelin that crashed into Potters Bar in 1916.

Norfolk

Banham Zoo
Norwich, Norfolk NR16 2HE
(01953) 887771
www.banhamzoo.co.uk
A 50-acre wildlife spectacular which will take you on a journey to experience tigers, leopards and zebra plus some of the world's most exotic, rare and endangered animals.

Blickling Hall, Gardens and Park
Norwich, Norfolk NR11 6NF
(01263) 738030
www.nationaltrust.org.uk/blickling-estate
A Jacobean redbrick mansion with a garden, orangery, parkland and lake. Spectacular long gallery, plasterwork ceilings and fine collections of furniture, pictures and books. You can walk across much of the 950 acres of woodland, parkland and historic countryside using waymarked routes and the estate also connects with other national paths.

Bressingham Steam and Gardens
Low Rd, Bressingham, Norfolk IP22 2AA
(01379) 686900
www.bressingham.co.uk
Where world renowned gardener and horticulturist Alan Bloom combined his passion for plants and gardens with his love of steam to create a truly unique experience for all the family.

Cromer Pier
Cromer, Norfolk NR27 9HE
www.cromer-pier.com
Cromer Pier is a Grade II listed, 12 year old, award winning, seaside pier on the north coast of Norfolk. The pier is the home of the Cromer Lifeboat Station and the Pavilion Theatre and absolutely the best crab fishing spot on the coast.

Fritton Lake Country World
Great Yarmouth, Norfolk NR31 9HA
(01493) 488288
A woodland and lakeside haven with a children's assault course, putting, an adventure playground, golf, fishing, boating, wildfowl, heavy horses, cart rides, falconry and flying displays.

Great Yarmouth Maritime Festival
September, Great Yarmouth, Norfolk
www.great-yarmouth.co.uk/maritime-festival
A mix of traditional and modern maritime vessels will be moored on South Quay for visitors to admire and go aboard.

Norwich Castle Museum and Art Gallery
Norfolk NR1 3JU
(01603) 493649
www.museums.norfolk.gov.uk
One of Norwich's most famous landmarks, the ancient Norman keep dominates the city and is one of the most important buildings of its kind in Europe. Explore the Castle's history as a palace and later as a prison, and enjoy the fabulous collections of fine art.

Royal Norfolk Show
June, Norwich, Norfolk
www.royalnorfolkshow.co.uk
The Royal Norfolk Show celebrates everything that's Norfolk. It offers 10 hours of entertainment each day from spectacular grand ring displays, traditional livestock and equine classes, to a live music stage, celebrity guests and over 650 stands.

Sainsbury Centre for Visual Arts
UEA, Norwich, Norfolk NR4 7TJ
(01603) 593199
www.scva.ac.uk
Containing a collection of world art, it was one of the first major public buildings to be designed by the architect Norman Foster.

Sandringham
King's Lynn, Norfolk PE35 6EN
(01485) 545400
www.sandringhamestate.co.uk
The Norfolk country retreat of H.M. The Queen and HRH The Duke of Edinburgh. A fascinating house, an intriguing museum and the best of the Royal gardens.

Suffolk

Aldeburgh Music Festival
June, Snape Maltings, Suffolk IP17 1SP
www.aldeburgh.co.uk
The Aldeburgh Festival of Music and the Arts offers an eclectic mix of concerts, operas, masterclasses, films and open air performances at different venues in the Aldeburgh/Snape area in Suffolk.

Gainsborough's House
Sudbury, Suffolk CO10 2EU
(01787) 372958
www.gainsborough.org
Gainsborough's House is the only museum situated in the birthplace of a great British artist. The permanent collection is built around the works of leading English painter Thomas Gainsborough, alongside other temporary exhibitions.

Go Ape! High Wire Forest Adventure - Thetford
Suffolk IP27 0AF (0845) 643 9215
www.goape.co.uk
Experience an exhilarating course of rope bridges, tarzan swings and zip slides... all set high in the trees above the forest floor.

Ickworth House, Park and Gardens
Bury St. Edmunds, Suffolk IP29 5QE
(01284) 735270
www.nationaltrust.org.uk/ickworth
Fine paintings, a beautiful collection of Georgian silver, an Italianate garden and stunning parkland.

Latitude Festival
July, Southwold, Suffolk
www.latitudefestival.com
Primarily a music festival but also has a full spectrum of art including film, comedy, theatre, cabaret, dance and poetry.

National Horseracing Museum and Tours
Newmarket, Suffolk CB8 8JH
(01638) 667333
www.nhrm.co.uk
Family-friendly venue embracing fine and decorative art, social history, archive material and photos. Discover the stories of racing from its early origins at Newmarket to its modern-day heroes.

RSPB Minsmere Nature Reserve
Saxmundham, Suffolk IP17 3BY
(01728) 648281
www.rspb.org.uk/minsmere
One of the UK's premier nature reserves, offering excellent facilities for people of all ages and abilities.

Smiths Row
Bury St Edmunds, Suffolk IP33 1BT
(01284) 762081
www.smithsrow.org
A contemporary art gallery and craft workshop; relax in The Art Lounge with an exhibition book, or take part in a workshop to develop your crafting skills.

Somerleyton Hall and Gardens
Lowestoft, Suffolk NR32 5QQ
(01502) 734901
www.somerleyton.co.uk
12 acres of landscaped gardens to explore including our famous 1864 Yew hedge maze. Guided tours of the Hall.

Suffolk Show
June, Ipswich, Suffolk
www.suffolkshow.co.uk
Animals, food and drink, shopping…there's lots to see and do at this popular county show.

Sutton Hoo
Woodbridge, Suffolk IP12 3DJ
(01394) 389700
www.nationaltrust.org.uk
Anglo-Saxon burial site set on a stunning 255 acre estate with breathtaking views over the River Debe.

Tourist Information Centres

When you arrive at your destination, visit the Tourist Information Centre for quality assured help with accommodation and information about local attractions and events, or email your request before you go.

Aldeburgh	48 High Street	01728 453637	atic@suffolkcoastal.gov.uk
Aylsham	Bure Valley Railway Station	01263 733903	aylsham.tic@broadland.gov.uk
Beccles	The Quay	01502 713196	admin@beccles.info
Bedford	St Pauls Square	01234 718112	touristinfo@bedford.gov.uk
Bishop's Stortford	2 Market Square	01279 655831	tic@bishopsstortford.org
Brentwood	Town Hall	01277 312500	
Burnham Deepdale	Deepdale Information	01485 210256	info@deepdalefarm.co.uk
Bury St Edmunds	6 Angel Hill	01284 764667	tic@stedsbc.gov.uk
Cambridge	Peas Hill	0871 226 8006	info@visitcambridge.org
Clacton-on-Sea	Town Hall	01255 686633	clactontic@tendringdc.gov.uk
Colchester	1 Queen Street	01206 282920	vic@colchester.gov.uk
Cromer	Louden Road	0871 200 3071	cromerinfo@north-norfolk.gov.uk
Diss	Meres Mouth	01379 650523	dtic@s-norfolk.gov.uk
Dunstable	Priory House	01582 891420	tic@dunstable.gov.uk
Ely	Oliver Cromwell's House	01353 662062	tic@eastcambs.gov.uk
Felixstowe	91 Undercliff Road West	01394 276770	ftic@suffolkcoastal.gov.uk
Great Yarmouth	25 Marine Parade	01493 846346	gab@great-yarmouth.gov.uk
Hertford	10 Market Place	01992 584322	tic@hertford.gov.uk
Holt	3 Pound House	0871 200 3071 / 01263 713100	holtinfo@north-norfolk.gov.uk
Hoveton	Station Road	01603 782281	hovetontic@broads-authority.gov.uk
Hunstanton	Town Hall	01485 532610	info@visithunstanton.info
Ipswich	St Stephens Church	01473 258070	tourist@ipswich.gov.uk
King's Lynn	The Custom House	01553 763044	kings-lynn.tic@west-norfolk.gov.uk
Lavenham	Lady Street	01787 248207	lavenhamtic@babergh.gov.uk
Letchworth Garden City	33-35 Station Road	01462 487868	tic@letchworth.com
Lowestoft	East Point Pavilion	01502 533600	touristinfo@waveney.gov.uk
Luton	Luton Central Library	01582 401579	tourist.information@lutonculture.com
Maldon	Wenlock Way	01621 856503	tic@maldon.gov.uk
Newmarket	63 The Guineas	01638 719749	tic.newmarket@forest-heath.gov.uk
Norwich	The Forum	01603 213999	tourism@norwich.gov.uk
Peterborough	9 Bridge Street	01733 452336	tic@peterborough.gov.uk
Saffron Walden	1 Market Place	01799 524002	tourism@saffronwalden.gov.uk
Sandy	Rear of 10 Cambridge Road	01767 682 728	tourism@sandytowncouncil.gov.uk
Sheringham	Station Approach	01263 824329	sheringhaminfo@north-norfolk.gov.uk
Skegness	Embassy Theatre	0845 6740505	skegnessinfo@e-lindsey.gov.uk
Southend-on-Sea	Pier Entrance	01702 215620	vic@southend.gov.uk
Southwold	69 High Street	01502 724729	southwold.tic@waveney.gov.uk
St Albans	Old Town Hall	01727 864511	tic@stalbans.gov.uk
Stowmarket	The Museum of East Anglian Life	01449 676800	tic@midsuffolk.gov.uk
Sudbury	Sudbury Library	01787 881320 / 372331	sudburytic@sudburytowncouncil.co.uk
Swaffham	The Shambles	01760 722255	swaffham@eetb.info
Waltham Abbey	6 Highbridge Street	01992 660336	tic@walthamabbey-tc.gov.uk
Wells-Next-The-Sea	Staithe Street	0871 200 3071 / 01328 710885	wellsinfo@north-norfolk.gov.uk
Whitlingham	Whitlingham Country Park	01603 756094	whitlinghamtic@broads-authority.gov.uk
Wisbech	2-3 Bridge Street	01945 583263	tourism@fenland.gov.uk
Witham	61 Newland Street	01376 502674	tic@witham.gov.uk
Woodbridge	Woodbridge Library	01394 446510 / 276770	felixstowetic@suffolkcoastal.gov.uk
Wymondham	Market Cross	01953 604721	wymondhamtic@btconnect.com

Regional Contacts and Information

For more information on accommodation, attractions, activities, events and holidays in the East of England, contact the following regional tourism organisation. Their website has a wealth of information.

Visit East Anglia
(0333) 302 4202
www.visiteastofengland.com

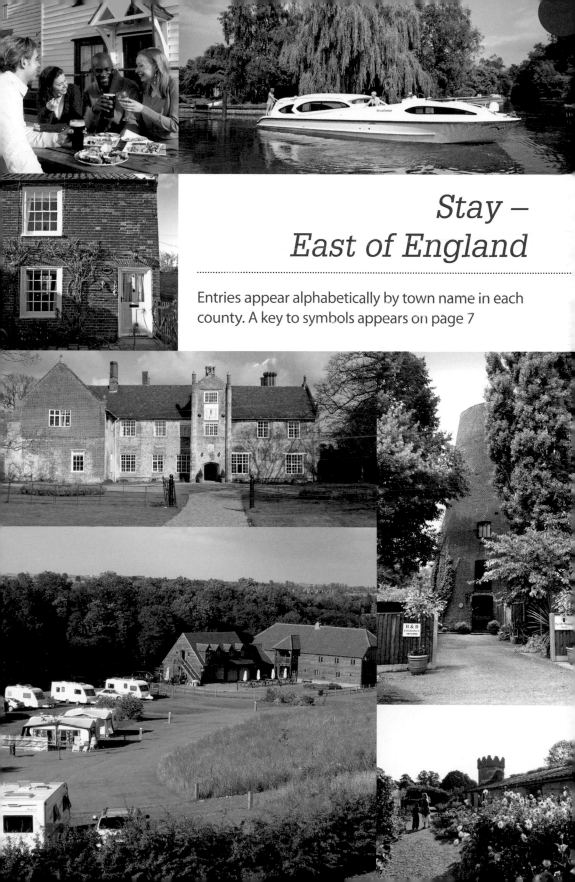

Stay –
East of England

Entries appear alphabetically by town name in each
county. A key to symbols appears on page 7

BEDFORD, Bedfordshire   Map ref 2D1   S

Dovecote Self-Catering

Contact: Ros and Ian Northern, Owners, Priory Farm, Lavendon Road, Harrold, Bedford MK43 7EE **T:** (01234) 720293 **E:** info@dovecoteselfcatering.co.uk
W: www.dovecoteselfcatering.co.uk

Units   3
Sleeps   1-11
PER UNIT PER WEEK
£385.00 - £600.00

Three comfortable self-catering cottages in the picturesque village of Harrold. The Dovecote is a range of traditional stone and brick built buildings set around a sunny courtyard. Each cottage has an individual character but they all have modern facilities. The countryside is on your doorstep, but we are near good pubs and shopping. We welcome families young and old as well as business people. **Open:** All year **Nearest Shop:** 350 metres **Nearest Pub:** 250 metres

Site: ☼ **P** Payment: 💷 Property: 🖥 📶 🛁 Children: 🍼 🎀 ♿ Unit: 📶 🛏 🖥 📷 🍽 📺 📀

CAMBRIDGE, Cambridgeshire   Map ref 2D1   S

Glebe Cottage

Contact: Mrs Fiona Key, Owner, 44 Main Street, Hardwick, Cambridge, Cambridgeshire CB3 7QS **T:** (01954) 212895 **E:** info@camcottage.co.uk
W: www.camcottage.co.uk   **£ BOOK ONLINE**

Units   1
Sleeps   2
PER UNIT PER WEEK
£400.00 - £450.00

Recently refurbished, the soft furnishings of velvet drapes and blinds bring a warm cosy feel. New kitchen with dishwasher. Upstairs brand new en suite bathroom to double bedroom. Views of over two acres of established garden with furniture and BBQ. A little bit of paradise and a quiet spot but close enough to the city and transport links.

Open: All year except Christmas - New Year
Nearest Shop: 0.5 miles
Nearest Pub: 300 yards

Site: ☼ **P** Leisure: 🚴 ♪ ⚑ ♻ Property: 🖥 🛁 Children: 🍼 Unit: 📶 🛏 🖥 📷 🍽 📺 📀 BBQ

Sign up for our newsletter

Visit our website to sign up for our e-newsletter and receive regular information on events, articles, exclusive competitions and new publications.

www.visitor-guides.co.uk

CAMBRIDGE, Cambridgeshire　Map ref 2D1　SatNav CB23 7DG　C

Highfield Farm Touring Park

Long Road, Comberton, Cambridge CB23 7DG
T: (01223) 262308 **F:** 01223 262308 **E:** enquiries@highfieldfarmtouringpark.co.uk
W: www.highfieldfarmtouringpark.co.uk

🚐 (60)	£15.00-£25.00	
🚍 (60)	£15.00-£25.00	
⛺ (60)	£13.50-£25.00	
120 touring pitches		

A popular, family-run park with excellent facilities close to the University City of Cambridge and Imperial War Museum, Duxford. Ideally situated for touring East Anglia and within easy access of the Cambridge park and rides. Prices for Caravans and motorvans are based on two people with electric included. Please view our website for further information.

Directions: From Cambridge take the A1303 to Bedford. After 3 miles, left at roundabout, follow sign to Comberton. From M11 jct 12, A603 to Sandy. Then B1046 to Comberton.

Open: April to October.

Site: ⛺🅿 Payment: € ☼ Leisure: ♪ ► ∪ Children: ⛷ ⚠ Catering: 🍴 Park: 🐕 🔒 ♿ ☂ Touring: ☎ 🖕 🔌 ⚡

HUNTINGDON, Cambridgeshire　Map ref 3A2　SatNav PE28 9AJ　C

Quiet Waters Caravan Park

Hemingford Abbots, Huntingdon, Cambridgeshire PE28 9AJ
T: (01480) 463405 **F:** 01480 463405 **E:** quietwaters.park@btopenworld.com
W: www.quietwaterscaravanpark.co.uk

🚐 (18)	£19.00-£23.00	
🚍 (18)	£19.00-£23.00	
⛺ (2)	£19.00-£23.00	
🏠 (9)	£320.00-£450.00	
18 touring pitches		

A quiet, family owned riverside park in the centre of a picturesque village. Fishing, boating & excellent walking area. Luxury holiday static caravans and touring pitches, seasonal pitches also available. Disabled facilities available. **Directions:** Junction 25 off the A14, 13 miles from Cambridge, 5 miles from Huntingdon. **Open:** 1st April to 30th October.

Site: ⛺🅿 Payment: 💳 ☼ Leisure: ♪ ► Children: ⛷ Park: 🐕 ♿ 🔒 ☂ Touring: ☎ 🖕 🔌 ⚡

HUNTINGDON, Cambridgeshire　Map ref 3A2　SatNav PE28 3DE　C

Stroud Hill Park

Fen Road, Pidley, Huntingdon, Cambridgeshire PE28 3DE
T: (01487) 741333 **E:** info@stroudhillpark.co.uk
W: www.stroudhillpark.co.uk

🚐	£25.00-£27.00
🚍	£25.00-£27.00
⛺	£25.00-£27.00
60 touring pitches	

Stroud Hill Park is a privately owned, exclusively adult, touring caravan site in Pidley, Cambridgeshire. The quiet, attractive, rural site provides a central Cambridgeshire location for touring caravans and campers. This premier site has been awarded many industry accolades in recognition of the high standard of the on-site facilities. **Open:** All Year.

Site: 📶 ⛺🅿 Payment: 💳 ☼ Leisure: ♪ ► ⚲ Catering: ✗ 🍴 Park: 🐕 ♿ 🔒 ☂ Touring: ☎ 🖕 🔌 ⚡

HUNTINGDON, *Cambridgeshire* Map ref 3A2 SatNav PE28 2AA C

VisitEngland
★★★★
HOLIDAY PARK

Wyton Lakes Holiday Park
Banks End, Wyton, HUNTINGDON, Cambridgeshire PE28 2AA
T: (01480) 412715 / 07785 294419 **E:** loupeter@supanet.com
W: www.wytonlakes.com

🚐 (60)	£20.00
🚗 (60)	£20.00
⛺ (20)	£17.00
🏠 (1)	£400.00-£500.00

80 touring pitches

Adult-only park. Some pitches beside the on-site carp and coarsefishing lakes. River frontage. Close to local amenities. Toilet and shower block, dishwashing, laundry. 2 Bedroomed chalet for weekly hire. Excellent local bus service. **Directions:** Exit 23 off A14. Follow signs A141 March. Go past 4 roundabouts. At 4th roundabout take A1123 to St Ives. Park approx 1 mile on right. **Open:** April to October.

Payment: 💳 Leisure: 🎣 Park: 🐾 ♿

PETERBOROUGH, *Cambridgeshire* Map ref 3A1 S

VisitEngland
★★★★
SELF CATERING

Common Right Barns
Contact: Teresa Fowler, Owner/proprietor, Plash Drove, Tholomas Drove, Wisbech St Mary, Cambridgeshire PE13 4SP **T:** (01945) 410424 / 07767600472
E: teresa@commonrightbarns.co.uk **W:** www.commonrightbarns.co.uk

Units	1
Sleeps	2-3

PER UNIT PER WEEK
£450.00 - £500.00

Flat access bungalow in converted Dairy farm buildings set in rural Fenland hamlet, perfect for relaxing or exploring. Facilities for those with mobility impairment. **Open:** All Year **Nearest Shop:** 2 miles **Nearest Pub:** 800 metres

Site: ♿ P Property: 🐾 ♿ 📶 🍴 Unit: 📺 📀 BBQ

BILLERICAY, Essex   Map ref 3B3   S

VisitEngland ★★★★★ SELF CATERING

VisitEngland Gold AWARD

Units   1
Sleeps   1-6

PER UNIT PER WEEK
£675.00 - £1550.00

SPECIAL PROMOTIONS
Price depends on number of bedrooms reserved. 5% discount for stays of 4 weeks or more against 2-3 bedroom options.

The Pump House Apartment

Contact: Mr John Bayliss, The Pump House Apartment, 132 Church Street, Great Burstead, Billericay, Essex CM11 2TR **T:** (01277) 656579 **F:** 01277 631160
E: enquiries@thepumphouseapartment.co.uk
W: www.thepumphouseapartment.co.uk **£ BOOK ONLINE**

The apartment is on two floors and luxuriously furnished, with air-conditioning. The accommodation comprises two living rooms, fitted kitchen/diner and the option of one, two or three bedrooms all with bath/shower rooms. Guests have use of heated pool (May to September), hot tub, gazebo and gardens, free Wi-Fi.

Open: All year
Nearest Shop: 0.5 miles
Nearest Pub: 0.5 miles

Site: ✿ P **Payment:** 🖃 € **Leisure:** ♨ ♫ ♪ ♪ ♪ **Property:** 🖥 🔲 🔳 **Children:** 🐕 🛏 🎎
Unit: ▯ ▯ ▣ ▣ ▧ 📺 🔊 📀 BBQ ☎

COLCHESTER, Essex   Map ref 3B2   SatNav CO5 8FE   C

VisitEngland ★★★★ HOLIDAY PARK

🚐 (30)   £18.00-£35.00
🚎 (30)   £18.00-£35.00
▲ (30)   £18.00-£35.00

Fen Farm Camping and Caravan Site

Moore Lane, East Mersea, Colchester, Essex CO5 8FE
T: (01206) 383275 **F:** 01206 386316 **E:** havefun@fenfarm.co.uk
W: www.fenfarm.co.uk

Celebrating 90 years of camping, peaceful family run caravan & camping park on the Essex Coast. Excellent for families. Modern facilities. No hire vans. We welcome tents, tourers and motorhomes of any size. Dogs welcome. **Directions:** Follow the B1025 to Mersea, take left fork onto Island. Follow road to 'Dog and Pheasant' pub, 1st turn on right leads to Fen Farm. **Open:** March - November.

Site: ▲🅿 **Payment:** 🖃 ☀ **Leisure:** ♪ ♪ **Children:** 🐕 ⛰ **Catering:** 🛒 **Park:** 🐕 🖃 🔲 🌳 **Touring:** 🚽 ↻ 🔌 ⚡

MERSEA ISLAND, Essex Map ref 3C3

Away Resorts Mersea Island

Contact: Reception, East Mersea CO5 8UA **T:** (01442) 50 88 50
E: mersea.island@away-resorts.com
W: www.awayresorts.co.uk

Units 14
Sleeps 2-6

PER UNIT PER WEEK
£265.00 - £750.00

Away Resorts Mersea Island is a beautiful, family-friendly park on the Essex coast offering luxury caravan accommodation among the trees, with spacious surroundings, a private beach and access to the nearby country park for walks and cycling. Set in 22 acres of coastal countryside, the park overlooks the stunning Blackwater Estuary. Our peaceful location provides a safe environment for all age groups to enjoy the countryside, beach and recreational areas. Facilities include a heated swimming pool, clubhouse, tennis court and a convenient on-site shop. New accommodation options available for 2016.

Open: 1st February - 31st December

Site: ✿ Payment: 💷 Leisure: 🎣 ⚲ ⚲ Property: 🐾 ⛺ 🏠 🍴 Children: 🛝 🍴 Unit: 📺 🛏 📺 📀

STANSTED MOUNTFITCHET, Essex Map ref 2D1

Walpole Farmhouse

Contact: Mrs Jill Walton, Proprietor, Walpole Farmhouse, Cambridge Road,
Stansted Mountfitchet CM24 8TA **T:** (01279) 812265 **E:** info@walpolefarmhouse.com
W: www.walpolefarmhouse.com **£ BOOK ONLINE**

Units 2
Sleeps 1-5

PER UNIT PER WEEK
£250.00 - £450.00

Charmingly converted single storey building with its own spacious private garden. Both the Cottage and Studio are tastefully decorated with all modern facilities, including Wi-Fi & ample parking. Ideal for both foreign and UK visitors. Close to Stansted Airport, the UK motorway network, and with easy access to London & Cambridge by train or car. The local train station is a 15 minute walk away. Frequent buses pass-by to Saffron Walden, a picturesque medieval town and to Bishop's Stortford for great shopping, the cinema, and accessing the main commuter railway station.

Open: All year (please call or email for booking)   **Units:** Please see our detailed floor maps &
Nearest Shop: 0.25 miles (& more in village)   descriptions on www.walpolefarmhouse.com
Nearest Pub: 0.5 miles (Pubs in Village)

Site: ✿ P Payment: 💷 Leisure: 🚶 Property: 🐾 ⛺ 🍴 Children: 🛝 🍴 Unit: 🛏 🛏 📺 🛏 ⚲ 📺 📀

BUNTINGFORD, Hertfordshire Map ref 2D1 S

VisitEngland ★★★★ SELF CATERING

Units 2
Sleeps 4
PER UNIT PER WEEK
£410.00 - £550.00

The Old Swan Tea Shop

Contact: Lynda Sullivan, Owner, Hare Street, Buntingford, Hertfordshire SG9 0DZ
T: (01763) 289265 **E:** sullivan@oldswanteashop.co.uk
W: www.oldswanteashop.co.uk

A picturesque 15th Century Hall House set in two acres of garden and orchard, situated on the B1368, the old London to Cambridge coach road, where you will always find a warm and friendly welcome from your hosts Lynda and Bill. Ideally located in the East Hertfordshire countryside to offer easy access to Cambridge, Saffron Walden and other local attractions. Double unit for B&B at £75/night or £55 for a single person also available.
Open: All year **Nearest Shop:** 2 miles

Site: P **Leisure:** **Property:** **Children:** **Unit:**

HODDESDON, Hertfordshire Map ref 2D1 SatNav EN11 0AS C

VisitEngland ★★★ TOURING & CAMPING PARK

caravan	(46)	£14.50-£22.50
motorhome	(46)	£14.50-£22.50
tent	(138)	£14.50-£22.50
holiday home	(12)	£70.00-£80.00

Lee Valley Caravan Park - Dobbs Weir

Charlton Meadows, Essex Road, Hoddesdon, Hertfordshire EN11 0AS
T: (03000) 030 619 **E:** dobbsweircampsite@vibrantpartnerships.co.uk
W: www.visitleevalley.org.uk/wheretostay **£ BOOK ONLINE**

Lee Valley Caravan Park, Dobbs Weir is nestled in the picturesque countryside of Hertfordshire and Essex and is perfect for a relaxing stay whether in a tent, caravan, motorhome or one of our pre-pitched tents or Wigwams! Your site fee includes free car parking near the local train station, which means you can be exploring the sights of London or Cambridge within an hour. Holiday homes are also available to purchase.

Directions: From the A10 take the Hoddesdon turn off, then at the second roundabout, turn left signposted Dobbs Weir. Lee Valley Caravan Park is on the right within 1 mile.

Open: From 1st March - 31st January.

Site: **Payment:** **Leisure:** **Children:** **Catering:** **Park:**
Touring:

SOUTH MIMMS, Hertfordshire Map ref 2D1 S

VisitEngland ★★★ SELF CATERING

Units 3
Sleeps 2-6
PER UNIT PER WEEK
£250.00 - £330.00

Black Swan

Contact: Mr William Marsterson, Black Swan, 64 Blanche Lane, South Mimms, Potters Bar EN6 3PD **T:** (01707) 644180 / 07932 181441 **F:** 01707 642344
E: wmarsterson@yahoo.co.uk

Cottage and self-contained flats, 16th century listed building. Rail connections at Potters Bar and London Underground at Barnet allow travel to London within 45 minutes.
Open: All year **Nearest Shop:** 0.25 miles **Nearest Pub:** 0.25 miles

Site: P **Property:** **Children:** **Unit:**

AYLSHAM, Norfolk Map ref 3B1 S

Units 1
Sleeps 1-6

PER UNIT PER WEEK
£550.00 - £1100.00

SPECIAL PROMOTIONS
Short breaks: 3 nights Low season £360 - £385. July or Sept £550 - £595. Under occupancy discounts available for 2 or 3 people - Please see our web site for more details. Flexible start days.

The Old Windmill, Aylsham

Contact: Janet Bower, Owner, Old Mill House, Cawston Road, Aylsham, Norfolk NR11 6NB
T: (01263) 732118 **E:** aylshamwindmill@outlook.com
W: www.aylshamwindmill.co.uk **£ BOOK ONLINE**

Halfway between the City of Norwich and the coast at Cromer. Aylsham's old corn mill was built in 1826 and converted in 2000.
The 3 bedroom accommodation is on 4 floors, with normal domestic style stairs:
On the ground floor is cloakroom and utility with washing machine,tumble dryer and freezer.
The first floor is an open plan lounge, kitchen, dining area.
Above, 1 double bedroom and a twin room with a shared en-suite shower room, and a larger double bedroom with bathroom.
Private patio, parking for 3 cars.
The old market town of Aylsham is an ideal central base for exploring North Norfolk.

Open: All year
Nearest Shop: 10 - 15 mins walk.
Nearest Pub: 10 mins walk

Units: Grd floor, utility & cloaks,1st floor,open plan lounge/diner & kitchen, 2nd floor double and twin rooms shared en suite, 3rd floor king with en suite.

Site: P Payment: ☒ Property: ☷ ⬚ Children: ↘ ⬚ ⚹ Unit: ⬚ ⬚ ⬚ ⬚ ⬚ ⬚ ⬚

BACTON, Norfolk Map ref 3C1 S

Units 1
Sleeps 2-6
PER UNIT PER WEEK
£445.00 - £745.00

Primrose Cottage

Contact: Paul and Claire Medd, Primrose Cottage, Cable Gap Holiday Park, Coast Road, Bacton, Norfolk NR12 0EW **T:** (01692) 650667 **E:** holiday@cablegap.co.uk
W: www.cablegap.co.uk **£ BOOK ONLINE**

Primrose Cottage is a spacious 2 bedroom bungalow designed to accommodate older and less mobile guests and part-time wheelchair users. It is 3 star self-catering accommodation and benefits from central heating, fully fitted kitchen, large level wet-room bathroom, with its own parking and direct access ramp.
Open: Mid March to Mid November **Nearest Shop:** 0.1 miles
Nearest Pub: 0.1 mile

 Site: P Payment: ☒ Leisure: ♪ ⚑ Property: ☷ ⬚ Children: ↘ ⬚ ⚹ Unit: ⬚ ⬚ ⬚ ⬚

The Official Tourist Board Guide to **Self Catering & Camping 2016**

BODHAM, Norfolk   Map ref 3B1   S

Rookery Farm Norfolk

Contact: Mrs Emma McNeil Wilson, Booking Enquiries, Rookery Farm Norfolk, Rookery Farm, West Beckham, Holt, Norfolk NR25 6NX **T:** (01263) 821232 **F:** 01263 822242 **E:** holiday@rookeryfarmnorfolk.com **W:** www.rookeryfarmnorfolk.com **£ BOOK ONLINE**

Units 7
Sleeps 2-32

PER UNIT PER WEEK
£385.00 - £3815.00

SPECIAL PROMOTIONS
Please refer to website for details.

The perfect holiday retreat, Rookery Farm offers comfortable, contemporary self-catering accommodation in a tranquil coastal location. We aim to combine luxury, character and everything you could possibly need for a stress free break.
Rookery Farm is tucked away but perfectly placed for all that's good about beautiful north Norfolk with its unspoilt beaches, rolling countryside and charming towns and villages. The barns are set round a garden courtyard; in addition each property has its own private garden with patio, lawn and herb garden. There is a small play area for younger children

Open: All year
Nearest Shop: 2.5 miles
Nearest Pub: 0.5 miles

Site: ❊ P **Payment:** 💷 **Leisure:** ► **Property:** ✦ 🐾 🖥 🍴 Children: 🛏 **Unit:** 📺 🔲 BBQ

CROMER, Norfolk   Map ref 3C1   S

Beverley House Holiday Apartments

Contact: Robert & Susan Collins, Beverley House Holiday Apartments, 17 Alfred Road, Cromer NR27 9AN **T:** 07960 796309 **F:** 01263 512787 **E:** sue@beverley-house.co.uk

Units 5
Sleeps 3-4

PER UNIT PER WEEK
£134.00 - £478.00

SPECIAL PROMOTIONS
Short breaks available from Oct-Mar, 2-night stay.

Very comfortable Victorian property. Six well-furnished, warm, cosy apartments, some with sea view. Retains many original period features. Shops, pubs, station all within ten minutes walk. Street parking.

Open: All year
Nearest Shop: 0.25 miles

Nearest Pub: 0.25 miles

Site: P **Leisure:** ► **Property:** 🐾 🖥 Children: 🛏 **Unit:** 📺

CROMER, Norfolk Map ref 3C1 S

Units 1
Sleeps 1-6
PER UNIT PER WEEK
£300.00

Cliff Hollow

Contact: Ms L Willins, Booking Enquiries, Cliff Haven, 35 Overstrand Road, Cromer
NR27 0AL **T:** (01263) 512447 **F:** 01263 512447 **E:** l.willins@btinternet.com

Cottage in a quiet loop road, 3-5 minutes from the beach, cliffs and town. Secluded garden with garden furniture. Bird watching, walking, golf, cycling all available. **Open:** April - October, Christmas & New Year, February half term **Nearest Shop:** 1 mile **Nearest Pub:** 1 mile

Site: P Leisure: Property: Children: Unit:

CROMER, Norfolk Map ref 3C1 S

Units 1
Sleeps 6
PER UNIT PER WEEK
£400.00 - £950.00

Coach Cottage

Contact: Kathryn Moore, Manor Cottage, 8 High St., Mundesley, Norfolk NR11 8AE
T: (01263) 722381 / 07710 046869 **E:** contact@coachcottagenorfolk.co.uk
W: www.coachcottagenorfolk.co.uk **£ BOOK ONLINE**

Sleeping 6 (plus cots) in 3 bedrooms (2 doubles & choice of double or twin), this single storey, non-smoking cottage is furnished to a high standard with underfloor heating, wood burner stove, wifi. Light and airy throughout, Coach Cottage is a "home away from home" and offers you a perfect base for a relaxing holiday. 3 WCs. Secure walled garden. Child, dog & mobility friendly. Parking for 2 cars. **Open:** All Year **Nearest Shop:** 500m **Nearest Pub:** 300m

Site: P Payment: € Leisure: Property: Children: Unit: BBQ

CROMER, Norfolk Map ref 3C1 S

Units 85
Sleeps 1-6

PER UNIT PER WEEK
£300.00 - £1414.00

SPECIAL PROMOTIONS
Visit our website or call today for seasonal discounts and great savings.

Cromer Country Club

Contact: 127 Overstrand Road, Cromer, Norfolk NR27 0DJ **T:** (0800) 358 6991
E: EuHotels@diamondresorts.com
W: www.DiamondResortsandHotels.com **£ BOOK ONLINE**

With views of the picturesque Norfolk coastline, Cromer Country Club is ideally placed for a delightful break in a pleasant Victorian seaside town. Apartments are equipped with practical and modern conveniences and are furnished to a very comfortable standard.

The extensive leisure facilities make the resort a lively family destination. There is a swimming pool, steam room, a pool-side whirlpool and spa area. The Amber Bar and Restaurant offers an extensive menu in pleasant surroundings. Daily specials are created using the best locally sourced ingredients.

Open: All year
Nearest Shop: 1 mile
Nearest Pub: On Site

Units: A choice of Studio, one and two bedroom apartments available. All apartments boast a full kitchen, modern bathroom and Television with DVD player.

Site: P Payment: Leisure: Property: Children: Unit:

FAKENHAM, Norfolk Map ref 3B1 S

2 Westgate Barns

Contact: Bettina Gresham, Wareham Road, Binham, Norfolk NR21 0DQ **T:** (01483) 473653
E: enquiries@westgatebarn.co.uk
W: www.westgatebarn.co.uk

Units 1
Sleeps 2-8
PER UNIT PER WEEK
£761.00 - £1380.00

Luxury self-catering accommodation sleeping up to eight people, situated close to the North Norfolk coast in the beautiful village of Binham. The barn is equipped to a high standard with under floor heated solid oak flooring throughout the ground floor and a wood burning stove in the living room. With many modern amenities the barn still retains it's charm and character. **Open:** All year **Nearest Shop:** 0.5 miles
Nearest Pub: 0.5 miles

Site: P Property: Children: Unit: BBQ

FAKENHAM, Norfolk Map ref 3B1 S

Moor Farm Stable Cottages

Contact: Paul Davis, Owner, Moor Farm, The Street, Foxley, Dereham NR20 4QP
T: (01362) 688523 **F:** 01362 688523 **E:** mail@moorfarmstablecottages.co.uk
W: www.moorfarmstablecottages.co.uk

Units 16
Sleeps 3-10
PER UNIT PER WEEK
£300.00 - £1100.00

Situated on a working farm a courtyard of 2/3/4 bedroomed converted stables and barns. Central for North Norfolk coast, Sandringham, Broads and Norwich. Fishing in owner's lakes. Indoor heated swimming pool and spa. **Open:** All Year including Christmas/New Year **Nearest Shop:** 1 mile **Nearest Pub:** 1 mile

Site: P Leisure: Property: Children: Unit: BBQ

FAKENHAM, Norfolk Map ref 3B1 S

Pollywiggle Cottage

Contact: Mrs Marilyn Farnham-Smith, Owner, 79 Earlham Road, Norwich, Norfolk NR2 3RE
T: (01603) 471990 / 07974 804039 **F:** 01603 612221 **E:** marilyn@pollywigglecottage.co.uk
W: www.pollywigglecottage.co.uk **£ BOOK ONLINE**

Units 1
Sleeps 1-7

PER UNIT PER WEEK
£390.00 - £990.00

SPECIAL PROMOTIONS
Short breaks available out of peak times and reductions for a couple sharing one bedroom.

This well equipped 4 bedroomed comfortable retreat is situated on the edge of a small village but close to many attractions. The mature gardens to the front and rear are laid to lawns with pretty flower beds and a small pond. There are attractive rural views and a stunning coast nearby.

There are two bathrooms, both with showers over, one upstairs and one downstairs. The cottage is ideally situated for families or a romantic twosome! There is parking for 4 cars & two cycle shelters for 8 bikes. Small-party reductions out of season and short breaks are available - min 3 nights off peak.

Open: All year
Nearest Shop: 4 miles
Nearest Pub: 3 miles

Units: This is a 1700s brick and flint cottage with some low ceilings and narrow stairs.

Site: P Payment: Leisure: Property: Children: Unit: BBQ

FIELD DALLING, Norfolk　Map ref 3B1　S

★★★★
SELF CATERING

Gold
AWARD

Units	3
Sleeps	1-2

PER UNIT PER WEEK
£255.00 - £415.00

SPECIAL PROMOTIONS
Weekend breaks from £175, low season or last minute.

Hard Farm Barns

Contact: Mrs Angela Harcourt, Hard Farm Barns, Hard Farm House, Little Marsh Lane, Field Dalling, Holt, Norfolk NR25 7LL　**T:** (01328) 830655 / 07790 631760
E: angela@hardfarm.co.uk　**W:** www.hardfarm.co.uk　**£ BOOK ONLINE**

Spacious 4* Gold Award barn conversions sleeping 2, beautifully furnished and equipped with pretty gardens. The ancient flint barns retain their character with original beams and offer warmth and comfort all year round with full central heating. Oak Barn is ground floor, Beech and Ash are over 2 floors. They offer twin or super king beds, all have spacious bathrooms. Hard Farm is the ideal peaceful location for Holt, Blakeney and North Norfolk Coast with its abundance of bird-watching and walking opportunities. A pet is welcome in Ash Barn only. WiFi. Personally supervised and a warm welcome.

Open: All year
Nearest Shop: 1.5 miles
Nearest Pub: 1.5 miles

Units: 3 Barns each sleeping 2 people, one ground floor.

Site: ✿ **P** **Property:** 🐾 🛏 🖥 **Unit:** 📱 📺 🎵

GREAT YARMOUTH, Norfolk　Map ref 3C1　SatNav NR29 3BL　C

VisitEngland
★★★★★
HOLIDAY PARK

🚐	(104)	£16.50-£41.00
🚍	(104)	£16.50-£41.00
⛺	(126)	£12.50-£41.00
🏠	(4)	£545.00-£1145.00
🚎	(11)	£335.00-£1565.00

125 touring pitches

Clippesby Hall

Hall Lane, Clippesby, Norfolk NR29 3BL
T: (01493) 367800　**F:** 01493 367809　**E:** holidays@clippesby.com
W: www.clippesby.com　**£ BOOK ONLINE**

 Clippesby Hall is a 5 star touring & camping holiday park in the heart of the Norfolk Broads, with Gold awards from David Bellamy Conservation and the Green Tourism Business Scheme. Family-friendly, with loads to do on and off site. **Directions:** From the A47, between Norwich & Great Yarmouth, take the A1064 at Acle (Caister-on-sea road), turn left at Clippesby on the B1152, turn first left. **Open:** All year (Easter - October for catering).

Site: 📷 ⛽🅿 **Payment:** 💷 ☼ **Leisure:** 🚲 🎣 🏹 **Children:** 🛝 🎠 **Catering:** ✗ 🍴
Park: 🐾 🛏 🖥 📞 📶 **Touring:** 🚰 💧 🚐 ♪

GREAT YARMOUTH, *Norfolk*   Map ref 3C1   **S**

Clippesby Hall Holiday Park

Contact: Chris Haycock, Park manager, Clippesby Hall, Clippesby, Norfolk NR29 3BL
T: (01493) 367800 **F:** 01493 367809 **E:** holidays@clippesby.com
W: www.clippesby.com **£ BOOK ONLINE**

Units   15
Sleeps   1-8

PER UNIT PER WEEK
£335.00 - £1565.00

SPECIAL PROMOTIONS
Short breaks of 3
nights available during
Spring, Autumn and
Winter, charged at 65%
of weekly price.

The self-catering accommodation at Clippesby Hall is located in the heart of the Norfolk Broads, at an award-winning, independent, family holiday park, suitable for all ages. There is a wide range of accommodation available, from one-bedroom apartments, two-bedroom cottages, and three-bedroom Pine Lodges, to four-bedroom houses. Fully fitted kitchens, bathrooms and all heating are included, together with bed linen. The holiday park has its own bar, restaurant, cafe, outdoor pool, tennis, mini-golf, cycle hire, bike trails, and childrens play areas. Great scenery and beaches.

Open: All year (cafe, bar, resturant and pool Apr-Oct)
Nearest Shop: 3 miles
Nearest Pub: 2 miles

Units: 1-4 bedroom apartments, cottages and lodges set in 34 acre holiday park.

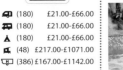

Site: ❀ **P Payment:** 💳 **Leisure:** 🚲 ⚓ ⚲ ⚲ **Property:** 🐾 🛏 📺 🍳 **Children:** 🛝 🎡 🚸
Unit: 🛏 🍽 🧺 📺 📀 BBQ ☎

GREAT YARMOUTH, *Norfolk*   Map ref 3C1   SatNav NR29 3QG **C**

The Grange Touring Park

Yarmouth Road, Ormesby St Margaret, Great Yarmouth, Norfolk NR29 3QG
T: (01493) 730306 **E:** info@grangetouring.co.uk
W: www.grangetouring.co.uk

🚗   £13.00-£26.00
🚐   £13.00-£26.00
⛺   £13.00-£26.00
70 touring pitches

In a sylvan setting three miles north of Great Yarmouth. 70 touring/tent/motorvan level grassy pitches with lighting, made-up roadways and high standard toilet/shower/disabled facilities. Graded four star/ticks with Quality in Tourism and the AA.
Directions: We are just five minutes drive from Great Yarmouth at the junction of the A149 and B1159. **Open:** Mid March - End September.

VisitEngland
★★★★
CAMPING PARK

Site: ⚠🅿 **Payment:** 💳 € **Leisure:** ▶ **Children:** 🛝 🎡 **Park:** 🚻 🛁 🚿 🛒 **Touring:** ☎ 🔌 ♪

GREAT YARMOUTH, *Norfolk*   Map ref 3C1   SatNav NR30 1TB **C**

Vauxhall Holiday Park

Acle New Road, Great Yarmouth, Norfolk NR30 1TB
T: (01493) 857231 **F:** 01493 331122 **E:** info@vauxhallholidays.co.uk
W: www.vauxhall-holiday-park.co.uk **£ BOOK ONLINE**

🚗 (180) £21.00-£66.00
🚐 (180) £21.00-£66.00
⛺ (180) £21.00-£66.00
🛖 (48)   £217.00-£1071.00
🏠 (386) £167.00-£1142.00
180 touring pitches

Five star Vauxhall Holiday Park in Great Yarmouth, Norfolk is a long established holiday park offering superb accommodation, camping mega pods and touring facilities. Offers family holidays, short breaks and music weekender events. **Directions:** Please contact us for directions. **Open:** All year.

VisitEngland
★★★★★
HOLIDAY &
TOURING PARK

Site: 📶 ⚠🅿 **Payment:** 💳 **Leisure:** 🚲 ▶ ⚓ ⚲ ⚲ **Children:** 🛝 🎡 **Catering:** ✕ 🍴 **Park:** ♪ 🚻 🛁 🚿 🛒
Touring: ☎ 🔌 ♪

HOLT, Norfolk *Map ref 3B1* S

VisitEngland ★★★ SELF CATERING

Units 1
Sleeps 3

6 Carpenters Cottages

Contact: Sally Beament, Owner, Norwich Road, Holt, Norfolk NR25 6SD
T: (02476) 545577 / 07787 992209 **E:** sallybeament@hotmail.com
W: www.6carpenterscottagesholt.co.uk

Pretty flint and pantiled terraced cottage on the edge of the lovely Georgian market town of Holt. All mod cons. Enclosed, flower filled, gravelled yard in front of cottage and dedicated parking behind. Coast is 3 miles away, excellent walks close by. **Open:** All year
Nearest Shop: 100 yards **Nearest Pub:** 100 yards

Site: P **Property:** **Unit:** TV DVD

HOLT, Norfolk *Map ref 3B1* S

VisitEngland ★★★★ SELF CATERING

Units 1
Sleeps 2-4
PER UNIT PER WEEK
£330.00 - £575.00

Garden Cottage

Contact: Rosemary Kimmins, Owner, Chequers, Bale Road, Sharrington, Norfolk NR24 2PG
T: (01263) 860308 / 07779 267330 **E:** rosemary@kimmins1.wanadoo.co.uk

This high quality conversion of an 18th century building overlooks a large garden in a quiet village convenient to Holt, Blakeney and the whole North Norfolk coast. Fitted and furnished to the highest standard with one double and one twin bedroom, bathroom with over bath shower, downstairs cloakroom, fully fitted kitchen. comfortable sitting room with digital TV, DVD and free Wi-Fi. No pets allowed.
Open: All year except Christmas and New Year
Nearest Shop: 1 mile **Nearest Pub:** 1.5 miles

Site: P **Leisure:** **Property:** **Unit:** TV DVD

HUNSTANTON, Norfolk *Map ref 3B1* S

VisitEngland ★★★★ SELF CATERING

Units 1
Sleeps 1-6

PER UNIT PER WEEK
£525.00 - £1045.00

SPECIAL PROMOTIONS
Short breaks (min 3 nights) available during school term time. Change over day is Saturday. Other days may be available out of season. Towels available. Contact owner to discuss your requirements.

Chilvers

Contact: Harriet Huntsman, Owner, Stockpot, 27 Hall Orchard Lane, Welbourn, Lincoln LN5 0NG **T:** (01400) 273474 / 07778 002858 **E:** hhuntsman@btinternet.com
W: www.chilverscosycottage.co.uk **£ BOOK ONLINE**

A charming Victorian cottage, modernised and well equipped with spectacular views and direct access onto the salt marsh. Downstairs comprises a sitting room with open fire, flatscreen TV and DVD player, a dining room and kitchen with hob, oven, microwave, fridge-freezer, dishwasher and washing machine. The twin, double and superking/twin bedrooms and bathroom are upstairs. Heated by electric oil filled wall mounted radiators. Outside is a BBQ and garden furniture. Ideally situated for sailing, walking, tennis, golf, bird watching, the Coast Hopper bus, excellent hostelries and dining out.

Open: All Year
Nearest Shop: 168 metres
Nearest Pub: 100 metres

Units: The double and superking/twin bedrooms plus the bathroom are on the first floor and the twin room is on the second floor.

Site: P **Property:** **Children:** **Unit:** TV DVD BBQ

HUNSTANTON, Norfolk   Map ref 3B1   **S**

Cornerside

Contact: Arthur Seebonn, Owner, 18 Roman Way, Irchester, Wellingborough, Northamptonshire NN29 7EG **T:** (01933) 358785

Units 1
Sleeps 1-4

Cornerside is on a small development at the south end of Hunstanton and has been recently refurbished. The property is on one level and is ideal for a family of four and anyone with mobility issues. It is close to the beach and other amenities and is an ideal base to explore from. There is parking adjacent to the property and a small shared grassed area for use of guests at the rear of property. Electricity included in price. Please contact for 2016 rates.

The lounge and dining area is open plan with comfortable seating and Freesat TV. The kitchen is fully equipped with cooker, refrigerator and microwave. A deposit of £50.00 is payable on booking and full balance is payable 4 weeks prior to arrival. Available Sat-Sat. Check in 2pm, Check out 10am. No Smoking, One pet allowed by arrangement.

Open: 1st March - 31st October.
Nearest Shop: 0.5 miles
Nearest Pub: 0.5 miles

Units: 2 bedrooms: 1 double and 1 twin with two 2'6" single beds. Bathroom is equipped with a mobility walk in bath/shower. Thermostatic heating throughout, wall mounted fan heater in bathroom. Bed linen and towels included.

Site: ✿ Leisure: ♪ ∪ Property: 🐾 🖼 Children: ⛄ Unit: ▣ 📺

HUNSTANTON, Norfolk   Map ref 3B1   SatNav PE36 5BB   **C**

Searles Leisure Resort

South Beach Road, Hunstanton PE36 5BB
T: (01485) 534211 **F:** 01485 533815 **E:** bookings@searles.co.uk
W: www.searles.co.uk **£ BOOK ONLINE**

🚐 (157)
🚗 (50)
🏕 (125)
🏠 (37)
📺 (122)

SPECIAL PROMOTIONS
Specialised themed breaks each Autumn, including Spectacular Fireworks, Legends Music weekend, Turkey & Tinsel, Sunny Hunny Soul. Please see website for details.

Searles Leisure Resort is a 5 star, award winning family resort that has been offering holidays on the Norfolk coast of Hunstanton for over 80 years.
Superb range of holiday homes and lodges as well as touring and camping pitches including family pods, all with free daily entertainment and free use of an indoor and outdoor swimming complex. Further activities include 27 hole golf course, fishing lake, bowls, tennis, Sea Tours and more, just 200 metres from a sandy beach with stunning sunsets.
The ideal base for exploring the Norfolk coast.

Directions: From King's Lynn take the A149 to Hunstanton. Upon entering Hunstanton follow B1161 to South Beach.

Open: Touring - all year, Holiday Hire - Feb to Nov & New Year.

Site: 📷 Payment: 💳 ☀ Leisure: ♿ ♪ ▶ ∪ ● ⚲ ⚲ ⚲ Children: ⛄ 🎡 Catering: ✕ 🍴
Park: 🐾 🎵 🖥 🔲 📱 🎬 Touring: 🚰 ⛽ 🚗 ♫

Seaescape Cottage

Contact: Valerie Daniels, Mill Farmhouse, Weybread, Diss IP21 5RS **T:** (01379) 586395
E: valerie@seaescapecottage.com
W: www.norfolkcottages.co.uk/cottage-details/1366 **£ BOOK ONLINE**

Units   1
Sleeps   1-4

PER UNIT PER WEEK
£378.00 - £539.00

SPECIAL PROMOTIONS
3 nights from £284.00 -
£404.00.

A newly refurbished, Victorian two storey end terrace cottage overlooking Gold Park in the centre of Mundesley, with two bedrooms sleeping up to four people. Kitchen, lounge, dining area, first floor bathroom with shower over bath. Patio doors from the kitchen leading to a small garden.

Open: All year
Nearest Shop: 0.25 miles
Nearest Pub: 0.25 miles

Site: ❋ P Leisure: ✦ Property: ▨ Children: ❧ Unit: ▯ ▣ ▨ ◔ ☥ ☤ BBQ

Kings Lynn Caravan & Camping Park

New Road, North Runcton, King's Lynn, Norfolk PE33 0RA
T: (01553) 840004 **E:** klcc@btconnect.com
W: www.kl-cc.co.uk **£ BOOK ONLINE**

🚐 (150)	£18.00
🚛 (150)	£18.00
⛺ (150)	£11.00
🏠 (4)	£350.00

150 touring pitches

Set in approximately ten acres of beautiful mature parkland, the site is situated on the edge of the village of North Runcton, one mile from the Hardwick roundabout where the A47, A10, A149 and A17 meet. Situated in a prime position for touring Norfolk and the Fens, which are both Areas of Outstanding Natural Beauty, it is also the nearest campsite to the historic port and market town of Kings Lynn. Fishing, golf, riding, bowling and clay pigeon shooting are a few of the sports available locally. Can also book by telephone

Directions: On arrival at Kings Lynn take the A47 Swaffham, Norwich road approx 1 mile from large roundabout where A10, A47 meet. Turning to North Runcton on right hand side, campsite entrance about 150 yards on the left.

Open: All year

f

Site: ▨ ⛺▣ Payment: ▤ € Leisure: ✦ ▶ ∪ Children: ❧ Catering: ▤ Park: ☗ ☲ ▯ ◫ ⋒ Touring: ▯ ◔ ⊙ ♪

NORWICH, Norfolk   Map ref 3C1   S

Units   14
Sleeps   2-6
PER UNIT PER WEEK
£215.00 - £735.00

Cable Gap Holiday Park

Contact: Coast Road, Bacton, Norfolk NR12 0EW **T:** (01692) 650667
E: holiday@cablegap.co.uk
W: www.cablegap.co.uk **£ BOOK ONLINE**

Cable Gap Holiday Park is a small holiday park situated next to the beach, open from mid-March to mid-November. With some vans enjoying a sea view you will be able to relax and enjoy your stay, with the majority having double glazing and central heating. We also welcome dogs in a select number of vans. **Open:** Mid March to Mid November.

Payment: 🔲 **Leisure:** ♪ ▶ **Property:** 🐕 ▭ ▣ 🏢 **Children:** 🛝

STALHAM, Norfolk   Map ref 3C1   S

Units   325
Sleeps   2-12
PER UNIT PER WEEK
£288.00 - £2300.00

Richardsons Boating Holidays

Contact: The Staithe, Stalham, Norfolk NR12 9BX **T:** (01692) 582277
E: boating@richardsonsgroup.net
W: www.richardsonsboatingholidays.co.uk **£ BOOK ONLINE**

Self-catering boating holidays on the Norfolk Broads, boats available to sleep 2-12. Pets welcome on selected boats. Weekly hire or short breaks. Richardson's has over 300 boats making it the largest operator on the Norfolk Broads. The Norfolk Broads are Britain's finest and best loved holiday boating location. A Richardson's boating holiday provides holidaymakers with unique scenery, fantastic pubs and restaurants and great fun family days out. No experience necessary - full trial run given. On board facilities include toilets, showers, equipped kitchen and sleeping quarters and TV.

Open: March-November

Units: Equipped kitchens and sleeping quarters plus toilet and shower. Buoyancy aids provided.

Site: P **Payment:** 🔲 **Property:** 🐕 ▣ 🍴 **Children:** 🛝 **Unit:** ▭ 📺 📀

THURSFORD, Norfolk   Map ref 3B1   S

Units   3
Sleeps   5-6
PER UNIT PER WEEK
£240.00 - £600.00

Station Farm Barn

Contact: Les Walton, Station Farm Barn, 32 Hall Street, Soham, Cambridgeshire CB7 5BW
T: (01353) 720419 / 07801 050267 **E:** enquiries@norfolk-barn-holidays.co.uk
W: www.norfolk-barn-holidays.co.uk **£ BOOK ONLINE**

Barn conversion providing one three-bedroomed and two two-bedroomed cottages. Fully equipped for self-catering family holidays. Well situated for exploring the whole of North Norfolk. 3 day weekend breaks available in off-peak periods at 65% of the weekly rate. Also available during peak on late availability basis. **Open:** All year **Nearest Shop:** 5 miles **Nearest Pub:** 0.10 miles

Site: ❀ P **Payment:** € **Property:** ▣ 🍴 **Children:** 🛝 🏏 🎣 **Unit:** ▭ ▭ ▣ 📺 🎛 📀 BBQ

WELLS-NEXT-THE-SEA, Norfolk   Map ref 3B1   S

Harbour View Cottage

Contact: Mrs Louise Evans-Evans, Harbour View Cottage, 48 Wingate Drive, Ampthill, Bedfordshire MK45 2XF **T:** (01525) 405494 **E:** cottageinwells@live.co.uk
W: www.cottageinwells.tripod.com **£ BOOK ONLINE**

Units   1
Sleeps   1-4

PER UNIT PER WEEK
£250.00 - £575.00

Refurbished in 2008, this warm and inviting cottage with Harbour views retains many original features and sleeps four. Modern bathroom and bespoke kitchen including washer and dishwasher, south facing garden. We will consider 3 or 4 night breaks depending on availability, please contact us for details.
Open: All year **Nearest Shop:** 0.30 miles **Nearest Pub:** 0.30 miles

Site: ✿ P Payment: € Leisure: ⅋ ♩ Property: ⬚ ▣ Children: ⬚2 Unit: ⬚ ▭ ⬚ ⬚ TV ⬚ ⬚

WICKMERE, Norfolk   Map ref 3B1   S

Church Farm Barns

Contact: Mr & Mrs Dom & Gill Boddington, Church Farm Barns, Regent Street, Wickmere, Norfolk NR11 7NB **T:** (01263) 577300 **E:** dom@churchfarmbarnsnorfolk.co.uk
W: www.churchfarmbarnsnorfolk.co.uk

Units   3
Sleeps   2-9

PER UNIT PER WEEK
£275.00 - £1180.00

SPECIAL PROMOTIONS
Please contact for short breaks or last minute bookings.

Weekend break for two from £196.00.

Discounts may be available for booking all 3 barns sleeping up to 17.

Lost in rustic and tranquil North Norfolk where time stands still, this luxurious accommodation offers a peaceful retreat for bird watchers, wildlife enthusiasts, dog owners, walkers and cyclists. Blickling (NT), Felbrigg (NT), Sheringham Park (NT), Wolterton and Mannington all within walking distance. Close to attractions: Broads National Park and North Norfolk coast. The smallest barn provides a cosy escape for two, while taken together the barns are a great venue for family parties and reunions. Friendly owners on site.

Open: All year
Nearest Shop: 1.25 miles
Nearest Pub: 0.75 miles

Units: Corner Barn: 2 double and 1 triple en-suite beds (1 ground floor) plus sofa bed. Owl Barn: 1 double and 2 twin beds. Bailey's Barn: 1 double.

Site: ✿ P Leisure: ⅋ ♩ ↑ ∪ ⚲ Property: ⑂ ▭ ⬚ ▣ Children: ⬚ ⌷ ⌁
Unit: ⬚ ⬚ ▭ ⬚ TV ⬚ ⬚ ∅ BBQ

3★ - 4★
SELF CATERING

Aldeburgh Bay Holidays

Contact: Aldeburgh Bay Holidays, Thorpeness Hotel, Lakeside Avenue, Thorpeness, Suffolk IP16 4NH **T:** (01728) 451031 **E:** sales@aldeburghbayholidays.co.uk
W: www.aldeburghbayholidays.co.uk **£ BOOK ONLINE**

Units	37
Sleeps	2-14

PER UNIT PER WEEK
£335.00 - £2750.00

SPECIAL PROMOTIONS
Short breaks, max 4 nights (incl Christmas and New Year, excl high season).

Located in the beautiful village of Thorpeness on the Suffolk coast, Aldeburgh Bay Holidays could not be better placed to offer you an idyllic holiday retreat.

We offer a unique and individual collection of self-catering holiday cottages, houses and apartments, many with stunning sea views. Choose from a beach side location or a cottage in the heart of the Suffolk countryside.
Each property has modern décor, fully equipped kitchens and spacious living areas.

With an abundance of local shops, attractions and areas of outstanding natural beauty, there really is plenty for everybody to enjoy.

Open: All year
Nearest Shop: 0.20 miles
Nearest Pub: 0.20 miles

Units: All have well equiped kitchen, living areas, some have gardens. Linen and services included in the price.

Site: ✿ P **Payment:** 🖃 **Leisure:** ⚒ ♪ ▶ ∪ ✎ **Property:** ▣ **Children:** ⛱ 🛏 ✠ **Unit:** 🗋 🗄 💻 🗳 🍳 📺

★★
SELF CATERING

Dial Flat

Contact: Mrs Pamela Harrison, Booking Enquiries, Dial Flat, 5 Dial Lane, Aldeburgh IP15 5AG **T:** (01728) 453212 **E:** p.harrison212@btinternet.com

Units	1
Sleeps	1-5

PER UNIT PER WEEK
£300.00 - £450.00

Comfortably furnished top floor flat with wonderful sea views overlooking Moot Green. 2 double bedrooms plus Z-bed. Living room with a colour TV with integral DVD player, kitchenette, bathroom with bath and walk in shower. Near to shops, restaurants, cinema and Jubilee Hall. Ideal for Snape, birdwatching, walking etc. Free Wi-Fi, electricity and garage parking included in rent.
Open: All year **Nearest Shop:** 2 mins **Nearest Pub:** 2 mins

Site: P **Leisure:** ▶ **Property:** 📺 ▣ **Unit:** 🗋 💻 📺 ◉ 📀

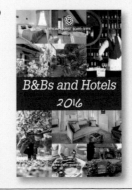

Orlando

Contact: Mr Peter Hatcher, Martlesham Hall, Church Lane, Martlesham IP12 4PQ
T: (01394) 382126 / 07860 567913 **F:** 01394 278600 **E:** peter@hatcher.co.uk
W: www.holidayhomealdeburgh.co.uk

Units   1
Sleeps   14

PER UNIT PER WEEK
£700.00 - £2900.00

SPECIAL PROMOTIONS
Weekend and midweek bookings welcome. Ideal for a family weekend at the seaside. Perfect to celebrate those special family occasions.

Orlando is a spacious, well-equipped six bedroom house adjacent to beach with magnificent, panoramic sea views. Friendly open kitchen with Aga. Ideal for three families or groups for that perfect seaside getaway. Free Wi-Fi broadband.

Open: All year
Nearest Shop: 0.01 miles
Nearest Pub: 0.01 miles

Site: **P** Payment: € Leisure: ♪ ▶ ∪ Property: ▦ ▣ ▦ Children: ⚘ ▥ ♀
Unit: ▯ ▤ ▣ ▦ ▧ ☏ TV ▥ ▥ ⌕ ☏

Culford Farm Cottages

Contact: Mr Steve Flack, Culford Farm Cottages, Home Farm, Culford, Bury St Edmunds, Suffolk IP28 6DS **T:** (01284) 728334 / 07725 201086 **E:** enquiries@homefarmculford.co.uk **W:** www.culfordfarmcottages.co.uk

Units 3
Sleeps 2-6

PER UNIT PER WEEK
£336.00 - £856.00

Unique, well-equipped farm cottages offering an indoor pool available all year, private hot tubs, and riverside walks on our peacefully located working farm with easy access to Bury St Edmunds and beyond. **Open:** All year **Nearest Shop:** 2 miles **Nearest Pub:** 2 miles

Site: ✿ P **Leisure:** ▶ ☆ **Property:** ✖ ⛾ 🗄 🖥 **Children:** 🛝 ⛺ ⚲ **Unit:** ⛾ 🗄 ▦ ▤ ⚲ 📺 📀 BBQ

Lackford Lakes Barns

Contact: Owner, Lackford Hall, Lackford, Nr Bury St Edmunds, Suffolk IP28 6HX **T:** (01284) 728041 **E:** emmaramsay22@gmail.com **W:** www.lackfordlakesbarns.co.uk **£ BOOK ONLINE**

Units 4
Sleeps 4-23

PER UNIT PER WEEK
£350.00 - £1200.00

SPECIAL PROMOTIONS
Weekly and short breaks of 3 or 4 nights with a flexible start date.

Situated within the picturesque and tranquil Lackford Lakes Nature Reserve, our charming accommodation is set in the heart of the beautiful Suffolk countryside, only 5 miles from historic and vibrant Bury St Edmunds, offering 4 self catering holiday cottages sleeping up to 23 guests.

Our grade 2 listed renovated barns are The Cart Lodge (sleeps 7), Holm Oak (sleeps 6), Lark Lodge (sleeps 6) and curlew Cottage (sleeps 4).

Open: All year round
Nearest Shop: 4 miles
Nearest Pub: 2 miles

Units: Grade 2 listed, converted barns of brick, flint and timber, insulated, double glazed, underfloor heating, comfortably furnished with modern bathrooms.

Site: ✿ P **Payment:** 💳 **Leisure:** ♪ ▶ ∪ ☆ **Property:** ∥ ⛾ 🗄 🖥 **Children:** 🛝 ⛺ ⚲ **Unit:** ⛾ 🗄 ▦ ▤ ⚲ 📺 📀 ⌀ BBQ

Rede Hall Farm Park

Contact: Mrs Christine Oakley, Partner, Rede Hall Farm Park, Rede Hall Farm, Chedburgh, Bury St Edmunds IP29 4UG **T:** (01284) 850695 **F:** 01284 850345 **E:** chris@redehallfarmpark.co.uk **W:** www.redehallfarmpark.co.uk **£ BOOK ONLINE**

Units 2
Sleeps 2-6

PER UNIT PER WEEK
£375.00 - £665.00

Country retreat in old-fashioned farmyard. Jenny Wren has two ground floor double bedrooms and galleried twin room. Nuthatch has two ground floor double en suite bedrooms and sofa bed. Also supplied is a shared Hot Spa Tub. We also have a Shepherds Hut that sleeps two in a private field with its own Hot Spa Tub. This is only available from March to end of September. Patio, BBQ, wood burner etc. **Open:** All year - Shepherds Hut April - Octo. **Nearest Shop:** 3 miles **Nearest Pub:** 1 miles

Site: ✿ P **Leisure:** ▶ **Property:** ✖ ⛾ 🗄 **Children:** 🛝 ⛺ ⚲ **Unit:** ⛾ 🗄 ▦ ▤ ⚲ 📺 📀 BBQ

EYE, Suffolk Map ref 3B2 S

VisitEngland ★★★★ SELF CATERING

VisitEngland Gold AWARD

Units 11
Sleeps 2-6

PER UNIT PER WEEK
£349.00 - £955.00

Log Cabin Holidays

Contact: Peter Havers, Owner, Athelington Hall, Horham, Eye, Suffolk IP21 5EJ
T: (01728) 628233 **E:** info@logcabinholidays.co.uk
W: www.logcabinholidays.co.uk

Enjoy 4* and 4* Gold Log cabins in an idyllic location in the beautiful North Suffolk countryside. The perfect reason to escape the pressures of urban life and embrace a well earned mini break in well appointed lodges, double glazed and central heated for year round comfort with outdoor hot tubs. **Open:** All year **Nearest Shop:** 1 mile **Nearest Pub:** 3 miles

Site: P **Payment:** **Leisure:** **Property:** **Children:** **Unit:** TV DVD BBQ

FELIXSTOWE, Suffolk Map ref 3C2 *SatNav IP11 2HB* C

VisitEngland ★★★★ TOURING & CAMPING PARK

(35)	£15.00-£50.00	
(35)	£15.00-£50.00	
(10)	£15.00-£33.00	
(209)		

45 touring pitches

Peewit Caravan Park

Walton Avenue, Felixstowe, Suffolk IP11 2HB
T: (01394) 284511 **E:** peewitpark@aol.com
W: www.peewitcaravanpark.co.uk

Family run and operated, Peewit Caravan Park is an oasis of peace and tranquility. Situated just 900 metres from Felixstowe's seafront, a short walk from the Edwardian town centre. **Directions:** Junction 62, A14 to Port of Felixstowe Dock Gate 1 roundabout. Entrance 100 yards on left. Site 500 yds up driveway. **Open:** Easter or April to 31st October.

PETS! WELCOME **Site:** **Payment:** **Leisure:** **Children:** **Park:** **Touring:**

KERSEY, Suffolk Map ref 3B2 S

VisitEngland ★★★★★ SELF CATERING

Units 1
Sleeps 2

PER UNIT PER WEEK
£360.00

SPECIAL PROMOTIONS
£60 per night - minimum of three nights.

Two nights are available at £180.

Wheelwrights Cottage

Contact: Doreen Gowan, The Forge, Kersey Upland, Kersey, Ipswich, Suffolk IP7 6EN
T: (01473) 829311 / 07785 572878 **E:** peter@pjgowan.net
W: www.wheelwrightscottage.co.uk

Wheelwrights is a cottage recently converted from an 18th century wheelwrights barn situated in the wilds of Suffolk, close to the picturesque village of Kersey. Wonderful countryside for walking or cycling. It consists of one bedroom with a 6ft bed, en suite bathroom with bath and shower, fully equipped kitchen and a large lounge with wood-burning stove.

Wheelwrights is situated in the grounds of a 16th century thatched cottage - 'The Forge' in Kersey Upland where the owners live. The villages of Hadleigh, Lavenham, Long Melford and Dedham are a short drive away and Felixstowe beach is only 40 mins.

Open: All year
Nearest Shop: 2.5 miles
Nearest Pub: 1 mile

Units: Large lounge with wood-burning stove. Fully fitted kitchen. Bedroom with king size bed and en suite bathroom.

WALKERS WELCOME CYCLISTS WELCOME

Site: P **Leisure:** **Property:** **Unit:** TV DVD

LAVENHAM, Suffolk   Map ref 3B2   S

Units 1
Sleeps 2
PER UNIT PER WEEK
£245.00 - £575.00

Staddles

Contact: Helen Burgess, Owner, The White Horse, 57-58 Water Street, Lavenham, Suffolk CO10 9RW **T:** (07827) 911539 **E:** helen424@btinternet.com
W: www.staddlescottage-lavenham.co.uk **£ BOOK ONLINE**

Lavenham is a historic medieval village boasting over 340 listed buildings. Lavenham has a long and colourful history, featuring at different times: Edward de Vere, 17th Earl of Oxford, one of those proposed as the real Shakespeare and Louis Napoleon in the 19th century. **Open:** All year **Nearest Shop:** 0.10 miles **Nearest Pub:** 0.10 miles

Site: ♿ P Leisure: ... Property: ... Unit: ... BBQ

LOWESTOFT, Suffolk   Map ref 3C1   S

Units 1
Sleeps 4
PER UNIT PER WEEK
£198.00 - £360.00

23 Alandale Drive

Contact: Karen Foster, Owner, Kessingland, Lowestoft, Suffolk NR33 7SD
T: (01223) 576874 / 07952 779046 **E:** karenfoster251@yahoo.co.uk

Holiday Bungalow in quiet village location, a very quick walk away from the beach. In Kessingland near Lowestoft, Southwold and Broads. Short breaks available. Guide dogs accepted, no pets. Great for walkers, cyclists and bird watchers, the property is located alongside the Suffolk Coastal Path. Buses run regularly to Southworld, Lowesoft and Great Yarmouth. 2 bedrooms, one double bed and an adult bunk bed. **Open:** 1st March - 4th January **Nearest Shop:** 1.5 miles **Nearest Pub:** 0.5 miles

Site: ♿ P Payment: € Leisure: ... Property: ... Children: ... Unit: ...

PIN MILL, Suffolk   Map ref 3C2   S

Units 1
Sleeps 1-4
PER UNIT PER WEEK
£275.00 - £460.00

Alma Cottage

Contact: Mr John Pugh, Alma Cottage, Culver End, Amberley, Stroud GL5 5AG
T: (01453) 872551 **E:** john.pugh@talk21.com

In centre of Pin Mill, 25m from high water, views over Orwell Estuary. A traditional sailing village, free public access to water, ideal for families, walkers, birdwatchers and painters. **Open:** All year **Nearest Shop:** 0.75 miles **Nearest Pub:** 0.10 miles

Site: ♿ P Payment: € Leisure: ... Property: ... Children: ... Unit: ...

Book your accommodation online

Visit our websites for detailed information, up-to-date availability and to book your accommodation online. Includes over 20,000 places to stay, all of them star rated.

www.visitor-guides.co.uk

Bruisyard Hall

Contact: Events Team, Bruisyard Hall, Bruisyard, Saxmundham, Suffolk IP17 2EJ
T: (01728) 639000 **E:** info@bruisyardhall.com
W: www.bruisyardhall.com

Units   12
Sleeps 10-24

PER UNIT PER WEEK
£6500.00 - £7500.00

SPECIAL PROMOTIONS
Call for last minute
offers!

Escape from it all with your very own 700 acre country estate and 5 star manor house set in the heart of the Suffolk countryside.

Whatever the occasion be it a family get together, a milestone birthday or anniversary, group of friends, Bruisyard Hall will ensure that everyone is under one roof so no-one is missing out. Accommodation for up to 24 people in the Main Hall and a further 4 people in the event barn, means nearest and dearest can all be together.

Open: All Year except Christmas and New Year
Nearest Shop: Waitrose, Saxmundham
Nearest Pub: White Horse, Rendham

Units: 12 bedroom, with 10 bathrooms. Mixture of double & twins.

Need more information?

Visit our websites for detailed information, up-to-date availability and to book your accommodation online. Includes over 20,000 places to stay, all of them star rated.

www.visitor-guides.co.uk

SOMERTON, Suffolk   Map ref 3B2   S

VisitEngland
★★★★
SELF CATERING

Units   2
Sleeps   2-4

PER UNIT PER WEEK
£245.00 - £485.00

SPECIAL PROMOTIONS
We also have 3 and 4
night breaks
throughout the year,
subject to availability.
Please phone for
prices.

Cartlodge & Granary

Contact: Mrs Sarah Worboys, Cartlodge and Granary, Worboys Farm Partners,
Francis Farm, Upper Somerton, Nr. Bury St Edmunds, Suffolk IP29 4BF **T:** (01284) 789241
F: 01284 789241 **E:** enquiries@francisfarmcottages.co.uk
W: www.francisfarmcottages.co.uk

Taking the name of, and built on, land once owned by French Benedictine Monks as far back as
1198, these sympathetically restored farm buildings offer accommodation with a great deal of
character. Set amidst rolling countryside, it is a working farm producing cereals. Cottages sleep 2/4.
The electricity in the cottages and the whole farm is serviced by a double bank of solar panels in the
meadow next to them.
(If using Sat Nav put in IP29 4ND and carry on down our lane.)

Open: All year
Nearest Shop: 5 miles
Nearest Pub: 2 miles

Units: An original Granary and Cartlodge
converted to a high 4* standard. The Cartlodge
and Granary are powered by Solar Panels to help
the environment.

Site: ✿ P Payment: 💷 Property: 🖳 Unit: 🗄 📺 🗲 🔾 📺 📀

SOUTHWOLD, Suffolk   Map ref 3C2   S

VisitEngland
★★★★
SELF CATERING

Units   1
Sleeps   2-4

PER UNIT PER WEEK
£360.00 - £590.00

SPECIAL PROMOTIONS
3 night weekend
breaks and 4 night
weekday breaks
available outside peak
seasons. Discount of
5% offered for party of
2 people only, using
one bedroom only, if
booking a full week.

Highsteppers at Blythview

Contact: Patricia Dowding, Owner, Highsteppers Holidays, Red Lodge Barn,
Middleton Moor, Saxmundham, Suffolk IP17 3LN **T:** (01728) 668100 / 07977 196156
E: pat_roy16@hotmail.com **W:** www.highsteppers-suffolk.co.uk

Highsteppers is a 2 storey apartment on the 1st and 2nd floors situated within a converted
Georgian Grade II listed building. Once a Workhouse but now an established and an ongoing
development. It also has the benefit of a shared indoor swimming pool, games room and mini-gym.
Fully equipped kitchen, good sized lounge and diner on first floor. Two double bedrooms, one en
suite and one separate bathroom.

Less than 10 miles from RSPB Minsmere as featured on Springwatch. Stunning views over the Blyth
Valley and only 5 miles from Southwold.

Open: All year
Nearest Shop: 1 mile
Nearest Pub: 1 mile

Units: A beautifully appointed apartment with
stunning views over the Blyth Valley. There are 2
double bedrooms, one with shower room and
en suite.

Site: P Leisure: 🐾 ♪ ⏵ ♉ ♠ 🕏 Property: 🖳 Children: 🕏 🏾 ⚲ Unit: 🗄 🗄 📺 🗲 🔾 📺 📀

SOUTHWOLD, Suffolk   Map ref 3C2   S

Solely Southwold

Contact: Kathy Oliver, Owner, 1 Sawyers Cottage, Norfolk Road, Wangford, Suffolk NR34 8RE **T:** (01502) 578383 **E:** kathy@solely-southwold.co.uk
W: www.solely-southwold.co.uk

Units   4
Sleeps   2-5
PER UNIT PER WEEK
£325.00 - £735.00

Well appointed central Southwold holiday homes, established in 1995. 2 cottages and 2 flats (1 on the ground floor). Convenient for beach, shops, pubs, restaurants and wonderful walks. Personally managed by the owners to high standards in home-from-home competitively priced accommodation. Free secure Wi-Fi. Book via phone or e-mail. **Open:** All year **Nearest Shop:** 10 metres **Nearest Pub:** 50 metres

Site: ❀ P Payment: € Property: 🐾 💻 ⬚ Children: 🐣 🍴 Unit: 🗋 🗋 📺 🗋 🍳 📺 📀 ⊘

THORPENESS, Suffolk   Map ref 3C2   S

House In The Clouds

Contact: Mrs Sylvia Le Comber, House In The Clouds, 4 Hinde House, 14 Hinde Street, London W1U 3BG **T:** (020) 7224 3615 / 07718455988 **F:** 020 7224 3615
E: houseintheclouds@btopenworld.com **W:** www.houseintheclouds.co.uk **£ BOOK ONLINE**

Units   1
Sleeps   12
PER UNIT PER WEEK
£2165.00 - £3235.00

Wonderfully-eccentric 'fantasy unmatched in England'. Five bedrooms, three bathrooms, unrivalled views from 'Room at the Top'. Billiards, snooker, table tennis, tennis, boules, bird watching. Sea, golf, Sailing on the Meare, music and walks. **Open:** All year **Nearest Shop:** 0.30 miles **Nearest Pub:** 0.30 miles

Site: ❀ P Leisure: ♿ 🏊 ♪ ↻ ♦ 🎾 Property: 🐾 ⬚ 🖼 Children: 🐣 🍴 🚼 Unit: 🗋 🗋 📺 🗋 🍳 📺 📀 BBQ ☎

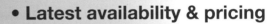

WOODBRIDGE, *Suffolk* *Map ref 3C2* **S**

Ore Valley Holiday Cottages

Contact: Justine Howe, Booking administrator, Sink Farm, Little Glemham, Woodbridge, Suffolk IP13 0BJ **T:** (01728) 602783 / 07796 148220 **E:** cottages@fridaystfarm.co.uk
W: www.orevalleyholidaycottages.co.uk **£ BOOK ONLINE**

Units   5
Sleeps   2-5
PER UNIT PER WEEK
£285.00 - £665.00

The Ore Valley Holiday Cottages are set amidst the rural Suffolk countryside. Just a short drive away from Suffolk's Heritage Coast, these five converted farm stables offer a 4 star self-catering stay for the keen explorer. All of the cottages give you the chance to take in a piece of the breathtaking views that make Suffolk the perfect getaway. **Open:** All year **Nearest Shop:** 3 miles
Nearest Pub: 1 mile

Site: ✿ P Payment: 💷 Leisure: ◆ Property: ∥ 🐾 🖥 🖲 Children: 🚼 🏬 ☂ Unit: 🍴 🍲 📺 🖨 ♒ 📺 📀 BBQ

WORTHAM, *Suffolk* *Map ref 3B2* **S**

Ivy House Farm

Contact: Mr Paul Bradley, Owner, Ivy House Farm Cottages, Long Green, Wortham, Diss, Norfolk IP22 1RD **T:** (01379) 898395 **E:** prjsbrad@aol.com
W: www.ivyhousefarmcottages.co.uk **£ BOOK ONLINE**

Units   3
Sleeps   4-11

PER UNIT PER WEEK
£280.00 - £1985.00

SPECIAL PROMOTIONS
Short breaks available:
please contact for
details.

This peaceful complex standing in spacious gardens is surrounded by common land in the heart of East Anglia. Consists of a 17th century farmhouse and two purpose-built cottages, one has facilities for the disabled. Indoor heated swimming pool, cosy barn with table tennis, pool table & piano. Snooker room and library. Bicycles to loan. Horse riding available. Masseurs onsite. No smoking. Owners on site.

Open: All year
Nearest Shop: 0.5 miles
Nearest Pub: 0.5 miles

Units: Farm house - sleeps 11, Owl Cottage (Mobility 2) - sleeps 7, Suffolk Punch - sleeps 4.

Site: ✿ P Payment: 💷 € Leisure: ♿ ♪ ▶ ♻ ◆ ⚲ Property: 🐎 🖥 🖲 Children: 🚼 🏬 ☂
Unit: 🍴 🍲 📺 🖨 ♒ 📺 📀 ⌀ BBQ

YOXFORD, *Suffolk* *Map ref 3C2* **S**

Rookery Park

Contact: Gemma Minter, Rookery Park LLC, Yoxford, Saxmundham, Suffolk IP17 3LQ
T: (01728) 668310 / 07984 864694 **E:** gemma@rookerypark.org
W: www.rookerypark.org

Units   1
Sleeps   4
PER UNIT PER WEEK
£360.00 - £460.00

Renovated in 2015. Attractively converted building. Ground floor open plan, downstairs bathroom, a twin and double bedroom upstairs. Stands alone, situated on a country estate. Convenient for the exploration of the beautiful Suffolk and Norfolk coast, as well as Yoxford itself offering a variety of restaurants/pubs and shops.
Open: All year **Nearest Shop:** 0.5 miles **Nearest Pub:** 0.5 miles

Site: ✿ P Leisure: ▶ Property: 🖥 🖲 Children: 🚼 Unit: 🍴 🍲 📺 🖨 ♒ 📺 📀 📀

For **key to symbols** see page 7

Don't Miss...

Burghley House
Stamford, Lincolnshire PE9 3JY
(01780) 752451
www.burghley.co.uk
Used in films Pride and Prejudice and The Da Vinci Code, the house boasts eighteen magnificent State Rooms and a huge collection of works and art, including one of the most important private collections of 17th century Italian paintings, the earliest inventoried collection of Japanese ceramics in the West and wood carvings by Grinling Gibbons and his followers.

Castle Ashby Gardens
Northamptonshire NN7 1LQ
(01604) 695200
www.castleashbygardens.co.uk
A haven of tranquility and beauty in the heart of Northamptonshire. Wander through these beautiful gardens, open 365 days of the year, and you are taking a walk through history. Set in the heart of a 10,000-acre estate, the 35 acres of extensive gardens are a combination of several styles including the romantic Italian Gardens, the unique Orangery and impressive Arboretum. The full Castle Ashby experience also involves a menagerie, children's play area, plant centre, tea room and gift shop.

Chatsworth
Bakewell, Derbyshire DE45 1PP
(01246) 565300
www.chatsworth.org
Chatsworth is a spectacular historic house set in the heart of the Peak District in Derbyshire, on the banks of the river Derwent. There are over 30 rooms to explore, including the magnificent Painted Hall and Sculpture Gallery. In the garden, discover water features, giant sculptures and beautiful flowers set in one of Britain's most well-known historic landscapes.

Sherwood Forest
Sherwood Forest Visitor Centre,
Edwinstowe, Nottinghamshire NG21 9HN
www.nottinghamshire.gov.uk
Once part of a royal hunting forest and legendary home of Robin Hood, Sherwood Forest National Nature Reserve covers 450 acres of ancient woodlands where veteran oaks over 500 years old grow, as well as being home to a wide variety of flora and fauna. Follow the waymarked trails amongst the leafy glades and spot birds including nightjars, woodlarks, hawfinches, marsh and willow tits. Marvel in the shadow of the historic Major Oak, browse the Visitor Centre shops or relax with a coffee in the Forest Table Restaurant.

Twycross Zoo
Hinckley, Leicestershire CV9 3PX
(01827) 880250
www.twycrosszoo.org
Set in more than 80 acres and renowned as a World Primate Centre, Twycross Zoo has around 500 animals of almost 150 species, including many endangered animals and native species in the Zoo's Nature Reserve. Pay a visit to meet the famous orangutans, gorillas and chimpanzees plus many other mammals, birds and reptiles.

East Midlands

Derbyshire, Leicestershire,
Lincolnshire, Northamptonshire,
Nottinghamshire, Rutland

The East Midlands is a region of historic castles and cathedrals, lavish houses, underground caves, a rich industrial heritage and spectacular countryside including the Peak District and the Lincolnshire Wolds. Climb to enchanting hilltop castles for breathtaking views. Explore medieval ruins and battlefields. Discover hidden walks in ancient forests, cycle across hills and wolds, or visit one of the regions many events and attractions.

Lincolnshire
Derbyshire
Nottinghamshire
Rutland
Leicestershire
Northamptonshire

Explore – East Midlands

Derbyshire

'There is no finer county in England than Derbyshire. To sit in the shade on a fine day and look upon verdure is the most perfect refreshment' according to Jane Austen. Derbyshire is the home of the UK's first National Park, the Peak District, which has been popular with holidaymakers for centuries. It forms the beginning of the Pennine Chain and its reservoirs and hills are second to none in beauty. This is excellent walking, riding and cycling country and contains plenty of visitor attractions and historic sites such as Gullivers Theme Park at Matlock Bath and the 17th century Palladian Chatsworth, seat of the Duke of Devonshire.

Leicestershire & Rutland

Leicester is a cathedral city with a 2000-year history, now host to a modern university and the county's pastures fuel one of its main exports: cheese. Foxton Locks is the largest flight of staircase locks on the English canal system with two 'staircases' of five locks bustling with narrowboats. Belvoir Castle in the east dominates its vale. Rockingham Castle at Market Harborough was built by William the Conqueror and stands on the edge of an escarpment giving dramatic views over five counties and the Welland Valley below. Quietly nestling in the English countryside, England's smallest county of Rutland is an idyllic rural destination with an array of unspoilt villages and two charming market towns, packed with rich history and character.

Lincolnshire

Lincolnshire is said to produce one eighth of Britain's food and its wide open meadows are testament to this. Gothic triple-towered Lincoln Cathedral is visible from the Fens for miles around, while Burghley House hosts the famous annual Horse Trials and is a top tourist attraction. The Lincolnshire Wolds, a range of hills designated an Area of Outstanding Natural Beauty and the highest area of land in eastern England between Yorkshire and Kent, is idyllic walking and cycling country. Also perfect for bird watchers and nature lovers, Lincolnshire's Natural Coast is one of this region's best kept secrets!

Northamptonshire

County town Northampton is famous for its shoe making, celebrated in the Central Museum and Art Gallery, and the county also has its share of stately homes and historic battlefields. Silverstone in the south is home to the British Grand Prix. Althorp was the birthplace and is now the resting place of the late Diana Princess of Wales.

Nottinghamshire

Nottingham's castle dates from 1674 and its Lace Centre illustrates the source of much of the city's wealth, alongside other fine examples of Nottinghamshire's architectural heritage such as Papplewick Hall & Gardens. Legendary tales of Robin Hood, Sherwood Forest and historic battles may be what the county is best known for, but it also hosts world class sporting events, live performances and cutting edge art, and there's plenty of shopping and fine dining on offer too. To the north, the remains of Sherwood Forest provide a welcome breathing space and there are plenty of country parks and nature reserves, including the beautiful lakes and landscape of the National Trust's Clumber Park.

Visit – East Midlands

Derbyshire

Buxton Festival
July, Buxton, Derbyshire
www.buxtonfestival.co.uk
A summer celebration of the best opera, music and literature, at the heart of the beautiful Peak District.

Creswell Crags
Chesterfield, Derbyshire S80 3LH
(01909) 720378
www.creswell-crags.org.uk
A world famous archaeological site, honeycombed with caves and smaller fissures. Stone tools and remains of animals found in the caves by archaeologists provide evidence for a fascinating story of life during the last Ice Age between 50,000 and 10,000 years ago. It is also home to Britain's only known Ice Age cave art.

Derby Museum and Art Gallery
Derby DE1 1BS
(01332) 641901
www.derbymuseums.org
Derby Museum and Art Gallery holds collections and displays relating to the history, culture and natural environment of Derby and its region.

Derbyshire Food & Drink Fair
May, Derby, Derbyshire
www.derbyshirefoodanddrinkfair.co.uk
Over 150 stalls will showcase the best local produce from Derbyshire and the Peak District region, as well as unique and exotic foods from further afield.

Gulliver's Kingdom Theme Park
Matlock Bath, Derbyshire DE4 3PG
(01629) 580540
www.gulliversfun.co.uk
With more than 40 rides & attractions, Gulliver's provides the complete family entertainment experience. Fun & adventure with Gully Mouse, Dora the explorer, Diego and "The Lost World".

Haddon Hall
Bakewell, Derbyshire DE45 1LA
(01629) 812855
www.haddonhall.co.uk
Haddon Hall is a stunning English Tudor and country house on the River Wye at Bakewell in Derbyshire, Haddon Hall is one of England's finest examples of a medieval manor.

Hardwick Hall
Chesterfield, Derbyshire S44 5QJ
(01246) 850430
www.nationaltrust.org.uk/hardwick
Owned by the National Trust, Hardwick Hall is one of Britain's greatest Elizabethan houses. The water-powered Stainsby Mill is fully functioning and the Park has a fishing lake and circular walks.

Heights of Abraham
Matlock, Derbyshire DE4 3NT
(01629) 582365
www.heightsofabraham.com
Country park and famous show caverns set in 60 acres of woodland and reached by cable car over deep limestone gorge in the Peak District.

Kedleston Hall
Derby DE22 5JH
(01332) 842191
www.nationaltrust.org.uk/kedleston-hall
A fine example of a neo-classical mansion built between 1759-65 by the architect Robert Adam and set in over 800 acres of parkland and landscaped pleasure grounds. Administered by The National Trust.

Renishaw Hall and Gardens
Dronfield, Derbyshire S21 3WB
(01246) 432310
www.renishaw-hall.co.uk
The Gardens are Italian in design and were laid out over 100 years ago by Sir George Sitwell. The garden is divided into 'rooms' with yew hedges, flanked with classical statues.

The Silk Mill - Museum of Industry and History
Derby DE1 3AF
(01332) 255308
www.derbymuseums.org
The Silk Mill was completed around 1723 and the re-built Mill now contains displays on local history and industry.

Speedwell Cavern and Peak District Cavern
Castleton, Hope Valley, Derbyshire S33 8WA
(01433) 623018
www.speedwellcavern.co.uk
Speedwell Cavern and Peak District Cavern offer the chance for amazing adventures in the heart of the Peak District, with unusual rock formations, the largest natural cave entrance in the British Isles and an incredible underground boat trip.

Sudbury Hall
Ashbourne, Derbyshire DE6 5HT
(01283) 585305
www.nationaltrust.org.uk/sudburyhall/
Explore the grand 17th Century hall with its richly decorated interior and see life below stairs. Learn about George Vernon, the young man who built the hall you see today at Sudbury in 1660.

Leicestershire & Rutland

Artisan Cheese Fair
April / May, Melton Mowbray, Leicestershire
www.artisancheesefair.co.uk
A chance to taste the huge range of cheeses that are made locally and further afield. Visitors to the Artisan Cheese Fair can sample and purchase many of the 250 popular and rare cheeses on show from 50 exhibitors including the leading names in UK artisan cheese production.

Ashby-de-la-Zouch Castle
Leicestershire LE65 1BR
(01530) 413343
www.english-heritage.org.uk/daysout/properties/ashby-de-la-zouch-castle
Visit Ashby-de-la-Zouch Castle where you will see the ruins of this historical castle, the original setting for many of the scenes of Sir Walter Scott's classic tale 'Ivanhoe'.

Bosworth Battlefield Heritage Centre
Market Bosworth, Leicestershire CV13 0AD
(01455) 290429
www.bosworthbattlefield.com
Delve into Leicestershire's fascinating history at Bosworth Battlefield Country Park - the site of the 1485 Battle of Bosworth.

Conkers Discovery Centre
Ashby-de-la-Zouch, Leicestershire DE12 6GA
(01283) 216633
www.visitconkers.com/thingstodo/discoverycentre
Enjoy the great outdoors and explore over 120 acres of the award winning parkland.

Easter Vintage Festival
March, Great Central Railway, Leicestershire
www.gcrailway.co.uk
A real treat for all this Easter with traction engines, classic cars and buses, fairground rides, trade stands, a beer tent as well as lots of action on the double track.

Great Central Railway
Leicester LE11 1RW
(01509) 632323
www.gcrailway.co.uk
The Great Central Railway is Britain's only double track main line steam railway. Enjoy an exciting calendar of events, a footplate ride or dine in style on board one of the steam trains.

Lincoln Castle
Castle Hill, Lincoln LN1 3AA
(01522) 554559
www.lincolncastle.com
Discover a site steeped in history spanning the centuries and experience nearly 1000 years of jaw-dropping history, from battles to the hanging of criminals and ghostly tales.

National Space Centre
Leicester LE4 5NS
(0845) 605 2001
www.spacecentre.co.uk
The award winning National Space Centre is the UK's largest attraction dedicated to space. From the moment you catch sight of the Space Centre's futuristic Rocket Tower, you'll be treated to hours of breathtaking discovery & interactive fun.

Rutland Water
Egleton, Oakham, Rutland LE15 8BT
(01572) 770651
www.rutlandwater.org.uk
There's plenty to keep everyone entertained at Rutland Water, with a huge range of watersports, fantastic fishing, an outdoor adventure centre and nature reserves teeming with wildlife.

Twinlakes Theme Park
Melton Mowbray, Leicestershire LE14 4SB
(01664) 567777
www.twinlakespark.co.uk
Twinlakes Theme Park - packed with variety, fun and endless adventures for every member of your family.

Lincolnshire

Ayscoughfee Hall Museum and Gardens
Spalding, Lincolnshire PE11 2RA
(01775) 764555
www.ayscoughfee.org
Ayscoughfee Hall Museum is housed in a beautiful wool merchant's house built in 1451 on the banks of the River Welland.

Belton House
Belton, Lincolnshire NG32 2LS
(01476) 566116
www.nationaltrust.org.uk/belton-house
Belton, is a perfect example of an English Country House. The mansion is surrounded by formal gardens and a series of avenues leading to follies within a larger wooded park.

Burghley Horse Trials
September, Burghley House, Lincolnshire
www.burghley-horse.co.uk
One of the most popular events in the British equestrian calendar.

Doddington Hall
Lincoln LN6 4RU
(01522) 694308
www.doddingtonhall.com
A Elizabethan mansion by the architect Robert Smythson. The hall stands today as it was completed in 1600 with walled courtyards, turrets and gatehouse.

Hardys Animal Farm
Ingoldmells, Lincolnshire PE25 1LZ
(01754) 872267
www.hardysanimalfarm.co.uk
Learn about the countryside and how a farm works. There are animals for the children to enjoy as well as the history and traditions of the countryside.

Lincolnshire Show
June, Lincolnshire Showground
www.lincolnshireshow.co.uk
Agriculture remains at the heart of the Lincolnshire Show with livestock and equine competitions, machinery displays and the opportunity to find out where your food comes from and to taste it too!

Lincolnshire Wolds Walking Festival
May, Louth, Lincolnshire
www.woldswalkingfestival.co.uk
Over 90 walks and bike rides, taking place in an Area of Outstanding Natural Beauty and surrounding countryside.

Normanby Hall Museum and Country Park
Scunthorpe, Lincolnshire DN15 9HU
(01724) 720588
xwww.normanbyhall.co.uk
Normanby Hall is a classic English mansion set in 300 acres of gardens, parkland, deer park, woods, ornamental and wild birds.

Tattershall Castle
Lincolnshire LN4 4LR
(01526) 342543
www.nationaltrust.org.uk/tattershall-castle
Tattershall Castle was built in the 15th Century to impress and dominate by Ralph Cromwell, one of the most powerful men in England. The castle is a dramatic red brick tower.

Northamptonshire

78 Derngate
Northampton NN1 1UH
(01604) 603407
The only house in England designed by Charles Rennie Mackintosh is ow a multi award-winning visitor attraction offering an unforgettable day out.

Althorp
Northampton NN7 4HQ
(01604) 770107
www.spencerofalthorp.com
*One of England's finest country houses, and
ancestral home of Diana, Princess of Wales.*

British Grand Prix
July, Silverstone, Northamptonshire
www.silverstone.co.uk
*The only place in the UK to see the world's best
Formula One drivers in action.*

Coton Manor Garden
Nr Guilsborough, Northants NN6 8RQ
(01604) 740219
www.cotonmanor.co.uk
*A beautiful Old English garden with luxuriant borders,
rose gardens, herb gardens, woodland and water
gardens enclosed by old yew and holly hedges.*

Lamport Hall and Gardens
Northamptonshire NN6 9II ID
(01604) 686272
www.lamporthall.co.uk
*Grade 1 listed building that was home to the Isham
family and their collections for over four centuries.*

**National Waterways Museum -
Stoke Bruerne**
Towcester, Northamptonshire NN12 7SE
(01604) 862229
www.canalrivertrust.org.uk
*Stoke Bruerne is an ideal place to explore the story
of our waterways.*

Prebendal Manor Medieval Centre
Nassington, Northamptonshire PE8 6QG
(01780) 782575
www.prebendal-manor.co.uk
*Visit a unique medieval manor and enjoy the largest
recreated medieval gardens in Europe.*

Rockingham Castle
Market Harborough, Northamptonshire LE16 8TH
(01536) 770240
www.rockinghamcastle.com
*Rockingham Castle stands on the edge of an
escarpment giving dramatic views over five
counties and the Welland Valley below.*

Salcey Forest
Hartwell, Northamptonshire NN17 3BB
(01780) 444920
www.forestry.gov.uk/salceyforest
*Wildlife and history are in abundance at Salcey,
so come and discover this ancient semi-natural
woodland and get a birds eye view on the
tremendous Tree Top Way.*

Sulgrave Manor
Northamptonshire OX17 2SD
(01625) 822447
www.sulgravemanor.org.uk
*Sulgrave Manor is the ancestral home of George
Washington's family with authentic furniture shown
by friendly guides.*

Wicksteed Park
Kettering, Northamptonshire NN15 6NJ
(01536) 512475
www.wicksteedpark.co.uk
*Wicksteed Park remains Northamptonshire's most
popular attraction and entertainment venue.*

Nottinghamshire

Armed Forces Weekend
June, Wollaton Park, Nottingham, Nottinghamshire
www.experiencenottinghamshire.com
*Nottingham welcomes the annual national event
celebrating our Armed Forces past and present.*

Attenborough Nature Centre
Attenborough, Nottingham, NG9 6DY
(01159) 721777
www.attenboroughnaturecentre.co.uk
*With a visionary eco-design, set against the
backdrop of the beautiful Attenborough Nature
Reserve, the Attenboroudgh Nature Centre provides
a place for visitors to look, learn and refresh.*

Festival of Words
October, Nottingham, Nottinghamshire
www. nottwords.org.uk
*Celebrating Nottingham's love of words, this
dazzling line up of events and diverse range of host
venues pay a fitting tribute to Nottinghamshire's
rich literary heritage.*

Galleries of Justice Museum
Nottingham NG1 1HN
(0115) 952 0555
www.galleriesofjustice.org.uk
There are many ways to explore the museum of Crime and Punishment, with free exhibitions, audio and performance-led tours plus an on-site café and gift shop. You will be delving in to the dark and disturbing past of crime and punishment.

Holme Pierrepont Country Park
Newark, Nottinghamshire NG24 1BG
(01636) 655765
www.nwscnotts.com
Set in 270 acres of beautiful parkland and home to the National Watersports Centre. With excellent water sports facilities, Family Fun Park, Life Fitness Gym and marvellous nature trails for cycling and walking.

Newark Air Museum
Nottinghamshire NG24 2NY
(01636) 707170
www.newarkairmuseum.org
The air museum is located on part of the former World War Two airfield of RAF Winthorpe. Displaying aircraft, helicopters, aeroplanes, aero engines and aviation exhibits. The museum is open to the public every day except December 24th, 25th, 26th and January 1st.

Newark Castle
Holme Pierrepont, Nottinghamshire NG12 2LU
(0115) 982 1212
www.newark-sherwooddc.gov.uk
At the heart of the town for many centuries the castle has played an important role in historical events. The gardens are pretty, formal gardens bordered by the remaining walls of Newark Castle.

The Newark International Antiques and Collectors Fair
February, Newark, Nottinghamshire NG24 2NY
www.iacf.co.uk/newark
(01636) 702 326
The largest event of its kind in Europe. It is the ultimate treasure hunting ground with 2,500 stands attracting thousands of dealers and buyers from around the globe.

Nottingham Castle
Nottingham NG1 6EL
(0115) 915 3700
www.nottinghamcastle.org.uk
Situated on a high rock, commanding spectacular views over the city and once rivalled the great castles of Windsor and the Tower of London.

Nottinghamshire County Show
May, Newark Showground, Nottinghamshire
www.newarkshowground.com
Promoting farming, food, rural life and heritage in Nottinghamshire and beyond.

Papplewick Hall & Gardens
Nottinghamshire NG15 8FE
(0115) 963 3491
www.papplewickhall.co.uk
A fine Adam house, built in 1787 and Grade I listed building with a landscape park, surrounded by tree belts and a woodland garden.

Robin Hood Beer Festival
October, Nottingham Castle, Nottinghamshire
www.beerfestival.nottinghamcamra.org
Set in the stunning grounds of Nottingham Castle, the Robin Hood Beer Festival offers the world's largest selection of real ales and ciders.

Robin Hood Festival
August, Sherwood Forest, Nottinghamshire
www.experiencenottinghamshire.com
Celebrate our most legendary outlaw in Sherwood Forest's medieval village with jousting tournaments, story tellers, comedy acts amd more.

Sherwood Forest Country Park
Nottinghamshire NG21 9HN
(01623) 823202
www.nottinghamshire.gov.uk/sherwoodforestcp
Sherwood Forest Country Park covers 450 acres and incorporates some truly ancient areas of native woodland.

Sherwood Pines Forest Park

Edwinstowe, Nottinghamshire NG21 9JL
(01623) 825411
www.forestry.gov.uk/sherwoodpines
The largest forest open to the public in the East Midlands and centre for outdoor activities.

Tourist Information Centres

When you arrive at your destination, visit the Tourist Information Centre for quality assured help with accommodation and information about local attractions and events, or email your request before you go.

Ashbourne	13 Market Place	01335 343666	ashbourneinfo@derbyshiredales.gov.uk
Ashby-de-la-Zouch	North Street	01530 411767	ashby.tic@nwleicestershire.gov.uk
Bakewell	Old Market Hall	01629 813227	bakewell@peakdistrict.gov.uk
Boston	Boston Guildhall	01205 356656 / 720006	ticboston@boston.gov.uk
Buxton	The Pavilion Gardens	01298 25106	tourism@highpeak.gov.uk
Castleton	Buxton Road	01433 620679	castleton@peakdistrict.gov.uk
Chesterfield	Rykneld Square	01246 345777	tourism@chesterfield.gov.uk
Derby	Assembly Rooms	01332 643411	tourism@derby.gov.uk
Glossop	Glossop One Stop Shop	0845 1297777	
Grantham	The Guildhall Centre, Council Offices	01476 406166	granthamtic@southkesteven.gov.uk
Horncastle	Wharf Road	01507 601111	horncastle.info@cpbs.com
Kettering	Municipal Offices	01536 315115	tic@kettering.gov.uk
Leicester	51 Gallowtree Gate	0844 888 5181	info@goleicestershire.com
Lincoln Castle Hill	9 Castle Hill	01522 545458	visitorinformation@lincolnbig.co.uk
Loughborough	Loughborough Town Hall	01509 231914	loughborough@goleicestershire.com
Louth	Cannon Street	01507 601111	louth.info@cpbs.com
Mablethorpe	Louth Hotel, Unit 5	01507 474939	mablethorpeinfo@e-lindsey.gov.uk
Melton Mowbray	The Library, Wilton Road	0116 305 3646	
Newark	Keepers Cottage, Riverside Park	01636 655765	newarktic@nsdc.info
Northampton	Sessions House, County Hall	01604 367997/8	tic@northamptonshire.gov.uk
Nottingham City	1-4 Smithy Row	08444 775 678	tourist.information@nottinghamcity.gov.uk
Retford	40 Grove Street	01777 860780	retford.tourist@bassetlaw.gov.uk
Rutland Water	Sykes Lane	01780 686800	tic@anglianwater.co.uk
Sherwood	Sherwood Heat	01623 824545	sherwoodtic@nsdc.info
Silverstone	Silverstone Circuit	0844 3728 200	Elicia.Bonamy@silverstone.co.uk
Spalding	South Holland Centre	01775 725468 / 764777	touristinformationcentre@sholland.gov.uk
Stamford	Stamford TI Arts Centre	01780 755611	stamfordtic@southkesteven.gov.uk
Swadlincote	Sharpe's Pottery Museum	01283 222848	gail.archer@sharpespotterymusuem.org.uk
Woodhall Spa	The Cottage Museum	01526 353775	woodhall.spainfo@cpbs.com

Regional Contacts and Information

For more information on accommodation, attractions, activities, events and holidays in the East Midlands, contact one of the following regional or local tourism organisations. Their websites have a wealth of information and many produce free publications to help you get the most out of your visit.

East Midlands Tourism
www.eastmidlandstourism.com

Experience Nottinghamshire
www.experiencenottinghamshire.com

Peak District and Derbyshire
www.visitpeakdistrict.com

Discover Rutland
(01572) 722577
www.discover-rutland.co.uk

Lincolnshire
(01522) 545458
www.visitlincolnshire.com

VisitNorthamptonshire
www.visitnorthamptonshire.co.uk

Leicestershire
0844 888 5181
www.goleicestershire.com

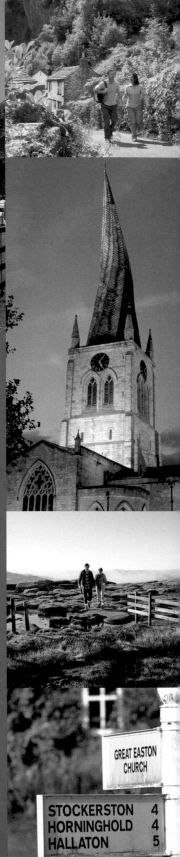

Stay – East Midlands

Entries appear alphabetically by town name in each
county. A key to symbols appears on page 7

VisitEngland
★★★★
HOLIDAY, TOURING
& CAMPING PARK

Rivendale Caravan & Leisure Park

Buxton Road, Nr Alsop En Le Dale, Ashbourne DE6 1QU
T: (01335) 310311 **F:** 01335 310100 **E:** enquiries@rivendalecaravanpark.co.uk
W: www.rivendalecaravanpark.co.uk **£ BOOK ONLINE**

🚐 (81)	£18.00-£27.00
🚎 (81)	£18.00-£27.00
🅰 (30)	£17.00-£27.00
🏠 (12)	£40.00-£90.00
🚐 (2)	£200.00-£895.00

111 touring pitches

SPECIAL PROMOTIONS
Stay Sunday - Thursday
& get 5 nights for the
price of 4.

Surrounded by spectacular Peak District scenery, convenient for Alton Towers, Chatsworth, Dove Dale and Carsington Water. Ideal for cyclists and ramblers with the Tissington Trail 100 metres away and footpaths running directly from site into Dove Dale. Choice of pitch surfaces. Yurts, Camping Pods, accessible Pine Lodges & bedroom suites. Fly fishing lake. Overnight holding area.

Directions: Rivendale is situated 6.5 miles north of Ashbourne, directly off the A515 Buxton road on the right-hand side, travelling north.

Open: All year except 3rd Jan - 28th Jan.

Site: 🏕 🅰🅿 **Payment:** 💷 ☀ **Leisure:** ♨ ♪ ⛳ **Children:** 🎠 ⛰ **Catering:** ✗ 🍴 **Park:** 🐕 🚌 🔲 📷 ⛪
Touring: 🚿 🚽 🔌 ♨

VisitEngland
★★★★
SELF CATERING

VisitEngland
Silver
AWARD

Rivendale Caravan & Leisure Park

Contact: Greg Potter, Director, Alsop Rivendale ltd, Buxton Road, Alsop-en-le-Dale,
Derbyshire DE6 1QU **T:** (01335) 310311 / 07850666648 **F:** 01335 310100
E: enquiries@rivendalecaravanpark.co.uk
W: www.rivendalecaravanpark.co.uk **£ BOOK ONLINE**

Units	1
Sleeps	1-6

PER UNIT PER WEEK
£490.00 - £900.00

SPECIAL PROMOTIONS
From £450 for a 4 night
mid-week break.

Luxurious 3 bedroom accessible lodge built to residential specification Bs3632 with gas central heating and double glazing designed for snug, year-round use. Ramp access to sun-deck & lodge, with profiling bed, shower-room wet -room, electric recliner chair provided, plus hoist etc available upon request. The lodge has a well-equipped kitchen with linen, towels provided and a parking space immediately in front. The ideal base to explore the Peak District & visit the local attractions. 2 bedroom lodge with hot-tub also available.

Open: All year except closes 2nd Jan - 31st Jan.
Nearest Shop: On site
Nearest Pub: On site plus 3 about 2.5 miles

Units: 1 double bedroom, 1 bunk bedroom (with 2 beds), twin room or single with hoist.

Site: P **Payment:** 💷 **Leisure:** ♪ ▶ ⛳ **Property:** 〰 🐕 🚌 🔲 🖥 **Children:** 🎠 🧍 **Unit:** 🔲 📺 🎬 📺 📀

ASHBOURNE, Derbyshire   Map ref 4B2   S

Sandybrook Country Park

Contact: Buxton Road, Ashbourne, Derbyshire DE6 2AQ **T:** (01335) 300000
F: 01335 342679 **E:** enquiries@sandybrook.co.uk
W: www.sandybrook.co.uk

Units   51
Sleeps   2-8
PER UNIT PER WEEK
£369.00 - £1589.00

Award winning Sandybrook Country Park has fantastic facilities including a swimming pool, restaurant and children's play area. Many of our luxury lodges include a private hot tub and the park is close to the picturesque market town of Ashbourne and Alton Towers. With its breathtaking views, Sandybrook is an ideal location for exploring the Peak District with an abundance of walks and cycle routes in the local area. **Open:** All year.

Site: P Payment: 💷 Leisure: 🏊 ⛶ ♨ Property: 🐕 🛏 🖥 🖨 Children: 🚼 🍴 👶 Unit: 🛏 🖥 🎬 📺 BBQ

ASHBOURNE, Derbyshire   Map ref 4B2   S

Throwley Hall Holiday Cottages

Contact: Mrs Sue Richardson, Throwley Hall Farm, Ilam, Nr Ashbourne, Derbyshire DE6 2BB **T:** (01538) 308224 **E:** throwleyhall@hotmail.com
W: www.throwleyhallfarm.co.uk

Units   2
Sleeps   2-13
PER UNIT PER WEEK
£240.00 - £1095.00

Throwley Hall Farm, (a working farm) is situated above the Manifold Valley, surrounded by stunning scenery and good walking country. Near to Alton Towers, Dovedale, and numerous other places of interest are within a few miles. Throwley Moor Farmhouse and Throwley Cottage are detached houses providing comfortable accommodation with open fires and south facing gardens, ideal for families & reunions. **Open:** All Year **Nearest Shop:** 2 miles **Nearest Pub:** 2 miles

Site: ❀ P Payment: 💷 Leisure: ♿ 🏊 ⛶ ♨ Property: 🐕 🛏 🖥 🖨 Children: 🚼 🍴 👶 Unit: 🛏 🖥 🎬 📺 BBQ

BUXTON, Derbyshire   Map ref 4B2   SatNav SK17 9TQ   C

Beech Croft Farm Caravan & Camping Park

Blackwell-in-the-Peak, Nr Buxton, Derbyshire SK17 9TQ
T: (01298) 85330 **E:** mail@beechcroftfarm.co.uk
W: www.beechcroftfarm.co.uk

🚐 (30)   £22.00-£24.50
🚚 (30)   £22.00-£24.50
⛺ (40)   £6.25-£18.00
30 touring pitches

SPECIAL PROMOTIONS
October - 'Reduced Season Rates for Tents' Please contact for details.

In the heart of the Peak District, Beech Croft is a small family run site, alongside their small sheep farm. Southerly facing with views towards the rolling Derbyshire hills. On the Pennine Bridleway with Monsal Trail & Limestone Way close by. All hardstandings have 16 amp EHU, water tap and TV aerial socket. Environmentally friendly underfloor heated toilet & shower block. Free Wi-Fi.

Directions: Midway between Buxton & Bakewell being 6 miles to each town. Signposted & easily accessible from the A6.

Open: All year.

Site: 🛖 Payment: 💷 ☀ Children: 🚼 Catering: 🍴 Park: 🐕 🖥 🖨 Touring: 🚿 🚽

BUXTON, Derbyshire Map ref 4B2 S

Units 1
Sleeps 4
PER UNIT PER WEEK
£200.00 - £320.00

Greens Farm

Contact: Mrs Sheila Kidd, Owner, Quarnford, Nr Buxton, Derbyshire SK17 0SS
T: (01298) 25172 **E:** skidd156@hotmail.com
W: www.simplicitywebsites.co.uk/greensfarm

Comfortable well equipped cottage sleeping four with enclosed garden. In relaxing surroundings with lots of wildlife to be seen all around.Lots of great walks from the door.Ideal for visiting many of the local attractions such as Alton Towers, Potteries and Chatsworth. The electricity ,bed linen,towels and dogs are all included in the price. **Open:** All year **Nearest Shop:** 1.5 miles
Nearest Pub: 1.5 miles

Site: ❀ P Property: 🐾 🔲 Children: ⛹ 🏢 Unit: 📺 🖥 🔥 ⚫ 📀

BUXTON, Derbyshire Map ref 4B2 SatNav SK17 0DT C

🚐 (73) £16.25-£21.75
🚙 (14) £16.25-£21.75
⛺ (30) £12.50-£17.50
95 touring pitches

Newhaven Caravan and Camping Park

Newhaven, Buxton SK17 0DT
T: (01298) 84300 **E:** newhavencaravanpark@btconnect.com
W: www.newhavencaravanpark.co.uk

Halfway between Ashbourne and Buxton in the Peak District National Park. Well-established park with modern facilities, close to the Tissington and High Peak trails, local towns and villages, historic houses and Derbyshire Dales. **Directions:** Half way between Ashbourne and Buxton on the A515 at junction with A5012. **Open:** March to October.

Site: 🅰🅿 Payment: 💷 ☀ Leisure: ♪ Children: ⛹ ⛰ Catering: 🛒 Park: 🐾 🖥 🌰 Touring: 🚿 🚻 🚐

BUXTON, Derbyshire Map ref 4B2 S

Units 1
Sleeps 1-2
PER UNIT PER WEEK
£295.00 - £410.00

Pyegreave Cottage

Contact: Mr & Mrs N C Pollard, Pyegreave Cottage, Pyegreave Farm, Combs, High Peak SK23 9UX **T:** (01298) 813444 **F:** 01298 815381 **E:** rita.pollard@allenpollard.co.uk
W: www.pyegreavecottage.com **£ BOOK ONLINE**

Character stone cottage maintained to a high standard, situated within the Peak District National Park. Spectacular views. Ideal for walking, golf, theatre, fishing, cycling and climbing. Idyllic and tranquil hideaway. **Open:** All year **Nearest Shop:** 3 miles
Nearest Pub: 1 mile

WALKERS / CYCLISTS Site: ❀ P Payment: 💷 € Leisure: 🚴 ♪ ▶ ∪ Property: 🖥 🔲 Children: ⛹ Unit: 🖥 🖨 📺 🔥 🔲 TV ⚫ 📀 BBQ ☎

CASTLETON, Derbyshire Map ref 4B2 S

Units 2
Sleeps 2-4
PER UNIT PER WEEK
£340.00 - £595.00

Riding House Farm Cottages

Contact: Mrs Denise Matthews, Owner, Riding House Farm, Castleton, Hope Valley, Derbyshire S33 8WB **T:** (01433) 620257 **E:** denise@riding-house-cottages.co.uk
W: www.riding-house-cottages.co.uk **£ BOOK ONLINE**

Newly converted farm cottages in the heart of the Peak District National Park. Both cottages are equipped to a very high standard, with charm, character and in a stunning location. Castleton caves and castle, Chatsworth House and Haddon Hall all nearby. **Open:** All year **Nearest Shop:** 1 mile **Nearest Pub:** 1 mile

WALKERS / CYCLISTS Site: ❀ P Leisure: 🚴 ♪ ▶ ∪ Property: 🐾 🖥 🔲 Children: ⛹ 🏢 ⚡ Unit: 🖥 🖨 📺 🔥 🔲 TV ⚫ 📀 BBQ

CHESTERFIELD, *Derbyshire* *Map ref 4B2* **S**

Pottery Flat Chesterfield

Contact: Janine Mannion-Jones, Potter and Landlady, JMJ Pottery, 140 Chatsworth Road, Brampton, Chesterfield S40 2AR **T:** (01246) 555461 / 07790 949583
E: orders@jmjpottery.com **W:** www.thepotteryflatchesterfield.co.uk **£ BOOK ONLINE**

Units	3
Sleeps	2-6

PER UNIT PER WEEK
£400.00 - £600.00

SPECIAL PROMOTIONS
Contact the owner.

Contemporary spacious self catering apartment, with single, double & twin bedrooms. Living room, fully fitted and equipped kitchen/dining room, shower room/separate toilet. Private parking. Within walking distance of town centre on the road into the Peak District. Graded 3 star gold.

Open: All year
Nearest Shop: 0.20 miles
Nearest Pub: 0.01 miles

Units: Short flight of steps access inside the property.

Site: ✿ P Payment: 🔄 Property: 🐾 📺 📷 📱 Children: 🚼 🛏 Unit: 📷 📱 📺 📷 📺 📀

HARTINGTON, *Derbyshire* *Map ref 4B2* **S**

1 Staley Cottage

Contact: Mr Joseph Oliver, Carr Head Farm, Penistone, Sheffield S36 7GA
T: (01226) /62387

Units	2
Sleeps	6-8

PER UNIT PER WEEK
£365.00 - £590.00

Spacious, well maintained, 3 bedrooms, double facilities, dining room, lounge, laundry room, large garden and parking. Owner maintained for 30 years to a high standard. Log fire, summer house and garden room. **Open:** All year **Nearest Shop:** 200 yards **Nearest Pub:** 200 yards

Site: ✿ P Leisure: 🚴 Property: 📺 📷 Children: 🛏 🚶 Unit: 📷 📱 📺 📷 🍳 BBQ ☎

HARTINGTON, *Derbyshire* *Map ref 4B2* **S**

Ash Tree Cottage

Contact: Mrs Clare Morson, Ash Tree Cottage, Nettletor Farm, Mill Lane, Hartington, NR Buxton SK17 0AN **T:** (01298) 84247 / 07517 220972 **E:** nettletorfarm@btconnect.com
W: www.nettletorfarm.co.uk

Units	1
Sleeps	4

PER UNIT PER WEEK
£300.00 - £500.00

Single storey cottage, sleeps four and private parking for two cars. Own contained patio and garden area. Ideally located for Hartington village and picturesque walks into the dales. **Open:** All year **Nearest Shop:** 5 min walk **Nearest Pub:** 5 min walk

Site: ✿ P Leisure: 🚴 🎣 ⛳ Property: 📷 Children: 🚼 🛏 🚶 Unit: 📷 📺 📷 📀 BBQ

MATLOCK, Derbyshire   Map ref 4B2   S

HOLIDAY PARK

Units   112
Sleeps   2-8
PER UNIT PER WEEK
£415.00 - £1965.00

Darwin Forest Country Park

Contact: Darley Moor, Two Dales, Matlock DE4 5PL **T:** (01629) 732428 **F:** 01629 735015
E: enquiries@darwinforest.co.uk
W: www.darwinforest.co.uk

Award winning Darwin Forest provides the perfect base for exploring the stunning Derbyshire Peak District. many of our luxury lodges include a private hot tub and our fabulous on-site facilities include a swimming pool, spa, gym, indoor and outdoor play areas and an award winning restaurant. Our 5 star park is close to Chatsworth House and an abundance of spectacular walking and cycling routes. **Open:** All year.

Site: P Payment: 🏧 **Leisure:** 🖢 ▶ ♀ ⚡ 🎣 🎾 **Property:** 🐾 🚩 📶 🏠 🍽 **Children:** 👶 🛏 🧍 **Unit:** 📺 📱 💻 📻 📻 📺 🎬 📀 BBQ

MATLOCK, Derbyshire   Map ref 4B2   S

SELF CATERING
3★ - 4★

Units   18
Sleeps   4-9
PER UNIT PER WEEK
£450.00 - £1600.00

Darwin Lake

Contact: Darwin Lake, Jaggers Lane, Darley Moor, Nr.Matlock DE4 5LH **T:** (01629) 735859
E: enquiries@darwinlake.co.uk
W: www.darwinlake.co.uk

Superb stone cottages, situated amongst beautiful countryside and natural wildlife of Darwin Lake. High standard of furnishings throughout. Excellent walking and outdoor pursuits. Cottages are all together in one small village location ideal for groups, reunions, weddings, and events as we do have a large hall with function rooms also. **Open:** All year **Nearest Shop:** 2 miles **Nearest Pub:** 0.5 miles

Site: P Payment: 🏧 **Leisure:** 🖢 ♪ ▶ ♀ **Property:** ✀ 🚩 📶 🏠 🍽 **Children:** 👶 🛏 🧍 **Unit:** 📺 📱 💻 📻 📻 📺 🎬 BBQ

NETHERSEAL, Derbyshire   Map ref 4B3   S

SELF CATERING

Units   2
Sleeps   1-12
PER UNIT PER WEEK
£309.00 - £992.00

Sealbrook Farm

Contact: Jane Kirkland, Sealbrook Farm, Grangewood, Swadlincote DE12 8BH
T: (01827) 373236 **E:** info@sealbrookfarmcottages.co.uk
W: www.sealbrookfarmcottages.co.uk **£ BOOK ONLINE**

Located in quiet hamlet. Local shops, pubs, attractions and walks. In the heart of the National Forest. Easy reach of motorway networks and airports. Private off-road parking, large lockable storage available. Wi-Fi.
Open: All year **Nearest Shop:** 2 miles **Nearest Pub:** 1.5 miles

WALKERS ✓ FAMILIES ✓ CYCLISTS ✓
WALKERS ✓ FAMILIES ✓ CYCLISTS ✓
WALKERS ✓ FAMILIES ✓ CYCLISTS ✓

Site: ✿ P Leisure: 🖢 ♪ **Property:** 📶 🏠 🍽 **Children:** 👶 🛏 🧍 **Unit:** 📺 📱 💻 📻 📻 📺 🎬 BBQ

Need more information?

Visit our websites for detailed information, up-to-date availability and to book your accommodation online. Includes over 20,000 places to stay, all of them star rated.

www.visitor-guides.co.uk

The Official Tourist Board Guide to **Self Catering & Camping 2016**

ASHBY-DE-LA-ZOUCH, Leicestershire   Map ref 4B3   **S**

Forest Lodge

Contact: Janice Pearson, Owner, The Rowans, Spring Lane, Packington,
Ashby de la Zouch, Leicestershire LE65 1WU **T:** (01530) 411984 / 07709 032390
E: hillfarmpackington@hotmail.co.uk **W:** www.hillfarmpackington.co.uk **£ BOOK ONLINE**

Units   1
Sleeps   4

PER UNIT PER WEEK
£500.00 - £600.00

SPECIAL PROMOTIONS
1 night stay £150, short
breaks available.

Luxury rural retreat located on the outskirts of a village in The National Forest. Near historic Ashby de la Zouch, major tourist attractions, off road cycle centre and country walks. Relaxing hot tub overlooks beautiful countryside. Rare breed animals and farm shop on site selling home produce. Clay Pigeon Shooting, Champneys Health Spa resort nearby (2 miles). Golf Courses within 5 miles, 2 leisure centres within 5 miles. Pony trekking / horse riding - we can accommodate your own horse on our livery yard. Children welcome from any age. The log cabin is furnished to a high standard and includes TV and DVD player, a music centre, washing machine and dishwasher, and a fully equipped kitchen. The cabin has 2 kingsize bedrooms, 1 of which can be spilt into single beds. There are 2 bathrooms, 1 of which is en suite. Linen and towels are provided.

Open: All year
Nearest Shop: 1 mile
Nearest Pub: 1 mile

Units: 1 unit, sleeps 4. Hot Tub and horse riding on site, kitchen has all mod cons. Parking available.

Site: ✿ P Leisure: ♿ ▶ ∪ Property: ∥ 🐾 🗟 🖭 Children: 🧒 Unit: 🗄 🗄 🖭 🗟 🍳 📺 📀

ASHBY-DE-LA-ZOUCH, Leicestershire   Map ref 4B3   **S**

Normans Barn

Contact: Mrs Isabel Stanley, Proprietor, F Stanley & Son, Ingles Hill Farm, Burton Road,
Ashby-de-la-Zouch LE65 2TE **T:** (01530) 412224 **E:** isabel_stanley@hotmail.com
W: www.normansbarn.co.uk

Units   1
Sleeps   2-5
PER UNIT PER WEEK
£370.00 - £560.00

Luxuriously appointed barn conversion incorporating minstrels' gallery. Both double bedrooms (one twin) en suite. On working farm including 130 acres of woodland walks. Easy access to M42, NEC, Calke Abbey and Castle Donington Park/Airport, Nottingham, Leicester and Derby. 1 mile from Ashby-de-la-Zouch. **Open:** All year plus Christmas and New Year **Nearest Shop:** 0.5 miles **Nearest Pub:** 0.5 miles

Site: ✿ P Leisure: ♿ ♪ ▶ ∪ Property: 🐾 🗟 🖭 Children: 🧒 Unit: 🗄 🗄 🖭 🗟 🍳 📺 📀 📟

BARROW UPON SOAR, Leicestershire   Map ref 4C3   **S**

Kingfisher Cottage

Contact: Mr David Petty, 8072 Little Britton Road, Yonges Island, South Carolina, U.S.A
29449 **T:** +1-843-889-1299 **F:** 1-843-889-1299 **E:** dvdpetty1@gmail.com

Units   1
Sleeps   4-6
PER UNIT PER WEEK
£400.00 - £600.00

Semi-detached roadside cottage comprising two reception rooms, two bedrooms, two bathrooms and rear garden to canal. Quiet part of village, convenient for shops and transport. Friendly pub nearby. **Open:** All year **Nearest Shop:** 0.25 miles **Nearest Pub:** 0.10 miles

Site: ✿ P Leisure: ♪ ∪ Property: 🖭 Children: 🧒 Unit: 🗄 🗄 🖭 🗟 🍳 📺 📀 📟 🍽 BBQ ☎

MELTON MOWBRAY, Leicestershire   Map ref 4C3   S

1 The Green

Contact: Lynn Lawton, Owner, 1 The Green, Muston, Nottinghamshire NG13 0FQ
E: lynnlawton@mac.com
W: www.onethegreen.co.uk

Units   1
Sleeps   2-6
PER UNIT PER WEEK
£360.00 - £635.00

4 bedroom detached cottage with front garden and patio. Off street parking. In quiet village in the Vale of Belvoir. Log fire, 2 single and 2 double bedrooms, bathroom, shower, downstairs toilet, Gas Central Heating and a lockable outside store for bikes. **Open:** All year **Nearest Shop:** 2 miles **Nearest Pub:** 0.6 miles

Site: ✿ P Leisure: ♪ ▶ ♘ Property: ♞ 🖵 🖩 🖳 Children: ⛱ 🛏 ✚ Unit: 🗄 🖵 🖩 📺 📼 🍴 BBQ 📞

MELTON MOWBRAY, Leicestershire   Map ref 4C3   S

Sycamore Farm Holidays

Contact: Waltham Road, Harby, Melton Mowbray, Leicestershire LE14 4DB
T: (01949) 860640 **E:** Jean.Stanley22@yahoo.com
W: www.sycamorefarmcottage.co.uk

Units   1
Sleeps   6
PER UNIT PER WEEK
£575.00

Sycamore Farm is set in open country side in the vale of Belvior, walks across our fields, three bedroom's one double ensuit two twin bedrooms bath room with bath and shower both are wet rooms. the cottage has under floor heating through out. And a 5/6 person hot tub with panoramic views over the vale. **Open:** All year **Nearest Shop:** 0.75 miles **Nearest Pub:** 0.75 miles

[f]

Site: P Leisure: ♪ ▶ ♘ Property: ♞ 🖵 🖩 🖳 Children: ⛱ 🛏 ✚ Unit: 🗄 🖥 🖵 🖩 🍴 📺 📼 BBQ

ALFORD, Lincolnshire Map ref 4D2 **S**

Units 4
Sleeps 2-6
PER UNIT PER WEEK
£240.00 - £590.00

Woodthorpe Hall Country Cottages

Contact: Alford, Lincolnshire LN13 0DD **T:** (01507) 450294
E: enquires@woodthorpeleisurepark.co.uk
W: www.woodthorpeleisurepark.co.uk

Cottages overlooking golf course, quiet location with all the modern amenities. One cottage has its own sauna, wet room and hot tub. There is fishing, golf, holistic salon and a restaurant and bar with garden and aquatic centres close by.
Short breaks available.
Open: All year **Nearest Shop:** 0.20 miles **Nearest Pub:** 0.20 miles

Site: ❀ P Payment: 🖃 Leisure: ♪ ▶ ♣ Property: 🐾 🖳 🗄 🖵 Children: 👶 Unit: 🗄 🗄 ☏ 🖭 📀

BOSTON, Lincolnshire Map ref 3A1 **S**

Units 2
Sleeps 2-5

SPECIAL PROMOTIONS
Minimum of 3 nights.

The Forge and The Smithy

Contact: Johanne Roberts, Chapel Road, Tumby Woodside, Boston, Lincolnshire PE22 7SP
T: (01526) 342943 **E:** enquiries@the4ge.co.uk
W: www.the4ge.co.uk

The Forge (sleeps 5) and the Smithy (sleeps 2) are detached self catering cottages located in rural Lincolnshire and situated within their own enclosed and quiet garden with secure private car parking. Both are (4*) Four Star Visit England plus awarded Highly Commended by Tastes of Lincolnshire. For recent visitor comments please refer to our website - www.the4ge.co.uk. Both cottages are fully equipped and include bedding and towels. Sorry no pets.
Please contact or see www.the4ge.co.uk for price list.

Open: All year

Nearest Shop: 3 miles
Nearest Pub: 2 miles

Units: The Forge - sleeps 5.
The Smithy - sleeps 2.

Site: ❀ P Leisure: ♪ Property: 🗄 🖵 Children: 👶 🖳 🚶 Unit: 🗄 🗄 🖵 🖭 ☏ 📺 📀

BRATTLEBY, Lincolnshire Map ref 4C2 **S**

Units 1
Sleeps 2-4
PER UNIT PER WEEK
£275.00 - £475.00

The Stable

Contact: Jerry Scott, Owner, The Stable Cottage, Sunnyside, East Lane, Brattleby, Lincoln LN1 2SQ **T:** (01522) 730561 / 07990 786931 **E:** jerry@lincolncottages.co.uk
W: www.lincolncottages.co.uk

200 year old stone and pantile cottage of character. In a quiet conservation village six miles (scenic drive) from the historic cathedral city of Lincoln. Tastefully furnished and decorated. Self-contained cottage garden with views over open fields. Great location for exploring Lincolnshire. **Open:** All year **Nearest Shop:** 1.5 miles **Nearest Pub:** 1 mile

Site: ❀ P Payment: € Property: 🐾 🖳 🗄 🖵 Children: 👶 🚶 Unit: 🗄 🖵 🖭 ☏ 📺 📀

GREAT CARLTON, Lincolnshire   Map ref 4D2   S

VisitEngland
★★★★
SELF CATERING

| Units | 1 |
| Sleeps | 1-5 |

PER UNIT PER WEEK
£200.00 - £400.00

SPECIAL PROMOTIONS
Short breaks in low season, ring for details.

Willow Farm

Contact: Jim Clark, Willow Farm, Lordship Road, Great Carlton LN11 8JT
T: (01507) 338540 / 07876 482738 **E:** willowfarmfishing@gmail.com
W: www.willowfarmfishing.co.uk

A cosy bungalow set in a peaceful, rural location on the outskirts of the market town of Louth. High standard of accommodation comprising of 3 bedrooms, sleeping 5. Paved patio area overlooking the beautiful countryside. Fly and coarse fishing available onsite. Within easy reach of coastal resorts, golf courses, Cadwell Park, Donna Nook and Louth market town.

Open: All year
Nearest Shop: 2 miles
Nearest Pub: 2 miles

Units: Two twin rooms, one single room, lounge, kitchen/diner, shower, electric heating, washing machine, electric cooker, microwave, TV, two toilets.

Site: ✿ P Leisure: ✦ Property: 🐕 🖳 Children: ⇗ Unit: 📷 🗄 📺

HOGSTHORPE, Lincolnshire   Map ref 4D2   S

VisitEngland
★★★★
SELF CATERING

| Units | 2 |
| Sleeps | 1-5 |

PER UNIT PER WEEK
£375.00 - £520.00

f t

Helsey House Holiday Cottages

Contact: Elizabeth Elvidge, Joint Owner, Helsey House Holiday Cottages, Helsey House, Helsey, Hogsthorpe, Skegness PE24 5PE **T:** (01754) 872927 **E:** info@helseycottages.co.uk
W: www.helseycottages.co.uk **£ BOOK ONLINE**

Situated in the private grounds of Helsey House. Each award winning cottage converted from original cattle stalls. Furnished to the highest standard. Single storey cottages with no steps. Rural location but close to quiet sandy beaches. Ample parking within the grounds. Large play area and heated outdoor pool (summer only). Special needs families, less mobile guests and pets are all welcome! **Open:** All year **Nearest Shop:** 3 miles
Nearest Pub: 3 miles

 Site: ✿ P Leisure: ✦ ⌖ ↻ ⚲ Property: 🐕 🖳 🗄 🖳 Children: ⇗ 🎠 ⚘ Unit: 📷 🗄 📺 🎧 📀 BBQ

INGOLDMELLS, Lincolnshire   Map ref 4D2   S

VisitEngland
★★★★
SELF CATERING

| Units | 3 |
| Sleeps | 5 |

PER UNIT PER WEEK
£335.00 - £550.00

f t

Skegness Water Leisure Park - Bungalows

Contact: Reception, Skegness Water Leisure Park, Walls Lane, Skegness PE25 1JF
T: (01754) 899400 **F:** 01754 897867 **E:** enquiries@skegnesswaterleisurepark.co.uk
W: www.skegnesswaterleisurepark.co.uk

Recently refurbished luxury holiday bungalows just ¼ mile from award winning beaches. Sited on award winning family friendly holiday park, just 10 minutes walk from golden beaches. **Open:** 1st March - 30th November each year **Nearest Shop:** 0.10 miles
Nearest Pub: 0.10 miles

Site: ✿ P Payment: 💷 Leisure: ✦ ⌖ ↻ Property: 🐕 🗄 🖳 🖳 Children: ⇗ 🎠 ⚘ Unit: 📷 🗄 🎧 📺 BBQ

LINCOLN, Lincolnshire   Map ref 4C2   S

Drws Nesaf, Metheringham

Contact: Alan and Nicola Jones, 86 Prince's Street, Metheringham, Lincolnshire LN4 3DE
T: (01526) 322558 **E:** nj.jones60@tiscali.co.uk

Our warm, comfortable bungalow is within easy reach of Lincoln, the Wolds, Lincolnshire's aviation heritage and the fens. It is set in a quiet location overlooking an old windmill. There is off-road car parking and established gardens at the front and back. The village pubs and shops are within easy walking distance. There is a village railway station and we are on the bus route. **Open:** All year except Christmas holidays **Nearest Shop:** 0.5 mile **Nearest Pub:** 0.5 mile

Units	1
Sleeps	1-3

PER UNIT PER WEEK
£200.00 - £300.00

Site: ❀ P Property: 🖵 Children: ➹ Unit: 🖵 📷 🛇 TV

LINCOLN, Lincolnshire   Map ref 4C2   SatNav LN6 0EY   C

Hartsholme Country Park

Skellingthorpe Road, Lincoln LN6 0EY
T: (01522) 873578 **E:** hartsholmecp@lincoln.gov.uk
W: www.lincoln.gov.uk/hartsholmecampsite

Our 3 star English Tourism rated site offers flat, level grassy pitches set in mature wooded parkland. Easy access to city centre and local attractions. **Directions:** Main entrance is on the B1378 (Skellingthorpe Road). It is signposted from the A46 (Lincoln Bypass) and from the B1003 (Tritton Road). **Open:** 1st March to 31st October.

🚐	£16.60-£22.00
🚚	£16.60-£22.00
⛺ (8)	£10.00-£22.00

26 touring pitches

Payment: 💷 ☼ Leisure: ♪ Children: ➹ ⚠ Catering: ✗ 🛒 Park: 🐕 🐾 Touring: 🚾 🚰

LINCOLN, Lincolnshire   Map ref 4C2   S

Old Vicarage Cottages

Contact: Susan Downs, Bluestone, 15 Crescent Close, Nettleham, Lincoln LN2 2SP
T: (01522) 750819 **E:** susan@oldvic.net
W: www.oldvic.net

Delightful stone cottages offering spacious, well equipped accommodation with free Wi-Fi. Both properties have private gardens and off road parking/garage. Located within five minutes walking distance of the centre of this attractive award winning village with shops, cafe, pubs which serve both lunch and evening meals, Village Green and picturesque Beckside. **Open:** All year **Nearest Shop:** 0.50 miles **Nearest Pub:** 0.50 miles

Units	2
Sleeps	2-4

PER UNIT PER WEEK
£335.00 - £475.00

Site: ❀ P Payment: 💷 Property: 🖵 📷 🖵 Children: ➹ Unit: 🖵 📷 🖵 📷 🛇 TV 📀

LOUTH, Lincolnshire   Map ref 4D2   S

Church Cottage

Contact: Pam Wallis, Owner, Biscathorpe Park, Biscathorpe, Louth, Lincolnshire LN11 9RA
T: (01507) 313203 / 07788 281419 **E:** info@churchcottagebiscathorpe.co.uk
W: www.churchcottagebiscathorpe.co.uk **£ BOOK ONLINE**

Self catering luxury holiday accommodation, recently refurbished, open plan ground floor with under floor heating and sleeps 6, all bedrooms are en suite. Situated in the beautiful Lincolnshire Wolds Area of Outstanding Natural Beauty. The cottage was awarded Finalist Status at 2014 LABC Building Excellence Awards. **Open:** All year **Nearest Shop:** 1 mile **Nearest Pub:** 1 mile

Units	1
Sleeps	2-6

PER UNIT PER WEEK
£475.00 - £1000.00

Site: ❀ P Leisure: ∪ Property: 🐕 🖵 📷 🖵 Children: ➹ 🏓 🚶 Unit: 🖵 📷 🖵 📷 🛇 TV 📀 ♨ BBQ

LOUTH, Lincolnshire   Map ref 4D2   S

Louth Barn

Contact: Ronnie & Louise Millar, Louth Barn, Grosvenor House, 74 Keddington Road, Louth, Lincolnshire LN11 0BA **T:** (01507) 609381 / 07986 524395
E: enquiries@louthbarn.com **W:** www.louthbarn.com **£ BOOK ONLINE**

Units   1
Sleeps   2-4
PER UNIT PER WEEK
£331.00 - £444.00

Situated on the edge of Louth our converted Victorian barn is adjacent to the main house. Relaxing, comfortable, well-equipped, super-king size bed, internet, shared mature garden, summerhouse, playhouse, swings, own patio, covered parking. Extensive DVD Library, Lego and Brio available, also outdoor table football, pool table and table tennis available. **Open:** All year **Nearest Shop:** 0.20 miles **Nearest Pub:** 0.20 miles

Site: ✿ P Property: ▭ ▯ Children: ➳ 🛏 🚶 Unit: ▯ ▯ ▭ ▯ ▯ 📺 🆅 BBQ

MABLETHORPE, Lincolnshire   Map ref 4D2   S

Dunes Cottage

Contact: Sheila Morrison, Bank House, Brickyard Lane, Theddlethorpe St Helen, Lincolnshire LN12 1NR **T:** (01507) 338342 **E:** sheila.a.morrison@btopenworld.com
W: www.dunesholidaycottage.co.uk

Units   1
Sleeps   1-6

PER UNIT PER WEEK
£300.00 - £475.00

Charming 19th century 2 bedroomed cottage nestling on the edge of a National Nature Reserve. Next to the dunes with sandy beach and wonderful views of the dunes to the wolds and out to sea. Offers visitors peace and tranquillity, a place to get away from stresses and strains of modern life.

Open: All year
Nearest Shop: 4 miles
Nearest Pub: 2 miles

Units: Two bedrooms, sitting room with sofa bed, dining room and large breakfast kitchen.

Site: ✿ P Property: 🐾 ▯ Children: ➳ 🚶 Unit: ▯ ▭ ▯ 📺 🆅 🆅 BBQ

MARKET RASEN, Lincolnshire   Map ref 4C2   S

Masondale Cottage

Contact: Mr Neil Cooper, Otby House Farm, Walesby, Lincolnshire LN8 3UU
T: (01673) 838530 / 07768 714281 **E:** n.cooper@otby-lake.co.uk
W: www.otby-lake.co.uk **£ BOOK ONLINE**

Units   1
Sleeps   6
PER UNIT PER WEEK
£400.00 - £575.00

Spacious peaceful farm cottage converted to high quality 4 star self catering accommodation. Perfect base for outdoor activities or a totally relaxing break. Panoramic views. Livery. Quite exceptional trout fishing. Masondale Cottage sits at the edge of the Lincolnshire Wolds with unrivalled panoramic views of the Vale of Ancholme looking across to Lincoln Cathedral prominent on the horizon.
Open: All year **Nearest Shop:** 4 miles **Nearest Pub:** 4 miles

Site: ✿ P Payment: 💳 Leisure: 🎵 ▸ ∪ ⚲ Property: ⫽ ▭ ▯ ▯ Children: ➳ 🛏 🚶 Unit: ▯ ▯ ▭ ▯ 📺 🆅 BBQ 📞

SKEGNESS, Lincolnshire Map ref 4D2
SatNav PE25 1JF **C**

Skegness Water Leisure Park
Walls Lane, Skegness PE25 1JF
T: (01754) 899400 **F:** 01754 897867 **E:** enquiries@skegnesswaterleisurepark.co.uk
W: www.skegnesswaterleisurepark.co.uk **£ BOOK ONLINE**

🚐	£18.00-£25.50
🚐	£18.00-£25.50
⛺	£18.00-£24.00
🏠 (11)	£35.00-£45.00
(3)	£315.00-£505.00

250 touring pitches

Family-orientated caravan and camping site 'Where the coast meets the countryside'. Ten-minute walk to award-winning beaches with scenic, rural views. Close to Butlins and Fantasy Island. **Directions:** A52 north from Skegness 2.5 miles. Turn left at Cheers pub into Walls Lane. Site entrance is 400 yards on the left hand side. **Open:** March to November.

Site: 🏷 A🅿 **Payment:** 💳 ☼ **Leisure:** 🎣 ♪ ▶ ♦ **Children:** 👶 ⚠ **Catering:** ✕ 🍴 **Park:** 🐾 ♫ 📺 **Touring:** 🚰 🔌 ♨ ⚒

STAMFORD, Lincolnshire Map ref 3A1
S

Elder Flower Cottage
Contact: Mr & Mrs P & D Wilkinson, Elderflower Cottage, Shepherds Walk, Belmesthorpe,
Nr Stamford Lincs PE9 4JF **T:** (01780) 757188 / 07711533204 / 07759666084
E: philipwdawn@btinternet.com **W:** www.elderflowercottage.co.uk **£ BOOK ONLINE**

Units   1
Sleeps   4

PER UNIT PER WEEK
£380.00 - £420.00

SPECIAL PROMOTIONS
Special rates for
Burghley Horse Trials.

Spacious, detached, high-quality bungalow close to the historic town of Stamford and Rutland Water. Decorated, furnished and equipped to a high standard. Situated between the villages of Ryhall and Belmesthorpe. The cottage is an ideal base for holidaymakers looking for a peaceful break in the countryside but within easy reach of Stamford, Peterborough and Oakham. The owners live nearby so are available if any queries arise.
A welcome pack of bread ,butter,milk, tea and coffee is provided for the arrival of guests.

Open: All year
Nearest Shop: 0.25 miles
Nearest Pub: 0.25 miles

Site: ✿ P **Leisure:** 🎣 ♪ ▶ **Property:** 🐾 📺 🖥 **Children:** 👶 🎮 🌳 **Unit:** 📻 🖥 📶 🌀 📺 📀

WEST BARKWITH, Lincolnshire Map ref 4D2
S

Glebe Farm Apartments
Contact: Stephen Campion, Glebe Farm Apartments, The Barn, Glebe Farm, West Barkwith
LN8 5LF **T:** (01673) 858919 **E:** enquiries@glebeapart.co.uk
W: www.glebeapart.co.uk **£ BOOK ONLINE**

Units   4
Sleeps   2-4
PER UNIT PER WEEK
£230.00 - £300.00

Converted farm buildings into cosy apartments in rural countryside. Large grounds to enjoy, including free fishing in well-stocked lake. Online booking. **Open:** All year **Nearest Shop:** 1 mile **Nearest Pub:** 1 mile

Site: ✿ P **Leisure:** 🎣 **Property:** 🐾 📺 🖥 **Children:** 👶 🎮 🌳 **Unit:** 📻 🖥 🌀 📺 📀 BBQ

Petwood Caravan Park

Stixwould Road, Woodhall Spa, Lincolnshire LN10 6QH
T: (01526) 354799 **E:** info@petwoodcaravanpark.co.uk
W: www.petwoodcaravanpark.co.uk

98 touring pitches

We are a 4 star family caravan park, offering superb facilities, set in the heart of the beautiful inland resort of Woodhall Spa. The village is just a 5 minute walk from the site and has a variety of excellent restaurants and shops. Please contact for 2016 Rates.

Open: 18th March to 16th October.

Site: ⚑🄿 Payment: 🄴 ☼ Children: ↘ Park: 🐕 🖥 🅗 🅟 Touring: 🅕 🕹

Woodhall Country Park

Stixwould Road, Woodhall Spa LN10 6UJ
T: (01526) 353710 **E:** info@woodhallcountrypark.co.uk
W: www.woodhallcountrypark.co.uk **£ BOOK ONLINE**

🚐 (100)   £20.00-£29.00
🚛 (100)   £20.00-£29.00
🅰 (35)   £16.00-£26.00
100 touring pitches

Woodhall Country Park is a unique 5 star camping and touring experience, set in tranquil woodlands in the heart of a conservation area in Lincolnshire. You will enjoy the natural surroundings of the park and feel close to nature, surrounded by woodland and wildlife. The new facilities offered here are ideal for touring caravans and tents – with Camping Pods also avaliable for hire.

Directions: Woodhall Country Park is located on the outskirts of Woodhall Spa, Lincolnshire.

Open: 1st March - 30th November.

Site: ⊚ ⚑🄿 Payment: 🄴 ☼ Leisure: ♿ 🕭 ▸ Children: ↘ Park: 🐕 🅗 🅟 Touring: 🅕 🕹 ⚒

CRANFORD, Northamptonshire   Map ref 3A2   S

VisitEngland
★★★
SELF CATERING

Units   1
Sleeps   2-6
PER UNIT PER WEEK
£360.00 - £460.00

No. 4 The Green

Contact: Mrs Emma Robinson, 36 Duck End House, Cranford, Kettering, Northamptonshire NN14 4AD **T:** (01536) 330608 **E:** no4thegreen@gmail.com

Charming 3 bed thatched cottage in the heart of the village. Fully modernised with all the home from home facilities you need. Close to major roads and train station. Pets welcome by arrangement.
Open: All year **Nearest Shop:** 3 miles **Nearest Pub:** 0.10 miles

Site: ✿ P Property: 🐾 🖥 🖪 🎱 Children: 🌊 🎮 🚲 Unit: 🛏 🖪 📺 🖨 🎽 📺 🎧 📀

GREAT DODDINGTON, Northamptonshire   Map ref 3A2   S

VisitEngland
★★★★★
SELF CATERING

Units   1
Sleeps   2-4
PER UNIT PER WEEK
£360.00 - £600.00

The Old Watermill

Contact: Mrs. Anne Newman, Hardwater Mill, Hardwater Road, Great Doddington, Wellingborough NN29 7TD **T:** (01933) 276870 / 07702 512022 **F:** 01933 276870
E: sales@watermillholidays.co.uk **W:** www.watermillholidays.co.uk **£ BOOK ONLINE**

A charming and historic former watermill, Grade II listed. The well equipped accommodation is on three floors. One four-poster double and one twin bedroom. Central heating Double glazed. Plenty of old elm beams and oak floors. Pets welcome, garden plus riverside walks. Special Christmas and New Year breaks available.
Open: All year **Nearest Shop:** 1 mile **Nearest Pub:** 1.5 miles

Site: ✿ P Leisure: ♪ ▶ Property: 🐾 🖪 🎱 Children: 🌊10 Unit: 🛏 🖪 📺 🖨 🎽 📺 🎧 📀 🖋

PETERBOROUGH, Northamptonshire   Map ref 3A1   S

VisitEngland
★★★★
SELF CATERING

VisitEngland
Gold
AWARD

Units   2
Sleeps   1-2

PER UNIT PER WEEK
£315.00 - £450.00

SPECIAL PROMOTIONS
Please contact us for prices.

Hall Farm Kings Cliffe

Contact: Ms Sarah Winfrey, Hall Farm Kings Cliffe - SC & GA, Hall Farm, Hall Yard, Kings Cliffe PE8 6XQ **T:** (01780) 470796 / 07906 502494 **E:** info@hallfarmkingscliffe.co.uk
W: www.hallfarmkingscliffe.co.uk **£ BOOK ONLINE**

Hall Farm Kings Cliffe is in a quiet village location within easy reach of Stamford, Oundle, Rutland Water and Peterborough and offers two types of self-catering accommodation each with its own private entrance and furnished to a high standard.

The Stables Cottage is on two floors in a 17th century stable block and faces into a courtyard. It provides stylish comfortable living with old oak beams and ancient stone.

The Archway Apartment is recently refurbished with windows overlooking the church and an old stone courtyard. With old oak beams and high ceilings it has a fresh modern style.

Open: All year except Christmas and New Year
Nearest Shop: 0.10 miles
Nearest Pub: 0.10 miles

Units: Both the Cottage and Apartment have a super-king size bed that can be separated to make two single beds if required.

Site: P Leisure: ♪ Property: 🖪 🎱 Children: 🌊12 🎮 Unit: 🖪 📺 🖨 🎽 📺 🎧 📀

LAMBLEY, *Nottinghamshire*   *Map ref 4C2*   S

Dickman's Cottage

Contact: Ros Marshall Smith, Owner, Dickman's Cottage, Springsyde, Birdcage Walk, Otley, West Yorkshire LS21 3HB **T:** (01943) 462719 **F:** 01943 850925
E: enquiries@dickmanscottage.co.uk **W:** www.dickmanscottage.co.uk **£ BOOK ONLINE**

Units   1
Sleeps   1-4
PER UNIT PER WEEK
£330.00 - £530.00

Five miles north east of Nottingham in the charming village of Lambley. Oak beamed cottage which combines original features with modern comfort. Fully fitted kitchen, pantry and bathroom with bath/shower. Two bedrooms - one double, one twin. TV/DVD, dishwasher, washer/dryer. Central heating. Lovely cottage garden. Private parking. Wifi. **Open:** All year **Nearest Shop:** 0.25 miles
Nearest Pub: 0.25 miles

Site: ✿ P Payment: £ € Property: ♌ 🖥 🔲 🔳 Children: ⏃ 🍴 ♿ Unit: ▯ ▤ ▣ ▨ ⚲ 📺 📀 BBQ 📞

NEWARK, *Nottinghamshire*   *Map ref 4C2*   S

Rose and Sweet Briar Cottages

Contact: Mrs Janet Hind, Owner, Rose and Sweet Briar Cottages, Hill Farm, Kersall, Newark, Nottinghamshire NG22 0BJ **T:** (01636) 636274 **E:** hind-hillfarm@hotmail.co.uk
W: www.roseandsweetbriar.co.uk

Units   2
Sleeps   2-4
PER UNIT PER WEEK
£130.00 - £285.00

Single storey cottages set in 1½ acre of private grounds of Hill farm in the hamlet of Kersall, Nr Newark (no longer working farm). Quiet location, beautiful views, large garden, off road parking. Close to Newark, Southwell, Ollerton, Edwinstowe and within easy travelling distance of Lincoln and Nottingham. Ideal location for exploring Sherwood Forest / Robin Hood country. Sorry no pets/no smoking.
Open: All year
Nearest Shop: 5 miles **Nearest Pub:** 1 mile

Site: ✿ P Leisure: ⛳ ♪ ► U Property: 🔲 Children: ⏃ Unit: ▯ ▣ ▨ ⚲ 📺 📀

NOTTINGHAM, Nottinghamshire   Map ref 4C2   S

Woodview Cottages

Contact: Jane Morley, Woodview Cottages, Newfields Farm, Owthorpe NG12 3GE
T: (01949) 81985 / 07949 973470 **F:** 01949 81580 **E:** enquiries@woodviewcottages.co.uk
W: www.woodviewcottages.co.uk

Units	2
Sleeps	1-4

PER UNIT PER WEEK
£400.00 - £575.00

A haven of tranquillity, two idyllic stone cottages in a beautiful setting 8 miles from Nottingham/Leicester. Picturesque gardens and beautiful woodland views. Each cottage is maintained by the owner ensuring high standards and comprises a well-equipped kitchen, comfortable living/dining-room with wood-burning stove and exposed beams; 2 bedrooms with exposed stone work, 1 double and 1 twin accommodating up to 4 people; bathroom/W.C. with shower cubicle. Ideal for nature lovers and wildlife enthusiasts.
Open: All year **Nearest Shop:** 3 miles **Nearest Pub:** 3 miles

Site: ✿ **P Payment:** 💷 **Leisure:** ♪ **Property:** 🖥 🗄 📱 **Children:** 🎠 **Unit:** 🗄 🍴 📟 🖥 🍳 📺 📻 📀

BROOKE, Rutland   Map ref 4C3   S

America Lodge

Contact: Mrs Lesley MacCartney, Proprietor, The Office, America Lodge, Brooke LE15 8DF
T: (01572) 723944 / 07850 937653 **F:** 01572 759399 **E:** americalodge@btconnect.com
W: www.americalodge.co.uk

Units	1
Sleeps	2-9

PER UNIT PER WEEK
£550.00 - £750.00

SPECIAL PROMOTIONS
Weekend breaks off-season or as late availability: 2 nights £375; 3 nights £405; 2 nights late departure Sunday (6pm) £399.

A lovely secluded farmhouse close to Rutland Water, just south of Oakham, the County Town of Rutland. Views over classic rolling English Countryside. Graded high 3 star. Private garden and grounds, large well appointed kitchen. Very central in UK. Will sleep 9 plus a cot. Refurbished December 2013 www.americalodge.co.uk.

Open: All year
Nearest Shop: 3 miles
Nearest Pub: 2 miles

Units: Farmhouse accommodation.

Site: ✿ **P Leisure:** 🚲 ♪ ▶ ∪ **Property:** 🐾 🖥 🗄 **Children:** 🐕 🎠 ♿ **Unit:** 🗄 🍴 📟 🖥 🍳 📺 📻 📀 🔥 BBQ

STRETTON, Rutland   Map ref 3A1   S

Stretton Lakes

Contact: Mrs Rachel Needham, Owner, Stretton Lakes, Clipsham Road, Stretton, Oakham, Rutland LE15 7QS **T:** (01780) 410507 **E:** info@strettonlakes.co.uk
W: www.strettonlakes.co.uk **£ BOOK ONLINE**

Units	6
Sleeps	2-4

PER UNIT PER WEEK
£430.00 - £955.00

Enjoy England Silver Award for Self Catering holiday of the year 2011. Six luxury log cabins overlooking fishing lakes surrounded by woodland, all with Hot Tubs, our 5* lodges also have a Sauna. Mini breaks available 3 or 4 nights prices start from £310 low season.
Open: All year **Nearest Shop:** 3 miles **Nearest Pub:** 1 mile

Site: ✿ **P Payment:** 💷 **Leisure:** 🚲 ♪ ▶ ∪ **Property:** 🖥 🗄 📱 **Children:** 🐕 🎠 ♿ **Unit:** 🗄 🍴 📟 🖥 🍳 📺 📻 📀 BBQ

Don't Miss...

Dudley Zoological Gardens

Dudley, West Midlands DY1 4QB
(01384) 215313
www.dudleyzoo.org.uk
DZG is unique - a zoo with hundreds of animals set around an 11th century castle incorporating the world's largest single collection of Tecton buildings and the country's only vintage chairlift – all sited on a 40-acre wooded hillside with a rich geological history. From lions and tigers to snakes and spiders, animal feeding, face painting, land train and fair rides, there's something for everyone.

Iron Bridge and Toll House

Telford, Shropshire TF8 7DG
(01952) 433424
www.ironbridge.org.uk
The Ironbridge Gorge is a remarkable and beautiful insight into the region's industrial heritage. Ten award-winning Museums spread along the valley beside the wild River Severn - still spanned by the world's first Iron Bridge, where you can peer through the railings and conjure a vision of sailing vessels heading towards Bristol and the trading markets of the world.

The Potteries Museum & Art Gallery

Stoke-on-Trent ST1 3DW
(01782) 232323
www.stokemuseums.org.uk/visit/pmag
Travel back in time and discover the history of The Potteries including the world's greatest collection of Staffordshire ceramics, a World War II Spitfire, decorative arts and natural history. A warm and friendly welcome awaits at one of Britain's leading museums where the unique combination of 'product and place' is celebrated in its outstanding displays.

Shakespeare's Birthplace Trust

Stratford-upon-Avon, Warwickshire CV37 6QW
www.shakespeare.org.uk
A unique Shakespeare experience with outstanding archive and library collections, inspiring educational and literary event programmes. Discover the Tudor town house that was Shakespeare's Birthplace. Visit Mary Arden's Farm, the childhood home of Shakespeare's mother. Explore the lavish rooms and tranquil gardens of Hall's Croft. Fall in love with romantic Anne Hathaway's Cottage, the quintessentially English thatched family home of Shakespeare's wife. Take in the period splendour of Nash's House and learn about Shakespeare's final home at New Place where he died in 1616.

Warwick Castle

Warwickshire CV34 4QU
0871 265 2000
www.warwick-castle.co.uk
Battlements, towers, turrets, History, magic, myth and adventure - Warwick Castle is a Scheduled Ancient Monument and Grade 1 listed building packed with things to do, inside and out.

Heart of England

Herefordshire, Shropshire,
Staffordshire, Warwickshire,
West Midlands, Worcestershire

The Heart of England: a name that defines this lovely part of the country so much better than its geographical name: The Midlands. Like a heart it has many arteries and compartments, from the March counties of Shropshire and Herefordshire, through Birmingham and the West Midlands, birthplace of the Industrial revolution. It is a region rich in history and character and you'll find pretty villages, grand castles and plenty of canals and waterways to explore.

Staffordshire

Shropshire

West Midlands

Warwick-shire   Worcester-shire

Herefordshire

Explore – Heart of England

Coventry & Warwickshire

From castles and cathedrals to art galleries, museums and exciting events, this region captivates visitors from all over the world.

A beautifully preserved Tudor town on the banks of the Avon and Warwickshire's most visited, Stratford-upon-Avon is the bard's birthplace with numerous theatres playing Shakespeare and other dramatists' work. The city of Warwick is dominated by its 14th century castle and its museums, and plenty of family activities are staged throughout the year. Historic Coventry has over 400 listed buildings and is most famous for its cathedrals, with the modern Church of St Michael sitting majestically next to the 'blitzed' ruins of its 14th century predecessor.

Herefordshire

Herefordshire's ruined castles in the border country and Iron Age and Roman hill-forts recall a turbulent battle-scarred past. Offa's Dyke, constructed by King Offa of Mercia in the 8th century marks the border with Wales but today the landscape is peaceful, with delightful small towns and villages and Hereford cattle grazing in pastures beside apple orchards and hop gardens.

Hereford has an 11th century cathedral and the Mappa Mundi while in the west, the Wye meanders through meadows and valleys. Hay-on-Wye is now best known for its annual Book Festival and plethora of second hand bookshops.

Shropshire

Tucked away on the England/Wales border, Shropshire is another March county that saw much conflict between English and Welsh, hostilities between warring tribes and invading Romans.

The Wrekin and Stretton Hills were created by volcanoes and in the south the Long Mynd rises to 1700 ft with panoramic views of the Severn plain. Ironbridge, near Telford, is said to be where the Industrial Revolution started. County town Shrewsbury was an historic fortress town built in a loop of the river Severn and these days joins Ludlow, with its 11th century castle, as one of the gastronomic high spots of Britain.

There are many splendid historic and architectural gems in Shropshire, from Jacobean coaching inns in the heart of picturesque market towns to Elizabethan manor houses such as the 16th Century Upton Cressett Hall, with its restored Great Hall dining room and spectacular gatehouse, set in the remote and unspoilt Shropshire countryside.

Staffordshire

Staffordshire, squeezed between the Black Country to the south and Manchester to the north, conceals many heritage treasures and an exciting industrial history. It is home to the Potteries, a union of six towns made famous by Wedgwood, Spode and other ceramic designers, celebrated at the many museums and visitor centres.

Lichfield, just north of Birmingham is the birthplace of Samuel Johnson and has a magnificent three-spired 13th century cathedral, while some of England's finest houses and most beautiful gardens are also to be found in the county. Fabulous examples include the award-winning landscaped gardens on the Trentham Estate and the 'Capability' Brown parklands at Weston Park, on the border with Shropshire. Meanwhile, the unspoilt ancient heathland of Cannock Chase, leafy woodlands of the National Forest and secluded byways of South Staffordshire all offer the chance to further enjoy the great outdoors.

West Midlands

The Industrial revolution of the 19th century led to the growth of Birmingham into Britain's second city - the city of a thousand trades. Its prosperity was based on factories, hundreds of small workshops and a network of canals, all of which helped in the production of everything from needles and chocolate to steam engines and bridges. Nowadays the city has one of the best concert halls in Europe, excellent shopping and a regenerated waterside café culture.

The West Midlands is an urban area which still represents the powerhouse of Central Britain. Wolverhampton has been called Capital of the Black Country, made famous through its ironwork and Walsall, birthplace of Jerome K Jerome, has three museums. Affluent Sutton Coldfield and Solihull have proud civic traditions and a number of pretty parks. Many of Solihull's rural villages sit along the Stratford-upon-Avon canal and offer plenty of picturesque pubs along the tow path from which to watch the gentle meander of passing narrow boats.

Worcestershire

The beautiful county of Worcestershire has a fantastic selection of historic houses and gardens to discover and Worcester itself has a famous cathedral, cricket ground, and 15th century Commandery, now a Civil war museum.

Great Malvern, still a Spa town, is famous as the birthplace of Sir Edward Elgar, who drew much of his inspiration from this countryside and who is celebrated at the annual Malvern Festival. The old riverside market town of Evesham is the centre of the Vale of Evesham fruit and vegetable growing area which, with the tranquil banks of the river Avon and the undulating hills and peaceful wooded slopes of the Cotswolds, offers some of the prettiest landscapes in the country.

Droitwich, known in Roman times as Salinae, still has briny water in its spa baths and can trace the origins of salt extraction in the area back to prehistoric times, it even holds an annual Salt Festival to celebrate this unique heritage.

Visit – Heart of England

Coventry & Warwickshire

Coventry Cathedral - St Michael's
West Midlands CV1 5AB
(024) 7652 1257
www.coventrycathedral.org.uk
*Glorious 20th century Cathedral, with stunning 1950's
art & architecture, rising above the stark ruins of the
medieval Cathedral destroyed by air raids in 1940.*

Compton Verney
Stratford-upon-Avon CV35 9HZ
(01926) 645500
www.comptonverney.org.uk
*Award-winning art gallery housed in a grade I listed
Robert Adam mansion.*

Godiva Festival
July, Coventry, Warwickshire
www.godivafestival.com
*The Godiva Festival is the UK's biggest free family
festival held over a weekend in the War Memorial Park,
Coventry. The event showcases some of the finest
local, national and International artists, live comedy,
family entertainment, Godiva Carnival, and lots more.*

Heart Park
Fillongley, Warwickshire CV7 8DX
(01676) 540333
www.heartpark.co.uk
*"We believe that the heart of our Park is the beach
and lake. But for those of you who'd like to try
out a few 'different' activities - we've got a great
assortment for you to try."*

Heritage Open Days
September, Coventry, Warwickshire
www.heritageopendays.org.uk
*Celebrating England's architecture and culture by
allowing visitors free access to interesting properties
that are either not usually open or would normally
charge an entrance fee. Also including tours, events and
activities that focus on local architecture and culture.*

Kenilworth Castle and Elizabethan Garden
Warwickshire CV8 1NE
(01926) 852078
www.english-heritage.org.uk/kenilworth
One of the most spectacular castle ruins in England.

Packwood House
Solihull, Warwickshire B94 6AT
(01564) 782024
www.nationaltrust.org.uk/packwood-house
*Restored tudor house, park and garden with
notable topiary.*

Ragley Hall
Stratford-upon-Avon, Warwickshire B49 5NJ
(01789) 762090
www.ragley.co.uk
*Ragley Hall is set in 27 acres of beautiful formal
gardens. If a fun family day out is what you're
looking for then Ragley Hall, Park & Gardens really
does have something for everyone!*

Ryton Pools Country Parks
Coventry, Warwickshire CV8 3BH
(024) 7630 5592
www.warwickshire.gov.uk/parks
*The 100 acres of Ryton Pools Country Park are just
waiting to be explored. The many different habitats
are home to a wide range of birds and other wildlife.*

Stratford River Festival
July, Stratford, Warwickshire
www.stratfordriverfestival.co.uk
*The highly successful Stratford-upon-Avon River
Festival brings the waterways of Stratford alive, with
boatloads of family fun, on the first weekend of July.*

Three Counties Show
June, Malvern, Warwickshire
www.threecounties.co.uk
*Three jam-packed days of family entertainment and
fun, all in celebration of the great British farming
world and countryside.*

Herefordshire

Eastnor Castle

Ledbury, Herefordshire HR8 1RL
(01531) 633160
www.eastnorcastle.com
Fairytale Georgian Castle dramatically situated in the Malvern Hills. Surrounded by a beautiful deer park, arboretum and lake, this award winning tourist attraction is a fun filled family day out.

Goodrich Castle

Ross-on-Wye, Herefordshire HR9 6HY
(01600) 890538
www.english-heritage.org.uk/goodrich
Come and relive the turbulent history of Goodrich Castle with our free audio and then climb to the battlements for breathtaking views over the Wye Valley.

The Hay Festival

May / june, Hay-on-Wye, Herefordshire
www.hayfestival.com
Some five hundred events see writers, politicians, poets, scientists, comedians, philosophers and musicians come together on a greenfield site for a ten day fesitval of ideas and stories at the Hay Festival.

Hereford Cathedral

Herefordshire HR1 2NG
(01432) 374202
www.herefordcathedral.org
Some of the finest examples of architecture from Norman times to the present day. Its most famous treasure is Mappa Mundi, a mediaeval map of the world dating from the 13th century.

Hereford Museum and Art Gallery

Herefordshire HR4 9AU
(01432) 260692
www.herefordshire.gov.uk
Hereford Museum and Art Gallery, housed in a spectacular Victorian gothic building, has been exhibiting artefacts and works of fine and decorative art connected with the local area since 1874. The Art Gallery hosts regularly changing exhibitions of contemporary and historic art and themed object displays

Hergest Croft Gardens

Kington, Herefordshire HR5 3EG
(01544) 230160
www.hergest.co.uk
The gardens extend over 50 acres, with more than 4000 rare shrubs and trees. With over 60 champion trees and shrubs it is one of the finest collections in the British Isles. With a Gift Shop and Tearooms the Gardens are the perfect place to explore and relax.

Ledbury Heritage Centre

Herefordshire, HR8 1DN
(01432) 260692
www.herefordshire.gov.uk
The story of Ledbury's past displayed in a timber-framed building in the picturesque lane leading to the church. Learn about the poets John Masefeild and Elizabeth Barrett Browning and try your hand at timber framing.

Shropshire

Bridgnorth Cliff Railway

Bridgnorth, Shropshire, WV16 4AH
(01746) 762124
www.bridgnorthcliffrailway.co.uk
Take a journey on the oldest and steepest funicular inland electric cliff railway in the country between High Town and Low Town. Visit spectacular shops, gardens, and enjoy the views that Charlies I named the finest in his kingdom.

The British Ironwork Centre

Oswestry, Shropshire SY11 4JH
(0800) 6888386
www.britishironworkcentre.co.uk
A treasure trove of magnificent animal sculptures and decorations, including of a 13ft-high gorilla made from an incredible 40,000+ spoons donated by people from all over the world.

Darby Houses (Ironbridge)

Telford, Shropshire TF8 7EW
(01952) 433424
www.ironbridge.org.uk
The Darby Houses are one of the ten Ironbridge Gorge Museums. Experience the everyday life of Coalbrookdale's ironmasters in the former homes of the Darby family.

Enginuity

Telford, Shropshire TF8 7DG
(01952) 433424
www.ironbridge.org.uk
Enginuity is one of the ten Ironbridge Gorge Museums. Enjoy a fun-filled family day out at this science and technology centre. At Enginuity you can turn the wheels of your imagination, test your horse power and discover how good ideas are turned in to real things.

English Haydn Festival

June, Bridgnorth, Shropshire
www.englishhaydn.com
Focusing on Joseph Haydn's music and his life in Vienna, in particular during the years leading up to his death in 1809 and his friendship and influence on Beethoven and Schubert, performed in St. Leonards Church, Bridgnorth.

Ludlow Food Festival

September, Ludlow, Shropshire
www.foodfestival.co.uk
More than 160 top quality independent food and drink producers inside Ludlow Castle.

Much Wenlock Priory

Shropshire TF13 6HS
(01952) 727466
www.english-heritage.org.uk/wenlockpriory
Wenlock Priory, a ruined 12th century monastery, with its stunning clipped topiary, has a pastoral setting on the edge of lovely Much Wenlock.

RAF Cosford Air Show

June, Shifnal, Shropshire
www.cosfordairshow.co.uk
This RAF-organised show usually features all the airshow favourites, classic and current British and foreign aircraft, exhibits and trade stalls all on this classic RAF airbase.

Royal Air Force Museum Cosford

Shifnal, Shropshire TF11 8UP
(01902) 376200
www.rafmuseum.org
The award winning museum houses one of the largest aviation collections in the United Kingdom along with being home to the National Cold War Exhibition. FREE Admission.

Severn Valley Railway – The Engine House

Highley, Shropshire
www.svr.co.uk/EngineHouse
The stunning Engine House Centre at Highley takes you on a fascinating journey behind the scenes. Marvel at the massive locomotives, delve into the intriguing history of Britain's railways, enjoy themed exhibitions and meet the engine that collided with a camel!

Shrewsbury Folk Festival

August, Shrewsbury, Shropshire
www.shrewsburyfolkfestival.co.uk
Shrewsbury Folk Festival has a reputation for delivering established artists from the UK alongside acts celebrating folk traditions from across the world who will take you on a voyage of discovery, bringing you ever-changing musical colours with their breath-taking performances.

Stokesay Castle

Craven Arms, Shropshire SY7 9AH
(01588) 672544
www.english-heritage.org.uk/stokesaycastle
Stokesay Castle, nestles in peaceful South Shropshire countryside near the Welsh Border. It is one of more than a dozen English Heritage properties in the county.

V Festival

August, Weston Park, Shropshire
www.vfestival.com
Legendary rock and pop festival held annually during the penultimate weekend in August.

Wenlock Olympian Games

July, Much Wenlock, Shropshire
www.wenlock-olympian-society.org.uk
The games that inspired the modern Olympic Movement.

Wroxeter Roman City

Shrewsbury, Shropshire SY5 6PH
(01743) 761330
www.english-heritage.org.uk/wroxeter
Wroxeter Roman City, or Viroconium, to give it its Roman title, is thought to have been one of the largest Roman cities in the UK with over 200 acres of land, 2 miles of walls and a population of approximately 5,000.

Staffordshire

Abbots Bromley Horn Dance
September, Abbots Bromley, Staffordshire
www.abbotsbromley.com
Ancient ritual dating back to 1226. Six deer-men, a fool, hobby horse, bowman and Maid Marian perform to music provided by a melodian player.

Aerial Extreme Trentham
Staffordshire ST4 8AX
0845 652 1736
www.aerialextreme.co.uk/index.php/courses/trentham-estate
Our tree based adventure ropes course, set within the tranquil grounds of Trentham Estate is a truly spectacular journey. All ages are guaranteed a bucket load of fun.

Etruria Industrial Museum
Staffordshire ST4 7AF
(01782) 233144
www.stokemuseums.org.uk
Discover how they put the 'bone' in bone china at the last working steam-powered potters mill in Britain. Includes a Bone and Flint Mill and family-friendly interactive exhibition.

Leek Food Festival
March, Staffordshire, ST13 5HH
www.leekfoodanddrink.co.uk
The Leek Food Festival is host over 70 stalls and hot vendors, a beer festival tent, and experience Leek's fabulous shops and pubs at the same time.

Lichfield Cathedral
Staffordshire WS13 7LD
(01543) 306100
www.lichfield-cathedral.org
A medieval Cathedral, one of the oldest places of Christian worship in Britain, with 3 spires in the heart of an historic City set in its own serene Close.

Midlands Grand National
March, Uttoxeter Racecourse, Staffordshire
www.uttoxeter-racecourse.co.uk
The biggest fixture in Uttoxeter's calendar and the second longest Steeplechase in the country at 4 miles and 1 1/2 furlongs.

National Memorial Arboretum
Lichfield, Staffordshire DE13 7AR
(01283) 792333
www.thenma.org.uk
150 acres of trees and memorials, planted as a living tribute to those who have served, died or suffered in the service of their Country.

The Roaches
Upper Hulme, Leek, Staffordshire ST13 8UB
www.staffsmoorlands.gov.uk
The Roaches (or Roches) is a wind-carved outcrop of gritstone rocks that rises above the waters or Tittesworth reservoir, between Leek in Staffordshire and Buxton in Derbyshire. It's impressive gritstone edges and craggy rocks are loved by walkers and climbers alike.

Stone Food & Drink Festival
October, Stone, Staffordshire
www.stonefooddrink.org.uk
Growing from humble beginnings in the town's Georgian High Street into one of the Midlands' biggest and busiest food festivals.

Tamworth Castle
Staffordshire B79 7NA
(01827) 709629
www.tamworthcastle.co.uk
The number one Heritage attraction located in the town. Explore over 900 years of history in the magnificent Motte and Bailey Castle.

Trentham Gardens
Stoke-on-Trent, Staffordshire, ST4 8JG
(01782) 646646
www.trentham.co.uk/trentham-gardens
Enjoy beautiful show gardens; take a woodland stroll along the mile-long lake, or get active in the adventure playground.

World of Wedgwood
Stoke-on-Trent, Staffordshire ST12 9ER
(01782) 282986
www.worldofwedgwood.com
Enjoy the past, buy the present and treasure the experience. The World of Wedgwood offers a unique chance to immerse yourself in the heritage of Britain's greatest ceramics company.

West Midlands

Barber Institute of Fine Arts
Edgbaston, West Midlands B15 2TS
(0121) 414 7333
www.barber.org.uk
British and European paintings, drawings and sculpture from the 13th century to mid 20th century, including Old Master and Impressionist collections. The Barber Institute also hosts an impressive range of concert programmes throughout the year.

Bewdley Museum
Bewdley, DY12 2AE
(01299) 403573
www.bewdleymuseum.co.uk
Set in a historic Butchers Shambles, Bewdley Museum offers a fascinating insight to the history of Bewdley with gardens, interesting displays and demonstrations using craft.

Birmingham Botanical Gardens
Edgbaston, Birmingham B15 3TR
(0121) 454 1860
www.birminghambotanicalgardens.org.uk
Visit the ornamental gardens and glasshouses spaning from tropical rainforest to arid desert climates. A lively birdhouse, wildlife trails and a seasonal butterfly house also sit attractively amongst the fifteen acres of flourishing gardens and foliage.

Birmingham Literature Festival
October, Birmingham, West Midlands
www.visitbirmingham.com
Celebrating the city's literature scene, the Birmingham Literature Festival takes places every year with its trademark mix of literature events, talks and workshops.

Birmingham International Jazz and Blues Festival
July, Birmingham, West Midlands
www.visitbirmingham.com
The festival presents around 175 performances each year in around 40 venues. Musicians and fans come to the city from every corner of the UK as well as from further afield and significantly, almost all of the events are free to the public.

Black Country Living Museum
Dudley, West Midlands DY1 4SQ
(0121) 557 9643
www.bclm.co.uk
Britain's friendliest open-air museum - visit original shops and houses, ride on fair attractions, take a look down the underground coalmine.

Frankfurt Christmas Market & Craft Fair
November-December, Birmingham, West Midlands
www.visitbirmingham.com
The largest authentic German market outside Germany and Austria and the centrepiece of the city's festive event calendar.

Great Malvern Priory
Malvern, WR14 2AY
(01684) 561020
www.greatmalvernpriory.org.uk
Great Malvern Priory was founded as Benedictine Priory in 1085 and has been changing and developing for centuries. See different stages of life and appreciate the beautiful architecture in this parish church dedicated to St Mary and St Michael.

Ikon Gallery
Brindley Place, Birmingham B1 2HS
(0121) 248 0708
www.ikon-gallery.org
Ikon is an internationally acclaimed contemporary art venue housed in the Grade II listed, neo-gothic former Oozells Street Board School, designed by John Henry Chamberlain in 1877.

Moseley Folk Festival
September, Birmingham, West Midlands
www.visitbirmingham.com
Offering an inner city Shangri-la bringing together people from all ages and backgrounds to witness folk legends playing alongside their contemporaries.

Thinktank-Birmingham Science Museum
West Midlands B4 7XG
(0121) 348 8000
www.thinktank.ac
Thinktank is Birmingham's science museum where the emphasis is firmly on hands on exhibits and interactive fun.

Worcestershire

The Almonry Museum & Heritage Centre
Evesham, Worcestershire WR11 4BG
(01386) 446944
www.almonryevesham.org
The 14th century house has 12 rooms of exhibits from 2000 years of Evesham history and pleasant gardens to the rear.

Greyfriars House
Worcester WR1 2LZ
(01905) 23571
www.nationaltrust.org.uk
The National Trust's Greyfriars House and Garden, Worcestershire, built in 1480 by a wealthy merchant, is a fine timbered Medieval merchants house and walled garden.

Hanbury Hall
Droitwich Spa, Worcestershire WR9 7EA
(01527) 821214
www.nationaltrust.org.uk/hanburyhall
Early 18th century house, garden & park owned by the Vernon family for nearly 300 years. Choose from one of the scenic walks and make the most of your day by exploring the estate and surrounding countryside.

West Midland Safari and Leisure Park
Bewdley, Worcestershire DY12 1LF
(01299) 402114
www.wmsp.co.uk
Are you ready to SAFARI and come face to face with some of the fastest, tallest, largest and cutest animals around? The park is home to some of the world's most beautiful and endangered exotic animal species. The leisure park features 28 rides and attractions, there is something here to suit the whole family.

Worcester Cathedral
Worcestershire WR1 2LA
(01905) 732900
www.worcestercathedral.co.uk
Worcester Cathedral is one of England's most magnificent and inspiring buildings, as it rises majestically above the River Severn. It has been place of prayer and worship for 14 centuries.

Worcester City Art Gallery & Museum
Worcestershire WR1 1DT
(01905) 25371
www.whub.org.uk
The art gallery & museum runs a programme of exhibitions/events for all the family. Explore the fascinating displays, exhibitions, café, shop and Worcestershire Soldier Galleries. The collections and exhibitions are many and varied, covering centuries of the county's history right up to the present day.

Tourist Information Centres

When you arrive at your destination, visit the Tourist Information Centre for quality assured help with accommodation and information about local attractions and events, or email your request before you go.

Bewdley	Load Street	0845 6077819	bewdleytic@wyreforestdc.gov.uk
Bridgnorth	The Library	01746 763257	bridgnorth.tourism@shropshire.gov.uk
Bromyard	The Bromyard Centre	01885 488133	enquiries@bromyard-live.org.uk
Church Stretton	Church Street	01694 723133	churchstretton.scf@shropshire.gov.uk
Droitwich Spa	St Richard's House	01905 774312	heritage@droitwichspa.gov.uk
Ellesmere, Shropshire	The Boathouse Visitor Centre	01691 622981	ellesmere.tourism@shropshire.gov.uk
Evesham	The Almonry	01386 446944	tic@almonry.ndo.co.uk
Hereford	1 King Street	01432 268430	reception@visitherefordshire.co.uk
Ironbridge	Museum of The Gorge	01952 433424 / 01952 435900	tic@ironbridge.org.uk
Kenilworth	Kenilworth Library	0300 5558171	kenilworthlibrary@warwickshire.gov.uk
Ledbury	38 The Homend	0844 5678650	info@vistledbury.info
Leek	1 Market Place	01538 483741	tourism.services@staffsmoorlands.gov.uk
Leominster	1 Corn Square	01568 616460	leominstertic@herefordshire.gov.uk
Lichfield	Lichfield Garrick	01543 412112	info@visitlichfield.com
Ludlow	Castle Street	01584 875053	ludlow.tourism@shropshire.gov.uk
Malvern	21 Church Street	01684 892289	info@visitthemalverns.org
Market Drayton	49 Cheshire Street	01630 653114	marketdrayton.scf@shropshire-cc.gov.uk
Much Wenlock	The Museum - Visitor Information Centre	01952 727679 / 01743 258891	muchwenlock.tourism@shropshire.gov.uk
Newcastle-Under-Lyme	Newcastle Library	01782 297313	tic.newcastle@staffordshire.gov.uk
Nuneaton	Nuneaton Library	0300 5558171	nuneatonlibrary@warwickshire.gov.uk
Oswestry (Mile End)	Mile End	01691 662488	oswestrytourism@shropshire.gov.uk
Oswestry Town	The Heritage Centre	01691 662753	ot@oswestry-welshborders.org.uk
Redditch	Palace Theatre	01527 60806	info.centre@bromsgroveandredditch.gov.uk
Ross-on-Wye	Market House	01989 562768 / 01432 260675	visitorcentreross@herefordshire.gov.uk
Royal Leamington Spa	Royal Pump Rooms	01926 742762	vic@warwickdc.gov.uk
Rugby	Rugby Art Gallery Museum	01788 533217	visitor.centre@rugby.gov.uk
Shrewsbury	Barker Street	01743 281200	visitorinformation@shropshire.gov.uk
Solihull	Central Library	0121 704 6130	artscomplex@solihull.gov.uk
Stafford	Stafford Gatehouse Theatre	01785 619619	tic@staffordbc.gov.uk
Stoke-On-Trent	Victoria Hall, Bagnall Street	01782 236000	stoke.tic@stoke.gov.uk
Stratford-Upon-Avon	Bridge Foot	01789 264293	tic@discover-stratford.com
Tamworth	Philip Dix Centre	01827 709581	tic@tamworth.gov.uk
Telford	The Telford Shopping Centre	01952 238008	tourist-info@telfordshopping.co.uk
Upton Upon Severn	The Heritage Centre	01684 594200	upton.tic@malvernhills.gov.uk
Warwick	Visit Warwick	01926 492212	info@visitwarwick.co.uk
Whitchurch (Shropshire)	Whitchurch Heritage Centre	01948 664577	heritage@whitchurch-shropshire-tc.gov.uk
Worcester	The Guildhall	01905 726311 / 722561	touristinfo@visitworcester.com
Coventry	St Michael's Tower, Coventry Cathedral Ruins	024 7622 5616	tic@coventry.gov.uk

Regional Contacts and Information

For more information on accommodation, attractions, activities, events and holidays in the Heart of England, contact one of the following regional or local tourism organisations. Their websites have a wealth of information and many produce free publications to help you get the most out of your visit.

Marketing Birmingham
(0844) 888 3883
www.visitbirmingham.com

Visit Coventy & Warwickshire
(024) 7622 5616
www.visitcoventryandwarwickshire.co.uk

Visit Herefordshire
(01432) 268430
www.visitherefordshire.co.uk

Shakespeare Country
(0871) 978 0800
www.shakespeare-country.co.uk

Shropshire Tourism
(01743) 261919
www.shropshiretourism.co.uk

Destination Staffordshire
(01785) 277397
www.enjoystaffordshire.com

Stoke-on-Trent
(01782) 236000
www.visitstoke.co.uk

Destination Worcestershire
(0845) 641 1540
www.visitworcestershire.org

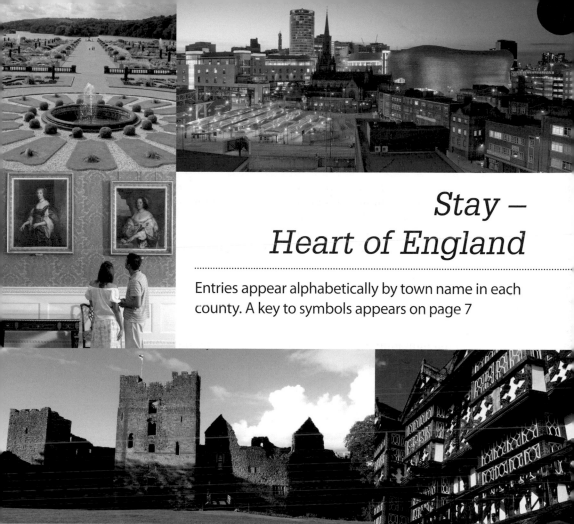

Stay –
Heart of England

Entries appear alphabetically by town name in each
county. A key to symbols appears on page 7

KINGTON, Herefordshire   Map ref 2A1   S

White Heron Properties

Contact: Jo Hilditch, Managing Director, Whittern Farms Ltd., Lyonshall, Kington HR5 3JA
T: (01544) 340241 **F:** 01544 340253 **E:** info@whiteheronproperties.com
W: www.whiteheronproperties.com **£ BOOK ONLINE**

Units   5
Sleeps   2-32

PER UNIT PER WEEK
£500.00 - £640.00

SPECIAL PROMOTIONS
We offer Friday to
Sunday, Friday to
Monday and Monday
to Friday as standard
stays.

We have five lovely properties in rolling Herefordshire countryside. They vary from pet friendly small cottages to large contemporary accommodation for house parties, all with en suite bedrooms. The largest has a swimming pool, sauna, hot tub, table tennis, cinema, Wii, Xbox and even a squash court.

We can host small conferences, weddings, hen parties or just provide luxurious accommodation for a romantic weekend away in the country. With great service from a friendly team we can offer full catering, or leave it all to you - the choice is yours, whichever you choose you will not be disappointed! Prices shown are based on a small unit. Please contact for larger unit rates.

Open: All year
Nearest Shop: 3 miles
Nearest Pub: 2 miles

Units: At White Heron properties we have a total of 23 bedrooms in 5 properties, some en suite.

Site: ❀ P Payment: 💳 Leisure: ⚓ ↑ ♺ ⚒ ⚲ Property: ∥ ⛺ 🅱 🖥 Children: 🐴 🏠 ⚹
Unit: ⬚ ▣ ▤ ⚲ 📺 🎧 📀 🔥 BBQ ☎

LEOMINSTER, Herefordshire   Map ref 2A1   S

Bellwood Lodges

Contact: Mrs Linda Stokes, Owner, Shobdon, Leominster, Herefordshire HR6 9NJ
T: (01568) 708642 **E:** info@bellwoodlodges.co.uk
W: www.bellwoodlodges.co.uk **£ BOOK ONLINE**

Units   2
Sleeps   1-12
PER UNIT PER WEEK
£420.00 - £490.00

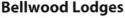

Holiday chalets set in the beautiful Herefordshire countryside. Well equipped, including one which is fully wheelchair accessible throughout. All linen and towels included. We also have a play area and plenty of space for children to enjoy and a hot tub available. One chalet has been graded by the AA as 4 star accommodation whilst the other received a 3 star grading. Walkers are welcome. **Open:** All year except November **Nearest Shop:** 1.5 miles **Nearest Pub:** 1.5 miles

Site: ❀ P Property: ∥ ↑ ⛺ 🖥 Children: 🐴 🏠 ⚹ Unit: ▣ 📺 📀 BBQ

ROSS-ON-WYE, Herefordshire   Map ref 2A1   S

Bramley Cottage

Contact: Lucy Snell, c/o Bramley House, Pencoyd, Harewood End, Hereford HR2 8JY
T: (01989) 730416 / 07747 041026 **E:** lucy@bramleyholidaycottage.co.uk
W: www.bramleyholidaycottage.co.uk

Units   1
Sleeps   1-4
PER UNIT PER WEEK
£310.00 - £520.00

Bramley Cottages lies in the heart of the Wye Valley. 5 miles from Ross on Wye and near the cathedral town of Hereford. It provides the perfect location from which to explore the stunning countryside, whether on foot along the banks of the Wye to Symonds Yat or on bikes in the Forest of Dean, or just canoeing gently down the river. **Open:** All year **Nearest Shop:** 2 miles **Nearest Pub:** 1.25 miles

Site: ❀ P Property: ↑ ⛺ 🅱 🖥 Children: 🏠 ⚹ Unit: ⬚ ▤ ▣ ⚲ 📺 📀 BBQ

ROSS-ON-WYE, Herefordshire   Map ref 2A1   S

Flanesford Priory

Contact: Kath Taylor-Jessup, General Manager, Flanesford Priory, Goodrich, Ross-on-Wye, Herefordshire HR9 6HZ **T:** (01600) 890 506 **F:** 01600 891019
E: info@flanesfordpriory.co.uk **W:** www.flanesfordpriory.co.uk **£ BOOK ONLINE**

Units   10
Sleeps   2-42
PER UNIT PER WEEK
£240.00 - £1200.00

Ten beautifully appointed self catering apartments and cottages, situated in the picturesque village of Goodrich in the Wye Valley; on the doorstep of the Forest of Dean. Ranging from 2 to 8 persons there is accommodation to suit every taste and budget, including the luxury and award winning 5 star Cider Mill. Fishing, cycling, canoeing walking and much more available locally. **Open:** All year **Nearest Shop:** 0.5 miles **Nearest Pub:** 0.5 miles

 Site: ✿ P Payment: 💷 Leisure: ♪ ▶ Property: ⚓ 🖼 🗄 🗐 Children: 🌣 🛏 🏃 Unit: 🗄 🗄 📺
🗃 📺 🎦 📀 🚿 BBQ

CHAPEL LAWN, Shropshire   Map ref 4A3   S

The Squire Farm Holiday Cottages

Contact: Mrs Becky Sherman, The Squire Farm, Chapel Lawn, Bucknell, Shropshire SY7 0BW **T:** (01547) 530530 **E:** becky@squirefarm.co.uk
W: www.squirefarm.co.uk **£ BOOK ONLINE**

Units   2
Sleeps   1-6
PER UNIT PER WEEK
£290.00 - £604.00

The Squire Farm has two unusual and interesting cottages; a Japanese themed barn conversion which sleeps two people and has a hot tub, the other is more traditional with a large open fireplace and sleeps four. With beautiful views and peaceful surroundings, you can enjoy walks right from your door and explore the historical Shropshire countryside. Please contact us for prices. **Open:** All year **Nearest Shop:** 3 miles **Nearest Pub:** 3 miles

 Site: ✿ P Payment: 💷 Leisure: 🚲 ♪ Property: ⚓ 🗐 Children: 🌣 🛏 Unit: 🗄 🗄 📺 🗃 🗃
📺 🎦 📀 🚿 BBQ

LUDLOW, Shropshire   Map ref 4A3   S

Castle House Lodgings

Contact: Sonja Belchere, The Custodian, Castle House Lodgings, Ludlow Castle, Castle Square, Ludlow, Shropshire SY8 1AY **T:** (01584) 874465 **F:** 01584 874465
E: info@ludlowcastle.com **W:** www.castle-accommodation.com **£ BOOK ONLINE**

Units   3
Sleeps   1-4

PER UNIT PER WEEK
£895.00 - £1230.00

SPECIAL PROMOTIONS
Three night weekend break
(Friday to Sunday)

Four night break
(Monday to Thursday)

Seven night break
(Friday to Thursday).

Castle House Lodgings comprise of three 4-5* self catering apartments, full of character features and finished to the highest of standards, set within the walls of Ludlow Castle. Each apartment provides a sitting room/dining room, fully equipped kitchen, two twin bedrooms and two bathrooms and a car parking space.

Open: All year
Nearest Shop: 0.10 miles
Nearest Pub: 0.10 miles

 Site: P Payment: 💷 Leisure: 🚲 ♪ ♺ Property: ⚓ 🖼 🗄 🗐 Children: 🌣 🛏 🏃
Unit: 🗄 🗄 📺 🗃 🗃 📺 🎦 📀 📞

Heart of England - Shropshire

LUDLOW, Shropshire   Map ref 4A3   S

Glebe Barn

Contact: Mr & Mrs Jones, Glebe Barn, Caynham, Ludlow, Shropshire SY8 3BN
T: (01584) 705027 **E:** info@glebebarnludlow.co.uk
W: www.glebebarnludlow.co.uk

Units   1
Sleeps   7

PER UNIT PER WEEK
£348.00 - £818.00

SPECIAL PROMOTIONS
Why not enjoy a relaxing weekend break! Available during off season & winter weekends Fri-Mon.

A delightful detached barn conversion in the picturesque rural village of Caynham, 3 miles from Ludlow. Superbly renovated to perfectly blend original character and contemporary fixtures and fittings, this lovely property boasts a wealth of exposed oak beams, trusses and doors, creating a lovely welcoming atmosphere.

Open: All year
Nearest Shop: 2.50 miles
Nearest Pub: 2.30 miles

Units: Two double bedrooms and one family bedroom i.e. double and single. Large kitchen and spacious living room.

Site: ✿ P Leisure: ▸ Property: 🖥 🔲 Children: 🛋 🛏 ⚲ Unit: 🔲 🔲 🔲 🔲 📶 🎧 📺 🍴 BBQ

LUDLOW, Shropshire   Map ref 4A3   S

The Silver Pear Apartments

Contact: Mr Christopher Tuffley, Director, Silver Pear Apartments, 68-69 Broad Street, Ludlow SY8 1NH **T:** (01584) 879096 **F:** 01584 879124 **E:** sales@silverpear.co.uk
W: www.silverpearapartments.co.uk

Units   2
Sleeps   2-6

Our apartments have been restored to the highest specification, utilising all the original features of such an important building, and much of the original oak features have been saved. **Open:** All year
Nearest Shop: 0.01 miles **Nearest Pub:** 0.02 miles

Payment: 💷 Leisure: 🚴 ♪ ▸ ⛵ Property: 🖥 🔲 Children: 🛋 🛏 ⚲ Unit: 🔲 🔲 🔲 🔲 📶 📺 🎧 📺

LUDLOW, Shropshire   Map ref 4A3   S

Sutton Court Farm Cottages

Contact: Mrs Jane Cronin, Sutton Court Farm, Little Sutton, Ludlow, Shropshire SY8 2AJ
T: (01584) 861305 **E:** enquiries@suttoncourtfarm.co.uk
W: www.suttoncourtfarm.co.uk

Units   6
Sleeps   2-6
PER UNIT PER WEEK
£245.00 - £580.00

6 comfortable cottages surrounding a peaceful, sunny courtyard, 5 miles from historic Ludlow in an Area of Outstanding Natural Beauty. Ironbridge, Shrewsbury, Hereford and the Welsh borders within easy reach. Breakfast packs, cream teas and evening meals available to order. Short breaks (min. 2 nights) all year round. Special offer from Nov to Mar (excl holidays), 3 nights for 2, 4 nights for 3. **Open:** All year **Nearest Shop:** 6 miles **Nearest Pub:** 3 miles

Site: ✿ P Leisure: 🚴 ♪ ▸ ⛵ Property: 🐾 🖥 🔲 🔲 Children: 🛋 🛏 ⚲ Unit: 🔲 🔲 🔲 📶 📺 🎧 🍴 BBQ ☎

ABBOTS BROMLEY, *Staffordshire*   *Map ref 4B3*   S

Units 6
Sleeps 2-10

PER UNIT PER WEEK
£200.00 - £995.00

SPECIAL PROMOTIONS
Short breaks available
Friday to Monday
or Monday to Friday.

Blithfield Lakeside Barns

Contact: Mrs Maxine Brown, Blithfield Lakeside Barns, St Stephens Hill Farm, Admaston, Rugeley, Staffordshire WS15 3NQ **T:** (01889) 500234
E: blithfieldlakesidebarns@hotmail.co.uk
W: www.blithfieldlakesidebarns.co.uk **£ BOOK ONLINE**

Superb lakeside barn conversions on organic dairy farm overlooking Blithfield Reservoir, 2 miles Abbots Bromley. Nr Peak District, Cannock Chase, National Forest, Drayton Manor and Alton Towers. Trout/carp fishing, walking, cycling. Pets welcome in 2 cottages. Excellent local pubs/restaurants.

Open: All year
Nearest Shop: 2 miles
Nearest Pub: 2 miles

Site: P Payment: Leisure: Property: Children: Unit: BBQ

ALTON, *Staffordshire*   *Map ref 4B2*   S

Units 1
Sleeps 2-6
PER UNIT PER WEEK
£527.00 - £727.00

Blythe Farmhouse

Contact: Mrs Irene Bullock, Booking Enquiries, Blythe Farmhouse, Riverside Road, Tean ST10 4JW **T:** (01538) 724061 / 07969 443869 **E:** irene@blythefarmhouse.co.uk
W: www.blythefarmhouse.co.uk

 Blythe Farmhouse is a grade II listed building. It has been extensively renovated retaining many of the original features. Fantastic views over the Staffordshire countryside. Accommodation equipped with quality fittings. **Open:** All year **Nearest Shop:** 1.5 miles **Nearest Pub:** 1.5 miles

Site: P Leisure: Property: Children: Unit: BBQ

BIDDULPH, *Staffordshire*   *Map ref 4B2*   S

Units 1
Sleeps 14
PER UNIT PER WEEK
£578.00 - £1113.00

Heritage Wharf Bungalow

Contact: Mike Dowse, Heritage Narrow Boats, The Marina, Scholar Green ST7 3JZ
T: (01782) 785700 **E:** email@heritagenarrowboats.co.uk
W: www.heritagenarrowboats.co.uk

 Large accommodation comprised of five bedrooms, three bathrooms (two en suite), fully equipped kitchen with electric 'range style' cooker, tall fridge/freezer, dishwasher and utility room with washing machine and dryers. The spacious lounge area has three large sofas and an armchair, a large open fireplace and a TV and DVD. Other features include large patio with picnic table and barbecue, overlooking a private marina to the front with a large secluded side garden for sunbathing in privacy. **Open:** All year **Nearest Shop:** 0.5 miles **Nearest Pub:** 0.25 miles

Site: P Property: Children: Unit: BBQ

VisitEngland
★★★★
SELF CATERING

Units   44
Sleeps   1-6

PER UNIT PER WEEK
£490.00 – £1267.00

SPECIAL PROMOTIONS
Visit our website or call today for seasonal discounts and great savings.

Wychnor Park Country Club

Contact: Wychnor Hall, Nr Barton-Under-Needwood, Staffordshire DE13 8BU
T: (0800) 358 6991   **E:** EuHotels@diamondresorts.com
W: www.DiamondResortsandHotels.com   **£ BOOK ONLINE**

Set in a private, peaceful estate, this country club has landscaped gardens and combines the best of old and new for a relaxing environment.

All beautiful accommodation at Wychnor Park Country Club offers a high standard of luxury. Guests may be allocated rooms in the historic main building, the coach house and courtyard buildings or spacious log cabins in the grounds. The superb gardens provide a host of sporting activities. Above all, Wychnor Park Country Club is an peaceful country retreat.

Open: All year
Nearest Shop: 3 miles
Nearest Pub: On Site

Units: A choice of one and two bedroom apartments available. All apartments boast a full kitchen, modern bathroom and Television with DVD player.

Site: ✿ P **Payment:** 💳 **Leisure:** ⚐ ⌇ ⚲ **Property:** 🏠 🗐 🗗 **Children:** 🐾 🛏 ☂
Unit: 🗎 🗄 🖳 🗄 🗄 📺 📀 ☎

DILHORNE, Staffordshire Map ref 4B2 S

VisitEngland ★★★★ SELF CATERING

Units 3
Sleeps 1-5
PER UNIT PER WEEK
£200.00 - £600.00

Little Summerhill Cottages

Contact: Mrs Beth Plant, Little Summerhill Farm, Tickhill Lane, Dilhorne ST10 2PL
T: (01782) 550967 / 07976 068560 **F:** 01782 550967
E: info@holidaycottagesstaffordshire.com **W:** www.holidaycottagesstaffordshire.com

Newly converted, one and two bedroomed cottages in Staffordshire Moorlands. Convenient for Peak District, Potteries and Alton Towers, yet a cosy, well equipped retreat with scenic views, on working smallholding. **Open:** All year **Nearest Shop:** 3 miles **Nearest Pub:** 2 miles

Site: P **Payment:** € **Property:** **Children:** **Unit:** BBQ

LEEK, Staffordshire Map ref 4B2 S

VisitEngland ★★★ SELF CATERING

Units 2
Sleeps 1-6
PER UNIT PER WEEK
£296.50 - £656.00

SPECIAL PROMOTIONS
Short breaks from two nights minimum available any day of the week.

Roaches Holiday Cottages

Contact: Karen Oliver, Paddock Farm, Upper Hulme, Leek, Staffordshire Moorlands ST13 8TY **T:** (01538) 300345 **E:** karen@roachescottages.co.uk
W: www.roachescottages.co.uk **£ BOOK ONLINE**

Family run ETB 3 Star, Farmhouse Holiday Cottages on the south-western edge of the Peak District National Park by the Roaches. Breathtaking views stretching far over valley, reservoir and beyond. Two cosy, open plan cottages, each sleeping up to six people. Bedding, central heating and water included. The award winning Roaches Tea Rooms is just across the courtyard open for breakfasts, lunches and afternoon teas.

Open: All year
Nearest Shop: 3 miles
Nearest Pub: 0.5 mile

Units: Each cottage has one double bedroom and two twin bedrooms. One twin bedroom on ground floor of each cottage.

Site: P **Payment:** **Property:** **Children:** **Unit:**

LEEK, Staffordshire Map ref 4B2 S

VisitEngland ★★★ SELF CATERING

Units 1
Sleeps 6
PER UNIT PER WEEK
£295.00 - £460.00

Rosewood Cottage

Contact: Lower Berkhamsytch Farm, Bottomhouse, Nr Leek, Staffordshire ST13 7QP
T: (01538) 308213 **E:** a.e.mycock@gmail.com
W: www.rosewoodcottage.co.uk

Set in picturesque Staffordshire Moorlands, bordering Peak District. Attractive three bedroomed cottage including four poster bed. Central to Alton Towers, Potteries and Peak District. Field available for pet walking and ball games. Indian restaurant and country café nearby. Free internet access.
Open: All year
Nearest Shop: 2 miles **Nearest Pub:** 2 miles

Site: P **Leisure:** **Property:** **Children:** **Unit:**

STONE, Staffordshire   Map ref 4B2   S

3★ - 4★
NARROWBOAT

Units   14
Sleeps   2-8

PER UNIT PER WEEK
£505.00 - £1784.00

SPECIAL PROMOTIONS
Please our website for
our special offers.

Canal Cruising Company Ltd

Contact: Mrs Karen Wyatt, Booking Enquiries, Canal Cruising Company Ltd, Crown Street,
Stone ST15 8QN **T:** (01785) 813982 **F:** 01785 819041 **E:** canalcruisingcoltd@aol.co.uk
W: www.canalcruising.co.uk **£ BOOK ONLINE**

Situated in the Heart of England, Stone is the ideal starting point for a different type of Holiday.
Canal Boating in the slow lane, an adventure, seeing England from a different view point. We have
several choices of routes including Four Counties Ring, The Caldon, The Cheshire Ring and
Llangollen.

We Offer Day Hire, Shortbreak, Weekly and longer. A week or more from Stone, you have several
choices of routes, for an energetic week you can do the Four Counties Ring visiting Shropshire,
Staffordshire, Cheshire and the Midlands. Alternately, for an easier week for example - The Caldon.
Gift Vouchers are available.

Open: Mid March to End October
Nearest Shop: 0.5 miles
Nearest Pub: 0.5 miles

Site: **P** Payment: ⬚£ € Leisure: ⚓ Property: 🐾 ⬚ Children: ⬚ ⬚ Unit: ⬚ 📺

WATERHOUSES, Staffordshire   Map ref 4B2   S

3★ - 4★
SELF CATERING

Units   2
Sleeps   1-6
PER UNIT PER WEEK
£225.00 - £520.00

Greenside Cottages

Contact: Mr & Mrs Terry & Sue Riley, Owner, Greenside Cottages, Brown End Farm,
Waterhouses, Staffordshire ST10 3JR **T:** (01538) 308313 / 07779 320975 **F:** 01538 308053
E: sriley01@gmail.com **W:** www.greenside-cottages.co.uk

2 delightful converted stone cottages in Peak District. Well
equipped, very welcoming and comfortable. Ideal base for walking
and cycling from doorstep. Historic houses and visitor attractions
are within easy reach. Alton Towers is only 15 minutes away. Day's
cycling for guests. **Open:** All year **Nearest Shop:** 0.40 miles
Nearest Pub: 0.40 miles

 Site: ✿ **P** Leisure: 🚴 ⚓ ∪ Property: ⬚ Children: ⬚ ⬚ ⚲ Unit: ⬚ ⬚ ⬚ ⬚ 📺 ⬚ ⬚ BBQ

SHIPSTON-ON-STOUR, Warwickshire   Map ref 2B1   S

⭐★★★
SELF CATERING

Units   1
Sleeps   1-2
PER UNIT PER WEEK
£340.00 - £450.00

Burmington View

Contact: Vanessa Barney, Burmington Grange Cottage, Cherington, Shipston on Stour,
Warwickshire CV36 5HZ **T:** (01608) 686526 **E:** vanessa@burmington-view.co.uk
W: www.burmington-view.co.uk

Situated in a lovely rural location, Burmington View is two miles
from the historic Shipston-on-Stour. Bright and comfortable, fully
equipped, one bedroom loft conversion with views over open
countryside. **Open:** All year **Nearest Shop:** 2 miles
Nearest Pub: 2 miles

Site: ✿ **P** Leisure: ⚓ ⚲ Property: ⫽ ⬚ ⬚ ⬚ Unit: ⬚ ⬚ ⬚ ⬚ 📺 ⬚ BBQ

STRATFORD-UPON-AVON, Warwickshire   Map ref 2B1   S

3★-4★ SELF CATERING

Units   1
Sleeps   1-3
PER UNIT PER WEEK
£320.00 - £435.00

As You Like It

Contact: Mr & Mrs Ian & Janet Reid, c/o Inwood House, New Road, Stratford-upon-Avon CV37 8PE **T:** (01789) 450266 / 07956 692015 **E:** ian@alderminster99.freeserve.co.uk
W: www.asyoulikeitcottage.co.uk **£ BOOK ONLINE**

'As You Like It' is a character cottage in central Stratford within easy walking distance of the theatres and the town's many attractions. It is located within the 'Old Town ' area close to the river and Holy Trinity Church, and ten minutes walk from the Royal Shakespeare Theatre. There is private parking provided. **Open:** All year
Nearest Shop: 0.25 miles **Nearest Pub:** 0.25 miles

Site: P Property: 🐕 ▦ 🖳 Unit: ▣ 🗄 🔦 📺 🎦 📞

STRATFORD-UPON-AVON, Warwickshire   Map ref 2B1   SatNav CV37 9SR   C

★★★ TOURING & CAMPING PARK

🚐 (50)   £19.00-£27.00
🚏 (15)   £19.00-£27.00
⛺ (50)   £18.00-£25.00
50 touring pitches

Dodwell Park

Evesham Road (B439), Dodwell, Stratford-upon-Avon CV37 9SR
T: (01789) 204957 **E:** enquiries@dodwellpark.co.uk
W: www.dodwellpark.co.uk

Small, family-run touring park 2 miles SW of Stratford-upon-Avon. Country walks to River Avon and Luddington village. Ideal for visiting Warwick Castle, Shakespeare properties and Cotswolds. Brochure on request. Rallies welcome. Over 50 years as a family business! **Directions:** Leaving Stratford-Upon-Avon take the B439 signposted 'B349 Bidford' (also signposted Racecourse) for 2 miles, we are on left (after going over a large hill). **Open:** All year.

Site: ▲🄿 Payment: 💷 ☼ Leisure: 🎣 🎵 ▸ Children: 🛝 Catering: 🛒 Park: 🐕 🌲 Touring: 🚽 🚿 🔌

WARWICK, Warwickshire   Map ref 4B3   S

★★★ SELF CATERING

Units   4
Sleeps   4-6
PER UNIT PER WEEK
£355.00 - £595.00

Bianca & Whitley Elm Cottages

Contact: Katherine Russell, Case Lane, Mousley End, Warwick CV35 7JE
T: (01926) 484577 / 07929 264386 **E:** enquiries@whitleyelmcottages.co.uk
W: www.whitleyelmcottages.co.uk

Four attractive cottages converted from 18th century barns, in the grounds of a Tudor manor house set in beautiful countryside.
Open: All Year **Nearest Shop:** 2 miles **Nearest Pub:** 0.75 mile

Site: ✿ P Property: 🐕 ▦ 🗄 🖳 Children: 🛝 ▦ 🚼 Unit: ▯ 🗄 ▣ 🔦 📺 🎦 BBQ

BEWDLEY, Worcestershire Map ref 4A3

VisitEngland ★★★★ SELF CATERING

Units 1
Sleeps 1-4
PER UNIT PER WEEK
£415.00 - £520.00

Fern Cottage

Contact: Jenny, Bewdley, Worcestershire DY12 2ER **T:** 07899 797535
E: bookings@ferncottagebewdley.co.uk
W: www.ferncottagebewdley.co.uk **£ BOOK ONLINE**

A cosy modern cottage. Conveniently situated, an easy walk from Bewdley's pubs, shops, restaurants, the River Severn and beautiful countryside. Sleeps 4 in two en suite bedrooms. Wi-Fi. Courtyard garden. Parking. Available for short lets. **Open:** All year **Nearest Shop:** 0.10 miles **Nearest Pub:** 0.20 miles

WALKERS WELCOME · FAMILIES WELCOME · CYCLISTS WELCOME

Site: P **Leisure:** **Property:** **Children:** **Unit:**

BEWDLEY, Worcestershire Map ref 4A3

VisitEngland ★★★★ SELF CATERING

Units 1
Sleeps 2-6
PER UNIT PER WEEK
£520.00 - £675.00

Fern View

Contact: Jenny, Bewdley, Worcestershire DY12 2ER **T:** 07899 797535
E: bookings@fernviewbewdley.co.uk
W: www.fernviewbewdley.co.uk **£ BOOK ONLINE**

Situated a short walk from Georgian Bewdley, this refurbished bungalow sleeps 6 in three bedrooms, two en suite. Ideal for families and the less mobile. Wi fi. Private garden. Parking. Available for short lets. **Open:** All year **Nearest Shop:** 0.10 miles **Nearest Pub:** 0.10 miles

Site: P **Leisure:** **Property:** **Children:** **Unit:**

BROMSGROVE, Worcestershire Map ref 4B3

VisitEngland 2★-3★ SELF CATERING

Units 7
Sleeps 4-6
PER UNIT PER WEEK
£354.00 - £450.00

Inkford Court Cottages

Contact: Alcester Road, Wythall, Nr. Bromsgrove B47 6DL **T:** (01564) 822304 / 07831 462 451 **E:** inkfordcourtcottages@hotmail.co.uk

Inkford court cottages is a collection of circa 18th century buildings set around a central courtyard. All cottages have been restored to provide the latest requirements whilst retaining the unique beauty of the buildings such as the oak beams and hand made bricks.
Inkford court is located on the borders of Warwickshire and Worcestershire and positioned within minutes from the M42 allowing easy access to a wide variety of destinations such as Birmingham, the NEC and Stratford upon Avon.

Open: All year
Nearest Shop: 1 mile
Nearest Pub: 300 yards

Units: All fully central heated and come with fully equipped kitchens, two or three bedrooms sleeping between four or six people, bathrooms with electric showers and televisions with freeview. All linen, electric and gas are included in the weekly fee.

Site: P **Leisure:** **Property:** **Children:** **Unit:**

MALVERN, Worcestershire   Map ref 2B1   S

★★★★
SELF CATERING
VisitEngland

Units   1
Sleeps   10
PER UNIT PER WEEK
£612.00 - £1452.00

Beesoni Lodge

Contact: Laura Smith, Owner, Beesoni, Hill End, Castlemorton, Malvern WR13 6BL
T: (01684) 830016 / 07557 353600 **E:** info@beesonilodge.co.uk
W: www.beesonilodge.co.uk

Fabulous spacious Four Star detached barn conversion, exceptional standard with exposed beams throughout. Sleeps ten, four bedrooms (one four-poster), three bathrooms (one with spa bath). Large fully equipped kitchen. Heating, Linen and Towels included. Set in private grounds. Stunning views of Malvern Hills and Cotswolds. Within easy reach of Malvern, Upton upon Severn, Cheltenham and Worcester. **Open:** All year **Nearest Shop:** 3 miles **Nearest Pub:** 2.5 miles

Site: ✿ P Property: ⫻ 🐾 🖥 🗄 📠 Children: 🐥 🛏 ⚲ Unit: 🖥 🔌 📺 🎬 🍖

MALVERN, Worcestershire   Map ref 2B1   S

★★★★
SELF CATERING
VisitEngland

Gold
AWARD
VisitEngland

Units   1
Sleeps   1-4
PER UNIT PER WEEK
£350.00 - £550.00

Holywell Suite

Contact: Andrea, Holywell Suite, Wells House, Holywell Road, Malvern, Worcestershire WR14 4LH **T:** 07905 827082 **E:** bookings@holywellsuite.co.uk
W: www.holywellsuite.co.uk **£ BOOK ONLINE**

Holywell Suite has an enviable, 4 Star Gold rated, specification throughout. Serviced by lift access, the third floor, award-winning apartment provides a private retreat with awesome, uninterrupted views across the Worcestershire countryside. The Malvern Hills are right on your doorstep. **Open:** All year **Nearest Shop:** 0.3 miles **Nearest Pub:** 0.1 miles

Site: ✿ P Payment: 💷 € Leisure: ⚓ ♪ ⚑ ∪ Property: ⫻ 🖥 🗄 📠 Unit: 🖥 🔌 📺 🎬

For **key to symbols** see page 7

MALVERN, Worcestershire Map ref 2B1 S

★★★★ SELF CATERING / VisitEngland Gold AWARD

Rhydd Barn

Contact: Miss Rosemary Boaz, Under Ley, Doverhay, Porlock, Somerset TA24 8LL
T: (01643) 862359 **E:** info@rhyddbarn.co.uk
W: www.rhyddbarn.co.uk

Units   1
Sleeps   1-2
PER UNIT PER WEEK
£320.00 - £440.00

Outstanding barn conversion with spacious accommodation on three floors and wonderful views of the Malvern Hills. Tiled and wooden floors, white walls interspersed with pine beams and black iron work. Commended finalist for the Best Self Catering Award - Visit Worcestershire Awards for Excellence 2013. **Open:** All year
Nearest Shop: 2 miles **Nearest Pub:** 0.25 miles

Site: ✿ **P Property:** 📶 **Unit:** 🍴 🔌 📺 📻 📺 📀

PERSHORE, Worcestershire Map ref 2B1 S

★★★★ SELF CATERING

Garth Cottage

Contact: Mrs Margaret Smith, 8 Pensham Hill, Pershore, Worcestershire WR10 3HA
T: (01386) 561213 / 07759 655717 **F:** 01386 561213 **E:** stephen.smith@homecall.co.uk
W: www.garthcottage.co.uk

Units   1
Sleeps   1-3
PER UNIT PER WEEK
£305.00 - £420.00

Delightful detached cottage in peaceful location, 10 minutes leisurely walk from Pershore. Large airy bedroom, double bed settee in lounge. Use of owners outdoor swimming pool (seasonal May to October weather dependent), by arrangement. Short breaks from £135. Special rates for Bank Holidays, Xmas, & New Year.
Open: All year **Nearest Shop:** 1 mile **Nearest Pub:** 0.75 miles

Site: ✿ **P Leisure:** 🎵 ⛳ ♘ ⚘ **Property:** 🐾 📶 🔌 🖥 **Children:** 🚼 ⛺ ♿ **Unit:** 🖥 🔌 📺 📻 📀 BBQ

SUTTON, Worcestershire Map ref 4A3 S

★★★★ SELF CATERING / VisitEngland Gold AWARD

Long Cover Cottage & The Coach House

Contact: Mrs Eleanor Van Straaten, Holiday Cottage, Fishpool Cottage, Kyre, Tenbury Wells WR15 8RL **T:** (01885) 410208 / 07725 972486
E: ellie_vanstraaten@yahoo.co.uk **W:** www.a-country-break.co.uk

Units   2
Sleeps   2-8
PER UNIT PER WEEK
£700.00 - £900.00

Long Cover Cottage: A retreat from the outside world with magnificent views in all directions over the Teme and Kyre Valleys. Exposed beams, oak/elm staircase, Aga, woodburning stove. Coach House: Retire to your own private viewpoint with its picture-postcard views across open pastures to the Teme and Kyre valleys.

Open: All year
Nearest Shop: 3 miles
Nearest Pub: 3 miles

Site: ✿ **Leisure:** 🎵 ⛳ ♘ ⚘ **Property:** 🐾 📶 🔌 🖥 **Children:** 🚼 ⛺ ♿ **Unit:** 🍴 🔌 📺 📻 📺 📀 🎵 BBQ

TENBURY WELLS, *Worcestershire* Map ref 4A3 S

Rochford Park Cottages

Contact: Mrs Jarka Robinson, Rochford Park, Nr Tenbury Wells, Worcestershire WR15 8SP
T: (01584) 781392 **F:** 01584 781392 **E:** cottages@rochfordpark.co.uk
W: www.rochfordpark.co.uk

Units	2
Sleeps	3-8

PER UNIT PER WEEK
£195.00 - £747.00

Former farm outbuildings, now stylish, comfortable cottages suitable for couples, families or groups of friends, situated in beautiful Teme valley. Restful places, full of character. Woodlands, lakes nearby. **Open:** All year **Nearest Shop:** 3 miles **Nearest Pub:** 1.5 miles

Site: ❋ P Leisure: ♿ 🏊 ♪ ↻ 🔍 Property: 🔲 🛏 Children: 🚼 🏕 🎠 Unit: 🚪 🔲 💻 🍽 📺 📀 🍴 BBQ

WORCESTER, *Worcestershire* Map ref 2B1 S

Hop Pickers Rural Retreats

Contact: Mrs Louise Wild, Owner, Pigeon House Farm, Dingle Road, Leigh, Worcestershire WR6 5JX **T:** (01886) 833668 / 07834 652132 **E:** enquiries@hoppickersbarn.co.uk
W: www.hoppickersbarn.co.uk

Units	3
Sleeps	2-5

PER UNIT PER WEEK
£450.00 - £845.00

SPECIAL PROMOTIONS
Short breaks available
from 2 nights. Please
call for details.

Award winning self-catering Rural Retreat. Hop Pickers offers a warm welcome in 3 very different properties. The old 17th century barn with original oak beams and high vaulted ceilings, the luxury log cabin nestled in the orchard and the lovingly hand crafted Shepherd's hut with exclusive hot tub tucked away in the woodland. The 9 acre smallholding is in a tranquil setting in the beautiful unspoilt Worcestershire countryside. Between Malvern and Worcester in an Area of Outstanding Natural Beauty it offers a perfect location for family and friend get togethers, get away from it all holidays and romantic breaks. Woodland walk and wildlife hide overlooking the oast ponds where you can spot badgers, bats and buzzards. High speed Internet now available. Proud winners for the 2nd year running of 2015 Destination Worcestershire self-catering award.

Open: All Year
Nearest Shop: 2 miles
Nearest Pub: 2.3 miles

Units: Pet friendly. Barn 2 bedrooms sleeps 5, Cabin 2 bedrooms sleeps 4 Suitable for limited mobility. Shepherd's Hut King size bed for 2, Shower room and private hot tub (no pets).

Site: ❋ P Leisure: ♿ 🏊 ♪ 🔍 ⚲ 🔍 Property: 🐾 🚆 🔲 🛏 Children: 🚼 🏕 🎠
Unit: 🚪 🔲 💻 🍽 📺 🎧 📀 BBQ

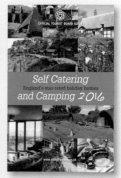

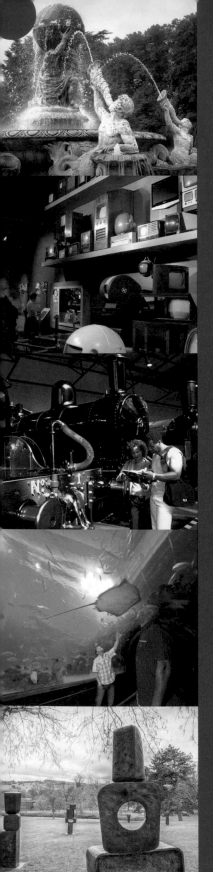

Don't Miss...

Castle Howard ❀
Malton, North Yorkshire YO60 7DA
(01653) 648444
www.castlehoward.co.uk
A magnificent 18th century house situated in breathtaking parkland, dotted with temples, lakes statues and fountains; plus formal gardens, woodland garden and ornamental vegetable garden. Inside the House guides share stories of the house, family and collections, while outdoor-guided tours reveal the secrets of the architecture and landscape.

National Media Museum
Bradford, West Yorkshire BD1 1NQ
0870 701 0200
www.nationalmediamuseum.org.uk
The National Media Museum is a fabulous free museum in Bradford, West Yorkshire devoted to film, photography & TV. Journey through popular photography, discover the past, present and future of television in Experience TV, watch your favourite film and TV moments in the BFI Mediatheque, play with light, lenses and colour in the Magic Factory, explore the world of animation and get gaming in the Games Lounge! The National Media Museum is also home to Yorkshire's only IMAX cinema, for an eye-opening, jaw-dropping 3D cinema experience.

National Railway Museum
York, North Yorkshire YO26 4XJ
0844 815 3139
www.nrm.org.uk
A fantastic day out for the whole family in York with over 300 years of fascinating history in York's only National Museum. Explore giant halls full of trains, railway legends including the majestic Duchess of Hamilton and the futuristic Japanese Bullet Train and marvel at the stunning opulence of the Royal Trains. Watch engineers at work in The Workshop, uncover hidden treasures in The Warehouse and make tracks to the outdoor area where children can let off steam in the play area or take a trip on the miniature railway rides.

The Deep ❀
Hull, East Riding of Yorkshire HU1 4DP
(01482) 381000
www.thedeep.co.uk
Full with over 3500 fish and more than 40 sharks, The Deep tells the amazing story of the world's oceans through stunning marine life, interactives and audio-visual presentations making it a fun-filled family day out for all ages.

Yorkshire Sculpture Park ❀
West Bretton, West Yorkshire WF4 4LG
(01924) 832631
www.ysp.co.uk
Showing work by British and international artists, including Henry Moore and Barbara Hepworth the Yorkshire Sculpture Park is an extraordinary place that sets out to challenge, inspire, inform and delight.

Yorkshire

Yorkshire, the largest county in England, is one of the most popular and boasts award-winning culture, heritage and scenery. There's cosmopolitan Leeds, stylish Harrogate and rural market towns full of charm and character. The wild moors and deserted dales of the Yorkshire Dales and North York Moors National Parks are majestic in their beauty and the county has a spectacular coastline of rugged cliffs and sandy beaches. The region also has a wealth of historic houses, ruined castles, abbeys and fortresses for visitors to discover.

Yorkshire

Explore – Yorkshire

North Yorkshire

Steeped in history, North Yorkshire boasts some of the country's most splendid scenery. Wherever you go in The Dales, you'll be faced with breathtaking views and constant reminders of a historic and changing past. In medieval days, solid fortresses like Richmond and Middleham were built to protect the area from marauding Scots. Ripley and Skipton also had their massive strongholds, while Bolton Castle in Wensleydale once imprisoned Mary, Queen of Scots. The pattern of history continues with the great abbeys, like Jervaulx Abbey, near Masham, where the monks first made Wensleydale cheese and the majestic ruins of Fountains Abbey in the grounds of Studley Royal. Between the Dales and the North York Moors, Herriot Country is named for one of the world's best loved writers, James Herriot, who made the area his home for more than 50 years and whose books have enthralled readers with tales of Yorkshire life.

Escape to the wild, deserted North York Moors National Park with its 500 square miles of hills, dales, forests and open moorland, neatly edged by a spectacular coastline. Walking, cycling and pony trekking are ideal ways to savour the scenery and there are plenty of greystone towns and villages dotted throughout the Moors that provide ideal bases from which to explore. From Helmsley, visit the ruins of Rievaulx Abbey, founded by Cistercian monks in the 12th century or discover moorland life in the Ryedale Folk Museum at Hutton-le-Hole. The Beck Isle Museum in Pickering provides an insight into the life of a country market town and just a few miles down the road you'll find Malton, once a Roman fortress, and nearby Castle Howard, the setting for Brideshead Revisited.

York

Wherever you turn within the city's medieval walls, you will find glimpses of the past. The splendours of the 600-year old Minster, the grim stronghold of Clifford's Tower, the National Railway Museum, the medieval timbers of the Merchant Adventurers' Hall and the fascinating Jorvik Viking Centre all offer an insight into the history of this charming city.

Throughout the city, statues and monuments remind the visitor that this was where Constantine was proclaimed Holy Roman Emperor, Guy Fawkes was born and Dick Turpin met his end.

Modern York is has excellent shopping, a relaxed cafe culture, first class restaurants and bars, museums, tours and attractions. Whether you visit for a romantic weekend or a fun-filled family holiday, there really is something for everyone.

Leeds & West Yorkshire

For centuries cloth has been spun from the wool of the sheep grazing in the Pennine uplands and the fascinating story of this industrial heritage can be seen in the numerous craft centres and folk museums throughout West Yorkshire.

Bradford was a major industrial centre and this can be seen in the number of converted wool, cotton and other textile mills in the area. Salts Mill is a Grade II Listed historic mill building built in 1853 by Sir Titus Salt along with the village to house his workers, in what is now an area of architectural and historical interest. Not far from Haworth is Bingley, where the Leeds & Liverpool canal makes its famous uphill journey, a route for the coal barges in days gone by, nowadays replaced by holidaymakers in gaily painted boats. Leeds itself is a vibrant city with its Victorian shopping arcades, Royal Armories Museum and lively arts scene.

Yorkshire Coastline

The Yorkshire coastline is one of the UK's most naturally beautiful and rugged, where pretty fishing villages cling to rocky cliffs, in turn towering over spectacular beaches and family-friendly seaside destinations.

At the northern end of the coastline, Saltburn is a sand and shingle beach popular with surfers and visitors can ride the Victorian tram from the cliff to the promenade during the summer. Whitby is full of quaint streets and bestowed with a certain Gothic charm. At Scarborough, one of Britain's oldest seaside resorts, the award-winning North Bay and South Bay sand beaches are broken by the rocky headland, home to the historic Scarborough Castle. Filey, with its endless sands, has spectacular views and a 40-mile stretch of perfect sandy beach sweeps south from the dramatic 400 ft high cliffs at Flamborough Head. Along this coastline you can find the boisterous holiday destination of Bridlington, or a gentler pace at pretty Hornsea and Withernsea.

East Yorkshire

From cosmopolitan Hull to the hills and valleys of the Yorkshire Wolds, East Yorkshire is wonderfully diverse. A landscape of swirling grasslands, medieval towns, manor houses and Bronze Age ruins contrasting with the vibrant energy and heritage of the Humber. The Wolds are only a stones throw from some great seaside resorts and Beverley, with its magnificent 13th century minster and lattice of medieval streets, is just one of the many jewels of architectural heritage to be found here. Hull is a modern city rebuilt since the war, linked to Lincolnshire via the impressive 1452 yd Humber Bridge.

South Yorkshire

The historic market town of Doncaster was founded by the Romans and has a rich horseracing and railway heritage. The area around Sheffield - the steel city - was once dominated by the iron and steel industries and was the first city in England to pioneer free public transport. The Industrial Museum and City Museum display a wide range of Sheffield cutlery and oplate. Today, Meadowhall shopping centre, with 270 stores under one roof, is a must-visit for shopaholics.

Visit – Yorkshire

 Attractions with this sign participate in the Visitor Attraction Quality Assurance Scheme.

North Yorkshire

Flamingo Land Theme Park and Zoo
Malton, North Yorkshire YO17 6UX
0871 911 8000
www.flamingoland.co.uk
One-price family funpark with over 100 attractions, 5 shows and Europe's largest privately-owned zoo.

The Forbidden Corner
Middleham, Leyburn, North Yorkshire DL8 4TJ
(01969) 640638
www.theforbiddencorner.co.uk
The Forbidden Corner is a unique labyrinth of tunnels, chambers, follies and surprises created within a four acre garden in the heart of Tupgill Park and the Yorkshire Dales.

Grassington Festival
June - July, Grassington, North Yorkshire
www.grassington-festival.org.uk
15 days of music and arts in the Yorkshire Dales.

Malton Food Lovers Festival
May, Malton, North Yorkshire
www.maltonyorkshire.co.uk
Fill up on glorious food and discover why Malton is considered 'Yorkshire's Food Town' with mountains of fresh produce.

North Yorkshire Moors Railway
Pickering, North Yorkshire YO18 7AJ
(01751) 473799
www.nymr.co.uk
Take a classic steam train from Pickering to Grosmont on the famous North Yorkshire Moors Railway for breathaking scenery.

Ripon International Festival
September, Ripon, North Yorkshire
www.riponinternationalfestival.com
A festival packed with music events, solo dramas, intriguing theatre, magic, fantastic puppetry, literary celebrities, historical walks - and more!

Scarborough Castle
Scarborough, North Yorkshire YO11 1HY
www.english-heritage.org.uk
(01723) 372451
One of the finest tourist attractions in Yorkshire, with its 3,000 year history, stunning location and panoramic views over the dramatic Yorkshire coastline.

Scarborough Jazz Festival
September, Scarborough, North Yorkshire
www.jazz.scarboroughspa.co.uk
A variety and range of jazz acts with a balanced programme of predominantly British musicians, with the addition of a few international stars.

Scarborough Seafest
July, Scarborough, North Yorkshire
www.discoveryorkshirecoast.com
Celebrating Scarborough's maritime heritage with seafood kitchen cooking demonstrations, exhibitor displays and musical performances.

Swaledale Festival
May - June, Various locations, North Yorkshire
www.swaledale-festival.org.uk
The award-winning Festival is an annual celebration of music and arts in the beautiful landscape of the three northernmost Yorkshire Dales - Swaledale, Wensleydale and Arkengarthdale. A Varied programme of top-quality events, individually ticketed, realistically priced, and spread over two glorious weeks.

The Walled Garden at Scampston
Malton, North Yorkshire YO17 8NG
(01944) 759111
www.scampston.co.uk
Set within the 18th century walls of the original kitchen garden for Scampston Hall, an exciting 4 acre contemporary garden. Created by Piet Oudolf, with striking perennial meadow planting as well as traditional spring/autumn borders.

Whitby Abbey
Whitby, North Yorkshire, YO22 4JT
(01947) 603568
www.english-heritage.org.uk/whitbyabbey
Perched high on a cliff, it's easy to see why the haunting remains of Whitby Abbey were inspiration for Bram Stoker's gothic tale of 'Dracula'. Recently named Britain's most romantic ruin, Whitby Abbey is bursting with history just waiting to be explored.

York

Fairfax House
York, North Yorkshire, YO1 9RN
(01904) 655543
www.fairfaxhouse.co.uk
Fairfax House is one of the finest Georgian houses in England, ready to transport you straight back to Georgian England with magnificent architect designed John Carr, changing exhibitions and a range of special events.

JORVIK Viking Centre
York, North Yorkshire YO1 9WT
(01904) 615505
www.jorvik-viking-centre.co.uk
Travel back 1000 years on board your time machine through the backyards and houses to the bustling streets of Jorvik. JORVIK Viking Centre also offers four exciting exhibitions and the chance to actually come face to face with a 'Viking'.

York Early Music Festival
July, York, North Yorkshire
www.ncem.co.uk
The 2015 festival takes as its starting point the 600th anniversary of the Battle of Agincourt and features cross-currents between France and England from the Middle Ages through to the Baroque.

York Boat Guided River Trips
North Yorkshire YO1 7DP
(01904) 628324
www.yorkboat.co.uk
Sit back, relax and enjoy a drink from the bar as the sights of York city and country sail by onboard a 1 hour Guided River Trip along the beautiful River Ouse with entertaining live commentary delivered by the local and knowledgeable skippers.

York Minster
York, North Yorkshire YO1 7JN
(0)1904 557200
www.yorkminster.org
Regularly voted one of the most popular things to do in York, the Minster is not only an architecturally stunning building but is a place to discover the history of York over the centuries, its artefacts and treasures.

Yorkshire Air Museum
York, North Yorkshire YO41 4AU
(01904) 608595
www.yorkshireairmuseum.org
The Yorkshire Air Museum is based on a unique WWII Bomber Command Station with fascinating exhibits and attractive award-winning Memorial Gardens. In addition to its role as a history of aviation museum, the Yorkshire Air Museum is also home to The Allied Air Forces Memorial.

Leeds & West Yorkshire

The Bronte Parsonage Museum
Haworth, West Yorkshire BD22 8DR
(01535) 642323
www.bronte.org.uk
Stop off at Haworth, home of the Bronte sisters, to visit The Bronte Parsonage museum and experience the rugged atmosphere of Wuthering Heights.

Eureka! The National Children's Museum
Halifax, West Yorkshire HX1 2NE
(01422) 330069
www.eureka.org.uk
Eureka! The National Children's Museum is a magical place where children play to learn and grown-ups learn to play.

Harewood House
Leeds, West Yorkshire LS17 9LG
(0113) 218 1010
www.harewood.org
Harewood House, Bird Garden, Grounds and Adventure Playground - The Ideal day out for all the family.

Haworth 1940's Weekend
May, Haworth, West Yorkshire
www.haworth1940sweekend.co.uk
A fabulous weekend celebrating and comemorating the 1940s.

The Henry Moore Institute
Leeds, LS1 3AH
(0113) 246 7467
www.henry-moore.org/hmi
Discover sculpture in Leeds. Feel inspired in three beautiful gallery spaces with an ever-changing programme of exhibitions accompanied by tours, talks and events which explore sculpture from ancient to modern.

Leeds City Museum
Leeds, LS2 8BH
(0113) 224 3732
www.leeds.gov.uk/museumsandgalleries/Pages/
Leeds-City-Museum
Leeds City Museums offers six galleries to visit and lots of fun, interactive learning for all the family.

Leeds Festival
August, Wetherby, Leeds
www.leedsfestival.com
From punk and metal, through rock, alternative and indie to dance, Leeds offers music fans a chance to see hot new acts, local bands, huge stars and exclusive performances.

Lotherton Hall & Gardens
Leeds, West Yorkshire LS25 3EB
(0113) 378 2959
www.leeds.gov.uk/lothertonhall
Lotherton is a charming Edwardian house and country estate set in beautiful grounds.

National Coal Mining Museum for England
Wakefield, West Yorkshire WF4 4RH
(01924) 848806
www.ncm.org.uk
Based at the site of Caphouse Colliery in Overton the National Coal Mining Museum offers an exciting and enjoyable insight into the working lives of miners through the ages.

Pontefract Liquorice Festival
July, Wakefield, West Yorkshire
www.yorkshire.com
The festival celebrates this unusual plant, the many wonderful products created from it and its historic association with the town.

Royal Armouries Museum
Leeds, West Yorkshire LS10 1LT
(0133) 220 1999
www.royalarmouries.org
Over 8,000 objects displayed in five galleries - War, Tournament, Oriental, Self Defence and Hunting. Among the treasures are Henry VIII's tournament armour and the world record breaking elephant armour. Regular jousting and horse shows.

Salt's Mill
Saltaire, West Yorkshire BD18 3LA
(01274) 531163
www.saltsmill.org.uk
Shopping, dining and art in one glorious building... Salt's Mill is an art gallery, shopping and restaurant complex inside a converted former mill, built by Sir Titus Salt.

Xscape Castleford
Castleford, West Yorkshire WF10 4TA
(01977) 664 794
www.xscape.co.uk
The ultimate family entertainment awaits! Dine, bowl, snow, skate, climb, movies, shop, dance on ice!

York Gate Garden
Leeds LS16 8DW
0113 267 8240
www.perennial.org.uk/garden/york-gate-garden
Tucked away behind the ancient church in Adel, on the northern outskirts of Leeds, York Gate is a garden of immense style and craftsmanship, widely recognised as one of the most innovative small gardens of the period.

East Yorkshire

East Riding Rural Life Museum
Beverley, East Yorkshire HU16 5TF
(01482) 392780
www.museums.eastriding.gov.uk
Working early 19th century four-sailed Skidby Windmill, the last working mill in Yorkshire, plus Museum of East Riding Rural Life.

RSPB Bempton Cliffs Reserve
Bridlington, East Riding of Yorkshire YO15 1JF
(01262) 422212
www.rspb.org.uk
A family favourite, and easily the best place in England to see, hear and smell seabirds! More than 200,000 birds (from April to August) make the towering chalk cliffs seem alive.

Skipsea Castle
Hornsea, East Riding of Yorkshire YO15 3NP
0870 333 1181
www.english-heritage.org.uk/daysout/properties/skipsea-castle/
The remaining earthworks of a motte-and-bailey castle dating from before 1086 and among the first raised in Yorkshire.

Treasure House and Art Gallery
Beverley, East Riding of Yorkshire HU17 8HE
(01482) 392790
www.museums.eastriding.gov.uk/treasure-house-and-beverley-art-gallery
Art gallery and museum with historic exhibitions. The Treasure House tower provides splendid views over the rooftops of Beverley.

Wilberforce House
Hull, East Riding of Yorkshire HU11NQ
(01482) 300300
www.hullcc.gov.uk/museums
Slavery exhibits, period rooms and furniture, Hull silver, costume, Wilberforce and abolition.

South Yorkshire

Barnsley Market
Barnsley, South Yorkshire, S70 1SX
(01226) 772238
www.barnsley.gov.uk
Barnsley Markey boats over 300 stalls including local butchers, fishmongers and grocers and a huge variety of craft, cosmetics, antiques and much more. Every day except Thursdays.

Brodsworth Hall and Gardens
Doncaster, South Yorkshire DN5 7XJ
(01302) 722598
www.english-heritage.org.uk/brodsworth
One of England's most complete surviving Victorian houses. Inside many of the original fixtures & fittings are still in place, although faded with time. Outside the 15 acres of woodland & gardens have been restored to their 1860's heyday.

Cannon Hall Farm
Barnsley, South Yorkshire, S75 4AT
(01226) 790427
www.cannonhallfarm.co.uk
Cannon Hall Farm is a family-run farm filled with animal magic. Watch out for special events, new arrivals, and one of the best farm shops around with both local and worldwide produce.

Doncaster Racecourse
Leger Way, Doncaster DN2 6BB
(01302) 304200
www.doncaster-racecourse.co.uk
The St Leger at Doncaster Racecourse is the oldest classic horse race in the world, and the town celebrates in style with a whole festival of events.

Magna Science Adventure Centre
Rotherham, South Yorkshire S60 1DX
(01709) 720002
www.visitmagna.co.uk
Magna is the UK's 1st Science Adventure Centre set in the vast Templeborough steelworks in Rotherham. Fun is unavoidable here with giant interactives.

RSPB Old Moor Nature Reserve
Barnsley, South Yorkshire S73 0YF
(01226) 751593
www.rspb.org.uk
Whether you're feeling energetic or just fancy some time out visit Old Moor to get closer to the wildlife.

Sheffield Botanical Gardens
South Yorkshire S10 2LN
(0114) 268 6001
www.sbg.org.uk
Extensive gardens with over 5,500 species of plants, Grade II Listed garden pavillion.

Sheffield: Millennium Gallery
South Yorkshire S1 2PP
(0114) 278 2600
www.museums-sheffield.org.uk
One of modern Sheffield's landmark public spaces, the Gallery always has something new to offer.

Tourist Information Centres

When you arrive at your destination, visit the Tourist Information Centre for quality assured help with accommodation and information about local attractions and events, or email your request before you go.

Aysgarth Falls	Aysgarth Falls National Park Centre	01969 662910	aysgarth@yorkshiredales.org.uk
Beverley	34 Butcher Row	01482 391672	beverley.tic@eastriding.gov.uk
Bradford	Brittainia House	01274 433678	bradford.vic@bradford.gov.uk
Bridlington	25 Prince Street	01262 673474 / 01482 391634	bridlington.tic@eastriding.gov.uk
Brigg	The Buttercross	01652 657053	brigg.tic@northlincs.gov.uk
Cleethorpes	Cleethorpes Library	01472 323111	cleetic@nelincs.gov.uk
Danby	The Moors National Park Centre	01439 772737	moorscentre@northyorkmoors.org.uk
Doncaster	Blue Building	01302 734309	tourist.information@doncaster.gov.uk
Filey	The Evron Centre	01723 383637	fileytic2@scarborough.gov.uk
Grassington	National Park Centre	01756 751690	grassington@yorkshiredales.gov.uk
Halifax	The Piece Hall	01422 368725	halifax@ytbtic.co.uk
Harrogate	Royal Baths	01423 537300	tic@harrogate.gov.uk
Hawes	Dales Countryside Museum	01969 666210	hawes@yorkshiredales.org.uk
Haworth	2/4 West Lane	01535 642329	haworth.vic@bradford.gov.uk
Hebden Bridge	New Road	01422 843831	hebdenbridge@ytbtic.co.uk
Holmfirth	49-51 Huddersfield Road	01484 222444	holmfirth.tic@kirklees.gov.uk
Hornsea	Hornsea Museum	01964 536404	hornsea.tic@eastriding.gov.uk
Horton-in-Ribblesdale	Pen-y-ghent Cafe	01729 860333	mail@pen-y-ghentcafe.co.uk
Huddersfield	Huddersfield Library	01484 223200	huddersfield.information@kirklees.gov.uk

Hull	1 Paragon Street	01482 223559	tourist.information@hullcc.gov.uk
Humber Bridge	North Bank Viewing Area	01482 640852	humberbridge.tic@eastriding.gov.uk
Ilkley	Town Hall	01943 602319	ilkley.vic@bradford.gov.uk
Ingleton	The Community Centre Car Park	015242 41049	ingleton@ytbtic.co.uk
Knaresborough	9 Castle Courtyard	01423 866886	kntic@harrogate.gov.uk
Leeds	The Arcade	0113 242 5242	tourinfo@leedsandpartners.com
Leeming Bar	The Yorkshire Maid, 88 Bedale Road	01677 424262	thelodgeatleemingbar@btconnect.com
Leyburn	The Dales Haven	01969 622317	
Malham	National Park Centre	01969 652380	malham@ytbtic.co.uk
Otley	Otley Library & Tourist Information	01943 462485	otleytic@leedslearning.net
Pateley Bridge	18 High Street	0845 389 0177	pbtic@harrogate.gov.uk
Reeth	Hudson House, The Green	01748 884059	reeth@ytbtic.co.uk
Richmond	Friary Gardens	01748 828742	hilda@richmondtouristinformation.co.uk
Ripon	Minster Road	01765 604625	ripontic@harrogate.gov.uk
Rotherham	40 Bridgegate	01709 835904	tic@rotherham.gov.uk
Scarborough	Brunswick Shopping Centre	01723 383636	scarborough2@scarborough.gov.uk
Scarborough (Harbourside)	Harbourside TIC	01723 383636	scarborough2@scarborough.gov.uk
Selby	Selby Library	0845 034 9540	selby@ytbtic.co.uk
Settle	Town Hall	01729 825192	settle@ytbtic.co.uk
Sheffield	Unit 1 Winter Gardens	0114 2211900	visitor@marketingsheffield.org
Skipton	Town Hall	01756 792809	skipton@ytbtic.co.uk
Sutton Bank	Sutton Bank Visitor Centre	01845 597426	suttonbank@northyorkmoors.org.uk
Todmorden	15 Burnley Road	01706 818181	todmorden@ytbtic.co.uk
Wakefield	9 The Bull Ring	0845 601 8353	tic@wakefield.gov.uk
Wetherby	Wetherby Library & TIC	01937 582151	wetherbytic@leedslearning.net
Whitby	Langborne Road	01723 383637	whitbytic@scarborough.gov.uk
Withernsea	Withernsea Lighthouse Museum	01964 615683 / 01482 486566	withernsea.tic@eastriding.gov.uk
York	1 Museum Street	01904 550099	info@visityork.org

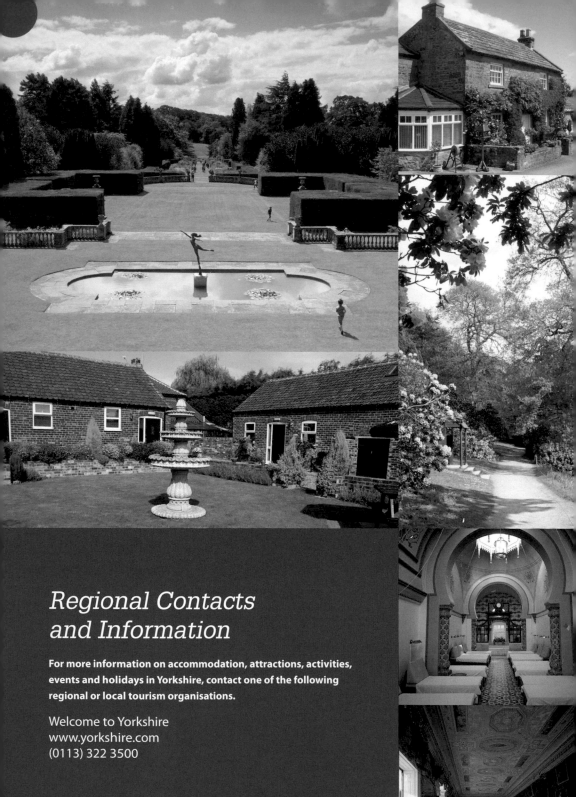

Regional Contacts and Information

For more information on accommodation, attractions, activities, events and holidays in Yorkshire, contact one of the following regional or local tourism organisations.

Welcome to Yorkshire
www.yorkshire.com
(0113) 322 3500

Stay – Yorkshire

Entries appear alphabetically by town name in each county. A key to symbols appears on page 7

BEVERLEY, East Yorkshire   Map ref 4C1   S

Heron Lakes

Contact: Mrs Lynne Lakin, Reception, Heron Lakes, Main Road, Routh, Beverley HU17 9SL
T: (01964) 545968 / 07966 805593 **E:** lynne@heron-lakes.co.uk
W: www.heron-lakes.co.uk

Units	5
Sleeps	4

PER UNIT PER WEEK
£430.00 - £850.00

SPECIAL PROMOTIONS
Please contact us for prices or view our website.

Peaceful and tranquil are some of the words that can only describe the wonderful lodge breaks here at Heron Lakes set in 75 acres of beautiful landscaped lakes and woodland. Heron lakes has been sympathetically designed to encourage wildlife and we are very proud of the fact that we have been given a Silver Award for Conservation from Professor David Bellamy and the Puffin Award from the Yorkshire Wildlife Trust.

Open: All year
Nearest Shop: 2 miles
Nearest Pub: 0.5 Miles

Units: All units have a twin room and a double with en suite, fully fitted kitchens and large decking areas.

Site: ✿ P **Payment:** 💷 **Leisure:** ♪ ▶ ∪ **Property:** 🐕 🖥 🔲 📶 **Children:** ⛳
Unit: 🔲 🔲 🖥 🔲 🍴 📺 🔲 📀

BEVERLEY, East Yorkshire   Map ref 4C1   S

Horseshoe Cottage & Bay Tree

Contact: Louise Martin, Owner/Manager, Fawley House, 7 Nordham, North Cave, East Yorkshire HU15 2LT **T:** (01430) 422266 / 07951745033 **E:** louisem200@hotmail.co.uk
W: www.nordhamcottages.co.uk

Units	2
Sleeps	2-5

PER UNIT PER WEEK
£305.00 - £795.00

Charming former gardener's cottages to Fawley House, with south facing courtyard garden. A memorable welcome assured from your helpful host. Instant access to stunning Wolds countryside. Shops & pubs close by. Coast, town, & city all in easy reach.
HORSESHOE & BAY TREE are on the quiet street of Nordham, N Cave, close to Beverley. H:sleeps 5 +2 with 2 baths, & B:2. Can interlink.2 mins off M62 **Open:** All year **Nearest Shop:** 240m
Nearest Pub: 390m

NORTH DALTON, *East Yorkshire* Map ref 4C1 **S**

★★★
SELF CATERING

| Units | 1 |
| Sleeps | 1-4 |

PER UNIT PER WEEK
£255.00 - £440.00

SPECIAL PROMOTIONS
Short breaks available, 2 nights (excluding Christmas, New Year, Easter and Bank Holidays - 4 days min).

Old Cobbler's Cottage

Contact: Ms Chris Wade, Waterfront Cottages, 2 Mere Cottages, Star Row, North Dalton, Driffield, East Yorkshire YO25 9UX **T:** (01377) 219901 / 07801 124264 **F:** 01377 217754 **E:** chris.wade@adastra-music.co.uk **W:** www.waterfrontcottages.co.uk **£ BOOK ONLINE**

19th century, mid-terraced, oak-beamed cottage on the edge of a picturesque pond in a peaceful and friendly farming village, between York and Yorkshire's Heritage Coast. The cottage has a small garden for sitting in with BBQ facilities. Dining area and main bedroom look directly over the pond - where the local ducks can be watched from! Open fire. Ideally located for walking, visiting the coast, historic houses, races at York and Beverley and Hockney country. Excellent pub serving meals adjacent, which welcomes dogs and children. Up to 2 pets welcome, free of charge. Parking at the cottage.

Open: All year
Nearest Shop: 3 miles
Nearest Pub: 0.10 miles

Units: Double bedroom and single bedroom (with opportunity for a Z Bed), Shower room and toilet on ground floor. Drying area in entrance.

Site: ✿ P Payment: 🖃 Leisure: ▶ Property: 🐾 🖥 🗄 🍳 Children: 🧸 🛏 🔔
Unit: 🖃 🗄 🍳 📺 ⊞ 📀 🏊 BBQ 📞

ALLERSTON, *North Yorkshire* Map ref 5D3 **S**

★★★★
SELF CATERING

| Units | 3 |
| Sleeps | 1-6 |

PER UNIT PER WEEK
£364.00 - £630.00

The Old Station

Contact: Carol Benson, Proprietor, The Old Station, Main Street, Allerston, Pickering YO18 7PG **T:** (01723) 859024 / 07799 766963 **E:** oldstationallerston@gmail.com **W:** www.theoldstationallerston.co.uk

Three railway carriage conversions at a former village station. Modern conveniences, countryside views, proprietors on hand in station house. This unique accommodation provides an excellent base from which to explore North Yorkshire's countryside, coast and attractions. Allerston is situated on the edge of the North York Moors National Park and Dalby Forest, just 12 miles from the coast.
Open: All year except January 2016 **Nearest Shop:** 3 miles **Nearest Pub:** 0.7 mile

Site: ✿ P Leisure: ▶ Property: 🗄 🍳 Children: 🧸 🛏 🔔 Unit: 🗄 🖃 🍳 📺 📀 BBQ

For **key to symbols** see page 7

DANBY, North Yorkshire   Map ref 5C3   S

VisitEngland
★★★
SELF CATERING

Clitherbecks Farm

Contact: Catherine Harland, Proprietor, Clitherbecks Farm, Danby, Whitby,
North Yorkshire YO21 2NT **T:** (01287) 660321 **E:** enquiries@clitherbecks.co.uk
W: www.clitherbecks.co.uk

Units	1
Sleeps	1-7

PER UNIT PER WEEK
£240.00 - £410.00

Dwelling mentioned in Doomsday Book. Present building built in 1780. Self-contained accommodation with separate entrance. Two bedrooms that can comfortably sleep 7 people. Shared bathroom.
Downstairs is one living room with central heating and coal fire adjoining a kitchen with electric cooker, microwave, and a fridge-freezer.
Towels and bedding are provided. Heating and electric are included in the price with the exception of coal and wood for which there will be an additional charge. You have your own entrance through a fenced in garden.

Open: All year
Nearest Shop: 1 mile (supermarket 3 miles)
Nearest Pub: 1 mile

Units: " bedrooms, 1 bathroom, Living room and kitchen. You have the run of one third of an old farmhouse with your own entrance & fenced in garden.

Site: ✿ P Property: ☆ 🚲 🔲 🍴 Children: ☇ Unit: 🔲 📺 🍴 BBQ

Crows Nest Caravan Park

Crows Nest Caravan Park, Gristhorpe, Filey, North Yorkshire YO14 9PS
T: (01723) 582206 **E:** enquiries@crowsnestcaravanpark.com
W: www.crowsnestcaravanpark.com **£ BOOK ONLINE**

🚐 (50)	£20.00-£35.00
🚏 (50)	£20.00-£35.00
⛺ (200)	£20.00-£35.00
🏠 (40)	£320.00-£630.00

Crows Nest Caravan Park is located on the beautiful Yorkshire coast between Scarborough and Filey, it is the ideal park to enjoy these two great seaside towns and their glorious sandy beaches.

Privately owned and operated by the Palmer family, this award winning park is the perfect base for families and couples wishing to explore one of England's finest holiday destinations.

Directions: 2 miles north of Filey, 5 miles south of Scarborough. Just off A165 main road, turn off at roundabout with Jet petrol station.

Open: March 1st - October 31st.

Site: 🅿️ **Payment:** ☀️ **Leisure:** ➤ 🎯 **Children:** 🐴 **Catering:** ✖️ **Park:** 🐕 🎵 **Touring:**

Filey Holiday Cottages

Contact: Amanda Robinson, Filey Holiday Cottages, West Flotmanby, Muston, Filey YO14 0HY **T:** 07981 371910 **E:** info@fileyholidaycottages.co.uk
W: www.fileyholidaycottages.co.uk **£ BOOK ONLINE**

Units   14
Sleeps   1-5

PER UNIT PER WEEK
£300.00 - £645.00

SPECIAL PROMOTIONS
3-4 night stays from
£180 - £350

Fourteen cottages converted from stables many with original beams. The cottages are located outside the village of Muston close to the coastal town of Filey overlooking the Vale of York. We have 6 cottages catering for families up to 4 people, 3 cottages catering for families up to 5 people, 4 cottages catering for families up to 3 people and 1 cottage for couples.

We have spacious, safe grassy areas for children to play alongside our play area and for older children we have a games room with a pool table and WiFi. We are pet friendly too and offer 4 of our cottages for guests with pets.

Open: All year
Nearest Shop: 3 miles
Nearest Pub: 3 miles

Units: All our cottages have open plan living areas

Site: P **Payment:** **Leisure:** ➤ 🔌 **Property:** 🐕 **Children:** 🐴 **Unit:** 📺 BBQ

FILEY, North Yorkshire *Map ref 5D3*   SatNav YO14 0PU **C**

Orchard Farm Holiday Village

Stonegate, Hunmanby, Filey YO14 0PU
T: (01723) 891582 / 07790 426129 **F:** 01723 891582
E: info@orchardfarmholidayvillage.co.uk **W:** www.orchardfarmholidayvillage.co.uk

⊟	£18.00-£26.00
⊟	£18.00-£26.00
Å (25)	£14.00-£26.00
⬛ (7)	£279.00-£989.00
60 touring pitches	

Family park in edge-of-village location with easy access to resorts of Filey, Scarborough and Bridlington. Amenities include children's play area, fishing lake and entertainment during peak season. **Directions:** From A165 from Scarborough take 1st right to Hunmanby under railway bridge 1st right. **Open:** March to October.

Site: 🏠 **Payment:** ☼ **Leisure:** ♪ ▶ ♪ ⚲ ☂ **Children:** ⛷ ⚠ **Catering:** ☕ **Park:** 🐾 ♫ ⬛ ⬛ 🔥
Touring: 🚽 🚿 🔌

GIGGLESWICK, North Yorkshire *Map ref 5B3*   **S**

Ivy Cottage (Giggleswick) Limited

Contact: David & Betty Hattersley, 22 Malvern Drive, Woodford Green IG8 0JW
T: (020) 8504 8263 **E:** info@ivycottagegiggleswick.co.uk
W: www.ivycottagegiggleswick.co.uk **£ BOOK ONLINE**

Units   1
Sleeps   6

PER UNIT PER WEEK
£295.00 - £595.00

SPECIAL PROMOTIONS
Short Breaks and Special Offers by arrangement.

A bright and well maintained stone cottage in the centre of Giggleswick village, sleeping 6 in two doubles and one twin-bedded room. The upstairs bathroom is by Villeroy & Bosch with a separate shower unit, whilst downstairs there is a second WC and a clothes drying area. There is also central heating, an open fire, private parking and a cycle store.

For your leisure there is a flat screen TV in both kitchen and lounge, Wi-Fi, an iPod dock and a library of local books and maps.

The ancient church and two inns with restaurants are close by and a walk into Settle takes around ten minutes.

Open: All year
Nearest Shop: 0.80 miles
Nearest Pub: 0.05 miles

Units: Ivy Cottage (Giggleswick) Limited is a family owned business established in 1987.

Site: ✿ P **Payment:** € **Leisure:** ♿ ▶ **Property:** ▦ ⬛ ▣ **Children:** ⛷⁵ **Unit:** ⬛ ⬛ 📺 ⬛ ⬛ ⌖ 📺 📀 ◿ ☎

GIGGLESWICK, North Yorkshire *Map ref 5B3*   **S**

Pendle View Holiday Apartment

Contact: Mrs Chris Chandler, Owner, Pendle View Holiday Apartment, 2 Pendle View, Giggleswick, Settle BD24 0AZ **T:** (01729) 822147 / 0787 9643878
E: pendleview@hotmail.com **W:** www.settleholiday.co.uk

Units   1
Sleeps   2-3
PER UNIT PER WEEK
£280.00 - £340.00

Pendle View is a spacious, self-contained, garden flat with a kitchen, living room, bedroom and shower room. It is the lower ground floor of a grade II listed early Victorian semi-detached house, stone-built in the local style. It has car parking and patio. **Open:** All year except Christmas and New Year **Nearest Shop:** 1 mile
Nearest Pub: 0.01 miles

Site: ✿ P **Property:** ▦ ▣ **Children:** ⛷ ▥ 🔥 **Unit:** ⬛ ⬛ 📺 ⬛ ⌖ 📺 📀

HARROGATE, *North Yorkshire* Map ref 4B1 **S**

VisitEngland ★★★★ SELF CATERING

Units 14
Sleeps 2-4
PER UNIT PER WEEK
£392.00 - £658.00

Ashness Apartments

Contact: Hazel Spinlove, Ashness Apartments, 15 St Marys Avenue, Harrogate HG2 0LP
T: (01423) 526894 **F:** 01423 700038 **E:** office@ashness.com
W: www.ashness.com **£ BOOK ONLINE**

High quality apartments, superbly situated in a nice, quiet road of fine Victorian townhouses very near the town centre of Harrogate. Well equipped with high speed wired and wireless internet throughout. Excellent shops, restaurants and cafes are a short walk away through Montpellier Gardens with the Stray, Valley Gardens, Royal Hall and Conference Centre just around the corner. **Open:** All year **Nearest Shop:** 0.10 miles **Nearest Pub:** 0.10 miles

Site: **P** Payment: ☒ Property: // ⚘ 🖥 📶 Children: ⛱ 🛏 ♿ Unit: 🖥 📺 🖥 🍴 TV 🎧 DVD 📞

HELMSLEY, *North Yorkshire* Map ref 5C3 **S**

VisitEngland ★★★★ SELF CATERING

Units 1
Sleeps 1-4
PER UNIT PER WEEK
£265.00 - £450.00

Townend Cottage

Contact: Mrs Margaret Begg, Owner, Townend Farmhouse, High Lane, Beadlam, Nawton, York YO62 7SY **T:** (01439) 770103 **E:** margaret.begg@ukgateway.net
W: www.townendcottage.co.uk

A very warm, comfortable, oak beamed stone cottage. Off main road 3 miles from charming market town of Helmsley. Ideal for walking/touring moors, coast and York. Cosy log fire. Special offers available for low season short breaks. Minimum stay 2 nights £120, 3 nights £180. **Open:** All year **Nearest Shop:** 3 miles **Nearest Pub:** 0.25 miles

Site: ⚘ **P** Leisure: 🎵 ▶ ⛳ Property: ⚘ 🖥 📶 Children: ⛱ 🛏 ♿ Unit: 🖥 🖥 📺 🖥 🍴 TV 🎧 DVD ✎

HELMSLEY, *North Yorkshire* Map ref 5C3 **S**

VisitEngland ★★★★ SELF CATERING

Units 1
Sleeps 1-4
PER UNIT PER WEEK
£395.00 - £495.00

Tykes Cottage

Contact: Mrs. Laura Barry, Proprietor, 8 Bondgate Mews, Bondgate, Helmsley, North Yorkshire YO62 5EU **T:** (0113) 2869735 / 07879448391 **E:** lpbarry@btinternet.com
W: www.tykescottage.co.uk

Superbly equipped modern 2 bedroom stone 'Mews' cottage, (sleeps 4) with gardens to the front and rear. BBQ seating and sun deck. Set in a quiet location 5 mins. stroll from the picturesque market square. Private parking, all linen and electric included. An ideal base from which to explore the area. **Open:** All year round **Nearest Shop:** 100 yards **Nearest Pub:** 400 yards

Site: ⚘ **P** Payment: ☒ Property: 🖥 📶 Children: ⛱ 🛏 ♿ Unit: 🖥 🖥 📺 🖥 🍴 TV 🎧 DVD BBQ

HUTTON-LE-HOLE, *North Yorkshire* Map ref 5C3 **S**

VisitEngland ★★★ SELF CATERING

Units 1
Sleeps 1-5
PER UNIT PER WEEK
£284.00 - £598.00

Primrose Hill Farmhouse

Contact: Nigel Custance, Booking Enquiries, Primrose Hill Farm, Hutton-le-Hole, North Yorkshire YO62 6UA **T:** (01751) 417752 / 07929 188661
E: nigel.custance@btinternet.com **W:** www.primrosehillfarmhouse.com **£ BOOK ONLINE**

Delightful cottage style farmhouse in a stunning village and overlooking the beck. From your parking and enclosed garden at the rear, enjoy the owner's fields with their sheep and horses. Great place to relax, walk, bike, visit the Moors & coast. Sleeps 5 in two bedrooms with Kingsize beds. Farmhouse kitchen with dishwasher, washing machine, tumble drier, cooker and microwave. Freesat TV & Wi-Fi.
Open: All year **Nearest Shop:** 3 miles **Nearest Pub:** 0.5 miles

Site: ⚘ **P** Payment: € Leisure: ♿ 🎵 ▶ ⛳ Property: ⚘ 🖥 📶 Children: ⛱ 🛏 ♿ Unit: 🖥 🖥 📺 🖥 🍴 TV 🎧 DVD ✎

INGLEBY GREENHOW, North Yorkshire   Map ref 5C3   S

Ingleby Manor

Contact: Christine Bianco, Ingleby Manor, Ingleby Greenhow, Great Ayton TS9 6RB
T: (01642) 722170 **E:** christine@inglebymanor.co.uk
W: www.inglebymanor.co.uk

Units   6
Sleeps   2-6

PER UNIT PER WEEK
£343.00 - £887.00

SPECIAL PROMOTIONS
Special winter breaks 4
nights for the
price of 3.

5% discount on
bookings confirmed
before Christmas.

5% discount on second
and subsequent weeks
of bookings in the
same summer season.

Ingleby Manor, once the home of a Courtier of Henry VIII, is an important 16th century Grade II*
Listed building in 50 acres of beautiful formal gardens and woodland, with a trout stream in a
peaceful hidden valley in the North York Moors National Park.

Spacious apartments and cottages individually designed with appropriate furnishings, log fires and
full central heating, fully equipped kitchens with dishwasher, clothes washer and dryer, etc. Ingleby
Manor has been awarded 5 Star Gold Award from VisitEngland for 'Exceptional quality of
accommodation and customer service'.

Open: All year
Nearest Shop: 3 miles
Nearest Pub: 0.5 miles

Units: 4 apartments in the Manor House itself, 3
ground floor and suitable for accompanied
disabled guests. 2 separate cottages sleep 4
each.

Site: ✿ P Payment: 💷 € Leisure: ⚓ ♪ ☋ Property: ◪ 🐾 🖼 🗄 🗐 Children: 🛝 🛏 ⚲
Unit: 🛏 🖥 📺 🌀 TV DVD 🔥 BBQ 📞

KIRKBYMOORSIDE, North Yorkshire   Map ref 5C3   S

Cowldyke Farm

Contact: Mrs Janet Benton, Owner, Salton Road, Great Edstone, Kirkbymoorside, York,
North Yorkshire YO62 6PE **T:** (01751) 431242 **E:** janetbenton@btconnect.com
W: www.cowldyke-farm.co.uk

Units   6
Sleeps   2-6
PER UNIT PER WEEK
£230.00 - £570.00

Our family cottages sleeping 2 or more, are all rated 4 star and are
very spacious. All are tastefully decorated, spotlessly clean, cosy,
and warm. Three cottages have the added attraction of an open fire
or a log burning stove in addition to the central heating. There is
plenty to see and do on the farm. Down by the river is a good place
for a bit of wildlife spotting. Bring your fly fishing rod.
Open: All Year **Nearest Shop:** 4 miles **Nearest Pub:** 4 miles

Site: ✿ P Leisure: ♪ Property: 🗐 🗄 Children: 🛝 Unit: 🛏 🖥 📺 🌀 TV DVD 🔥 BBQ

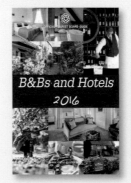

4★ - 5★
SELF CATERING

Surprise View Cottage, Field Barn Cottage & Lowna Farmhouse

Contact: Mrs Ruth Wass, Surprise View Cottages, Sinnington Lodge, Sinnington, York YO62 6RB **T:** (01751) 431345 **E:** info@surpriseviewcottages.co.uk
W: www.surpriseviewcottages.co.uk **£ BOOK ONLINE**

Units	3
Sleeps	1-8

PER UNIT PER WEEK
£310.00 - £1260.00

SPECIAL PROMOTIONS
Short breaks available all year round in the farmhouse except for school holidays, 3 day breaks in the smaller cottages November, December, January & February.

Lowna Farmhouse and 2 Barn conversions; historic location, originally old mill and tannery, giving panoramic views over moorland edge and immediate access to field and woodland walks. Warm, roomy accommodation with quality furnishings and fittings. A wealth of beams and original stone and brick features. 'Comfort' is the key word. Tranquillity is assured at Surprise View Cottages; in the heart of the countryside yet central for touring, walking, cycling. Whether it's history, scenery, wildlife, pub life or farm activities - you'll find it here!

Open: All year
Nearest Shop: 3 miles
Nearest Pub: 1 mile

Units: Three cottages, two smaller units sleeping 4, large farmhouse sleeping up to 8.

Site: ❋ P Leisure: 🎣 🏌 ⛵ 🚣 Property: 🐕 ⌨ 📺 📶 Children: 🍼 🛏 🚼
Unit: 🚪 🍽 📺 📶 📺 ④ 📀 🔥 BBQ 📞

★★★★
SELF CATERING

Old Reading Room

Contact: The Wood Family, Proprietor, Lastingham Grange, Lastingham, North Yorkshire YO62 6TH **T:** (01751) 417345 **F:** 01751 417358 **E:** reservations@lastinghamgrange.com
W: www.lastinghamgrange.com **£ BOOK ONLINE**

Units	1
Sleeps	1-5

PER UNIT PER WEEK
£300.00 - £500.00

SPECIAL PROMOTIONS
Please phone us or visit our website.

A three bedroom holiday cottage located in the historic village of Lastingham, a peaceful backwater in the heart of the North York Moors National Park. Lastingham is a perfect centre for the Moors and the Dales, ruined abbeys and castles, the ancient city of York and the coast, with its smugglers' coves and its long sandy Beaches, a mere twenty or so miles away.

The Cottage has a ground floor sitting room, dining room and kitchen then on the first floor, two double bedrooms and one single bedroom and bathroom with bath and walk in shower. Linen and towels are provided.

Open: All year
Nearest Shop: 5 miles
Nearest Pub: 0.10 miles

Units: Ground floor sitting room, dining room and kitchen. First floor, three bedrooms (2 double, 1 single) and bathroom with bath and walk in shower.

Site: P Payment: 💳 Leisure: ⛵ 🚣 Property: ⌨ 📺 📶 Children: 🍼 🛏 🚼 Unit: 🚪 🍽 📺 📶 📺 📀 📞

LITTLE BARUGH, North Yorkshire   Map ref 5C3   S

Stainers Farm Cottages

Contact: Jackie Smith, Stainers Farm Cottages, Stainers Farm, Little Barugh YO17 6UY
T: (01653) 668224 / 07879 636979 **E:** info@stainersfarm.co.uk
W: www.stainersfarm.co.uk **£ BOOK ONLINE**

Units   5
Sleeps 4-10
PER UNIT PER WEEK
£295.00 - £1150.00

Renovated country cottages with individual character and charm in a peaceful rural setting with wonderful views of open countryside. 1 pet allowed by arrangement, friendly cottage, Wi-Fi available.
Open: All year **Nearest Shop:** 5 miles
Nearest Pub: 1.5 miles

Site: ❀ Property: ▦ ▤ ▦ Children: ⛱ ▥ ⚲ Unit: ▯ ▤ ▣ ▣ ▣ ∅ BBQ

MALTON, North Yorkshire   Map ref 5D3   S

Home Farm Holiday Cottages

Contact: Mrs Rachel Prest, Owner, The Old Fold, Railway Street, Slingsby, York YO62 4AL
T: (01653) 628277 / 07803 186941 **E:** rachelprest@yahoo.co.uk
W: www.yorkshire-holiday-cottage.co.uk

Units   2
Sleeps 4-6
PER UNIT PER WEEK
£345.00 - £630.00

Attractive single storey, ground floor, stone barn conversions in a lovely village setting. The spacious cottages are furnished and equipped to a very high standard with the inclusion of antique and mellow pine and co ordinating fabrics and furnishings. Ideally situated for moors, coast and York. Three miles from Castle Howard.
Open: All Year **Nearest Shop:** 400m **Nearest Pub:** 100m

Site: ❀ P Property: ▦ ▤ ▦ Children: ⛱ ▥ ⚲ Unit: ▯ ▤ ▣ ▣ ▣ ▣ ∅ ☎

Walnut Garth

Contact: Cas Radford, Proprietor, Walnut Garth, c/o Havendale, High Street, Swinton, Malton YO17 6SL **T:** (01653) 691293 / 07766 208348 **F:** 01653 691293
E: cas@walnutgarth.co.uk **W:** www.walnutgarth.co.uk

Units 1
Sleeps 1-4

PER UNIT PER WEEK
£227.00 - £447.00

SPECIAL PROMOTIONS
£25 discount for stays
of 2 weeks or longer.

Tastefully decorated, two-bedroom cottage furnished to a high standard with all modern conveniences. Set in owner's grounds at edge of Swinton village, yet only 2 miles from market town of Malton with excellent selection of local amenities and attractions. Easy access to York, coast and Moors. Gym on site. £25 discount for stays of 2 weeks or longer. Christmas cake, pudding & 'Winter Warmer' for Christmas weeks.

Open: All year
Nearest Shop: 0.25 miles
Nearest Pub: 0.25 miles

Units: All rooms are on the ground floor - floor plan available on website for further information.

Site: ✿ P Leisure: ♪ ∪ Property: ★ 🖥 🅱 🖳 Children: 🛏 ♿ ☖ Unit: 🗄 🖿 📠 🛢 🔌 📺 🅰 📀 BBQ 📞

Blackthorn Gate

Contact: Mrs Rita Corrigan, Blackthorn Gate, Eastfields Farm, Nunthorpe, Nr Stokesley, North Yorkshire TS7 0PB **T:** (01642) 324496 **E:** info@blackthorngate.co.uk
W: www.blackthorngate.co.uk **£ BOOK ONLINE**

Units 4
Sleeps 1-5

PER UNIT PER WEEK
£396.00 - £865.00

SPECIAL PROMOTIONS
Weekend and
midweek breaks
available. Friday to
Monday or Monday to
Friday.

Four Swedish designed two bedroomed log Lodges set in 230 acres of beautiful open farmland with stunning views of Roseberry Topping. A tranquil haven for your holiday, perfect for spotting wildlife and bird watching. Private on site fishing with 3 fully stocked ponds. Games Room with table tennis, bar football and pool table. Ideally situated for touring and walking in North Yorkshire and the Tees Valley. Larger Lodges wheelchair friendly with downstairs bathroom with wet room style shower.

Open: All year
Nearest Shop: 2 miles
Nearest Pub: 1.5 miles

Units: Living/dining room, fully fitted kitchen, master en suite, separate bathroom with sauna. Each Lodge has a bbq, veranda with garden furniture.

Site: ✿ P Payment: 💷 € Leisure: ♪ ▶ ∪ 🎣 Property: ★ 🖥 🅱 🖳 Children: 🛏 ♿ ☖
Unit: 🗄 🖿 📠 🔌 📺 📀 BBQ

PATELEY BRIDGE, North Yorkshire   Map ref 5C3   **S**

Helme Pasture Lodges & Cottages

Contact: Mrs Rosemary Helme, Helme Pasture Lodges & Cottages, Hartwith Bank, Summerbridge, Harrogate HG3 4DR **T:** (01423) 780279 **E:** info@helmepasture.co.uk **W:** www.helmepasture.co.uk

Units   4
Sleeps   2-10
PER UNIT PER WEEK
£225.00 - £795.00

Enjoy a comfortable stay in one of our genuine Scandinavian lodges or converted cottage. Situated in natural tranquil woodland. David Bellamy & Friends of the A.O.N.B. awards. Endless country walks. Markets, villages, abbeys and castles. Visit York, Harrogate, Skipton and Ripon. Warm welcome. **Open:** All year
Nearest Shop: 0.30 miles **Nearest Pub:** 0.30 miles

Site: ✿ P Payment: 🗜 € Leisure: 🎣 ⌚ ↻ Property: 🐾 🖥 🖳 Children: 🧸 Unit: 🍳 🍽 🖥 🗑 TV DVD BBQ 📞

PICKERING, North Yorkshire   Map ref 5D3   **S**

Kale Pot Cottage

Contact: Diane & Mike Steele, Kale Pot Cottage, Kale Pot Hole, Newtondale, Pickering, North Yorkshire YO18 8HU **T:** (01751) 476654 **E:** enquiries@northyorkmoorscottage.co.uk **W:** www.northyorkmoorscottage.co.uk

Units   1
Sleeps   2-5

PER UNIT PER WEEK
£325.00 - £625.00

SPECIAL PROMOTIONS
Weekend and mid week short breaks available November to February.

Comfortable, spacious, individual cottage situated in our paddock in beautiful Newtondale. A converted 18th century barn, the cottage is well equipped and completely restored. Stunning views of forest and the North York Moors. An ideal base for walking and mountain biking or just relaxing, with the North York Moors steam railway nearby. We are remote, but the market town of Pickering is just 10 miles away, Whitby and the coast 15 miles and historic York 35 miles. Owners living nearby.

Open: All year
Nearest Shop: 10 miles
Nearest Pub: 3 miles

Units: Kitchen, lounge and dining areas upstairs to take advantage of the views, double bedroom en suite, twin room with space for third bed, has its own wetroom.

Site: ✿ P Payment: € Leisure: 🚲 🎣 ↻ Property: 🐾 🖥 🖳 Children: 🧸 🛏 ⚲
Unit: 🍳 🍽 🖥 🗑 🎛 TV 🕐 DVD 🍷 BBQ 📞

RICHMOND, North Yorkshire   Map ref 5C3   **S**

Mount Pleasant Farm Cottages

Contact: Alison Pittaway, Owner, Whashton, Richmond, North Yorkshire DL11 7JP **T:** (01748) 822784 **E:** info@mountpleasantfarmhouse.co.uk **W:** www.mountpleasantfarmhouse.co.uk

Units   3
Sleeps   4
PER UNIT PER WEEK
£320.00 - £700.00

Mount Pleasant Farm is situated in the heart of lovely rolling countryside, with superb views over the Vale of York. The Parlour and The Dairy are two beautifully converted cottages, each with two bedrooms. For somewhere really special why not try The High Barn - set in its own grounds in a spectacular location, with breathtaking panoramic views, yet within walking distance of two beautiful villages. **Open:** Open all year **Nearest Shop:** 3 miles
Nearest Pub: 1 mile

Site: ✿ P Leisure: 🚲 🎣 ⌚ ↻ Property: 🚶 🐾 🖥 🖳 Children: 🧸 🛏 ⚲ Unit: 🍳 🍽 🖥 🗑 🍷 TV 🕐 DVD
BBQ

RICHMOND, North Yorkshire   Map ref 5C3   S

Natural Retreats - Yorkshire Dales

Contact: Aislabeck Plantation, Hurgill Road, Richmond, North Yorkshire DL10 4SG
T: (01625) 416 430 **E:** info@naturalretreats.com
W: www.naturalretreats.com **£ BOOK ONLINE**

Units	18
Sleeps	2-6

PER UNIT PFR WEEK
£525.00 - £1712.00

SPECIAL PROMOTIONS
Offers only available at
www.naturalretreats.
com

An ideal location for family holidays and just a stroll away from the quaint town of Richmond, Natural Retreats offer award-winning three bedroom lodges nestled into the rich green hills of the Yorkshire Dales, offering unbeatable views of the Swale Valley. Highlights include floor to ceiling windows, luxurious interiors and furnishings and wood burning stoves. Every guest also receives a complimentary welcome hamper containing delicious local produce such as bread, cheese and wine.

Open: All Year
Nearest Shop: 1.5 miles
Nearest Pub: 1.5 miles

Units: Open plan, three bedroom, ground floor residences, some have en suites for every bedroom, others family bathroom

Site: P Payment: ⊞ Leisure: ♪ ⚐ Property: ⫽ ⅋ ▦ ◨ ▣ Children: ⛾ ▦ ⚲
Unit: ▯ ⊟ ▣ ⊟ ⬚ ◉ ⊙ ⌀

ROSEDALE ABBEY, North Yorkshire   Map ref 5C3   S

Rosedale Abbey Holiday Cottages

Contact: Rosedale Abbey Caravan Park, Pickering, North Yorkshire YO18 8SA
T: (01723) 584311 **E:** info@flowerofmay.com
W: www.flowerofmay.com **£ BOOK ONLINE**

Units	5
Sleeps	2-4

PER UNIT PER WEEK
£258.00 - £540.00

SPECIAL PROMOTIONS
Short breaks are available, Friday to Monday or Monday to Friday. Short breaks from £194. Please visit the website or call us to check prices and availability.

The cottages and apartment are immaculately presented, beautifully furnished and equipped to a very high standard. In a peaceful village setting nestling in the North York Moors National Park. Ideal walking country within easy reach of Yorkshire's Heritage Coast. Many guests comment that they cannot wait to return to our cosy, comfortable cottages.

Open: All year
Nearest Shop: 0.05 miles
Nearest Pub: 0.10 miles

Site: ✿ P Payment: ⊞ Property: ⅋ ▦ ◨ ▣ Children: ⛾ ▦ ⚲ Unit: ▯ ▣ ◨ ▣ 📺 ⊙ ☏

Cayton Village Caravan Park Ltd

Mill Lane, Cayton Bay, Scarborough YO11 3NN
T: (01723) 583171 **E:** info@caytontouring.co.uk
W: www.caytontouring.co.uk

🚐 (235)	£14.00-£36.00
🚟 (20)	£16.00-£36.00
⛺ (55)	£14.00-£29.00
310 touring pitches	

Playground, recreation field, dog walk, shop and bus service from park entrance. Seasonal pitches, winter storage, caravan sales. Super sites, Hardstanding and grass pitches. Beach 0.5m, Scarborough 3m. Adjoining village with fish shop & pub.
Directions: From A64 take B1261 to Filey. In Cayton turn left onto Mill Lane. From A165 turn inland at Cayton Bay roundabout onto Mill Lane. 0.5m on RHS. **Open:** 1st March to 31st October.

f 𝕏

Site: ⚿🅿 **Payment:** 💳 ☼ **Leisure:** 🎵 ⮞ **Children:** ⛷ ⚠ **Catering:** 🛒 **Park:** 🐕 🚾 🔋 🅬
Touring: 🚰 🕒 🔌 ⚡

Flower of May Holiday Park

Flower of May Holiday Park, Lebberston, Scarborough, North Yorkshire YO11 3NU
T: (01723) 584311 **F:** 01723 585716 **E:** info@flowerofmay.com
W: www.flowerofmay.com **£ BOOK ONLINE**

🚐 (300)	£22.00-£28.00
🚟 (20)	£22.00-£28.00
⛺ (60)	£22.00-£28.00
🏠 (20)	£240.00-£690.00

SPECIAL PROMOTIONS
Early booking offer available please refer to be website. Short breaks also available.

Excellent family-run park. A family friendly indoor pool, adventure playground, bar complex, mini-market, fish & chip shop, cafe and more. Ideal for coast and country. Touring and Camping prices per pitch, per night includes four people and one car.

Luxury caravans for hire. Seasonal serviced pitches. Glamping Pods available for a unique experience (please check our website for prices).

Directions: From A64 take the A165 Scarborough/Filey coast road. Well signposted at Lebberston.   **Open:** Easter to October.

f 𝕏

Site: 🏕 ⚿🅿 **Payment:** 💳 ☼ **Leisure:** 🎵 🎣 🎿 **Children:** ⛷ ⚠ **Catering:** ✕ 🛒 **Park:** 🐕 🎵 🚾 🔋 🅬 🅿
Touring: 🕒 🔌 ⚡

Harbourside Apartments

Contact: Victoria Corrigan, Director, 16-18 Sandside, Scarborough, North Yorkshire YO11 1PE **T:** (01723) 500045 **E:** enquiries@escape2thesands.com
W: www.scarboroughapartments.co.uk

Units	5
Sleeps	2-4
PER UNIT PER WEEK	
£500.00 - £1000.00	

Harbourside apartments offer a traditional seaside holiday wrapped in wonderful contemporary luxury. These 4* Gold Apartments offer stunning views over Scarborough South bay and harbour. Within walking distance to the town centre and just a stones throw from the Beach. Harbourside Apartments are ideally located for couples or family holiday. **Open:** All year **Nearest Shop:** 0.5 miles **Nearest Pub:** 0.25 miles

Payment: 💳 **Leisure:** ⮞ **Property:** 🚾 🔋 🅬 **Children:** ⛷ 🛏 🧍 **Unit:** 🔋 🅬 🍳 📺

Jasmine Park

Cross Lane, Snainton, Scarborough YO13 9BE
T: (01723) 859240 **E:** enquiries@jasminepark.co.uk
W: www.jasminepark.co.uk **£ BOOK ONLINE**

VisitEngland
★★★★★
HOLIDAY, TOURING
& CAMPING PARK

🚐	(74)	£22.00-£37.00
🚑	(74)	£22.00-£37.00
⛺	(20)	£17.00-£37.00
🏠	(30)	£450.00-£700.00

94 touring pitches

Family-owned, tranquil park in picturesque countryside setting between Scarborough (8 miles) and Pickering. Superbly maintained facilities including our fantastic children's play area. Yorkshire Coast Caravan Park of the Year 2010. Tents and tourers welcome. Seasonal pitches and storage available. Luxury caravans for hire.

Directions: Turn south off the A170 in Snainton opposite the junior school at traffic lights. Signposted.

Open: March to October.

Payment: 💷 ☼ **Leisure:** 🚲 ♪ ▶ ∪ **Children:** 🐎 ⚠ **Catering:** 🍴 **Park:** 🐕 🖥 📶 📦 🔌 **Touring:** 🚰 🚿 ♨ ⚡ ♨

VisitEngland
★★★★★
SELF CATERING

VisitEngland
Gold
AWARD

The Sands Sea Front Apartments

Contact: Reservations Team, Escape 2 The Sands Ltd, The Sands, Scarborough, N Yorkshire YO12 7TN **T:** (01723) 364714 **F:** 01723 352364 **E:** enquiries@escape2thesands.com
W: www.escape2thesands.com **£ BOOK ONLINE**

Units	67
Sleeps	2-6

PER UNIT PER WEEK
£500.00 - £2500.00

SPECIAL PROMOTIONS
Out of season special offers available.

Stylish and contemporary, these 5-star luxury apartments have a magnificent location on Scarborough's North Bay, on Yorkshire's rugged and beautiful East Coast. The Sands award-winning apartments and have been given a 5-star Gold rating by VisitBritain. All apartments have unrivalled stunning sea views from your own private balcony, modern 5-star furnishings, flat-screen TVs, DVD players and designer kitchens. Internet access and car parking are available. Perfect for families, friends or couples.

Open: All year

Nearest Shop: 0.10 miles

Nearest Pub: 0.3 miles

Site: P Payment: 💷 **Leisure:** 🚲 ♪ ∪ **Property:** 🖥 📶 📺 📋 **Children:** 🐎 🛏 🧍
Unit: 🚿 🍴 📺 ♨ 🔌 📺 💿 📀

Units   3
Sleeps   1-5

PER UNIT PER WEEK
£320.00 - £740.00

White Acre & White Gable

Contact: David Squire, Manager, JG Squire Ltd, 15 Victoria Park, Scarborough, North Yorkshire YO12 7TS **T:** (01723) 374220 **E:** david@scarborough.co
W: www.scarborough.co **£ BOOK ONLINE**

Large, self-contained flats in the heart of the holiday area. Close to the beach and most holiday attractions. Own off street parking.

White Acre is well situated in the heart of the holiday area, near to the beach and Peasholm Park. The property stands alongside decorative gardens and enjoys lovely views of the Peasholm area. White Gable is quietly situated in one of the most desirable districts of Scarborough, directly opposite the golf course at Scalby Mills, close to the Sea-Life centre, sea-front promenade, beach, miniature railway and the open air theatre. White Gable has Wi-Fi.

Open: All year
Nearest Shop: 200m & 600m
Nearest Pub: 200m

Units: Each flat has own entrance; two bedrooms with flat-screen TV; lounge with 42 inch Plasma HD TV; Fitted Kitchen; Bathroom. No extras.

Site: P Property: 🏠 🔌 **Children:** ⌇ 🎠 ☂ **Unit:** 🛏 🖵 🔲 🍴 📺 📀

🚐 (38)   £20.00-£28.00
🚙 (38)   £20.00-£28.00
⛺ (38)   £15.00-£25.00
🏠 (15)   £195.00-£515.00
38 touring pitches

SPECIAL PROMOTIONS
Loyalty card available
for campers.

Robin Hood Caravan Park

Slingsby, York YO62 4AP
T: (01653) 628391 **F:** 01653 628392 **E:** info@robinhoodcaravanpark.co.uk
W: www.robinhoodcaravanpark.co.uk **£ BOOK ONLINE**

An award winning, privately owned park set in the heart of picturesque Ryedale. Peaceful and tranquil, a perfect base for families and couples wishing to explore the stunning countryside of North Yorkshire. Within easy reach of York, Castle Howard, Flamingoland and the coastal resorts of Scarborough, Whitby and Filey. Overnight holding area available.

Directions: Situated on the edge of Slingsby with access off the B1257 Malton to Helmsley road.

Open: March to October.

f 🐦

Payment: 💳 ☼ **Leisure:** 🎣 ☾ **Children:** ⌇ 🎢 **Catering:** 🛒 🍴 🍺 ☕ **Park:** 🐕 📧 🔲 ♿ 🛎 **Touring:** 🚿 ♿ 🚐

★★★ SELF CATERING
VisitEngland

| Units | 1 |
| Sleeps | 1-5 |

PER UNIT PER WEEK
£325.00 - £630.00

SPECIAL PROMOTIONS
Short breaks on request - mainly in Low Season or at short notice.

Pennysteel Cottage

Contact: Ms Chris Wade, Waterfront Cottages, 2 Mere Cottages, Star Row, North Dalton, Driffield, East Yorkshire YO25 9UX **T:** (01377) 219901 / 07801 124264 **F:** 01377 217754 **E:** chris.wade@adastra-music.co.uk **W:** www.waterfrontcottages.co.uk **£ BOOK ONLINE**

Old fisherman's cottage with original character and features, including beamed ceilings and wood panelled walls. All rooms and terrace overlooking the attractive harbour of Staithes and its lifeboat station. Sit and relax with the comfort of a log burning stove and watch the ships go past. Perfect for those with a romantic love of the past. Located off the main High Street in a quiet corner, just a couple of minutes from the beach, pubs, restaurant and shops. Ideal for walking (on the Cleveland Way long distance footpath) and the coast. Close to Whitby, Heartbeat Country, and the Moors.

Open: All year
Nearest Shop: 0.10 miles
Nearest Pub: 0.10 miles

Units: Kitchen, living and dining room on ground floor. Double bedroom, single bedroom and toilet on first floor. Twin attic room, shower and bathroom on second floor.

Site: ✿ **Payment:** 💷 **Leisure:** ♪ **Property:** 🐕 🖼 🔲 🔳 🔲 **Children:** 🐾 🛏 ⚹
Unit: 🔲 🔲 📺 🔲 🔳 📺 📀 ♪ BBQ ☎

For **key to symbols** see page 7

Yorkshire - North Yorkshire

Croft Farm Holiday Cottages

Contact: Emma Carpenter, Owner, Croft Farm, Ruswarp, Whitby, North Yorkshire YO21 1NY **T:** (01947) 825853 **E:** emma@croftfarm.com
W: www.croftfarm.com

Units 3
Sleeps 1-16
PER UNIT PER WEEK
£270.00 - £620.00

These superb cottages in the village of Ruswarp near Whitby are furnished to a very high standard with private parking and a friendly welcome. Short breaks are available and pets by arrangement. **Open:** Open all year. **Nearest Shop:** 50m
Nearest Pub: 150m

Site: **P** Property: Unit:

Fayvan Holiday Apartments

Contact: Benita and Michael Nicholson, 43 Crescent Avenue, West Cliff, Whitby, North Yorkshire YO21 3EQ **T:** (01947) 604813 / 07808 340871
E: fayvan.apartments@btinternet.com **W:** www.fayvan.co.uk **£ BOOK ONLINE**

Units 3
Sleeps 5
PER UNIT PER WEEK
£520.00 - £620.00

Fayvan Self-Catering Apartments all have stunning sea views and views of Crescent Gardens. These high quality apartments have been awarded 4 stars by VisitBritain and provide a perfect location for all Whitby has to offer. **Open:** All year round **Nearest Shop:** 400m **Nearest Pub:** 400m

Payment: Leisure: Property: Children: Unit:

Flask Inn Holiday Home Park

Contact: Blacksmiths Hill, Robin Hood's Bay, Whitby, North Yorkshire YO22 4QH **T:** (01947) 880592 **F:** 01947 880592 **E:** info@flaskinn.com
W: www.flaskinn.com

Units 10
Sleeps 4
PER UNIT PER WEEK
£290.00 - £520.00

Small, family-run 5 star site for over 30 years, in the North York Moors. All our holiday homes have central heating and double glazing throughout. All have a double bedroom en suite, Freeview TV, DVD, full kitchen with fridge/freezer and microwave. All holiday homes have outside decking and seating. Situated in the North Yorkshire Moors on the A171, 7 miles to Whitby, 12 miles to Scarborough and 4 miles to Robin Hood's Bay. **Open:** March to November.

Payment: Leisure: Property: Children:

WHITBY, *North Yorkshire* Map ref 5D3 **S**

Forest Lodge Farm

Contact: Peter & Kate Stannard, Owners, Forest Lodge Cottages, Castleton, Whitby, North Yorkshire YO21 2DZ **T:** (01287) 660024 / 07980 159071 **E:** pandkstannard@aol.com **W:** www.forestlodgecottages.co.uk **£ BOOK ONLINE**

Units 3
Sleeps 2-18

PER UNIT PER WEEK
£450.00 - £1300.00

SPECIAL PROMOTIONS
Friday to Monday and Monday to Friday breaks available. For other breaks please contact us. All 3 cottages can be booked together to sleep 18 plus infants.

In the North York Moors National Park, Forest Lodge is an organic farm with three luxury 5* Gold Award, Grade 2 Listed cottages around a flagged courtyard. Each cottage has its own garden/sitting area with table/chairs/BBQ and is surrounded by our meadows and open moorland with footpaths and bridleway from the farm. There is also a 2 acre field with slide/swings/play area with goalpost and badminton net and plentiful car parking on site. Beautiful sandy beaches are a short drive away at Whitby, Robin Hoods Bay, Runswick Bay and Saltburn. NYM Railway steam trains run from Whitby to Pickering.

Open: All year
Nearest Shop: 0.75 miles
Nearest Pub: 0.75 miles

Units: Dale House (8) 4 double, 2 and shower ground floor. North Range (6) 3 double, 1 ground floor. Coltus (4) 2 double, 1 en suite. All with underfloor heating.

Site: ✿ **P** Payment: 💳 Leisure: ▶ Property: 🖥 📖 🍴 Children: 🦮 🏊 🚸
Unit: 🛏 🍽 📺 🎞 📻 📺 💿 📀 🚿 **BBQ**

WHITBY, *North Yorkshire* Map ref 5D3 **S**

Lemon Cottage

Contact: Andy Martin, Park Manager, Northcliffe & Seaview Holiday Parks, Bottoms Lane, High Hawsker, Whitby YO22 4LL **T:** (01947) 880477 **E:** enquiries@northcliffe-seaview.com **W:** www.northcliffe-seaview.com **£ BOOK ONLINE**

Units 1
Sleeps 1-4
PER UNIT PER WEEK
£405.00 - £735.00

Lemon Cottage is a Gold Award 4 Star Holiday Cottage situated on our 5 Star Seaview Holiday Park. Sleeping 4 with 2 En suite bedrooms, a stunning interior and private sun terrace. Ground floor accommodation. Fabulous location with easy access to the beautiful Heritage Coast & Cinder Cycle Path. 3 Night weekend breaks from £250 & 4 night mid week breaks from £280. Free Wi-Fi
Open: 1st March - 7th November **Nearest Shop:** 1m
Nearest Pub: 800m

Site: **P** Payment: 💳 Leisure: ▶ 🏹 🎣 Property: 🍴 Children: 🦮 🏊 🚸 Unit: 🛏 🍽 📺 🎞 📻 📺 💿 📀

WHITBY, North Yorkshire   Map ref 5D3   **S**

Northcliffe & Seaview Holiday Parks

Contact: Northcliffe & Seaview Holiday Parks, Bottoms Lane, High Hawsker, Whitby, North Yorkshire YO22 4LL **T:** (01947) 880477 **E:** enquiries@northcliffe-seaview.com **W:** www.northcliffe-seaview.com **£ BOOK ONLINE**

Units 9
Sleeps 2-4

PER UNIT PER WEEK
£215.00 - £735.00

SPECIAL PROMOTIONS
Visit our website to view our new caravans for sale, check availability & book your holiday.

Register your email address to receive our 'special offers' by email.

These award winning parks are situated on the beautiful Heritage Coast twixt Whitby and RHB. Both Gold Award Conservation parks have fabulous countryside and coastal views with access to superb walks and a cycle track.

We sell and hire luxurious caravans, have a 4 Star Gold Award cottage and an exclusive seasonal only touring park. Facilities include free Wi-fi, play parks, football pitches and lots more.

Open: March 1st until November 7th.

Payment: ⊞ **Leisure:** ♿ ♪ ↑ ∪ ♣ **Property:** 🖥 🗄 **Children:** 🛝

YORK, North Yorkshire   Map ref 4C1   **S**

44 Postern Close

Contact: Mrs Christine Turner, Booking Enquiries, 44 Postern Close, Meadowcroft, Millfield, Willingham, Cambridge CB24 5HD **E:** 44posternclose@gmail.com **W:** www.yorkholidayflat.co.uk

Units 1
Sleeps 1-2
PER UNIT PER WEEK
£325.00 - £450.00

One double-bedroomed apartment, within the prestigious Bishops Wharf Riverside development. Five minutes walking distance from city centre. Sitting/dining room, kitchen, bathroom, small balcony and parking space. No smoking. **Open:** All year **Nearest Shop:** 5 mins walk **Nearest Pub:** 2 mins walk

Site: P Payment: ⊞ **Leisure:** ♿ ♪ ↑ **Property:** ∥ 🖥 🗄 **Unit:** 🗄 🖥 🗄 🗄 📺 📀

YORK, North Yorkshire   Map ref 4C1   SatNav YO61 1RY   **C**

Alders Caravan Park

Home Farm, Monk Green, Alne nr Easingwold, York YO61 1RY
T: (01347) 838722 **E:** enquiries@homefarmalne.co.uk
W: www.alderscaravanpark.co.uk

🚐 (87)   £20.00-£22.00
🚏   £20.00-£22.00
⛺   £20.00
🛖 (4)   £40.00-£45.00
87 touring pitches

A working farm in historic parkland where visitors may enjoy peace and tranquillity. York (on bus route), Moors, Dales and coast nearby. Tastefully landscaped, adjoins village cricket ground. Woodland walk.
Camping pods availabile.
Directions: From A19 exit at Alne sign, in 1.5 miles turn left at T-junction, 0.5 miles park on left in village centre.
Open: March to October.

Site: 🏕 **Payment:** ⊞ ☼ **Leisure:** ♪ ↑ ∪ **Children:** 🛝 **Catering:** 🍴 **Park:** 🐕 🗄 🛎 🛒 **Touring:** 🚿 🚻 ♨

YORK, North Yorkshire Map ref 4C1 S

The Blue Rooms

Contact: Mrs Kirsty Wheeldin, Executive Manager, The Blue Rooms, 4 Franklins Yard, Fossgate, York YO1 9TN **T:** (01904) 673990 **F:** 01904 658147 **E:** info@thebluebicyle.com **W:** www.thebluebicyle.com **£ BOOK ONLINE**

Units   6
Sleeps   1-4
PER UNIT PER WEEK
£875.00 - £1400.00

Beautifully decorated apartments, some with wood beam ceilings, four poster beds and views over the River Foss. Guests will be welcomed on arrival with a complimentary bottle of champagne and fruit basket. Guests also receive a breakfast platter for each morning of their stay which they prepare at their leisure in the fully fitted kitchen in each apartment. Each apartment also includes a fridge full of complimentary mixers, fruits juices, soft drinks, beers and milk. **Open:** All year **Nearest Shop:** 0.10 miles **Nearest Pub:** 0.10 miles

Site: P Payment: ⊞ **Leisure:** 🚴 ♪ ▶ ∪ **Property:** 🖥 **Children:** 🎠 **Unit:** 🗄 🗄 📺 🖨 🔧 📺 🎦 📀 ☎

YORK, North Yorkshire Map ref 4C1 SatNav YO61 1ET C

Goosewood Holiday Park

Sutton on the Forest, York, North Yorkshire YO61 1ET
T: (01347) 810829 **F:** 01347 811498 **E:** info@flowerofmay.com
W: www.flowerofmay.com **£ BOOK ONLINE**

🚐 (90)   £22.00-£28.00
🚅 (10)   £22.00-£28.00
🏠 (5)   £369.00-£1099.00
🚐 (14)   £193.00-£820.00

SPECIAL PROMOTIONS
Early booking offer available please refer to be website. Short breaks also available.

A quiet, peaceful park with fishing lake, children's adventure play area and leisure complex with indoor pool, bar and games room. Luxury holiday lodges and lodge-style holiday homes, many with hot tubs available to hire. A perfect place to relax and ideal for visiting the historic city of York and surrounding beauty spots of Yorkshire. A warm welcome. For bookings please call 01723 584311 or book online

Directions: North of York. Follow route to Strensall.

Open: March - 2nd January.

Site: 🏕 🅰🄿 **Payment:** ⊞ ☼ **Leisure:** ♪ 🎣 🎯 **Children:** 🎠 🎢 **Catering:** ✕ 🍴 **Park:** 🐕 🍴 🖨 🛢 🔥 **Touring:** 🚽 🚿 ⚡ 🚿

YORK, North Yorkshire Map ref 4C1 S

Manor Farm Cottages

Contact: Liz Stephenson, Owner, SP Stephenson Ltd, Manor Farm, Goodmanham, York YO43 3JA **T:** (01430) 873510 / 07779 246214 **E:** info@manorfarm-cottages.co.uk **W:** www.manorfarm-cottages.co.uk

Units   2
Sleeps   1-6
PER UNIT PER WEEK
£350.00 - £600.00

Deep in the heart of rural East Yorkshire, Manor Farm Cottages are beautiful retreats overlooking the stunning Yorkshire Wolds. The single storied cottages have adjacent parking with level access. **Open:** All year **Nearest Shop:** 1 mile **Nearest Pub:** 0.20 miles

Site: ⚘ **P Property:** 🖥 🖨 🖥 **Children:** 🎠 🪑 🪜 **Unit:** 🗄 🗄 📺 🖨 🔧 📺 📀 BBQ

Minster's Reach Apartments

Contact: Jill Aspin, Minster's Reach, High Newbiggin Street, York YO31 7RD
T: 07793 942003 **E:** jill@yorkcityholidaylets.co.uk
W: www.yorkcityholidaylets.co.uk **£ BOOK ONLINE**

Units   4
Sleeps   1-5

PER UNIT PER WEEK
£400.00 - £800.00

SPECIAL PROMOTIONS
We offer weekly stays
and short weekend or
midweek breaks.

We are very flexible, so
please get in touch
and we can arrange
your stay!

Regular special offers
can be found on our
website.

Minster's Reach is our collection of beautifully luxurious, 4 Star Gold holiday apartments, centrally located in York within our private walled courtyard. They provide a private, relaxing setting for your visit to York - everything you need for a home from home experience, and all in reach of York Minster.

Choose between our ground floor apartments with their private garden areas, or our first floor loft style apartments. Each apartment has been decorated to a high standard, with modern fittings and furniture throughout. Situated in the midst of everything the Historical City of York has to offer.

Open: All year
Nearest Shop: Less than 50 metres
Nearest Pub: Less than 50 metres

Units: All apartments within a private courtyard. Two have 1 bedroom (sleep 4), and two have 2 bedrooms (sleep 5), all have modern bathrooms and kitchens.

Site: ✿ Payment: 💳 Property: ∥ 🖥 📶 🛜 Children: 🧒 🛏 🎢 Unit: 📺 🗄 📺 🍽 📶 📺 📀 BBQ ☏

Pavilion Cottage

Contact: Heidi Whitaker, Pavilion Cottage, Shipton Road, York YO30 5RE
T: (01904) 639258 / 07974 853876 **F:** 01904 636051 **E:** handiwhitaker5@gmail.com
W: www.pavilioncottage-holidayinyork.co.uk **£ BOOK ONLINE**

Units   1
Sleeps   4-10
PER UNIT PER WEEK
£1100.00 - £1300.00

A warm welcome with flowers and a tea tray on arrival awaits you at Pavilion Cottage. The cottage sleeps ten adults comfortably, has wonderful views over neighbouring cricket pitches and open countryside, yet lies close enough to walk to York city centre. The cottage also benefits from free parking for up to three cars. Staying here is like being in the countryside with the benefits of a city.
Open: All year **Nearest Shop:** 0.5 miles **Nearest Pub:** 0.5 miles

Site: ✿ P Payment: € Leisure: 🚴 ⚓ ♨ Property: 🐕 🖥 📶 🛜 Children: 🧒 🛏 🎢 Unit: 📺 🗄
📺 🍽 📶 📺 📀 BBQ

The Riverside York

Contact: Patrick Lavers, 8/8a Peckitt Street, York YO1 9SF **T:** (01904) 623008 / 07734 554755 **F:** 01904 656588 **E:** relax@riverside-york.co.uk
W: www.riverside-york.co.uk **£ BOOK ONLINE**

Units   2
Sleeps   2-8
PER UNIT PER WEEK
£590.00 - £1390.00

Situated in the heart of historic York, our beautiful 5-star Victorian riverside townhouse and apartment offers the perfect luxury self-catering base. The Riverside House offers three double bedrooms and spacious living with Digital Freeview, DVD, Wii console and free parking. The Riverside Apartment has one large kingsize bedroom, with generous ground floor living space, bathroom and kitchen.
Open: All year **Nearest Shop:** 300 yards **Nearest Pub:** 150 yards

Site: P Payment: 💳 Property: ∥ 🖥 📶 🛜 Children: 🧒 🛏 🎢 Unit: 📺 🗄 📺 🗄 🍽 📶 📺 📀

YORK, North Yorkshire   Map ref 4C1   S

York Lakeside Lodges

Contact: Mr Neil Manasir, Booking Enquiries, York Lakeside Lodges, Moor Lane, York YO24 2QU **T:** (01904) 702346 / 07831 885824 **E:** neil@yorklakesidelodges.co.uk
W: www.yorklakesidelodges.co.uk

Units   16
Sleeps   2-7
PER UNIT PER WEEK
£260.00 - £895.00

Lodges and cottages around a large fishing lake, in parkland yet two miles from the city centre with Tesco and a coach service to city centre just over the road. **Open:** All year **Nearest Shop:** 0.10 miles **Nearest Pub:** 0.60 miles

Site: ❁ P Leisure: ♪ ∪ Property: ♞ ⌨ ▦ Children: ⛱ ▦ ☂ Unit: ▦ ▦ TV ◉ BBQ ✆

PENISTONE, South Yorkshire   Map ref 4B1   S

Moor Royd House

Contact: Janet Hird, Booking Enquiries, Moor Royd House, Manchester Road, Millhouse Green, Sheffield S36 9FG **T:** (01226) 763353 **F:** 01226 763353
E: info@moorroydhouse.co.uk **W:** www.moorroydhouse.co.uk

Units   3
Sleeps   1-8

'The Other Side' and 'The Old Farmhouse' are at Moor Royd House, as is the guest suite which can take two more people. Peak District National Park only one mile away. **Open:** All year
Nearest Shop: 1 mile **Nearest Pub:** 1 mile

Site: ❁ P Leisure: ♿ ♪ ∪ Property: ♞ ⌨ ▦ Children: ⛱ ▦ ☂ Unit: ▦ ▦ ▦ TV ◉ BBQ

SHEFFIELD, South Yorkshire   Map ref 4B2   S

Pat's Cottage

Contact: John & Robbie Drakeford, 110 Townhead Road, Dore, Sheffield S17 3GB
T: (01142) 366014 / 07850 200711 **E:** johnmdrakeford@hotmail.com
W: www.patscottage.co.uk **£ BOOK ONLINE**

Units   1
Sleeps   4-6
PER UNIT PER WEEK
£295.00 - £470.00

An attractive 18th century stone cottage, sympathetically refurbished, retaining original features including black beams. Use of owners swimming pool included in season. On the edge of the Peak District and the city of Sheffield.
Open: All year **Nearest Shop:** 0.30 miles **Nearest Pub:** 0.30 miles

Site: ❁ P Leisure: ♪ ∪ ⚒ Property: ♞ ⌨ ▦ Children: ⛱ ▦ Unit: ▦ ▦ TV BBQ

HALIFAX, West Yorkshire   Map ref 4B1   S

Windmill Court Cottages

Contact: Keighley Road, Ogden, Halifax, West Yorkshire HX2 8YB **T:** (01422) 244941
E: info@windmillcourt.co.uk
W: www.windmillcourt.co.uk

Units   4
Sleeps   4-6
PER UNIT PER WEEK
£400.00 - £650.00

An ideal base for exploring Yorkshire, a cosy and comfortable welcome awaits. Set in semi rural setting. Close to local beauty spots Ogden water for walking. Open views. Lots of good parking. Near to Haworth Bronte Country-Skipton-York-Yorkshire Dales-Halifax. Horse riding golf fishing walking. Also do two and three day break - please email or ring for a quote. Goose Cottage rated 4*.
Open: All year **Nearest Shop:** 1.5 miles **Nearest Pub:** 100 yards

Site: ❁ P Payment: £ € Leisure: ♿ ♪ ► ∪ Property: ⁄⁄ ♞ ⌨ ▦ Children: ⛱ ▦ ☂ Unit: ▦ ▦ ▦ TV BBQ

Don't Miss...

Blackpool Illuminations
Sept-Nov, Blackpool
www.illuminations.visitblackpool.com
This world famous display lights up Blackpool's promenade with over
1 million glittering lights that will make you oooh and aaah in wonder.
Head for the big switch on or buy tickets for the Festival Weekend.
There's also Blackpool Zoo, the Pleasure Beach Resort and fabulous
entertainment at the Blackpool tower. Whether you're nine or 90, there
are plenty of things to do in Blackpool day and night, all year round.

Chester Zoo
Cheshire CH2 1LH
(01244) 380280
www.chesterzoo.org
Over 12000 animals and 400 different species, including some of the
most exotic and endangered species on the planet in 125 acres of award-
winning zoological gardens. Chester Zoo is one of the world's top zoos,
and the UK's number one wildlife attraction, with over the 1.4 million
visitors every year..

Jodrell Bank Discovery Centre
Macclesfield, Cheshire SK11 9DL
(01477) 571766
www.jodrellbank.net
A great day out for all the family, explore the wonders of the universe
and learn about the workings of the giant Lovell Telescope. Start your
visit in the Planet Pavillion by exploring our place in the universe with
the clockwork Orrery. Discover how Jodrell Bank scientists use radio
telescopes to learn more about distant objects in space in the Space
Pavilion exhibition, listen to the sound of the Big Bang, and find out
about 'Big Telescopes' via a range of hands-on activities.

Muncaster Castle
Ravenglass, Cumbria CA18 1RQ
(01229) 717614
www.muncaster.co.uk
Medieval Muncaster Castle is a treasure trove of paintings,
silver, embroideries and more in acres of Grade 2 woodland gardens,
famous for rhododendrons and breathtaking views of the
Lake District. The Great Hall, octagonal library and elegant dining room
must not be missed. Elegant rooms, historic furnishings, superb works of
art, yet still a lived-in home. The audio tour, narrated by the Pennington
family, whose ancestors have been at Muncaster for 8 centuries, enlivens
the castle, bringing the past to the present.

Tate Liverpool
Merseyside L3 4BB
(0151) 702 7400
www.tate.org.uk/liverpool
Housing the national collection of modern art in the North in beautiful
light filled galleries, Tate Liverpool is one of the largest galleries of
modern and contemporary art outside London. Major exhibitions in
recent years have included the work of Jackson Pollock, Andy Warhol
and René Magritte. Free to visit except for special exhibitions. The Tate
Liverpool café offers a range of refreshments with views of the historic
Albert Dock.

North West

Cheshire, Cumbria, Lancashire,
Greater Manchester, Merseyside

The breathtaking scenery of the Lake District dominates the North West, but urban attractions such as cosmopolitan Manchester and Liverpool, with its grand architecture and cultural credentials, have much to recommend them. Further afield, you can explore the Roman and Medieval heritage of Chester, discover Lancashire's wealth of historic houses and gardens, or make a date for one of the huge variety of events that take place in this region throughout the year.

Cumbria

Lancashire

Greater Manchester

Merseyside

Cheshire

Explore – North West

Cheshire

The charms of the old walled city of Chester and the picturesque villages that dot Cheshire's countryside contrast sharply with the industrial towns of Runcorn and Warrington. Iron age forts, Roman ruins, Medieval churches, Tudor cottages and elegant Georgian and Victorian stately homes are among the many attractive sights of the county. South Cheshire, like Cumbria to the north, has long been the home of the wealthy from Manchester and Liverpool and boasts a huge selection of of excellent eateries. It also has peaceful, pretty countryside, and is within easy reach of the wilder terrain of the Peak District and North Wales.

Cumbria

In this lovely corner of England, there is beauty in breathtaking variety. The area is loved by many who come back time and again to its inspirational magic, brilliant blue lakes and craggy mountain tops. The central Lake District with its mountains, lakes and woods is so well known that there is a tendency to forget that the rest of Cumbria contains some of the most varied and attractive landscape in Britain. In the east of the county, the peaceful Eden Valley is sheltered by the towering hills of the Pennines, with charming little red sandstone villages and reminders of the Roman occupation everywhere. Alston, with its cobbled streets is the highest town in England, and has been used for numerous TV location sets.

Cumbria's long coastline is full of variety with rocky cliffs, sea birds, sandy estuaries, miles of sun-trap sand dunes and friendly harbours. In Autumn the deciduous woodlands and bracken coloured hillsides glow with colour. In Winter, the snow covered mountain tops dazzle magnificently against blue skies. In Spring, you can discover the delights of the magical, constantly changing light and the joy of finding carpets of wild flowers.

The Lake District is an outdoor enthusiasts paradise offering everything from walking and climbing to orienteering, potholing, cycling, riding, golf, sailing, sailboarding, canoeing, fishing and waterskiing. A great way to take in the beauty of this unique area is to plan your own personal route on foot, or cycle one of the many formal trails such as the Cumbria Cycle Way.

The Cumbrian climate is ideal for gardens and the area is famous for the rhododendrons and azaleas which grow here in abundance.

If you fancy a break from the great outdoors there is a wealth of historic houses, from small cottages where famous writers have lived to stately homes, that have seen centuries of gracious living and architectural importance.

Lancashire

Lancashire's Forest of Bowland is an area of outstanding natural beauty with wild crags, superb walks, streams, valleys and fells.

Blackpool on the coast has been the playground of the North West for many years and still draws millions of holiday makers every year, attracted to its seven miles of beach, illuminations, Pleasure Beach Amusement Park and golf. Morecambe, Southport, Lytham St Annes and Fleetwood also offer wide beaches, golf and bracing walks.

Lancaster, a city since Roman times, has fine museums, a castle and an imitation of the Taj Mahal, the Ashton Memorial.

Manchester

Manchester's prosperity can be traced back to the 14th century when Flemish weavers arrived to transform a market town into a thriving boom city at the forefront of the Industrial Revolution.

Now known as The Capital of the North, the city is rich in culture with plenty of galleries, museums, libraries and theatres. The City Art Gallery displays its famous pre-Raphaelite collection while the Halle Orchestra regularly fills the Bridgewater Hall.

At Granada Studios you can still tour the set of Coronation Street and you can find quality shopping locations and sporting (particularly football) traditions. Cosmopolitan Manchester makes a great place to stay for a spot of retail therapy too!

Merseyside

Liverpool was an important city long before The Beatles emerged from their Cavern in the Swinging Sixties. It grew from a village into a prosperous port, where emigrants sailed for the New World and immigrants arrived from Ireland. Today the ocean going liners are fewer, but the revitalised dock complex ensures that the city is as vibrant as ever. Liverpool's waterfront regeneration flagship is the Albert Dock Village, which includes the Maritime Museum and Tate Gallery Liverpool. The city has two modern cathedrals, a symphony orchestra, plenty of museums and Britain's oldest repertory theatre The Playhouse.

In recent years, Liverpool has seen the opening of an extensive range of cafés, restaurants and accommodation to suit all tastes and budgets, as well as becoming a mecca for serious shoppers with locations such as the Metquarter and Liverpool ONE, the huge open-air shopping district that is home to more than 160 famous high street shops, cool independent boutiques, cafés and restaurants in the heart of the city centre.

Visit – North West

 Attractions with this sign participate in the Visitor Attraction Quality Assurance Scheme.

Cheshire

Anson Engine Museum
Macclesfield, Cheshire SK12 1TD
(01625) 874426
www.enginemuseum.org
Recognised as one of the Country's leading specialist museums; see exhibitions of engines of all sizes, as well as craft demonstrations, working machinery and local history exhibitions. A must-see for both enthusiasts and non-enthusiasts.

Arley Hall & Gardens
Northwich, Cheshire CW9 6NA
(01565) 777353
www.arleyhallandgardens.com
The Gardens are outstanding for their vitality, variety and historical interest and are particularly celebrated for the magnificent double herbaceous border. The Hall is an impressive example of a Victorian country house built in the Elizabethan style.

Catalyst Science Discovery Centre
Widnes, Cheshire WA8 0DF
(0151) 420 1121
www.catalyst.org.uk
Interactive science centre whose aim is to make science exciting and accessible to people of all ages.

Chester Cathedral
Cheshire CH1 2HU
(01244) 324756
www.chestercathedral.com
A must-see for Chester, a beautiful cathedral with a fascinating history.

Cholmondeley Castle Gardens
Malpas, Cheshire SY14 8AH
(0182) 720383
www.cholmondeleycastle.com
Visitors can enjoy the tranquil Temple Water Garden, Ruin Water Garden, memorial mosaic, Rose garden & many mixed borders.

Forest Live
July, Delamere Forest Cheshire, CW8 2JD
www.forestry.gov.uk
Hosted in seven different forest venues, Forest Live hosts some of the biggest names in the music industry. A fantastic outdoor concert for any music lover.

Go Ape! Hire Wire Forest Adventure - Delamere
Northwich, Cheshire CW8 2JD
(0845) 643 9215
www.goape.co.uk
Take to the trees and experience an exhilarating course of rope bridges, tarzan swings and zip slides.

Grosvenor Park Open Air Theatre
July-August, Grosvenor Park, Chester, Cheshire
www.grosvenorparkopenairtheatre.co.uk
The award winning Grosvenor Park Open Air Theatre is the greatest open air theatre experience outside of London. 2016 guarantees another summer of exciting performances.

Hare Hill Gardens
Macclesfield, Cheshire SK10 4PY
(01625) 584412
www.nationaltrust.org.uk/harehill
A small but perfectly formed and tranquil woodland garden, surrounded by parkland, with a delightful walled garden at its heart.

National Waterways Museum
Ellesmere Port, Cheshire CH65 4FW
(0151) 335 5017
www.canalrivertrust.org.uk
Unlock the wonders of our waterways at the National Waterways Museum, a fun and informative day out for all ages.

RHS Flower Show Tatton Park
July, Tatton Park, Knutsford, Cheshire
www.rhs.org.uk
A fantastic display of flora and fauna and all things garden related in stunning Cheshire countryside.

Cumbria

Great North Swim
June, Windermere, Cumbria
www.greatswim.org
Europe's biggest open water swim series comes to the Lake District.

Grizedale Forest Visitor Centre
Hawkshead, Cumbria LA22 0QJ
(01229) 860010
www.forestry.gov.uk/northwestengland
Grizedale Forest offers a range of activities for all ages through the year, from mountain biking to relaxing walks, Go-Ape to the sculpture trails.

Holker Hall & Gardens
Grange-over-Sands, Cumbria LA11 7PL
(01539) 558328
www.holker.co.uk
Home to Lord and Lady Cavendish, Victorian wing, glorious gardens, parkland and woodlands.

Hutton-in-the-Forest
Penrith, Cumbria CA11 9TH
(017684) 84449
www.hutton-in-the-forest.co.uk
A beautiful house surrounded by magnificent woodland of the medieval forest of Inglewood. Both the interior and exterior show a wide variety of architectural and decorative styles from the 17th century to the present day.

Museum of Lakeland Life
Kendal, Cumbria LA9 5AL
(01539) 722464
www.lakelandmuseum.org.uk
This award-winning museum takes you and your family back through time to tell the story of the Lake District and its inhabitants.

Penrith Castle
Cumbria CA11 7HX
(01912) 691200
www.english-heritage.org.uk/daysout/properties/penrith-castle/
The mainly 15th Century remains of a castle begun by Bishop Strickland of Carlisle and developed by the Nevilles and Richard III.

Ravenglass & Eskdale Railway
Cumbria CA18 1SW
(01229) 717171
www.ravenglass-railway.co.uk
Heritage steam engines haul open-top and covered carriages from the Lake District coastal village of Ravenglass to the foot of England's highest mountains.

South Lakes Safari Zoo
Dalton-in-Furness, Cumbria LA15 8JR
(01229) 466086
www.southlakessafarizoo.com
The ultimate interactive animal experience. Get close to wildlife at Cumbria's top tourist attraction.

Ullswater Steamers
Cumbria CA11 0US
(01768) 482229
www.ullswater-steamers.co.uk
The 'Steamers' create the opportunity to combine a cruise with some of the spectacular walks in the lake District.

Windermere Lake Cruises, Lakeside
Newby Bridge, Cumbria LA12 8AS
(01539) 443360
www.windermere-lakecruises.co.uk
Steamers and launches sail daily between Ambleside, Bowness and Lakeside.

The World of Beatrix Potter
Bowness, Cumbria LA23 3BX
(01539) 488444
www.hop-skip-jump.com
A magical indoor attraction that brings to life all 23 Beatrix Potter's Peter Rabbit tales.

Lancashire

Blackpool Dance Festival
May, Blackpool, Lancashire
www.blackpooldancefestival.com
The world's first and foremost festival of dancing.

Blackpool Pleasure Beach
Blackpool, Lancashire FY4 1EZ
(0871) 222 1234
www.blackpoolpleasurebeach.com
The UK's most ride intensive theme park and home to the legendary Big One and Valhalla.

The Blackpool Tower
Blackpool, Lancashire FY1 4BJ
(0871) 222 9929
www.theblackpooltower.com
Built in 1894, The Blackpool Tower is one of Britain's best loved landmarks. There are plenty of experiences on offer at The Blackpool Tower to ensure you have an unparalleled Blackpool experience.

Clitheroe Food Festival
August, Clitheroe, Lancashire
www.clitheroefoodfestival.com
Celebrating the very finest Lancashire food and drink produces. Includes chef demos, tastings and cookery workshops.

Farmer Ted's Farm Park
Ormskirk, Lancashire L39 7HW
(0151) 526 0002
www.farmerteds.com
An interactive children's activity park, sited on a working farm within the beautiful Lancashire countryside.

Garstang Walking Festival
May, Garstang, Lancashire
www.visitlancashire.com
A celebration of springtime in the stunning countryside of Garstang and the surrounding area. Guided walks and activities for all the family.

Lytham Proms Festival
August, Lytham & St Annes, Lancashire
www.visitlancashire.com
Summer proms spectacular with shows from leading performers.

Ribchester Roman Museum
Preston, Lancashire PR3 3XS
(01254) 878261
www.ribchesterromanmuseum.org
Lancashire's only specialist Roman museum, located on the North bank of the beautiful River Ribble.

Sandcastle Waterpark
Blackpool, Lancashire FY4 1BB
(01253) 343602
www.sandcastle-waterpark.co.uk
The UK's Largest Indoor Waterpark and with 18 slides and attractions.

Thornton Hall Farm Country Park
Lancashire BD23 3TS
(01282) 841148
www.thorntonhallcountrypark.co.uk
Come rain or shine, a fun filled family day out is always guaranteed at Thornton Hall Farm. Get involved with hands-on activities, make friends with the farm animals and visit the new tearoom while the little ones burn off the remainder of their energy in the huge fun filled Wizzick Play Barn.

Wyre Estuary Country Park
Thornton Lancashire FY5 5LR
(01253) 863100
www.wyre.gov.uk
The award winning Wyre Estuary Country Park offers year-round activities and events for all the family including ranger-led walks, environmentally themed activities and annual events like the Family Sculpture Day.

Manchester

East Lancashire Railway
Bury, Greater Manchester BL9 0EY
(0161) 764 7790
www.eastlancsrailway.org.uk
The beautifully restored East Lancashire Railway takes you on a captivating journey to discover the region's rich transport heritage.

Greater Manchester Marathon in Trafford
April, Trafford, Manchester
www.greatermanchestermarathon.com
The UK's flattest, fastest and friendliest Marathon with a superfast course, great entertainment, outstanding crowd support and glorious finish at Manchester United Football Club.

The Lowry
Pier 8, Salford Quays M50 3AZ
(0843) 208 6000
www.thelowry.com
Set in a stunning waterside location at the heart of the redeveloped Salford Quays in Greater Manchester, The Lowry is an architectural gem that brings together a wide variety of performing and visual arts, including the works of LS Lowry and contemporary exhibitions.

Manchester Art Gallery
Greater Manchester M2 3JL
(0161) 235 8888
www.manchestergalleries.org
Houses one of the country's finest art collections in spectacular Victorian and Contemporary surroundings. With changing exhibitions and a programme of events and a host of free family friendly resources.

Manchester Histories Festival
June, Various city centre locations
www.manchesterhistoriesfestival.org.uk
The ten-day MHF celebrates the heritage and history of Manchester across numerous city centre venues. The festival offers a fantastic opportunity to explore and learn this great city and is a great event for old and young alike.

Manchester Museum
Greater Manchester M13 9PL
(0161) 275 2648
www.manchester.ac.uk/museum
Found on Oxford Road, on The University of Manchester campus (in a very impressive gothic-style building). Highlights include Stan the T.rex, mummies, live animals such as frogs and snakes, object handling and a varied programme of events.

Manchester United Museum & Tour Centre
Greater Manchester M16 0RA
(0161) 868 8000
www.manutd.com
The story of Manchester United is unlike any other club in the world. Beginning more than a century ago, it combines eras of total English and European domination. The official museum and tour offers every football fan a unique insight into Manchester United Football Club and a fantastic day out.

National Football Museum
Urbis Building, Manchester M4 3BG
0161 605 8200
www.nationalfootballmuseum.com
The world's biggest and best football museum. Drama, History, Skill, Art, Faith, Style, Passion is what we're all about at the National Football Museum. More than 140,000 football-related items plus a kids' discovery zone and skills-testing simulators.

People's History Museum
Greater Manchester M3 3ER
(0161) 838 9190
www.phm.org.uk
National centre for the collection, conservation, interpretation and study of material relating to the history of working people in Britain.

Ramsbottom Chocolate Festival
March / April, Ramsbottom, Greater Manchester
www. ramsbottomchocolatefestival.com
Two-day chocolate market, with interactive workshops, activities for adults and children, music, competitions, Giant Easter Egg display, and much more.

Saddleworth and District Whit Friday Brass Band Contest
May, Oldham, Greater Manchester
www.whitfriday.brassbands.saddleworth.org
Brass bands compete in contests at venues scattered around the moorland villages and towns on the western edge of the Pennines.

Whitworth Art Gallery
Manchester M15 6ER
(0161) 275 7450
www.manchester.ac.uk/whitworth
Home to an famous collection of British watercolours, textiles and wallpapers.

Merseyside

'Another Place' by Antony Gormley
Crosby Beach, Liverpool L23 6SX
www.antonygormley.com
100 cast-iron, life-size figures spread out along three kilometres of the foreshore on Crosby beach in Liverpool, stretching almost one kilometre out to sea. The spectacular sculptures - each one weighing 650 kilos - are made from casts of the artist's own body standing on the beach, all of them looking out to sea, staring at the horizon in silent expectation.

Beatles Story
Liverpool, Merseyside L3 4AD
(0151) 709 1963
www.beatlesstory.com
A unique visitor attraction that transports you on an enlightening and atmospheric journey into the life, times, culture and music of the Beatles.

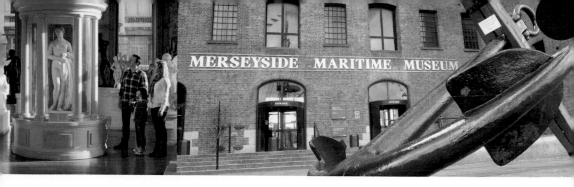

Birkenhead Festival of Transport
September, Birkenhead, Merseyside
www.bheadtransportfest.com
A fantastic week-end of activities for all the family. Featuring classic cars, steam engines and other modes of vintage transport.

Croxteth Hall & Country Park
Liverpool, Merseyside L12 0HB
(0151) 233 3020
www.liverpoolcityhalls.co.uk/croxteth-hall/
Situated in a beautiful Country Park setting and one of Liverpool's most important heritage sites. The Country Park is also home to a real working Home Farm, a Victorian Walled Garden and a 500 acre nature reserve - all open to the public.

The Gallery Liverpool
Merseyside L8 5RF
(0151) 709 2442
www.thegalleryliverpool.co.uk
Set in the heart of Liverpool's Independent Cultural District, the gallery occupies the entire upper floor of the industrial premises of John O'Keeffe and Son Ltd.

Grand National
April, Aintree, Merseyside
www.aintree.co.uk
The most famous horse race over jumps takes place over the challenging Aintree fences.

Knowsley Safari Park
Merseyside L34 4AN
(0151) 430 9009
www. knowsleysafariexperience.co.uk
Enjoy a 5 mile safari through 450 acres of parkland.

Liverpool Football Club
Merseyside L4 0TH
(0151) 260 6677
www.liverpoolfc.com
Meet an LFC Legend; get your photograph with one of our many trophies or indulge yourself in one of our award winning Experience Days.

Liverpool Sound City
May, Bramley Moore Dock, Liverpool
www.liverpoolsoundcity.co.uk
A 3-day festival of incredible live music and arts.

Mersey Ferries
Woodside Ferry Terminal, Merseyside, L3 1DP
(0151) 330 1444
www.merseyferries.co.uk
Step aboard to see Liverpool's stunning waterfront. The decks of the Mersey Ferry offer the best way to see the city's world-famous skyline. Our River Explorer Cruise takes you on a 50 minute trip where you'll be captivated by Liverpool's fascinating history.

Merseyside Maritime Museum
Liverpool Waterfront, Liverpool L3 4AQ
www.liverpoolmuseums.org.uk
(0151) 478 4499
Discover objects rescued from the Titanic among the treasures, one of the venues of the National Museums Liverpool, a group of free museums and galleries.

Speke Hall, Gardens & Estate
Liverpool, Merseyside L24 1XD
(0151) 427 7231
www.nationaltrust.org.uk/spekehall
One of the most famous half timbered houses in Britain. The Great Hall and priest hole date from Tudor times, while the Oak Parlour and smaller rooms, some with William Morris wallpapers, illustrates the Victorian desire for privacy and comfort.

Walker Art Gallery
Liverpool, Merseyside L3 8EL
(0151) 478 4199
www.liverpoolmuseums.org.uk/walker
Home to outstanding works by Rubens, Rembrandt, Poussin, Gainsborough and Hogarth, the Walker Art Gallery is one of the finest art galleries in Europe

Wirral Folk on the Coast Festival
June, Wirral, Merseyside
www.wirralfolkonthecoast.com
All-on-one-site friendly festival at Whitby Sports & Social Club, with fine music real ale and good food being served plus many more visitor attractions.

World Museum Liverpool
Merseyside L3 8EN
(0151) 478 4393
www.liverpoolmuseums.org.uk/wml
Extensive collections from the Amazonian Rain Forest to the mysteries of outer space.

Tourist Information Centres

When you arrive at your destination, visit the Tourist Information Centre for quality assured help with accommodation and information about local attractions and events, or email your request before you go.

Accrington	Town Hall	01254 380293	information@leisureinhyndburn.co.uk
Alston Moor	Town Hall	01434 382244	alston.tic@eden.gov.uk
Altrincham	20 Stamford New Road	0161 912 5931	tourist.information@trafford.gov.uk
Ambleside	Central Buildings	015394 32582	tic@thehubofambleside.com
Appleby-in-Westmorland	Moot Hall	017683 51177	tic@applebytown.org.uk
Barnoldswick	Post Office Buildings	01282 666704 / 661661	tourist.info@pendle.gov.uk
Barrow-in-Furness	Forum 28	01229 876543	touristinfo@barrowbc.gov.uk
Blackburn	Blackburn Market	01254 688040	visit@blackburn.gov.uk
Blackpool	Festival House, The People's Promenade	01253 478222	tic@blackpool.gov.uk
Bolton	Central Library Foyer	01204 334321 / 334271	tourist.info@bolton.gov.uk
Bowness	Glebe Road	015394 42895	bownesstic@lakedistrict.gov.uk
Brampton	Moot Hall	016977 3433 / 01228 625600	bramptontic@gmail.co.uk
Broughton-in-Furness	Town Hall	01229 716115	broughtontic@btconnect.com
Burnley	Regeneration and Planning Policy	01282 477210	tic@burnley.gov.uk
Bury	The Fusilier Museum	0161 253 5111	touristinformation@bury.gov.uk
Carlisle	Old Town Hall	01228 625600	tourism@carlisle.gov.uk
Chester (Town Hall)	Town Hall	0845 647 7868	welcome@chestervic.co.uk
Clitheroe	Platform Gallery & VIC	01200 425566	tourism@ribblevalley.gov.uk
Cockermouth	4 Old Kings Arms Lane	01900 822634	cockermouthtouristinformationcentre@btconnect.com
Congleton	Town Hall	01260 271095	congletontic@cheshireeast.gov.uk
Coniston	Ruskin Avenue	015394 41533	mail@conistontic.org
Discover Pendle	Boundary Mill Stores	01282 856186	discoverpendle@pendle.gov.uk
Egremont	12 Main Street	01946 820693	lowescourt@btconnect.com

Ellesmere Port	McArthur Glen Outlet Village	0151 356 5562	enquiries@cheshiredesigneroutlet.com
Garstang	1 Cherestanc Square	01995 602125	garstangtic@wyrebc.gov.uk
Glenridding Ullswater	Bekside Car Park	017684 82414	ullswatertic@lakedistrict.gov.uk
Grange-Over-Sands	Victoria Hall	015395 34026	council@grangeoversands.net
Kendal	25 Stramongate	01539 735891	info@kendaltic.co.uk
Keswick	Moot Hall	017687 72645	keswicktic@lakedistrict.gov.uk
Kirkby Stephen	Market Square	017683 71199	visit@uecp.org.uk
Lancaster	The Storey	01524 582394	lancastervic@lancaster.gov.uk
Liverpool Albert Dock	Anchor Courtyard	0151 233 2008	jackie.crawford@liverpool.gov.uk
Liverpool John Lennon Airport	Information Desk	0151 907 1058	information@liverpoolairport.com
Lytham St Annes	c/o Town Hall	01253 725610	touristinformation@fylde.gov.uk
Macclesfield	Town Hall	01625 378123 / 378062	karen.connon@cheshireeast.gov.uk
Manchester	45-50 Piccadilly Plaza	0871 222 8223	touristinformation@visitmanchester.com
Maryport	The Wave Centre	01900 811450	info@thewavemaryport.co.uk
Millom	Millom Council Centre	01946 598914	millomtic@copelandbc.gov.uk
Morecambe	Old Station Buildings	01524 582808	morecambevic@lancaster.gov.uk
Nantwich	Civic Hall	01270 537359	nantwichtic@cheshireeast.gov.uk
Northwich	Information Centre	01606 288828	infocentrenorthwich@cheshirewestandchester.gov.uk
Oldham	Oldham Library	0161 770 3064	tourist@oldham.gov.uk
Pendle Heritage Centre	Park Hill	01282 677150	pendleheritagecentre@htnw.co.uk
Penrith	Middlegate	01768 867466	pen.tic@eden.gov.uk
Preston	The Guildhall	01772 253731	tourism@preston.gov.uk
Rheged	Redhills	01768 860015	tic@rheged.com
Rochdale	Touchstones	01706 924928	tic@link4life.org
Rossendale	Rawtenstall Queens Square	01706 227911	rawtenstall.library@lancashire.gov.uk
Saddleworth	Saddleworth Museum	01457 870336	saddleworthtic@oldham.gov.uk
Salford	The Lowry, Pier 8	0161 848 8601	tic@salford.gov.uk
Sedbergh	72 Main Street	015396 20125	tic@sedbergh.org.uk
Silloth-on-Solway	Solway Coast Discovery Centre	016973 31944	sillothtic@allerdale.gov.uk
Southport	112 Lord Street	01704 533333	info@visitsouthport.com
Stockport	Staircase House	0161 474 4444	tourist.information@stockport.gov.uk
Ulverston	Coronation Hall	01229 587120 / 587140	ulverstontic@southlakeland.gov.uk
Windermere	Victoria Street	015394 46499	info@ticwindermere.co.uk

Regional Contacts and Information

For more information on accommodation, attractions, activities, events and holidays in North West England, contact one of the following regional or local tourism organisations. Their websites have a wealth of information and many produce free publications to help you get the most out of your visit.

Visit Chester
www.visitchester.com

Cumbria Tourism
T (01539) 822 222
E info@cumbriatourism.org
www.golakes.co.uk

Visit Lancashire
T (01257) 226600 (Brochure request)
E info@visitlancashire.com
www.visitlancashire.com

Visit Manchester
T 0871 222 8223
E touristinformation@visitmanchester.com
www.visitmanchester.com

Visit Liverpool
T (0151) 233 2008 (information enquiries)
T 0844 870 0123 (accommodation booking)
E info@visitliverpool.com (accommodation enquiries)
E liverpoolvisitorcentre@liverpool.gov.uk
(information enquiries)
www.visitliverpool.com

Stay – North West

Entries appear alphabetically by town name in each county. A key to symbols appears on page 7

North West - Cheshire

CHESTER, Cheshire　Map ref 4A2　S

4* Gold Wharton Lock Apartment

Contact: Mrs Sandra Jeffrey, Owner / Manager, Chester City Centre, Cheshire CH2 3DH
T: (01258) 817 816 / 07454 379933 **E:** rentals@stayinchester.com
W: www.stayinchester.com **£ BOOK ONLINE**

Units 1
Sleeps 1-4
PER UNIT PER WEEK
£450.00 - £630.00

Luxury canalside apartment, private lounge balcony overlooking lock gates, peaceful location, short walk to city centre. Hypnos beds, granite kitchen, lounge with 'Living Art' fire, kingsize bedroom, twin bedroom, two bathrooms, free allocated parking and free Wi-Fi. Romantic breaks, family holidays, business trips. 2/3 night weekends from £310, 4 night midweeks from £310, weeks from £450. **Open:** All year **Nearest Shop:** 0.25 miles **Nearest Pub:** 0.2 miles

Site: ✿ P Payment: 💷 Leisure: ♨ ♪ ♦ ♦ Property: ⚡ 🖥 🚭 🍴 Children: ≿ Unit: 🛏 🧺 🖥 🍳 TV DVD

CONGLETON, Cheshire　Map ref 4B2　S

Broomfield Barns

Contact: Mrs Anita Lockett, Landlady, Broomfield Barns, Broomfield House, Trap Road, Congleton, Cheshire CW12 2LT **T:** (01260) 224581/514 **E:** info@broomfieldbarns.co.uk
W: www.broomfieldbarns.co.uk

Units 1
Sleeps 2-6
PER UNIT PER WEEK
£655.00 - £750.00

Broomfield Barn provides self-catering accommodation for two to six people. 3 bedrooms, 1 double, 1 triple and 1 single. Double/twin rooms £65 per night. Located in the heart of the Cheshire countryside with easy access to the Derbyshire hills, lovely gardens, Stately Homes, award winning country pubs and nearby Clonter Theatre.
Guide dogs only.
Open: All year **Nearest Shop:** 5 miles **Nearest Pub:** 0.5 miles

Site: ✿ P Leisure: ♨ ♪ ♦ ♦ Property: 🚭 🍴 Children: ≿ Unit: 🛏 🍳 TV 🎧

MACCLESFIELD, Cheshire　Map ref 4B2　S

Cheshire Hunt Holiday Cottages

Contact: Mrs Anne Gregory, Owner, Cheshire Hunt Holiday Cottages, Hedge Row, Off Spuley Lane, Rainow Macclesfield, Cheshire SK10 5DA **T:** (01625) 572034 / 07506 825480 **E:** enquiries@cheshirehuntholidaycottages.co.uk
W: www.cheshirehuntholidaycottages.co.uk

Units 2
Sleeps 2-11
PER UNIT PER WEEK
£595.00 - £890.00

Situated on a small track which winds through a valley, each cottage has its own unique character and both enjoy wonderful views over open countryside but are within walking distance of the local village and amenities. Both cottages have separate facilities and share the use of a games room. There is also the flexibility of hiring both properties for extended family holidays and weddings. **Open:** All year **Nearest Shop:** 1 mile **Nearest Pub:** 0.5 miles

Site: ✿ P Leisure: ♨ ♦ Property: 🐾 🚭 🍴 Children: ≿ 🍴 ☂ Unit: 🛏 🧺 🖥 🍳 TV DVD 🎧

ALLONBY, Cumbria   Map ref 5A2   S

Crookhurst Farm Cottages

Contact: Brenda Wilson, Bowscale Farm, Allonby CA15 6RB **T:** 07773 047591
E: brenda@crookhurst.com
W: www.crookhurst.com **£ BOOK ONLINE**

Units   3
Sleeps   2-15

PER UNIT PER WEEK
£375.00 - £1400.00

SPECIAL PROMOTIONS
Short break prices
available on request.

Crookhurst Farm & Cottages is set in lovely open countryside and situated half a mile to Allonby, on the Solway coast. Spacious 5 bedroomed House suitable for limited mobility with wheelchair access. Private garden and ample parking. Sleeps 12 plus cots, adjoining cottages sleeping 2-3.

Bowscale View is nestled within beautiful valleys and fields, a half mile from Allonby and the beach. This is Dog friendly. Spacious, luxury self-catering accommodations suitable for those looking for a rural, tranquil and peaceful getaway, surrounded by beautiful scenery. Suitable for limited mobility with wheelchair access.

Open: All year
Nearest Shop: 0.5 miles
Nearest Pub: 0.5 miles

Units: Weekly prices available on website. Open over Christmas and New Year. Wi-Fi Available.

Site: ❄ P Leisure: ♪ ► ∪ ⚲ Property: 🐾 🗏 🖳 Children: ↘ ▥ ⚹ Unit: 🗄 🗄 🖥 ⚲ 📺 🎧 📀 ☎

AMBLESIDE, Cumbria   Map ref 5A3   S

Cuckoo's Nest

Contact: Anthony or Christine Harrison, Compston Road, Ambleside, Cumbria LA22 9DJ
T: (01539) 432330 **E:** enq@cottagesambleside.co.uk
W: www.cottagesambleside.co.uk **£ BOOK ONLINE**

Units   1
Sleeps   2

PER UNIT PER WEEK
£375.00 - £525.00

SPECIAL PROMOTIONS
Minimum stay of 3
nights, accepted 2
weeks before the
arrival date, please
telephone to enquire.

The Cuckoos Nest is cosy and comfortable and ideally situated in the heart of Ambleside although the hustle and bustle outside does not spoil the privacy and romantic atmosphere inside.
Just a short walk takes you to all the amenities of Ambleside, restaurants, pubs and shops.
The surrounding fells are within easy walking distance as are Windermere & Rydal water, so much to do and so easily accessible.

Being on the bus route makes it also very convenient if you dont have a car or want to leave it behind for the day.
Use of nearby spa included, with swim & gym facilities

Open: All year round

Units: The kitchen is on the ground floor, the bedroom, lounge and bathroom are all on the first floor.

Site: P Payment: 💳 € Leisure: ► Property: 🖳 🖳 Unit: 🗄 🗄 🖥 ⚲ 📺 📀

The Lakelands

Contact: Janine Wagstaff, Site Coordinator, Lower Gale, Ambleside, Cumbria LA22 0BD
T: (015394) 33777 **E:** admin@resort-solutions.co.uk
W: www.the-lakelands.com

Sleeps   2-8

PER UNIT PER WEEK
£260.00 - £1050.00

Comfortable self-catering apartments and a separate four bedroomed house, all with access to a leisure centre on the site. We are situated in a unique position overlooking the popular town of Ambleside. The Lakelands offers superb, unspoilt views of the town, Lakeland countryside and the fells beyond - and enjoys easy access to the many delights of the area.

Popular Ambleside offers an excellent selection of shops, restaurants and friendly inns. While walkers are spoilt for choice with a number of pathways directly accessed from the town.

Open: All year

Units: Designed and furnished to a high standard, one- and two-bedroom apartments and a separate four bedroomed house, all self contained and fully-equipped.

Site: ✿ P Payment: 📧 Leisure: 🏊 Property: 📺 ⬚ ⬚ Children: 🐾 🛏 ☝ Unit: ⬚ 📺 🍴 📺 📀

Over Brandelhow

Contact: Kath Manners, T manners & Sons Ltd, 2 Dovecote hill, South Church Enterprise Park, Bishop Auckland, Co. Durham DL14 6XW **T:** 07711 592156
E: info@overbrandelhow.com **W:** www.overbrandelhow.com

Units   1
Sleeps   6

PER UNIT PER WEEK
£550.00 - £1065.00

The views down the Borrowdale valley from the cottage must be some of the best in the area. The location is so peaceful and has great walks from the doorstep. The cottage benefits from a very social open plan living area and the use of natural materials. There is a terrace for alfresco dining and from there is a view of the lake.
Open: All year **Nearest Shop:** 4 miles
Nearest Pub: 2 mile

Site: ✿ P Property: 🐾 📺 ⬚ Children: 🐾 🛏 ☝ Unit: ⬚ ⬚ 📺 ⬚ 🍴 📺 📀 BBQ

Burnside Park

VisitEngland
★★★★
SELF CATERING

Contact: Lisa Holden, Resort Manager, Hapimag Resorts & Residences UK Ltd,
The Lodge, Burnside Park, Kendal Road, Bowness-on-Windermere LA23 3EW
T: (01539) 446624 **F:** 01539 447754 **E:** bowness@hapimag.com
W: www.burnsidepark.co.uk **£ BOOK ONLINE**

Units   46
Sleeps   2-6

PER UNIT PER WEEK
£460.00 - £1180.00

SPECIAL PROMOTIONS
Short breaks are
available throughout
the year starting from
£240 for minimum 2
nights in a sleep 4.

Luxury self catering apartments 300m from Lake Windermere and Bowness centre. Sleeping 2-6 guests.Your stay here includes use of the leisure facilities at Parklands Country Club (Burnside Hotel). Complimentary Wi-Fi. Our apartments are let on a weekly basis Saturday to Saturday, short breaks available on a minimum 2 night stay.

Open: All year
Nearest Shop: 0.5 miles
Nearest Pub: 0.5 miles

Units: 2 room apartments have a double bedroom en-suite & a twin bedroom with a separate shower room & the 1 room apartments have a double room & bathroom

Site: ❀ P **Payment:** 🔳 **Leisure:** ♪ ∪ ❦ **Property:** 🐾 ⊟ ▣ 🖳 🖵 **Children:** 🚼 🛏 🚶
Unit: ⊟ ⬛ 🖳 📺 🎛 🆅 ☎

EXPLORE
two heritage visitor attractions in the
LAKE DISTRICT

ULLSWATER 'STEAMERS'

RAVENGLASS RAILWAY
L'AAL RATTY
AND ESKDALE

© Shane Turnball

© Brian Sherwen

Explore Ullswater onboard the 'Steamers', that link to some of the most famous and spectacular walking routes in the National Park or climb aboard La'al Ratty and take a journey from the coast to the mountains. Visit one and get 50% off the other*

*on full fare day tickets only

01229 717171 ravenglass-railway.co.uk   017684 82229 ullswater-steamers.co.uk

BROUGHTON-IN-FURNESS, Cumbria   Map ref 5A3   S

Thornthwaite

Contact: Mrs Jean Jackson, Thornthwaite, Woodland, Broughton in Furness, Cumbria
LA20 6DF **T:** (01229) 716340 **E:** info@lakedistrictcottages.co.uk
W: www.lakedistrictcottages.co.uk **£ BOOK ONLINE**

Units   6
Sleeps   1-6

PER UNIT PER WEEK
£180.00 - £650.00

SPECIAL PROMOTIONS
Short breaks available
all year round. Please
email for further
details.

Situated in the unspoilt Woodland Valley, there are five cottages and a luxury Log Cabin with stunning views of the Lakeland fells. Ideally situated for walking, cycling or just relaxing, with many walks from your cottage, we even have our own private fishing lake. Guests can enjoy going badger watching at dusk, see the fox cubs playing or catch a glimpse of the barn owls out hunting. Within easy reach of the main attractions. However if you need to get away from it all and relax in a friendly atmosphere, our farm is perfect.

Open: All year
Nearest Shop: 3 miles
Nearest Pub: 3 miles

Site: P Leisure: Property: Children: Unit: BBQ

CARLISLE, Cumbria   Map ref 5A2   S

Brackenhill Tower & Jacobean Cottage

Contact: Mrs Jan Ritchie, Manageress, Brackenhill Estates, Brackenhill, Longtown, Carlisle, Cumbria CA6 5TU **T:** (01461) 800285 / 07779 138 694
E: enquiries@brackenhilltower.co.uk **W:** www.brackenhilltower.co.uk **£ BOOK ONLINE**

Units   2
Sleeps   2-16
PER UNIT PER WEEK
£700.00 - £3000.00

A 16thC castle with wow factor! Stated luxury and comfort in a real historic landmark of character and authentic clan Graham Reiver stronghold.
Jacuzzi onsite.
Nearest Shop: Longtown **Nearest Pub:** Longtown

Site: P Payment: Property: Children: Unit: BBQ

Sign up for our newsletter

Visit our website to sign up for our e-newsletter and receive regular information on events, articles, exclusive competitions and new publications.
www.visitor-guides.co.uk

GRANGE-OVER-SANDS, Cumbria   Map ref 5A3   SatNav LA11 6HR   C

Greaves Farm Caravan Park

c/o Nether Edge, Field Broughton, Grange-over-Sands, Cumbria LA11 6HR
T: (01539) 536587 **E:** info@greavesfarmcaravanpark.co.uk
W: www.greavesfarmcaravanpark.co.uk

(10)	£18.00-£20.00
(10)	£18.00-£20.00
(10)	£16.00-£18.00
(2)	£250.00-£460.00
20 touring pitches	

Small quiet park in pleasant rural location 2.5m north of Cartmel. Family owned and supervised. Ideal base for exploring the South Lakes within easy reach of Windermere, Kendal, Furness Peninsula and Morecambe Bay. Conveniently situated for many places of interest and easy walks on the lower fells. Two well-equipped 4 berth luxury holiday caravans for hire. Spacious touring and camping park, level grass tent pitches in 4acre meadow, hard standings and electric hook ups (6amp) available, indoor washing up facilities.

Directions: Exit 36 off M6. Follow A590 signed Barrow. After Meathop roundabout continue on A590 for further 4.5miles, just after end of dual carriageway take left hand road signed Cartmel and Holker. Continue 1.5m. Site is signed.

Open: Early March to End October

Payment: ☀ **Leisure:** ♪ ▶ ☺ **Children:** ☛ **Park:** 🐾 🎣 ⛳ **Touring:** ♨ ♿ 🏧

HIGH LORTON, Cumbria   Map ref 5A3   S

Holemire Barn Cottage

Contact: Mrs Angela Fearfield, Holemire Barn, c/o Holemire House, High Lorton, Cockermouth CA13 9TX **T:** (01900) 85225 **E:** enquiries@lakelandbarn.co.uk
W: www.lakelandbarn.co.uk **£ BOOK ONLINE**

Units 1
Sleeps 2
PER UNIT PER WEEK
£400.00 - £500.00

Traditional Lakeland barn with exposed beams, converted to high quality accommodation. Close to Keswick. Warm, light and sunny. In superb walking country. Ospreys nesting close by. Red squirrels in garden. **Open:** All year **Nearest Shop:** 0.25 miles
Nearest Pub: 0.25 miles

Site: ✿ P **Leisure:** 🚲 ♪ ▶ ☺ **Property:** 🏠 🍴 **Unit:** 🛏 💻 🚿 🍳 📺 🐕 📀

KENDAL, Cumbria   Map ref 5B3   S

Shaw End Mansion

Contact: Mr & Mrs Edward & Karlyn Robinson, Shaw End Holidays, Haveriggs Farm, Whinfell, Kendal LA8 9EF **T:** (01539) 824220 / 07778596863 **F:** 01539 824220
E: info@shawend.co.uk **W:** www.shawend.co.uk **£ BOOK ONLINE**

Units 4
Sleeps 2-18
PER UNIT PER WEEK
£275.00 - £500.00

Shaw End Mansion is set on 200-acres of farm and woodland in a beautiful location. Shaw End - a restored Georgian house - contains spacious and elegant apartments with fantastic views and walks from the doorstep. Why not rent the whole house, which is ideal for weddings and parties. **Open:** All year **Nearest Shop:** 3 miles
Nearest Pub: 3 miles

Site: ✿ P **Payment:** 💳 **Leisure:** ♪ ☺ **Property:** 🏠 🍴 **Children:** ☛ 🍴 🧸 **Unit:** 🛏 💻 🚿 🍳 📺 🐕 📀 ♿

Waters Edge Caravan Park

Crooklands, Kendal, Cumbria LA7 7NN
T: (01539) 567708 **E:** stay@watersedgecaravanpark.co.uk
W: www.watersedgecaravanpark.co.uk

🚐 (26)	£17.35-£24.90	
🚃 (26)	£17.35-£24.90	
⛺ (6)	£10.00-£27.50	
26 touring pitches		

Friendly site in open countryside. Lake District, Morecambe and Yorkshire Dales nearby. All hardstanding pitches. Lounge, bar, pool room and patio area. Shower block with laundry. Local pub/restaurant within 300yds. Overnight holding area available. **Directions:** Leave M6 at jct 36, take A65 toward Kirkby Lonsdale for approx 100 yds, then left on A65 toward Crooklands. Site approx 1 mile on the right. **Open:** 1st March to 14th November.

Site: 🏧 🅰🄿 **Payment:** 💷 ☼ **Leisure:** ♪ ⌐ ∪ ✦ **Children:** ⛄ **Catering:** 🍴 **Park:** 🐕 🚾 🛂 📵
Touring: 🚽 🕐 🚐

Brewery Lane Holiday Cottages

Contact: The Heads, Keswick, Cumbria CA12 5ER **T:** (017687) 72750 **E:** info@brewery-lane.co.uk
W: www.brewery-lane.co.uk **£ BOOK ONLINE**

Units	4
Sleeps	2-4
PER UNIT PER WEEK	
£330.00 - £670.00	

Superior, centrally situated, comfortable cottages with either 2 double bedrooms or 1 double and 1 twin bedroom. Private parking in enclosed landscaped courtyard area. Keswick town centre's shops, pubs and restaurants are within easy walking distance as is Derwentwater and The Theatre by the Lake. All cottages are well equipped and owner maintained to a high standard. Quality Cumbria Assessed. **Open:** All Year

Site: ✿ **P** **Property:** 🚾 🅿 **Children:** ⛄ 🎮 🚸 **Unit:** 🛏 🍴 💻 📺 📀

Castlerigg Hall Caravan & Camping Park

Castlerigg Hall, Keswick, Cumbria CA12 4TE
T: (01768) 774499 **E:** info@castlerigg.co.uk
W: www.castlerigg.co.uk / www.foodatjiggers.co.uk

🚐 (65)	£19.75-£33.00	
🚃 (65)	£19.75-£33.00	
⛺ (120)	£16.40-£23.40	
🏠 (12)	£295.00-£550.00	

Our elevated position commands wonderful panoramic views of the surrounding fells. Formerly a Lakeland hill farm, Castlerigg Hall has been sympathetically developed into a quality touring park. Facilities include Campers store, Food at Jiggers and Castlerigg Gallery. **Directions:** Head out of Keswick on the A591 direction Windermere. At the top of the hill turn right at the brown tourist sign indicating Castlerigg Hall. **Open:** 11th March - 9th November.

Payment: 💷 **Leisure:** ♪ ⌐ **Children:** ⛄ **Catering:** ✗ **Park:** 🐕 🚾 🛂 📵

High Rigg

Contact: Tom Sayer, Fasnakyle, Oldhill Wood, Studham, Beds LU6 2NF **T:** (01582) 872574 / 07512 744593 **E:** tom.sayer@lineone.net
W: www.highrigg.co.uk

Units	1
Sleeps	1-6
PER UNIT PER WEEK	
£290.00 - £630.00	

High Rigg is a comfortable and well equipped house, sleeping 6. The River Greta and Fitz Park are nearby, the town centre and Derwentwater a short walk away. There are 4 bedrooms, bathroom, shower room, living room, dining room and kitchen. **Open:** All year **Nearest Shop:** 350m **Nearest Pub:** 600m

Site: ✿ **Property:** 🐕 🛂 🅿 **Children:** ⛄ 🚸 **Unit:** 🛏 🍴 💻 🛁 🍳 📀 ☎

KESWICK, Cumbria Map ref 5A3 S

Latcrag Caravan

Contact: High Row Farm, Threlkeld, Keswick, Cumbria CA12 4SF **T:** (017687) 79256

Latcrag caravan is situated by a small working farm with outstanding views from the Blencathra hillside. It is a 6 berth well equipped caravan with mod cons and panel heaters in all rooms.

Units   1
Sleeps   6
PER UNIT PER WEEK
£250.00 - £340.00

Site: P Leisure: ♪ ▶ Property: 🏠 Children: ♨ 🍴 ⚱ Unit: 🛏 🍳 📺 📀

KESWICK, Cumbria Map ref 5A3 S

VisitEngland
★★★★
SELF CATERING

Latcrag Cottage

Contact: Mrs Benson, High Row, Threlkeld, Keswick, Cumbria CA12 4SF **T:** (017687) 79256

Latcrag is a superbly presented and fully equipped cottage situated on the slopes of Blencathra with stunning views of the valley and fells. Superb base for walkers and cyclists from the door or to just chill out. Owner maintained and tastefully furnished, clean and comfortable with central heating and all mod cons. Parking for 2 cars with garage. Latcrag has a double bedroom and a family room, living room with suite, tv, dvd and radio. Kitchen has fridge freezer, washer dryer and a microwave. 2 small dogs are welcome by arrangement. All linen and towels are included in tariffs.
Open: All year **Nearest Shop:** 5 miles **Nearest Pub:** 1 mile

Units   1
Sleeps   1-5
PER UNIT PER WEEK
£270.00 - £450.00

Site: ✿ P Leisure: ▶ Property: 🐕 🏠 🖥 Children: ♨ 🍴 ⚱ Unit: 🛏 🍳 📺 📀

KESWICK, Cumbria Map ref 5A3 S

VisitEngland
★★★★
SELF CATERING

Peter House Cottages

Contact: Valerie & Cerita Trafford, Owners, Peter House Farm, Bassenthwaite, Keswick, Cumbria CA12 4QX **T:** (01768) 776018 / 07743 898729 **E:** info@peterhousecottages.co.uk **W:** www.peterhousecottages.co.uk **£ BOOK ONLINE**

Units   2
Sleeps   2-5

PER UNIT PER WEEK
£385.00 - £495.00

SPECIAL PROMOTIONS
Short breaks available.
Minimum stay 3 nights.
Please contact for
information.

Peterhouse cottage and Pembroke cottage are situated on a lakeland hill farm with wonderful scenery. Situated in a peaceful location at the foot of Skiddaw, with Dash Falls, Ullock Pike and Binsey literally on the doorstep.

Close by is the village of Bassenthwaite and the market town of Keswick. The cottages are spacious, comfortable and well equipped and are an ideal base for either walking, cycling or relaxing. Private off road parking.

Open: March - December
Nearest Shop: 2 mile
Nearest Pub: 2 mile

Units: Both cottages have two bedrooms sleeping 5 and 4, electric hob/ovens, microwave, kettle, toaster, fridge/freezer. Linen, towels & heating inclusive. Electric showers over bath, toilet & wash basin. TV/DVD player and electric storage heating.

Site: ✿ P Leisure: ▶ Property: 🐕 🏠 🖥 Children: ♨ 🍴 ⚱ Unit: 🛏 🍳 🍽 📺 📀

KESWICK, Cumbria   Map ref 5A3   S

San Ging Keswick

Contact: Helen Ball, Owner Manager, 5 Grange Park, Keswick, 5 Grange Park CA12 4AY
T: (017687) 75890 / 07720 034494 **E:** helen@sangingkeswick.co.uk
W: www.sangingkeswick.co.uk **£ BOOK ONLINE**

Units   1
Sleeps   1-8
PER UNIT PER WEEK
£750.00 - £1995.00

San Ging is a modern split level house built into the hillside just above Keswick town centre with stunning views towards Bassenthwaite lake. The house provides comfortable accommodation for up to 8 people and is ideally suited to groups and families. With easy access to all parts of the Lake District it makes a good base for many outdoor activities and other attractions. See website for details. **Open:** All year **Nearest Shop:** 1 mile **Nearest Pub:** 1 mile

Site: ✿ **P Property:** 🍴🅱️🍳 **Children:** 🐴🏠🚶 **Unit:** 🍴🍴🖥️🍴🍳📺🎦📀🌀BBQ📞

KIRKBY LONSDALE, Cumbria   Map ref 5B3   SatNav LA6 2SE C

Woodclose Park

Chapel House Lane, High Casterton, Kirkby Lonsdale LA6 2SE
T: (01524) 271597 **F:** 01524 272301 **E:** info@woodclosepark.com
W: www.woodclosepark.com **£ BOOK ONLINE**

🚐 (17)   £15.00-£27.00
🚚 (14)   £15.00-£27.00
⛺ (5)   £14.50-£18.00
52 touring pitches

Enjoy England award winning park, set in the beautiful Lune valley between the Yorkshire Dales and the Lake District National Park, walking distance to Kirkby Lonsdale Town. Tourers, camping, self catering Wigwams and holiday homes and lodges for sale. Holiday Home extended season until January. **Directions:** M6 jct 36, follow A65 for approx 6 miles. The park entrance can be found just past Kirkby Lonsdale on the left-hand side, up the hill. **Open:** 1st March - 31st October. Holiday Homes until 1st January.

Payment: 💷☀ **Leisure:** 🎣♪➤U **Children:** 🐴⚂ **Catering:** 🛒 **Park:** 🐕🅱️🚶🎦🌀 **Touring:** 🚽🚿🚰🚿

LONGSLEDDALE, Cumbria   Map ref 5B3   S

The Coach House

Contact: Jenny Farmer, The Coach House, c/o Capplebarrow House, Kendal, Longsleddale, Cumbria LA8 9BB **T:** (01539) 823686 **E:** jenyfarmer@aol.com
W: www.capplebarrowcoachhouse.co.uk **£ BOOK ONLINE**

Units   1
Sleeps   1-2
PER UNIT PER WEEK
£160.00 - £300.00

Stone-built, converted coach house with ground-floor shower room, bedroom and open staircase to first-floor kitchen and lounge. Excellent views. Located in peaceful, picturesque valley. Log burner and super-king bed. Pets welcome. **Open:** All year **Nearest Shop:** 6 miles **Nearest Pub:** 7 miles

Site: ✿ **P Property:** 🐕🍴🅱️🍳 **Children:** 🐴🏠🚶 **Unit:** 🖥️📺🎦📀🌀BBQ

NEWBY BRIDGE, Cumbria   Map ref 5A3   S

Newby Bridge Country Caravan Park

Contact: Canny Hill, Newby Bridge, Cumbria LA12 8NF **T:** (015395) 31030
E: newbybridge@lakedistrictestates.com
W: www.newbybridgepark.co.uk

Units   8
Sleeps   2-6
PER UNIT PER WEEK
£250.00 - £660.00

Newby Bridge Caravan Country Park is a perfect location surrounded by woodlands. The Park provides a tranquil setting with an abundance of wildlife, excellent facilities and easy access to a variety of walking and cycling routes, water based activities, restaurants, inns and local visitor attractions. Located near the Southern shore of Windermere at the edge of the Lake District National Park and within easy distance to the ancient village of Cartmel.

Site: **P Payment:** 💷€ **Leisure:** ♪➤U **Property:** //🐕🅱️🍽️🍳🌀 **Children:** 🐴🏠🚶 **Unit:** 🍴🖥️📺📀

PENRITH, Cumbria Map ref 5B2

Flusco Wood
Flusco, Penrith CA11 0JB
T: (01768) 480020 **E:** info@fluscowood.co.uk
W: www.fluscowood.co.uk

🚐 (26) £21.00-£24.00
🚐 (10) £21.00-£24.00
36 touring pitches

A high-standard, quiet woodland touring caravan park with fully serviced pitches and centrally heated amenity building. Short drive to many attractions and places of interest in the Lake District. Overnight holding area available. **Directions:** M6 jct 40, travel west on A66 towards Keswick. After about 4 miles turn right (signposted Flusco). Entrance along lane on the left. **Open:** Easter to November.

Payment: 💳 ☼ **Leisure:** 🚲 ♪ ♿ **Children:** 🛝 ⚠ **Catering:** 🍴 **Park:** 🐕 🗑 📞 ☕ **Touring:** 📞 🚿 🚽

PENRITH, Cumbria Map ref 5B2
S

Sycamore Cottage
Contact: Nicky Godfrey-Evans, Owner, Ellonby, Penrith, Cumbria CA11 9SJ
T: 07949 149759 **E:** info@cumbriandiscoveries.co.uk
W: www.sycamorecottage.info

Units 1
Sleeps 2-3
PER UNIT PER WEEK
£260.00 - £425.00

A peaceful and delightful small single storey cottage set in the courtyard of the owner's 18th century farmhouse, in the quiet hamlet of Ellonby on the edge of the Lake District National Park and the Eden Valley. The guest's private patio and small garden overlook a pond. Excellent for walking, cycling or sightseeing. The owner is a Blue Badge Tourist Guide with a wealth of local knowledge. **Open:** All year **Nearest Shop:** 3.6 miles **Nearest Pub:** 1 mile

Site: ❄ P **Payment:** € **Leisure:** ► **Property:** // 🐕 🗑 📞 **Children:** 🛝 🏊 **Unit:** 🗑 📺 BBQ

SILLOTH, Cumbria Map ref 5A2

Stanwix Park Holiday Centre
Greenrow, Silloth, Wigton, Cumbria CA7 4HH
T: (016973) 32666 **F:** 016973 32555 **E:** enquiries@stanwix.com
W: www.stanwix.com

🚐 (127) £93.00-£118.00
🏕 (127) £93.00-£118.00
🏠 (4) £30.00-£50.00

Caravan holiday homes for hire. Large leisure centre. Swimming pools, ten-pin bowling and amusement arcade, family entertainment, disco and adult cabaret. Situated on the Solway Coast, popular destination to explore the Lake District. Tents & touring prices are per week. Camping Pod prices are per night. **Directions:** Please contact for directions. **Open:** All year

f 🐦

Site: 🅿 **Payment:** 💳 ☼ **Leisure:** 🚲 ♪ ► 🎱 **Children:** 🛝 ⚠ **Catering:** ✕ 🍴 **Park:** 🐕 🎵 🗑 📞 ☕ **Touring:** 📞 🚿 🚽

TROUTBECK, Cumbria Map ref 5A3
S

Troutbeck Inn Holiday Cottages
Contact: Rowan Mahon, Booking Enquiries, Troutbeck Inn & Holiday Cottages, Troutbeck, Penrith CA11 0SJ **T:** (01768) 483635 **E:** info@troutbeckinn.co.uk
W: www.thetroutbeckinn.co.uk **£ BOOK ONLINE**

Units 3
Sleeps 2-4
PER UNIT PER WEEK
£295.00 - £565.00

Our three self catering cottages were originally converted from stone barns and are all very spacious. The one bedroom cottage has a king size sleigh bed and both of the two bedroom cottages have an upstairs sitting room taking advantage of the wonderful fell views. **Open:** All year **Nearest Shop:** 6 miles

Site: P **Payment:** 💳 **Property:** 🐕 🗑 📞 **Children:** 🛝 **Unit:** 📺 📺

ULLSWATER, *Cumbria* *Map ref 5A3* **S**

Elm How, Cruck Barn & Eagle Cottage

Contact: Patterdale, Glenridding, Ullswater, Cumbria CA11 0PU **T:** (01539) 445756
E: info@matsonground.co.uk
W: www.matsonground.co.uk

Units   3
Sleeps   2-8
PER UNIT PER WEEK
£345.00 - £1450.00

Near Patterdale and Glenridding, we have 3 self-catering holiday cottages all offering quiet, comfortable accommodation. Elm How, sleeps 8 and Cruck Barn, sleeps 2 are in the Grisedale Valley above Patterdale, near Ullswater.
Open: All year **Nearest Shop:** 2 miles **Nearest Pub:** 2 miles

Site: ✿ **P Payment:** 💷 **Leisure:** ⚲ ☋ **Property:** ∥ ☊ 🖥 📶 🖳 **Children:** ♨ 🛏 ☗ **Unit:** 🗄 🗄 📺 📟 🖌 📺 🎬 📀 ∅ BBQ ☎

ULLSWATER, *Cumbria* *Map ref 5A3* **S**

Hartsop Fold Holiday Lodges

Contact: Peter Sewell, Manager, Lyon Leisure, Crossgate Lane, Hartsop, Patterdale, Cumbria CA11 0NZ **T:** 07917 784977 / 07917784977 **E:** info@hartsop-fold.co.uk
W: www.hartsop-fold.co.uk **£ BOOK ONLINE**

Units   12
Sleeps   2-6
PER UNIT PER WEEK
£495.00 - £775.00

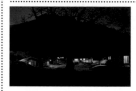

Between Ullswater and Windermere. Scandanavian style lodges on a secluded site, in a quiet corner of the Lakes. Sleep up to six in all Lodges. Week, mid-week & weekend breaks available. Equipped with fitted kitchen, colour TV & free Wi-Fi. **Open:** All Year **Nearest Shop:** 3 **Nearest Pub:** 1

Site: P Leisure: ♪ ⚑ **Property:** ☊ 🖥 📶 🖳 **Children:** ♨ 🛏 ☗ **Unit:** 🗄 📺 🖌 📺 📀 ☎

ULLSWATER, *Cumbria* *Map ref 5A3* *SatNav CA10 2LT* **C**

Hillcroft Holiday Park

Roe Head Lane, Pooley Bridge, Penrith, Cumbria CA10 2LT
T: (017684) 86363 **E:** info@hillcroftpark.co.uk
W: www.hillcroftpark.co.uk

🚐	(14)	£20.00-£33.00
🚐	(14)	£20.00-£33.00
⛺	(64)	£15.00-£27.00
🏠	(16)	£40.00-£60.00
🏕	(14)	£305.00-£599.00
🛖	(5)	£249.00-£465.00

A warm and friendly welcome awaits you when you visit Hillcroft Park, Ullswater in the northern part of the Lake District. Hillcroft Park is the perfect holiday retreat, especially for those who love the outdoor life. Various pitches, lodges & caravans available, Some with Hot Tubs! Please see website for further details.
Directions: Please see website.
Open: Camping & Pods: 1st March – 15th November. Static Caravans & lodges: 1st March to 6th January.

Site: 🏕 🅰🄿 **Payment:** 💷 ☀ **Leisure:** ⚲ ♪ ⚑ ☋ **Children:** ♨ ⚠ **Catering:** 🍴
Park: ☊ 🖥 📺 🅿 🄵 **Touring:** 🚻 🚽 🚰 ⚡

ULLSWATER, *Cumbria* *Map ref 5A3* *SatNav CA11 0JF* **C**

Waterfoot Caravan Park

Pooley Bridge, Penrith, Ullswater CA11 0JF
T: (017684) 86302 **F:** 017684 86728 **E:** info@waterfootpark.co.uk
W: www.waterfootpark.co.uk **£ BOOK ONLINE**

🚐	(34)	£15.50-£28.00
🚐	(34)	£15.50-£28.00
	34 touring pitches	

Set in the grounds of a Georgian mansion overlooking Ullswater. Waterfoot Park is a 5 star holiday park with excellent facilities for touring and self catering wigwam holidays. David Bellamy Conservation Gold Award. Holiday Homes for sale. **Directions:** M6 jct40, follow signs marked Ullswater Steamers. West on A66 1 mile. Left at roundabout A592 (Ullswater). Park located on right. Satnav not compatable. **Open:** 1st March to 14th November.

Site: 🏕 🅰🄿 **Payment:** 💷 ☀ **Leisure:** ⚲ ♪ ⚑ ☋ **Children:** ♨ ⚠ **Catering:** 🍴 **Park:** ☊ 🖥 📺 🅿 🄵
Touring: 🚻 🚽 ⚡

WIGTON, *Cumbria* Map ref 5A2 **S**

Units   1
Sleeps   1-8

PER UNIT PER WEEK
£295.00 - £625.00

SPECIAL PROMOTIONS
Please contact for
short breaks
information.

Foxgloves

Contact: Mrs Janice Kerr, Foxgloves, Greenrigg Farm, Westward, Wigton, Cumbria
CA7 8AH **T:** (01697) 342676 **E:** kerr_greenrigg@hotmail.com
W: www.foxgloves.moonfruit.com

Spacious, extremely well-equipped, comfortable cottage with Aga, offering a high standard of
accommodation. Superlative setting and views. Large, safe garden. Guests are welcome to explore
the farm and fields where a variety of wildlife can be seen. Within easy reach of Lake District,
Scottish Borders and Roman Wall. Children and Pets very welcome.

Open: All year
Nearest Shop: 1 mile
Nearest Pub: 1 mile

Site: ✿ P Leisure: ♨ ♪ ▶ ♺ Property: ⌂ ⊟ 🖳 Children: ⛛ 🛏 ♿ Unit: ⊟ ⊟ 🖳 ⊟ ℗ 📺 ⓓ 📀 ∅ BBQ

WINDERMERE, *Cumbria* Map ref 5A3 **S**

Units   20
Sleeps   2 10
PER UNIT PER WEEK
£497.00 - £2537.00

Graythwaite Cottages

Contact: Graythwaite, Newby Bridge, Ulverston, Nr Windermere, Cumbria LA12 8BQ
T: (01244) 352 336 **E:** cottages@graythwaite.com
W: www.graythwaite.com

Thirteen cottages and barn conversion are located within a
secluded courtyard. The original Victorian farmstead of the estate
was skillfully converted in the early 1990's. **Open:** All Year

Site: ✿ P Leisure: ♪ ♦ Property: ⌂ ⊟ ⊟ 🖳 Children: ⛛ 🛏 ♿ Unit: ⊟ ⊟ 🖳 ⊟ ℗ ⓓ 📀 ∅ BBQ

WINDERMERE, *Cumbria* Map ref 5A3 SatNav LA12 8NR **C**

🚐 (43)   £21.00-£41.00
🚍 (43)   £21.00-£41.00
🏠 (3)   £325.00-£595.00
43 touring pitches

Hill of Oaks Park

Tower Wood, Windermere LA12 8NR
T: (015395) 31578 **F:** 015395 30431 **E:** enquiries@hillofoaks.co.uk
W: www.hillofoaks.co.uk **£ BOOK ONLINE**

Hill of Oaks is a 5 star award-winning park, located on the shores of
Windermere. Excellent facilities include boat launching slipway and
jetties, electric car hire and woodland walks. Self catering
properties on weekly let and Holiday Homes & Lodges.
Directions: M6 jct 36, west on A590 towards Barrow and Newby
Bridge. At roundabout turn right, onto A592. Park is approx 3 miles
on left-hand side. **Open:** 1st March to Mid November.

Site: ▲🅿 Payment: ⊞ ☼ Leisure: ♪ Children: ⛛ ⚠ Catering: 🛒 Park: ⌂ ⊟ ⊟ ⊞ ℟ Touring: ⊟ ⟳
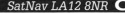

WINDERMERE, *Cumbria* Map ref 5A3   S

VisitEngland
★★★★
SELF CATERING

Hill of Oaks Park

Contact: Christopher & Maureen Dodds, Park Managers, Lake District Estates, Newby Bridge Road, Windermere, Cumbria LA12 8NR **T:** (015395) 31578
E: enquiries@hillofoaks.co.uk **W:** www.hillofoaks.co.uk **£ BOOK ONLINE**

Units   3
Sleeps   2-4
PER UNIT PER WEEK
£375.00 - £695.00

This five star award winning Park has a selection of self catering properties available for weekly rental. Located on over a kilometre of Windermere shoreline, the Parks excellent facilities include private jetties and moorings, fabulous lake views from each property, on site shop, woodland walks, children's play area and shuttle ferry to Lakeside. Free Wi-Fi for self catering holidays.
Open: March to Mid November **Nearest Shop:** On Site
Nearest Pub: 2 miles

Site: **P** Payment: ⛽ Leisure: ♪ ▶ Property: 🚇 🅱 🔲 Children: ⛷ 🏃 Unit: 🍴 🍽 🔲 🔌 📺 📀

WINDERMERE, *Cumbria* Map ref 5A3   SatNav LA23 3PG C

VisitEngland
★★★★★
HOLIDAY, TOURING
& CAMPING PARK

VisitEngland
Gold AWARD

Park Cliffe Camping & Caravan Estate

Birks Road, Windermere LA23 3PG
T: (015395) 31344 **F:** 015395 31971 **E:** info@parkcliffe.co.uk
W: www.parkcliffe.co.uk **£ BOOK ONLINE**

🚐 (60)   £27.00-£34.00
🚗 (60)   £27.00-£34.00
⛺ (80)   £21.00-£33.00
🛖 (3)   £186.00-£644.00
60 touring pitches

The winner of many top-quality awards, Park Cliffe is set in 25 acres of picture-postcard countryside above the eastern shores of Windermere with sweeping views across the lake. Tourer & camping pitches, caravans & camping pods for hire.
Camping pods - £44-£52. **Directions:** Do not follow SatNav - M6 jct 36, follow A590 towards Barrow. At Newby Bridge take A592 towards Windermere. After 3.6 miles turn right into Birks Road.
Open: 1st March to 13th November.

Site: 🏕 ⛺🅿 Payment: ⛽ ☼ Leisure: ▶ 🎣 Children: ⛷ ⛰ Catering: ✕ 🛒 Park: 🐕 🚌 🅱
🏠 🔥 Touring: 📶 🚿 💡 ⚡

OLDHAM, *Greater Manchester* Map ref 4B1   SatNav OL3 5UN C

VisitEngland
★★★★
HOLIDAY, TOURING
& CAMPING PARK

Moorlands Caravan Park

Ripponden Road, Denshaw, Oldham OL3 5UN
T: (01457) 874348 **E:** moorlandscp@aol.com
W: www.moorlandscp.co.uk

🚐 (40)   £18.00-£24.00
🚗 (40)   £18.00-£24.00
⛺ (20)   £8.00
40 touring pitches

Newly refurbished, 4 star park on the moors of Saddleworth. Ideal for walkers, horse riders, or just a family stay. Half a mile from the Pennine Way and Pennine Bridal Way. Short walk to pub and stunning views for tents, caravans and camping pods. Limited winter availability. **Directions:** Junction 22 of the M62, 2 miles in the direction of Saddleworth. **Open:** All year.

Site: ⛺🅿 Payment: ⛽ ☼ Leisure: ♪ ▶ ∪ Children: ⛷ Park: 🐕 🅱 🔥 Touring: 📶 🚿 💡 ⚡

ROCHDALE, *Greater Manchester* Map ref 4B1   SatNav OL15 0AS C

VisitEngland
★★★
HOLIDAY, TOURING
& CAMPING PARK

Hollingworth Lake Caravan Park

Roundhouse Farm, Hollingworth Lake, Littleborough OL15 0AT
T: (01706) 378661 **E:** info@hollingworthlakecaravanpark.com
W: www.hollingworthlakecaravanpark.com

🚐 (30)
🚗 (10)
⛺ (10)
50 touring pitches

A popular, five-acre park adjacent to Hollingworth Lake. At the foot of the Pennines, within easy reach of many local attractions. Backpackers walking the Pennine Way are welcome at this family-run park. Hardstanding and grass areas. Excellent train service into Manchester Victoria. 20 minutes from Littleborough/Smithybridge. Overnight holding area available. Restaurant/cafe within 1m of site. Please contact for 2016 rates. **Directions:** From M62. Jct 21 Milnrow. Follow Hollingworth signs to Fishermans Inn/The Wine Press. Take Rakewood Road then 2nd on right. **Open:** All year.

Payment: ☼ Leisure: ♪ ∪ Catering: 🛒 Park: 🅱 🏠 🔥 Touring: 📶 🚿 💡 ⚡

BLACKPOOL, Lancashire   Map ref 4A1   S

★★
SELF CATERING

Units   10
Sleeps   2-6

PER UNIT PER WEEK
£150.00 - £450.00

SPECIAL PROMOTIONS
Massive savings of up to 50% off high season rates! Low/mid season early bird discounts. (Terms & Conditions apply).

Lynton Apartments

Contact: Iggy or Koko, Lynton Apartments, 227 Promenade, Blackpool FY1 5DL
T: (01253) 624 296 **E:** info@lyntonapartments.co.uk
W: www.lyntonapartments.co.uk

Lynton Apartments offer spacious, self-catering holiday flats at the heart of the Promenade located halfway between Blackpool Tower and the Pleasure Beach with stunning sea views, fully equipped kitchens & private bathrooms. Our units are refurbished annually to very high standards & have flat screen colour TV's with Freeview in all lounges & free Wi-Fi throughout the building.

Open: All year
Nearest Shop: 0.10 miles
Nearest Pub: 0.10 miles

Payment: ⊞ **Property:** 🖥 🗄 **Children:** 🍼 🍴 🏃 **Unit:** 🗓 💻 📺

CARNFORTH, Lancashire   Map ref 5B3   S

3★-4★
SELF CATERING

Units   4
Sleeps   4-6

PER UNIT PER WEEK
£280.00 - £620.00

SPECIAL PROMOTIONS
70% of the weekly booking charge; minimum charge of 3 nights.

Brackenthwaite Holiday Cottages

Contact: Matthew, Brackenthwaite Farm, Yealand Redmayne, Near Carnforth, Lancashire LA5 9TE **T:** (015395) 63276 **E:** info@brackenthwaite.com
W: www.brackenthwaite.com

Relax comfortably in one of our four holiday cottages based in the stunning Arnside and Silverdale designated Area of Outstanding Beauty (AONB). There are lots of lovely activities close-by such as bird watching at Leighton Moss RSPB reserve (2 miles away), golf in Silverdale and water sports at Carnforth. With an abundance of footpaths, the area is a haven for walkers and also cyclists. Nature lovers will find a wealth of flora and fauna, especially at the nearby Gaitbarrows National Nature Reserve. The Lake District, coast and Yorkshire Dales are all easily accessible by either the A6 or M6.

Open: All Year: short breaks taken from Nov - Easter
Nearest Shop: 2 miles
Nearest Pub: 1.5 miles at Beetham

Units: We have four holiday cottages, two which sleep up to six and two which sleep up to four. One is 4 star graded and the other three are 3 star graded.

Site: ⚘ P **Payment:** ⊞ **Leisure:** ⚑ **Property:** 🐕 🖥 🗄 🗄 **Children:** 🍼 🍴 🏃
Unit: 🗓 💻 🗄 ⚙ 📺 ④ 🕹 BBQ

CARNFORTH, Lancashire   Map ref 5B3   S

Units   1
Sleeps   5
PER UNIT PER WEEK
£170.00 - £395.00

Deroy Cottage

Contact: Mr Colin Cross, The Heights, Hawk Street, Carnforth, Lancashire LA5 9LA
T: (01524) 733196   **E:** colin@cross00.orangehome.co.uk
W: www.colincross.co.uk

At The Heights we offer excellent self-catering accommodation with use of a summerhouse and BBQ and magnificent views over Morecambe Bay to the Lakeland fells. We are ideally situated for Lancaster Canal, Ingleton Waterfalls and Arnside. **Open:** All year **Nearest Shop:** 100 yards **Nearest Pub:** 100 yards

Site: ✿ P Property: 🐾 🖵 Children: 🚼 🎫 ♿ Unit: ☐ ▣ ♨ 📺 📀 BBQ

CARNFORTH, Lancashire   Map ref 5B3   S

Units   124
Sleeps   1-6

PER UNIT PER WEEK
£419.00 - £1267.00

SPECIAL PROMOTIONS
Visit our website or call today for seasonal discounts and great savings.

Pine Lake Resort

Contact: Dock Acres, Carnforth, Lancashire LA6 1JZ   **T:** (0800) 358 6991
E: EuHotels@diamondresorts.com
W: www.DiamondResortsandHotels.com **£ BOOK ONLINE**

These unique Scandinavian-style Lodges lie in a tranquil location by Pine Lake near Carnforth. Guests can enjoy water skiing, sailing and canoeing and there is also an indoor swimming pool, fitness centre and spa. The on site restaurant provides a varied menu including children's options and evening entertainment is available in the bar area.

Each 2 bedroom lodge or studio comes with a fully equipped kitchen and some have lake views. Complimentary toiletries, a flat-screen TV and a DVD player are all included, Wi-Fi can be purchased as extra.

Open: All year
Nearest Shop: On Site
Nearest Pub: On Site

Units: A choice of Studios and two bedroom apartments available. All apartments boast a modern bathroom, kitchen and Television with DVD player.

Site: ✿ P Payment: 💳 Leisure: ▶ 🎣 🏊 ⚲ Property: 🚾 ▣ 🖵 Children: 🚼 🎫 ♿ Unit: ▣ ♨ 📺 📀 📞

LANCASTER, Lancashire   Map ref 5A3   SatNav LA2 9HH   C

🚐 (36)   £16.00-£18.00
🚗 (4)   £16.00-£18.00
⛺ (8)   £13.00-£15.00
40 touring pitches

New Parkside Farm Caravan Park, Lancaster

Denny Beck, Caton Road, Lancaster LA2 9HH
T: (01524) 770723   **E:** enquiries@newparksidefarm.co.uk
W: www.newparksidefarm.co.uk

Peaceful, family-run park on a working farm on the edge of the Forest of Bowland. Extensive views of the Lune Valley and Ingleborough. Excellent base for exploring the Lakes, Dales and unspoilt coast and countryside of North Lancashire. **Directions:** Leave M6 at junction 34, A683 east towards Caton/Kirkby Lonsdale, caravan park entrance 1 mile from motorway junction on the right (signposted). **Open:** 1st March to 31st October.

Site: ⛺▣ Payment: ☀ Leisure: 🎵 Children: 🚼 Park: 🐾 🔥 Touring: 🚽 🚿 🚐

LANCASTER, Lancashire   Map ref 5A3   S

Thurnham Hall

Contact: Thurnham, Nr Lancaster, Lancashire LA2 0DT **T:** (0800) 358 6991
E: EuHotels@diamondresorts.com
W: www.DiamondResortsandHotels.com **£ BOOK ONLINE**

Units   60
Sleeps   1-6

PER UNIT PER WEEK
£280.00 - £1267.00

SPECIAL PROMOTIONS
Visit our website or call today for seasonal discounts and great savings.

With an elegant Jacobean Great Hall, this resort a features a leisure centre and traditional restaurant. Thurnham Hall is a 12th-century country estate, set in nearly 30 acres of grounds in scenic Lancashire. The stylish, self-catering accommodation is set in either the historic main house or in modern courtyard buildings. All apartments and studios have a satellite TV and a private bathroom.

The leisure centre at Thurnham Hall has a large indoor swimming pool and a state-of-the-art fitness suite. Guests can relax in the sauna and spa bath, or enjoy treatments in the beauty salon.

Open: All year
Nearest Shop: 2 miles
Nearest Pub: 2 miles

Units: A choice of Studio, one and two bedroom apartments available. All apartments boast a full kitchen, modern bathroom and Television with DVD player.

Site: ❀ P **Payment:** 💳 **Leisure:** 🎵 ⛳ **Property:** 🏢 **Children:** 🧸 **Unit:** 📺 💿 ☎

LYTHAM ST. ANNES, Lancashire   Map ref 4A1   SatNav FY8 4LR   C

Eastham Hall Caravan Park

Saltcotes Road, Lytham St Annes, Lancashire FY8 4LS
T: (01253) 737907 **E:** info@easthamhall.co.uk
W: www.easthamhall.co.uk

🚐 (140)   £20.00-£35.00
🚐   £20.00-£35.00
🏠 (150)   £2430.00
140 touring pitches

SPECIAL PROMOTIONS
Please see website for discounts throughout the year.

Eastham Hall Caravan Park has been owned and managed by the Kirkham family for 50 years. Whether you buy a holiday home on the park or visit with your touring caravan, you can share our lovely rural retreat in a highly sought after location. The park has an on-site shop which is open seven days a week selling essential items including bread, milk, ice cream and newspapers (a newspaper ordering service is provided).

We have a children's adventure playground, extensive playing fields and a dedicated dog exercise area and a dog walk. Touring Pitches: 100 Seasonal, 40 nightly.

Prices based on up to 4 people.

Directions: Please see website.

Open: Touring: 1st March - 1st December
Holiday Homes: 20th February - 3rd January.

Site: ⚠P **Payment:** 💳 ☀ **Children:** 🧸 **Catering:** 🍴 **Park:** **Touring:** 🚿

ORMSKIRK, Lancashire   Map ref 4A1   S

Martin Lane Farm Holiday Cottages

Contact: Owner, Martin Lane Farm Holiday Cottages, 5 Martin Lane, Burscough, Ormskirk, Lancashire L40 8JH **T:** (01704) 893527 / 07803 049128 **E:** cottages@btinternet.com **W:** www.martinlanefarm-holidaycottages.co.uk **£ BOOK ONLINE**

Units   4
Sleeps   1-6
PER UNIT PER WEEK
£315.00 - £630.00

Four beautiful, award-winning country cottages, one fully accessible for guests with disabilities. Nestling in the peaceful, arable farmland of West Lancashire, a haven of rest and tranquility. For those who don't want a 'quiet life' we are just 4 miles from Southport's seaside attractions and the quaint market town of Ormskirk. Martin Mere Wildfowl Trust and Rufford Old Hall, just 2 miles away. **Open:** All year **Nearest Shop:** .50 mile **Nearest Pub:** 0.25 miles

Site: ⚘ P **Payment:** ££ € **Leisure:** ♪ ↑ ∪ **Property:** ▦ ▤ ▥ **Children:** ☡ ♨ ☂ **Unit:** ▯ ▤
▣ ▣ ▦ ♒ TV ◉ DVD BBQ

POULTON-LE-FYLDE, Lancashire   Map ref 4A1   S

Hardhorn Breaks

Contact: Nicholas Pawson, Owner, High Bank Farm, Fairfireld Road, Poulton-le-fylde, Lancashire FY6 8DN **T:** (01253) 890422 / 07563 723058 **E:** blackpoolnick@btinternet.com **W:** www.highbank-farm.com

Units   4
Sleeps   2-20
PER UNIT PER WEEK
£225.00 - £560.00

A complex of 4 recently converted cottages, in the pretty village of Hardhorn, near Poulton-le-Fylde, with Blackpool a short drive away. We are also ideally located for convenient access to a whole host of trip destinations, from the natural splendour of the Lake District and Yorkshire Dales to the urban metropolis of Manchester and several traditional North West textile towns all within easy reach. **Open:** All year **Nearest Shop:** 0.5 miles **Nearest Pub:** 0.5 miles

Site: ⚘ P **Payment:** ££ **Property:** ↑ ▦ ▤ ▥ **Children:** ☡ ♨ ☂ **Unit:** ▯ ▣ ▤ ♒ TV DVD BBQ

PRESTON, Lancashire   Map ref 4A1   S

Crabtree Narrowboat Hire

Contact: Robert Foulkes, Owner, Crabtree Farm, Hagg Lane, St Michael's On Wyre, Preston, Lancashire PR3 0UJ **T:** (01995) 671 712 / 07572 664949 **E:** info@crabtreenarrowboathire.com **W:** www.crabtreenarrowboathire.com

Units   4
Sleeps   2-6
PER UNIT PER WEEK
£700.00 - £1200.00

Crabtree Narrowboat Hire is a friendly, family run narrowboat hire company based on the beautiful, lock-free Lancaster Canal.
We operate 4 luxury boats from our base at Barton Grange Marina – "Willow" (44ft), "Linden" (44ft), "Cedar" (45ft) and "Mulberry" (57ft). All our boats have been assessed and awarded 5 Stars by VisitEngland and we are the only hire company in England to have been awarded a 2015 VisitEngland ROSE Award in Recognition Of Service Excellence.
For a family holiday, short break or a romantic, relaxing getaway you will find a warm welcome with Crabtree Narrowboat Hire.

Open: March to November
Nearest Shop: 25 Yards
Nearest Pub: 1 Mile

Site: P **Payment:** ££ **Property:** ↑ ▥ **Children:** ☂ **Unit:** ♒ TV DVD

TEWITFIELD, *Lancashire* *Map ref 5B3* **S**

Tewitfield Marina

Contact: Shirley Dennison, Bookings Office, 2 Lapwing House, Tewitfield Marina, Chapel Lane, Carnforth LA6 1GP **T:** (01524) 782092 **F:** 01524 782461
E: info@tewitfieldmarina.co.uk **W:** www.tewitfieldmarina.co.uk **£ BOOK ONLINE**

Sleeps 1-7

PER UNIT PER WEEK
£245.00 - £725.00

SPECIAL PROMOTIONS
1 night break (£75.00 - £125.00), Weekend breaks (£150.00-£325.00), special promotions all year round please ring/email for details.

Tewitfield Marina offers a home from home environment in its luxury 1, 2, 3 and 4 bedroom self-catering holiday homes. All properties are furnished to the highest standard with linen/towels on arrival, majority have a balcony view. Kitchens are fully equipped, inc washing machine, dishwasher, fridge freezer, microwave & oven. TV's in lounge and bedroom area. Free parking and play area. Pub and Restaurant on site.

Open: All year
Nearest Shop: Less than 1 mile
Nearest Pub: On site

Site: ❀ P Payment: 📧 **Leisure:** 👣 ♪ ▶ ♻ **Property:** 🐾 🖾 🖾 🖾 **Children:** 🛏 🛋 ♿
Unit: 🖾 🖾 🖾 🖾 🖾 🖾 🖾 🖾

WADDINGTON, *Lancashire* *Map ref 4A1* **S**

Blackbird Cottage

Contact: Ms Joanne Bywood, Blackbird Cottage, Waddington BB7 3HP **T:** (00352) 498014
E: blackbird.cottage@yahoo.co.uk
W: www.blackbirdcottage.weebly.com **£ BOOK ONLINE**

Units 1
Sleeps 1-4
PER UNIT PER WEEK
£350.00 - £500.00

Providing comfortable, centrally-heated accommodation for up to 4 people, Blackbird Cottage has one double bedroom, one bedroom with bunkbeds, fully fitted kitchen and comfortable living room with TV and DVD player. **Open:** All year **Nearest Shop:** 0.01 miles **Nearest Pub:** 0.01 miles

Payment: € **Property:** // 🐾 🖾 🖾 **Children:** 🛏 **Unit:** 🖾 🖾 🖾 🖾 🖾 🖾

WORSTON, *Lancashire* *Map ref 4A1* **S**

Angram Green Holiday Cottages

Contact: John Haworth, Angram Green Holiday Cottages, Angram Green Cottage, Worston, Clitheroe, Lancashire BB7 1QB **T:** (01200) 441455 / 07782 215984
E: info@angramgreen.co.uk **W:** www.angramgreen.co.uk

Units 3
Sleeps 1-6
PER UNIT PER WEEK
£280.00 - £580.00

Farm-based cottages in rural Lancashire. Stunning views across open countryside. Ideal base for walkers and cyclists. One double bedroom, one pair of child-size bunks in smaller units. Two double bedrooms and one twin room in the larger unit. Also dishwasher and washing machine in larger unit. Pets in Pendleside only. Restaurant and bar within walking distance. **Open:** All year **Nearest Shop:** 2 miles **Nearest Pub:** 0.5 miles

Site: ❀ P Leisure: ♪ ▶ **Property:** 🐾 🖾 **Children:** 🛏 🛋 ♿ **Unit:** 🖾 🖾 🖾 🖾 🖾 🖾

VisitEngland
★★★★★
HOLIDAY & TOURING PARK

Willowbank Holiday Home and Touring Park

Coastal Road, Ainsdale, Southport PR8 3ST
T: (01704) 571566 **E:** info@willowbankcp.co.uk
W: www.willowbankcp.co.uk

🚐 (87) £16.00-£21.20
🚙 (87) £16.00-£21.20
🚐 (228)
87 touring pitches

SPECIAL PROMOTIONS
Please see our web site
for offers.

Willowbank Holiday Home & Touring Park offers an easily accessible location, convenient for Southport & Liverpool with well maintained modern facilities in a quiet and relaxed atmosphere. The park is open from 14th Feb to 31st January for holiday homes, touring caravans, motor homes and trailer tents. Last check in 9.00pm. Check out 12.00pm. No Commercial vehicles. Please note we do not let out holiday homes.

Directions: From M6 jct 26 for M58, from the M62 jct for M57. A5036 & A5207 leading to A565 towards Southport, RAF Woodvale, Coastal Rd.

Open: 14th February to 31st January.

Payment: 💳 ☼ **Leisure:** 🛁 ♪ ▶ ∪ **Children:** 🧒 **Park:** 🐾 🚮 🗑 🧴 🎋 **Touring:** 🛡 ⚙ ⚡ ♨

Book your accommodation online

Visit our websites for detailed information, up-to-date availability and to book your accommodation online. Includes over 20,000 places to stay, all of them star rated.

www.visitor-guides.co.uk

The Official Tourist Board Guide to **Self Catering & Camping 2016**

SOUTHPORT, Merseyside   Map ref 4A1

SatNav PR9 8DF **C**

Riverside Holiday Park

Southport New Road, Banks, Southport, Merseyside PR9 8DF
T: (01704) 228886 **F:** 01704 505886 **E:** reception@harrisonleisureuk.com
W: www.harrisonholidays.com **£ BOOK ONLINE**

🚐 (150)	£17.00-£40.00
🚍 (150)	£17.00-£40.00
🏕 (60)	£295.00-£635.00

150 touring pitches

Riverside Holiday Park, located in Banks, Southport is an award winning Holiday Park. A warm welcome awaits you, with luxury self catering holiday homes and touring areas with standard and fully serviced pitches. **Open:** All year.

Site: 🏕 🅰🅿 **Payment:** 💷 ☼ **Leisure:** 🚴 🎣 🎱 🎯 **Children:** 🐴 🎢 **Catering:** ✗ 🍴 **Park:** 🐕 🎵 🗑 🌳
Touring: 🚽 🔌 🚐

SOUTHPORT, Merseyside   Map ref 4A1

S

Sandy Brook Farm

Contact: Mrs W Core, Sandy Brook Farm, 52 Wyke Cop Road, Scarisbrick, Southport
PR8 5LR **T:** (01704) 880337 / 07719 468712 **E:** sandybrookfarm@gmail.com
W: www.sandybrookfarm.co.uk **£ BOOK ONLINE**

Units	5
Sleeps	2-6

PER UNIT PER WEEK
£215.00 - £405.00

SPECIAL PROMOTIONS
Last minute short breaks available. Please ring for details.

Our converted barn stands in peaceful countryside, offering five superbly equipped and traditionally furnished self-catering holiday apartments. The comfortable apartments sleep 2/4/6 and 'The Dairy' is equipped for disabled guests. The seaside town of Southport is 3.5 miles away and the historic town of Ormskirk is 5 miles away.
Liverpool, Manchester, and Blackpool are all within easy reach. Rufford Old Hall and Martin Mere Wildfowl Trust plus many other places of interest are also close by.

Open: All year
Nearest Shop: 2 miles
Nearest Pub: 1 mile

Units: Fully equipped apartments, with one or two bedrooms and sofa beds in the lounge. Sleeps 2/4/6.

Site: ✿ P **Leisure:** 🎣 ⛳ ৩ **Property:** 🖥 🗑 🌐 **Children:** 🐴 🍴 🎯 **Unit:** 📺 🗑 🍴 📺

WIRRAL, Merseyside   Map ref 4A2

S

Port Sunlight Holiday Cottages

Contact: Port Sunlight Village Trust, 23 King George's Drive, Port Sunlight, Wirral
CH62 5DX **T:** (0151) 644 4800 **E:** accommodation@portsunlightvillage.com
W: www.portsunlightvillage.com

Units	3
Sleeps	1-6

PER UNIT PER WEEK
£650.00 - £795.00

Port Sunlight Village Trust are proud to present for hire, three outstanding Grade II Listed holiday cottages. One 5 star and two 4 star accredited by Visit England Quality Assured, a guarantee of quality fittings and furnishings. Come and enjoy this 19th century village with 21st century home comforts.
Prices correct at time of print.
Open: All year **Nearest Shop:** 0.5 miles **Nearest Pub:** 0.5 miles

Site: ✿ P **Payment:** 💷 **Leisure:** 🎣 ⛳ ৩ **Property:** 🖥 🌐 **Children:** 🐴 🍴 🎯 **Unit:** 📺 🗑 🖥 📺 📀
BBQ

Don't Miss...

The Alnwick Garden
Alnwick, Northumberland NE66 1YU
(01665) 511350
www.alnwickgarden.com
Be inspired by the most exciting contemporary garden developed in the last century, The Alnwick Garden. The inspiration of the Duchess of Northumberland, this fascinating garden features the Grand Cascade as its centrepiece to create spellbinding water displays. Explore the Rose Garden, Ornamental Garden, Serpent Garden with eight water sculptures nestling in the coils of a topiary serpent, Bamboo Labyrinth and don't miss the Poison Garden which holds dangerous plants and their stories. The garden is also home to the and one of the world's largest tree houses, with rope bridges, walkways in the sky and a fantastic place to eat.

BALTIC Centre for Contemporary Art
Gateshead, Tyne and Wear NE8 3BA
(01914) 781810
www.balticmill.com
Housed in a landmark industrial building on the south bank of the River Tyne in Gateshead, BALTIC is a major international centre for contemporary art and is the biggest gallery of its kind in the world. It presents a dynamic, diverse and international programme of contemporary visual art, ranging from blockbuster exhibitions to innovative new work and projects created by artists working within the local community.

Beamish Museum
County Durham DH9 0RG
(01913) 704000
www.beamish.org.uk
Beamish - The Living Museum of the North, is a world-famous open air museum vividly recreating life in the North East in the early 1800's and 1900's. It tells the story of the people of North East England during the Georgian, Victorian, and Edwardian periods through a costumed cast, engaging exhibits and an exciting programme of events including The Great North Festival of Transport, a Georgian Fair, The Great North Festival of Agriculture.

Durham Cathedral
County Durham DH1 3EH
(0191) 3864266
www.durhamcathedral.co.uk
Durham Cathedral is perhaps the finest example of Norman church architecture in England or even Europe. Set grandly on a rocky promontory next to the Castle with the medieval city huddled below and the river sweeping round, it is a World Heritage Site and houses the tombs of St Cuthbert and The Venerable Bede.

Lindisfarne Priory
Holy Island, Northumberland TD15 2RX
(01289) 389200
www.english-heritage.org.uk/lindisfarnepriory
Lying just a few miles off the beautiful Northumberland coast, Holy Island contains a wealth of history and is home to one of the region's most revered treasures, Lindisfarne Priory. The epicentre of Christianity in Anglo Saxon times and once the home of St Oswald, it was the birthplace of the Lindisfarne Gospels, one of the world's most precious books and remains a place of pilgrimage today. NB: watch the tides as the causeway is only open at low tide.

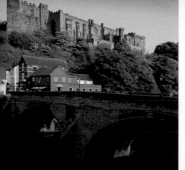

North East

County Durham, Northumberland,
Tees Valley, Tyne & Wear

The North East contains two Areas of Outstanding Natural Beauty, a National Park, Hadrian's Wall, the dynamic city of Newcastle, and County Durham, with its fine cathedral and castle. This region is awash with dramatic hills, sweeping valleys, vast expanses of dune-fringed beaches and ragged cliffs with spectacular views. Littered with dramatic castles, ruins and historic houses, there are plenty of exciting family attractions and walking routes galore.

Northumberland

Tyne & Wear

County Durham

Tees Valley

Explore – North East

County Durham & Tees Valley

Durham Cathedral, the greatest Norman building in England, was once a prison and soars grandly above the Medieval city and surrounding plain. Famed for its location as much as for its architecture, it is the burial place of both St Cuthbert, a great northern saint, and the Venerable Bede, author of the first English history.

The Vale of Durham is packed full of award-winning attractions including Locomotion: The National Railway Museum at Shildon and Beamish – The Living Museum of the North, the country's largest open air museum. Auckland Castle was the palace of Durham's unique Prince Bishops for more than 900 years. Part of the North Pennines Area of Outstanding Natural Beauty, the Durham Dales including Teesdale and Weardale, is a beautiful landscape of hills, moors, valleys and rivers, with numerous picturesque villages and market towns.

Comprising miles of stunning coastline and acres of ancient woodland, Tees Valley covers the lower, flatter area of the valley of the River Tees. This unique part of the UK, split between County Durham and Yorkshire, has nearly a hundred visitor attractions, including Preston Hall and Saltholme Nature Reserve, which can both be found in Stockton-on-Tees.

The Durham Heritage Coast, from Sunderland to Hartlepool, is one of the finest in England. The coastal path that runs along much of its length takes you on a spectacular journey of natural, historical and geological interest, with dramatic views along the shore and out over the North Sea. The historic port city of Hartlepool has award-winning attractions, a fantastic marina, beaches and countryside.

Newcastle & Tyne And Wear

Newcastle-upon-Tyne, once a shipbuilding centre, is a rejuvenated city of proud civic tradition with fine restaurants, theatres, and one of the liveliest arts scenes outside London. As well as the landmark Baltic, there's the Laing Art Gallery, the Great North Museum and The Sage concert venue. The Theatre Royal is the third home of the Royal Shakespeare Company and a venue for major touring companies. The Metro Centre in neighbouring Gateshead attracts shoppers from all over the country with more than 300 outlets and 11 cinema screens.

Northumberland

Northumbria, to use its ancient name, is an undiscovered holiday paradise where the scenery is wild and beautiful, the beaches golden and unspoiled, and the natives friendly. The region is edged by the North Sea, four national parks and the vast Border Forest Park. Its eastern sea boundary makes a stunning coastline, stretching 100 miles from Staithes on the Cleveland boundary, to Berwick-on-Tweed, England's most northerly town, frequently fought over and with the finest preserved example of Elizabethan town walls in the country. In between you'll find as many holiday opportunities as changes of scenery.

Step back in time 2,000 years along Hadrian's Wall, explore the hills, forests and waterfalls of the National Parks, and discover historic castles, splendid churches and quaint towns. Visitors can trace man's occupation of the region from prehistoric times through rock carvings, ancient hill forts, Saxon churches, Norman priories, medieval castles, and a wealth of industrial archaeology. Housesteads Roman Fort at Haydon Bridge is the most complete example of a British Roman fort. It features magnificent ruins and stunning views of the countryside surrounding Hadrian's Wall.

The region has a rich maritime heritage too. Ruined coastal fortifications such as Dunstanburgh and fairy-tale Lindisfarne are relics of a turbulent era. Agriculture is also one of the region's most important industries. Take a trip on the Heatherslaw Light Railway, a narrow gauge line operating from Etal Village to Heatherslaw Mill, a restored waterdriven corn mill and agricultural museum near the delightful model village of Ford.

Visit – North East

County Durham & Tees Valley

Adventure Valley
Durham, County Durham DH1 5SG
(01913) 868291
www.adventurevalley.co.uk
*Split into six Play Zones (with three under cover), you'll
find the very best in family fun come rain or shine.*

Billingham International Folklore Festival
August, Billingham, County Durham
www.billinghamfestival.co.uk
*A festival of traditional and contemporary world
dance, music and arts.*

Bishop Auckland Food Festival
April, Bishop Auckland, County Durham
www.bishopaucklandfoodfestival.co.uk
*Be inspired by cookery demonstrations and
entertained by performers.*

The Bowes Museum
Barnard Castle, County Durham DL12 8NP
(01833) 690606
www.thebowesmuseum.org.uk
*A collection of outstanding European fine and
decorative arts offering an acclaimed exhibition
programme, special events and children's activities.*

Durham Book Festival
October/November, Durham, County Durham
www.durhambookfestival.com
*With writers covering everything from politics to
poetry, and fiction to feminism, there's something
for everyone at the Durham Book Festival. See
website for dates and full programme.*

Durham Castle
County Durham DH1 3RW
(01913) 343800
www.durhamworldheritagesite.com
*Durham Castle is part of the Durham City World
Heritage Site and has enjoyed a long history of*

*continuous use. Along with Durham Cathedral, it
is among the greatest monuments of the Norman
Conquest of Britain and is now home to students of
University College, Durham. Entrance is by guided
tour only, please telephone opening and tour times.*

East Durham Heritage and Lifeboat Centre
County Durham, SR7 7EE
www.seahamlifeboats.oneuk.com
*Take a look at exhibitions with themed displays on
the area's maritime, industrial and social heritage
dating back from before the 8th Century.*

Hall Hill Farm
Durham, County Durham DH7 0TA
(01388) 731333
www.hallhillfarm.co.uk
*Award-winning farm attraction set in attractive
countryside, see and touch the animals at
close quarters.*

Hamsterley Forest
Bishop Auckland, County Durham DL13 3NL
(01388) 488312
www.forestry.gov.uk/hamsterleyforest
*A 5,000 acre mixed woodland open to the public
all year.*

Hartlepool Art Gallery
Hartlepool, Tees Valley TS24 7EQ
(01429) 869706
www.hartlepool.gov.uk
*Former church building also includes the
TIC and a bell tower viewing platform looking
over Hartlepool.*

Hartlepool's Maritime Experience
Tees Valley TS24 0XZ
(01429) 860077
www.hartlepoolsmaritimeexperience.com
*A superb re-creation of an 18th century seaport and
a fantastic place to visit. It brings to life the time of
Nelson, Napoleon and the Battle of Trafalgar.*

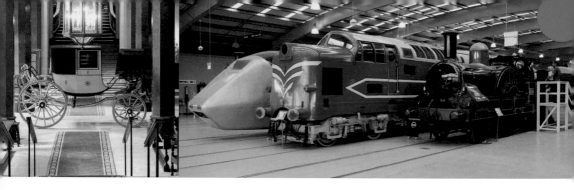

Hartlepool Museum
Maritime Avenue, Hartlepool TS24 0XZ
(01429) 860077
www.hartlepoolsmaritimeexperience.com
Situated beside Hartlepool Historic Quay, includes local historical exhibits, PSS Wingfield Castle and the original lighthouse light.

Head of Steam
Tees Valley DL3 6ST
(01325) 405060
www.darlington.gov.uk/Culture/headofsteam/welcome
Restored 1842 station housing a collection of exhibits relating to railways in the North East of England, including Stephenson's Locomotion, call for details of events.

High Force Waterfall
Middleton-in-Teesdale, County Durham DL12 0XH
(01833) 622209
www.highforcewaterfall.com
Discover the force of nature at High Force, one of the most spectacular waterfalls in England. Enjoy a picnic or take a walk along many way marked routes.

HMS Trincomalee
Hartlepool, Tees Valley TS24 0XZ
(01429) 223193
www.hms-trincomalee.co.uk
HMS Trincomalee, built in 1817, is one of the oldest ship afloat in Europe. Come aboard for a unique experience of Navy life two centuries ago.

Killhope, The North of England
Lead Mining Museum
Bishop Auckland, County Durham DL13 1AR
(01388) 537505
www.killhope.org.uk
Fully restored Victorian lead mine and the most complete lead mining site in Great Britain.

Locomotion: The National Railway Museum at Shildon
Shildon, County Durham DL4 1PQ
(01388) 931232
www.nrm.org.uk/locomotion
The first National Museum in the North East. Free admission. View over 60 vehicles, children's play area and interactive displays.

mima
Middlesbrough, Tees Valley TS1 2AZ
(01642) 726720
www.visitmima.com
mima, Middlesbrough Institute of Modern Art, is a £14.2m landmark gallery in the heart of Middlesbrough. mima showcases an international programme of fine art and applied art from the 1900s to the present day.

Preston Hall Museum and Park
Stockton-on-Tees, Tees Valley TS18 3RH
(01642) 527375
www.prestonparkmuseum.co.uk
A Georgian country house set in beautiful parkland overlooking the River Tees. A Museum of social history with a recreated Victorian street and working craftsmen.

Raby Castle
Staindrop, County Durham DL2 3AH
(01833) 660202
www.rabycastle.com
Home of Lord Barnard's family since 1626, includes a 200 acre deer park, gardens, carriage collection, adventure playground, shop and tearoom.

Saltburn Smugglers Heritage Centre
Saltburn-by-the-Sea, Tees Valley TS12 1HF
(01287) 625252
www.thisisredcar.co.uk/visit/saltburn-smugglers-heritage-centre
Step back into Saltburn's past and experience the authentic sights, sounds and smells.

Saltholme Wildlife Reserve
Middlesbrough, Tees Valley TS2 1TU
(01642) 546625
www.rspb.org.uk/reserves/guide/s/saltholme
An amazing wildlife experience in the Tees Valley.

Weardale Railway
County Durham, DL13 2YS
(01388) 526203
www.weardale-railway.org.uk
The Weardale Railway follows the path of the River Wear and passes through spectacular scenery. A good time is to be had by all on these heritage locomotives.

Newcastle & Tyne And Wear

Arbeia Roman Fort and Museum
South Shields, Tyne and Wear NE33 2BB
(01912) 771410
www.twmuseums.org.uk/arbeia
Arbeia is the best reconstruction of a Roman fort in Britain and offers visitors a unique insight into the every day life of the Roman army, from the soldier in his barrack room to the commander in his luxurious house.

BBC Tours Newcastle
Newcastle upon Tyne, NE2 4NS
www.bbc.co.uk/showsandtours/tours/newcastle
Take a tour of the broadcasting house for an in depth behind the scenes look into what it's like to be a director and presenter for the BBC. Take a seat in the director's chair, or ask questions that have always been a mystery.

Centre for Life
Newcastle-upon-Tyne, Tyne and Wear NE1 4EP
(01912) 438210
www.life.org.uk
The Centre for Life is an award-winning science centre where imaginative exhibitions, interactive displays and special events promote greater understanding of science and provoke curiosity in the world around us.

Discovery Museum
Newcastle-upon-Tyne, Tyne and Wear NE1 4JA
(01912) 326789
www.twmuseums.org.uk/discovery
A wide variety of experiences for all the family to enjoy.

Evolution Emerging
May, Newcastle, Tyne and Wear
www.evolutionemerging.com
The North East's premier music event, taking place over a Bank Holiday.

Great North Museum: Hancock
Newcastle-upon-Tyne, Tyne and Wear NE2 4PT
(0191) 208 6765
www.twmuseums.org.uk/great-north-museum
See major new displays showing the wonder of the animal and plant kingdoms, objects from the Ancient Greeks and a planetarium and a life-size T-Rex.

Hatton Gallery
Newcastle-upon-Tyne, Tyne and Wear NE1 7RU
(01912) 226059
www.twmuseums.org.uk/hatton
Temporary exhibitions of contemporary and historical art. Permanent display of Kurt Schwitters' Merzbarn.

Laing Art Gallery
Newcastle-upon-Tyne, Tyne and Wear NE1 8AG
(01912) 327734
www.twmuseums.org.uk/laing
The Laing Art Gallery is home to an important collection of 18th and 19th century painting, which is shown alongside temporary exhibitions of historic and contemporary art.

Namco Funscape
Gateshead, Tyne and Wear, NE11 9XY
(0191) 406 1066
Find fun in 38, 000 sq ft of state-of-the-art arcade games, tenpin bowling, fantastic bars and the fastest dodgem track in Europe.

National Glass Museum
Liberty Way, Sunderland, SR6 0GL
(01915) 155555
www.nationalglasscentre.com
Overlooking the River Wear, enjoy an ever-changing programme of exhibitions, live glass blowing, and banqueting and a stunning restaurant.

Newcastle Theatre Royal
Newcastle upon Tyne NE1 6BR
(0844) 811 2121
www.theatreroyal.co.uk
The Theatre Royal is a Grade I listed building situated on historic Grey Street in Newcastle-upon-Tyne. It hosts a variety of shows, including ballet, contemporary dance, drama, musicals and opera in a restored 1901 Frank Matcham Edwardian interior.

Sage Gateshead
Gateshead Quays, Gateshead NE8 2JR
(0191) 443 4661
www.sagegateshead.com
A concert venue and centre for musical education on the south bank of the River Tyne. It stages a varied and eclectic programme in state-of-the-art halls.

Segedunum Roman Fort, Baths & Museum

Wallsend, Tyne and Wear NE28 6HR
(0191) 278 4217
www.twmuseums.org.uk/segedunum
Segedunum Roman Fort is the gateway to Hadrian's Wall. Explore the excavated fort site, visit reconstructions of a Roman bath house, learn about the history of the area in the museum and enjoy the view from the 35 metre viewing tower.

Tyneside Cinema

Newcastle upon Tyne, Tyne and Wear NE1 6QG
(0191) 227 5500
www.tynesidecinema.co.uk
Showing the best films in beautiful art deco surroundings, Tyneside Cinema's programme ranges from mainstream to arthouse and world cinema. As the last surviving Newsreel theatre still operating full-time in the UK, this Grade II-listed building is a must-visit piece of lovingly restored heritage.

WWT Washington Wetland Centre

Washington, Tyne and Wear NE38 8LE
(01914) 165454
www.wwt.org.uk/visit/washington
45 hectares of wetland, woodland and wildlife reserve. Home to wildfowl, insects and flora with lake-side hides, wild bird feeding station, waterside cafe, picnic areas, sustainable garden, playground and events calendar.

Northumberland

Alnwick Beer Festival

September, Alnwick, Northumberland
www.alnwickbeerfestival.co.uk
If you enjoy real ale, or simply want to enjoy a fantastic social event, then make sure you pay this festival a visit.

Alnwick Castle

Northumberland NE66 1NQ
(01665) 511100
www.alnwickcastle.com
A significant visitor attraction with lavish State Rooms and superb art collections, as well as engaging activities and events for all ages, and all set in beautiful landscape by Northumberland-born 'Capability' Brown. Potter fans will recognise Alnwick as Hogwarts from the Harry Potter films.

Bailiffgate Museum

Alnwick, Northumberland NE66 1LX
(01665) 605847
www.bailiffgatemuseum.co.uk
Bailiffgate Museum brings to life the people and places of North Northumberland in exciting interactive style.

Bamburgh Castle

Northumberland NE69 7DF
(01668) 214515
www.bamburghcastle.com
A spectacular castle with fantastic coastal views. The stunning Kings Hall and Keep house collections of armour, artwork, porcelain and furniture.

Belsay Hall, Castle & Gardens

Nr Morpeth, Northumberland NE20 0DX
(01661) 881636
www.english-heritage.org.uk
Lose yourself at Belsay with its unique combination of Grecian architecture, medieval ruins, formal terraces and lush jungle-esque Quarry Garden. Enjoy wonderful views from the top of the castle tower and a tasty treat at the tempting Victorian tearoom.

Chillingham Castle

Northumberland, NE66 5NJ
01668 215359
www.chillingham-castle.com
A remarkable Medieval fortress with Tudor additions, torture chamber, shop, dungeon, tearoom, woodland walks, furnished rooms and topiary garden.

Cragside House, Gardens & Estate

Morpeth, Northumberland NE65 7PX
(01669) 620333
www.nationaltrust.org.uk/cragside/
*Built on a rocky crag high above Debdon Burn,
the house is crammed with ingenious gadgets
and was the first in the world to be lit electrically.
The gardens are breathtaking with 5 lakes, one of
Europe's largest rock gardens, and over 7 million
trees and shrubs.*

Haydon Bridge Festival

July, Haydon Bridge, Northumberland
www.haydonbridgefestival.co.uk
Annual celebration of the finest real ales and wines.

Hexham Abbey Festival

September-October, Hexham, Northumberland
www.hexhamabbey.org.uk
*An exciting array of events to capture the
imagination, bringing the very best world-class
musicians and artists to Hexham.*

Hexham Old Gaol

Northumberland NE46 1XD
(01670) 624523
www.hexhamoldgaol.org.uk
Step into the oldest purpose-built prison in
England. *Tour the Old Gaol, 1330AD, by glass lift.
Meet the gaoler to learn about the treatment of
criminals then put yourself in the prisoners' shoes
and try on costumes.*

Kielder Castle Forest Park Centre

Northumberland NE48 1ER
(01434) 250209
www.forestry.gov.uk/kielder
*Features include forest shop, information centre,
tearoom and exhibitions. Bike hire available.*

Lindisfarne Castle

Northumberland TD15 2SH
(01289) 389244
www.nationaltrust.org.uk/lindisfarne-castle/
*Rising from the sheer rock face at the tip of Holy
Island off the Northumberland coast, Lindisfarne
Castle was built to defend a harbour sheltering
English ships during skirmishes with Scotland.*

Northumberland National Park

Northumberland, NE66 4LT
(01665) 578890
www.northumberlandnationalpark.org.uk
*Covering 405 acres of breathtaking landscape rich
in wildlife, heritage and picturesque valleys.*

RNLI Grace Darling Museum

Bamburgh, Northumberland NE69 7AE
(01668) 214910
www.rnli.org.uk/gracedarling
*A museum dedicated to Grace Darling and her
family, as well as all those who Save Lives at Sea.*

Warkworth Castle

Warkworth, Northumberland NE65 0UJ
(01665) 711423
www.english-heritage.org.uk/warkworthcastle
*This hill-top fortress and hermitage offers a
fantastic family day out. The magnificent cross-
shaped keep was once home to 'Harry Hotspur',
immortalised as a rebel lord by Shakespeares.*

Whalton Manor Gardens

Northumberland, NE61 3UT
(01670) 775205
www.whaltonmanor.co.uk
*Experience a first-hand insight into nature's true
beauty with a guided tour from the owner. Why not
stay for home-cooked lunch and a cream tea as well?*

Tourist Information Centres

When you arrive at your destination, visit the Tourist Information Centre for quality assured help with accommodation and information about local attractions and events, or email your request before you go.

Alnwick	2 The Shambles	01670 622152 / 01670 622151	alnwick.tic@northumberland.gov.uk
Amble	Queen Street Car Park	01665 712313	amble.tic@northumberland.gov.uk
Bellingham	Station Yard	01434 220616	bellinghamtic@btconnect.com
Berwick-Upon-Tweed	106 Marygate	01670 622155 / 625568	berwick.tic@northumberland.gov.uk
Bishop Auckland	Town Hall Ground Floor	03000 269524	bishopauckland.touristinfo@durham.gov.uk
Corbridge	Hill Street	01434 632815	corbridge.tic@northumberland.gov.uk
Craster	Craster Car Park	01665 576007	craster.tic@northumberland.gov.uk
Darlington	Central Library	01325 462034	crown.street.library@darlington.gov.uk
Durham Visitor Contact Centre	1st Floor	03000 262626	visitor@thisisdurham.com
Gateshead	Central Library	0191 433 8420	libraries@gateshead.gov.uk
Guisborough	Priory Grounds	01287 633801	guisborough_tic@redcar-cleveland.gov.uk
Haltwhistle	Westgate	01434 322002	haltwhistle.tic@northumberland.gov.uk
Hartlepool	Hartlepool Art Gallery	01429 869706	hpooltic@hartlepool.gov.uk
Hexham	Wentworth Car Park	01434 652220	hexham.tic@northumberland.gov.uk
Middlesbrough	Middlesbrough Info. Centre & Box Office	01642 729900	tic@middlesbrough.gov.uk
Middleton-in-Teesdale	10 Market Place	01833 641001	tic@middletonplus.myzen.co.uk
Morpeth	The Chantry	01670 623455	morpeth.tic@northumberland.gov.uk
North Shields	Unit 18	0191 2005895	ticns@northtyneside.gov.uk
Once Brewed	National Park Centre	01434 344396	tic.oncebrewed@nnpa.org.uk
Otterburn	Otterburn Mill	01830 521002	tic@otterburnmill.co.uk
Saltburn by Sea	Saltburn Library	01287 622422 / 623584	saltburn_library@redcar-cleveland.gov.uk
Seahouses	Seafield Car Park	01665 720884 / 01670 625593	seahouses.tic@northumberland.gov.uk
South Shields	Haven Point	0191 424 7788	tourism@southtyneside.gov.uk
Stockton-On-Tees	High Street	01642 528130	visitorinformation@stockton.gov.uk
Whitley Bay	York Road	0191 6435395	susan.clark@northtyneside.gov.uk
Wooler	The Cheviot Centre	1668 282123	wooler.tic@northumberland.gov.uk

Regional Contacts and Information

For more information on accommodation, attractions, activities, events and holidays in North East England, contact one of the regional or local tourism organisations. Their websites have a wealth of information and many produce free publications to help you get the most out of your visit.

www.visitnortheastengland.com

www.thisisdurham.com
www.newcastlegateshead.com
www.visitnorthumberland.com
www.visithadrianswall.co.uk
www.visitnorthtyneside.com
www.visitsouthtyneside.co.uk
www.seeitdoitsunderland.co.uk

Stay – North East

Entries appear alphabetically by town name in each county. A key to symbols appears on page 7

BISHOP AUCKLAND, Co Durham   Map ref 5C2   S

New Cottage

Contact: Margaret Partridge, Owner, Hollymoor Farm, Cockfield DL13 5HF
T: (01388) 718567 **E:** margandpatpartridge@tiscali.co.uk
W: www.hollymoorfarm.co.uk

Units	1
Sleeps	2

PER UNIT PER WEEK
£266.00 - £275.00

New Cottage is on a working farm in County Durham, on the borders of the beautiful Durham Dales, Teesdale and Weardale. With its elevated position it is surrounded by beautiful views. The panoramic views from the lounge are a never-ending source of delight - they are stunning. The sunsets are truly magnificent.
Open: All Year **Nearest Shop:** 1 Mile **Nearest Pub:** 1 Mile

Site: ✿ P Property: 🔲 🖵 Unit: 🔲 📺 🔾 📺 BBQ

BOWES, Co Durham   Map ref 5B3   S

Mellwaters Barn

Contact: Mr Andrew Tavener, Mellwaters Barn, East Mellwaters Farm, Stainmore Road, Bowes, Barnard Castle DL12 9RH **T:** (01833) 628181 **E:** mellwatersbarn@aol.com
W: www.mellwatersbarn.co.uk **£ BOOK ONLINE**

Units	4
Sleeps	2-4

PER UNIT PER WEEK
£294.00 - £525.00

SPECIAL PROMOTIONS
3 nights short breaks from £126, small cottage, £225 large cottage

We would like to welcome you to Mellwaters Barn Cottages in Beautiful Teesdale centrally placed in Northern England within easy reach of the Lake District, Yorkshire Dales, Durham and York. Auckland Castle, Beamish and Bowes Museum are all places of interest and are easy to reach. Mellwaters Barn is an ideal visitor centre in beautiful countryside with clean air, these award-winning spacious luxury cottages are designed for a perfect relaxing holiday. All cottages are fully equipped and prices include all accommodation costs. Open all year. Arrival / departure any day of the week.

Open: All year, short breaks available
Nearest Shop: Barnard Castle
Nearest Pub: Bowes

Units: Two cottages fully wheelchair accessible,sleep four people, bedrooms on the ground floor . Two smaller cottages sleep 2 people bedrooms upstairs.

Site: P Property: ▦ 🔲 🖵 Unit: 🔲 📺 📺 🔾 🔾 📀

CORNRIGGS, Co Durham   Map ref 5B2   S

Cornriggs Cottages

Contact: Mrs Janet Elliott, Low Cornriggs Farm, Cowshill in Weardale, Bishop Auckland, Durham DL13 1AQ **T:** (01388) 537600 / 07760 766794 **E:** cornriggsfarm@btconnect.com
W: www.cornriggsfarm.co.uk **£ BOOK ONLINE**

Units	2
Sleeps	2-6

PER UNIT PER WEEK
£399.00 - £495.00

Both luxury cottages have, spectacular views. Easy access to Durham, Beamish and The Lakes. Three large accessible bedrooms, two WC's with shower and bathroom. Dining kitchen very well equipped, large lounge with fire and big comfy sofas, Satellite TV & Garden. Working farm with Hereford cattle and beautiful wild flower meadows/birds. Breakfast is available. Near to the village of Cowshill **Open:** All year **Nearest Shop:** 1.5 miles
Nearest Pub: 1 mile

  Site: ✿ P Payment: 💳 € Leisure: ♿ 🎣 ▶ ♻ 🔾 Property: 🔲 🖵 Children: 🚼 🏠 🧒 Unit: 📺 🔲
🔲 🔾 📺 📀 📀

MIDDLETON-IN-TEESDALE, Co Durham   Map ref 5B3   **S**

Firethorn Cottage

Contact: Mrs Clare Long, Firethorn Cottage, 53 Union Street, Fairview, Cheltenham, Gloucestershire GL52 2JN **T:** (01242) 700308 / 07780 951162
E: Firethorncottage@hotmail.co.uk

Units 1
Sleeps 2
PER UNIT PER WEEK
£200.00 - £275.00

A delightful Grade II listed, detached stone-built lead miner's cottage. One up/one down with flagstone floor, lounge diner, open fire, traditional rag rugs and beamed ceiling. Modern bathroom upstairs with bath and shower over and heated towel rail. Double bedroom with storage. Outside a small cottage garden with views. Night storage heaters throughout. Superb walking and fishing close by. **Open:** All year **Nearest Shop:** 200 yards **Nearest Pub:** 300 yards

Site: Property: Unit:

ALLENDALE, Northumberland   Map ref 5D2   **S**

Fell View Cottage

Contact: Mr & Mrs Colin & Carole Verne-Jones, Owners, 69 Buckinghamshire Road, Belmont, Durham DH1 2BE **T:** (0191) 3869045 / 0780 7473749
E: info@fellviewcottage.co.uk **W:** www.fellviewcottage.co.uk **£ BOOK ONLINE**

Units 1
Sleeps 1-7
PER UNIT PER WEEK
£450.00 - £850.00

Rebuilt barn, now detached, three-bedroom stone cottage in designated Area of Outstanding Natural Beauty with wonderful unrestricted views of the Allendale Valley and beyond. Built to the highest possible standards of a traditional Northumberland cottage, it has a large master bedroom with a king-size bed, two further twin bedrooms and Wi-Fi. **Open:** All year **Nearest Shop:** 1.5 miles **Nearest Pub:** 1.5 miles

 Site: P Payment: Leisure: Property: Children: Unit: BBQ

ALLENHEADS, Northumberland   Map ref 5B2   **S**

Molecatcher's Cottage

Contact: Miss Andrea Cowie, Bookings Administrator, Springboard Sunderland Trust, Unit 1 Rivergreen Industry Centre, Pallion, Sunderland, Tyne and Wear SR4 6AD
T: (01915) 5155320 **E:** acowie@springboard-ne.org **W:** www.molecatcherscottage.co.uk

Units 1
Sleeps 1-4
PER UNIT PER WEEK
£240.00 - £450.00

SPECIAL PROMOTIONS
Weekend, short breaks and special offers available.

Mole Catchers is a cosy cottage with a contemporary twist in the heart of the secret North Pennines, in the village of Allenheads. Beamed throughout, the cottage has one double and one twin bedroom, a living room with wood burning stove a charming modern kitchen and bathroom and a walled garden. The cottage provides a fantastic base to explore the surrounding countryside. Weekend, short breaks and special offers available, please see our website for details.

Open: All year
Nearest Shop: 6 miles
Nearest Pub: 0.5 miles

Site: P Leisure: Property: Children: Unit: BBQ

ALNWICK, *Northumberland*   Map ref 5C1   S

VisitEngland
★★★★
SELF CATERING

27 Pottergate

Contact: Mr Richard Evans, 3 Longdyke Steading, Shilbottle, Alnwick, Northumberland
NE66 2HQ **T:** (01665) 581188 / 07878 756732 **E:** enquiries@alnwickpottergate.co.uk
W: www.alnwickpottergate.co.uk

Units   1
Sleeps   1-6

PER UNIT PER WEEK
£650.00 - £950.00

Architect designed four bedroom town house just round the corner
from Alnwick Castle and short walk to Alnwick Garden. Surrounded
by lovely countryside Alnwick is three miles from the coast.
Open: All year **Nearest Shop:** 0.10 miles **Nearest Pub:** 0.10 miles

Site: ✿ **P** Payment: € Leisure: ♿ ⌿ ▶ ↻ Property: ⫽ ☐ ⊡ Children: ⛺ ▥ ⚲ Unit: ☐ ☐ ▣ ☐ ℚ ⏷
⊡

BAMBURGH, *Northumberland*   Map ref 5C1   S

VisitEngland
4★ - 5★
SELF CATERING

VisitEngland
Gold
AWARD

Outchester & Ross Farm Cottages

Contact: John and Heather Sutherland, Outchester & Ross Farm Cottages, The Farmhouse,
Ross, Belford, Northumberland NE70 7EN **T:** (01668) 213336 **E:** stay@rosscottages.co.uk
W: www.rosscottages.co.uk **£ BOOK ONLINE**

Units   17
Sleeps   2-6

PER UNIT PER WEEK
£300.00 - £1050.00

SPECIAL PROMOTIONS
Special offers from
time to time. Discounts
for under occupancy.
Please look on the
website.

Enjoy a peaceful break in spacious, warm cottages with private gardens and ample parking in lovely
Northumbrian coastal locations near Lindisfarne and Farne Islands. Close to walking and cycling
routes. Three of our cottages permit dogs. Free use of telescopes and star gazing shelter for guests.
Surrounded by unspoilt countryside, magnificent castles and beautiful beaches. Our well-equipped
cottages sleep 2-6, or you can enjoy a romantic break in our 5-star Ducket, an 18th century stone
tower with 21st century facilities.

Open: All year
Nearest Shop: 3 miles
Nearest Pub: 3 miles

[f] [y]

Site: ✿ **P** Payment: ⊞ Leisure: ♿ ▶ ↻ Property: ▤ ☐ ⊡ Children: ⛺ ▥ ⚲
Unit: ☐ ☐ ▣ ☐ ℚ ⏷ ▣ ⊡ ☎

Need more information?

Visit our websites for detailed
information, up-to-date availability
and to book your accommodation
online. Includes over 20,000 places
to stay, all of them star rated.

www.visitor-guides.co.uk

Point Cottages

3★ - 4★
SELF CATERING

Contact: Mrs Elizabeth Sanderson, Point Cottages, 30 The Oval, Benton, Newcastle-upon-Tyne NE12 9PP **T:** (01912) 662800 **F:** 01912 151630 **E:** info@bamburgh-cottages.co.uk
W: www.bamburgh-cottages.co.uk **£ BOOK ONLINE**

| Units | 5 |
| Sleeps | 2-6 |

PER UNIT PER WEEK
£295.00 - £1350.00

SPECIAL PROMOTIONS
3 night winter breaks from £190. Please contact for details.

A cluster of one, two and three bedroom cottages in a superb location next to a beautiful links golf course at the edge of historic Bamburgh overlooking magnificent sandy beaches. Large shared garden. Views to Farne Islands, Lindisfarne & Bamburgh Castle. Ten car parking spaces, two per cottage. Guest comments: really cosy - beautiful - comfortable - peaceful - very enjoyable - great beds - will return.

Open: All year
Nearest Shop: 1 mile
Nearest Pub: 1 mile

Units: All ground floor except Aiden. Cuthbert/Bede interconnectable (10 person), shared laundry at rear of cottages. £1 coin metre only pay for the electricity you use.

Site: ✿ P Leisure: 🚴 🏊 ⛳ ⛵ Property: 🐕 📺 🖥 🎱 Children: 🐎 ⛏ 👶 Unit: ▣ 🍳 📺 📀 🍴 BBQ

Seal Waters

★★★
SELF CATERING

Contact: Mr Peter Carr-Seaman, Owners, Seal Waters, Aydon South Farm, Corbridge, Northumberland NE45 5PL **T:** (01434) 632839 **F:** 01434 632849 **E:** info@sealwaters.com
W: www.sealwaters.com **£ BOOK ONLINE**

| Units | 1 |
| Sleeps | 4 |

PER UNIT PER WEEK
£575.00 - £990.00

An outstanding location with spectacular views overlooking Budle Bay and Holy Island. The beach is just a short "hop" through the dunes and there is a lovely walk from the cottage to Bamburgh and the Castle. The golf course is close by and Budle Bay is also a very popular spot for bird watching. Good safe parking outside the door. Many guests say that the cottage has the 'wow' factor.

Open: All year
Nearest Shop: 2 miles
Nearest Pub: 2 miles

Units: Single storey cottage with double bedroom and a small twin bedded room, separate bathroom and shower room, dining conservatory and kitchen.

Site: ✿ P Leisure: ⛳ Property: 🐕 📺 🖥 Unit: ▣ 📺 📀 🍴 📞

North East - Northumberland

VisitEngland

★ ★ ★ ★
HOLIDAY, TOURING
& CAMPING PARK

🚐 (144)   £18.50-£25.00
🚎 (144)   £18.50-£25.00
⛺ (30)   £9.75-£22.00
🚐 (27)   £260.00-£640.00
144 touring pitches

SPECIAL PROMOTIONS
Please see website for
special offers and
details of our wigwams
too!

Waren Caravan and Camping Park

Waren Mill, Bamburgh, Northumberland NE70 7EE
T: (01668) 214366 **F:** 01668 214224 **E:** waren@meadowhead.co.uk
W: www.meadowhead.co.uk **£ BOOK ONLINE**

Waren Caravan and Camping Park is nestled in coastal countryside with spectacular views to Holy Island and Bamburgh Castle. On site facilities include restaurant and bar, splash-pool, shop and children's play area. Our welcoming environment means you have all you need if you wish to stay on-site but we also make a great base from which to explore Northumberland's coast and castles. Please contact us for up to date prices.

Directions: Follow B1342 from A1 to Waren Mill towards Bamburgh. By Budle turn right, follow Meadowhead's Waren Caravan and Camping Park signs.

Open: 7th March to 1st November.

Site: 📶 **Payment:** 💷 € ☼ **Leisure:** 🎣 ⚓ ⚲ **Children:** 🧸 ⚴ **Catering:** ✖ 🍴 **Park:** 🐎 🚉 🗄 🗃 🎭 **Touring:** 🚻 🚾 🔌 🔧

BELLINGHAM, Northumberland   Map ref 5B2   S

Riverdale Court

Contact: Simon Irving, Manager, Riverdale Hall Hotel, Bellingham, Hexham, Northumberland NE48 2JT **T:** (01434) 220254 **E:** reservations@riverdalehallhotel.co.uk **W:** www.riverdalehallhotel.co.uk

Units   4
Sleeps   1-5

PER UNIT PER WEEK
£160.00 - £490.00

SPECIAL PROMOTIONS
Please see website for current special offers.

Set in the grounds of the Riverdale Hall Hotel, Riverdale Court consists of four self-catering apartments with splendid river views and ample parking. The two first-floor apartments, Blakey and Graham, have balconies. The ground-floor apartments, Abrahams and Milburn have patio areas. All overlooking the cricket field, the North Tyne River and bridge and Dunterley Fell (Pennine Way). Guests enjoy free use of pool, sauna and amenities. Fishing, golf, cricket, walking and mountain biking all near by. Please see website for further details.

Open: All year.
Nearest Shop: 1 Mile.
Nearest Pub: 1 Mile.

Units: The Abrahams, Blakey and Graham all have two bedrooms. The Milburn has one large bedroom. All apartments have open plan lounges and a kitchen with dishwasher.

Site: ✿ **P** **Payment:** 🔢 **Leisure:** 🚴 ⚓ ► ∪ ९ **Property:** ∥ 🐾 ▣ 🔲 **Children:** 🍼 🛏 ⚐
Unit: ▢ ▤ ▭ ▨ ९ TV ④ DVD ℓ

BERWICK-UPON-TWEED, Northumberland   Map ref 5B1   S

Broadstone Cottage - Norham

Contact: Mr Edward Chantler, Broadstone Farm, Grafty Green, Maidstone ME17 2AT **T:** (01622) 850207 **E:** davidchantler@btconnect.com

Units   1
Sleeps   1-5
PER UNIT PER WEEK
£175.00 - £375.00

Village cottage. Ideal centre for touring, walking and fishing holidays. 20 minutes to beach. Shops and pubs nearby. Full central heating. Bathroom with shower. One double, one twin. Good sized secure garden.
Open: All year **Nearest Shop:** 0.05 miles **Nearest Pub:** 0.05 miles

Site: ✿ **P** **Property:** 🐾 🔲 **Children:** 🍼 🛏 **Unit:** ▢ ▭ ▨ ९ TV

BERWICK-UPON-TWEED, Northumberland   Map ref 5B1   S

Marlborough Cottage

Contact: Mr Peter Adamson, Proprietor, Marlborough House, 133 Main Street, Spittal, Berwick-upon-Tweed TD15 1RP **T:** (01289) 305293 / 07443 953857
E: marlboroughcottage@live.co.uk **W:** www.marlboroughcottage.info

Units   1
Sleeps   1-5
PER UNIT PER WEEK
£300.00 - £600.00

Superior two-bedroomed cottage, impressive seafront location, fully equipped kitchen, shower-room with double-sized cubicle provided with grips & anti-slip mats. Ramped access to Cottage, all on one level, wheelchair-accessible, off-road parking. Freshly-laundered bedding & towels provided.
Open: All year **Nearest Shop:** 0.25 miles **Nearest Pub:** 0.25 miles

Site: ✿ **P** **Leisure:** 🚴 ⚓ ► ∪ **Property:** 🖼 ▣ 🔲 **Children:** 🍼 🛏 **Unit:** ▢ ▤ ▭ ▨ ९ TV ④ DVD

For **key to symbols** see page 7

BERWICK-UPON-TWEED, Northumberland   Map ref 5B1   S

Seaview Cottage

Contact: Brenda Crowcroft, Owner, Berwick Cottage Holidays, Cow Road, Spittal, Berwick-upon-Tweed TD15 2QS **T:** (01289) 304175 **E:** b.crowcroft@talk21.com **W:** www.berwickcottageholidays.co.uk

Units 1
Sleeps 6
PER UNIT PER WEEK
£375.00 - £575.00

Charming, stone built cottage, sleeps six in comfort. Wood-burner, patio garden, stunning sea views and easy access A1 Newcastle and Edinburgh. Access to lovely beaches. **Open:** All year **Nearest Shop:** 1 mile **Nearest Pub:** 1 mile

CRASTER, Northumberland   Map ref 5C1   S

Craster Tower Penthouse Apartment

Contact: Mrs Fiona Craster, Craster Tower Penthouse Apartment, Craster Tower, Alnwick, Northumberland NE66 3SS **T:** (01665) 576674 **E:** stay@crastertower.co.uk **W:** www.crastertower.co.uk **£ BOOK ONLINE**

Units 1
Sleeps 1-8
PER UNIT PER WEEK
£650.00 - £1840.00

Spacious comfortable apartment encompassing the whole top floor of historic Craster Tower, beside picturesque fishing village producing world famous kippers. Elegantly furnished, with spectacular sea views. Ideal for beaches, walkers, golfers and history lovers. Comprehensively equipped kitchen, comfortable sitting room with flat screen TV, log burner and Wi-Fi, 18th century drawing room and tennis. **Open:** All year including Christmas and New Year **Nearest Shop:** 0.10 miles **Nearest Pub:** 0.5 miles

HALTWHISTLE, Northumberland *Map ref 5B2* S

VisitEngland ★★★★ SELF CATERING

Units 5
Sleeps 3-28
PER UNIT PER WEEK
£299.00 - £845.00

Lambley Farm Cottages

Contact: Lambley Farm Cottages, Lambley CA8 7LQ **T:** 07967 274286
E: stay@lambleycottages.co.uk
W: www.lambleycottages.co.uk **£ BOOK ONLINE**

This cluster of barn conversions are set within 90 acres. Close to the South Tyne River. Outside space is not in short supply here, as our guests are welcome to explore all of the 100-acre Lambley Country Estate. From the cottages, there are spectacular views along the salmon-rich River South Tyne and down the valley towards Lambley Viaduct. Sauna facilities now available and indoor games room. **Open:** All year **Nearest Shop:** 4 miles **Nearest Pub:** 1.5 miles

Site: P **Payment:** € **Leisure:** **Property:** **Children:** **Unit:** BBQ

HEXHAM, Northumberland *Map ref 5B2* *SatNav NE48 2JY* C

VisitEngland ★★★★★ TOURING & CAMPING PARK

(50) £12.00-£45.00
(43) £12.00-£45.00
(25) £7.00-£45.00
(4) £45.00
70 touring pitches

Bellingham Camping and Caravanning Club

Brown Rigg, Bellingham, Hexham, Northumberland NE48 2JY
T: (01434) 220175 **E:** bellingham.site@thefriendlyclub.co.uk
W: www.campingandcaravanningclub.co.uk/bellingham **£ BOOK ONLINE**

Set in the glorious Northumberland National Park, Bellingham is a perfect base for exploring this undiscovered part of England. Visitors can enjoy beautiful walks or cycle rides from the site and explore some of the major attractions in the vicinity, for example, Kielder Water, Hadrian's Wall and Cragside. The North Tyne, one of England's best salmon rivers, is a short walk away, while the campsite is within the largest Dark Skies Park in Europe and is perfect for stargazing. **Open:** 1st March - 4th January.

Site: **Payment:** **Leisure:** **Children:** **Catering:** **Park:** **Touring:**

HEXHAM, Northumberland *Map ref 5B2* S

VisitEngland ★★★★ SELF CATERING

Units 1
Sleeps 5
PER UNIT PER WEEK
£220.00 - £415.00

Braemar

Contact: Mrs Cynthia Bradley, Owner, Edenholme, John Martin Street, Haydon Bridge, Northumberland NE47 6AA **T:** (01434) 684622 / 07949 369222
E: edenholme@btinternet.com **W:** www.edenholme.co.uk **£ BOOK ONLINE**

Delightful two-bedroomed bungalow with large garden to front and back. Sleeping 4/5 it is located in a small village with shops, pub and restaurant 100yds away. Ideal location for visiting Hadrian's Wall, Northumberland, Kielder Water, Metro Centre, Durham, Carlisle, Lakes and Scotland. **Open:** All year
Nearest Shop: 100 Yards **Nearest Pub:** 100 Yards

Site: P **Leisure:** **Property:** **Children:** **Unit:** BBQ

HEXHAM, Northumberland *Map ref 5B2* *SatNav NE46 2JP* C

VisitEngland ★★ TOURING & CAMPING PARK

(50) £15.00-£18.00
(30) £15.00-£18.00
(10) £11.00
50 touring pitches

Hexham Racecourse Caravan Site

High Yarridge, Yarridge Road, Hexham NE46 2JP
T: (01434) 606847 **F:** 01434 605814 **E:** hexrace.caravan@btconnect.com
W: www.hexham-racecourse.co.uk

Grass area, sloping in parts. Most pitches with electrical hook-up points. Separate area for tents. **Directions:** From Hexham take the B6305 Allendale Road for 3 miles turn left at T Junction, site 1.5 miles on the right. **Open:** May to September.

Site: **Payment:** **Leisure:** **Children:** **Park:** **Touring:**

For **key to symbols** see page 7

Farne View House, Farne Court Cottage & Farne View Cottage

Contact: Mr George Farr / Mrs Barbara Milnes, Pallinsburn House, Cornhill-on-Tweed, Northumberland TD12 4SG **T:** (01890) 820233 / 820579 **F:** 01890 820233
E: pallinsburn@yahoo.co.uk **W:** www.holyislandaccommodation.co.uk

Units   3
Sleeps   1-8

PER UNIT PER WEEK
£356.00 - £886.00

SPECIAL PROMOTIONS
Short breaks usually out of season but can accommodate in high season if booked less than 3 weeks before start date.

FVHouse sleeps 7/8: 2 x s/k zip/link doubles, 1 with en suite shower, 1 single room with 3 singles & z bed if needed. Top floor family bathroom, ground floor cloakroom.
Cottages sleep 4 each: FCC: 1 x double, 1 x s/k zip/link double, FVC: 2 x s/k zip/link doubles.
Bathrooms: on first floor (toilet, hand basin, bath & shower).
FVH Kitchen: Open fire, private garden across road. FCC: Woodburner. FVC. Electric fire. Private garden + shared courtyard garden with FCC. Elec. storage heating included all 3 props. Parking. One pet by arrangement. No pets FVC. Views of castle and coast (not FCC)

Open: All year
Nearest Shop: 0.10 miles
Nearest Pub: 0.10 miles

Units: FVH: 2nd floor 2 rooms-3 singles+1 zbed & 1 x s/kdouble.1st floor s/kdouble+ ensuite shower rm. FCC:1 x double & 1 x s/k double. FVC: 2 x s/k doubles.

Site: ✿ P Leisure: ♪ ▸ ♻ Property: 🐾 🏢 Children: 🧸 🎪 🏃 Unit: 📱 🍴 📺 🍳 📺 📀 ⌀

Book your accommodation online

Visit our websites for detailed information, up-to-date availability and to book your accommodation online. Includes over 20,000 places to stay, all of them star rated.

www.visitor-guides.co.uk

LOW NEWTON-BY-THE-SEA, Northumberland   Map ref 5C1   **S**

4 Coastguard Cottages

Contact: Ms Susan Jarratt, 3 Moorcourt Drive, Cheltenham, Gloucestershire GL52 2QL
T: (01242) 517772 **E:** susanmjarratt@hotmail.com

Our warm and comfortable three-bedroom holiday cottage is well equipped for six people and overlooks the sea and Dunstanburgh Castle. The long sandy beach is less than 200 yards from the garden gate. Sorry, no pets. **Open:** All year **Nearest Shop:** 2 miles **Nearest Pub:** 300 yds

| Units | 1 |
| Sleeps | 6 |

PER UNIT PER WEEK
£450.00 - £700.00

Site: ✿ **P** Leisure: ♪ ► ∪ Property: ▭ ▯ Children: ≿ Unit: ▯ ▯ ▭ ▯ ▯ TV ▯ ∂

MORPETH, Northumberland   Map ref 5C2   SatNav NE65 9QH   **C**

Felmoor Park

Eshottheugh, Felton, Morpeth, Northumberland NE65 9QH
T: (01670) 787790 **E:** info@felmoorpark.com
W: www.felmoorpark.com   **£ BOOK ONLINE**

🚐 (22)	£500.00-£980.00
🚏 (10)	£500.00-£650.00
⛺ (5)	£150.00-£480.00

Felmoor Holiday Park is set in 40 acres of Northumbrian woodland. We have luxury log cabins, lodges and static caravans to rent, most with hot tubs. Park facilities include Gym, Sauna, Steam room, Swim Spa and hot tub. Felmoor Park is centrally located for all of Northumberland's historical and natural attractions. We also have new and pre-loved homes available for sale.

Directions: 6 miles North of Morpeth or 9 miles South of Alnwick on the East side of the A1.   **Open:** All year

Site: ▦ **A**▯ Payment: ▦ ☼ Leisure: ♿ ► ♠ Children: ≿ ⚠ Park: ⌇ ▭ ▯

NEWTON-BY-THE-SEA, Northumberland Map ref 5C1 S

Link House Farm Holiday Cottages

Contact: Mrs Kathleen Thompson, Owner, Link House Farm, Newton-by-the-Sea, Alnwick, Northumberland NE66 3ED **T:** (01665) 576820 **E:** stay@linkhousefarm.co.uk
W: www.linkhousefarm.com

Units	13
Sleeps	2-8

PER UNIT PER WEEK
£165.00 - £1600.00

Northumbrian Luxury coastal cottages, located on our farm between the fishing villages of Craster & Beadnell. Each property is completely self contained and equipped to a high standard with their own garden area and seating. Also, a large adventure play ground and football area. Ideal for families, couples, walkers, cyclists and bird watchers or for those who deserve and crave a peaceful holiday on our beautiful picturesque coastline. No pets.
Open: All Year **Nearest Shop:** 2.5 Miles **Nearest Pub:** 0.5 Miles

Site: **P** Payment: ⬛ Leisure: 🏊 ▶ ∪ Property: ⬛ ⬛ Children: 🚼 Unit: ⬛ 🔌 TV DVD

NEWTON-BY-THE-SEA, Northumberland Map ref 5C1 S

Sea Winds

Contact: Mrs Jo Leiper, Sea Winds, Bygate, Black Heddon, Newcastle-upon-Tyne NE20 0JJ
T: (01661) 881506 / 07720 051201 **E:** stay@seawinds-lownewton.co.uk
W: www.seawinds-lownewton.co.uk

Units	1
Sleeps	2-6

PER UNIT PER WEEK
£425.00 - £950.00

Situated within the picturesque village of Low Newton-by-the-Sea, this former fisherman's cottage is just 200m from a beautiful sandy beach which is part of Northumberland's Heritage Coast. High-quality and offering many home comforts make it an exceptional family base to discover the secrets of the surrounding area.
Open: All year **Nearest Shop:** 3 miles **Nearest Pub:** 0.25 miles

Site: ❀ **P** Leisure: 🔥 Property: 🐕 ⬛ ⬛ Children: 🚼 🎠 ⚡ Unit: ⬛ ⬛ ⬛ 🔌 TV ⬛ DVD ∅ BBQ 📞

SEAHOUSES, Northumberland Map ref 5C1 S

1, 2 & 3 The Old Bakery

Contact: Susan Parker, Owner, No's 1, 2 & 3 The Old Bakery, Crown Street, Seahouses, Northumberland NE68 7TQ **T:** (01484) 665633 / 07833 357974
E: susanparker400@btinternet.com **W:** www.oldbakeryseahouses.co.uk

Units	3
Sleeps	2

PER UNIT PER WEEK
£255.00 - £430.00

SPECIAL PROMOTIONS
Short break information available upon request.

Numbers 1, 2 & 3 The Old Bakery are 3 separate one double-bedroomed properties converted from the old bakery in Seahouses. Each cottage is individually and tastefully furnished and offers excellent accommodation with private parking for a couple wishing to be based on the Northumbria Coast. The harbour and village amenities are a few minutes walk away, with another 10 minute walk to the beach. No2 The Bakery is a member of Seahouses Ocean Club.

Open: All year
Nearest Shop: 2 minute walk
Nearest Pub: 4 minute walk

Units: 3 x 1 double-bedroomed cottages with bath & over bath shower, lounge, kitchen/diner and private parking.

Site: **P** Payment: € Leisure: 🚲 🏊 ▶ ∪ Property: ⬟ 🖥 ⬛ ⬛ ⬛ Unit: ⬛ ⬛ ⬛ 🔌 TV DVD

NEWCASTLE UPON TYNE, *Tyne and Wear* *Map ref 5C2*   **S**

★★★
SELF CATERING

Units   1
Sleeps   1-4
PER UNIT PER WEEK
£280.00 - £350.00

135 Audley Road Self Catering Flat

Contact: Miss Linda Wright, 137 Audley Road, South Gosforth, Newcastle-upon-Tyne NE3 1QH **T:** (0191) 2856374 / 07733 617784 **E:** lkw@audleyroad.co.uk
W: www.audleyroad.co.uk

Self-contained flat, accommodates four people, close to shops and Metro, with easy access to city centre. All amenities. Short lets accepted, price on enquiry. Approximately 2.5 miles from city centre and 6.5 miles from Newcastle Airport. Ideal as a base to visit the North East for leisure or work-related trips. **Open:** All year
Nearest Shop: 0.20 miles **Nearest Pub:** 0.20 miles

Property: ⌨ 🖥 📶 **Children:** 🚼 🧒 **Unit:** 🛏 🚿 📺 🍳 📺 ☎

SOUTH SHIELDS, *Tyne And Wear* *Map ref 5C2*   **S**

★★★★
SELF CATERING

Units   1
Sleeps   1-4
PER UNIT PER WEEK
£380.00 - £540.00

Embla

Contact: Jon & Sue, Westoe Crown Village, South Shields, Tyne and Wear NE33 3ND
T: (08442) 327805 **E:** embla@fastmail.co.uk
W: www.selfcateringapartmentnortheast.co.uk

A unique 2 bedroom luxury apartment, free Wi-Fi. Just a few metres from the parks & beaches of South Shields. Perfect for anyone wanting to relax, walk, enjoy culture, shopping, history etc. We are unique in that there is no one below and no one above, so guests don't have to suffer noise from people below or above them. Private covered parking. Beautifully decorated throughout to a very high standard, ideal for anyone who demands comfort and modern surroundings. Strictly no smoking & no pets. **Open:** All year
Nearest Shop: 500 metres **Nearest Pub:** 500 metres

Site: ♿ **P** **Payment:** 💷 **Leisure:** 🏊 🚶 ⛳ **Property:** ⌨ 📶 **Unit:** 🛏 🚿 📺 🍳 📺 📀

SOUTH SHIELDS, *Tyne And Wear* *Map ref 5C2*   **S**

★★★★
SELF CATERING

Units   1
Sleeps   2-5
PER UNIT PER WEEK
£500.00

Hill Head Farm

Contact: William & Margaret Stewart, Owners, Lizard Lane, South Shields, Tyne and Wear SR6 7NN **T:** (0191) 295248 / (0191) 292076 - tearoom / 07786 534250
E: hillheadm@aol.com **W:** www.hillheadfarm.co.uk

2 bedroom farm bungalow, newly decorated to very high standard, in beautiful countryside overlooking the sea. Weekly price is based on couple sharing. Extra £50 charge per person per week for parties over 2. Onsite Tearoom is closed 22nd Dec - 5th Jan. **Open:** All Year
Nearest Shop: 0.25 miles **Nearest Pub:** 0.25 miles

Site: ♿ **P** **Property:** 🖥 📶 **Children:** 🚼 🏞 🧒 **Unit:** 🛏 📺 🍳 🧺 📺 📀

For **key to symbols** see page 7

Map 1

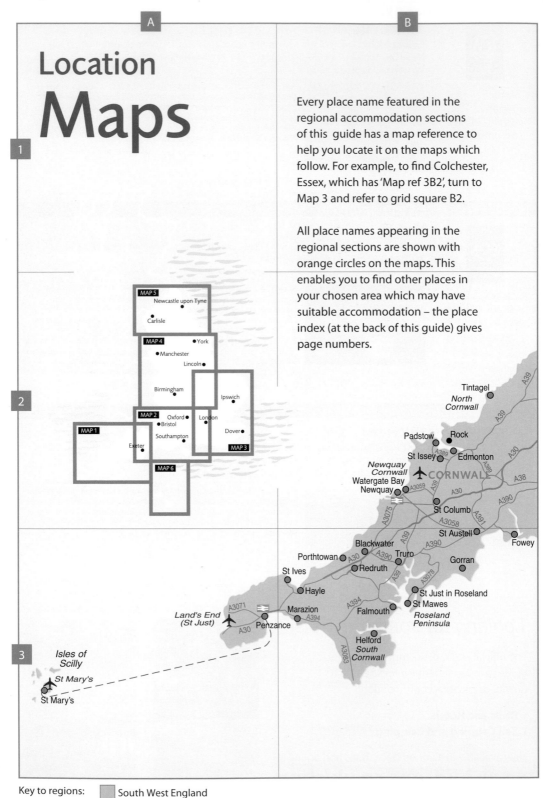

Location
Maps

Every place name featured in the regional accommodation sections of this guide has a map reference to help you locate it on the maps which follow. For example, to find Colchester, Essex, which has 'Map ref 3B2', turn to Map 3 and refer to grid square B2.

All place names appearing in the regional sections are shown with orange circles on the maps. This enables you to find other places in your chosen area which may have suitable accommodation – the place index (at the back of this guide) gives page numbers.

Key to regions: ▢ South West England

Map 1

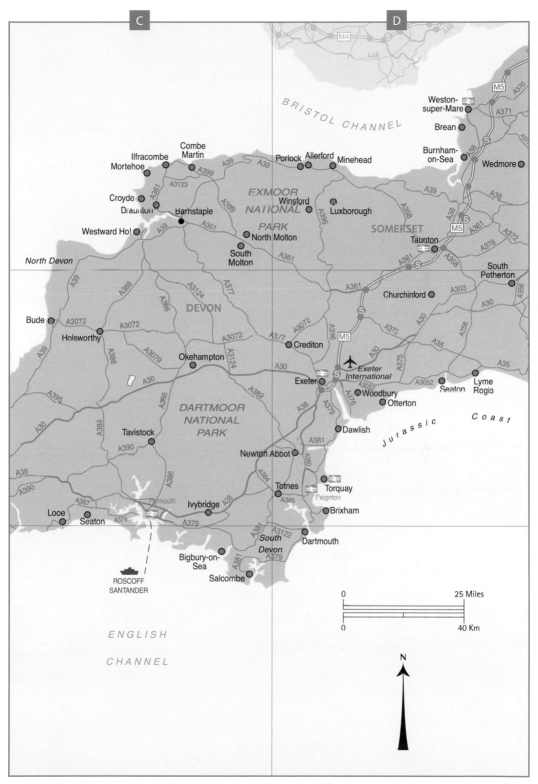

Orange circles indicate accommodation within the regional sections of this guide

Map 2

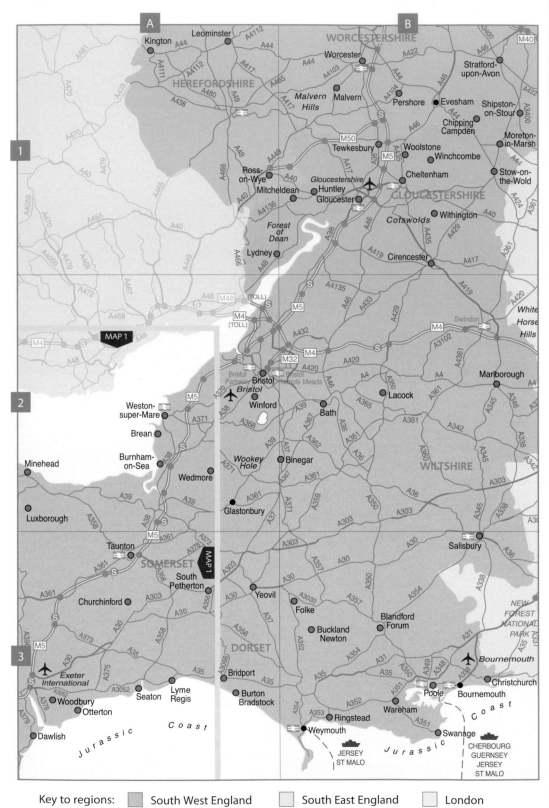

Key to regions: ▢ South West England ▢ South East England ▢ London

Map 2

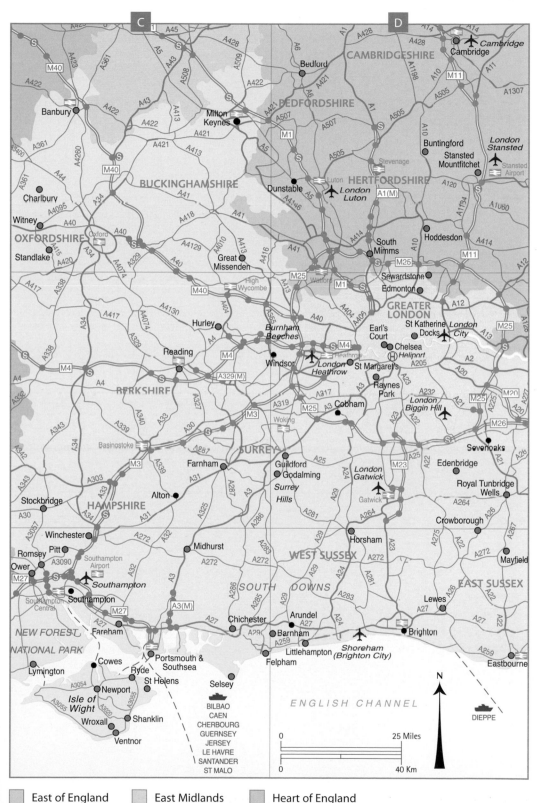

East of England   East Midlands   Heart of England

Orange circles indicate accommodation within the regional sections of this guide

Map 3

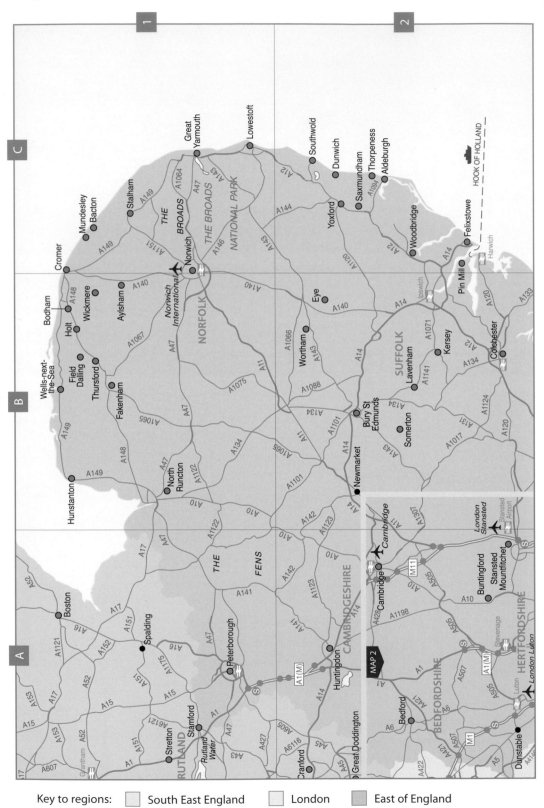

Key to regions: South East England   London   East of England

Map 3

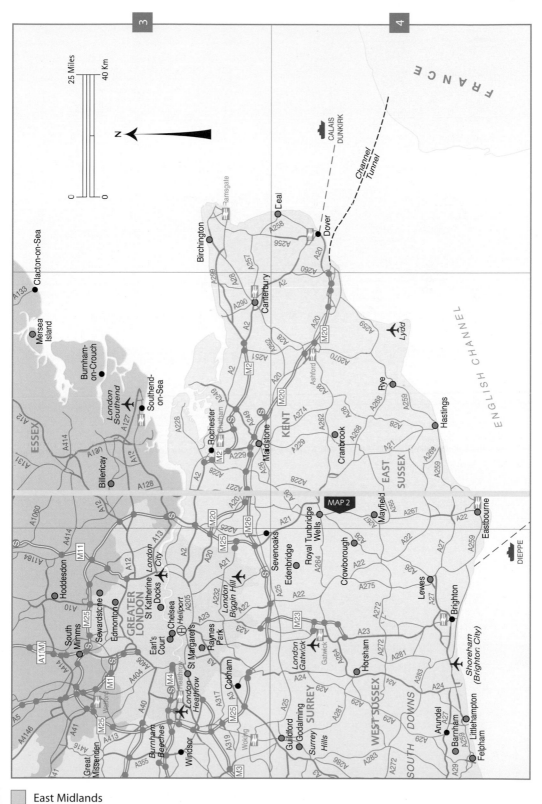

East Midlands

Orange circles indicate accommodation within the regional sections of this guide

Map 4

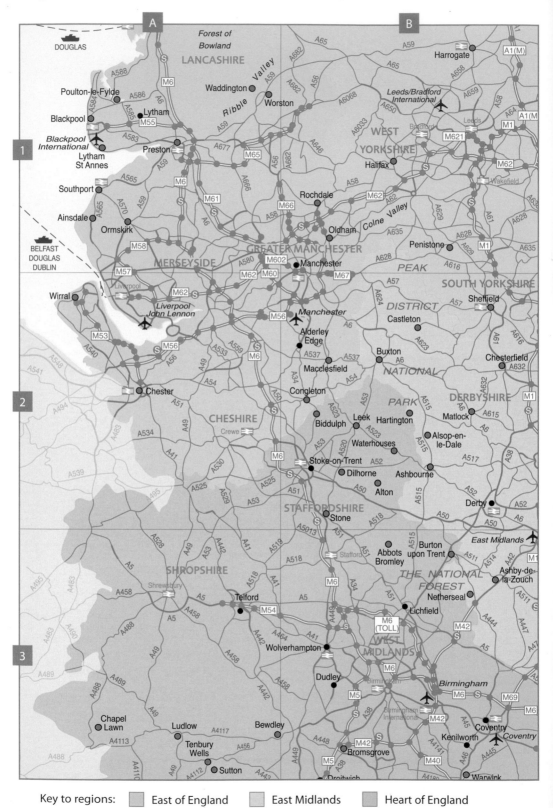

Key to regions: ⬜ East of England ⬜ East Midlands ⬜ Heart of England

Map 4

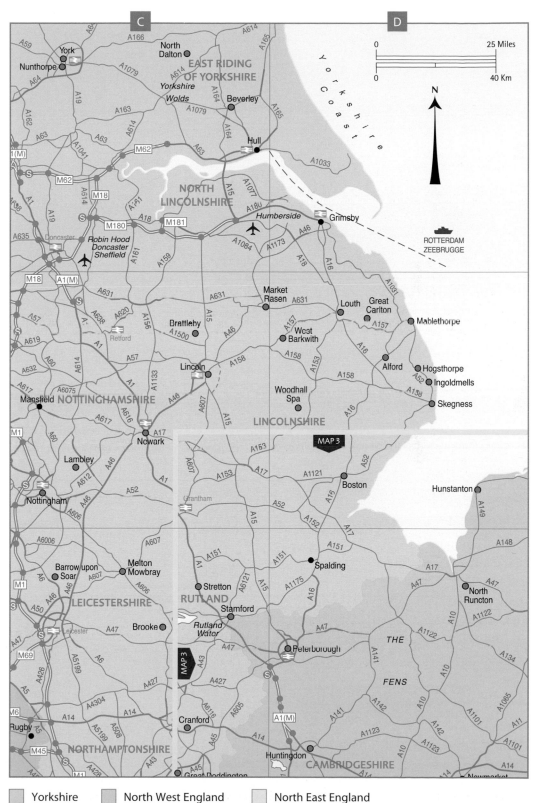

Yorkshire   North West England   North East England

Orange circles indicate accommodation within the regional sections of this guide

Map 5

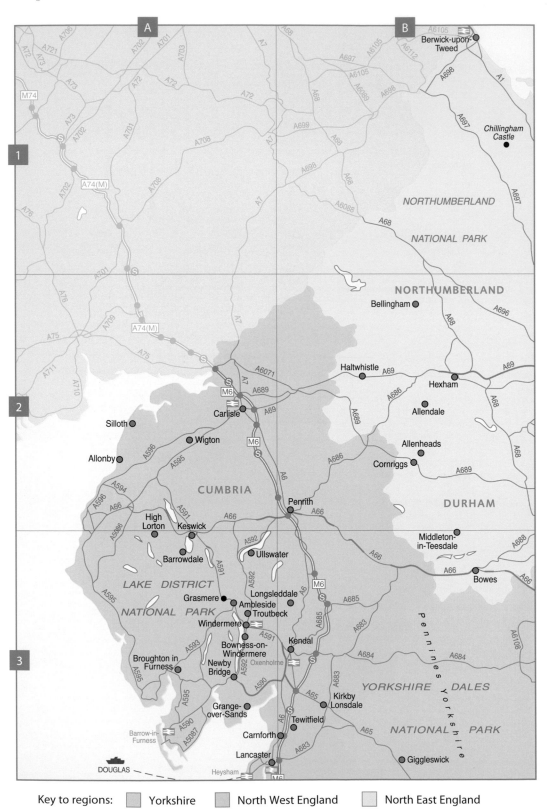

A706 A721 A72 A73 A702 A701 A702 A703 A7 A68 A6105 A6112 A6105 A6105 A6089 A698 A6105 A6112 A698 A1 A697 A698

Berwick-upon-Tweed

M74 A72 A72 A72 A701 A708 A72 A7 A699 A68 A698 A68

A74(M) A697

Chillingham Castle ●

1

A76 A701 A708 A7 A698 A68 **NORTHUMBERLAND**

A76 A709 **A74(M)** A7 A6071 A6088 A68 **NATIONAL PARK**

A75 A711 A75 A7 **S** A6071 A689 A68 A696

Bellingham ●

2

A710 **S** **M6** A7 A689 A69 Haltwhistle ● A69 Hexham ●

A686

Silloth ● Carlisle ● A69 A689 Allendale ●

Wigton ● **M6** A686

NORTHUMBERLAND

Allonby ● A596 **S** A6 A686 Allenheads ●

A595 A596 Cornriggs ●

CUMBRIA A689 **DURHAM**

A594 A66 Penrith ● A66

A596 A66 A5086 A591 High Lorton A66 Middleton-in-Teesdale ● A688 A66

Keswick ● A592 A66 Bowes ● A66

Barrowdale ● Ullswater A685 A66

LAKE DISTRICT A591 A592 **M6** A6108

A595 Grasmere ● Longsleddale **S**

NATIONAL PARK Ambleside ● A685 A683 A684

Windermere Troutbeck A685

Broughton in Furness ● A593 Bowness-on-Windermere Kendal ● A684 *Pennines Yorkshire* A684

Newby Bridge A592 Oxenholme A591 **S** A683 **YORKSHIRE DALES**

3 A595 A590 A65 Kirkby Lonsdale ●

Grange-over-Sands ● A6 Tewitfield A683 **NATIONAL PARK**

Barrow-in-Furness A5087 Carnforth ● A65

A590 Lancaster ● A683 Giggleswick ●

DOUGLAS Heysham **M6**

A A B

Key to regions: ▮ Yorkshire ▮ North West England ▮ North East England

338

Map 5

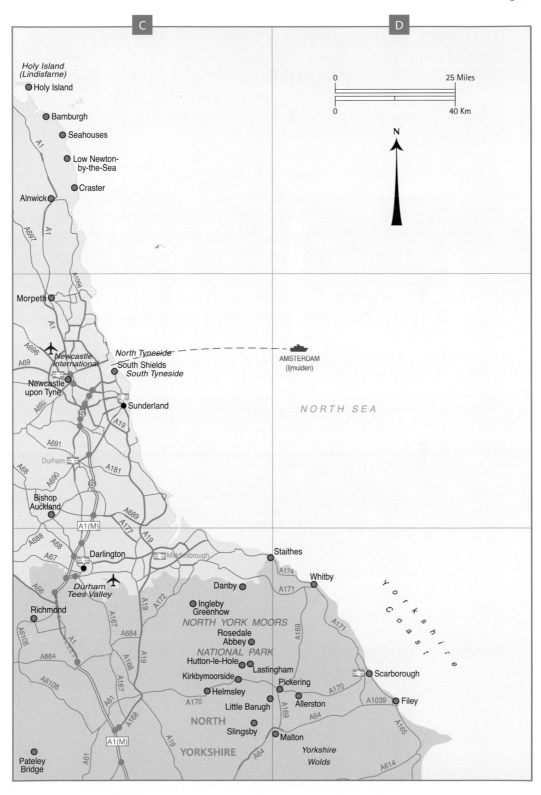

C	D

Holy Island
(Lindisfarne)
● Holy Island

● Bamburgh

● Seahouses

● Low Newton-
by-the-Sea

● Craster

Alnwick ●

A1
A697
A1

Morpeth ●

A1

A696
A69
A692
A691
A68
A690

✈ Newcastle
International

North Tyneside
South Shields
South Tyneside

Newcastle
upon Tyne

S

A19

● Sunderland

0   25 Miles
0   40 Km

N

AMSTERDAM
(Ijmuiden)

NORTH SEA

Durham

A181

S

Bishop
Auckland ●

A1(M)
A177
A19
A689

A688 A68
A67
A66

Darlington ●

A172
A19

Durham
Tees Valley ✈

Richmond ●

A167
A684
A6108
A684
A6108

A61
A168
A167
A19

Middlesbrough

Staithes ●

A174

Whitby ●

Danby ●

A171

● Ingleby
Greenhow

NORTH YORK MOORS

Rosedale
Abbey ●

NATIONAL PARK

A169
A171

Hutton-le-Hole ●
Kirkbymoorside ●

● Lastingham

● Helmsley

A170

Little Barugh ●

NORTH

Slingsby ●

Pickering ●

A170
A64

Allerston ●

A1039

Scarborough ●

● Filey

Pateley ●
Bridge

A61
A19
A1(M)

YORKSHIRE

A64

● Malton

Yorkshire
Wolds

A169

A185
A614

Yorkshire
Coast

77th EDITION

SIGNPOST HOTELS

SIGNPOST
SELECTED PREMIER HOTELS 2015

Every hotel featured in this guide has that something special no run-of-the-mill hotels included

•

Available from Signpost hotels and all good book shops

•

Visit our website for up-to-date special offers and a chance to win a weekend stay at a Signpost hotel

'Gem of a guide... covers hotels of character'
EXECUTARY NEWS

'For anyone doing any extensive motoring in Britain, this guide would seem invaluable'
NEW YORKER MAGAZINE

'The British Hotel guide for the discerning traveller'
PERIOD LIVING

www.signpost.co.uk

Map 7
London

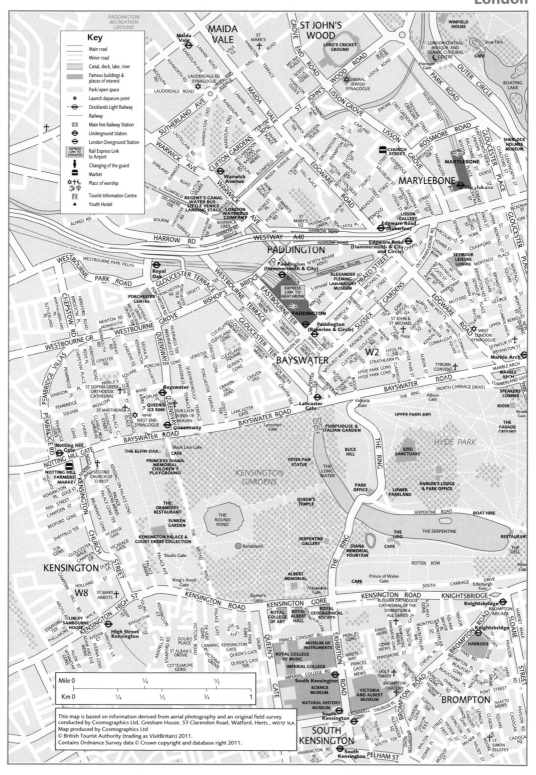

Map 8
London

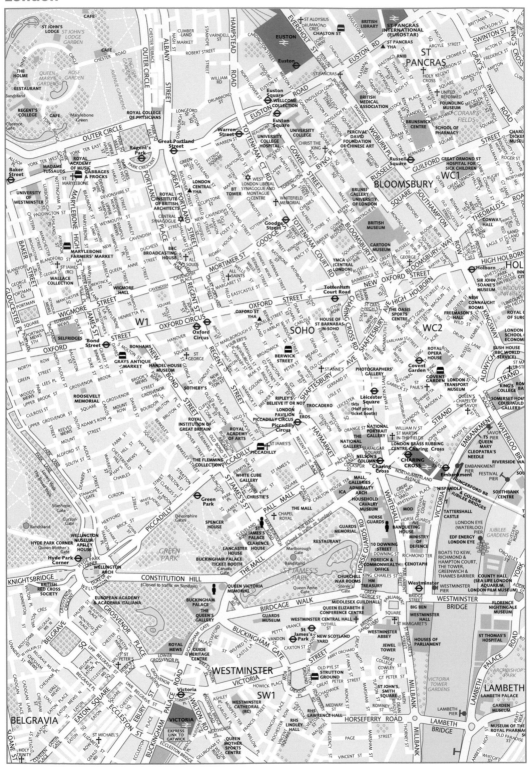

Map 8
London

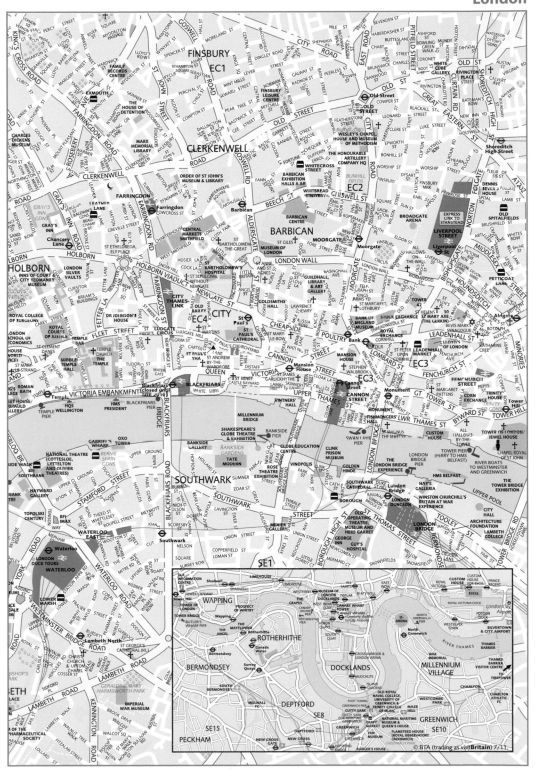

MOTORWAY
SERVICE AREA

Motorway Service
Area Assessment Scheme

Something we all use and take for granted but how good are they?

The star ratings cover over 250 different aspects of each operation, including cleanliness, the quality and range of catering and also the quality of the physical aspects, as well as the service. It does not cover prices or value for money.

OPERATOR: EXTRA

Baldock	★★★★
Beaconsfield	★★★★★
Blackburn	★★★★★
Cambridge	★★★★
Cobham	★★★★★
Cullompton	★★★
Peterborough	★★★★

OPERATOR: MOTO

Birch E	★★★
Birch W	★★★
Bridgwater	★★★
Burton in Kendal	★★★
Cherwell Valley	★★★★
Chieveley	★★★
Doncaster N	★★★★
Donington Park	★★★★
Exeter	★★★
Ferrybridge	★★★★
Frankley N	★★★
Frankley S	★★★★
Heston E	★★★
Heston W	★★★
Hilton Park N	★★★
Hilton Park S	★★★
Knutsford N	★★★★
Knutsford S	★★★★
Lancaster N	★★★★
Lancaster S	★★★★
Leigh Delamere E	★★★★
Leigh Delamere W	★★★★
Medway	★★★
Pease Pottage	★★★
Reading E	★★★★
Reading W	★★★
Severn View	★★★
Southwaite N	★★★
Southwaite S	★★★★

Stafford N	★★★★
Tamworth	★★★
Thurrock	★★★★
Toddington N	★★★★
Toddington S	★★★★
Trowell N	★★★
Trowell S	★★★
Washington N	★★★
Washington S	★★★
Wetherby	★★★★
Winchester N	★★★★
Winchester S	★★★★
Woolley Edge N	★★★★
Woolley Edge S	★★★★

OPERATOR: ROADCHEF

Chester	★★★★
Clacket Lane E	★★★★
Clacket Lane W	★★★★
Durham	★★★
Killington Lake	★★★
Maidstone	★★★★
Northampton N	★★★
Northampton S	★★★
Norton Canes	★★★★
Rownhams N	★★★
Rownhams S	★★★
Sandbach N	★★★
Sandbach S	★★★
Sedgemoor S	★★★
Stafford S	★★★
Strensham N	★★★
Strensham S	★★★
Taunton Deane N	★★★
Taunton Deane S	★★★
Tibshelf N	★★★
Tibshelf S	★★★

Watford Gap N	★★★
Watford Gap S	★★★

OPERATOR: WELCOME BREAK

Birchanger Green	★★★★
Burtonwood	★★★
Charnock Richard N	★★★★★
Charnock Richard S	★★★
Corley E	★★★
Corley W	★★★
Fleet N	★★★★
Fleet S	★★★★
Gordano	★★★★
Hartshead Moor E	★★★
Hartshead Moor W	★★★
Hopwood Park	★★★★
Keele N	★★★
Keele S	★★★★
Leicester Forest East N	★★★
Leicester Forest East S	★★★
London Gateway	★★★★
Membury E	★★★
Membury W	★★★★
Michaelwood N	★★★★
Michaelwood S	★★★★
Newport Pagnell S	★★★
Newport Pagnell N	★★★
Oxford	★★★★
Sedgemoor N	★★★
South Mimms	★★★★
Telford	★★★
Warwick N	★★★
Warwick S	★★★★
Woodall N	★★★
Woodall S	★★★

OPERATOR: WESTMORLAND

Tebay N	★★★★★
Tebay S	★★★★★
Gloucester N	★★★★★

HIGHWAYS AGENCY

Motorway Service Areas on the Strategic Road Network

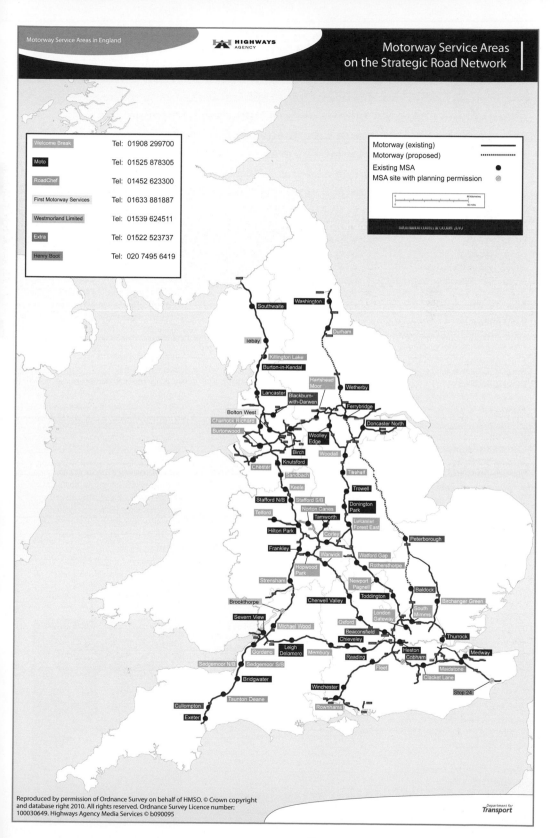

Welcome Break	Tel: 01908 299700
Moto	Tel: 01525 878305
RoadChef	Tel: 01452 623300
First Motorway Services	Tel: 01633 881887
Westmorland Limited	Tel: 01539 624511
Extra	Tel: 01522 523737
Henry Boot	Tel: 020 7495 6419

Motorway (existing)
Motorway (proposed)
Existing MSA
MSA site with planning permission

Information correct at October 2010

Southwaite
Washington
Durham
Tebay
Killington Lake
Burton-in-Kendal
Hartshead Moor
Wetherby
Lancaster
Blackburn-with-Darwen
Ferrybridge
Bolton West
Charnock Richard
Doncaster North
Burtonwood
Woolley Edge
Woodall
Birch
Chester
Knutsford
Tibshelf
Sandbach
Keele
Trowell
Stafford N/B
Stafford S/B
Donington Park
Telford
Norton Canes
Leicester Forest East
Tamworth
Hilton Park
Corley
Peterborough
Frankley
Warwick
Watford Gap
Hopwood Park
Rothersthorpe
Strensham
Newport Pagnell
Baldock
Brookthorpe
Cherwell Valley
Toddington
Birchanger Green
Severn View
London Gateway
South Mimms
Michael Wood
Oxford
Beaconsfield
Thurrock
Leigh Delamere
Chieveley
Heston
Gordano
Membury
Reading
Cobham
Medway
Sedgemoor N/B
Sedgemoor S/B
Fleet
Maidstone
Bridgwater
Clacket Lane
Winchester
Stop 24
Cullompton
Taunton Deane
Rownhams
Exeter

Department for Transport

Official tourist board guide **Self Catering and Camping**

Self-catering agencies

All of the self-catering agencies listed below offer a selection of cottages and holiday homes over particular geographical areas. Many of the agencies only promote properties that are assessed annually by VisitEngland, however some only promote a percentage of properties that have a star rating. To avoid disappointment, you are advised to check if your desired accommodation has a VisitEngland star rating before booking. Agencies that promote the highest percentage of quality assessed accommodation at the time of publishing feature at the top of the list.

Cottages4you
0345 268 0760
www.cottages4you.co.uk
Properties throughout the country.

Welcome Cottages
0345 268 0816
www.welcomecottages.com
Properties across the UK.

English Country Cottages
0345 268 0785
www.english-country-cottages.co.uk
Hand-picked holiday cottages in England.

Cumbrian Cottages
01228 599 960
www.cumbrian-cottages.co.uk
A collection of holiday properties in Cumbria and the Lake District.

Ingrid Flute's Yorkshire Holiday Cottages
01947 600 700
www.yorkshireholidaycottages.co.uk
info@yorkshireholidaycottages.co.uk
Holiday homes across Yorkshire.

Lakelovers
01539 488 855
www.lakelovers.co.uk
enquiries@lakelovers.co.uk
Individual properties in Cumbria.

Coast & Country Cottages
01548 843 773
www.coastandcountry.co.uk
Properties in Salcombe, Dartmouth and South Devon.

Norfolk Country Cottages
01263 715 779
www.norfolkcottages.co.uk
info@norfolkcottages.co.uk
Over 400 properties in Norfolk.

Suffolk Secrets
01502 722 717
www.suffolk-secrets.co.uk
holidays@suffolk-secrets.co.uk
Family-owned, with over 350 properties across Suffolk.

Marsdens Devon Cottages
01271 813 777
www.marsdens.co.uk
devon@marsdens.co.uk
Over 350 holiday cottages in North Devon and Exmoor.

Dream Cottages
01305 789 000
www.dream-cottages.co.uk
admin@dream-cottages.co.uk
Providing cottages across Dorset, Devon, and Somerset.

Cornish Horizons Holiday Cottages
01841 533 331
www.cornishhorizons.co.uk
cottages@cornishhorizons.co.uk
Providing a large portfolio of properties in North Cornwall.

Kent & Sussex Holiday Cottages
01580 720 770
www.kentandsussexcottages.co.uk
info@kentandsussexcottages.co.uk
Over 250 cottages throughout Kent and Sussex.

Dorset Coastal Cottages
0800 980 4070
www.dorsetcoastalcottages.com
hols@dorsetcoastalcottages.com
Self catering on the Dorset coast.

Marsdens Cornish Cottages
01503 289 289
www.cornish-cottages.co.uk
cornwall@marsdens.co.uk
Self-catering accommodation throughout Cornwall.

Harbour Holidays, Padstow
01841 533 402
www.padstow-self-catering.co.uk
contact@harbourholidays.co.uk
A wide range of self-catering accommodation in and around Padstow and the Seven Bays Cornwall.

Carbis Bay Holidays
0800 012 2241
www.carbisbayholidays.co.uk
enquiries@carbisbayholidays.co.uk
Self-catering accommodation in Carbis Bay and St Ives, Cornwall.

The Cornish Collection Ltd
01503 262 736
www.cornishcollection.co.uk
enquiries@cornishcollection.co.uk
A selection of properties in Looe and across South East Cornwall.

Lakeland Cottage Company
01539 538 180
www.lakeland-cottage-company.co.uk
info@lakeland-cottage-company.co.uk
A large range of cottages in the Lake District.

**The Coppermines &
Coniston Lake Cottages**
01539 441 765
www.coppermines.co.uk
info@coppermines.co.uk
*A wide range of cottages set in
the Lake District.*

Roseland Holiday Cottages
01872 580 480
www.roselandholidaycottages.co.uk
enquiries@
roselandholidaycottages.co.uk
*A selection of cottages in St
Mawes and Portscatho, Cornwall.*

Estuary & Rock Holidays
01208 863 399
www.rockholidays.co.uk
info@naturalretreats.com
*A collection of accommodation
in Cornwall.*

Birds Norfolk Holiday Homes
01485 534 267
www.norfolkholidayhomes-birds.co.uk
shohol@birdsnorfolkholidayhomes.co.uk
*Self-catering accommodation
along the North West Norfolk Coast.*

Keswick Cottages
01768 780 088
www.keswickcottages.co.uk
info@keswickcottages.co.uk
*Cottages in and around Keswick,
the Lake District.*

Linstone Chine Holiday Services
01983 755 933
www.linstone-chine.co.uk
enquiries@linstone-chine.co.uk
*Offering accommodation on the
isle of Wight.*

Campden Cottages
01386 852 462
www.campdencottages.co.uk
campdencottages@icloud.com
*Self-catering accommodation
throughout the Cotswolds.*

Askrigg Cottage Holidays
01969 650 022
www.askrigg.com
stay@askrigg.com
*Holiday cottages in the Yorkshire
Dales National Park.*

Island Cottage Holidays
01929 481 555
www.islandcottageholidays.com
mail@islandcottageholidays.com
*Providing a wide collection of
cottages on the Isle of Wight.*

Whitby Holiday Cottages
01947 603 010
www.whitby-cottages.net
enquiries@whitby-cottages.net
*Offering a large collection of
cottages in and around Whitby.*

Portscatho Holidays
01326 270 900
www.portscathoholidays.co.uk
info@portscathoholidays.co.uk
*Offering accommodation in the
Roseland Peninsula, including St Mawes
and Portscatho in South Cornwall.*

Holiday Homes and Cottages SW
01803 299 677
www.swcottages.co.uk
iain@swcottages.co.uk.
*Holiday cottages and apartments
across Devon and Cornwall.*

Coquet Cottages
01665 710 700
www.coquetcottages.co.uk
info@coquetcottages.co.uk
*Self-catering accommodation
based in Northumberland.*

Milkbere Holiday Cottages
01297 20729
www.milkberehols.com
info@milkberehols.com
*Accommodation in Devon
and Dorset.*

Dorset Cottage Holidays
01929 481 547
www.dhcottages.co.uk
enq@dhcottages.co.uk
*A collection of cottages and
apartments in Dorset.*

Lakeland Cottage Holidays
01768 776 065
www.lakelandcottages.co.uk
info@ lakelandcottages.co.uk
*Self-catering accommodation in
the Lake District.*

Porthleven Harbour Cottages
01326 563 198
www.cornishhideaways.co.uk
info@cornishhideaways.com
*Self-catering holiday
accommodation in the Porthleven
and Rinsey area of West Cornwall.*

Bath Holiday Rentals
01225 482 225
www.bathholidayrentals.com
alexa@bathholidayrentals.com
*Self-catering apartments and
cottages in and around Bath.*

Wight Locations
01983 617 322
www.wightlocations.co.uk
enquiries@wightlocations.co.uk
Cottages on the Isle of Wight.

Home from Home Holidays
01983 532 385
www.homefromhomeiow.co.uk
htromh@crldirect.co.uk
*A selection of self-catering
properties on the Isle of Wight.*

Holiday Cottages Cornwall
01525 402 204
www.holidaycottagescornwall.com
*Cottages and apartments in the
coastal resorts of South Cornwall.*

Scilly Self Catering
01720 422 082
www.scillyselfcatering.com
Self-catering on the Isles of Scilly.

Country Hideaways
01969 663 559
www.countryhideaways.co.uk
info@countryhideaways.co.uk
*Cottages and apartments
throughout the Yorkshire Dales.*

The Good Life Cottage Company
01539 437 417
www.thegoodlifecottageco.co.uk
stay@thegoodlifecottageco.co.uk
*Holiday cottages in the heart of the
Lake District.*

 The following agencies have been accredited by VisitEngland following an annual assessment of their policies and procedures. Individual accommodation that these agencies promote may not be part of the VisitEngland Quality Assessment Scheme. However, if the agency is part of the VisitEngland Quality Accredited Agency Scheme the agency should have their own programme of inspections in place, ensuring the accommodation they promote is rated to a comparable standard.

Aspects Holidays
01736 754 242
www.aspects-holidays.co.uk
hello@aspects-holidays.co.uk
Over 400 holiday cottages in West Cornwall, St Ives and Carbis Bay.

Blue Chip Holidays
0333 3317 724
www.bluechipholidays.co.uk
Accommodation available in Cornwall, Devon, Dorset, the Isle of Wight, and Yorkshire.

Cadgwith Cove Cottages
01326 290 162
www.cadgwithcovecottages.co.uk
info@cadgwithcovecottages.co.uk
Self-catering in Cadgwith Cove and surrounds on the Lizard peninsula in coastal Cornwall.

Classic Cottages
01326 555 555
www.classic.co.uk
Self-catering accommodation in The Southwest.

Coast & Country Cottages
01548 843 773
www.coastandcountry.co.uk
salcombe@coastandcountry.co.uk
Self Catering Holiday Homes in Salcombe, Dartmouth and South Devon.

Cornish Cottage Holidays
01326 573 808
www.cornishcottageholidays.co.uk
enquiry@
cornishcottageholidays.co.uk
Holiday cottages in Cornwall.

Cornish Horizons Holiday Cottages
01841 533 331
www.cornishhorizons.co.uk
cottages@cornishhorizons.co.uk
Holiday cottages throughout Cornwall.

Cornish Riviera Holidays
01736 797 891
www.cornishrivieraholidays.co.uk
info@cornishrivieraholidays.co.uk
St Ives fisherman's cottages and harbour side flats on the North Cornwall coast.

Cornish Traditional Cottages
01208 821 666
www.corncott.com
bookings@corncott.com
Coastal and countryside self-catering holiday cottages in Cornwall.

Cottages4you
0345 268 0760
www.cottages4you.co.uk
*Accommodation throughout
the country.*

Dorset Coastal Cottages
0800 980 4070
www.dorsetcoastalcottages.com
hols@dorsetcoastalcottages.com
Self-catering on the Dorset coast.

Dream Cottages
01305 789000
www.dream-cottages.co.uk
admin@dream-cottages.co.uk
*Providing cottages across Dorset,
Devon and Somerset.*

English Country Cottages
0345 268 0785
www.english-country-cottages.co.uk
*Hand-picked holiday cottages
in England.*

holidaycottages.co.uk
01237 459 888
www.holidaycottages.co.uk
*Over 2,000 holiday cottages in
popular destinations across the UK.*

**Ingrid Flute's
Yorkshire Holiday Cottages**
01947 600 700
www.yorkshireholidaycottages.co.uk
info@yorkshireholidaycottages.co.uk
Holiday homes across Yorkshire.

John Bray Cornish Holidays
01208 863 206
www.johnbraycornishholidays.co.uk
lettings@johnbray.co.uk
*Cornish holiday cottages in Rock,
Daymer Bay, Polzeath and Port Isaac.*

Kent & Sussex Holiday Cottages
01580 720 770
www.kentandsussexcottages.co.uk
info@kentandsussexcottages.co.uk
Over 250 cottages in Kent and Sussex.

Lakelovers
01539 488 855
www.lakelovers.co.uk
enquiries@lakelovers.co.uk
*Properties to suit every occasion
throughout the southern and
central Lake District.*

Lyme Bay Holidays
01297 443 363
www.lymebayholidays.co.uk
email@lymebayholidays.co.uk
*Holiday homes in Lyme Regis
and the surrounding coast and
countryside areas.*

Marsdens Cornish Cottages
01503 289 289
www.cornish-cottages.co.uk
cornwall@marsdens.co.uk
*Self-catering accommodation
throughout Cornwall.*

Marsdens Devon Cottages
01271 813 777
www.marsdens.co.uk
devon@marsdens.co.uk
*Over 350 cottages throughout
North Devon and Exmoor.*

Miles & Son
01929 423 333
www.milesandson.co.uk
property@milesandson.co.uk
*Self-catering accommdation in
Swanage and the surrounding
villages on the Isle of Purbeck.*

Milkbere Holiday Cottages
01297 20729
www.milkberehols.com
info@milkberehols.com
*Accommodation in Devon and
Dorset.*

New Forest Cottages
01590 679 655
www.newforestcottages.co.uk
*Self-catering holiday cottages in
the New Forest area.*

Norfolk Country Cottages
01263 715 779
www.norfolkcottages.co.uk
info@norfolkcottages.co.uk
Over 400 properties in Norfolk.

**Northumbria Coast
& Country Cottages**
01665 830 783
www.northumbria-cottages.co.uk
bookings@nccc-ltd.co.uk
*Holiday cottages throughout
Northumberland.*

Rumsey Holiday Homes
01202 707 357
www.rhh.org
office@rhh.org
*Central south coast houses, flats
and bungalows in the Poole,
Bournemouth and South Dorset area.*

**Salcombe & Dartmouth
Holiday Homes**
01548 843 485
www.salcombe.com
shh@salcombe.org
*Properties within Salcombe and
rural farm ares in the South Hams.*

Suffolk Secrets
01502 722 717
www.suffolk-secrets.co.uk
holidays@suffolk-secrets.co.uk
*Family owned, with over 350
properties across Suffolk.*

Toad Hall Cottages
01548 202 020
www.toadhallcottages.co.uk
thc@toadhallcottages.co.uk
*Rural and waterside cottages in the
South West.*

Welcome Cottages
0345 268 0816
www.welcomecottages.com
Properties across the UK.

There are hundreds of "Green" places to stay and visit in England from small bed and breakfasts to large visitor attractions and activity holiday providers. Businesses displaying this logo have undergone a rigorous verification process to ensure that they are sustainable (green) and that a qualified assessor has visited the premises.

We have indicated the accommodation which has achieved a Green award... look out for the 🌱 symbol in the entry.

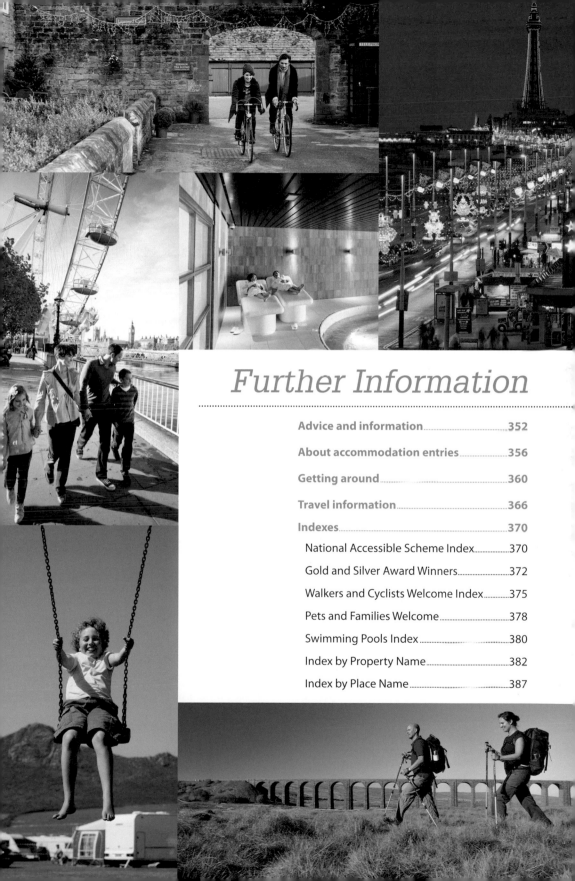

Further Information

Advice and information

Making a booking

When enquiring about accommodation, make sure you check prices, the quality rating and other important details. You will also need to state your requirements clearly and precisely, for example:

- Arrival and departure dates, with acceptable alternatives if appropriate;
- The accommodation you need;
- The number of people in your party and the ages of any children;
- Special requirements, such as ground-floor bathroom, garden, cot.

Confirmation

Misunderstandings can easily happen over the telephone, so do request a written confirmation, together with details of any terms and conditions that apply to your booking.

Deposits

When you book your self-catering holiday, the proprietor will normally ask you to pay a deposit immediately, and then to pay the full balance before your holiday date.

The reason for asking you to pay in advance is to safeguard the proprietor in case you decide to cancel at a late stage, or simply do not turn up. He or she may have turned down other bookings on the strength of yours, and may find it hard to re-let if you cancel.

In the case of caravan, camping and touring parks and holiday villages, the full charge often has to be paid in advance. This may be in two instalments – a deposit at the time of booking and the balance by, say, two weeks before the start of the booked period.

Cancellations

Legal contract

When you accept accommodation that is offered to you, by telephone or in writing, you enter into a legally binding contract with the proprietor. This means that if you cancel your booking, fail to take up the accommodation or leave early, you will probably forfeit your deposit and may expect to be charged the balance at the end of the period booked if the place cannot be re-let. You should be advised at the time of the booking of what charges would be made in the event of cancelling the accommodation or leaving early, which is usually written into the property's terms and conditions. If this is not mentioned, you should ask the proprietor for any cancellation terms that apply before booking your accommodation to ensure any disputes are avoided. Where you have already paid the full amount before cancelling, the proprietor is likely to retain the money. However if the accommodation is re-let, the proprietor will make a refund to you which normally excludes the amount of the deposit.

Tourist information centres throughout Britain are able to give campers and caravanners information about parks in their areas. Some tourist information centres have camping and caravanning advisory services that provide details of park availability and often assist with park booking.

Electric hook-up points

Most parks now have electric hook-up points for caravans and tents. Voltage is generally 240v AC, 50 cycles. Parks may charge extra for this facility, and it is advisable to check rates when making a booking.

Avoiding peak season

In the summer months of June to September, parks in popular areas such as North Wales, Cumbria, the West Country or the New Forest in Hampshire may become full. Campers should aim to arrive at parks early in the day or, where possible, should book in advance. Some parks have overnight holding areas for visitors who arrive late. This helps to prevent disturbing other campers and caravanners late at night and means that fewer visitors are turned away. Caravans or tents are directed to a pitch the following morning.

Other caravan and camping places

If you enjoy making your own route through Britain's countryside, it may interest you to know that the Forestry Commission operates campsites in Britain's Forest Parks as well as in the New Forest. Some offer reduced charges for youth organisations on organised camping trips and all enquiries about them should be made well in advance of your intended stay to the Forestry Commission.

Travelling with pets

Dogs, cats, ferrets and some other pets can be brought into the UK from certain countries without having to undertake six months' quarantine on arrival, provided they meet the requirements of the Pet Travel Scheme (PETS).

For full details, visit the PETS website at
w www.gov.uk/take-pet-abroad
or contact the PETS Helpline
t +44 (0)370 241 1710
e pettravel@ahvla.gsi.gov.uk
Ask for fact sheets which cover dogs and cats, ferrets or domestic rabbits and rodents.

There are no requirements for pets travelling directly between the UK and the Channel Islands. Pets entering Jersey or Guernsey from other countries need to be Pet Travel Scheme compliant and have a valid EU Pet Passport.
For more information see www.jersey.com or www.visitguernsey.com.

Remember, if you book by telephone and are asked for your credit card number, you should check whether the proprietor intends to charge your credit card account, should you later cancel your reservation. A proprietor should not be able to charge your credit card account with a cancellation fee without your consent unless you agreed to this at the time of your booking. However, to avoid later disputes, we suggest you check whether this is the intention before providing your details.

Insurance

There are so many reasons why you might have to cancel your holiday, which is why we strongly advise people to take out a cancellation insurance policy. In fact, many self-catering agencies now advise their customers to take out a policy when they book their holiday.

Arrival time

If you know you will be arriving late in the evening, it is a good idea to say so when you book. If you are delayed on your way, a telephone call to say that you will be late is often appreciated.

It is particularly important to liaise with the proprietor about key collection as he or she may not be on site.

Finding a park

Tourist signs similar to the one shown here are designed to help visitors find their park. They clearly show whether the park is for tents or caravans or both.

353

What to expect

The proprietor/management is required to undertake the following:

Prior to booking
- To describe accurately in any advertisement, brochure, or other printed or electronic media, the facilities and services provided;
- To make clear to guests in print, electronic media and on the telephone exactly what is included in all prices quoted for accommodation, including taxes and any other surcharges. Details of charges for additional services/facilities should also be made clear, for example breakfast, leisure etc;
- To provide information on the suitability of the premises for guests of various ages, particularly for the elderly and the very young;
- To allow guests to view the accommodation prior to booking if requested.

At the time of booking
- To clearly describe the cancellation policy to guests i.e. by telephone, fax, internet/email as well as in any printed information given to guests;
- To adhere to and not to exceed prices quoted at the time of booking for accommodation and services;
- To make clear to guests if the accommodation offered is in an unconnected annexe or similar, and to indicate the location of such accommodation and any difference in comfort and/or amenities from accommodation at the property.

On arrival
- To welcome all guests courteously and without discrimination in relation to gender, sexual orientation, disability, race, religion or belief.

During the stay
- To maintain standards of guest care, cleanliness, and service appropriate to the type of establishment;
- To deal promptly and courteously with all enquiries, requests, bookings and correspondence from guests;
- To ensure complaints received are investigated promptly and courteously to an outcome that is communicated to the guest.

On departure
- To give each guest, on request, details of payments due and a receipt, if required/requested.

General
- To give due consideration to the requirements of guests with special needs, and make suitable provision where applicable;
- To ensure the accommodation, when advertised as open, is prepared for the arrival of guests at all times;
- To advise guests, at any time prior to their stay, of any changes made to their booking;
- To have a complaints handling procedure in place to deal promptly and fairly with all guest complaints;
- To hold current public liability insurance and to comply with all relevant statutory obligations including legislation applicable to fire, health and safety, planning and food safety;
- To allow, on request, VisitEngland representatives reasonable access to the establishment, to confirm that the Code of Conduct is being observed or in order to investigate any complaint of a serious nature;

Comments and complaints

Information

Other than rating information, the proprietors themselves supply descriptions of their properties and other information for the entries in this book. They have all signed a declaration to confirm that their information accurately describes their accommodation business. The publishers cannot guarantee the accuracy of information in this guide, and accept no responsibility for any error or misrepresentation. All liability for loss, disappointment, negligence or other damage caused by reliance on the information contained in this guide, or in the event of bankruptcy or liquidation or cessation of trade of any company, individual or firm mentioned, is hereby excluded. We strongly recommend that you carefully check prices and other details before you book your accommodation.

Quality signage

All establishments displaying a quality sign have to hold current membership of VisitEngland's Quality Assessment Scheme.

When an establishment is sold, the new owner has to re-apply and be re-assessed. In certain circumstances the rating may be carried forward before the property is re-assessed.

Problems

Of course, we hope you will not have cause for complaint, but problems do occur from time to time. If you are dissatisfied with anything, make your complaint to the management immediately. Then the management can take action by investigating the matter in attempts to put things right. The longer you leave a complaint, the harder it is to deal with it effectively.

In certain circumstances, the national tourist board may look into your complaint. However, they have no statutory control over establishments or their methods of operating and cannot become involved in legal or contractual matters such as financial compensation.

If you do have problems that have not been resolved by the proprietor and which you would like to bring to their attention, please write to: Quality in Tourism, 1320 Montpellier Court, Pioneer Way, Gloucester Business Park, Gloucester, Gloucestershire GL3 4AH

About the accommodation entries

Entries

All accommodation featured in this guide has been assessed or has applied for assessment under a quality assessment scheme.

Start your search for a place to stay by looking in the 'Where to Stay' sections of this guide, where proprietors have paid to have their establishment featured in either a standard entry (includes photograph, description, facilities and prices) or an enhanced entry (photograph(s) and extended details).

Locations

Places to stay are listed by town, city or village. If a property is located in a small village, you may find it listed under a nearby town (providing it is within a seven-mile radius).

Within each region, counties run in alphabetical order. Place names are listed alphabetically within each county, and include interesting county information and a map reference.

Complete addresses for self-catering rental properties are not given and the town(s) listed may be a distance from the actual property. Please check the precise location before booking.

Map references

These refer to the colour location maps at the back of the guide. The first figure shown is the map number, the following letter and figure indicate the grid reference on the map. Place names that have a standard or enhanced entry appear on the maps. Some standard or enhanced entries were added at the last minute and therefore they do not appear on the maps.

Telephone numbers

Booking telephone numbers are listed below the contact address for each entry. Area codes are shown in brackets.

Prices

The prices printed are to be used as a guide only; they were supplied to us by proprietors in summer 2015.

Remember, changes may occur after the guide goes to press, therefore we strongly advise you to check prices before booking your accommodation.

Prices are shown in pounds sterling, including VAT where applicable. For self-catering accommodation, pries are per unit per week. Touring pitch prices are based on the minimum and maximum charges for one night for two persons, car and caravan or tent. (Some parks may charge separately for a car, caravan or tent and for each person and there may be an extra charge for caravan awnings.) Minimum and maximum prices for caravan holiday homes are given per week.

Prices often vary throughout the year and may be significantly lower outside of peak periods. You can get details of other bargain packages that may be available from the establishments themselves, regional tourism organisations or your local Tourist Information Centre (TIC). Your local travel agent may also have information and can help you make your booking.

Opening period

If an entry does not indicate an opening period, please check directly with the proprietor.

Symbols

The at-a-glance symbols included at the end of each entry show many of the services and facilities available at each property. You will find the key to these symbols on page 7.

Smoking

In the UK and the Channel Islands, it is illegal to smoke in enclosed public spaces and places of work. Smoking may be allowed in self-contained short-term rental accommodation, such as holiday cottages, flats or caravans, if the owner chooses to allow it.

If you wish to smoke, we advise you to check the proprietor's smoking policy before you book.

Pets

Many places accept guests with dogs, but we advise that you check this with the proprietor before booking, remembering to ask if there are any extra charges or rules about exactly where your pet is allowed. The acceptance of dogs is not always extended to cats and it is strongly advised that cat owners contact the property well in advance of their stay.

Some establishments do not accept pets at all. Pets are welcome by arrangement where you see this symbol ⚐. The quarantine laws have changed and now dogs, cats and ferrets are able to come into Britain and the Channel Islands from over 50 countries. For details of the Pet Travel Scheme (PETS) please turn to page 353.

Payments accepted

The types of payment accepted by an establishment are listed in the payment accepted section. If you plan to pay by card, check that the establishment will accept the particular type of card you own before booking. Some proprietors will charge you a higher rate if you pay by credit card rather than cash or cheque. The difference is to cover the charges paid by the proprietor to the credit card company.

When you book by telephone, you may be asked for your credit card number as confirmation. Remember, the proprietor may then charge your credit card account if you cancel your booking. See details of this under Cancellations on page 352.

Awaiting confirmation of rating
At the time of going to press some properties featured in this guide had not yet been assessed therefore their rating for this year could not be included. The term 'Rating Applied For' indicates this throughout your guide.

Useful contacts

British Holiday & Home Parks Association

Chichester House, 6 Pullman Court,
Great Western Road, Gloucester GL1 3ND
t (01452) 526911 (enquiries and brochure requests)
w parkholidayengland.org.uk

Professional UK park owners are represented by the British Holiday and Home Parks Association. Over 2,700 parks are members, and each year welcome millions of visitors seeking quality surroundings in which to enjoy a good value stay.

Parks provide caravan holiday homes and lodges for hire and pitches for your own touring caravan, motor home or tent. On many, you can opt to buy your own holiday home.

A major strength of the UK's park industry is its diversity. Whatever your idea of holiday pleasure, there's sure to be a park which can provide it. If your preference is for a quiet, peaceful holiday in tranquil rural surroundings, you'll find many idyllic locations.

Alternatively, many parks are to be found at our most popular resorts – and reflect the holiday atmosphere with plenty of entertainment and leisure facilities. For more adventurous families, parks often provide excellent bases from which to enjoy outdoor activities.

Literature available from BH&HPA includes a guide to parks which have this year achieved the David Bellamy Conservation Award for environmental excellence.

The Camping and Caravanning Club

Greenfields House, Westwood Way,
Coventry CV4 8JH
t 024 7647 5448
t 024 76475426 (advance bookings)
w campingandcaravanningclub.co.uk

Discover the peace and quiet of over 100 award-winning club sites. Experience a different backdrop to your holiday every time you go away, with sites in the lakes and mountains, coastal and woodland glades or cultural and heritage locations.

The Club is proud of its prestigious pedigree and regularly achieves awards for spotless campsites, friendly service and caring for the environment – a guarantee that you will enjoy your holiday.

Non-members are welcome at the majority of our sites and we offer special deals for families, backpackers, overseas visitors and members aged 55 and over. Recoup your membership fee in just six nights and gain access to over 1,300 Certificated Sites around the country.

For more details, please refer to our entries listed at the back of this publication or if you require any more information on what The Friendly Club can offer you then telephone 024 7647 5448, or call to request your free guide to The Club.

The Caravan Club

East Grinstead House, East Grinstead,
West Sussex RH19 1UA
t (01342) 326944
w caravanclub.co.uk
The Caravan Club offers 200 sites in the UK and
Ireland. These include city locations such as
London, Edinburgh, York and Chester, plus sites
near leading heritage attractions such as Longleat,
Sandringham, Chatsworth and Blenheim Palace. A
further 30 sites are in National Parks.

Virtually all pitches have an electric hook-up point.
The toilet blocks and play areas are of the highest
quality. Friendly, knowledgeable site wardens are
on hand too.

Most Caravan Club Sites are graded four or five stars
according to The British Graded Holiday Parks Scheme,
run by the national tourist boards, so that you can be
assured of quality at all times. Over 130 sites are open
to non-members, but why not become a member and
gain access to all sites, plus a further 2,500 certificated
locations – rural sites for no more than five vans.
Tent campers are welcome at over 60 sites.

Join The Club and you can save the cost of your
subscription fee in just five nights with member
discounts on site fees!

Forest Holidays

Bath Yard, Moira, Derbyshire DE12 6BA
t 03330 110 495
w forestholidays.co.uk

Forest Holidays, a new partnership between
the Forestry Commission and the Camping
and Caravanning Club, have over 20 camping
and caravan sites in stunning forest locations
throughout Great Britain in addition to three cabin
sites. Choose from locations such as the Scottish
Highlands, the New Forest, Snowdonia National
Park, the Forest of Dean, or the banks of Loch
Lomond. Some sites are open all year and dogs are
welcome at most. Advance bookings are accepted
for many sites.

For a unique forest experience, call Forest Holidays for
a brochure on 03330 110 495 or visit their website.

The Motor Caravanners' Club Ltd

1st Floor, Woodfarm Estate, Marlbank Road,
Welland, Malvern WR13 6NA
t (0) 1684 311677
e info@motorcaravanners.eu
w motorcaravanners.eu
The Motor Caravanners' Club is authorised to
issue the Camping Card International (CCI). It also
produces a monthly magazine, Motor Caravanner,
for all members. Member of The Federation
Internationale de Camping et de Caravanning (FICC).

The National Caravan Council

The National Caravan Council,
Catherine House, Victoria Road,
Aldershot, Hampshire
GU11 1SS
t (01252) 318251
w thencc.org.uk

The National Caravan Council (NCC) is the trade
body for the British caravan industry – not just
touring caravans and motorhomes but also caravan
holiday homes. It has in its membership parks,
manufacturers, dealers and suppliers to the industry
– all NCC member companies are committed
continually to raise standards of technical and
commercial excellence.

So, if you want to know where to buy a caravan,
where to find a caravan holiday park or simply
need advice on caravans and caravanning, see the
website thencc.org.uk where there is lots of helpful
advice including:

- How to check whether the caravan, motorhome
  or caravan holiday home you are buying complies
  with European Standards and essential UK health
  and safety regulations (through the Certification
  scheme that the NCC operates).
- Where to find quality parks to visit on holiday.
- Where to find approved caravan and motorhome
  workshops for servicing and repair.

Caravan holidays are one of the most popular
choices for holidaymakers in Britain – the NCC
works closely with VisitBritain to promote caravan
holidays in all their forms and parks that are part of
the British Graded Holiday Parks Scheme.

Getting around

London transport

Each London Underground line has its own unique colour, so you can easily follow them on the Underground map. Most lines run through central London, and many serve parts of Greater London. Tube services run every day from around 5.30am to around 1am. From Autumn 2015 some services will run all night on Fridays and Saturdays. Buses are a quick, convenient way to travel around London, providing plenty of sightseeing opportunities along the way. There are over 6,500 buses in London operating 700 routes every day. You will need to buy a ticket or Travel Pass before you board the bus.

London's National Rail system stretches all over London. Many lines start at the main London railway stations (Paddington, Victoria, Waterloo, Kings Cross) with links to the tube. Trains mainly serve areas outside central London, and travel overground.

Children usually travel free, or at reduced fare, on all public transport in London.

Oyster cards

The Visitor Oyster Card is a pay-as-you-go smartcard. It's a quick and easy way to pay for journeys on bus, Tube, tram, DLR, London Overground, TfL Rail and most National Rail services in London.

A Visitor Oyster card costs £3 (plus postage) and is pre-loaded with pay as you go credit for you to spend on travel. You can choose how much credit to add to your card: £10, £15, £20, £25, £30, £35, £40, or £50. As a guide a £20 card will usually cover a return journey from Heathrow plus travel around Central London for one 1 or 2 days. If you are visiting for 3-4 days, get a £30 card or if you are here for a week and you will be travelling lots every day, then a £50 card is a good option, The credit on your card never expires - it stays there until you use it. If you run out of credit on your card, it's easy to top it up and use it again. Children under 11 travel free, but children over 11 need their own travel ticket. There is no child version of the Oyster card, but there is a child Travelcard

For further information or to buy cards visit www.visitbritainshop.com/world/london-visitor-oyster-card or www.tfl.gov.uk/travel-information/visiting-london/visitor-oyster-card

London congestion charge

The congestion charge is £11.50 daily charge to drive in central London at certain times. Check if the congestion charge is included in the cost of your car before booking. If your car's pick up point is in the congestion-charging zone, the company may pay the charge for the first day of your hire.

Low Emission Zone

The Low Emission Zone is an area covering most of Greater London, within which the most polluting diesel-engine vehicles are required to meet specific emissions standards. If your vehicle does not, you will be required to pay a daily charge.

Vehicles affected by the Low Emission Zone are older diesel-engine lorries, buses, coaches, large vans, minibuses and other heavy vehicles such as motor caravans and motorised horse boxes. This also includes vehicles registered outside of Great Britain. Cars and motorcycles are not affected by this scheme. For more information visit www.tfl.gov.uk

Rail and train travel

Britain's rail network covers all main cities and smaller regional towns. Trains on the network are operated by a few large companies running routes from London to stations all over Britain. Therefore smaller companies that run routes in regional areas. You can find up-to-the-minute information about routes, fares and train times on the National Rail Enquiries website (www.nationalrail.co.uk). For detailed information about routes and services, refer to the train operators' websites (see page 293).

Railway passes
BritRail offer a wide selection of passes and tickets giving you the freedom to travel on all National Rail services. Passes can also include sleeper services, city and attraction passes and boat tours. Passes can usually be purchased from travel agents outside Britain or by visiting the BritRail website www.britrail.net.

Bus and coach travel

Public buses
Every city and town in Britain has a local bus service. These services are privatised and managed by separate companies. The largest bus companies in Britain are First (www.firstgroup.com/ukbus), Stagecoach (www.stagecoachbus.com) and Arriva (www.arrivabus.co.uk), and run buses in most UK towns. Outside London, buses usually travel to and from the town centre or to the busiest part of town. Most towns have a bus station, where you'll be able to find maps and information about routes. Bus route information may also be posted at bus stops.

Tickets and fares
The cost of a bus ticket normally depends on how far you're travelling. Return fares may be available on some buses, but you would usually need to buy a 'single' ticket for each individual journey.

You can also buy your ticket when boarding a bus by telling the driver where you are going. One-day and weekly travel cards are available in some towns, and these can be purchased from either the driver or from an information centre at the bus station. Tickets are valid for each separate journey rather than for a period of time, so if you get off the bus you'll need to buy a new ticket when getting on another.

Domestic flights

Flying is a time-saving alternative to road or rail when it comes to travelling around Britain. Domestic flights are fast and frequent and there are 33 airports across Britain that operate domestic routes. You will find airports marked on the maps at the front of this guide.

Domestic flight advice
Photo ID is required to travel on domestic flights. However it is advisable to bring your passport as not all airlines will accept other forms of photo identification. Please be aware of the high security measures at all airports in Britain which include include restrictions on items that may be carried in hand luggage. It is important that you check the restrictions in place with your airline prior to travel, as these can vary over time and don't forget to allow adequate time for check-in and boarding on arrival.

Cycling

Cycling is a great way to see some of England's iconic scenery and there are many networks of cycling routes available across England. The National Cycle Network offers over 10,000 miles of walking and cycling routes details for connecting towns and villages, countryside and coast across England. For more information and view these routes see page 289 or visit Sustrans at www.sustrans.co.uk.

Think green

If you'd rather leave your car behind and travel by 'green transport' to some of the attractions highlighted in this guide you'll be helping to reduce congestion and pollution as well as supporting conservation charities In their commitment to green travel.

The National Trust encourages visits made by non-car travellers and it offers admission discounts or a voucher for the tea room at a selection of its properties if you arrive on foot, cycle or public transport (you may need to produce a valid bus or train ticket if travelling by public transport.).

More information about The National Trust's work to encourage car-free days out can be found at www.nationaltrust.org.uk.

If you have
access needs…

Guests with hearing, visual or mobility needs can feel confident about booking accommodation that participates in the National Accessible Scheme (NAS).

Look out for the NAS symbols which are included throughout the accommodation directory. Using the NAS could help make the difference between a good holiday and a perfect one!

For more information on the NAS and tips & ideas on holiday travel in England, go to: www.visitengland.com/accessforall

Here are just some of the most popular long distance routes on the 12,000 mile Sustrans National Cycle Network. To see the Network in it's entirety and to find routes near you, visit **www.sustrans.org.uk**

Sustrans is the UK's leading sustainable transport charity working on practical projects to enable people to choose to travel in ways which benefit their health and the environment.

68 National Cycle Network Route Number
  Long Distance Routes
  (1) Coast & Castles Cycle Route
  (2) Pennine Cycleway - North Pennines
  (3) Hadrian's Cycleway
  (4) Sea to Sea
  (5) Pennine Cycleway - South Pennines & the Dales
  (6) Derby to York
  (7) Hull to Fakenham
  (8) East of England
  (9) South Midlands Cycle Route
  (10) Thames Valley Cycle Route
  (11) Garden of England
  (12) Downs & Weald Cycle Route
  (13) Devon Coast to Coast
  (14) The Cornish Way
  (15) The West Country Way
  (16) The Severn & Thames

Map reproduced from Ordnance Survey material with the permission of Ordnance Survey on behalf of the Contoller of Her Majesty's Stationery Office © Crown copyright. Unauthorised reproduction infringes Crown copyright and may lead to prosecution or civil proceedings.
Licence number 100020852 (2009)

By car and by train

Distance chart

The distances between towns on the chart below are given to the nearest mile, and are measured along routes based on the quickest travelling time, making maximum use of motorways or dual-carriageway roads. The chart is based upon information supplied by the Automobile Association.

To calculate the distance in kilometres multiply the mileage by 1.6
For example: Brighton to Dover
82 miles x 1.6 =131.2 kilometres

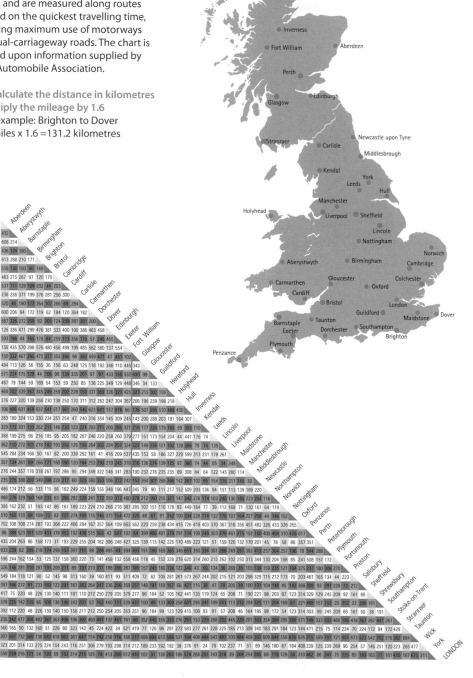

Aberdeen
Aberystwyth — 472
Barnstaple — 608 214
Birmingham — 436 124 180
Brighton — 613 288 210 171
Bristol — 518 130 100 90 169
Cambridge — 463 215 267 97 120 170
Cardiff — 537 111 128 109 202 44 203
Carlisle — 236 236 371 199 376 281 256 300
Carmarthen — 520 48 190 172 264 107 266 68 284
Dorchester — 600 206 94 172 119 62 184 120 364 182
Dover — 587 326 272 208 82 205 124 239 381 301 200
Edinburgh — 126 336 471 299 476 381 333 400 100 386 463 458
Exeter — 593 198 44 165 178 84 259 113 356 175 57 248 455
Fort William — 156 435 570 398 576 480 456 499 199 485 562 580 137 554
Glasgow — 150 332 467 295 472 377 333 396 96 382 459 477 47 451 102
Gloucester — 484 113 126 56 155 36 150 63 248 125 118 192 346 110 445 343
Guildford — 571 224 175 128 44 106 96 139 335 201 97 97 433 150 532 430 99
Hereford — 487 79 144 59 189 54 153 59 250 85 126 225 349 129 448 346 34 133
Holyhead — 464 102 339 167 345 249 259 202 228 150 331 369 326 323 425 323 215 302 156
Hull — 376 227 320 139 258 230 138 250 170 311 312 262 247 304 367 266 196 239 198 218
Inverness — 106 496 631 459 637 541 517 561 260 546 623 641 157 616 66 176 507 595 510 488 430
Kendal — 283 189 324 153 330 234 251 254 47 240 316 354 145 309 245 143 200 288 203 181 164 307
Leeds — 329 173 301 120 262 211 146 230 123 224 293 271 200 285 321 219 177 220 179 165 59 383 110
Lincoln — 388 199 275 98 216 185 95 205 182 267 246 220 258 260 379 277 151 173 154 204 44 441 176 74
Liverpool — 362 110 272 101 278 182 193 202 126 158 264 302 224 257 324 222 148 236 151 102 128 386 79 74 139
Maidstone — 545 284 234 166 50 167 82 200 339 262 161 41 416 209 537 435 153 58 186 327 220 599 313 231 178 261
Manchester — 357 134 261 89 266 171 160 190 120 184 253 290 219 245 318 216 136 224 139 125 97 380 74 44 85 34 248
Middlesbrough — 276 244 357 176 318 267 197 286 95 294 349 322 146 341 283 190 232 276 235 89 308 84 64 122 145 280 114
Newcastle — 235 275 388 207 349 298 229 317 60 325 380 353 106 372 242 153 264 307 266 266 142 267 102 95 154 176 311 145 39
Northampton — 486 174 212 56 133 115 56 162 249 224 159 155 348 196 447 345 79 90 111 217 152 509 203 136 94 151 113 139 189 220
Norwich — 488 278 329 160 168 233 63 266 282 328 241 172 359 313 480 378 212 160 215 201 147 542 276 174 103 240 130 185 223 254 118
Nottingham — 395 162 232 51 193 142 86 161 189 223 224 210 266 216 387 285 107 151 110 178 93 449 164 77 39 112 168 71 130 161 64 119
Oxford — 510 160 170 68 109 73 32 107 274 169 115 146 373 154 472 370 48 67 81 242 190 534 228 174 132 176 74 167 258 44 146 102
Penzance — 702 308 108 274 287 193 368 222 466 284 167 357 564 109 663 562 220 259 238 434 415 726 419 403 370 367 318 356 451 482 326 433 326 265
Perth — 86 398 523 351 529 433 378 453 152 438 515 503 42 507 102 64 399 486 401 379 291 114 199 245 303 278 461 275 192 150 400 404 310 426 617
Peterborough — 435 204 263 86 158 173 37 193 229 255 204 162 306 248 427 325 139 115 142 225 110 489 223 121 51 159 120 132 170 201 45 78 58 86 357 351
Plymouth — 633 239 62 205 218 124 299 153 397 215 98 288 495 44 594 493 151 190 169 365 346 657 350 334 301 296 249 287 382 413 257 364 257 196 78 544 288
Portsmouth — 596 244 154 53 125 137 158 360 220 73 141 458 132 558 456 118 45 152 328 276 620 314 260 215 262 102 250 313 344 130 204 188 85 241 508 157 172
Preston — 326 146 281 110 287 191 209 211 89 197 273 311 188 266 287 195 157 245 160 138 122 344 35 36 269 35 139 159 25 121 184 375 237 180 306 270
Salisbury — 549 184 118 121 90 52 145 98 313 160 39 160 411 93 511 409 72 62 105 281 261 573 267 244 202 215 121 203 298 329 115 212 173 70 203 461 165 134 44 223
Sheffield — 397 166 272 91 233 182 192 201 161 263 264 247 236 256 359 257 148 191 150 154 88 421 115 38 47 79 205 39 100 131 104 198 6 93 297 228 73 212
Shrewsbury — 417 75 220 48 226 130 140 111 181 110 212 250 279 205 379 277 96 184 52 105 162 441 135 119 124 65 208 71 190 221 90 163 87 123 314 329 129 245 209 92 161 88
Southampton — 578 225 142 135 66 106 136 140 342 201 53 152 440 111 539 437 100 49 133 309 258 601 295 241 199 243 113 232 294 325 111 204 169 67 221 489 157 152 20 252 23 209 191
Stoke-on-Trent — 392 112 220 48 210 130 110 110 150 211 212 250 204 205 353 251 96 184 99 123 129 415 109 93 99 59 207 46 164 195 98 152 54 123 314 300 66 161 50 38 191 245 209 66
Stranraer — 235 342 477 305 482 387 363 406 106 392 469 487 132 461 181 86 352 440 355 276 261 153 229 288 232 245 229 201 163 354 388 295 380 571 148 333 502 466 195 418 267 287 447 261
Taunton — 560 165 50 132 160 51 226 54 424 422 34 521 419 72 496 471 215 75 114 374 254 586 281 290 340 183 291 184 213 411 215 94 172 429
Wick — 207 597 732 560 738 642 618 662 361 647 724 742 258 716 166 277 608 695 610 588 531 104 408 484 543 487 700 484 409 307 609 644 550 635 826 215 589 757 721 451 673 523 542 702 516 362 684
York — 323 201 314 133 275 224 154 243 116 251 306 279 193 298 314 212 189 233 192 138 32 376 91 24 79 102 237 71 51 89 146 180 87 184 408 230 125 339 269 96 254 57 146 210 120 223 265 477
LONDON — 550 239 216 121 54 120 59 153 314 215 125 78 413 200 512 410 102 31 136 282 186 574 268 201 143 216 39 204 254 285 68 118 129 56 310 462 86 241 75 225 85 169 163 71 161 420 167 675 211

Map labels: Inverness, Fort William, Aberdeen, Perth, Edinburgh, Glasgow, Stranraer, Carlisle, Newcastle upon Tyne, Middlesbrough, Kendal, York, Leeds, Hull, Manchester, Holyhead, Liverpool, Sheffield, Lincoln, Nottingham, Norwich, Aberystwyth, Birmingham, Cambridge, Carmarthen, Gloucester, Oxford, Colchester, Cardiff, Bristol, London, Guildford, Maidstone, Dover, Barnstaple, Taunton, Southampton, Dorchester, Brighton, Plymouth, Penzance

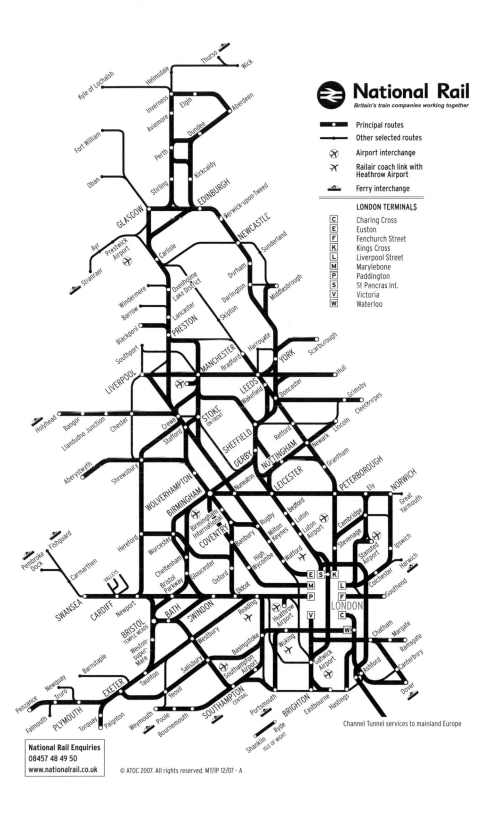

National Rail
Britain's train companies working together

●━━	Principal routes
━━	Other selected routes
⊗	Airport interchange
✈	Railair coach link with Heathrow Airport
⛴	Ferry interchange

LONDON TERMINALS

C	Charing Cross
E	Euston
F	Fenchurch Street
K	Kings Cross
L	Liverpool Street
M	Marylebone
P	Paddington
S	St Pancras Int.
V	Victoria
W	Waterloo

Channel Tunnel services to mainland Europe

National Rail Enquiries
08457 48 49 50
www.nationalrail.co.uk

© ATOC 2007. All rights reserved. MT/IP 12/07 - A

Travel information

General travel information

Streetmap	www.streetmap.co.uk	
Transport for London	www.tfl.gov.uk	0843 222 1234
Travel Services	www.departures-arrivals.com	
Traveline	www.traveline.info	0871 200 2233

Bus & coach

Megabus	www.megabus.com	0900 160 0900
National Express	www.nationalexpress.com	08717 818 178
WA Shearings	www.shearings.com	0844 824 6351

Car & car hire

AA	www.theaa.com	0800 085 2721
Green Flag	www.greenflag.com	0845 246 1557
RAC	www.rac.co.uk	0844 308 9177
Alamo	www.alamo.co.uk	0871 384 1086*
Avis	www.avis.co.uk	0844 581 0147*
Budget	www.budget.co.uk	0844 544 3407*
Easycar	www.easycar.com	
Enterprise	www.enterprise.com	0800 800 227*
Hertz	www.hertz.co.uk	0870 844 8844*
Holiday Autos	www.holidayautos.co.uk	0871 472 5229
National	www.nationalcar.co.uk	0871 384 1140
Thrifty	www.thrifty.co.uk	01494 751500

Air

Air Southwest	www.airsouthwest.com	0870 043 4553
Blue Islands (Channel Islands)	www.blueislands.com	08456 20 2122
BMI	www.flybmi.com	0844 848 4888
BMI Baby	www.bmibaby.com	0905 828 2828*
British Airways	www.ba.com	0844 493 0787
British International (Isles of Scilly to Penzance)	www.islesofscillyhelicopter.com	01736 363871*
CityJet	www.cityjet.com	0871 663 3777
Eastern Airways	www.easternairways.com	08703 669100
Easyjet	www.easyjet.com	0843 104 5000
Flybe	www.flybe.com	0871 700 2000*
Jet2.com	www.jet2.com	0871 226 1737*
Manx2	www.manx2.com	0871 200 0440*
Ryanair	www.ryanair.com	0871 246 0000
Skybus (Isles of Scilly)	www.islesofscilly-travel.co.uk	0845 710 5555
Thomsonfly	www.thomsonfly.com	0871 231 4787

Train

National Rail Enquiries	www.nationalrail.co.uk	0845 748 4950
The Trainline	www.trainline.co.uk	0871 244 1545
UK train operating companies	www.rail.co.uk	
Arriva Trains	www.arriva.co.uk	0191 520 4000
c2c	www.c2c-online.co.uk	0845 601 4873
Chiltern Railways	www.chilternrailways.co.uk	0845 600 5165
CrossCountry	www.crosscountrytrains.co.uk	0844 811 0124
East Midlands Trains	www.eastmidlandstrains.co.uk	0845 712 5678
Eurostar	www.eurostar.com	08432 186 186*
First Capital Connect	www.firstcapitalconnect.co.uk	0845 026 4700
First Great Western	www.firstgreatwestern.co.uk	0845 700 0125
Gatwick Express	www.gatwickexpress.com	0845 850 1530
Heathrow Connect	www.heathrowconnect.com	0845 678 6975
Heathrow Express	www.heathrowexpress.com	0845 600 1515
Hull Trains	www.hulltrains.co.uk	0845 071 0222
Island Line	www.islandlinetrains.co.uk	0845 600 0650
London Midlands	www.londonmidland.com	0121 634 2040
Merseyrail	www.merseyrail.org	0151 702 2071
National Express East Anglia	www.nationalexpresseastanglia.com	0845 600 7245
National Express East Coast	www.nationalexpresseastcoast.com	0845 722 5333
Northern Rail	www.northernrail.org	0845 000 0125
ScotRail	www.scotrail.co.uk	0845 601 5929
South Eastern Trains	www.southeasternrailway.co.uk	0845 000 2222
South West Trains	www.southwesttrains.co.uk	0845 600 0650
Southern	www.southernrailway.com	0845 127 2920
Stansted Express	www.stanstedexpress.com	0845 600 7245
Translink	www.translink.co.uk	(028) 9066 6630
Transpennine Express	www.tpexpress.co.uk	0845 600 1671
Virgin Trains	www.virgintrains.co.uk	08450 008 000*

Ferry

Ferry Information	www.discoverferries.com	0207 436 2449
Condor Ferries	www.condorferries.co.uk	0845 609 1024*
Steam Packet Company	www.steam-packet.com	08722 992 992*
Isles of Scilly Travel	www.islesofscilly-travel.co.uk	0845 710 5555
Red Funnel	www.redfunnel.co.uk	0844 849 9988
Wight Link	www.wightlink.co.uk	0871 376 1000

Phone numbers listed are for general enquiries unless otherwise stated.
* Booking line only

David Bellamy
Conservation Award

BRONZE   SILVER   GOLD

Parks wishing to enter for a David Bellamy Conservation Award must complete a detailed questionnaire covering different aspects of their environmental policies, and describe what positive conservation steps they have taken. The park must also undergo an independent audit from a local wildlife or conservation body which is familiar with the area. Final assessments and the appropriate level of any award are then made personally by Professor Bellamy.

Parks with a current 2015/16 Bellamy Award offer a variety of accommodation from pitches for touring caravans, motor homes and tents, to caravan holiday homes, holiday lodges and cottages for

rent or to buy. Holiday parks with these awards are not just those in quiet corners of the countryside. Amongst the winners are much larger centres in popular holiday areas that offer a wide range of entertainments and attractions.

The parks listed on the following pages all have a detailed entry in this guide and have received a Gold, Silver or Bronze David Bellamy Conservation Award. Use the Index by Property Name starting on page 382 to find the page number.

A full list of award-winning parks is available at www.bellamyparks.co.uk or www.ukparks.com

Wooda Farm Holiday Park	Gold	Bude	South West
Cofton Country Holidays	Gold	Dawlish	South West
Lady's Mile Touring and Camping Park	Gold	Dawlish	South West
Whitemead Forest Park	Gold	Lydney	South West
Ladram Bay Holiday Park	Gold	Otterton	South West
Porlock Caravan Park	Gold	Porlock	South West
Tehidy Holiday Park	Gold	Redruth	South West
Stonehenge Campsite	Gold	Salisbury	South West
Trethem Mill Touring Park	Gold	St. Just in Roseland	South West
Langstone Manor Holiday Park	Gold	Tavistock	South West
Watergate Bay Touring Park	Gold	Watergate Bay	South West

Halse Farm Caravan & Tent Park	Gold	Winsford	South West
Harrow Wood Farm Caravan Park	Silver	Christchurch	South West
Wheel Farm Cottages	Silver	Combe Martin	South West
Oakcliff Holiday Park	Silver	Dawlish	South West
Castle Brake Holiday Park	Silver	Woodbury	South West
Shearbarn Holiday Park	Gold	Hastings	South East
Hurley Riverside Park	Gold	Hurley	South East
Whitefield Forest Touring Park	Gold	Ryde	South East
Appuldurcombe Gardens Holiday Park	Gold	Ventnor	South East
Clippesby Hall	Gold	Clippesby	East of England
Fen Farm Camping and Caravan Site	Gold	Colchester	East of England
Peewit Caravan Park	Gold	Felixstowe	East of England
Vauxhall Holiday Park Ltd	Gold	Great Yarmouth	East of England
Searles Leisure Resort	Gold	Hunstanton	East of England
Rivendale Caravan & Leisure Park	Gold	Ashbourne	East Midlands
Beech Croft Farm Caravan & Camping Park	Gold	Buxton	East Midlands
Darwin Forest Country Park	Gold	Matlock	East Midlands
Skegness Water Leisure Park	Gold	Skegness	East Midlands
Cayton Village Caravan Park Ltd	Gold	Scarborough	Yorkshire
Northcliffe & Seaview Holiday Parks	Gold	Whitby	Yorkshire
Castlerigg Hall Caravan & Camping Park	Gold	Keswick	North West
Woodclose Caravan Park	Gold	Kirkby Lonsdale	North West
Eastham Hall Caravan Park	Gold	Lytham St. Annes	North West
Flusco Wood	Gold	Penrith	North West
Willowbank Holiday Park	Gold	Southport	North West
Hillcroft Holiday Park	Gold	Ullswater	North West
Waterfoot Caravan Park	Gold	Ullswater	North West
Hill Of Oaks & Blake Holme Caravan Estate	Gold	Windermere	North West
Park Cliffe Camping & Caravan Estate	Gold	Windermere	North West
Newby Bridge Country Caravan Park	Silver	Newby Bridge	North West
Moorlands Caravan Park	Silver	Oldham	North West
Riverside Holiday Park	Bronze	Southport	North West
Waren Caravan & Camping Park	Gold	Bamburgh	North East

National Accessible Scheme index

Establishments with a detailed entry in this guide who participate in the National Accessible Scheme are listed below. At the front of the guide you can find information about the scheme. Establishments are listed alphabetically by place name.

370

♿ Mobility level 2

Ainsdale, North West	**Willowbank Holiday Home and Touring Park ★★★★★**	304
Ashbourne, East Midlands	**Rivendale Caravan & Leisure Park ★★★★**	194
Bacton, East of England	**Primrose Cottage ★★★**	162
Bowes, North East	**Mellwaters Barn ★★★★Gold**	318
Cromer, East of England	**Coach Cottage ★★★★Gold**	164
Maidstone, South East	**Coldblow Farm ★★★-★★★★**	116
Minehead, South West	**Woodcombe Lodges & Cottages ★★★★**	86
Pateley Bridge, Yorkshire	**Helme Pasture Lodges & Cottages ★★★★**	260
Peterborough, East of England	**Common Right Barns ★★★★**	158
Southport, North West	**Sandy Brook Farm ★★★**	305

♿ Mobility level 3 - Independent

Bowes, North East	**Mellwaters Barn ★★★★Gold**	318
Haltwhistle, North East	**Lambley Farm Cottages ★★★★**	325
Ormskirk, North West	**Martin Lane Farm Holiday Cottages ★★★★-★★★★★**	302

♿ Mobility level 3 - Assisted

Bowes, North East	**Mellwaters Barn ★★★★Gold**	318
Cornriggs, North East	**Cornriggs Cottages ★★★★★**	318

🔊 Hearing impairment level 1

Ashbourne, East Midlands	**Rivendale Caravan & Leisure Park ★★★★**	194
Cornriggs, North East	**Cornriggs Cottages ★★★★★**	318

🔊 Hearing impairment level 2

Halifax, Yorkshire	**Windmill Court Cottages ★★★★**	271

👁 Visual impairment level 1

Ainsdale, North West	**Willowbank Holiday Home and Touring Park ★★★★★**	304
Ashbourne, East Midlands	**Rivendale Caravan & Leisure Park ★★★★**	194
Canterbury, South East	**Broome Park Golf and Country Club ★★★★**	114

Gold Award winners

Establishments with a detailed entry in this guide that have achieved recognition of exceptional quality are listed below. Establishments are listed alphabetically by place name.

South West

Bath, **Greyfield Farm Cottages** ★★★-★★★★★	83
Binegar, **Spindle Cottage Holidays** ★★★★	83
Bude, **Tamar Valley Cottages** ★★★★	44
Bude, **Whalesborough Cottages & Spa** ★★★★★	45
Bude, **Wooldown Holiday Cottages** ★★★-★★★★★	46
Cirencester, **The Stable**s ★★★★★	79
Falmouth, **Budock Vean Cottages &**	
Holiday Homes ★★★-★★★★★	47
Gorran, Owls roost ★★★★	49
Helford, **Mudgeon Vean Farm**	
Holiday Cottages ★★-★★★★	49
Holsworthy, **Woodford Bridge Country Club** ★★★★	65
Lacock, **Piccadilly Caravan Park Ltd** ★★★★	90
Luxborough, **Westcott Farm Holiday Cottages** ★★★	85
Mitcheldean, **Holme House Barn** ★★★★	80
Moreton-In-Marsh, **Summer Cottage** ★★★★	81
Okehampton, **Peartree Cottage** ★★★★	68
Padstow, **Sunday & School Cottages** ★★★★	51
Padstow, **Yellow Sands Cottages** ★★★-★★★★★	52
Porthtowan, **Rosehill Lodges** ★★★★★	53
Ringstead, **Upton Grange Holiday Cottages** ★★★★	77
Seaton,	
Mount Brioni Holiday Apartments ★★★-★★★★	54
St. Austell, **Natural Retreats - Trewhiddle** ★★★★★	54

St. Columb, **Cornish Holiday Lodges** ★★★-★★★★★	55
St. Issey, **Trewince Farm Holiday Park** ★★★★	55
St. Just in Roseland,	
Trethem Mill Touring Park ★★★★★	56
St. Mawes, **Roundhouse Barn Holidays** ★★★★★	57
Stow-on-the-Wold, **Broad Oak Cottages** ★★★★	81
Torquay, **Long Barn Luxury Holiday Cottages** ★★★★	71
Totnes, **Aish Cross Holiday Cottages** ★★★★★	72
Wedmore, **Pear Tree Cottages** ★★★★	88

South East

Chichester, **Honer Cottage** ★★★	120
Chichester, **Laneside** ★★★★	120
Crowborough, **Hodges** ★★★★★	121
Edenbridge, **Medley Court - Hever Castle** ★★★★	115
Pitt, **South Winchester Lodges** ★★★★★	110
Portsmouth and Southsea,	
Admiralty Apartments ★★★-★★★★★	110
Stockbridge,	
Larch Loft Self Catering Apartment ★★★★	111

London

London SW3,	
The Apartments - Chelsea & Marylebone ★★★★	140
St Margaret's, **Twickenham, 20 The Baron**s ★★★★	141

Walkers and cyclists welcome

Look out for quality-assessed accommodation displaying the Walkers Welcome and Cyclists Welcome signs.

Participants in these schemes actively encourage and support walking and cycling. In addition to special meal arrangements and helpful information, they'll provide a water supply to wash off the mud, an area for drying wet clothing and footwear, maps and books to look up cycling and walking routes and even an emergency puncture-repair kit! Bikes can also be locked up securely undercover.

The standards for these schemes have been developed in partnership with the tourist boards in Northern Ireland, Scotland and Wales, so wherever you're travelling in the UK you'll receive the same welcome.

Walkers Welcome & Cyclists Welcome

Establishments participating in the Walkers Welcome and Cyclists Welcome schemes provide special facilities and actively encourage these recreations. Accommodation with a detailed entry in this guide is listed below. Place names are listed Alphabetically.

Walkers Welcome & Cyclists Welcome

Allendale, North East	**Fell View Cottage ★★★★**	319
Allonby, North West	**Crookhurst Farm Cottages ★★★★**	287
Ashbourne, East Midlands	**Rivendale Caravan & Leisure Park ★★★★**	194
Ashby-de-la-Zouch, East Midlands	**Forest Lodge ★★★★**	199
Beverley, Yorkshire	**Horseshoe Cottage & Bay Tree ★★★★ Gold**	250
Bewdley, Heart of England	**Fern Cottage ★★★★**	232
Bodham, East of England	**Rookery Farm Norfolk ★★-★★★★ Gold**	163
Brooke, East Midlands	**America Lodge ★★★**	209
Buxton, East Midlands	**Pyegreave Cottage ★★★★ Gold**	196
Castleton, East Midlands	**Riding House Farm Cottages ★★★★★ Gold**	196
Chapel Lawn, Heart of England	**The Squire Farm Holiday Cottages ★★★★**	225
Chesterfield, East Midlands	**Pottery Flat Chesterfield ★★★ Gold**	197
Cromer, East of England	**Coach Cottage ★★★★ Gold**	164
Dawlish, South West	**Cofton Country Holidays ★★★★**	62
Dawlish, South West	**Lady's Mile Touring and Camping Park ★★★★**	63
Dawlish, South West	**Oakcliff Holiday Park ★★★★**	64
Dawlish, South West	**The Eastdon Estate ★★★-★★★★**	63
Fakenham, East of England	**Pollywiggle Cottage ★★★★**	165
Fareham, South East	**Cowes View Coastguard Cottage ★★★★**	109
Farnham, South East	**Bentley Green Farm ★★★★★**	118
Field Dalling, East of England	**Hard Farm Barns ★★★★ Gold**	166
Giggleswick, Yorkshire	**Ivy Cottage (Giggleswick) Limited ★★★★**	254
Great Yarmouth, East of England	**Clippesby Hall ★★★★★**	166
Great Yarmouth, East of England	**Clippesby Hall Holiday Park**	167
Halifax, Yorkshire	**Windmill Court Cottages ★★★★**	271
Helford, South West	**Mudgeon Vean Farm Holiday Cottages ★★★-★★★★ Gold**	49
Horsham, South East	**Ghyll Cottage ★★★★**	122
Kersey, East of England	**Wheelwrights Cottage ★★★★★**	176
Lincoln, East Midlands	**Drws Nesaf, Metheringham ★★★ Gold**	203
Louth, East Midlands	**Church Cottage ★★★★ Gold**	203
Louth, East Midlands	**Louth Barn ★★★★ Gold**	204
Ludlow, Heart of England	**Glebe Barn ★★★★ Gold**	226
Ludlow, Heart of England	**Sutton Court Farm Cottages ★★★-★★★★**	226
Ludlow, Heart of England	**The Silver Pear Apartments ★★★★ Gold**	226
Luxborough, South West	**Westcott Farm Holiday Cottages ★★★★ Gold**	85

🔲 Walkers Welcome

Welcome Pets!

Want to travel with your faithful companion? Look out for accommodation displaying the **Welcome Pets!** sign. Participants in this scheme go out of their way to meet the needs of guests bringing dogs, cats and/or small birds. In addition to providing water and food bowls, torches or nightlights, spare leads and pet washing facilities, they'll buy in food on request, and offer toys, treats and bedding. They'll also have information on pet-friendly attractions, pubs, restaurants and recreation. Of course, not everyone is able to offer suitable facilities for every pet, so do check if there are any restrictions on type, size and number of animals when you book.

Look out for the following symbol in the entry.

Families and Pets Welcome

Establishments participating in the Families Welcome or Welcome Pets! schemes provide special facilities and actively encourage families or guests with pets. Accommodation with a detailed entry in this guide is listed below. Place names are listed alphabetically.

Families and Pets Welcome

Allonby, North West	Crookhurst Farm Cottages ★★★★	287
Ashby-de-la-Zouch, East Midlands	Forest Lodge ★★★★	199
Beverley, Yorkshire	Heron Lakes ★★★★ Gold	250
Bodham, East of England	Rookery Farm Norfolk ★★-★★★★ Gold	163
Brooke, East Midlands	America Lodge ★★★	209
Cromer, East of England	Coach Cottage ★★★★ Gold	164
Dawlish, South West	Lady's Mile Touring and Camping Park ★★★★	63
Louth, East Midlands	Church Cottage ★★★★ Gold	203
Lydney, South West	Whitemead Forest Park ★★★★	79
Macclesfield, North West	Cheshire Hunt Holiday Cottages ★★★★	286
Maidstone, South East	Coldblow Farm ★★★-★★★★	116
Mitcheldean, South West	Holme House Barn ★★★★ Gold	80
Nunthorpe, Yorkshire	Blackthorn Gate ★★★★ Gold	259
Okehampton, South West	Peartree Cottage ★★★★ Gold	68
Shanklin, South East	Luccombe Villa Holiday Apartments ★★★★	112
Windermere, North West	Park Cliffe Camping & Caravan Estate ★★★★ Gold	298

Families Welcome

Beverley, Yorkshire	Horseshoe Cottage & Bay Tree ★★★★ Gold	250
Bewdley, Heart of England	Fern Cottage ★★★★	232
Binegar, South West	Spindle Cottage Holidays ★★★★ Gold	83
Carlisle, North West	Brackenhill Tower & Jacobean Cottage ★★★★-★★★★★ Gold	290
Chesterfield, East Midlands	Pottery Flat Chesterfield ★★★ Gold	197
Dawlish, South West	Oakcliff Holiday Park ★★★★	64
Edenbridge, South East	Medley Court - Hever Castle ★★★★★ Gold	115
Fakenham, East of England	2 Westgate Barns ★★★★ Gold	165
Fakenham, East of England	Pollywiggle Cottage ★★★★	165
Hastings, South East	14 Old Humphrey Avenue ★★★	122
Horsham, South East	Ghyll Cottage ★★★★	122
Leek, Heart of England	Roaches Holiday Cottages ★★★	229
London SW20, London	Thalia Holiday Home ★★★★	140
Louth, East Midlands	Louth Barn ★★★★ Gold	204
Ludlow, Heart of England	The Silver Pear Apartments ★★★★ Gold	226
Luxborough, South West	Westcott Farm Holiday Cottages ★★★★ Gold	85
Midhurst, South East	Long Meadow ★★★★	123
Netherseal, East Midlands	Sealbrook Farm ★★★★	198

Otterton, South West	**Ladram Bay Holiday Park ★★★★★**	69
Pin Mill, East of England	**Alma Cottage ★★**	177
Scarborough, Yorkshire	**The Sands Sea Front Apartments ★★★★★ Gold**	263
Slingsby, Yorkshire	**Robin Hood Caravan Park ★★★★★**	264
St. Austell, South West	**The Old Inn, Pentewan ★★★**	54
St. Columb, South West	**Cornish Holiday Lodges ★★★-★★★★ Gold**	55
St. Issey, South West	**Trewince Farm Holiday Park ★★★★ Gold**	55
Stretton, East Midlands	**Stretton Lakes ★★★★-★★★★★ Gold**	209
Torquay, South West	**Long Barn Luxury Holiday Cottages ★★★★ Gold**	71
Whitby, Yorkshire	**Forest Lodge Farm ★★★★★ Gold**	267
York, Yorkshire	**Minster's Reach Apartments ★★★★ Gold**	270
York, Yorkshire	**Pavilion Cottage ★★★★**	270

🐾 Pets Welcome

Bamburgh, North East	**Waren Caravan and Camping Park ★★★★**	322
Felixstowe, East of England	**Peewit Caravan Park ★★★★**	176
Field Dalling, East of England	**Hard Farm Barns ★★★★ Gold**	166
Looe, South West	**Talehay Cottages ★★★★**	50
North Dalton, Yorkshire	**Old Cobbler's Cottage ★★★**	251
Pateley Bridge, Yorkshire	**Helme Pasture Lodges & Cottages ★★★★**	260
Peterborough, East of England	**Common Right Barns ★★★★**	158
Poole, South West	**Wychcott ★★**	76
Scarborough, Yorkshire	**Cayton Village Caravan Park Ltd ★★★★★**	262
Skegness, East Midlands	**Skegness Water Leisure Park ★★★**	205
Staithes, Yorkshire	**Pennysteel Cottage ★★★**	265
Truro, South West	**The Valley ★★★★★**	58
Ullswater, North West	**Hillcroft Holiday Park ★★★★**	296
Worcester, Heart of England	**Hop Pickers Rural Retreats ★★★★ Gold**	235

Swimming Pools index

If you're looking for accommodation with swimming facilities use this index to see at a glance detailed accommodation entries that match your requirement. Establishments are listed alphabetically by place name.

🏊 Indoor pool

Allonby, North West	Crookhurst Farm Cottages ★★★★	287
Ambleside, North West	The Lakelands ★★★★	288
Ashbourne, East Midlands	Sandybrook Country Park ★★★★★	195
Bellingham, North East	Riverdale Court ★★★	323
Bigbury-on-Sea, South West	Apartment 5, Burgh Island Causeway ★★★★★	59
Bowness-on-Windermere, North West	Burnside Park ★★★★	289
Bude, South West	Whalesborough Cottages & Spa ★★★★★ Gold	45
Bude, South West	Woodland Lodge Holidays ★★★★	46
Burton Upon Trent, Heart of England	Wychnor Park Country Club ★★★★	228
Bury St. Edmunds, East of England	Culford Farm Cottages ★★★★-★★★★★	175
Canterbury, South East	Broome Park Golf and Country Club ★★★★	114
Carnforth, North West	Pine Lake Resort ★★★★	300
Chipping Campden, South West	Walnut Tree ★★★★	78
Combe Martin, South West	Wheel Farm Cottages ★★★-★★★★	60
Cromer, East of England	Cromer Country Club ★★★★	164
Dawlish, South West	Cofton Country Holidays ★★★★	62
Dawlish, South West	Cofton Country Holidays ★★★★	62
Dawlish, South West	Lady's Mile Touring and Camping Park ★★★★	63
Dawlish, South West	Welcome Family Holiday Park ★★★★	65
Deal, South East	Kingsdown Park Holiday Village ★★★★★	115
Fakenham, East of England	Moor Farm Stable Cottages ★★★-★★★★	165
Falmouth, South West	Budock Vean Cottages & Holiday Homes ★★★★-★★★★★ Gold	47
Filey, Yorkshire	Crows Nest Caravan Park ★★★★	253
Filey, Yorkshire	Orchard Farm Holiday Village ★★★★★	254
Folke, South West	Folke Manor Farm Cottages ★★★★	75
Great Yarmouth, East of England	Vauxhall Holiday Park ★★★★	167
Hastings, South East	Shearbarn Holiday Park ★★★★	122
Holsworthy, South West	Woodford Bridge Country Club ★★★ Gold	65
Hunstanton, East of England	Searles Leisure Resort ★★★★★	169
Lancaster, North West	Thurnham Hall ★★★★	301
Lydney, South West	Whitemead Forest Park ★★★★	79
Matlock, East Midlands	Darwin Forest Country Park ★★★★★	198
Moreton-In-Marsh, South West	Old Market Way ★★★★	80
Newquay, South West	Riverside Holiday Park ★★★★	51
Otterton, South West	Ladram Bay Holiday Park ★★★★★	69
Scarborough, Yorkshire	Flower of May Holiday Park ★★★★★	262
Selsey, South East	Green Lawns Holiday Park (Bunn Leisure) ★★★★★	124
Selsey, South East	Warner Farm Camping & Touring Park ★★★★★	124
Selsey, South East	West Sands Holiday Park (Bunn Leisure) ★★★★	125
Selsey, South East	White Horse Holiday Park (Bunn Leisure) ★★★★	125
Silloth, North West	Stanwix Park Holiday Centre ★★★★★	295
Southport, North West	Riverside Holiday Park ★★★	305
Southwold, East of England	Highsteppers at Blythview ★★★★	179

⤴ Outdoor pool

Index by property name

Accommodation with a detailed entry in this guide is listed below.

385

Index by place name

The following places all have detailed accommodation entries in this guide. If the place where you wish to stay is not shown the location maps (starting on page 312) will help you to find somewhere to stay in the area.

Index to display advertisers

w411b.

HUDSON'S MEDIA LIMITED

Published by: Hudson's Media Ltd
35 Thorpe Road, Peterborough, PE3 6AG
Tel: 01733 296910 Fax: 01733 209292

On behalf of: VisitBritain, Sanctuary Buildings, 20 Great Smith Street, London SW1P 3BT

Editor: Deborah Coulter
Editorial Contributor: Neil Pope
Production team: Deborah Coulter, Rhiannon McCluskey,
Rebecca Owen-Fisher and Sophie Studd

Creative: Jamieson Eley
Advertising team: Ben Piper, Matthew Pinfold, Seanan McGrory, James O'Rawe
Email: VEguides@hudsons-media.co.uk Tel: 01733 296913
Production System: NVG – leaders in Tourism Technology. www.nvg.net
Printer: Stephens & George, Merthyr Tydfil
Retail Sales: Compass – Tel: 020 8996 5764